ANNALS OF THE NEW YORK ACADEMY OF SCIENCES

Volume 462

EDITORIAL STAFF

Executive Editor

BILL BOLAND

Associate Editor

SHEILA KATES TREITLER

The New York Academy of Sciences
2 East 63rd Street
New York, New York 10021

ELECTROCONVULSIVE THERAPY
Clinical and Basic Research Issues

ANNALS OF THE NEW YORK ACADEMY OF SCIENCES
Volume 462

ELECTROCONVULSIVE THERAPY
Clinical and Basic Research Issues

Edited by Sidney Malitz and Harold A. Sackeim

The New York Academy of Sciences
New York, New York
1986

Library of Congress Cataloging in Publication Data

Electroconvulsive therapy.

(Annals of the New York Academy of Sciences, ISSN 0077-8923; v. 462)
Papers from a conference held from Jan. 16 to Jan. 18, 1985 in New York, sponsored by the New York Academy of Sciences and the National Institute of Mental Health.
Includes bibliographies and indexes.
1. Electric shock therapy—Congresses. I. Malitz, Sidney, 1923– . II. Sackeim, Harold A. III. New York Academy of Sciences. IV. National Institute of Mental Health (U.S.) V. Series.
Q11.N5 vol. 462 500 s 86-2471
[RC485] [616.89'122]
ISBN 0-89766-319-5
ISBN 0-89766-320-9 (pbk.)

SP
Printed in the United States of America
ISBN 0-89766-319-5 (Cloth)
ISBN 0-89766-320-9 (Paper)
ISSN 0077-8923

ANNALS OF THE NEW YORK ACADEMY OF SCIENCES

Volume 462
March 14, 1986

ELECTROCONVULSIVE THERAPY[a]

Clinical and Basic Research Issues

Editors and Conference Organizers
SIDNEY MALITZ and HAROLD A. SACKEIM

CONTENTS

[a]This volume is the result of a conference entitled Electroconvulsive Therapy: Clinical and Basic Research Issues held from January 16 to January 18, 1985 in New York, N.Y., sponsored by The New York Academy of Sciences and the National Institute of Mental Health.

Part III: Biochemical and Neuroendocrinological Effects 2

Part IV. Neurophysiological Effects 1

Part V. Neurophysiological Effects 2

Part VI. Neuropsychological Effects

Part VII. Mechanisms of Action

Major funding for this conference was provided by:

- THE NATIONAL INSTITUTE OF MENTAL HEALTH

Financial assistance was received from:

- AMERICAN CYANAMID COMPANY, MEDICAL RESEARCH DIVISION
- HOECHST-ROUSSEL PHARMACEUTICALS INC.
- MECTA CORPORATION
- MERCK SHARP & DOHME RESEARCH LABORATORIES
- MERRELL DOW RESEARCH INSTITUTE
- NORWICH EATON PHARMACEUTICALS, INC.
- NOVO DIAGNOSTIC SYSTEMS
- THE UPJOHN COMPANY

Preface

Convulsive therapy has been in use for more than 50 years. Electroconvulsive therapy (ECT) will reach the half-century mark in 1988. Despite its longevity, ECT is probably the most controversial form of somatic treatment in psychiatry. Also in spite of the many years it has been utilized, research centering on ECT has been undergoing a significant revitalization.

Why the renewed interest in ECT? The current increased commitment to biological approaches to psychiatric disturbance may be a contributory factor. However, the case of ECT is somewhat unique. The introduction of psychotropic agents in the 1950s, 1960s, and 1970s diminished the clinical role of ECT and captured the attention of a generation of new investigators. The impact of the introduction of these agents was extraordinary, and altered the priority of research efforts to the detriment of ECT. Increasingly, however, as we have learned more about the limitations of psychotropics, both in terms of efficacy and long-term side effects, ECT has once again assumed a more secure position as a therapeutic modality.

This renewed research interest has also been fueled by developments within the ECT field. ECT has undergone intensive scrutiny regarding its short-term therapeutic properties. In the last decade we have witnessed a series of British studies evaluating the role of the seizure in the therapeutic process. In the last two decades, there have been more than 35 clinical trials contrasting unilateral and bilateral ECT. Current research efforts are identifying the technical aspects of the ECT stimulus that impact on efficacy and side effects and are challenging long held views about how ECT works.

Parallel to these developments have been technological advances. It is now possible to visualize and quantify basic physiological processes within the brain. Significant progress has also been made in our capacity to assess the integrity of biochemical systems. ECT has often been an area of first application of technological advancement to the realm of psychiatry. In part, this may be due to the discrete nature of the treatment making for greater methodological purity. Also, the magnitude of the physiological changes that accompany the seizure and the postseizure period may make ECT a useful testing ground for new techniques. However, increasingly it is also recognized that ECT provides an alternate arena for identifying the neural processes that are deranged in specific psychiatric disturbances and which are apparently altered by somatic treatment.

This volume is the product of an international conference cosponsored by The New York Academy of Sciences and the National Institute of Mental Health. The conference was aimed at providing a forum for new research efforts, highlighting critical issues regarding the efficacy of the treatment and its impact on neurochemistry, neurophysiology, neuroanatomy, and cognition. Another aim of the conference was to present a multidisciplinary view of the effects of seizure elicitation. Procedures much like ECT in the human are used routinely in animal models of epilepsy. Topics relevant to the field of ECT, such as the neuropsychological consequences of treatment, the determinants of seizure threshold, and the neurophysiology of seizure propagation and termination, are also of inherent relevance to problems of human epilepsy. Perhaps reflecting the fractionation between neurology and psychiatry, since the days of Grey Walter and Foster Kennedy, neurologists have manifested little inclination to utilize the human ECT circumstance for studying the seizure. We hope that this conference has helped to stimulate such interdisciplinary exchange.

An enterprise of this sort reflects the contributions of many people. We wish to express our gratitude and appreciation to them at this time. Dr. Jack Blaine represented the National Institute of Mental Health and participated in the planning and organizing of the meeting from its inception. Ms. Ellen A. Marks, Conference Director of The New York Academy of Sciences, guided the meeting from the initial submission process through its instantiation. Drs. William Cain and Kurt Salzinger provided counsel regarding the structure of the program. Ms. Sheila Kates Treitler admirably supervised the editing of this volume. Rose Mary Colorafi, William Lancaster, and Shirley Chalke were responsible for communicating with speakers. Without generous financial support, meetings of this type could not be held. We thank the organizations that provided financial assistance. Finally, we thank the participants and audience who attended this conference. Many traveled from distant places to spend three blustery days in New York in January to share in what has been learned about ECT. We hope that what they gleaned from the meeting made their long and arduous journeys worthwhile.

HAROLD A. SACKEIM
SIDNEY MALITZ

History of Convulsive Therapy[a]

LOTHAR B. KALINOWSKY[b]

Department of Psychiatry
New York Medical College
Valhalla, New York 10595

Like all biological treatments in psychiatry, electric convulsive therapy (ECT) was discovered on the basis of clinical observations. None of those treatments originated from any understanding of the etiology of the illnesses for which they were invented.

Cerletti and Bini as the originators of ECT embarked on their animal experimentation[1] in Rome, Italy, after they were told that in Budapest, Hungary, the psychiatrist Von Meduna had applied pharmacological convulsive treatment to schizophrenics.[2] Cerletti was primarily a neurologist who had done work in experimental epilepsy for many years. Therefore, it was understandable that he raised the question of why Von Meduna had not used electricity as the easiest way to induce seizures. Cerletti did, however, have doubts about the feasibility of using electricity in humans because of the high fatality rate in his animal experiments with the electrical provocation of seizures for the purpose of studying anatomical changes in epilepsy. Cerletti's associate, Bini, who had no training in psychiatry when he joined Cerletti's staff, must be given credit for eliminating the danger of fatalities in the animal experiments and for the technical work of building the first ECT machine.

Von Meduna's idea of convulsive therapy was based on the frequent observation that catatonics and other schizophrenic patients would temporarily lose their psychotic symptomatology after spontaneous seizures whatever their cause. Such spontaneous seizures may occur after alcohol intake and head injury and, most frequently, when barbiturates are withdrawn. We observed this in a group of chronic patients who had received amybarbital as a treatment for a year, when it was suddenly discontinued. We also observed that clouded states and other psychiatric symptoms in epileptics clear up after one or two spontaneous seizures. A second reason for Meduna's undertaking was some studies suggesting antagonism between epilepsy and schizophrenia. Prior to Meduna's work, other Hungarian psychiatrists, Nyiro and Jablonski, had injected blood of schizophrenics into epileptics in order to reduce their seizures.[3] Von Meduna came to the opposite conclusion—that seizures would reduce schizophrenic symptomatology—and he realized that actual seizures had to be induced in his patients for this purpose. He decided on camphor in oil by intramuscular injection, and the first treatment was given on January 23, 1934. Apparently he had not been aware that camphor by mouth had already been given successfully by a Dr. W. Oliver, as published in the *London Medical Journal* in 1785.[4] Since camphor in oil led to seizures only after 15 to 20 minutes, during which time the patient felt very uncomfortable, Von Meduna replaced it with intravenous injection of pentylenetetrazol (Metrazol) which led to an immediate convulsion. It was this technique that led to the wide use of convulsive therapy four years before electric convulsive therapy was introduced.

Only recently an autobiography by Von Meduna, which had not been published for 50 years, was found by Max Fink.[5] In it, Meduna writes about the strong opposition on

[a] To Prof. Hanns Hippius, Munich, on his 60th birthday.
[b] Address correspondence to 155 East 76th Street, New York, N.Y. 10021.

the part of his teacher, Karl Schaffer, who saw schizophrenia as an untreatable, hereditary disease. Schaffer's antagonism led Meduna to leave Hungary and come to the United States. Here, Meduna did not pursue further work in convulsive therapy, but later experimented with carbon dioxide as a treatment for the neuroses.

It was a strange coincidence that in three subsequent years, the first three widely used treatments of the functional psychoses, primarily schizophrenia, were introduced: insulin coma therapy by Sakel in 1933,[6] convulsive therapy by Von Meduna in 1934, and psychosurgery by Moniz in 1935.[7] However, it must be emphasized that there was no connection whatsoever between these three discoveries. Contrary to statements by Sakel there was no relationship between his discovery and Meduna's. It is true that hypoglycemia from insulin treatment can lead to epileptic seizures, but Sakel clearly warned against seizures as a complication of hypoglycemia with the words *Caveat Medicus,* although he later claimed that he had discovered convulsive therapy. Sakel showed great hostility towards Meduna and continued to attack both pharmacological and electric convulsive therapy.

Cerletti and Bini's introduction of ECT—of which I was fortunate in having been an eyewitness—is surrounded by several misconceptions. There was no connection with the use of electrical eels by the Romans or the therapeutic application of electric current in the past for many types of patients including psychiatric ones. Cerletti's experiments were based on the work of physiologists and pathologists studying the brain in epilepsy. He used a technique by which he applied electrodes in mouth and rectum. It was Bini who realized that the numerous fatalities in animals were due to the current going through the heart, and he demonstrated that fatalities could be eliminated by applying both electrodes to the temples of the dogs he used for his experiments. In order to establish whether the duration of exposure to the current or the intensity of the voltage was more dangerous, Cerletti found that even high voltage has no untoward effect but that current applied for a longer period of time could lead to a fatality,[8] probably due to prolonged respiratory suppression. Antipsychiatrists used this finding as an argument against ECT, although such long exposure to the current has no resemblance to the technique used in ECT of psychiatric patients.

In 1937 an international meeting was organized by the Swiss psychiatrist Max Müller in Münsingen. It was there that Bini first reported his experiments in animals.[9] Cerletti was still hesitant to go ahead with the first treatment in humans. The statement that Cerletti got the idea of ECT from the killing of animals by electricity in the slaughterhouses of Rome is completely wrong. Actually this delayed the first treatment because, when Cerletti heard about it, he went to the slaughterhouse. There he found that the animals were not killed by the electric current, but that the current was used to make them unconscious and spare them the pain. The animals had a convulsion and were killed while unconscious.

The first treatment was given in April 1938 to a mute patient whose identity was unknown when he was hospitalized. He had been wandering the streets of Rome. The researchers' fear of giving too much current led to a painful sensation on the part of the patient, who did not lose consciousness during the first application with a minimal current. A second stimulus with a slightly higher voltage made the patient unconscious but did not lead to a convulsion. Only the third stimulus was followed by a complete seizure, after which the patient began to talk. He had a good remission after a series of treatments and could be followed for two years. Accornero, who was part of the closest team, gave a detailed report of these events in 1970 after both Cerletti and Bini had died.[10] In his later years, Cerletti thought that convulsions could be eliminated by applying seizures to animals and injecting the brain of such animals into the patient.[11] His theory was that substances—which he called Acroagonine—develop in such animals which could have an antipsychotic therapeutic effect and would spare the patient the seizure. Actually this method turned out to be ineffective, but some statements made by Cerletti were used by antipsychiatrists as an argument against the use of ECT.

Meduna as well as Cerletti and Bini applied their method originally to schizophrenics, and only later was it seen that it even gave better results in depressions. This historical fact proves that ECT is not a specific treatment for depression as is frequently claimed. Actually ECT is still widely used in schizophrenic patients, but it is a known fact that those psychiatric disorders that have a fairly good spontaneous prognosis also respond best to treatment. It is, therefore, not surprising that results in depressions are better and that in schizophrenics only those subtypes that have a fairly good prognosis respond to treatment. Still better are results in deliriums, where ECT is rarely used in this country; but the Scandinavian experience has shown that even a single ECT in such cases of delirium tremens can be life saving.

The best proof for the efficacy of convulsive therapies was their general acceptance in spite of the frequent complication of fractures. It is most interesting that a psychiatrist, A. E. Bennett, has done pioneer work[12] in extracting the muscle relaxant curare from *Chondodendron tomentosum* with which South American hunters paralyzed the animals they wanted to catch alive. Bennett, who had first suggested spinal anesthesia for the prevention of ECT fractures, recommended curare and later various synthetic curare preparations which were also introduced in surgical anesthesia. Although the antidote Prostigmine was routinely used in ECT, numerous unexplained fatalities occurred, and in 1951 succinyl choline became available as a safe muscle relaxant in ECT. To save the patient distress from the paralysis of the respiratory muscles, barbiturate anesthesia must be given prior to the muscle relaxant.

In this historical survey it should be mentioned that an American contribution to convulsive therapy consisted in a return to pharmacological convulsive therapy by means of an inhalant. In 1957, the pharmacologist Krantz, while studying fluorinated ethers for use in anesthesiology, found that hexafluorinated diethylether, when inhaled, caused a convulsion.[13] It was manufactured for psychiatric use under the trade name of Indoklon and introduced by way of a mask and with a vaporizer. It first caused some myoclonic movements identical to what is seen in Metrazol treatment. This was followed by the usual tonic and clonic phase of any seizure. First used without anesthesia, it was later modified with barbiturate and the muscle relaxant succinyl choline. Frequent nausea after the treatment had to be counteracted with Compazine. Therapeutically Indoklon was equal to ECT, and the impression of some of us was that it seemed somewhat more effective in patients who had responded poorly to ECT. By the way, it has also been claimed but not statistically proven that Metrazol-induced convulsions were therapeutically more effective than ECT. One of the advantages of Indoklon was the avoidance of the frightening term "electric shock." Unfortunately, the manufacturers of Indoklon discontinued this preparation because it was not financially rewarding.

At the end of the 1950s, the use of ECT decreased considerably with the introduction of antidepressant medication. This had already been the case some years earlier, when the neuroleptics ushered in the new era of psychopharmacotherapy. Also research supported by drug companies far exceeded research in ECT, where early clinical and basic science studies had been disappointing. It was only recently realized that the therapeutic results of psychotropic drugs had been overestimated. On the other hand, the side effects of both neuroleptics and antidepressants became increasingly problematic. Lately the use of ECT has increased considerably and at the same time clinical evaluation as well as studies regarding the mode of action have become more extensive as evidenced by this volume.

The antipsychiatry movement also contributed to an increase of studies in ECT. Criticism that we are still treating psychiatric disorders of which we do not know the causes with treatments whose mechanisms we do not understand led to greater efforts to increase our knowledge. It is more and more realized that convulsive therapy is in its clinical efficacy one of the most predictable treatments in medicine. The question is often asked why none of the originators of the so-called shock treatments received the Nobel prize. The special problem of biological treatments in psychiatry had been demonstrated already in the 1920s, when Wagner von Jauregg was considered for the Nobel prize but received it only after several years because the psychiatrist on the Nobel Prize Committee objected persistently to awarding the prize to a colleague who is so cruel as to give a patient suffering from a severe illness like general paresis a second illness like malaria. Similar objections were made in connection with shock treatments.

One must seriously question whether any grant application for experimenting on humans with artificially induced convulsions would have been approved in this country. Also it cannot be denied that research in psychiatry looked unscientific in the sense that the discovery of the treatment discussed in this volume was based purely on clinical observations of patients not in research centers but in mental institutions which today are ill reputed, although they contributed much to the therapeutic progress in our field.

REFERENCES

1. Cerletti, U. & L. Bini. 1938. L'elettroshock. Arch. Gen. Neuro. Psichiat. Psicoanal. **19:** 266.
2. Meduna, L. J. 1937. Die Konvulsionstherapie der Schizophrenie. Carl Marhold. Halle, Germany.
3. Nyiro, J. & A. Jablonski. 1929. Einige Daten zur Prognose der Epilepsie. Psychiatr. Neurol. Wochenschr. **31:** 547.
4. Oliver, W. 1785. Account of the effects of camphor in a case of insanity. London Med. J.: 120.
5. Fink, M. 1984. Meduna and the origins of convulsive therapy. Am. J. Psychiatry **141:** 1034.
6. Sakel, M. 1938. Nature and origin of the hypoglycemic treatment of psychoses. Am. J. Psychiatry **94** (Suppl. 24).
7. Moniz, E. 1936. Tentatives operatoires dans le traitement de certaines psychoses. Masson et Cie. Paris, France.
8. Cerletti, U. 1940. Le alterazioni istopatologiche del sistema nervoso nell'elettroshock. Riv. Spec. Freniat. **64:** 2.
9. Bini, L. 1938. Experimental researches on epileptic attacks induced by the electric current. Am. J. Psychiatry **94** (Suppl. 172).
10. Accornero, F. 1970. Testimonianzo oculare sulla scoperta dell'elettroshock. Pagine de Storia della Medicina **14:** 38.
11. Cerletti, U. 1950. Old and new information about electroshock. Am. J. Psychiatry **107:** 87.
12. Bennett, A. E. 1940. Preventing traumatic complications in convulsive shock therapy by curare. J. Am. Med. Assoc. **141:** 322.
13. Kranz, J. C., Jr., E. B. Truitt, Jr., L. Speers & A. S. C. Ling. 1957. New pharmacoconvulsive agent. Science **126:** 353.

PART I. EFFICACY

Electroconvulsive Therapy

Indications and Contraindications

MAX HAMILTON

Psychiatry Annex
University of Leeds
30 Clarendon Road
Leeds LS2 9NZ, England

INTRODUCTION

Although convulsive therapy was first introduced for the treatment of schizophrenia, clinical experience soon showed that it was much more effective for depressive illness (melancholia) in particular and affective disorders in general. The unpleasantness of the treatment was greatly moderated by the replacement of drug induction of convulsions by electrical methods and minimized by the use of anesthetics. Soon after the war, an attempt was made to modify the convulsions with curare, but it was the introduction of short-acting muscle relaxants that finally eliminated convulsion-induced bone injuries.

Since then, the treatment has become widely accepted by psychiatrists on the grounds that it is effective, gives better and quicker results than antidepressant drugs, is safe and has very few contraindications, and, finally, side effects are usually only minor. Despite this, electroconvulsive therapy (ECT) has become a subject for intense controversy and opposition, chiefly by civil rights groups, radicals, and sundry eccentric sects. The criticism has been made not so much on the abuse of the treatment (of which there has been plenty, as with treatments in other branches of medicine) as on its use under any circumstances. Regrettably, some psychologists and social workers have also opposed its use, largely because they are against the use of biological treatments of mental disorder on theoretical grounds.

The more rational critics of convulsive therapy have claimed that it has never been adequately tested by controlled trials. These critics do not complain that controlled trials have never been carried out for psychoanalytic and other psychotherapies, osteopathy, homeopathy, ecological medicine, herbalism, etc. There have never been public outcries for properly controlled trials of "fringe medicine." In fact, the critics are quite mistaken, as was pointed out by Barton.[1] One could add to his list the trials by Fink *et al.*,[2] Wilson *et al.*,[3] Freeman *et al.*,[4] West,[5] and Brandon *et al.*,[6] all of which were favorable to the treatment, and those of Lambourn and Gill[7] and Johnstone *et al.*,[8] which were equivocal. These trials will not be considered in detail here.

CLINICAL INDICATIONS: DEPRESSIONS

By and large, such researches as have been carried out on the indications for ECT in the depressions have confirmed clinical experience. This is not all that common in the world of medicine. As regards "types" of depression, it is generally agreed that it is the "endogenous" one that responds best. The symptoms that are most closely associated with a good response are the presence of marked depressive mood, psychomotor retardation, delayed insomnia (early morning wakening), guilt, diurnal variation of symptoms (worse in the morning). One could add also loss of appetite, loss of weight, and agitation when accompanied by marked biological symptoms. A clinical history of previous attacks is also a favorable sign.

Real convulsive therapy is clearly better than sham treatment for depressive illness associated with delusions,[8] and as antidepressant drugs are much less effective in this case, the presence of this symptom is an important indication for convulsive treatment. Nevertheless, it is less effective when delusions are present, as was first pointed out many years ago[9] and since then confirmed by others.[10]

Poor results can be expected if there is a history of behavioral disturbances in childhood and abnormal personality in inadequate, hypochondriacal, and hysterical types. It is noteworthy that these are not symptoms but background features.

Concerning the "type," it is my opinion that insufficient attention has been paid to the important distinction between a true depressive illness and a depressive reaction to the stresses of life, especially to the experience of loss. In such circumstances, it is normal to feel depressed. People become depressed when they lose a friend or a dear relative, when they lose their job or fail in an examination. The loss may be of something merely anticipated: an expected promotion or rise in income. The depression can be clearly seen to be directly related to the extent of the loss, but this must be judged from the point of view of the subject: what may be of great importance to one person may be trivial to another. The clinician must seek the inner significance of the loss.

The extent of the reaction must also be assessed in terms of the personality. Not all people are of the quiet, stolid, unemotional type which seems to be the ideal of so many psychiatrists. Many are emotionally sensitive and reactive vigorously to their circumstances. When things go well they are "up in the clouds" and when things go ill they swing into the depths; but however extreme their complaints and "symptoms," they are not suffering from a depressive illness.

The important criterion for the distinction is that a normal depressive reaction is closely related to the real world. The parents of a soldier who is reported to have been killed will be extremely depressed, but their mood will change instantly if they hear that he is alive after all. On the contrary, a depressive illness will continue on its course according to its own inner dynamics, regardless of the circumstances that may have precipitated it. The melancholic who is convinced he is bankrupt will be unaffected by evidence that all is well with his business.

The more clearly a patient's condition resembles the traditional subtype of "endogenous" depression, the better the response. Attempts have been made to determine if other subtypes would indicate the response to treatment, but this has yielded, by and large, only negative results. The distinction between the subtypes of *Diagnostic and Statistical Manual III* and of the *Research Diagnostic Criteria* is not related to outcome,[11] and this applies also to the subtypes of Paykel[12] and the more important distinction between unipolar and bipolar depression.[13] The response is the same for both sexes,[14] and in the presence of derealization.[15] The presence of psychological precipitants is related to poor outcome, and the more obvious they are the worse the result.[16] This is in line with the distinction made above. The response to treatment is slower in older patients.[17] There is some evidence that outcome is correlated positively with the duration of convulsions,[18] but some of the work on this confounds duration with number of treatments.

It has been pointed out that when patients do not respond to convulsive treatment, their spontaneous recovery is usually not earlier than six months afterwards.[19] This suggests that the treatment is relatively ineffective until it is given in the last six months of the acute phase. As the majority of patients have an illness that is less than six months in duration,[20] this is not a serious problem but it may explain an unexpectedly poor response. Obviously, the duration of an acute phase can be estimated only if the patient has experienced a previous attack.

CLINICAL INDICATIONS: MANIA

Until the introduction of the neuroleptics, the only effective treatment for mania was convulsive therapy. The use of these drugs and of lithium has made this treatment almost obsolete. Nonetheless it still has a use when the patient is severely disturbed and requires a treatment that will produce a rapid response.

CLINICAL INDICATIONS: SCHIZOPHRENIA

It is generally accepted that convulsive therapy is useless in chronic schizophrenia but that it is effective in breaking up catatonic stupor and excitement. As these are very rare, it is of no great practical importance. It is also used for acutely ill patients who are not eating or drinking and where the response to neuroleptics is greatly delayed. In fact there has been very little research in this field chiefly because the introduction of neuroleptic drugs has effectively replaced all other treatments. One trial of drugs plus convulsive therapy against drugs and sham showed that the actively treated group was significantly better than the control series up to 8 weeks but that the controls had "caught up" with the others by 16 weeks.[21] This confirms that the treatment is of temporary effect but that it can be helpful when a quick change is urgently required.

It is known that the schizoaffective illnesses and, expecially, the cycloid disorders are particularly responsive to antidepressive treatment rather than the neuroleptic drugs. The greater the prominence of suicidal ideas and guilt, the better the response to convulsive therapy.[22] It is possible that convulsive treatment might be useful when neuroleptics and antidepressant drugs, including lithium, have failed.

CLINICAL INDICATIONS: OTHER

There are some situations in which although antidepressant drugs would otherwise be adequate, there are special reasons why they should not be used. The first and most obvious is during early pregnancy, and even when it is merely a possibility. Old people are particularly liable to suffer from the side effects of antidepressants, and this is a good reason for preferring convulsive treatment. The same applies in the presence of cardiac, cardiovascular, hepatic, and renal disease, in all of which drug metabolism and excretion are impaired.

If the patient has a history of previous attacks that have not responded to drugs but have to convulsive therapy, it would be a kindness to the patient to go straight on to the treatment that is known to be effective. Even greater is the call for a humane approach if the patient is suffering from a very severe illness or is actively suicidal. Only those who have seen the agony of such patients can appreciate the cruelty of those individuals who are determined to protect the patients from convulsive therapy at all costs—the patients' costs.

CONTRAINDICATIONS

It is customary to point out that the treatment should not be given in the presence of such uncommon conditions as raised intracranial pressure, cerebral or aortic aneurisms, and also when there is a history of cerebral hemorrhage. In fact modification of the treatment by muscle relaxants and anesthetic has rendered it so safe that there are scarcely any contraindications for its use. It can and has been given to patients soon after a coronary infarction, to pregnant women, to those suffering from pulmonary tuberculosis, diabetes mellitus, bone fractures, and even a stitched-up cut throat.

A special case is that of the patient suffering from hypertension. The convulsion is usually accompanied by a brief rise in blood pressure and as there is some evidence that it is this that is associated with cognitive impairment,[23] it is necessary to weigh carefully the relative demerits of the two kinds of treatment. It has been recommended that for such patients, a ganglion blocker would diminish the risks of treatment (though increasing the effects of polypharmacy).

PREDICTION OF RESPONSE

From the earliest days of convulsion therapy, attempts have been made to improve the selection of suitable cases, i.e., to predict which ones would show a good response to treatment. The methods can be classified into three types, based upon psychological tests, physiological tests, and psychopathology (predictive scales).

PSYCHOLOGICAL TESTS

Very little work in this field appears to have been carried out. The most interesting is that using the Rorschach test.[24] It was found that those with good outcome showed few responses; little variety of content; no shading, movement, or color responses; a high proportion of whole, form, and popular responses. This was interpreted as "a basically conventional and unimaginative personality, generally lacking in empathy, introspectiveness or facility for verbal communication."[25] Patients with a high score on the California F scale (which implies a rigid, conventional, stereotyped, obsessional personality) did better than those with a low score.[25] The same workers found that sociological factors also played a part: better responses were more likely to be found among the older patients, those who had had less schooling and were more likely to be foreign born.[26]

PHYSIOLOGICAL TESTS

One of the earliest attempts to predict response to convulsive therapy was the Funkenstein test. The patients were given injections of methyl-acetyl choline and also of adrenaline, and the cardiovascular response measured (pulse rate and blood pressure). These were recorded, and the resulting curves were classified into different types. Some types were alleged to predict a good response to treatment. On the whole it was not possible to replicate the original findings. Examination of the results in detail indicated that the prediction was based on a differentiation between the older patients, who were chiefly depressives, and the younger ones, who were usually schizophrenics.

The sedation threshold test was introduced by Shagass as an objective measure of anxiety.[27] Sodium amylobarbitone is slowly injected intravenously, and the amount required to produce blurring in the speech of the patient is recorded. Alternatively an EEG measure may be used. The lower the threshold, the more likely a good response to convulsive therapy.[28] Confirmation of these results showed only a moderate correlation (in female patients) between threshold and outcome, amounting to 0.49 at one month and 0.42 at three months follow-up.[29] A related test consists of the injection of methedrine and noting the reaction of the patients. The drug may either intensify the symptoms or diminish them (normalizing reaction). The normalizing group was significantly worse at follow-up three months after.[28] It would appear that this group consisted largely of "neurotic" and the "intensifying" group of "psychotic" depressives.

None of these tests has survived in clinical practice. The most important physiological test currently being investigated is Carroll's dexamethasone suppression test. It was introduced as a method of differentiating between "endogenous" and other types of depression[30] (from the present point of view, of differentiating between a true depressive illness and a depressive reaction to stress), and on this basis could be a useful predictor for response to treatment.[31] It can be said that on the whole, patients who show an abnormal response (nonsuppression) are more likely to respond well to treatment.

PREDICTIVE SCALES

The first of these was that produced by Feldman.[32] It was derived from items in the Minnesota Multiphasic Personality Inventory and confirmed by cross-validation. Others failed to do so, obtaining only nonsignificant correlations with outcome[29] or none.[33] It is worth considering this in detail. It has been pointed out that the efficacy of the scale was based largely on the difference between schizophrenics and depressives and that prediction based on the diagnosis alone gave highly significant results.[34] In fact, the scale predicted outcome equally well for treatment with insulin and even brief psychotherapy. The items of the scale are concerned with personality, and the criterion of improvement was based on follow-up of one year, so the scale is related to general prognosis.

The Hobson scale is a considerable advance.[35] It is based on features of the illness that were related to outcome, but even then it has had variable success, ranging from correlations of about 0.7[29] to small, nonsignificant ones.[36]

An index that consists of a simple count of the number of items, present for a particular patient, is a crude approximation to a properly weighted sum of items based on multiple correlation. The first use of this method included a physiological test with clinical features,[10] but later ones confined themselves to clinical features including symptoms. The Newcastle scale,[37] a modified version,[38] and the Mendels scale[39] are the best known of such. Unfortunately, although they have had successes, they have also had failures.[36] Examination of the content of these scales shows that the items correspond well with those that distinguish between "endogenous" depression and other types.

The lack of success of predictive formulae needs to be considered carefully. It may well be that the factors leading to a good response to treatment bear little relation to those that determine the clinical features of the illness. If this should be so, it will be necessary to look elsewhere for predictive variables; but it is very likely that the most important difficulty is that concerned with selection.

If one starts with a mixed bag of diagnostic groups together with depressives, it is easy to find a prediction formula that will show that the last group contains the higher proportion of successes; but if this formula is then applied to a group of depressives, it must obviously fail. The clinical indications for convulsive therapy, when used properly, already give a high proportion of successes; in consequence, there is not much room for further improvement. There are many other subtle problems involved but they cannot be considered here.

SUMMARY

The indications for convulsive treatment are such that, when it is properly used, it is one of the most effective treatments in the whole of medicine. Its chief indication is for depressive illness that shows predominantly biological features. It is particularly useful for patients who have not responded to other treatments and for those who are actively suicidal. Research on the prediction of response has yielded very little information beyond that already based on clinical experience. In the right conditions it is remarkably safe and has few contraindications. In a way it corresponds to a "surgical" treatment and, therefore, it is to be hoped that when its mode of action is adequately elucidated, it will be replaced by "medical" treatments.

REFERENCES

1. Barton, J. L. 1977. ECT in depression: the evidence of controlled studies. Biol. Psychiatry **12:** 687–695.
2. Fink, M., R. L. Kahn & M. Green. 1958. Experimental studies of the electroshock process. Dis. Nerv. Syst. **19:** 113–118.
3. Wilson, I. C., J. T. Vernon, T. Guin & M. G. Sandifer. 1963. A controlled study of treatments of depression. J. Neuropsychiatry **4:** 331–337.
4. Freeman, C. P. L., J. V. Basson & A. Crighton. 1978. A double blind controlled trial of electroconvulsive therapy (ECT) and simulated ECT in depressive illness. Lancet **i:** 738–740.
5. West, E. D. 1981. Electroconvulsive therapy in depression: a double blind controlled trial. Br. Med. J. **282:** 355–357.
6. Brandon, S., P. Cowley, C. McDonald, P. Neville, R. Palmer & S. Wellstood-Eason. Electroconvulsive therapy: results in depressive illness from the Leicestershire trial. Br. Med. J. **288:** 22–25.
7. Lambourn, J. & D. Gill. 1978. A controlled comparison of simulated and real ECT. Br. J. Psychiatry **133:** 514–519.
8. Johnstone, E. C., J. F. W. Deakin, P. Lawler, C. D. Frith, M. Stevens, K. McPherson & T. J. Crow. 1980. The Northwick Park ECT trial. Lancet **ii:** 1317–1320.
9. Chodoff, P., D. Legault & W. Freeman. 1950. Ambulatory shock therapy. Dis. Nerv. Syst. **11:** 1–8.
10. Hamilton, M. & J. White. 1960. Factors related to outcome of depression treated with ECT. J. Ment. Sci. **106:** 1030–1040.
11. Rich, C. L., D. G. Spiker, S. W. Jewell & J. F. Neil. 1984. DSM III, RDC and ECT: depressive subtypes and immediate response. J. Clin. Psychiatry **45:** 14–18.
12. Paykel, E. S., G. L. Klerman & B. A. Prusoff. 1974. Prognosis of depression and the endogenous-neurotic distinction. Psychol. Med. **4:** 57–64.
13. Abrams, R. & M. A. Taylor. 1974. Unipolar and bipolar depressive illness. Phenomenology and response to electro-convulsive therapy. Arch. Gen. Psychiatry **30:** 320–321.
14. Zetin, M., G. J. Sklansky & M. Cramer. 1984. Sex differences in inpatients with major depression. J. Clin. Psychiatry **45:** 257–259.

15. Ackner, B., Q. A. F. R. Grant & A. E. Maxwell. 1960. The prognostic significance of depersonalization in depressive illnesses treated with electro-convulsive therapy. J. Neurol. Neurosurg. Psychiatry **23:** 242–245.
16. Rose, J. T. 1963. Reactive and endogenous depressions—response to ECT. Br. J. Psychiatry **109:** 213–217.
17. Rich, C. L., D. G. Spikles, S. W. Jewell, J. F. Neil & N. A. Black. 1984. The efficiency of ECT. 1. Response rate in depressive episodes. Psychiatr. Res. **11:** 167–176.
18. Ottosson, J-O. 1962. ECT of endogenous depression: an analysis of various factors on the efficacy of the therapy. J. Ment. Sci. **108:** 694–703.
19. Kukopulos, A., D. Reginaldi, L. Tondo, A. Bernabei & B. Calieri. 1977. Spontaneous length of depression and response to ECT. Psychol. Med. **7:** 625–629.
20. Angst, J. 1980. Verlauf unipolar depressiver, bipolar manischdepressiver und schizo-affectiver Erkrankungen and Psychosen. Ergebnisse einer prospektiven Studie [Course of unipolar depressive, bipolar manic-depressive and schizo-affective illnesses and psychoses]. Fortschr. Neurol. Psychiatr. **48:** 3–30.
21. Taylor, P. J. & J. J. Fleminger. 1980. ECT for schizophrenia. Lancet **i:** 1380–1382.
22. Folstein, M., S. Folstein & P. R. McHugh. 1973. Clinical predictors of improvement after electroconvulsive therapy of patients with schizophrenia, neurotic reactions and affective disorders. Biol. Psychiatry **7:** 147–152.
23. Hamilton, M., M. J. Stoker & C. M. Spencer. 1979. Post-ECT cognitive defect and elevation of blood pressure. Br. J. Psychiatry **135:** 77–78.
24. Kahn, R. L. & M. Fink. 1960. Prognostic value of Rorschach criteria in clinical response to convulsive therapy. J. Neuropsychiatry **1:** 242–245.
25. Kahn, R. L. & M. Pollack. 1959. Prognostic application of psychological techniques in convulsive therapy. Dis. Nerv. Syst. (Mon. Suppl.) **20**(5).
26. Fink, M., R. L. Kahn & M. Pollack. 1959. Psychological factors affecting individual differences in behavioral responses to convulsive therapy. J. Nerv. Ment. Dis. **128:** 243–248.
27. Shagass, C. 1954. The sedation threshold: a method for estimating tension in psychiatric patients. EEG Clin. Neurophysiol. **6:** 221–233.
28. Shagass, C. & A. L. Jones. 1958. A neurophysiological test for psychiatric diagnosis: results in 750 patients. Am. J. Psychiatry **114:** 1002–1010.
29. Roberts, J. M. 1959. Prognostic factors in the electroshock treatment of depressive states. II. The application of specific tests. J. Ment. Sci. **105:** 703–713.
30. Carroll, B. 1982. The dexamethasone suppression test for melancholia. Br. J. Psychiatry **140:** 292–304.
31. Brown, W. A., R. Johnston & D. Mayfield. 1979. The 24-hour dexamethasone suppression test in a clinical setting: relationship to diagnosis, symptoms and response to treatment. Am. J. Psychiatry **136:** 543–547.
32. Feldman, M. J. 1951. A prognostic scale for shock therapy. Psychol. Monogr. (65: No.d 10) No. 327.
33. Pumroy, D. K. & W. S. Kogan. 1958. A validation of measures that predict the efficacy of shock therapy. J. Clin. Psychol. **14:** 46–47.
34. Bannister, D. & H. R. Beech. 1961. An evaluation of the Feldman prognosis scale for shock therapy. J. Ment. Sci. **107:** 503–508.
35. Hobson, R. F. 1953. Prognostic factors in ECT. J. Neurol. Neurosurg. Psychiatry **16:** 275–281.
36. Abrams, R., M. Fink & S. Feldstein. 1973. The prediction of clinical response to ECT. Br. J. Psychiatry **122:** 457–460.
37. Carney M. W. P., M. Roth & R. F. Garside. 1965. The diagnosis of depressive syndromes and the prediction of ECT response. Br. J. Psychiatry **111:** 659–674.
38. Kerr, T. A., C. Gurney, K. Schapira & M. Roth. 1970. Measurement and prediction of outcome in affective disorders. Proc. R. Soc. Med. **63:** 235–238.
39. Mendels, J. 1967. The prediction of response to electro-convulsive therapy. Am. J. Psychiatry **124:** 153–159.

Controlled Trials of Electroconvulsive Therapy

TIMOTHY J. CROW AND EVE C. JOHNSTONE

Division of Psychiatry
Clinical Research Center
Northwick Park Hospital
Harrow HA1 3UJ, England

Electroconvulsive therapy, like every physical treatment in psychiatry with the exception of penicillin for GPI, was introduced on an entirely empirical basis. It became widely adopted before systematic evidence on its efficacy had been collected, and a clinical lore on its indications was built upon a minimal background of objectivity. Slowly a body of evaluation through clinical trials has accumulated, focusing first upon the procedure as a whole and more recently upon the element—the convulsion—that is widely believed to be necessary for the therapeutic effect.

MAJOR CLINICAL TRIALS

Two trials in the 1960s established the efficacy of electroconvulsive therapy (ECT) in depression relative to the then recently introduced antidepressant drugs. One trial in the United States[1] and one in the United Kingdom[2] each examined ECT relative to imipramine, a monoamine oxidase inhibitor, and placebo in a series of at least 250 inpatients with depression. The inclusion criteria of Greenblatt *et al.*[1] were probably somewhat wider than those of Cawley *et al.*[2] (TABLE 1), and the duration of the trial was longer, but the results were remarkably similar. Thus at the end of the first trial 91% were judged at least "moderately improved" and 76% "markedly" so on ECT, and in the second trial 84% were judged "improved" and 71% with no or only slight symptoms. The comparisons with the percentage of patients improved on placebo show advantages for ECT significant at the 1% level. There are also significant differences in favor of ECT with respect to the drug treatments, although in each trial one drug comparison (with phenelzine in Greenblatt *et al.*[1] and with imipramine in Cawley *et al.*[2]) is not significant at the "moderately improved" and "improved" level. Together the trials yield a concensus conclusion that ECT is at least as effective as antidepressant medication and perhaps more rapid in its action.

However it must be noted that neither trial was conducted blind with respect to ECT in the sense that they were blind with respect to the tablets (antidepressant or placebo) administered. Both clinicians and patients knew which patients had received electroconvulsive therapy.

Thus these trials did not eliminate the possibility that some aspect of the treatment procedure other than the induction of the convulsion was responsible for the therapeutic effect. For example there is evidence that the circumstances in which a treatment is administered affect placebo response rates,[3] and the history of the introduction, widespread use, and subsequent decline of insulin coma therapy suggests that in the past the psychological effects of an elaborate physical procedure have been underestimated.[4] For these reasons and also to understand the mechanism of action, a more precise evaluation of the role of the convulsion is desirable.

TABLE 1. Major Random-Allocation (Nonblind) Controlled Trials

		Diagnoses Included	Total Trial Entrants	Group Size	Treatments	Outcome at 8 Weeks: Percent Markedly Improved	p vs. ECT	Percent Markedly + Moderately Improved	p vs. ECT
Greenblatt, Grosser & Wechsler[1]	1964	Depression occurring in psychoneurosis (18%), manic-depression (27%), involutional melancholia (18%), schizoaffective reactions (20%), and character disorders (16%)	281	63	ECT (>9)	76	—	92	—
				73	Imipramine 200–250 mg	49	<0.01	74	<0.02
				38	Phenelzine 60–75 mg	50	<0.01	79	N.S.
				68	Isocarboxazid 40–45 mg	28	<0.001	56	<0.001
				39	Placebo	46	<0.01	59	<0.01
						Outcome at 4 weeks: Percent None or Slight Symptoms	**p vs. ECT**	**Percent Improved**	**p vs. ECT**
MRC trial Cawley *et al.*[2]	1965	Primary depression in patients aged 40–69 years of duration less than 18 months without adequate previous treatment	250	65	ECT (4–8)	71	—	84	—
				63	Imipramine 200 mg	52	<0.05	72	N.S.
				61	Phenelzine 60 mg	30	<0.01	38	<0.01
				61	Placebo	39	<0.01	45	<0.01

There have been two phases of interest in this question. A number of studies between 1953 and 1966 incorporated designs in which ECT was either compared with simulated (sham) ECT or was compared with other treatments in such a way as to cast light on the role of the convulsion. Since 1978 there has been further interest in this issue (particularly in the United Kingdom), and five trials have been conducted specifically to assess the role of the electrically induced convulsion.

TRIALS BETWEEN 1953 AND 1966

Data for trials between 1953 and 1966 are shown in TABLE 2. Two of the earliest studies included groups of patients treated with electroconvulsions unmodified by anesthesia or muscle relaxants,[5,6] in one case in comparison with pentothal anesthesia and subconvulsive stimulation under anesthesia,[5] in the other with groups treated with electroconvulsions modified by muscle relaxant and thiopental, and treated with thiopental or nitrous oxide alone.[6] Although the designs were unexceptionable and substantial improvements were seen in all groups in each trial, no significant advantages for convulsive over subconvulsive regimes were seen. However these trials included patients with schizophrenia, a diagnosis that would not now be considered the primary indication for the use of ECT. Thus the trial of Miller *et al.* was confined to chronic institutionalized patients originally diagnosed catatonic schizophrenic,[5] and the study of Brill *et al.* included 67 patients described as suffering from schizophrenic reactions, 14 with schizoaffective disorders, and 16 with depressive reactions.[6] In the latter study the 30 patients with depressive illnesses were analyzed separately; although there was a 67% overall clinical improvement in the shock-treated patients in this group compared to 44% in the nonshock patients, this difference did not reach statistical significance. For size of sample, rigor of design and analysis, and range of assessments employed, the study of Brill *et al.* has hardly been equalled in the literature. The authors' conclusion that "for groups comparable to this one, the more traumatic components of ECT (electricity, convulsions) might be abolished without reducing therapeutic effectiveness"[6] has received less subsequent attention than it deserved.

Some studies which have focused more directly on depression have included smaller sample sizes. Thus in the study of Harris and Robin more patients on ECT improved than those in the comparison groups treated with hexobarbitone and phenelzine or placebo[7] but the trial was not fully blind and the groups were too small for statistical analysis. McDonald *et al.* included a group of four patients treated with simulated ECT in their control group but these patients were not separately analyzed.[8] In the trial of Wilson *et al.* a significant difference in Hamilton scores ($p < 0.05$) was observed between the two groups of patients treated with electroshock and two given anesthetics, but the differences between individual groups were not significant and the shock vs. imipramine group differences disappeared in a second phase of the trial in which the drug dose was increased.[9] A larger study of depressions of moderate severity compared electroconvulsive therapy with thiopental-induced sleep and showed a difference in favor of the former,[10] but this difference was not significant and the patients were not blind to the nature of the treatments.

Two studies that appear to give a favorable result with respect to the therapeutic effect of the convulsion include faults of design with respect to random allocation.[11,12] Thus the study of Ulett *et al.* compared photoconvulsive and electroconvulsive treatments with subconvulsive photic stimulation and quinalbarbitone sedation.[11]

Although the outcome in the convulsive groups together was significantly superior to that in the two nonconvulsive groups together, allocation to groups was achieved by a mixture of matching and random allocation; in addition it is not clear to what extent the patients were aware of the differences between the treatments.

In a brief report of a trial comparing 16 patients treated with biweekly anesthetics and imipramine tablets and 15 patients treated with ECT and placebo tablets, Robin and Harris present clinical findings (TABLE 2) that show a significant ($p < 0.01$) advantage for the latter after two weeks of treatment.[13] Symptom ratings (data not presented) also apparently showed advantages for ECT, but nurses' ratings did not. The design of this study (similar in some respects to that of Wilson *et al.*)[9] is of interest in that it is of potential value in assessing the relative efficacy of tricyclic antidepressants and ECT with respect to different types of depressive illness, although neither trial included sufficient numbers of patients to make this possible.

RECENT TRIALS

Although between 1966 and 1978 no studies bearing directly upon the role of the convulsion have appeared, since that time five studies in which real ECT (modified by anesthesia) has been compared with simulated (sham) ECT (i.e., the induction of anesthesia and muscle relaxation as for ECT but without the passage of current) have been published (see TABLE 3). Major interest attaches to the question of the extent to which the results of these trials are in conflict or agreement. Since there are substantial differences in trial design and conduct, each must be separately discussed.

Freeman, Basson, and Crichton, 1978

Freeman *et al.* adopted an experimental design in which patients with a diagnosis of primary depressive illness were randomly allocated either to a course of real ECT or to a course of ECT in which the first two treatments were simulated.[14] Outcome was assessed both by depression ratings obtained at weekly intervals throughout the course of treatment and by the decision of the clinician (who was blind to treatment) to terminate the course. The authors concluded that "ECT is significantly superior to simulated ECT in the treatment of depressive illness"[14] on the basis that there were significant differences in Hamilton ratings after two treatments, and that the number of treatments administered to the simulated group was significantly greater.

However there are obstacles to accepting this conclusion without qualification. These arise partly from the design which permitted flexibility with respect to number of treatments administered but also attempted to assess the effects of different treatment schedules as if this had been an independent variable. Criticisms that may be made of the two outcome criteria are:

1. *Number of ECTs prescribed.* The principal difficulty here is that unequal numbers of patients were lost for reasons other than satisfactory response from the two groups: 2 were lost from the simulated ECT group because they developed hypomania, but a total of 6 were lost from the real ECT group—2 for hypomania, 2 because they refused further treatment, and 2 because they had an "inadequate response." Obviously this imbalance makes the use of "number of ECT to satisfactory response" problematic. Presumably the 2 patients who developed hypomania in each group can be eliminated, but the remaining 4 (20% of the randomized sample) lost from the real ECT group must be taken

TABLE 2

Authors	Year	Diagnoses Included[a]	Treatment Comparisons[b]	Group Sizes	Allocation	Assessments	Outcome	Significance
Miller, Clancy & Cumming[5]	1953	Catatonic schizophrenia	ECT (× 15) Pentothal (A) Pentothal (A) + subconvulsive shock	10 10 10	Random	2/4 raters blind	All groups showed behavioral improvements	No significant between-group differences
							No. recovered / No. markedly improved	
Ulett, Smith & Gleser[11]	1956	Involutional psychotic (18), manic-depressive (8), psychotic depressive (20) & psychoneurotic depressive (8) reactions; 1st episode catatonic and schizoaffective psychoses (20)	Photoconvulsive shock Subconvulsive photic shock ECT (12–15) Quinalbarbitone (S)	21 21 21 21	Matched/ random (i.e., not fully random)	Raters blind	7 / 5 1 / 3 5 / 2 2 / 3	ECT group not significantly different from other 3 groups: 2 convulsive groups superior to 2 nonconvulsive groups
							Percent improvement	
Brill, Crumpton, Eiduson, Grayson, Hellman & Richards[6]	1959	Schizophrenic reactions (67), depressive reactions (30)	ECT (× 20) ECT + scoline ECT + thiopental (A) Thiopental (A) N_2O (A)	19 20 20 20 18	Random	Raters blind	63, 60, 35 } shock: 53% 35, 55 } no shock: 47%	No significant differences between groups, between shock and no-shock groups or between the shock (67% improvement, $n = 21$) and no-shock (44% improvement, $n = 9$) depressive subgroups
							No. slightly or greatly improved after 2 weeks	
Harris & Robin[7]	1960	Depressive reactions	ECT (× 4) + hexobarbital (S) Hexobarbital (S) Hexobarbital (S) + phenelzine	4 4 4	Random	Not fully blind	4 1 —	Sample size too small for statistical analysis

Cronholm & Ottosson[12]	1960	Endogenous depression	ECT (× 6) ECT shortened by lidocaine	24 23	Sequential (i.e., not random)	Not fully blind			Significantly less improvement in group receiving lidocaine
							Withdrawn/ slight or no improvmt.	Mod. or marked improvmt.	
Robin & Harris[13]	1962	Depression	ECT (× 6) + placebo Anesthesia + imipramine	15 16	Random	Blind	3 13	12 3	$p < 0.01$
							No. improved/recovered		
Fahy, Imlah & Harrington[10]	1962	Nonreactive depression	ECT (× 6) Imipramine Thiopental anesthesia	20 20 20	Random	Patients not blind	12 10 8		Between-group differences not significant
							No. of responders		
Wilson, Vernon, Guin & Sandifer[9,c]	1963	Manic-depressive, involutional and reactive depression	ECT (× 6) + imipramine ECT (× 6) + placebo Thiopental (A) + imipramine Thiopental (A) + placebo	4 6 6 6	Random	2/3 raters blind	4 6 5 3		Between-group differences not significant
							Adjusted percent improvement		
McDonald, Perkins, Marjerrison & Podilsky[8]	1966	Depression	Amitriptyline ECT (× 8) Placebo/sham ECT	10 12 4 + 4	Random	Blind	29 36 15		ECT-sham ECT differences not separately analyzed

[a]Brackets indicate numbers of patients with each diagnosis.

[b]ECT, brackets indicate numbers of treatments; drugs, A indicates anesthesia, S indicates sedation.

[c]In Wilson *et al.*'s study, convulsive/nonconvulsive differences were present but these disappeared in phase 2 when imipramine dosage was increased.

[**Note added in proof:** Fink (1982. Br. J. Psychiatry **141:** 213–214) gives brief details of a comparison of convulsing with subconvulsive shock in a group of mixed psychotic patients, with greater therapeutic effects in the convulsive group.]

TABLE 3

Author	Year	Sample Assessed for Entry	Selection Criteria	Comparison Groups	Trial Sample: Starters	Trial Sample: Withdrawn	Trial Sample: <4 ECT	Trial Sample: Unacctd. for	Trial Sample: Completors
Freeman, Basson & Crichton[14]	1978	Not stated	Primary depression (Hamilton & Beck >15)	2 sham } + real 2 real } ECT	20 20	6 2			14 18
Lambourn & Gill[19]	1978	38 patients referred for ECT	Depressive psychoses	6 sham ECT 6 real ECT	16 16	— —			16 16
West[20,21]	1981	Not stated	Primary depression (Feighner criteria)	6 sham ECT 6 real ECT	12 13	1 2			11 11
Northwick Park[17,22]	1980, 1984	128 depressed inpatients[a]	MRC 1965 Newcastle and Feighner criteria	8 sham ECT 8 real ECT	35 35	4 4			31 31
					Starters	Withdrawn	<4 ECT	Unacctd. for	Completors
Leicester[27]	1984	143 depressed inpatients[b]	Patients referred for ECT including those with retardation, delusions & neurotic depression	Up to 8 sham ECT Up to 8 real ECT	42 53	10 6	2 0	1 4	29 43

[a]19 patients did not meet trial diagnostic criteria; 6 outside age range; 13 had ECT in previous 6 months; 12 refused; 2 detained; 6 poor anesthetic risk.
[b]48 patients did not give consent for various reasons.

into account. If the 2 patients can be assumed to have had an unsatisfactory response, the proportion of 4 of 18 in the real as compared to 0 of 18 in the simulated ECT group (Fisher's exact test $p = 0.052$) might support the paradoxical conclusion that real ECT is less effective than simulated ECT.[15] Freeman *et al.* adopted the strategy of excluding the two patients who refused further treatment and calculated that the number of ECTs given to the real ECT group (presumably including the two patients who were withdrawn because of "inadequate response," but whether or not including the patients who became hypomanic is unclear) is significantly less ($p < 0.05$) than the number given to the group given simulated ECT.[14] The data presented in the paper do not allow other assessments (e.g., with the inadequate responders excluded) of this variable to be made. It would seem that if the treatment course could be terminated either by satisfactory or by inadequate response, the number of treatments given is not a suitable dependent variable.

2. *Rating scale assessments.* Significant differences ($p < 0.05$) between the groups after two treatments in favor of real ECT were noted on Hamilton, Wakefield,

TABLE 3 (*continued*)

Type of ECT	Fit Ascertainmt.	Blind Procedure Adopted	Previous ECT	Previous Depression	Medication during Trial: TADs[c]	Medication during Trial: Benzodiaz	Dependent Variables	Follow-up
Ectron Mk 4 bilateral 400 V sine-wave 1.5S	Not stated	Yes	22/40	28/40	Yes	Yes	Hamilton, Beck + visual analogue scales, clinicians decision to administer more ECT	None
Ectron Mk 4 unilateral pulse	Yes	Yes	21/32	26/32	No	Yes	Hamilton scale, global assessment, treatment in follow-up period	26/32 at 1 month
Transycon double-sided unrectified	Yes	No details given	13/22	15/22	Yes	Yes	Clinicians VAS, Beck ratings, nurses' ratings	None
Ectron chopped sine-wave 195V, 1.7S bifrontal	Inflated cuff method	Yes	15/70	47/70	No	Yes	Hamilton scale, Leeds self-rating, nurses' ratings	57/62 at 1 month and 6 months
Ectron chopped sine-wave bitemporal	Yes	Yes	57/95	2.5 mean admissions/patient	No	Yes	Hamilton scale, clinician's decision to discontinue ECT	70/77 at 1 month; 69/77 at 6 months

[c]TAD is tricyclic antidepressant.

and visual analogue self-rating scales but not on the Beck scale. A significant difference between the groups was not present at later points. The presence of a significant ECT effect at so early a point in time is somewhat unexpected in view of earlier trial results (e.g., References 2 and 16) and later findings (e.g., Reference 17) which suggest that when ECT effects are demonstrable they emerge over a time course of two to three weeks. Moreover patients in this trial were all receiving antidepressant medication and those on simulated ECT would have been expected to benefit from this even if they lacked the postulated benefits of the convulsion. In view of the differential later loss of patients from the two groups, it must be asked whether such patients were included in these early assessments; Freeman has confirmed that this was the case.[18] A further question concerning the interpretation of this trial is why, if the response after two (i.e., two real against two simulated) treatments is recorded as evidence for an effect of the convulsion, the lack of significant differences after four and six treatments is not taken into account in the opposite sense. The lack of a difference (as assessed by the independent raters) after six treatments is surprising in view of the fact that at this point the clinician in charge of the case made a decision to continue with treatment in 12 patients in the simulated group but only 6 patients in the real ECT group.

For these reasons the findings of this trial cannot be as firmly interpreted as the authors have suggested.

Lambourn and Gill, 1978

Lambourn and Gill randomly allocated 32 patients referred with a diagnosis of depressive psychosis to a two-week course of six real or six simulated unilateral brief-pulse ECTs.[19] Antidepressant medication was discontinued, and clinical state was assessed by Hamilton ratings before and after the course of treatment and at one month follow-up. In the follow-up period some patients in each group received further antidepressant medication or real ECT. In Hamilton ratings there was a 66% decrease in scores in the group receiving real ECT and a 42% decrease in the simulated group, the difference being statistically insignificant. In the follow-up period similar numbers of patients in each group received extra ECT or antidepressant medication, and at the final assessment the scores of the two groups were closely similar.

One explanation considered by the authors for the lack of positive outcome (i.e., significant superiority for real ECT) is the use of unilateral rather than bilateral electrode placement. However a bilateral convulsion was noted on each occasion. The authors also consider whether their treatment group was less depressed than those usually treated with ECT. Two outpatients were included (both were randomized to the simulated treatment group), but the pretrial Hamilton ratings suggest that the patients in this trial were as depressed as those in the trial of Freeman *et al.*,[18] and the authors note that all but six of the patients treated with ECT at that center in the course of the trial were included. The results of this trial, which by its design of six real vs. six simulated ECTs and its eschewal of antidepressant medication (but not by choice of unilateral electrode placements) constitutes a more exacting test of the therapeutic effects of the convulsion, stand in contrast to the conclusions of Freeman *et al.*[18]

West, 1981

West randomly allocated 22 patients with primary depressive illness to six real or six simulated ECTs delivered over a period of three weeks and assessed outcome by a psychiatrist's visual analogue scale, Beck's scale, and a nine-point scale applied by nursing staff.[20,21] On all three assessments the patients receiving real ECT are reported as significantly, often highly significantly, more improved than those receiving simulated ECT. After six treatments the trial design allowed patients to be switched on the decision of the clinician in charge to the alternative form of treatment. In the event, 10 of the 11 patients receiving simulated but none of those receiving real ECT were so switched ($p < 0.005$). The results of this trial were therefore interpreted by the author as strong evidence for the efficacy of the convulsion.

Brandon *et al.* expressed reservations about this trial on grounds of "the sample size (22 cases), the unusually unequivocal result (all patients given simulated treatment improved on crossover to real treatment), problems of selection, and doubts about the extent to which blindness was achieved."[27] The latter point is of particular concern since there was apparently only one investigator. No details of the procedures adopted for randomization and blind assessment are given in the final report,[21] although in an earlier publication a research worker is mentioned (but not named) who apparently was involved both in randomization and administering the Beck scales.[20] These uncertainties diminish the weight that can be attached to the findings.

The Northwick Park ECT Trial

The Northwick Park ECT trial was designed to establish the role of the convulsion in a well-defined population of patients with endogenous depression, to examine predictors of response, and to determine whether the therapeutic effects of the convulsion, if present, are of long duration.[17,22] Seventy patients aged between 30 and 69 years were selected if they met each of three separate sets of criteria—the criteria for depressive illness of the MRC 1965 trial, the Feighner criteria for primary depressive illness, and the Newcastle criteria for endogenous depressive illness and for predicting good outcome to ECT. After consent had been obtained from both patients and relatives, those eligible were stratified by the presence or absence of delusions, agitation, or retardation before randomization to eight real or eight simulated ECTs given over the course of four weeks. Bilateral chopped sine-wave stimulation was applied to the real ECT group, the occurrence of a convulsion being monitored by the inflated cuff method. Particular attention was paid to maintaining the blind procedure in that neither psychiatrist nor anesthetist, nor any member of nursing staff, involved in administering ECT or randomizing patients to treatments was concerned with clinical care or assessment. Outcome was assessed by the Hamilton rating scale administered by clinicians the day before the next treatment was due (to avoid observing the amnesic effects of the last treatment) by Leeds self-rating and nurses' rating scales. Antidepressant medication was not administered during the four-week trial period, but every patient received nitrazepam nighttime sedation and some received additional diazepam during the day. In the follow-up period, with assessments at one and six months after trial completion, additional ECT or tricyclic medication was administered by the clinician in charge who remained blind to the trial treatment the patient had received.

Patients in both groups improved considerably during the course of treatment, but the improvement was greater in the real ECT group ($p < 0.01$ at the end of the fourth week, $p < 0.05$ taking into account the difference in depression ratings before trial entry). Similar trends were seen in terms of Leeds self-ratings and nurses' ratings, but the differences between the groups were never significant. In the one month following the trial, the amounts of extra medication and ECT administered to the groups were closely similar and the difference between the ratings of the two groups had disappeared at this time. On a battery of memory tests, the effects of ECT were clearly apparent but there was no evidence of persisting memory deficit at six months. A more detailed analysis of the nature of the deficits induced by ECT indicated that real ECT induced impairments of concentration, short-term memory, and learning but facilitated access to remote memories.[23] With recovery from depression memory function improved in patients treated with both real and sham ECT.

The conclusions drawn from the findings were that "the improvement in terms of psychiatrists' ratings in the group of patients given real ECT was significantly greater ($p < 0.01$) than that in those given simulated ECT, but the difference between the two groups was small in relation to the considerable improvement of both groups over the 4-week treatment period. . . . the therapeutic benefits of electrically induced convulsions in depression were of lesser magnitude and were more transient than has sometimes been claimed."[17]

Two main criticisms have been directed at this conclusion:

1. *That the patients in the trial were not representative of those who would be treated with ECT in some centers.* This criticism was made by Sandifer,[24] Birley,[25] and particularly by Kendell.[26] It should be noted however that the criteria for selection were in certain respects more rigorous than those of the

trials reviewed already and of the Leicester trial.[27] Patients were selected from a group of 128 patients admitted to hospital for treatment of a depressive episode during the course of the trial by application of three sets of criteria (the MRC 1965 trial criteria,[2] the Feighner criteria for primary depressive illness, and the Newcastle criteria both for endogenous depression and predicting response to ECT). Too little information is provided in the papers of Freeman *et al.*[14] and West[21] to allow any comparison of the samples assessed for those studies with those of the Northwick Park trial. The sample of Lambourn and Gill[19] as that of the Leicester study[27] was defined by clinicians' decision to refer for ECT rather than by independent criteria, but the proportion of patients entering the trial to those considered is comparable in the Leicester and Northwick Park trials (TABLE 3). Moreover an analysis of the trial sample according to various earlier predictive scales indicates that the mean of the trial sample was very comfortably within the recommended range for ECT according to the scales of Hobson,[28] Roberts,[29] and Mendels[30] as well as those of Carney *et al.*[31] (the Newcastle scales). According to his own scale, on which Kendell considers that a higher score predicts likelier response to ECT, the sample had a mean of 15.2 $\pm$ 10.9 compared to Kendell's sample of manic depressive patients (International Classification of Diseases 301) in a depressed phase (mean score 9.5) and melancholic (ICD 302) patients (mean score 9.7—see CRC Division of Psychiatry,[22] Table IV). A further misapprehension arises from Kendell's calculation that only 21% of the Northwick Park sample had received ECT previously compared to 55% in the Freeman study,[14] 66% in Lambourn and Gill's,[19] and 59% in West's,[21] from which he argues that "many patients would not normally have received ECT."[26] However this calculation overlooks that one of the entry criteria was that patients should not have received ECT in the previous six months. When the appropriate correction is applied the proportion rises to 37%. It is argued[22] that the discrepancy between this figure and those of other trials is more likely to have arisen from the known and relatively low previous usage of ECT in this part of London than from otherwise inapparent "overgenerous inclusion criteria"[26] which Kendell postulates. He goes on to attribute the lack of difference between the real and simulated ECT groups at one and six months follow-up to a "high relapse rate"[26] attributable to failure to use tricyclic antidepressants routinely in the follow-up period. This criticism overlooks that the lack of difference between the groups at follow-up (with similar amounts of treatment given) was due mainly to the fact that the simulated ECT group had further improved to catch up with the real ECT group in the month after trial completion. For these reasons we consider Kendell's criticisms[26] of the Northwick Park trial to be without substance.

2. *That the use of benzodiazepines diminished a therapeutic effect which would otherwise have been apparent.* This point was made by Lennox and Weaver[32] and d'Elia.[33] For reasons that we have already given,[34] we consider that the supposition that a relationship between seizure duration and therapeutic effect has been established rests on a mistaken interpretation of such evidence as is available. It is the case that such trials as have so far been conducted have not attempted to avoid sedative medication,[35] and in most trials substantial and often uncontrolled amounts have been given. For example in Cronholm and Ottosson's study, 31 of the 87 cases received phenobarbitone 25 mg + 0.16 g opium tincture three times a day.[12] We think it likely that current clinical practice is seldom based upon the premise that any sedative antagonizes the therapeutic effect of ECT and that most clinicians allow their patients to receive at least benzodiazepine hypnotics.

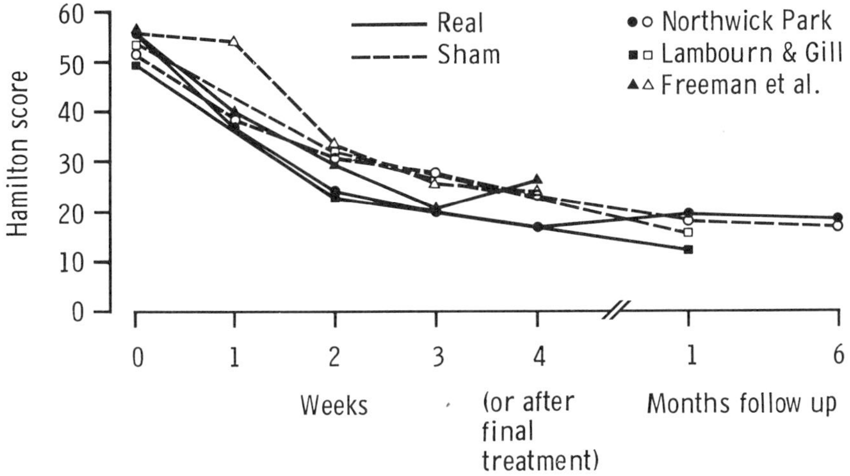

FIGURE 1. A comparison of Hamilton scores in the trials of Freeman *et al.*,[14] Lambourn and Gill,[19] and the Northwick Park trial (Johnstone *et al.*).[17] Groups treated with simulated ECT are shown with dashed lines. The simulated ECT group in the Freeman *et al.* trial received two simulated treatments before going on to real ECT, the total number of treatments being determined by the clinician.[14] Scores after the final treatment in that trial are compared with scores after the fourth week in the Northwick Park trial.

A Comparison of the Freeman et al., Lambourn and Gill, and Northwick Park Trials

West's trial[21] did not use the Hamilton scale,[36] but the other three trials did. Although the scale may not be used by different authors in the same way, some sort of comparison between trials can be made (FIGURE 1).

A number of interesting points emerge:

1. In spite of differences in design and selection criteria, before-treatment scores in the three trials are remarkably similar.
2. The time course of improvement in the different groups is similar. Thus whereas two groups of patients (the simulated groups in the Northwick Park[17] and Lambourn and Gill[19] trials) have received no convulsions at the three- and four-week points respectively, their rates of improvement are not substantially different from the real ECT treated groups (i.e., both groups in the Freeman study[14] and the real ECT groups in the Lambourn and Gill[19] and Northwick Park trials).[17,22]
3. For these reasons extrapolation of the trend in the simulated treatment group in the Freeman *et al.* study beyond two treatments would not be justified.
4. The findings in the Northwick Park and Lambourn and Gill studies at follow-up are closely similar.

The Leicester Trial

The Leicester study was mounted in the wake of the preceding trials to evaluate their apparently discrepant findings. Patients with a wide range of diagnoses (including some who were not depressed) referred for ECT were considered, but only those with depression as assessed on Present State Examination were included.[27] Since no specific criteria for endogenous depression or predicted response to ECT were applied, the sample is diagnostically wider than that of the Northwick Park trial.[17,22] Rigorous steps were taken to maintain the blindness of the procedure, and patients were randomly allocated to real or simulated ECT, the stimulation in the former group being of the same form as that given in the Northwick Park trial. As in the Northwick Park and Lambourn and Gill[19] studies, tricyclic antidepressant medication was excluded during the trial, but not in the follow-up. In contrast to these two trials, the length of treatment course was variable. Patients received up to eight real or simulated treatments, the decision to terminate earlier than eight being in the hands of the responsible clinician. Outcome was assessed both in terms of number of treatments given and Hamilton rating scales.

Ninety-five patients (compared to 70 in the Northwick Park trial) entered the study, and 72 (compared to 62) completed it. In a significantly ($p = 0.017$) greater number of cases, the course was terminated earlier than the eighth treatment in the

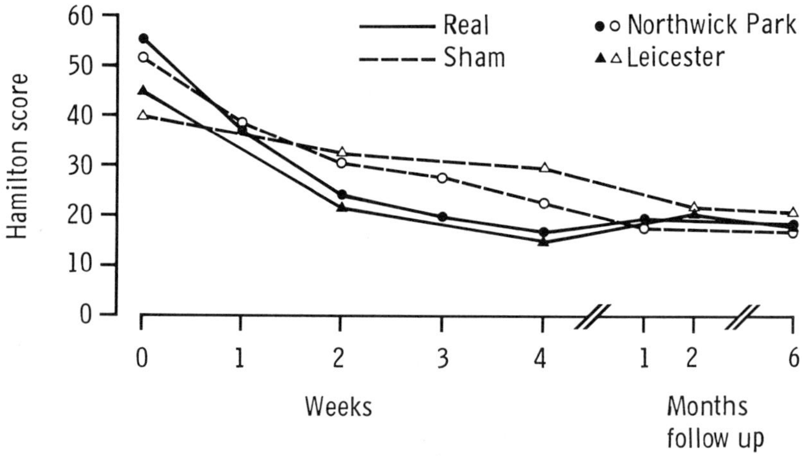

FIGURE 2. A comparison of Hamilton scores in the Northwick Park[17] and Leicester[27] trials.

real ECT group. Moreover on Hamilton rating scores, differences were present between the groups which were significant at the end of the second week ($p = 0.014$) and fourth week ($p = 0.0001$). These differences were not present at 12 and 28 weeks follow-up.

Comparison of the Hamilton scores with those of the Northwick Park study is instructive (FIGURE 2). The pretrial scores of the patients in the Leicester trial are somewhat less than those of the Northwick Park patients, and this is perhaps explained by differences in selection criteria. The rate of improvement in the real ECT groups in the two trials is approximately similar. The main difference between the trials lies in the less good response in the simulated ECT group in the Leicester trial. Again this may be due to differences in the circumstances in which the two trials were conducted—the Northwick Park trial being carried out in a relatively small and well-staffed research ward, while the Leicester study appears to have been conducted in more diverse and perhaps less-well-supervised clinical conditions. If this surmise is correct it may be supposed that nonspecific therapeutic effects (e.g., due to increased medical and nursing attention) were maximized in the Northwick Park trial.

Although the authors of the Leicester trial interpret their results as indicating that "the difference in outcome in favour of real treatment at two and four weeks was greater than that in the Northwick Park trial,"[27] a reservation concerning this conclusion must be expressed. This is that the number of noncompletors is rather large [23 (24%) compared to 8 (11%) in the Northwick Park trial,[17] 3 (25%) in West's trial,[21] 0 in the Lambourn and Gill trial,[19] and 8 (20%) in the Freeman *et al.* study[14]] and the effects of this cannot easily be assessed from the published account. Thus 16 patients (10 in the simulated and 6 in the real ECT groups) were withdrawn for specified reasons, but a further 2 patients (both in the simulated group) received fewer than four treatments, and were excluded from the analysis. Moreover a further 5 patients (4 in the real ECT and 1 in the simulated group) cannot be accounted for in the numbers included in the Hamilton ratings. If these patients were doing badly (and were not included because for example they were difficult to rate properly), this could affect the size of the difference between the groups. Similarly inclusion of the two patients in the simulated group excluded for receiving less than four treatments could diminish the significance of the between-group difference in treatments administered. Insufficient data have been presented to allow these comparisons to be made. Even without such corrections, the comparison in FIGURE 2 suggests that the similarities between the findings of the Northwick Park and Leicester trials are more striking than the differences.

PREDICTION OF RESPONSE TO ECT

A number of scales have been devised to predict response to ECT, e.g., References 28–31 and 37. However none has been devised on the basis of a comparison of real with simulated ECT and thus all are open to the objection that the clinical observations on which they are based have led them to predict general rather than ECT-specific treatment responsiveness, or even tendency to spontaneous remission. In the Northwick Park trial an attempt was made to examine the ability of each of these scales and other clinical variables to predict response to real rather than simulated ECT.[22] In general the outcome was disappointing. Response to ECT was not predicted by the endogenous stereotype. The most consistent predictor of response was the presence of delusions, which along with agitation and retardation had been used to stratify the sample. Some patients have both delusions and retardation, and when this overlap was allowed for, retardation by itself did not predict response to ECT.

The findings of the Leicester trial appear compatible with this conclusion. Both deluded and retarded subgroups showed significant real-simulated ECT outcome differences but since each of these features has not been examined in the absence of the other, it cannot be determined whether, as in the Northwick Park study, the presence of delusions is the critical factor. If this finding can be replicated, it raises the possibility that delusional depression is, as other workers have suggested, a distinct entity which responds specifically to ECT.

TRIALS OF ECT IN SCHIZOPHRENIA

Some nonblind controlled trials have suggested that ECT has beneficial effects in schizophrenia. Thus Smith *et al.* found that patients with acute episodes of schizophrenia treated with a combination of ECT and neuroleptics recovered more quickly than a group treated with neuroleptics alone;[38] and in May's study, patients treated with ECT alone did better than those treated with milieu therapy or psychotherapy but in general not so well as those treated with neuroleptics.[39]

Two trials illuminate the role of the convulsion. Miller, Clancy and Cumming in a study already referred to in chronic institutionalized patients found improvements in behavior in those treated with anesthetics as well as those treated with real ECT, and with anesthesia and subconvulsive shock, and no difference between the treatments.[5] By contrast, Taylor and Fleminger found that a group of schizophrenic patients on relatively low doses of neuroleptic medication (chlorpromazine 300 mg or trifluoperazine 15 mg daily, flupenthixol 40 mg or fluphenazine 25 mg monthly) showed greater improvement on a course of 8 to 12 real ECTs than on simulated ECT.[40] Four weeks after the treatment course the difference between the groups had diminished, and 12 weeks later it had largely disappeared. Although the numbers in this trial are small ($n = 20$), the results offer support for the view that the convulsion has some value in the treatment of schizophrenic symptoms. The differences between the findings of Taylor and Fleminger[40] and Miller *et al.*[5] are plausibly attributed to differences in patient populations, the former trial being concerned with a less chronic sample; but the negative findings of Brill *et al.* on more acutely ill patients, the majority of whom suffered from schizophrenic illnesses, must also be borne in mind.[6] It remains to be clearly established that electrically induced convulsions contribute a therapeutic effect which cannot be achieved by neuroleptic medication, but the fact that some symptoms of schizophrenia as well as delusions occurring in the course of depression respond (albeit in the short term) raises the possibility that the indication for ECT is delusional thinking rather than mood change.

OUTSTANDING ISSUES

An issue that has not been addressed by recent trials is whether ECT contributes a therapeutic effect that cannot be achieved by other means. The findings of the Northwick Park and Leicester trials suggest that a requirement for a rapid response is certainly one reason for considering ECT. It remains to be fully investigated whether there are types of depression (e.g., "delusional depression") that respond to ECT but less well to tricyclic medication. A trial design in which this issue could be ethically investigated is that adopted by Robin and Harris[13] and Wilson *et al.*,[9] i.e., that patients are allocated to groups receiving sham ECT and tricyclic medication, on the one hand, and real ECT and placebo, on the other. Such a trial should take into account the effective dose of antidepressant,[9] and might also be designed to address the question of whether neuroleptic medication is of value in deluded depression.

Related to this question is the issue of whether there are types of depressive illness that do not respond to other types of treatment but benefit from ECT over a longer period of time than is apparent in recent studies. These studies have given little support to the notion arising from the retrospective analysis of the literature of Avery and Winokur[41] that the mortality of depressive illness is increased in those not adequately treated with ECT or antidepressant medication. For if, as in the Northwick Park[17] and Leicester[27] trials, differences between the groups are inapparent at one month and six months after a course of treatment, it is difficult to believe that there are long-term benefits beyond this. However perhaps the question deserves further scrutiny in the group of deluded depressed patients, although to obtain a sufficient sample size and duration of follow-up presents difficulties.

Because none of the recent trials has included a comparison group that did not receive repeated anesthetics, they provide no information on the contribution of the nonconvulsive elements of the procedure.

CONCLUSIONS

1. The efficacy of the ECT procedure in the treatment of depressive illness of sufficient severity to require inpatient admission was established in the controlled but nonblind trials of Greenblatt *et al.*[1] and the MRC (Cawley *et al.*).[2]

2. Although the role of the electrically induced convulsion in the therapeutic effect was examined in a series of trials conducted between 1953 and 1966, these studies provided no unequivocal evidence that this was the critical element. Some studies yielded negative findings, or nonsignificant differences between groups treated with real and some form of simulated ECT, while others have defects of design (e.g., nonrandom allocation, failure to establish a blind procedure) which diminish the weight that can be attached to their conclusions.

3. A recent revival of interest in this issue has generated five further trials in which real ECT has been compared with simulated ECT. Although the findings are apparently diverse and criticisms, some pertinent, have been leveled at each study, the following conclusions are probably justified:

a. Depressed patients treated with simulated ECT show substantial improvements over a three- to four-week course of treatment (as shown by Lambourn and Gill,[19] and the Northwick Park[17] and Leicester[27] trials, and contested only in the findings of the small study of West[21]).
b. Patients receiving a course of real ECT improve to a significantly greater extent than those receiving simulated ECT (as demonstrated by Hamilton ratings in the Northwick Park[17] and Leicester[27] trials). Although this now appears to be a finding that can be accepted it should be noted that it is not always demonstrable and did not emerge in the study of Lambourn and Gill[19] or in the patient self-ratings and nurses' ratings in the Northwick Park trial.
c. Some limitations of the studies of Freeman *et al.*[14] and West[21] as indicators of the size of the effect attributable to the convulsion have been noted.

4. The findings of all those studies that have included a follow-up assessment (the Northwick Park[17] and Leicester[27] trials, and the Lambourn and Gill[19] study) are in agreement that the effects of the convulsion are of limited duration.

5. On the evidence available, the most consistent predictor of response to ECT is the presence of delusions. The reliability of this finding, and whether or not retardation is an independent predictor, remain to be established.

6. Whether electrically induced convulsions exert therapeutic effects in certain types of depression that cannot be achieved by other means has yet to be clearly established, as also has the contribution, if any, of nonconvulsive elements of the procedure.

REFERENCES

1. Greenblatt, M., G. H. Grosser & H. Wechsler. 1964. Differential response of hospitalized depressed patients to somatic therapy. Am. J. Psychiatry **120:** 935–943.
2. Medical Research Council, Cawley, R. H., *et al.* 1965. Clinical trial in the treatment of depressive illness. Br. Med. J. **i:** 881–886.
3. Lowinger, P. & S. Dobie. 1969. What makes the placebo work? A study in placebo response rates. Arch. Gen. Psychiatry **20:** 84–88.
4. Ackner, B., A. Harris & A. J. Oldham. 1957. Insulin treatment in schizophrenia: a controlled study. Lancet **i:** 607–611.
5. Miller, D. H., J. Clancy & E. Cumming. 1953. A comparison between unidirectional current non-convulsive electrical stimulation given with Reiter's machine, standard

alternating current electroshock (Cerletti method) and pentothal in chronic schizophrenia. Am. J. Psychiatry **109:** 617–621.
6. BRILL, N. Q., E. CRUMPTON, S. EIDUSON, H. M. GRAYSON, L. I. HILLMAN & P. A. RICHARDS. 1959. Relative effectiveness of various components of electroconvulsive therapy. Arch. Neurol. Psychiatry **81:** 627–635.
7. HARRIS, J. A. & A. A. ROBIN. 1960. A controlled trial of phenelzine in depressive reactions. J. Ment. Sci. **106:** 1432–1437.
8. MCDONALD, I. M., M. PERKINS, G. MARJERRISON & M. PODILSKY. 1966. A controlled comparison of amitriptyline and electroconvulsive therapy in the treatment of depression. Am. J. Psychiatry **112:** 1427–1431.
9. WILSON, I. C., J. T. VERNON, T. GUIN & M. G. SANDIFER. 1963. A controlled study of treatments of depression. J. Neuropsychiatry **4:** 331–337.
10. FAHY, P., N. IMLAH & J. HARRINGTON. 1963. A controlled comparison of electroconvulsive therapy, imipramine and thiopentone sleep in depression. J. Neuropsychiatry **4:** 310–314.
11. ULETT, G. A., K. SMITH & G. C. GLESER. 1956. Evaluation of convulsive and subconvulsive shock therapies utilizing a control group. Am. J. Psychiatry **112:** 795–802.
12. CRONHOLM, B. & J. O. OTTOSSON. 1960. Experimental studies of the therapeutic action of electroconvulsive therapy in endogenous depression. Acta Psychiatr. Scand. Suppl. **35**(145): 69–101.
13. ROBIN, A. A. & J. A. HARRIS. 1962. A controlled trial of imipramine and electroplexy. J. Ment. Sci. **106:** 217–219.
14. FREEMAN, C. P. L., J. V. BASSON & A. CRICHTON. 1978. Double-blind controlled trial of electroconvulsive therapy (ECT) and simulated ECT in depressive illness. Lancet **i:** 738–740.
15. CROW, T. J., C. D. FRITH & E. C. JOHNSTONE. 1978. How does ECT work? Lancet **i:** 1151 (letter).
16. HERRINGTON, R. N., A. BRUCE, E. C. JOHNSTONE & M. H. LADER. 1974. Comparative trial of L-tryptophan and ECT in severe depressive illness. Lancet **ii:** 731–734.
17. JOHNSTONE, E. C., J. F. W. DEAKIN, P. LAWLER, C. D. FRITH, M. STEVENS, K. MCPHERSON & T. J. CROW. 1980. The Northwick Park electroconvulsive therapy trial. Lancet **ii:** 1317–1320.
18. FREEMAN, C. P. L. 1978. How does ECT work? Lancet **i:** 1305 (letter).
19. LAMBOURN, J. & D. GILL. 1978. A controlled comparison of simulated and real ECT. Br. J. Psychiatry **133:** 514–519.
20. WEST, E. D. 1981. Randomised double blind controlled trial of ECT. *In* Electroconvulsive Therapy: An Appraisal. R. L. Palmer, Ed.: 202–213. Oxford University Press. Oxford, England.
21. WEST, E. D. 1981. Electroconvulsive therapy in depression: a double blind controlled trial. Br. Med. J. **282:** 355–357.
22. CLINICAL RESEARCH CENTRE DIVISION OF PSYCHIATRY. 1984. The Northwick Park ECT trial: predictors of response to real and simulated ECT. Br. J. Psychiatry **144:** 227–237.
23. FRITH, C. D., M. STEVENS, E. C. JOHNSTONE, J. F. W. DEAKIN, P. LAWLER & T. J. CROW. 1983. Effects of ECT and depression on various aspects of memory. Br. J. Psychiatry **142:** 610–617.
24. SANDIFER, M. G. 1981. The Northwick Park ECT trial. Lancet **i:** 98 (letter).
25. BIRLEY, J. L. T. 1981. Northwick Park ECT trial. Lancet **i:** 222 (letter).
26. KENDELL, R. E. 1981. The present status of electroconvulsive therapy. Br. J. Psychiatry **139:** 265–283.
27. BRANDON, S., P. COWLEY, C. MCDONALD, P. NEVILLE, R. PALMER & S. WELLSTOOD-EASON. 1984. Electroconvulsive therapy: results in depressive illness from the Leicestershire trial. Br. Med. J. **288:** 22–25.
28. HOBSON, R. F. 1953. Prognostic factors in electric convulsive therapy. J. Neurol. Neurosurg. Psychiatry **16:** 275–281.
29. ROBERTS, J. M. 1959. Prognostic factors on the electroshock treatment of depressive states. I. Clinical features from history and examination. J. Ment. Sci. **105:** 693–702.
30. MENDELS, J. 1967. The prediction of response to electroconvulsive therapy. Am. J. Psychiatry **124:** 153–159.

31. Carney, M. W. P., M. Roth & R. F. Garside. 1968. The diagnosis of depression syndromes and prediction of ECT response. Br. J. Psychiatry **111:** 659–674.
32. Lenox, R. H. & L. A. Weaver. 1981. Northwick Park ECT trial. Lancet **i:** 841–842 (letter).
33. d'Elia, G. 1981. Benzodiazepines and effectiveness of ECT. Br. J. Psychiatry **140:** 322–323 (letter).
34. Johnstone, E. C., T. J. Crow, J. F. W. Deakin, C. D. Frith, K. McPherson, P. G. Lawler & M. Stevens. 1981. Northwick Park ECT trial. Lancet **i:** 842–843 (letter).
35. Johnstone, E. C., J. F. W. Deakin, P. Lawler, C. D. Frith, M. Stevens, K. McPherson & T. J. Crow. 1982. Benzodiazepines and effectiveness of ECT. Br. J. Psychiatry **141:** 314–315 (letter).
36. Hamilton, M. 1967. Development of a rating scale for primary depressive illness. Br. J. Soc. Clin. Psychol. **6:** 278–296.
37. Hamilton, M. 1974. Prediction of response to ECT in depressive illness. *In* Classification and Prediction of Outcome of Depression. J. Angst, Ed. Schlattauer Verlag. Stuttgart, FRG.
38. Smith, K., W. R. P. Surphlis, M. D. Gynther & A. M. Shimkunas. 1967. ECT-chlorpromazine and chlorpromazine compared in the treatment of schizophrenia. J. Nerv. Ment. Dis. **144:** 284–290.
39. May, P. R. A. 1968. Treatment of Schizophrenia. Science House. New York, N.Y.
40. Taylor, P. & J. J. Fleminger. 1980. ECT for schizophrenia. Lancet **i:** 1380–1383.
41. Avery, D. & G. Winokur. 1976. Mortality in depressed patients treated with electroconvulsive therapy and antidepressants. Arch. Gen. Psychiatry **33:** 1029–1037.

Neuroendocrine Predictors of Electroconvulsive Therapy Outcome[a]

Dexamethasone Suppression Test and Prolactin

MAX FINK

Department of Psychiatry and Behavioral Science
School of Medicine
State University of New York
Stony Brook, New York 11794

There is much interest in biological markers in mental illness for diagnosis and classification, treatment selection, and prediction of outcome. This interest is not a new development, for many markers have been studied in the past quarter century. In the 1950s, we were interested in the blood pressure response to epinephrine and methacholine ("Funkenstein test"), which was used to select patients with good outcome in electroconvulsive therapy (ECT) and lobotomy. The fast frequency EEG response to amobarbital, the "sedation threshold," was used to separate patients with high degrees of anxiety and panic from those who were depressed and demented. Then various monoamine measures were studied, and in the past decade, neuroendocrine tests, particularly measures of cortisol, thyroid stimulating hormone (TSH), and prolactin, have captured our interest.

While the literature is complex, a few themes emerge that are relevant to the convulsive therapy process. Neuroendocrine dysregulation is a frequent finding in patients with severe mood disorders, particularly those with melancholia. So much so, that many authors consider a blunted TSH response to thyrotropin releasing hormone (TRH), elevated plasma cortisol levels with failure to suppress after dexamethasone, and impaired growth hormone response to insulin, apomorphine, or clonidine as markers of endogenous mood disorders. The measures normalize with clinical improvement, either in response to treatment or even when the illness abates spontaneously, as mood disorders often do.

In this report, I would like to review two aspects of neuroendocrine studies which have received much recent attention—the evidence for the dexamethasone suppression test (DST) as a predictor of clinical outcome, and prolactin release as an index of the centrencephalic activity of treatments.

DST AS PREDICTOR OF CLINICAL OUTCOME

Cortisol dysregulation characterizes the active phase of many psychiatric patients, particularly those who are severely depressed with melancholia. The changes in cortisol measures with clinical course have come under extensive study, and both Carroll[9] and Baldessarini and Arana[6] have summarized these findings. Carroll writes: "As patients improve with treatment their DST responses gradually approach normal values. When

[a]Aided, in part, by grants from the International Association for Psychiatric Research, Inc., St. James, New York 11780.

the test results convert to normal before significant clinical change is evident, this is usually a good prognostic sign that the patient will eventually respond."[9] He summarizes seven studies of DST conversion in relation to clinical response. All cases had abnormal DSTs on admission. Of 102 patients, 35 still had abnormal DST tests on discharge, and of these, 83% had a poor outcome even though treatment was continued in most cases. In two studies, suicides were recorded among the patients with persistently abnormal DSTs. In contrast, 90% of the patients whose DSTs normalized had a good short-term response to treatment and were free of relapse for up to six months. (See TABLE 1.)

Baldessarini and Arana reach a similar conclusion. They summarize the data of 13 reports in patients with severe depression.[6] Of 136 depressed patients who were DST nonsuppressors at initial assessment, 88 (65%) became cortisol suppressors to dexamethasone either during their treatment course or at follow-up (several weeks to six months). They write: "Among depressed patients whose DST normalized, only 17/88 (19.3%) had a poor clinical outcome. In contrast, 38/48 (79.2%) of the patients who persisted as DST(+) cortisol non-suppressors were found to have a poor clinical outcome with recrudescence of symptoms, rehospitalization or, in several cases, attempted or successful suicides ($X^2y = 44$; 1 df, $p = 0.0001$)."[6] (See TABLE 2.)

TABLE 1. DST Normalization and Clinical Outcome[a]

	DST Normalized		DST Not Normalized	
	Poor Outcome	Good Outcome	Poor Outcome	Good Outcome
Carroll 1972	—	—	7	0
Greden, 1980	2	8	4	0
Papakostas, 1981	0	5	3	1
Holsboer, 1982	0	16	4	0
Targum, 1982	3	16	3	3
Yerevanian, 1983	0	4	10	0
Nemeroff, 1983	2	11	5	2
TOTALS	7	60	36	6
	Chi squared p = 0.0001			

[a]Data from Reference 9.

ECT has been a feature in only a few of these studies, since most patients have been treated with tricyclic antidepressants. Yet, some reports exist. Albala *et al.* studied the effects of ECT in 6 unipolar depressed patients with abnormal DSTs on admission to the hospital.[2] Five of 6 converted, and these had a satisfactory clinical outcome; in 1 patient, the test did not normalize and this subject had a poor clinical outcome. In another report from this group, Greden *et al.* compared the clinical results in 10 unipolar or bipolar depressed patients who had an abnormal DST on admission and a normal test on discharge with 4 patients whose abnormal DST on admission had not normalized at discharge.[16] On all measures, those patients whose DST failed to normalize showed substantially less improvement. Four patients were treated with ECT; in 3 the tests normalized, and the response was evaluated as favorable. In 1 patient, the DST did not normalize, and she was readmitted within six weeks, treated with ECT again, and this time the DST normalized. (Further outcome was not reported.)

The findings were the same in our study.[25] In a sample of 50 hospitalized male veteran patients, we identified 14 with unipolar depression and melancholia who were treated with ECT. Ten exhibited abnormal DSTs before treatment. With ECT, symptoms of depression were reduced in all patients. The DST tests normalized in 8. In follow-up to nine months after treatment, 6 of the 8 remained well, and 2 had relapsed. Of the 6 patients with abnormal DSTs at the end of treatment, 3 were discharged from the hospital, but 2 were readmitted and 1 died in suicide within two months of discharge; and 3 were not dischargeable from the hospital.

Coryell examined the DST response in 42 depressed patients treated with ECT and reported that 21 patients with an initially abnormal DST response had better outcomes according to global ratings at the end of treatment than did patients with initially normal DSTs.[12] But the outcome was not poor in either group, with only 3 patients with initially normal DSTs being rated as unimproved at discharge. In a six-month follow-up of these patients, Coryell and Zimmerman failed to find any differences among the suppressors and nonsuppressors.[13] Indeed, they reported that the 9 patients whose DSTs had converted at discharge from abnormal to normal were less likely to have a sustained remission than were the 6 patients whose DSTs remained abnormal.

In a study of 18 severely depressed psychiatric inpatients with a positive DST on admission, Nemeroff and Evans treated 6 with ECT.[22] In each the DST normalized, and each was rated as asymptomatic at follow-up. Of the 12 patients treated with medications alone, 5 were nonsuppressors at the end of treatment and all required either further inpatient care or were symptomatic within 2 weeks to 4 months. Of the

TABLE 2. Clinical Outcome and DST Status on Follow-up of Depression[a]

		Rate of Poor Clinical Outcome	
Study (ref.)	Year	DST Normalized	DST Remained or Again Became (+)
TOTALS (%)	(n = 13 reports, 136 subjects)	17/88[b] (19.3%)	38/48[b] (79.2%)

[a]Data from Reference 6.
[b]$p < 0.0001$ by chi squared.

suppressors, 2 were readmitted within 2 months, and 5 were rated as asymptomatic in follow-up to 13 months. The authors concluded that continued cortisol nonsuppression was associated with poor clinical response or high risk of relapse.

Ames *et al.* studied 90 patients with primary depressive illness and reported that among 13 patients treated with ECT, they found the same degree of improvement in the Hamilton scale for the 6 nonsuppressors and the 7 suppressors at the time of first testing.[3] These authors do not provide data as to outcome, but in their discussion they write: "It is our present practice to continue ECT in non-suppressors until normal suppression occurs. Further studies are needed to see whether this will help prevent the relapses that are common after ECT treatment."[3]

Similar results were reported by Yerevanian *et al.* who reported DST and clinical results in 14 patients with Research Diagnostic Criteria (RDC) diagnoses of major depressive disorders with nonsuppressing DSTs on admission.[30] Four of the patients received courses of ECT; of these, the DST tests normalized in 2 and they were doing very well on follow-up; 2 failed to normalize—1 was readmitted within two weeks and 1 was persistently anhedonic and unable to work. The findings among the drug-treated patients were similar with all nonnormalizers doing poorly on follow-up, and 3 committing suicide. Similar observations and conclusions were reached by Holsboer *et al.*,[18] Greden *et al.*,[17] and Katona and Aldridge.[19]

While the prognosis for good outcome after a course of ECT is unrelated to the state of the pretreatment DST, the failure of the DST to normalize in a depressed patient is a cause for clinical concern and the serious consideration of further treatment.

PROLACTIN RESPONSE TO ECT

Plasma prolactin levels are another neuroendocrine measure of interest. There is a sharp increase in plasma prolactin after a grand-mal seizure, with peak activity about 30 minutes after the seizure and a rapid fall to baseline levels within 1 to 2 hours. This finding is so characteristic, that Trimble suggested that this increase be used to differentiate an epileptic fit from hysteria.[29] Similar increases occur after complex partial seizures[26] and during each seizure in convulsive therapy, both in patients with schizophrenia[5,8,21] and in depressive disorders.[23,24] The increase is found despite basal high levels which occur with the administration of chlorpromazine[20] or neuroleptic medication;[7] and the increase is not influenced by benzodiazepines.[4,7]

The significance of the prolactin release for the ECT process remains unclear. Does the plasma prolactin increase reflect a nonspecific release of humoral substances secondary to the physical stress of a seizure? Or does the prolactin release reflect a specific aspect of the seizure, with significance for the convulsive therapy process? When these increases in prolactin with seizures were first described, many sought for the persistence of plasma prolactin levels during the course of ECT, paralleling the clinical course perhaps. But no relationship between the level or the amount of prolactin released in successive seizures and the clinical course was found. The amount of prolactin released after the fifth or sixth seizure seemed to be the same as after the first, with the same time course, and with the levels returning to baseline within one to two hours after the seizure.

In the Northwick Park ECT and sham-ECT study, prolactin (PRL), cortisol, growth hormone (GH), and TSH serum levels were measured before and 15 minutes after the first and the last treatments in 62 patients receiving either eight real or eight sham treatments. Prolactin levels increased in the patients with real seizures, with the degree of effect attenuated by about 30% by the end of the treatment course. Cortisol increased without attenuation in the series, and no changes were noted for growth hormone and TSH.[14] A similar decrease in the prolactin response to seizures with successive treatments is reported by Abrams and Swartz.[1]

Skrabenek *et al.* reported differences in time course of release for GH, follicle stimulating hormone (FSH), PRL, and luteinizing hormone (LH), but not for TRH and substance P, and concluded that the release of these substances was best interpreted as a nonspecific stress response.[27] But Whalley *et al.* found differences in release rates for three neuroendocrine substances (prolactin, nicotine-stimulated neurophysin, and estrogen-stimulated neurophysin) and concluded that hormone release was a specific effect of seizures.[31] Differential effects on neuroendocrine release were also reported by Christie *et al.* and Coppen *et al.*[10,11]

Balldin found elevations in serum prolactin at 15 minutes after ECT seizures in 35 of 37 patients.[7] The increase in serum prolactin was statistically related to the duration of the seizure but not to the duration of the stimulus. Swartz and Abrams report that postictal serum prolactin levels tend to be greater for seizures through bilateral electrode placements than after unilateral electrode placement, concluding that the differences reflected greater hypothalamic stimulating effects of bilateral seizures.[28] In another report, Abrams and Swartz find an inverse relationship between the mean prolactin release for the first four treatments and outcome ratings, with the larger prolactin response associated with a slower treatment response.[1]

DISCUSSION

What can we make of these observations? These two indices of neuroendocrine function, cortisol regulation and prolactin release, are clearly of interest in the ECT process. The various findings reflect dramatic changes in the hypothalamic-pituitary neuroendocrine systems as a result of seizures.

Studies of cortisol seem to bear on clinical issues, particularly on the severity of the symptomatology and the resolution of the depressive illness. In our own practice, we are encouraged to repeat DST measures in our patients at biweekly intervals during a course of ECT, and failure of the test to normalize by the end of our course of treatment causes us considerable concern. But the studies are clearly incomplete, and we are left with many questions. Does the DST have prognostic significance, or is its merit chiefly as an index of the severity of the depressive disorder? Is normalization of the DST a valid end point to a course of therapy? If the DST does not normalize, should treatments continue? What is the significance, if any, of a normal DST at the initial evaluation for ECT treatment?

Prolactin levels seem unrelated to issues of mood or severity of depressive symptoms, but bear relationships to the seizure itself. Plasma prolactin level at 15 to 45 minutes after a seizure is an index to the intensity of the seizure. At the minimum, prolactin levels provide yet another index of a cerebral seizure. Further study may help us resolve the questions of therapeutic efficacy and equivalence among seizures induced by different currents or through different electrode placements. As with the studies of cortisol, the studies are incomplete and we are left with many questions. Is prolactin release a specific effect of seizures and their duration or is the release a nonspecific stress effect? Do the levels or do changes in the levels bear relations to the clinical outcome, or to the brain changes induced by the course of treatment? What is the relation of prolactin release to the release of other pituitary and hypothalamic peptides, and do measures of other peptides bear relations to clinical issues in the ECT process?

These studies help our understanding of the antidepressant activity of ECT. At the time that we were first studying the relationship between DST and TRH measures and the ECT process, much interest was being shown in the behavioral effects of peptides and peptide fragments, notably $ACTH_{4-10}$, $ACTH_{4-9}$, vasopressin, des-Tyr-gamma-endorphin, and beta-endorphin. These reports, and our experience with the DST and TRH tests, led Jan-Otto Ottosson and myself to suggest that neuroendocrine dysregulation may be a hallmark of syndromes responsive to convulsive therapy.[15] We proposed that the antidepressant efficacy of ECT depended on the release of peptides or other behaviorally active substances from centrencephalic (hypothalamic) stores. The recent experiences with cortisol and prolactin are encouraging, and further study of the pathophysiology and behavioral effects of brain peptides is clearly warranted, not only for an understanding of the ECT process, but of mood disorders as well.

REFERENCES

1. Abrams, R. & C. M. Swartz. 1985. ECT and prolactin release: relation to treatment response in melancholia. Convulsive Ther. **1:** 38–42.
2. Albala, A. A., J. F. Greden, J. Tarika & B. J. Carroll. 1981. Changes in serial

dexamethasone suppression tests among unipolar depressives receiving electroconvulsive treatment. Biol. Psychiatry **16:** 551–560.
3. Ames, D., G. Burrows, B. Davies, K. Maguire & T. Norman. 1984. A study of the dexamethasone suppression test in hospitalized depressed patients. Br. J. Psychiatry **144:** 311–313.
4. Arato, M. & G. Bagdy. 1982. Neuroendocrine study of the mechanism of action of electroconvulsive therapy. Neuropsychobiology **8:** 162–168.
5. Arato, M., A. Erdos, M. Kurcz, I. Vermes & M. Fekete. 1981. Studies on the prolactin response induced by electroconvulsive therapy in schizophrenics. Acta Psychiatr. Scand. **61:** 239–244.
6. Baldessarini, R. & G. W. Arana. 1985. Does the dexamethasone suppression test have clinical utility in psychiatry? J. Clin. Psychiatry **42:** 25–29.
7. Balldin, J. 1982. Factors influencing prolactin release induced by electroconvulsive therapy. Acta Psychiatr. Scand. **65:** 365–369.
8. Carchedi, F., P. Falaschi, M. Casacchia, A. Rocco, G. Meco, R. Cerbo, M. Saini & G. Frajese. 1978. Modificazioni della prolattina ematica in corso di terapia elettroconvulsivante (changes in blood prolactin during electroconvulsive therapy). Boll. Soc. Ital. Biol. Sper. **54:** 709–711.
9. Carroll, B. J. 1984. Dexamethasone suppression test. Adv. Biochem. Psychopharmacol. **39:** 179–188.
10. Christie, J. E., L. J. Whalley, N. S. Brown & H. Dick. 1982. Effect of ECT on the neuroendocrine response to apomorphine in severely depressed patients. Br. J. Psychiatry **140:** 268–273.
11. Coppen, A., V. A. Rao, M. Bishop, M. T. Abou-Saleh & K. Wood. 1980. Neuroendocrine studies in affective disorders. I. Plasma prolactin response to thyrotropin-releasing hormone in affective disorders: effect of ECT. J. Affective Dis. **2:** 311–315.
12. Coryell, W. 1982. Hypothalamic-pituitary-adrenal axis abnormality and ECT response. Psychiatry Res. **6:** 283–291.
13. Coryell, W. & M. Zimmerman. 1983. The dexamethasone suppression test and ECT outcome: a six-month follow-up. Biol. Psychiatry **18:** 21–27.
14. Deakin, J. F., I. N. Ferrier, T. J. Crow, E. C. Johnstone & P. Lawler. 1983. Effects of ECT on pituitary hormone release: relationship to seizure, clinical variables and outcome. Br. J. Psychiatry **143:** 618–624.
15. Fink, M. & J.-O. Ottosson. 1980. A theory of convulsive therapy in endogenous depression: significance of hypothalamic functions. Psychiatry Res. **2:** 49–61.
16. Greden, J. F., A. A. Albala, R. F. Haskett, N. M. James, L. Goodman, M. Steiner & B. J. Carroll. 1980. Normalization of the dexamethasone suppression test: a laboratory index of recovery from endogenous depression. Biol. Psychiatry **15:** 449–458.
17. Greden, J. F., R. Gardner, D. King, B. Grunhaus, B. J. Carroll & Z. Kronfol. 1983. Dexamethasone suppression tests in antidepressant treatment of melancholia. Arch. Gen. Psychiatry **40:** 493–500.
18. Holsboer, F., R. Liebl & E. Hofschuster. 1982. Repeated dexamethasone suppression test during depressive illness: normalisation of test result compared to clinical improvement. J. Affective Dis. **4:** 93-101.
19. Katona, C. L. & C. R. Aldridge. 1984. Prediction of ECT response. Neuropharmacology **23:** 281–283.
20. Klimes, I., M. Vigas, J. Jurcovicova & V. Wiedermann. 1978. Serum prolactin after electroconvulsive therapy in man. Endokrinologie **72:** 371–373.
21. Meco, G., M. Casacchia, F. Carchedi, P. Falaschi, A. Rocco & G. Frajese. 1978. Prolactin response in repeated electroconvulsive therapy in acute schizophrenia. Lancet **1:** 999.
22. Nemeroff, C. B. & D. L. Evans. 1984. Correlation between the dexamethasone suppression test in depressed patients and clinical response. Am. J. Psychiatry **141:** 247–249.
23. O'Dea, J. P., D. Gould, M. Hallberg & R. G. Wieland. 1978. Prolactin changes during electroconvulsive therapy. Am. J. Psychiatry **135:** 609–611.

24. ÖHMAN, R., J. WALINDER, J. BALLDIN & L. WALLIN. 1976. Prolactin response to electroconvulsive therapy. Lancet **2:** 936–937.
25. PAPAKOSTAS, Y., M. FINK, J. LEE, P. IRWIN & L. JOHNSON. 1981. Neuroendocrine measures in psychiatric patients: course and outcome with ECT. Psychiatry Res. **4:** 55–64.
26. PRITCHARD, P. B., III, B. B. WANNAMAKER, J. SAGEL, R. NAIR & C. DEVILLIER. 1983. Endocrine function following complex partial seizures. Ann. Neurol. **14:** 14–27.
27. SKRABANEK, P., A. BALFE, M. WEBB, J. MAGUIRE & D. POWELL. 1981. Electroconvulsive therapy (ECT) increases plasma growth hormone, prolactin, luteinising hormone and follicle-stimulating hormone but not thyrotropin or substance P. Psychoneuroendocrinology **6:** 261–267.
28. SWARTZ, C. & R. ABRAMS. 1984. Prolactin levels after bilateral and unilateral ECT. Br. J. Psychiatry **144:** 643–645.
29. TRIMBLE, M. R. 1978. Serum prolactin in epilepsy and hysteria. Br. Med. J. **2:** 1682.
30. YEREVANIAN, B. I., H. OLAFSDOTTIR, E. MILANESE, J. RUSSOTTO, P. MALLON, G. BACIEWICZ & E. SAGI. 1983. Normalization of the dexamethasone suppression test at discharge from the hospital: its prognostic value. J. Affective Dis. **5:** 191–197.
31. WHALLEY, L. J., R. ROSIE, H. DICK, G. LEVY, A. G. WATTS, W. J. SHEWARD, J. E. CHRISTIE & G. FINK. 1982. Immediate increases in plasma prolactin and neurophysin but not other hormones after electroconvulsive therapy. Lancet **2:** 1064–1068.

Electroconvulsive Therapy in the Treatment of Manic Episodes

JOYCE G. SMALL, VICTOR MILSTEIN,
MARIETTA H. KLAPPER, JEFFREY J. KELLAMS,
MARVIN J. MILLER, AND IVER F. SMALL

Department of Psychiatry
Indiana University School of Medicine
Larue D. Carter Memorial Hospital
1315 West Tenth Street
Indianapolis, Indiana 46202

INTRODUCTION

The use of electroconvulsive therapy (ECT) in the treatment of mania has been studied much less than in either depression or schizophrenia. Nevertheless, clinicians have relied upon ECT for relieving symptoms during acute manic episodes and maintenance ECT has been used occasionally to prevent recurrences. Task force reports and surveys of practicing psychiatrists indicate that ECT is still widely accepted as a treatment for mania and that mania is the third most common indication cited for ECT.[1–8]

In the predrug era literature, there was disagreement about the usefulness of ECT in the management of manic states. Some psychiatrists judged ECT to be as effective for the treatment of mania as it was for depression, whereas others considered it less so, requiring more seizures or daily or multiple daily ECT to produce remission. Overall efficacy was estimated from 62% to 75%, suggesting that ECT was not as effective in mania as in severe depression but perhaps more effective than in schizophrenia.[9,10] There was also controversy about whether or not ECT-treated manics were more vulnerable to relapse or early recurrence, although opposite viewpoints were also expressed. Later, retrospective studies compared ECT with neuroleptic medications and with no definitive treatment, showing that both somatic therapies were superior to no treatment, with minimal differences between ECT and neuroleptics.[11–13]

Thus far there have been no prospective studies comparing ECT and neuroleptics or ECT with lithium, now the standard treatment for manic illness. Recently interest has also been expressed in the place of carbamazepine (CBZ), and it has been suggested that ECT and CBZ may share common therapeutic mechanisms, wherein anticonvulsant effects of both treatments act to stabilize limbic system dysfunctions.[14] Concern is still expressed about whether ECT may or may not increase the risk of recurrence or induce rapid cycling in bipolar illnesses.[15,16] (In this regard, tricyclic and other antidepressant drugs have also been implicated in aggravating mood swings but CBZ in particular has not.) Other issues of importance are possible toxic interactions between lithium and ECT which preclude the use of the two treatments simultaneously.[17,18]

METHODS AND SUBJECTS

The data to be reported are from an ongoing randomized controlled trial comparing lithium and ECT in the treatment of mania. This study was initiated in

January 1982 at Larue D. Carter Memorial Hospital, which is a tertiary care facility with primary responsibilities for teaching and research based on the Indiana University School of Medicine campus. It is the only public institution in the state that offers ECT. Patients are referred from community mental health centers, private psychiatrists, and family physicians throughout the state after failure of ambulatory or short-term hospital treatment.

The subjects of this study were newly admitted adult patients with bipolar disorders presenting in manic or mixed phases. Inclusion criteria required *Diagnostic and Statistical Manual,* third edition (DSM III) diagnostic criteria for a manic episode, with or without admixtures of depression, and a history of at least one previous affective episode within the past two and a half years. Thus all patients had bipolar I disorders as defined by Research Diagnostic Criteria.[19] Diagnoses were established by semistructured psychiatric interviews which included the Mini–Mental State examination.[20] Relatives were interviewed independently by a social worker who used the Structured Interview for Affective Disorders and Schizophrenia—SADS-L[19] to corroborate the diagnosis. Patients with other DSM III diagnoses were excluded as were individuals with significant medical problems, affective episodes secondary to some other disorder, or physical contraindications to either lithium or ECT. Patients or their legal guardians were required to give written informed consent. In addition to these requirements, the patients had to have a score of 7 or more on the manic subsection of the Severity of Depression and Mania Scale (SDMS)[21] and a score of 60 or less on the Global Adjustment Scale (GAS).[22]

Patients who met the above criteria were withdrawn from lithium; neuroleptics were tapered, and any other psychotropic medications were discontinued. After 10 to 14 days, baseline evaluations were completed which included physical examination, laboratory studies including assessments of electrolytes and thyroid, renal, hepatic, and hematologic status as well as EEG, EKG, and the Halstead-Reitan neuropsychological test battery.[23] Clinical ratings of psychopathology were done by a clinician who did not have direct treatment responsibilities for the patients. These assessments include the Bech-Rafaelsen Manic Rating Scale (MRS),[24] the Hamilton Depression Scale (HDS),[25] the Brief Psychiatric Rating Scale (BPRS),[26] and the Clinical Global Impression Scale (CGI).[27] The Shopsin-Gershon Social Behavior Checklist, which focuses on interpersonal behaviors typical of manic patients, was completed by research nurses.[28] Interviews of the patients were preserved on videotape for later "time blind" analysis.[29]

Although lithium was withdrawn in all patients and every effort was made to maintain the patient drug free until the baseline evaluations could be completed, neuroleptic medications were permitted for the management of psychotic manifestations, to control potentially dangerous behavior, and to facilitate compliance with treatment. This provision in the protocol was mandated after an earlier attempt to study lithium vs. ECT alone in manic patients without such medications, which resulted in dropout of all four patients because none could maintain compliance long enough for either treatment to become effective.

Following completion of the baseline evaluations, patients were randomly assigned to treatment with either lithium or ECT. At first, unilateral nondominant ECT was the form of treatment prescribed with options for the clinician to switch over to bilateral treatment if therapeutic response was judged as inadequate. However, the first six patients on the study demonstrated little or no therapeutic benefit and some actually worsened with unilateral ECT, although they responded very rapidly when switched to bilateral treatment. At that point the design was changed so that bilateral ECT was administered to patients from the start of treatment. (A retrospective survey of the total hospital population also found that patients exhibiting manic symptoms did not respond well to unilateral treatment.)[30]

ECT was administered three times weekly with methohexital anesthesia, succinylcholine chloride relaxation and intravenous glycopyrrolate. The instrument used was the Monitored ECT Apparatus (MECTA), and stimulating electrodes were positioned with measured Lancaster placements for unilateral ECT[31] and bitemporal placements for bilateral induction. All seizures were EEG monitored with multichannel recordings during the first and the fifth or sixth treatments, and with the single-channel MECTA monitor at other treatments.

Lithium treatment was conducted in standard clinical fashion. Lithium carbonate was given in two or more daily doses to achieve plasma lithium levels of 0.6 to 1.2 mmol/l. In the ECT group, lithium was withheld until termination of ECT and then instituted in the same manner.

In the first eight weeks of treatment the clinical ratings and evaluations were repeated weekly. At the end of the eight weeks the neuropsychological testing, EEGs, and videotapes were obtained again. Throughout this period of time the only concomitant medications permitted were neuroleptics, which were used as sparingly as possible. In all patients efforts were made to withdraw neuroleptics altogether, but they were reinstated if the patient's clinical status deteriorated or if compliance with treatment was compromised.

After eight weeks of treatment, lithium was continued in all patients in doses to maintain plasma levels at or above 0.6 mmol/l. Clinical ratings and plasma lithium levels were obtained monthly thereafter with a projected follow-up period of two years.

RESULTS

As of December 1984, 33 patients were enrolled in the study after meeting intake criteria and giving signed informed consent. Seventeen were randomly assigned to receive ECT and 16 lithium. However, 3 patients in the ECT-assigned group were dropped during the baseline evaluation period because of remission in 2 patients and cycling to depression in the other. There were no dropouts during the baseline period in the lithium patients. At the point of initiation of treatment, 5 individuals refused to participate, despite giving consent earlier! Three patients objected to ECT, and 2 patients refused lithium. There was no further attrition in the first eight weeks of the study, and there were no missing data. However, a few dropouts occurred later. Two patients in the ECT group refused to take lithium any longer, and 1 patient in the lithium group was switched to ECT because of persistent manic symptoms unresponsive to combinations of lithium, neuroleptics, and carbamazepine.

For purposes of this paper, data were analyzed from all patients who had completed at least eight weeks of the study as of October 1984. At that time there were 10 patients who had been treated with ECT and 11 with lithium.

TABLE 1 shows the demographic data, which indicate that the groups were very similar. There was a preponderance of males in both groups which probably represents a referral bias towards patients that present with aggressive behavior or other management difficulties. Both groups of patients were in their mid to late 30s and had graduated from high school. Half had been married, but most were single at the time of the study.

TABLE 2 summarizes some of the historical information. Age at onset was in the

TABLE 1. Demographic Data

Assigned Treatment	n	Sex M	Sex F	Age ($\bar{X}$ years)	Education ($\bar{X}$ years)	Marital Status: Married	Marital Status: Ever Married	Marital Status: Single
ECT	10	7	3	35.7	14.1	2	3	5
Li	11	8	3	38.4	12.5	3	4	4

mid-20s in both groups and numbers of previous episodes were similar. The length of the current episode prior to entry in the study was 14.3 weeks for the ECT patients and 9.2 weeks for lithium, a nonsignificant difference. The 1.2 ratio of manic to depressive attacks in both groups indicates the same degree of manic proneness. None of the patients were rapid cyclers, defined as four or more episodes per year. Scores on the SADS-L items assessing social relationships, healthiest and sickest levels of functioning, and outcome of the last episode were nearly identical in the two groups. However, the patients assigned to ECT had had ECT more frequently in the past than did patients who were randomized to lithium. Nearly all of the ECT-treated patients had had such treatment before, whereas less than half of the lithium-treated patients had experienced ECT, although this difference was not statistically significant ($p > 0.05$). All patients were taking neuroleptics, and most were on lithium at the time of admission.

Mean scores on the battery of clinical ratings done at baseline showed no statistically significant differences between the two treatment groups (see TABLE 3). The GAS indicated major impairment in multiple areas of functioning, and the CGI scores denote ratings of markedly ill.

The prestudy neuropsychological test data revealed only three significant group differences with probabilities of less than 0.05, which was not much more than chance expectation. Two of these favored the ECT group, namely, better scores on the Location part of the Tactile Performance Test (TPT) and scores on the Benton Visual Retention Test. However, the lithium-assigned patients had significantly faster reaction times with the right hand on the TPT than did the ECT patients. The remaining 41 scores were similar in the two groups. Findings on the baseline Mini–Mental State examinations revealed no essential group differences, with average scores of 26.8 for the ECT patients and 24.9 for the lithium patients. Only one patient had a score below 20. The clinical EEG examinations yielded normal findings in half of the patients and mostly mild, nonspecific abnormalities compatible with the effects of neuroleptic medications and/or lithium in the remainder. There were no differences between the treatment groups.

The ECT patients received a mean series of 10.6 seizures. The patients who started on unilateral treatment had an average of 5.8 (range 4–9) right-sided treatments followed by 4.4 (range 2–11) bilaterally induced seizures. Mean seizure duration was

TABLE 2. History of Illness

Assigned Treatment	Age at Onset ($\bar{X}$ years)	Number of Previous Episodes: Manic 1–4	Manic 5–9	Manic ≥10	Depressed 1–4	Depressed 5–9	Depressed ≥10	Ratio Manic: Depressed	Previous ECT
ECT	25.7	6	3	1	7	2	1	1.2	9
Li	25.8	6	2	3	8	1	2	1.2	4

51 seconds in the patients who were switched from right to bilateral ECT and 54 seconds for those on bilateral treatment. Average duration of epileptiform activity for the entire treatment series was 536 seconds for the unilateral-switched-to-bilateral group and 586 seconds for those who received only bilateral ECT. None of the group differences were statistically significant.

FIGURE 1a displays mean scores on the CGI item no. 1, which rates severity of illness with lower values indicating less psychopathology. Average scores for patients on ECT were better than for those receiving lithium at all observation points except for baseline. These differences were significant at weeks 3, 6, and 7. Analysis of the GAS data revealed similar mean profiles favoring the ECT group (FIGURE 1b). At the end of eight weeks, GAS scores were 70 or above and global ratings were no more than mildly ill in 80% of the index ECT group and 55% of patients initially assigned to lithium.

FIGURES 2–5 summarize the clinical rating scale data. These data were examined using a two-way analysis of variance (ANOVA) for repeated measures. In no case did a significant group by time interaction arise. Where the main effects of group (ECT and lithium) and time (prestudy and the eight weekly ratings) were significant at $p < 0.05$, the two treatment groups were compared at each time of assessment.

TABLE 3. Baseline Evaluations

	Mean Score		
Rating Scales	ECT	Li	p
Global Assessment Scale	36.2	39.3	—
Clinical Global Impression no. 1	4.9	5.1	—
Symptoms of mania	10.3	11.2	—
Symptoms of depression	4.1	3.4	—
Manic Rating Scale	17.5	18.2	—
Hamilton Psychiatric Rating Scale for Depression	36.4	32.4	0.099
Brief Psychiatric Rating Scale	43.9	43.8	—
Behavior Check List	26.3	30.5	—

FIGURE 2 shows the Bech-Rafaelsen Manic Rating Scale with the 11 individual items listed. Statistically significant differences are indicated with upper and lower case E's, meaning the ECT group was better than the lithium group with a probability of less than 0.05 and 0.10 respectively. Differences favoring lithium would have been indicated by upper and lower case L's, but in fact there were none. The ECT group was rated at some point in time as better on all items except for hostility/destructiveness and disturbed sleep.

FIGURE 3 shows similar analyses of the BPRS data listing the individual items and total scores. Only E's, indicating significant differences favoring ECT, were present during the first eight weeks of therapy. These changes were especially prominent in week 6. The first item, somatic concern, showed the most consistent group differences favoring ECT.

FIGURE 4 contains the HDS data. This time there were a few differences favoring the lithium group, such as less agitation at baseline and less weight loss at eight weeks. Otherwise, the ECT group did better, particularly at week 7.

FIGURE 5 shows the results of comparisons of the BPRS and HDS factors, which again favored the ECT patients.

FIGURE 6 displays the Shopsin-Gershon Social Behavior Checklist data, which

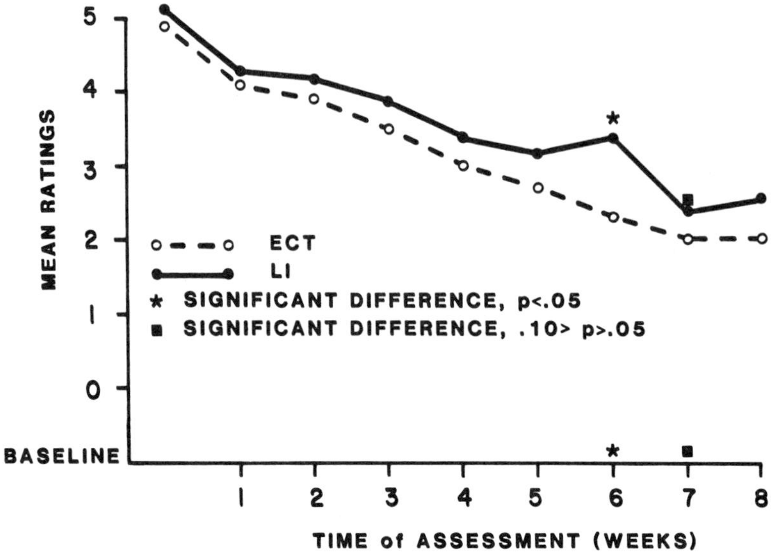

FIGURE 1a. Clinical Global Impression Scale, item no. 1.

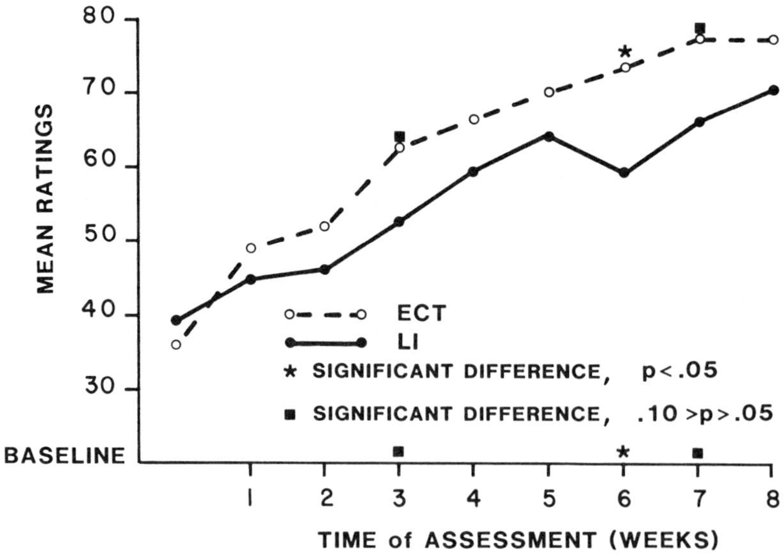

FIGURE 1b. Global Assessment Scale.

were gathered by research nurses. Findings were similar to results on the other rating scales, which were done independently by a different observer. All significant differences favored ECT, especially at week 6 when the ECT patients were rated as less angry, argumentative, and contentious than were their lithium-treated counterparts.

We were particularly concerned about the influence of neuroleptic medications, since differential use of these drugs could confound the therapeutic results. However, there were no statistically significant differences between ECT and lithium. One patient in each group was maintained without neuroleptics, and another pair received Prolixin Decanoate 12.5 mg intramuscularly every two to six weeks. The remainder were treated with oral neuroleptics in relatively low dosages for a little over a month.

ITEMS	Baseline	1	2	3	4	5	6	7	8
1. Activity (motor)				E					
2. Activity (verbal)			e					e	e
3. Flight of thoughts				e			E	e	
4. Voice/Noise level		E		E					
5. Hostility/Destructiveness									
6. Mood (feelings of well-being)		e							
7. Self-esteem									e
8. Contact		e		E					
9. Sleep (average of last 3 nights)									
10. Sexual interest							E		
11. Work							e	e	

Time of Assessment (weeks)

L = Lithium better ECT, $p<.05$
l = Lithium better ECT, $.10>p>.05$
E = ECT better Lithium, $p<.05$
e = ECT better Lithium, $.10>p>.05$

FIGURE 2. Bech-Rafaelsen Manic Rating Scale.

The mean daily chlorpromazine equivalent dosage was 350 mg (range 86–664) in the ECT patients and 238 mg (range 91–405) for lithium, a nonsignificant difference. Neuroleptics were discontinued before eight weeks in half of the ECT patients and two-thirds of the lithium-treated patients. FIGURE 7 displays these results graphically showing that drug dosages progressively declined over time.

Time-blind visual assessments of waking EEG background and paroxysmal characteristics before and after eight weeks of treatment revealed no significant group or time differences. Likewise, the neuropsychological test scores did not change after treatment in either group. However, findings on the Weschler Adult Intelligence Scale were interesting. TABLE 4 shows that there were no differences between the treatment groups at baseline or at the end of eight weeks, but there were striking changes after

ITEMS	Baseline	1	2	3	4	5	6	7	8
1. Somatic concern			e	e	e	E		E	
2. Anxiety							e		
3. Emotional withdrawal		e							
4. Conceptual disorganization									
5. Guilt feelings			e				E		
6. Tension						e		E	
7. Mannerisms and posturing									
8. Grandiosity									e
9. Depressive mood									
10. Hostility							e		
11. Suspiciousness							e	E	
12. Hallucinatory behavior									
13. Motor retardation									
14. Uncooperativeness							e		
15. Unusual thought content									
16. Blunted affect		E							
17. Excitement				E					
18. Disorientation									
19. Elevated mood									
Total Score		e					E	E	

Time of Assessment (weeks)

L = Lithium better ECT, $p<.05$
l = Lithium better ECT, $.10>p>.05$
E = ECT better Lithium, $p<.05$
e = ECT better Lithium, $.10>p>.05$

FIGURE 3. Brief Psychiatric Rating Scale.

treatment, all in the direction of improvement. This was true of both verbal and nonverbal test scores with significant increases in performance and full-scale IQs in both ECT and lithium groups.

Since this study has been ongoing for two years, the patients enrolled earlier have been followed as outpatients for several months. Estimates of patient compliance with taking lithium were based on serial plasma lithium determinations. Fifty percent of ECT and 80% of lithium patients appeared to be dependable about taking lithium with consistent plasma levels at or above 0.6 mmol/l. Differences between the groups were not significant.

These long-term patients also provided a preliminary indication of long-term outcome. For purposes of this study, recurrence was defined as a reappearance of symptoms after an asymptomatic period (SDMS score of 5 or less, GAS above 70) of at least two months during which there had been no changes in medications. To meet our definition of recurrence, the patients once again had to achieve SDMS scores of 7 or greater, scores on the GAS of less than 60 and meet DSM III criteria for a manic, mixed, or depressive episode. We also required that these observations be verified on two occasions. Patients with recurrences so defined could usually be managed as outpatients with increases in lithium and addition of neuroleptic or antidepressant medications or CBZ. If symptoms were very severe or the patient's behavior was unmanageable, rehospitalization was instituted.

At the time the data were analyzed, there were eight patients in each treatment group who had achieved remission as previously defined. Nine of these patients, three in the ECT group and six from the lithium group, experienced a total of 13 recurrences. Four individuals, two treated with ECT and two with lithium, had 2 recurrences. The five other patients had 1. Recurrences were predominantly manic (9 manic, 4 depressed) and occurred twice as often in the lithium-treated patients ($n = 6$) as in the

ITEMS	Baseline	1	2	3	4	5	6	7	8
1. Depressed mood									
2. Feelings of guilt				l	l				
3. Suicide									
4. Insomnia - early									
5. - middle									
6. - late									
7. Work & activities	l						e	e	
8. Retardation									
9. Agitation	L								
10. Anxiety-psychic							e		
11. -somatic					E	E		E	
12. Somatic symptoms - GI	e								
13. - general			e			E		e	
14. Genital symptoms								e	
15. Hypochondriasis									
16. Loss of weight - by hx									
17. - by scale									L
18. Insight									
19. Diurnal variation - A.M.									
20. - P.M.									
21. Depersonalization									
22. Paranoid symptoms									
23. Obsessive/compulsive symptoms									
24. Helplessness								e	E
25. Hopelessness							E		e
26. Worthlessness									
Total Score	l						e	E	

Time of Assessment (weeks)

L = Lithium better ECT, $p < .05$
l = Lithium better ECT, $.10 > p > .05$
E = ECT better Lithium, $p < .05$
e = ECT better Lithium, $.10 > p > .05$

FIGURE 4. Hamilton Depression Scale.

ECT group ($n = 3$), taking place in an average of 43 weeks for ECT and 47 weeks for lithium (range 13–81 weeks). Rehospitalization was necessary in four patients, one in the index ECT group and three on lithium. None of these differences between the treatment groups were statistically significant.

SUMMARY AND CONCLUSIONS

The results of this ongoing study confirm that either lithium or ECT followed by lithium are effective interventions in the treatment of manic episodes. In the

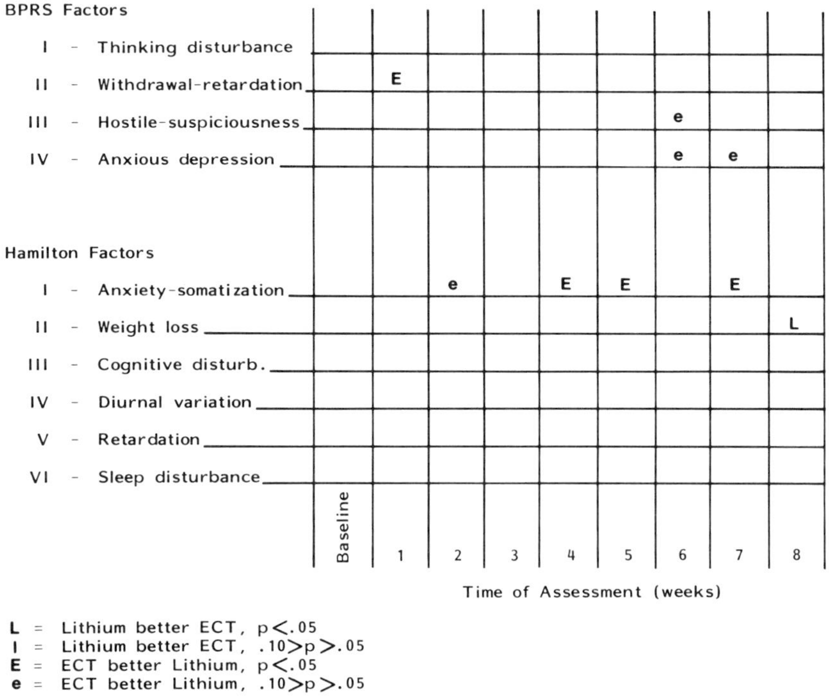

FIGURE 5. Brief Psychiatric Rating Scale and Hamilton Depression Scale factors.

population studied, neuroleptics were also required in the majority of patients early in the course of treatment. Both groups of patients demonstrated marked improvement during the first eight weeks of the study. No significant side effects or morbidity was encountered in either group. EEG and neuropsychological test data showed no differences between the two groups, and there were no significant changes or evidence of deterioration with either treatment. In fact, the WAIS improved significantly after eight weeks of treatment in both groups.

Analysis revealed that the two groups were equivalent in terms of demographic and historical data and baseline ratings of psychopathology. The weekly behavioral ratings for the first eight weeks revealed numerous significant group differences, all of which

ITEMS	Baseline	1	2	3	4	5	6	7	8
1. Angry							e		
2. Sullen									
3. Irritable									
4. Contentious							e		
5. Feelings easily hurt		e					e		
6. Doesn't get along with - staff									
- patients					E				
7. Angry with spouse/family		E					E	e	
8. Wants divorce									
9. Litigious					e				
10. Uses telephone excessively									
11. Consumates - unreal business									
- spends money									
- argumentative						E	E		
12. Writes letters							e	e	
13. Sexual - preoccupation									
- provocativeness									
14. Impulsive									
15. Antisocial acts				e					
16. Bragging									
17. Interest in gaudy/loud clothing									
Total Score							e		

Time of Assessment (weeks)

L = Lithium better ECT, $p < .05$
l = Lithium better ECT, $.10 > p > .05$
E = ECT better Lithium, $p < .05$
e = ECT better Lithium, $.10 > p > .05$

FIGURE 6. Shopsin-Gershon Ward Behavior Checklist.

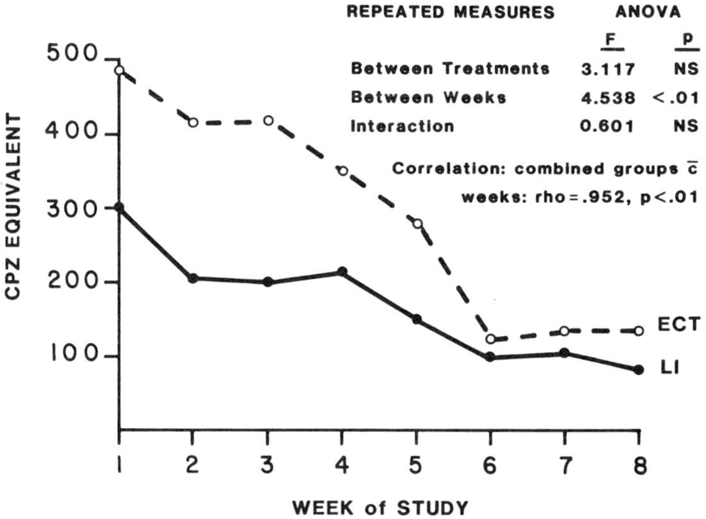

FIGURE 7. Concomitant neuroleptics.

favored the ECT patients. Neuroleptics were used similarly and conservatively in both groups, with reduction in dosages over time and discontinuation in most patients before the end of eight weeks of treatment. Preliminary long-term data indicate similar remission and dropout rates with ECT and lithium, but the ECT patients experienced fewer recurrences and rehospitalizations.

We conclude that ECT is a viable treatment alternative in the management of manic states with some short-term therapeutic advantages. We did not find any evidence that manic patients require extraordinary numbers of treatments or that ECT is associated with early or more frequent relapse. Continuation of the study should establish whether or not ECT exerts significant positive or negative effects on long-term outcome.

TABLE 4. Weschler Adult Intelligence Scale

	Baseline-T_1		After 8 Weeks-T_2		p
Subtests	ECT	Li	ECT	Li	(T_1 vs. T_2)
Information	9.7	9.8	10.8	10.2	NS
Comprehension	8.0	6.5	9.5	8.7	0.018
Arithmetic	8.7	7.7	10.6	9.6	0.038
Similarities	7.3	7.8	9.8	9.7	0.006
Digit span	8.2	7.6	7.9	8.5	NS
Vocabulary	9.8	8.1	10.2	9.3	NS
Digit symbol	6.3	6.6	7.4	7.2	0.047
Picture completion	6.0	7.4	7.9	9.5	0.019
Block design	8.3	6.8	9.6	8.8	0.025
Picture arrangement	5.7	6.3	6.6	7.8	NS
Object assembly	6.7	6.7	9.1	7.3	NS
Verbal IQ	93.0	88.7	99.4	96.9	NS
Performance IQ	86.4	84.9	92.9	93.8	0.029
Full scale IQ	91.0	86.5	96.6	95.4	0.031

REFERENCES

1. American Psychiatric Association, Eds. 1978. Electroconvulsive Therapy. Task Force Report 14. American Psychiatric Association. Washington, D.C.
2. Royal College of Psychiatrists, Eds. 1977. The Royal College of Psychiatrists' memorandum on the use of electroconvulsive therapy. Br. J. Psychiatry **131:** 261–272.
3. FINK, M., Ed. 1979. Convulsive Therapy: Theory and Practice. Raven Press. New York, N.Y.
4. LAMBOURN, J. & A. J. MURRILLS. 1978. Actual practice of ECT in a health region of Britain. Br. J. Psychiatry **133:** 520–523.
5. HESHE, J. & E. ROEDER. 1976. Electroconvulsive therapy in Denmark. Br. J. Psychiatry **128:** 241–245.
6. FREDERIKSEN, S-O. & G. D'ELIA. 1979. Electroconvulsive therapy in Sweden. Br. J. Psychiatry **134:** 283–287.
7. ASNIS, G. M., M. FINK & S. SAFERSTEIN. 1978. ECT in metropolitan New York hospitals: a survey of practice, 1975–76. Am. J. Psychiatry **135:** 479–482.
8. WEINER, R. D. & D. G. POWER. 1980. The use of ECT within the Veterans Administration Hospital system. Compr. Psychiatry **21:** 22–29.
9. SCHIELE, B. C. & R. A. SCHNEIDER. 1949. The selective use of electroconvulsive therapy in manic patients. Dis. Nerv. Syst. **10:** 291–297.

10. TAYLOR, M. A. 1982. Indications for ECT. *In* Electroconvulsive Therapy, Biological Foundations and Clinical Applications. A. Abrams & W. B. Essman, Eds.: 7–39. SP Medical and Scientific Books. New York, N.Y.
11. MCCABE, M. S. 1976. ECT in the treatment of mania: a controlled study. Am. J. Psychiatry **133:** 688–691.
12. MCCABE, M. S. & B. NORRIS, 1977. ECT versus chlorpromazine in mania. Biol. Psychiatry **12:** 245–254.
13. THOMAS, J. & B. REDDY. 1982. The treatment of mania. J. Affective Disord. **4:** 85–92.
14. POST, R. M., T. W. UHDE, F. W. PUTNAM, J. C. BALLENGER & W. H. BERRETTINI. 1982. Kindling and carbamazepine in affective illness. J. Nerv. Ment. Dis. **170:** 717–731.
15. KUKOPULOS, A., B. CALIARI, A. TUNDO, G. MINNAI, G. FLORIS, D. REGINALDI & L. TONDO. 1983. Rapid cyclers, temperament and antidepressants. Compr. Psychiatry **24:** 249–258.
16. POTTER, W. Z., D. L. MURPHY, T. A. WEHR, M. LINNOILA & F. K. GOODWIN. 1982. Clorgyline. Arch. Gen. Psychiatry **39:** 505–510.
17. SMALL, J. G., J. J. KELLAMS, V. MILSTEIN, & I. F. SMALL. 1980. Complications with electroconvulsive treatment combined with lithium. Biol. Psychiatry **15:** 103–111.
18. LERER, B., M. STANLEY & R. H. BELMAKER. 1984. ECT and lithium: parallels and contrasts in receptor mechanisms. *In* ECT: Basic Mechanisms. B. Lerer, R. D. Weiner & R. H. Belmaker, Eds.: 67–78. John Libbey & Company. London, England.
19. SPITZER, R. L. & J. ENDICOTT. 1977. Schedule for affective Disorders and Schizophrenia—Lifetime Version (SADS-L). New York State Psychiatric Institute. New York, N.Y.
20. FOLSTEIN, M. F., S. E. FOLSTEIN & P. R. MCHUGH. 1975. "Mini–mental state": a practical method for grading the cognitive state of patients for the clinician. J. Psychiatr. Res. **12:** 189–198.
21. RASKIN, A., J. SCHULTERBRANDT, N. REATIG & J. MCKEON. 1969. Replication of factors of pathology in interview, ward behavior, and self-report ratings of hospitalized depressives. J. Nerv. Ment. Dis. **148:** 87–98.
22. ENDICOTT, J., R. L. SPITZER, J. L. FLEISS & J. COHEN. 1976. Global Assessment Scale (GAS). Arch. Gen. Psychiatry **33:** 766–771.
23. REITAN, R. M. 1966. Problems and prospects in studying the psychological correlates of brain lesions. Cortex **2:** 127–154.
24. BECH, P., T. G. BOLWIG, P. KRAMP & O. J. RAFAELSEN. 1979. The Bech-Rafaelsen Mania Scale and the Hamilton Depression Scale. Acta Psychiatr. Scand. **59:** 420–430.
25. HAMILTON, M. A. 1960. A rating scale for depression. J. Neurol. Neurosurg. Psychiatry **23:** 56–62.
26. OVERALL, J. E. & D. R. GORHAM. 1962. The brief psychiatric rating scale. Psychol. Rep. **10:** 798–812.
27. GUY, W., R. R. BONATO. 1970. Manual for the ECDEU Assessment Battery, 2nd rev. U.S. Department of Health and Human Services. Washington, D.C.
28. SHOPSIN, B., Ed. 1979. Manic Illness. Raven Press. New York, N.Y.
29. RENFORDT, E. & H. BUSCH. 1976. Time-blind analysis of TV-stored interviews: an objective method to study antidepressive drug-effects. Int. Pharmacopsychiatry **11:** 129–134.
30. SMALL, J. G., I. F. SMALL, V. MILSTEIN, J. J. KELLAMS & M. H. KLAPPER. 1985. Manic symptoms: an indication for bilateral ECT. Biol. Psychiatry **20:** 125–134.
31. LANCASTER, N. P., R. R. STEINERT & I. FROST. 1958. Unilateral electroconvulsive therapy. J. Ment. Sci. **104:** 221–227.

Is Unilateral Electroconvulsive Therapy Really the Treatment of Choice in Endogenous Depression?

RICHARD ABRAMS

Department of Psychiatry and Behavioral Sciences
The Chicago Medical School
3333 Green Bay Road
North Chicago, Illinois 60064

INTRODUCTION

Although Lancaster *et al.* were not the first to apply electroconvulsive therapy (ECT) treatment electrodes over the nondominant hemisphere, they gave the method its present name, unilateral ECT (U/ECT), and were the first to systematically compare its cognitive and therapeutic effects with those of conventional bilateral ECT (B/ECT).[1] In a random assignment study using blind assessments of depression and orientation, they found that 4 B/ECT reduced depression scores by 71%, compared with 54% for U/ECT (not significant), and that recovery of orientation was significantly faster after U/ECT. These authors recommended that B/ECT be given to involutional depressives, patients who were actively suicidal, depressed patients who failed to show substantial improvement after 6 U/ECT, and catatonic schizophrenics who were "dangerously impulsive."

In general, these original observations were repeated in many later studies: U/ECT induced substantially less cognitive dysfunction than did B/ECT; the two methods frequently appeared therapeutically equivalent when compared objectively; but the subjective clinical and anecdotal impressions of many investigators were that B/ECT was therapeutically more active than U/ECT.

By 1975, d'Elia and Raotma could find 29 comparisons of U/ECT and B/ECT which they tabulated for research findings and clinical impressions.[2] If one corrects their misidentification of the study of Martin *et al.*[3] as showing U/ECT to be "decidedly more effective" (it was equal to B/ECT), and of Strain *et al.*[4] as showing U/ECT to be "somewhat less effective according to clinical impression" (it was significantly less effective according to objective measures), 15 studies reported the two methods to be equally effective, 13 reported an advantage for B/ECT, and 1 reported an advantage for unilateral ECT ($p < 0.001$).

These clinical observations took various forms, and were characterized by assertions that B/ECT worked faster; could be given less frequently; worked better in severely disturbed, agitated, manic, catatonic, suicidal, or endogenously depressed patients; resulted in fewer symptoms at the end of the treatment course; required fewer treatments; or produced greater depression scale score reductions.[5]

For example, the study of Cronin *et al.*, described by d'Elia and Raotma as showing U/ECT "somewhat less effective according to clinical impression,"[2] actually reported that 6 B/ECT reduced Beck Depression Inventory scores in endogenous depressives by 72% compared to 35% for U/ECT.[6] Much smaller differences were found in their patients with reactive depression, confirming the dictum that ECT is not indicated in this disorder.

Unilateral ECT is not used as widely as might be expected. When surveyed in 1978, 75% of American psychiatrists used B/ECT exclusively.[7] In England, 50% of senior consultants preferred B/ECT,[8] and 80% of clinics rarely or never used U/ECT.[9] U/ECT is probably used most widely in the Scandinavian countries, but even there, Frederiksen and d'Elia found that only half of the Swedish centers surveyed used U/ECT exclusively.[10]

The results from sham ECT studies are also pertinent. I found 12 comparisons of the efficacy of genuine vs. sham ECT in the treatment of depression. Eleven of these used B/ECT and found an advantage for genuine ECT. The only study that failed to show such an advantage used U/ECT (exact probability = 0.08).[11]

Six controlled studies have shown a statistically significant advantage for B/ECT over U/ECT, and a seventh has shown such an advantage for flurothyl convulsive therapy, as follows.

Strain *et al.* randomly assigned 96 hospitalized depressives to receive U/ECT ($n = 50$) or B/ECT ($n = 46$) and assessed the outcome under double-blind conditions.[4] The U/ECT group required a mean of one more treatment than for B/ECT ($p < 0.01$), and stayed an extra two days in the hospital. Forty percent of the U/ECT group required 10–12 treatments, compared with 17% of the B/ECT group ($\chi^2 = 5.4$, $p < 0.01$); and the B/ECT group scored significantly more improved than the U/ECT group on the two Clyde mood scale factors found to be the most valid indicators of depression: "unhappy" ($p = 0.008$) and "dizzy" ($p = 0.065$).

Abrams and Taylor randomly assigned 20 endogenous depressives to receive B/ECT ($n = 9$) or simultaneously administered left-sided and right-sided U/ECT.[12] After six treatments the B/ECT group exhibited significantly lower blindly rated Hamilton depression scale scores ($p < 0.05$). Following the first six treatments 91% of the U/ECT group required additional ECT, compared with only one-third of the B/ECT group ($\chi^2 = 4.9$, $p < 0.05$).

Reichert *et al.* randomly assigned 50 patients with varied diagnoses to B/ECT ($n = 27$) or U/ECT ($n = 23$) and found a significant advantage for the former method on the self-rated Hildreth Mood Scale at several points in the treatment course; significantly more patients in the U/ECT group also required an additional course of ECT within a month after treatment.[13]

Heshe *et al.* randomly assigned 51 endogenous depressives to receive B/ECT ($n = 24$) or U/ECT ($n = 27$) and blindly rated them on a three-point global outcome scale one week and three months after a mean course of 9 ECT.[14] My analysis of their published tables shows that one week after ECT more than a third of patients in the U/ECT group were rated as "unimproved," compared with none so rated in the B/ECT group (exact probability = 0.01). No between-group differences were found at three months post-ECT. When the sample was limited to patients over 60 years of age, more than half of the U/ECT subjects rated were "unimproved" a week after ECT compared with none of the B/ECT subjects (exact probability = 0.003); and at three months, 75% of the U/ECT patients were "unimproved" compared with only 30% of the B/ECT group (exact probability = 0.003). For unknown reasons, this study is quoted as showing little difference between the two methods.[15]

Abrams *et al.* randomly assigned 51 melancholics to B/ECT ($n = 24$) or U/ECT ($n = 27$); all treatments were monitored by EEG.[16] Blindly obtained Hamilton depression scale scores were reduced by 81% after 6 B/ECT vs. 56% after 6 U/ECT ($p = 0.004$). Moreover, patients receiving U/ECT required a mean of almost three more treatments ($p = 0.002$), more often required over 9 ECT ($p = 0.0007$), and were more frequently switched to the alternate form of treatment ($p = 0.008$).

Malitz *et al.* randomly assigned 52 primary major depressives to U/ECT ($n = 25$) or B/ECT ($n = 27$), both administered with a low-dose (just over threshold) titration technique.[17] Blindly administered Hamilton depression scale ratings showed a 69% reduction with B/ECT and a 34% reduction with U/ECT ($p < 0.001$); the distribution of treatment responses was similarly skewed: 70% of the B/ECT group were "responders" vs. 28% in the U/ECT group ($p = 0.002$).

Sebag-Montefiore randomly assigned 104 primary depressives to receive either U/ECT ($n = 51$) or flurothyl ($n = 53$), with and without antidepressants.[18] Blind Hamilton scale ratings after four treatments revealed no significant drug effects, but a highly significant advantage for flurothyl over U/ECT ($p < 0.005$). (It is generally accepted that flurothyl and B/ECT are equally effective in melancholia.)[19]

Thus, a number of methodologically sound studies report a therapeutic advantage for B/ECT over U/ECT, with a trend for the more recent studies to show such a difference more frequently than the older ones. I found nine controlled trials published since d'Elia and Raotma's paper,[2] of which five favored B/ECT.[12–14,16,17] Moreover, of seven controlled studies that report an advantage for one or the other method, six favor B/ECT and one U/ECT ($\chi^2 = 3.57$, $p < 0.10$).

DISCUSSION

The controversy over the comparative efficacy of U/ECT and B/ECT in melancholia derives primarily from the conflicting results of controlled trials. The following considerations may have contributed to the discordant observations and should be taken into account in the design of future studies.

Diagnosis. Endogenous depression (melancholia) is the primary indication for ECT, and patients with this syndrome should constitute the best population for comparing U/ECT and B/ECT. Cronin *et al.*, for example, found B/ECT to induce substantially more improvement than U/ECT in melancholics, but not in reactive depressives.[6] Unfortunately, few investigators have limited their samples to patients with melancholia.

Age. In her 1973 monograph, Strömgren found a statistically significant advantage for B/ECT over U/ECT in relieving depression in patients over 44 years old,[20] a result later confirmed by Heshe *et al.*[14] Older patients, of course, have a higher seizure threshold, and may possibly require the greater and more diffuse electrical stimulation of B/ECT in order to exhibit maximum benefit from treatment.

Sex. Malitz *et al.* report that seizure threshold is higher in men than in women by 50–100%.[17] Although no one to my knowledge has demonstrated a specific sex-related difference in ECT responsivity, the same considerations as already discussed for older depressives may also apply to samples of men.

Electrical stimulation. Although Ottosson reported no significant therapeutic effects attributable to the electrical stimulation alone,[21] there was nonetheless a trend for an effect that was separate from the seizure.[22] In their study of B/ECT vs. simultaneous left- and right-sided U/ECT,[12] Abrams and Taylor suggested that the greater antidepressant properties they found for the former method resulted from a direct therapeutic effect of the electrical stimulus on diencephalic (specifically, hypothalamic) structures, and quoted Weaver *et al.'s* model[23] in support of this hypothesis. More recently, Robin and de Tissera found a greater therapeutic effect for high-energy than low-energy stimulation in their sample of patients, although stimulus waveform was not controlled for.[22] The therapeutic advantage reported for B/ECT in treating older depressives may result from the fact that in raising the stimulus energy to overcome the higher threshold in these patients the physician is providing more direct electrical stimulation of critical brain areas than in younger patients, and thereby a greater therapeutic effect.

Technique considerations. Can the multiple clinical impressions tabulated by Abrams[5] and d'Elia and Raotma[2] of a therapeutic advantage for B/ECT be explained by the possibility that, with suboptimal technique, it is harder to get a seizure with U/ECT? In other words, are there more missed, shortened, or abortive seizures with U/ECT (as a function of poor technique coupled with failure to monitor seizures), resulting in an apparent advantage for B/ECT? Probably not. Such an explanation cannot account for the fact that so many investigators who found U/ECT and B/ECT equally effective using objective outcome measures nonetheless were convinced of some important therapeutic advantage for B/ECT. If their technique was adequate to demonstrate equivalence under controlled conditions, how could it simultaneously provide biased clinical observations in the same patients?

Finally, there are a variety of data that demonstrate substantially different effects of U/ECT and B/ECT on various measures of brain function.

Electroencephalograph. Several investigators have reported large differences between the two methods on the interictal resting EEG.[24–27] In general, post-ECT slow activity is greater with B/ECT and is significantly lateralized with U/ECT to the side of treatment electrode placement. Small *et al.* have also reported evoked potential differences between the methods.[27]

Memory. There is an extensive literature, recently summarized by Squire[28] and by Price,[29] that documents very substantial differences in amnesic effects between the two treatments.

Prolactin release. The anterior pituitary hormone, prolactin, is released by seizures whatever their cause.[30] Our own data[31,32] and those of others[33] demonstrate that B/ECT releases more prolactin than does U/ECT, suggesting differential hypothalamic stimulation with the two methods.

Cerebral metabolic activity. Cerebral blood flow and brain electrical activity mapping data both demonstrate large differences between U/ECT and B/ECT on postictal cerebral functioning.[34,35]

In my view, which is frankly biased in favor of a relation between brain and behavior, it would be unusual if two procedures with such different effects on brain functioning would nevertheless have identical effects on yet another aspect of brain (dys)function: the melancholic syndrome.

In their influential review, d'Elia and Raotma concluded that U/ECT was "the treatment of choice in endogenous depression,"[2] a belief echoed at least in part by several subsequent investigators. The present review suggests that such an assertion is premature, and does not correspond with objective data. Recent reports from Weiner[25] and Squire,[36] documenting persistent amnesia with B/ECT but not U/ECT, make a risk/benefit assessment of the two methods more critical than ever in choosing the best treatment for each patient. In this regard, an accurate perception of the relative therapeutic effects of the two methods is no less important than that for their amnesic effects, for if a patient who might have recovered with B/ECT commits suicide after failing to respond to U/ECT, any cognitive advantages of the latter treatment will also have been lost.

REFERENCES

1. LANCASTER, N. P., R. R. STEINERT & I. FROST. 1958. Unilateral electro-convulsive therapy. J. Ment. Sci. **104:** 221–227.
2. D'ELIA, G. & H. RAOTMA. 1975. Is unilateral ECT less effective than bilateral ECT? Br. J. Psychiatry **126:** 83–89.
3. MARTIN, W., H. F. FORD, E. C. MCDONALD & M. L. TOWLER. 1965. Clinical evaluation of unilateral EST. Am. J. Psychiatry **121:** 1087–1090.

4. Strain, J. J., L. Brunschwig, J. P. Duffy, D. P. Agle, A. L. Rosenbaum & T. G. Bidder. 1968. Comparison of therapeutic effects and memory changes with bilateral and unilateral ECT. Am. J. Psychiatry **125:** 294–304.
5. Abrams, R. 1972. Recent clinical studies in ECT. Semin. Psychiatry **4:** 3–12.
6. Cronin, D., P. Bodley, L. Potts, M. D. Mather, R. K. Gardner & J. C. Tobin. 1970. Unilateral and bilateral ECT: a study of memory disturbance and relief from depression. J. Neurol. Neurosurg. Psychiatry **33:** 705–713.
7. American Psychiatric Association. 1978. Task Force Report No. 14: Electroconvulsive Therapy: 6. APA. Washington, D.C.
8. Gill, D. & J. Lambourn. 1979. Indications for electric convulsion therapy and its use by senior psychiatrist. Br. Med. J. **1:** 1169–1171.
9. Pippard, J. & L. Ellam, Eds. 1981. Electroconvulsive Treatment in Great Britain. Gaskell (Royal College of Psychiatrists). London, England.
10. Frederiksen, S. O. & G. d'Elia. 1979. Electroconvulsive therapy in Sweden. Br. J. Psychiatry **134:** 283–287.
11. Lambourn, J. & D. Gill. 1978. A controlled comparison of simulated and real ECT. Br. J. Psychiatry **133:** 514–519.
12. Abrams, R. & M. A. Taylor. 1976. Diencephalic stimulation and the effects of ECT in endogenous depression. Br. J. Psychiatry **129:** 482–485.
13. Reichert, H., J. Benjamin, D. Keegan & G. Marjerrison. 1976. Bilateral and non-dominant unilateral ECT. I. Therapeutic efficacy. Can. Psychiatr. Assoc. J. **21:** 69–78.
14. Heshe, J., E. Röder & A. Theilgaard. 1978. Unilateral and bilateral ECT. Acta Psychiatr. Scand. Suppl. No. 275.
15. Strömgren, L. S. 1984. Is bilateral ECT ever indicated? Acta Psychiatr. Scand. **69:** 484–490.
16. Abrams, R., M. A. Taylor, R. Faber, T. Ts'o, R. Williams & G. Almy. 1983. Bilateral versus unilateral electroconvulsive therapy: efficacy in melancholia. Am. J. Psychiatry **140:** 463–465.
17. Malitz, S., H. A. Sackeim, P. Decina, M. Kanzler & B. Kerr. 1986. The efficacy of electroconvulsive therapy: dose-response interactions with modality. Ann. N.Y. Acad. Sci. (This volume.)
18. Sebag-Montefiore, S. E. 1974. Fluorothyl (Indoklon) in depression. Br. J. Psychiatry **124:** 616–617.
19. Fink, M. 1979. Convulsive Therapy: Theory and Practice: 203–204. Raven Press. New York, N.Y.
20. Strömgren, L. S. 1973. Unilateral versus bilateral electroconvulsive therapy. Acta Psychiatr. Scand. Suppl. No. 240.
21. Ottosson, J.-O. 1960. Experimental studies of the mode of action of electroconvulsive therapy. Acta Psychiatr. Neurol. Scand. **35**(Suppl. 145): 1–141.
22. Robin, A. & S. deTissera. 1982. A double-blind controlled comparison of the therapeutics effects of low and high energy electroconvulsive therapies. Br. J. Psychiatry **141:** 357–366.
23. Weaver, L., R. Williams & S. Rush. 1976. Current density in bilateral and unilateral ECT. Biol. Psychiatry **11:** 303–312.
24. Abrams, R., J. Volavka, R. Dornbush, J. Roubicek & M. Fink. 1970. Lateralized EEG changes after unilateral and bilateral electroconvulsive therapy. Dis. Nerv. System GWAN Suppl. **31:** 28–33.
25. Weiner, R. D., H. J. Rogers, J. R. T. Davidson & L. R. Squire. 1986. Effects of stimulus parameters on cognitive side effects. Ann. N.Y. Acad. Sci. (This volume.)
26. Sackeim, H. A., P. Decina, I. Prohovnik, S. Portnoy, M. Kanzler & S. Malitz. 1986. Dosage, seizure threshold, and efficacy. Ann. N.Y. Acad. Sci. (This volume.)
27. Small, J. G. 1974. EEG and neurophysiological studies of convulsive therapies. *In* Psychobiology of Convulsive Therapy. M. Fink, S. Kety, J. McGaugh & T. A. Williams, Eds.: 47–63. V. H. Winston and Sons. Washington, D.C.
28. Squire, L. 1982. Neuropsychological effects of ECT. *In* Electroconvulsive Therapy: Biological Foundations and Clinical Applications. R. Abrams & W. B. Essman, Eds.: 169–186. Spectrum Publications. New York, N.Y.

29. PRICE, T. R. P. 1982. Short- and long-term cognitive effects of ECT. I. Effects on memory. Psychopharmacol. Bull. **18:** 81–91.
30. TRIMBLE, M. A. 1978. Serum prolactin in epilepsy and hysteria. Br. Med. J. **ii:** 1682.
31. SWARTZ, C. & R. ABRAMS. 1984. Prolactin levels after unilateral and bilateral ECT. Br. J. Psychiatry **144:** 643–645.
32. ABRAMS, R. & C. M. SWARTZ. 1985. ECT and prolactin release. I. Effects of stimulus parameters. Convulsive Ther. **1:** 115–119.
33. PAPAKOSTAS, Y., C. STEFANIS, A. SINOURI, G. TRIKKAS, G. PAPADIMITRIOU & S. PITTOULIS. 1984. Increases in prolactin levels following bilateral and unilateral ECT. Am. J. Psychiatry **141**(12): 1623–1624.
34. SILFVERSKIÖLD, P., L. GUSTAFSON, J. RISBERG & I. ROSÉN. 1986. Acute and late effects of electroconvulsive therapy. Ann. N.Y. Acad. Sci. (This volume.)
35. PROHOVNIK, I., H. A. SACKEIM, P. DECINA & S. MALITZ. 1986. Acute reductions of regional cerebral blood flow following electroconvulsive therapy. Ann. N.Y. Acad. Sci. (This volume.)
36. SQUIRE, L. R. 1986. Memory functions as affected by electroconvulsive therapy. Ann. N.Y. Acad. Sci. (This volume.)

The Efficacy of Electroconvulsive Therapy[a]

Dose-Response Interactions with Modality

SIDNEY MALITZ,[b,c] HAROLD A. SACKEIM,[b,c,d] PAOLO DECINA,[b,c,d] MAUREEN KANZLER,[b,c] AND BARBARA KERR[b]

[b]Department of Biological Psychiatry
New York State Psychiatric Institute
722 West 168 Street
New York, New York 10032

[c]Department of Psychiatry
College of Physicians and Surgeons
Columbia University
722 West 168 Street
New York, New York 10032

[d]Department of Psychology
New York University
6 Washington Place
New York, New York 10003

A criticism often raised about electroconvulsive therapy (ECT) is that it, like other somatic treatments in psychiatry, has no rational basis.[1] We are ignorant of "how" and "why" ECT is so powerful as an antidepressant agent. In the case of ECT, however, this charge, in important respects, is wrong. Largely following the work of Ottosson,[2] for a quarter century it has been accepted that the elicitation of a generalized seizure is essential to the therapeutic process.

In depressed patients, chemical or electrical inductions of generalized seizure appear to be equivalent in producing strong therapeutic results.[3–5] Using bilateral ECT, Ottosson reported that there was no difference in rates of therapeutic response when a traditional electrical dosage was compared to a more intense, supramaximal dosage.[2] Blockade of the seizure discharge with an anticonvulsant medication or the use of subconvulsive electrical dosage is known to be nontherapeutic.[2,6–8] On the basis of this evidence, the most widely accepted view has been that the elicitation of a generalized seizure provides both the necessary and sufficient conditions for the antidepressant properties of the treatment.[9,10] Furthermore, there have been long-standing indications that electrical dosage and/or waveform characteristics are related to the cognitive side effects of ECT.[2,11,12] Configurations requiring greater electrical intensity are generally associated with more profound side effects.[13] d'Elia and colleagues recently summarized this view, stating: "An optimal therapeutic effect depends on the occurrence of a generalized, tonic-clonic seizure. . . . On the other hand, supraliminal stimulation does not enhance the therapeutic effect. The organic

[a]This research was supported in part by National Institute of Mental Health Grant No. MH35636.

syndrome, however, as measured by retrograde and anterograde dysmnesia, is aggravated by supraliminal stimulation. The aim is therefore to induce generalized seizure activity with a minimum of electrical energy."[10]

This view clearly has implications for clinical practice, particularly when coupled with the long series of studies contrasting the efficacy of bilateral and right unilateral ECT. Despite the continuing controversy, virtually all reviewers of the now more than 35 studies contrasting these two modalities have concluded that they are equivalent or near equivalent in therapeutic efficacy, often with the caveat that the more methodologically sound the study, the smaller the difference between the modalities in outcome measures.[14–16] For instance, Fink has suggested that impressions of differences in efficacy may emerge under conditions in which seizures are not monitored given the possibility that missed seizures are more frequent with unilateral ECT.[17] Aside from theoretical value, it may be questioned whether the significant differences in efficacy reported to date between bilateral and right unilateral ECT are of primary clinical significance. Such differences have been small in magnitude. For instance, the recent trial conducted by Abrams and colleagues resulted in perhaps the largest such difference.[18] Yet the decided advantage for bilateral ECT was reflected in a mean difference of only four points on the Hamilton Rating Scale for Depression. In this light, strong recommendations have frequently been made to rely principally on the right unilateral electrode placement and to minimize electrical dosage to that necessary to elicit generalized seizures.

The aims of the present study, in part, were to contrast the affective and cognitive consequences of right unilateral and bilateral ECT using an administration procedure designed to titrate electrical dosage to just above seizure threshold.[19] From a research vantage point, a titration procedure was important because there were indications that the modalities may differ in dosage necessary to elicit seizure.[20] Previous investigations have typically administered the same electrical intensity to all patients regardless of modality. If the modalities differ in seizure threshold, this practice introduces a confound in the extent to which dosage exceeds seizure threshold for each modality. Therefore, one purpose of the titration procedure was to equate the modalities with respect to the dosage necessary to elicit generalized seizure. A second purpose was to quantify seizure threshold for each patient and track it across the treatment course. Standard research and clinical procedures have generally involved use of a single dosage value for nearly all patients. The extent to which such procedures may involve excessive stimulus intensities can only be determined by assessing the range of seizure threshold in ECT patients. Thirdly, by titrating dosage to the minimum necessary to produce seizure and using a relatively efficient stimulus waveform, it was hoped that some of the traditional cognitive side effects of ECT might be moderated.

METHODS

Subjects

The sample was composed of 52 inpatients (34 female) presenting with primary, major depressive disorder. As is seen in TABLE 1, patients who received ECT in the past year, or with a history of organic brain syndrome or substance abuse, were excluded. Diagnosis was established according to the Research Diagnostic Criteria (RDC)[21] on the basis of interviews using the Schedule for Affective Disorders and Schizophrenia (SADS).[22] Patients were randomly assigned to right unilateral ECT ($n = 25$) or bilateral ECT ($n = 27$) conditions. The groups were equivalent with respect to the

TABLE 1. Inclusion and Exclusion Criteria

Inclusion
1. Primary, major depressive disorder.
2. Minimum Hamilton Score of 18.
3. ECT indicated.
4. Able to tolerate medication washout.
5. Willing to provide informed consent.
Exclusion
1. ECT in the past year.
2. History of organic brain syndrome.
3. History of substance abuse.
4. Pregnancy.

distribution of sex, age, education, socioeconomic status (SES), IQ, and handedness, as well as with respect to length of current episode, number of previous affective episodes, number of previous psychiatric hospitalizations, age at first episode, and history of previous ECT. The percentage of patients meeting the RDC for psychotic depression was also equivalent between the groups. The sample was largely composed of elderly patients (mean age = 61.33 years, standard deviation = 13.14) with recurrent mood disorder (mean number of prior episodes = 3.85, SD = 3.13) who met conservative criteria for lack of response to an adequate medication trial.

Treatment Procedures

At least five days prior to ECT, patients were withdrawn from all psychotropic medication except lorazepam (1 mg PRN Q12H). Patients received either methohexital (0.75 mg/kg) or thiopental (1.9 mg/kg) as the anesthetic, with random within-patient assignment to either agent at each treatment session. Atropine (0.4 mg intravenously) was administered prior to the anesthetic, and succinylcholine (0.5 mg/kg) served as the muscle relaxant. Patients were oxygenated from after the administration of the muscle relaxant to the recovery of spontaneous respiration. The standard bifrontotemporal electrode placement and the d'Elia placement[23] were used for bilateral and right unilateral ECT, respectively.

The MECTA device was used to elicit seizures. This device puts out a bidirectional, square wave, brief pulse stimulus. During each pulse, an 800 mA constant current is passed. A method of limits procedure was used to titrate dosage to just above seizure threshold. At the first treatment session, a set dosage was administered that rarely elicited a seizure (8 of 52 patients, 15.38%). Following a subconvulsive administration a minimum interval of 40 seconds intervened prior to restimulation at a higher intensity. In virtually all patients, a generalized seizure was elicited by the third stimulation. In the second treatment session, the dosage level that previously elicited a seizure was again administered. If a generalized seizure resulted with this single administration, the dosage was reduced at the next session. This procedure was followed throughout the course of treatment.

The frequency of pulses was the primary dosage factor that was manipulated. In patients with high thresholds, however, duration of the pulse train was also varied. The general aim was to have subconvulsive administrations in approximately 40 to 50% of sessions. On average, patients received 1.55 electrical administrations (SD = 0.28) per treatment session. The average percent of sessions with one or more subconvulsive administrations was 44.40% (SD = 0.17). Seizure duration was recorded both with a left frontal electroencephalograph (EEG) lead and by motor manifestations using the tourniquet method. A criterion of at least 25 seconds of generalized motor manifestation was required for an adequate seizure. The motor manifestations of seizures appeared to be all-or-none to the extent that nongeneralized Jacksonian seizure or seizures lasting less than 25 seconds in motor manifestations were rare. In such cases a 90 second interval was required prior to restimulation.

Average seizure durations did not differ for the bilateral and right unilateral groups, either when assessed by EEG or by motor manifestation. For both measures, seizure length was in the range reported for traditional, higher dosage forms of ECT administration. Across the sample the EEG measure of seizure duration averaged 60.53 seconds (SD = 19.94), while motor manifestations averaged 47.80 seconds (SD = 13.46).

The length of the ECT course was determined on a double-blind basis by a clinical evaluation team, and based on clinical response. The team interviewed patients and completed Hamilton ratings at pretreatment, and following the first, third, fifth, and then every subsequent treatment. A minimum of 10 treatments was required for patients to be classified as nonresponders to a modality, unless patients refused further ECT and had received at least 5 treatments. The modalities did not differ in average number of treatments (bilateral ECT: mean = 9.30, SD = 2.52; right unilateral ECT: mean = 9.40, SD = 2.26). Following the treatment course, patients were classified as responders if they evidenced at least a 60% reduction from pretreatment in Hamilton depression scores, had a maximum score of at most 16 on the 24-item version of the Hamilton scale, and maintained the reduction medication free for at least one week following the final treatment. Other patients were classified as nonresponders.

RESULTS

The electrical dosage (in units of charge or milliampere-seconds) that elicited the seizure was averaged for each patient across their treatments. The range in seizure threshold was greater than 12-fold (36–459 mA-seconds). Further, the wide variability in seizure threshold was not random.

Marked differences in the minimal stimulus intensity necessary to produce seizure were observed as a function of modality and sex. As seen in TABLE 2, seizure threshold was greater with bilateral than unilateral ECT, $F(1, 48) = 21.93$, $p < 0.001$. At the beginning of the ECT course, the minimal dosage value for bilateral ECT exceeded

TABLE 2. Seizure Threshold (in mA-sec) as a Function of Electrode Placement and Period during the ECT Course

Time Point	Bilateral ECT ($n = 27$)	Unilateral ECT ($n = 25$)	T-Test	Significance
Beginning of course	132.85 (68.11)	79.60 (39.33)	3.35	0.002
ECT No. 6–7	205.46 (127.35)	107.20 (62.31)	3.42	0.002
End of course	242.52 (157.07)	114.16 (66.07)	3.71	<0.001
Mean of all treatments	192.32 (94.63)	113.27 (52.63)	3.61	<0.001

that of unilateral ECT by 67% ($p = 0.002$). As expected, there was a marked increase in seizure threshold over the course of treatment, averaging 65% (SD = 53%, $p < 0.001$) across all patients. Critically, the proportional increase in seizure threshold was greater in the bilateral ECT group (87%) than in the right unilateral ECT group (40%), ($p = 0.001$).

Independent of modality there were marked sex differences. Throughout the course of ECT, males required on average 59% greater dosage than did females, $F(1, 48) = 12.13$, $p = 0.002$. Nonetheless, the proportionate increase in seizure threshold over the course of treatment was identical in the two sexes. On the basis of three variables, modality, sex, and age, 47% of the variance in seizure threshold (assessed across treatment) could be accounted for, $F(3, 48) = 14.24$, $p < 0.001$.

TABLE 3 presents mean Hamilton scores for assessments at pretreatment, following the sixth ECT, and at posttreatment. A repeated measures analysis of variance indicated main effects of modality, time of assessment, and a significant interaction (all $p \leq 0.005$). The two modalities were equivalent at the outset in depression scores. The bilateral group evidenced considerably greater therapeutic response than did the right unilateral ECT group. The reduction in Hamilton scores averaged 70% for the bilateral group and 37% for the right unilateral group. At the end of the trial, the difference between the two groups averaged 11 points.

The groups also differed when patients were classified dichotomously as responders or nonresponders. Among the bilateral ECT group, 19 of 27 patients or 70.37% were deemed responders, while only 7 of 25 patients or 28% of the right unilateral group were so classified ($p = 0.002$). This sharp differentiation in rates of response was not an artifact of an arbitrary cutoff score. As indicated in TABLE 4, at posttreatment, bilateral and unilateral responders had equivalent reductions in Hamilton depression scores. The bilateral nonresponder group had significantly greater reduction in scores than did the unilateral nonresponder group ($p = 0.01$).

DISCUSSION

The findings regarding efficacy were clear-cut. A decided advantage for bilateral ECT was obtained both when amount of change in depression scores and dichotomous classification of patients as ECT responders and nonresponders were examined. Further, patients classified as nonresponders to bilateral ECT showed greater clinical improvement relative to nonresponders in the right unilateral ECT condition.

The magnitude of the difference in efficacy was large and not in the range of prior comparisons of unilateral and bilateral ECT. As noted earlier, the large bulk of studies

TABLE 3. Hamilton Rating Scale for Depression Scores as a Function of Electrode Placement and Time Point in Treatment

Time Point	Bilateral ECT ($n = 27$)	Unilateral Right ECT ($n = 25$)	T-Test	Significance
Pretreatment	30.68 (6.97)	31.54 (8.37)	0.40	NS
ECT No. 6	14.23 (7.39)	20.78 (10.65)	2.54	0.02
Posttreatment	9.33 (7.41)	19.96 (11.66)	3.88	<0.001

TABLE 4. Percentage Change in Hamilton Depression Scores from Pretreatment to Posttreatment [(POST − PRE)/PRE] as a Function of Electrode Placement and Response Classification

	Electrode Placement			
Response Classification	Bilateral ECT	Unilateral Right ECT	T-Test	Significance
ECT responder				
Mean	0.82	0.84	0.36	NS
SD	0.14	0.12		
n	19	7		
ECT Nonresponder				
Mean	0.34	0.07	2.78	0.01
SD	0.17	0.25		
n	8	18		

in this area have not obtained significant differences between the two modalities.[14–16] Why, then, the divergence?

Currently, the duration of ECT-induced generalized seizure is the index most often discussed as reflecting the adequacy of the treatment. We used the conservative criterion of requiring at least 25 seconds of generalized motoric manifestation to certify a successful elicitation. The two treatment groups did not differ in seizure duration as assessed by motor or EEG manifestations. We did not observe the type of dissociated seizure pattern at times reported with ultra–brief pulse forms of administration.[11] On the basis of clinical observation, the convulsive manifestations of both groups were indistinguishable. Further, analyses of seizure-induced changes in cardiovascular measures, the increase in heart rate and in diastolic and systolic pressures, failed to reveal differences. Apparently, generalized seizures were induced in both groups, yet a marked divergence was obtained in efficacy.

In our view the aspect of the trial most likely to account for the specification centers on the issue of dosage. At titrated, relatively low dosage, bilateral ECT was a powerful antidepressant treatment. At titrated, relatively low dosage, right unilateral ECT was therapeutically weak. Previous comparisons of bilateral and right unilateral ECT have relied principally on traditional higher dosage administration. We suggest that, at least with brief pulse, constant current stimulation, dosage may be more critical to the therapeutic efficacy of unilateral ECT than of bilateral ECT. This view suggests that a therapeutic window characterizes right unilateral ECT. At dosages just above threshold, generalized seizures may be elicited with the d'Elia placement, have durations comparable to bilaterally induced seizures or high dosage elicitations, and yet be nontherapeutic. As dosage exceeds seizure threshold, we can expect greater therapeutic response with right unilateral ECT.

This view is compatible with the findings reported by Robin and DeTissera concerning bilateral ECT.[24] They randomly assigned patients to three different waveforms that differed markedly in dosage. The higher dosage conditions resulted in faster therapeutic response, contributing to the efficiency of the treatment. An obvious difficulty in work of this type is the confounding of waveform characteristics with dosage levels. Nonetheless, such findings suggest that stimulus features may contribute to the speed of response with bilateral ECT. Our data indicate that dosage factors may be critical as to whether or not therapeutic response will be obtained at all, particularly in the context of right unilateral ECT.

This view may aid in interpreting a variety of findings in the literature. It is noteworthy, for instance, that the Lambourn and Gill sham ECT trial stands out as an enigma in failing to show an advantage for real vs. sham ECT.[25] In this study, patients received right unilateral ECT, with a relatively low dosage technique.

Our findings with respect to the differences between the modalities in minimum stimulus intensity necessary to produce seizure suggest a confound in previous work contrasting bilateral and right unilateral ECT. With the form of stimulation we used, seizure threshold was consistently lower in the unilateral group. This indicates that when a single high dosage with brief pulse, constant current stimulation is administered to all patients, dosage relative to seizure threshold may be greater with right unilateral as compared to bilateral ECT. To the extent that dosage in excess of threshold contributes to efficacy, previous work has been based on designs favoring right unilateral ECT.

Some of the variability in results of previous efficacy trials may also relate to dosage issues. We observed that there was a marked sex difference in the stimulus intensity necessary to produce generalized seizures. Males required on average 59% greater stimulus intensity than did females. Age was also a factor found to be related to seizure threshold. Given the view that dosage in excess of threshold contributes to efficacy, particularly with the unilateral placement, variations among studies in sample composition with respect to sex and age may determine whether or not modality differences in efficacy are obtained. For instance, the recent report by Abrams and colleagues of a significant therapeutic advantage for bilateral ECT was based on a sample composed exclusively of males, except for one patient.[18] Had females been treated at the same single dosage, our results suggest that the extent to which threshold was exceeded would have been considerably greater and may have been of consequence for the response rate in the unilateral condition.

The findings of this study also indicate that there is a wide range of individual differences in seizure threshold. In a relatively homogenous group of depressed patients we found the range to be 12-fold. Clinically, we have observed that this range may be extended further when other age and diagnostic groups are considered. This suggests that when a constant, single dosage method is used to elicit seizures in all patients, dosage at each treatment may in some cases exceed seizure threshold by 1000 to 4000%, particularly when an inefficient seizure-inducing waveform is used. There is ample evidence that dosage in excess of threshold contributes to cognitive side effects.[2,11,13] Further, it would seem unlikely that any dosage-related therapeutic window would extend to several hundred percent above seizure threshold. Therefore, by not administering stimulus intensity relative to threshold, some patients may be exposed to unnecessarily high dosage and consequent cognitive disruption. By sharply minimizing dosage relative to threshold in patients receiving right unilateral ECT, there may be a loss of efficacy.

To test the view we have presented, we have just begun a new study involving random assignment of depressed patients to unilateral and bilateral ECT conditions, each at two dosage levels. The first dosage level is titrated to just above seizure threshold and the second level is titrated to 150% in excess of seizure threshold. In light of the wide individual differences in seizure threshold, it is noteworthy that conditions involving an intensity two and a half times the threshold dose nonetheless are less intense in absolute terms than many traditional, single dosage techniques. Given the findings of the present study, the most compelling comparison clinically may be between titrated, low dosage bilateral ECT and higher dosage right unilateral ECT. If, indeed, under these conditions there is equivalence in efficacy, the issue of the choice of modality may center on differential side effect profiles when bilateral and right unilateral are each administered at their respective optimal therapeutic dosage levels.

Finally, the findings of this study contradict the notion that elicitation of a generalized seizure, in and of itself, provides the necessary and sufficient conditions for the therapeutic process.[2,9,10] The poor rate of response in the right unilateral group, despite equivalence in seizure parameters, suggests that the generalized seizure may be necessary but not sufficient for antidepressant response. Elsewhere in this volume we present our thoughts on the neurophysiological factors that may have distinguished the seizures induced with each modality and why increased dosage may contribute to the efficacy of right unilateral ECT.[26]

The finding of poor clinical response with dosage titration and minimization and the use of the right unilateral placement was disappointing to us. At the outset of our trial, we had hoped, as had been recommended in the literature, that such a combination would prove efficacious while minimizing adverse effects. We note, however, that titrated, low dosage bilateral ECT appears to be an effective technique. Further, the findings that generalized seizures can be elicited with weak therapeutic properties may provide a method for isolating the neurophysiological and biochemical factors that contribute to the efficacy of ECT over and above those associated purely with seizure elicitation.

REFERENCES

1. CLARE, A. 1976. Psychiatry in Dissent. Tavistock Publications. London, England.
2. OTTOSSON, J.-O. 1960. Experimental studies of the mode of action of electroconvulsive therapy. Acta Psychiatr. Scand. **145**(Suppl. 35): 1–141.
3. FINK, M., R. L. KAHN, E. KARP, M. POLLACK, M. GREEN, B. ALAN & H. J. LEFKOWITS. 1961. Inhalant-induced convulsions: significance for the theory of the convulsive therapy process. Arch. Gen. Psychiatry **4:** 259–266.
4. LAURELL, B. & C. PERRIS. 1970. Seizure and postseizure electroencephalographic pattern. Acta Psychiatr. Scand. **213**(Suppl.): 8–21.
5. SMALL, I. F. 1974. Inhalant convulsive therapy. *In* Psychobiology of Convulsive Therapy. M. Fink, S. Kety, J. McGaugh & T. A. Williams, Eds.: 65–77. V. H. Winston & Sons. Washington, D.C.
6. FINK, M., R. L. KAHN & M. GREEN. 1958. Experimental studies of the electroshock process. Dis. Nerv. Syst. **19:** 113–118.
7. OTTOSSON, J.-O. 1962. Seizure characteristics and therapeutic efficiency in electroconvulsive therapy: an analysis of the antidepressive efficiency of grand mal and lidocaine-modified seizures. J. Nerv. Ment. Dis. **135:** 239–251.
8. ULETT, G. A., K. S. SMITH & G. C. GLESER. 1956. Evaluation of convulsive and subconvulsive shock therapies utilizing a control group. Am. J. Psychiatry **112:** 795–802.
9. FRASER, R. M. 1982. ECT: A Clinical Guide. John Wiley & Sons. Chichester, England.
10. D'ELIA, G., J.-O. OTTOSSON & L. S. STROMGREN. 1983. Present practice of electroconvulsive therapy in Scandinavia. Arch. Gen. Psychiatry **40:** 577–581.
11. CRONHOLM, B. & J.-O. OTTOSSON. 1963. Ultrabrief stimulus technique in electroconvulsive therapy. I. Influence on retrograde amnesia of treatments with the Elther ES electroshock apparatus, Siemens Konvulsator III and of lidocaine-modified treatment. J. Nerv. Ment. Dis. **137:** 117–123.
12. VALENTINE, M., K. M. G. KEDDIE & D. DUNNE. 1968. A comparison of techniques in electroconvulsive therapy. Br. J. Psychiatry **114:** 989–996.
13. WEINER, R. D. 1984. Does electroconvulsive therapy cause brain damage? Behav. Brain Sci. **7:** 1–53.
14. American Psychiatric Association. 1978. Electroconvulsive Therapy: Task Force Report 14. APA. Washington, D.C.
15. D'ELIA, G. & H. RAOTMA. 1975. Is unilateral ECT less effective than bilateral ECT? Br. J. Psychiatry **126:** 83–89.
16. FINK, M. 1979. Convulsive Therapy: Theory and Practice. Raven Press. New York, N.Y.
17. FINK, M. 1983. Missed seizures and the bilateral-unilateral electroconvulsive therapy controversy. Am. J. Psychiatry **140:** 198–199.

18. ABRAMS, R., M. A. TAYLOR, R. FABER, T. O. T. TSO, R. A. WILLIAMS & G. ALMY. 1983. Bilateral vs. unilateral electroconvulsive therapy: efficacy in melancholia. Am. J. Psychiatry **140:** 463–465.
19. MALITZ, S., H. A. SACKEIM & P. DECINA. 1982. ECT in the treatment of major affective disorders: clinical and basic research issues. Psychiatr. J. Univ. Ottawa **7:** 126–134.
20. WEINER, R. D. 1980. ECT and seizure threshold: effects of stimulus wave form and electrode placement. Biol. Psychiatry **15:** 225–241.
21. SPITZER, R. L., J. ENDICOTT & E. ROBINS. 1978. Research Diagnostic Criteria: rationale and reliability. Arch. Gen. Psychiatry **35:** 773–782.
22. ENDICOTT, J. & R. L. SPITZER. 1978. A diagnostic interview: the Schedule for Affective Disorders and Schizophrenia. Arch. Gen. Psychiatry **35:** 837–844.
23. D'ELIA, G. 1970. Unilateral electroconvulsive therapy. Acta Psychiatr. Scand. **215**(Suppl.): 5–98.
24. ROBIN, A. & S. DETISSERA. 1982. A double-blind controlled comparison of the therapeutic effects of low and high energy electroconvulsive therapies. Br. J. Psychiatry **141:** 357–366.
25. LAMBOURN, J. & D. GILL. 1978. A controlled comparison of simulated and real ECT. Br. J. Psychiatry **133:** 514–519.
26. SACKEIM, H. A., P. DECINA, I. PROHOVNIK, S. PORTNOY, M. KANZLER & S. MALITZ. 1986. Dosage, seizure threshold, and the antidepressant efficacy of electroconvulsive therapy. Ann. N.Y. Acad. Sci. (This volume.)

Electroconvulsive Therapy and Animal Models of Depression[a]

WILLIAM T. McKINNEY

Department of Psychiatry
University of Wisconsin School of Medicine
Clinical Sciences Center
600 Highland Avenue
Madison, Wisconsin 53792

INTRODUCTION

Electroconvulsive therapy studies in animals can be divided into two categories. First, there are those studies that are oriented toward the investigation of underlying mechanisms. Many of the remaining papers in this volume will deal with this category of studies; therefore, this paper will focus on the second category. These include those studies in which electroconvulsive therapy is given to animals to help test the empirical validity of a given animal model of depression.

KINDS OF ANIMAL MODELS

Animal models are basically experimental preparations developed in one species for the purpose of studying phenomena occurring in another species. There are four general kinds of animal models:

1. Those designed to simulate specific signs or symptoms of the human disorder. In this approach to animal modeling, one tries to produce, in animals, certain specific aspects of the human disorder. The primary intent is not to evaluate either a specific etiological theory or treatment responsiveness. Obviously, these are important questions even in this kind of modeling but are not the primary focus. In this context, the validity of the model is judged by how closely it approximates the human condition in terms of signs and/or symptoms. The reason for developing these kinds of models is to focus on the study of a particular symptom or on a cluster of symptoms. The methods used to induce the behavior may or may not be how such behaviors are produced in humans.
2. Those designed to test a specific etiological theory. These are sometimes called "theory-driven models" and are distinguished from the previous kind of models which involve behavioral similarities but are more atheoretical. These kinds of models are indeed theory driven in the sense that a theory drives the development of the paradigm but not theory driven in the sense that one must assume the validity of the theory to value the research.

[a]The preparation of this paper was supported in part by National Institute of Mental Health Research Grant MH-21892. It was also prepared, in part, while the author was a Fellow at the Center for Advanced Study in the Behavioral Sciences, Stanford, California. I am grateful for financial support provided by the John D. and Katherine T. McArthur Foundation.

3. Those models designed to study underlying mechanisms. As mentioned before, these models will be the focus of much of the remainder of this volume and involve the development of animal preparations that will permit the study of underlying mechanisms. They are not theory driven or developed necessarily on the basis of behavioral similarities.
4. Those designed to permit the testing of treatment techniques. This relates to the "empirical validity" of models and will be the subject of the remainder of this paper.

Before reviewing the studies of electroconvulsive therapy in the various proposed animal models of depression, it should be kept in mind that there is no such thing as a comprehensive model for any psychiatric syndrome nor is it likely that there ever will be. Such a quest is fruitless. However, animal preparations have been and can continue to be developed to study specific aspects of a number of psychiatric syndromes, including the evaluation of treatment techniques.

ANIMAL MODELS OF DEPRESSION

There are at least eight different proposed animal models of depression. They include:

1. Behavioral despair.
2. Changes in dominance hierarchy.
3. Chronic stress.
4. Conditioned motionlessness.
5. Intracranial self-stimulation.
6. Pharmacological.
7. Separation.
8. Uncontrollability.

Electroconvulsive therapy trials have been conducted in the behavioral despair model, in the chronic stress model, in the separation model, and in the uncontrollability models.

BEHAVIORAL DESPAIR MODEL

The paradigm for this model involves having rats or mice do forced swimming in a restricted space, i.e., water in a beaker from which there is no escape. In phase 1 they are placed in the cylinder for 15 minutes during which time they initially engage in vigorous activity followed by immobility. In phase 2 they are placed in the cylinder for 5 minutes and exhibit the characteristic immobility. A variety of psychoactive and other drugs have been tried, and, while there are both false positives and false negatives, in general, the model has high empirical validity in terms of being a screen for antidepressants.

Electroconvulsive treatments have also been tried.[1] In this study, three treatments were given over the 24 hours preceding phase 2 (30 mA; 50 Hz; 1 second). Ear clip electrodes were used as was a Grason Stadler 700 Constant Shock Generator. This kind of paradigm resulted in a significant decrease of immobility when the rats or mice were subjected to the behavioral despair paradigm.

UNCONTROLLABILITY MODELS

The basic paradigm in these models involves exposure to inescapable shock in phase 1 followed by exposure to escapable shock in the second phase. Animals that are initially exposed to a period of inescapable shock do not easily learn to escape in the second phase even when escape is possible if they do certain things. In other words, there is impaired responding when animals are exposed to the escapable shock.

In one of the first electroconvulsive therapy studies in this model, Dorworth and Wermier, using dogs as subjects, gave a series of six treatments over three days (120 V. a.c.; 60 Hz; 0.18 second).[2] They were administered bitemporally and produced seizures of "marked intensity." This resulted in significant improvement four days later in escape/avoidance learning in the electroconvulsive therapy group but not in the sham group. These results are generally consistent with drug trials in this kind of paradigm where tricyclic antidepressants, atypical antidepressants, and monoamine oxidase inhibitors are all effective, but anxiolytics, stimulants, and sedative drugs are not.

In another study using Sprague-Dawley rats and a learned helplessness paradigm, the subjects were given electroconvulsive therapy.[3] Random shock (0.7 mA) was given via a grid floor for a single 40-minute training session. The rats were tested on day 5 when pulsed shock (0.8 mA) was given for 40 msec and then was off for 360 msec and then on again. Shock could be terminated by lever press after 100 seconds without a press. A yellow cue light went on with each shock cycle, and there was a 24-second intertrial interval. The response latency to escape from shock was measured, and a success was defined as responding in less than 20 seconds. Electroconvulsive treatments were given two times per day beginning on day 1 for four days (100 mA; 0.25 second). Earclip electrodes were used, and there were clonic-tonic seizures of at least 10 seconds duration. Controls received subconvulsive shock (40 mA for 0.25 second). A marked reversal of learned helplessness was found, both in terms of a markedly shortened response latency and in the fact that very few animals remained helpless after electroconvulsive treatments as compared to the sham controls or to the helpless controls.

CHRONIC STRESS

In the chronic stress model, using rats, subjects are exposed to unpredictable aversive stimulation over 21 days. Stressors include such things as shock, food deprivation, water deprivation, cold stress, shaker stress, light/dark reversal, switching of cage mates, etc. This is known as the chronic stress phase. Generally, rats, in response to an acute stress, will show increased activity in an open field. However, exposure to the kind of chronic stress paradigm described above eliminated the increased response to an acute stress. That is, the dependent measure is the stress-induced activation in open field testing following acute stress.

Electroconvulsive therapy treatments have been tried in this model using transpinate electrodes (0.2 sec train or 400 V at 60 Hz). Treatments were given every 48 hours for seven treatments and were interspersed in the chronic stress protocol. Open field testing was done 24–48 hours after the last treatments. Electroconvulsive therapy treatments were effective in restoring the stress-induced activation which had been virtually eliminated as a result of exposure to the chronic stress. In general, antidepressants, but not other psychoactive drugs, are also effective in this paradigm.[4]

SEPARATION AND SOCIAL DEPRIVATION ANIMAL MODELS

Experimental studies of separation are numerous and mostly involve nonhuman primates. The rationale for studying separation arises from its possible role as a risk factor for human depressions as well as from its being a paradigm for the investigation of the interaction between stressful events and neurobiological functioning. There are a variety of behavioral and neurobiological effects, and, in general, antidepressants alleviate the separation response and depressants make it worse. Electroconvulsive therapy has not been tried in any systematic fashion but, hopefully, will in the future. In one situation where infant rhesus monkeys were undergoing maternal separation as part of another study, the infants were close to death (as can happen sometimes in separation studies), and electroconvulsive therapy was tried as a last resort. It worked dramatically. The infants began eating, became active again, and returned to their usual behaviors.

The only primate behavioral study in which electroconvulsive therapy has been systematically tried is early social deprivation.[5] In this study, rhesus monkeys were reared in early partial social isolation and exhibited marked self-disturbance behaviors, impairment in sociability, and diminished environmental activity. Electroconvulsive therapy treatments were given three times per week for four weeks. (90–100 V; 0.5 sec; Medcraft, Model B24). Premedications included Ketamine, 35 mg intravenously, and succinylcholine, 1–4 mg. Treatments were given bitemporally and resulted in tonic-clonic seizures. A control group was given sham electroconvulsive therapy. Playroom testing was done two times per day throughout the study, just before ECT treatment and five hours after a treatment. The socially deprived group exhibiting the abnormal, self-directed behaviors showed marked improvements in their social activity, decrease in their self-disturbance behaviors, and increased, but appropriate, aggression. The socially deprived group given sham electroconvulsive therapy showed no significant changes.

FUTURE RESEARCH PRIORITIES

I have been asked to conclude this presentation by making a few comments regarding important areas of investigation for the future.

1. As should be apparent, electroconvulsive therapy studies have been done in very few of the proposed animal models of depression. Therefore, there is a need to conduct such studies across different models in an empirical validity context.
2. There is a need to complement the use of rodents with the use of phylogenetically higher order animals to investigate electroconvulsive therapy mechanisms. For example, nonhuman primates could be an important bridge between rodent and human research. Longitudinal monitoring of a number of neurobiological parameters can potentially be done in a way not possible in humans or rodents. Such studies could be combined with serial assessment of learning and memory functions as well as the effects of electroconvulsive therapy on complex social behaviors, an area barely explored in human research yet of considerable importance.
3. Though this paper has been about depression, it would be of some interest to conduct electroconvulsive therapy studies in other proposed animals model systems, e.g., animal models of schizophrenia.

REFERENCES

1. Porsolt, R. D., G. Anton, N. Blavet & M. Jalfre. 1978. Behavioral despair in rats: a new model sensitive to antidepressant treatments. Eur. J. Pharmacol. **47:** 379–391.
2. Dorworth, T. R. & J. B. Overmier. 1977. On learned helplessness: the therapeutic effects of electroconvulsive shocks. Physiol. Psychol. **5:** 355–358.
3. Sherman, A. D., J. L. Sacquitine & F. Petty. 1982. Specificity of the learned helplessness model of depression. Pharmacol. Biochem. Behav. **16:** 449–454.
4. Katz, R. J. 1981. Animal model of depression: effects of electroconvulsive shock therapy. Neurosci. Biobehav. Rev. **5:** 273–277.
5. Lewis, J. & W. T. McKinney. 1976. The effect of electrically induced convulsions on the behavior of normal and abnormal monkeys. Dis. Nerv. Syst. **37:** 687–693.

The Efficacy of Electroconvulsive Therapy[a]

Discussion of Part I

HAROLD A. SACKEIM

Department of Psychology
New York University
6 Washington Place
New York, New York 10003

Department of Biological Psychiatry
New York State Psychiatric Institute
722 West 168 Street
New York, New York 10032

For decades, a major focus of clinical research in electroconvulsive therapy (ECT) has centered on the question of efficacy in the acute treatment of depressive illness. Given the wealth of clinical experience derived from the 52-year history of convulsive therapy and the findings of studies examining predictors of ECT outcome and those contrasting the efficacy of "real" vs. "sham" ECT, ECT vs. antidepressant medication, and ECT electrode placements, it can be stated categorically that ECT is a powerful, perhaps the most powerful, antidepressant available in psychiatry. The question as to whether ECT is an efficacious antidepressant has been addressed, confirmed, and is no longer at issue. Indeed, as Hamilton indicated,[1] one of the difficulties confronting research examining predictors of ECT outcome in depression is restriction in the variability of the dependent measure. When distributions are skewed such that often 80% of depressed patients are classified as responders, the likelihood of identifying significant predictors is compromised.

While the short-term antidepressant efficacy of ECT appears certain, the papers in this session directly or indirectly raised a host of issues that are of clinical and research concern. Some of these issues are discussed below.

IS SHAM ECT A PLACEBO OR AN ACTIVE TREATMENT?

Crow and Johnstone reviewed the controlled trials evaluating the antidepressant efficacy of ECT and concentrated on the sham vs. real ECT studies.[2] In general, this work has indicated superior acute therapeutic effects for real vs. sham ECT, with some variation among studies in the magnitude of this effect. Inspection of these studies indicates remarkably close uniformity in rates of response to real ECT, with the suggestion that differences between studies pertain largely to variability in outcome associated with sham ECT.

The rate of reduction in depressive symptomatology observed in sham-treated

[a]The preparation of this paper was supported in part by National Institute of Mental Health Grant No. MH 35636.

groups in the Freeman *et al.*,[3] Lambourne and Gill,[4] and Northwick Park[5] trials was noteworthy, averaging approximately 40%. The acute reduction in Hamilton scores of the sham groups in the Leicester study[6] and the recent Nottingham study[7] appeared to average 20% and 30% respectively. One must question why sham ECT results in at least some studies in rather large antidepressant effects and why there is such variability in this effect among studies.

One possibility is that repeated administration of anesthetic agents is an active form of antidepressant treatment. From this perspective, it is inappropriate to view sham conditions as equivalent to administration of placebo. Rather, sham vs. real ECT studies only address the relative contribution of seizure elicitation to the efficacy of ECT. The suggestion that repeated anesthesia may have antidepressant properties may not be outlandish. Later in this volume, the view is raised that the antidepressant and anticonvulsant properties of ECT may be related,[8,9] perhaps with both reflecting enhanced inhibitory neurotransmission.[10,11] In this context, it is of interest that the Northwick Park trial involved administration of 1.5 mg/kg methohexitol,[5] in contrast to 1.0 mg/kg in the Leicester study.[6]

The rate of response to sham ECT is all the more surprising when placebo response rates in double-blind, random-assignment trials with antidepressant medications are considered. We have come to expect generally that approximately one-third of depressed patients will show good response to placebo in medication trials.[12] Yet, in most centers in the United States, the large majority of patients referred for ECT have failed to respond to active medication trials for the same episode. One might expect that were such patients to have a placebo response, they would have done so during pre-ECT pharmacotherapy. Therefore, typical ECT selection procedures may screen out most potential placebo responders. Indeed, in our comparison of bilateral and unilateral right ECT at titrated low dosage, the unilateral right ECT group averaged only a 34% acute reduction in Hamilton scores, with the difference in efficacy between bilateral and unilateral ECT as large or larger than that commonly observed in the real vs. sham studies. The sample we studied was largely medication resistant, and it was not atypical for patients to be referred for ECT only after failing multiple medication trials. One wonders, therefore, whether the relative strong rate of therapeutic response to sham ECT in some trials conducted in England is related to use of ECT as a first-line treatment and whether variability in sham response rates is a function in part of sampling differences, particularly in relation to pre-ECT medication practices. This possibility is strengthened by the fact pointed out by Gregory *et al.*[7] that 86.5% of depressed patients admitted to the Northwick Park clincal unit entered the sham ECT study.[5] Likewise, Brandon *et al.* reported that only 41% of their study patients met unspecified criteria for an adequate course of antidepressants prior to the trial.[6]

This perspective suggests that an important issue that remains to be examined is the predictors of "therapeutic" response to sham ECT. Furthermore, in some of the sham-real trials, factors were identified that were said to be associated with response or lack thereof to real ECT. For instance, in the Leicester study neurotic depression was claimed to be associated with poor outcome as sham and real groups did not differ in recovery scores.[6] One might inquire, however, whether neurotic depression predisposed to good outcome with sham ECT.

LONG-TERM CLINICAL EFFECTS OF ECT

There has been significant misinterpretation of the sham-real ECT studies in terms of long-term therapeutic effects. These studies have generally observed that a few months after completion of the trial, outcome differences between sham and real groups disappear. The importance of the follow-up data is questionable, however, since sham and real patients went on, in each study, to be administered somatic treatments, including ECT, after completion of the trial.

This point indicates that the sham-real studies hardly address the issue of long-term clinical effects of ECT. Indeed, with the exception of the Small *et al.* study in mania,[13] the papers in this session, like virtually all recent ECT research, concentrated on short-term efficacy. From a clinical vantage point, perhaps the most significant issue facing ECT concerns relapse rates following successful acute treatment.

ECT stands as a marked exception to general clinical practice in the somatic therapy of affective disorders in that the treatment is almost always stopped when patients become euthymic. Medications, e.g., tricyclic antidepressants, are typically administered for a period of months following symptomatic remission to prevent relapse within the same episode.

It is established that when depressed patients go untreated following ECT, relapse is common, with estimates on the order of 50% within two months of the end of the ECT course.[14] This indicates that ECT, like psychotropic medications, acts to suppress transiently expression of depressive episodes. It is generally accepted that in unipolar illness following a course of successful treatment, antidepressant medications should be administered as "continuation" therapy, with the belief that relapse rates may be reduced to 20% in the months following the ECT course.

This practice requires reevaluation. Only three prospective, controlled investigations have examined the utility of antidepressants in preventing early relapse after ECT.[15–17] These studies were conducted in England in the 1960s. Patients were not selected for being resistant to antidepressant medication during the acute phase of illness. The bulk of patients in these studies were treated with both ECT and antidepressant medications during the acute phase and only randomized to drug or placebo after the ECT trial. As such, an unknown proportion of patients may have responded to medications during the acute phase. In this subgroup medications would be expected to be helpful in preventing relapse.

As mentioned earlier, at least in the United States, it appears that the majority of depressed ECT patients are individuals who fail to respond to antidepressant medications during the acute phase of illness. Current practice is based on the notion that these same medications are useful in preventing relapse in these patients. To my knowledge, there are no data in the ECT field that explicitly support this possibility. Likewise, to my knowledge, there are no data from clinical psychopharmacology supporting the efficacy of an antidepressant for continuation therapy following failure to respond to that antidepressant during the acute phase.

This issue is both of primary clinical concern and of relevance to mechanism of action issues. If, indeed, previously medication-resistant patients benefit from post-ECT antidepressant continuation therapy, one must question whether ECT has altered the biochemical substrate for the action of the antidepressant medication or whether the requisite substrates differ for acute and continuation therapies.

EFFICACY IN OTHER CONDITIONS

The patient group most likely to receive ECT presents with major depressive disorder. Acute efficacy in major depression is beyond question, and it is noteworthy, as McKinney reviewed,[18] that ECS appears to reverse deficits in virtually all animal models of depression in which it has been tested. In this circumstance, it is not unreasonable that the focus of attention with respect to the clinical effects of ECT centers on depressive disorder.

The paper by Small *et al.* presents the first prospective controlled study of the use of ECT to treat acute manic episodes.[13] The findings indicated that bilateral ECT was an effective treatment and perhaps more so than lithium carbonate. While suggesting that right unilateral ECT may be therapeutically weak, this study did not address the issue of the clinical utility of left unilateral ECT, which on theoretical grounds might be hypothesized to be more efficacious in mania than right unilateral ECT.[19]

The Small *et al.* results indicate that the range of conditions in which ECT is effective extends beyond depression. While there is a paucity of controlled investigations outside of depression and mania, one might include in this range catatonic states, toxic deliriums, alcohol and barbiturate withdrawal syndromes, and organic psychoses. This wide range of conditions amenable to ECT suggests reevaluation of some theoretical approaches to investigating biochemical mechanisms of action. As indicated in later papers in this volume, a common approach has been to examine similarities and differences in the biochemical effects of ECT and antidepressant medications, with the view that commonalities are likely to be of consequence to explicating the therapeutic mode of action of both forms of treatment. Two basic clinical facts suggest greater caution in attributing significance to such commonalities. First, it is clear that ECT is a highly efficacious treatment in depressed patients who are resistant to adequate trials of antidepressants. Why, then, should antidepressants and ECT act at the same biochemical substrate? Secondly, there are no grounds as of yet to determine whether the mode of action of ECT is the same or different in the various conditions for which it is effective. If, indeed, there is commonality in the mode of action of ECT in depression, mania, and catatonia, it is noteworthy that antidepressants are not effective in the latter two conditions.

THE UNILATERAL-BILATERAL ECT CONTROVERSY

The controversy as to whether right unilateral ECT and bilateral ECT differ in antidepressant efficacy has not been laid to rest despite now over 30 comparative trials. Abrams[20] reexamined this literature and appropriately noted that the hallmark review by d'Elia and Raotma[21] contained a number of errors. Nonetheless, it still appears to be the case that a fair number of studies have failed to detect differences, a fair number of studies have reported nonsignificant trends in favor of bilateral ECT, and a smaller number have reported statistically significant differences favoring bilateral ECT.

One comes away from this literature impressed by the marked variability in methodological rigor that has characterized much of the research. Of particular concern for ECT clinical trials is the notion of an adequate course of treatment, the classification of treatment responders and nonresponders, and the distinction between rates of patient response (i.e., efficacy) and speed of response (i.e., efficiency). It has become common practice in psychopharmacological clinical trials to stipulate a minimum length of treatment prior to designation as a treatment failure. Commonly in ECT trials, number of treatments is left in the hands of blind ward physicians who may often differ in thresholds for insisting on treatment termination or modification. In such circumstances, it may be impossible to determine whether patients were nonresponsive to a given type of ECT or were slow in response and prematurely terminated. Further, it is not common practice to adopt a priori criteria designating patients as ECT responders or not. Outcome data contrasting modalities are usually analyzed only in terms of changes in depression scores. While the use of such continuous measures enhances the power of statistical comparisons, there remain two drawbacks. First, the clinical significance of modality effects cannot be easily established. It should be of more consequence to know whether, for instance, an efficacy difference pertains to a greater relative response rate in 5, 20, or 40% of patients than pertaining only to a mean difference of 2, 4, or 6 points in Hamilton scores.

Secondly, it is still unclear whether recovery is speedier with bilateral ECT or whether outcome differences characterize only rates and/or depth of response. Part of this unclarity is due to the practice of reporting mean number of treatments for each modality, regardless of response rates. Certainly, speed of recovery should only be at issue for patients who indeed respond. The number of treatments administered to nonresponders is irrelevant to this type of outcome measure and likely to be arbitrarily determined. Indeed, one can imagine circumstances in which treatment is terminated or altered sooner in an unchanged patient relative to one who has partial but inadequate response.

These methodological reservations aside, the Abrams[20] and Malitz *et al.*[22] papers suggest that the standard conclusion is no longer tenable that without qualification bilateral ECT and unilateral right ECT are equal in therapeutic properties. It appears that the more critical issue is determining under what circumstances unilateral right ECT achieves therapeutic equivalence. Weiner has suggested that unilateral electrode placements may differ in associated efficacy due to variability in interelectrode distance resulting in different degrees of current shunting.[23] The Malitz *et al.* study reported a profound difference in response rates as a function of unilateral/bilateral modality, even though the d'Elia placement with a large interelectrode distance was used. The observation here was that at dosage just above seizure threshold unilateral right ECT became largely ineffective, whereas the therapeutic properties of bilateral ECT seemed maintained. If, indeed, these suggestions are accurate future studies might consider contrasting bilateral and unilateral modalities under conditions predetermined to be most favorable to each, e.g., low-dosage bilateral vs. high-dosage unilateral. Were therapeutic equivalence reestablished under these conditions, relative side effect profiles might be considered as determinative for clinical recommendations.

REFERENCES

1. HAMILTON, M. 1986. Electroconvulsive therapy: indications and contraindications. Ann. N.Y. Acad. Sci. (This volume.)
2. CROW, T. J. & E. C. JOHNSTONE. 1986. Controlled trials of electroconvulsive therapy. Ann. N.Y. Acad. Sci. (This volume.)
3. FREEMAN, C. P. L., J. V. BASSON & A. CRIGHTON. 1978. Double-blinded controlled trial of electroconvulsive therapy (ECT) and simulated ECT in depressive illness. Lancet **1:** 738–740.
4. LAMBOURN, J. & D. GILL. 1978. A controlled comparison of simulated and real ECT. Br. J. Psychiatry **133:** 514–519.
5. JOHNSTONE, E. C., P. LAWLER, J. STEVENS, J. F. W. DEAKIN, C. D. FIRTH, K. MCPHERSON & T. J. CROW. 1980. The Northwick Park electroconvulsive therapy trial. Lancet **2:** 1317–1320.
6. BRANDON, S., P. COWLEY, C. MCDONALD, P. NEVILLE, R. PALMER & S. WELLSTOOD-EASON. 1984. Electroconvulsive therapy: results in depressive illness from the Leicestershire trial. Br. Med. J. **228:** 22–25.
7. GREGORY, S., C. R. SHAWCROSS & D. GILL. 1985. The Nottingham ECT study: a

double-blind comparison of bilateral, unilateral and simulated ECT in depressive illness. Br. J. Psychiatry **146:** 520–524.
8. POST, R., F. PUTNAM, T. W. UHDE & S. R. B. WEISS. 1986. Electroconvulsive therapy as an anticonvulsant: implications for its mechanism of action in affective illness. Ann. N.Y. Acad. Sci. (This volume.)
9. SACKEIM, H. A., P. DECINA, I. PROHOVNIK, S. PORTNOY, M. KANZLER & S. MALITZ. 1986. Dosage, seizure threshold, and the antidepressant efficacy of electroconvulsive therapy. Ann. N.Y. Acad. Sci. (This volume.)
10. GREEN, A. R. 1986. Changes in γ-aminobutyric acid biochemistry and seizure threshold. Ann. N.Y. Acad. Sci. (This volume.)
11. HOLADAY, J. W., F. C. TORTELLA, J. B. LONG, G. L. BELENKY & R. J. HITZEMANN. 1986. Endogenous opioids and their receptors: evidence for involvement in the postictal effects of electroconvulsive shock. Ann. N.Y. Acad. Sci. (This volume.)
12. KLEIN, D., R. GITTELMAN, F. QUITKIN & A. RIFKIN. 1980. Diagnosis and Drug Treatment of Psychiatric Disorders: Adults and Children. Williams and Wilkins. Baltimore, Md.
13. SMALL, J. G., V. MILSTEIN, M. H. KLAPPER, J. J. KELLAMS, M. J. MILLER & I. F. SMALL. 1986. Electroconvulsive therapy in the treatment of manic episodes. Ann. N.Y. Acad. Sci. (This volume.)
14. SNAITH, R. P. 1981. How much ECT does the depressed patient need? *In* Electroconvulsive Therapy: An Appraisal. R. L. Palmer, Ed.: 61–64. Oxford University Press. Oxford, England.
15. INLAH, N. W., E. RYAN & J. A. HARRINGTON. 1965. The influence of antidepressant drugs on the response to electroconvulsive therapy and on subsequent relapse rates. Neuropharmacology **4:** 438–442.
16. KAY, D. W. K., T. FAHY & R. F. GARSIDE. 1970. A seven-month double-blind trial of amitriptyline and diazepam in ECT-treated depressed patients. Br. J. Psychiatry **117:** 667–711.
17. SEAGER, C. P. & R. L. BIRD. 1962. Imipramine and electrical treatment in depression: a controlled trial. J. Ment. Sci. **108:** 704–707.
18. MCKINNEY, W. T. 1986. Electroconvulsive therapy and animal models of depression. Ann. N.Y. Acad. Sci. (This volume.)
19. SACKEIM, H. A., M. S. GREENBERG, A. L. WEIMAN, R. C. GUR, J. P. HUNGERBUHLER & N. GESCHWIND. 1982. Hemispheric asymmetry in the expression of positive and negative emotions: neurological evidence. Arch. Neurol. **39:** 210–218.
20. ABRAMS, R. 1986. Is unilateral electroconvulsive therapy really the treatment of choice in endogenous depression? Ann. N.Y. Acad. Sci. (This volume.)
21. D'ELIA, G. & H. RAOTMA. 1975. Is unilateral ECT less effective than bilateral ECT? Br. J. Psychiatry **126:** 83–89.
22. MALITZ, S., H. A. SACKEIM, P. DECINA, M. KANZLER & B. KERR. 1986. The efficacy of electroconvulsive therapy: dose-response interactions with modality. Ann. N.Y. Acad. Sci. (This volume.)
23. WEINER, R. D. 1984. Does ECT cause brain damage? Behav. Brain Sci. **7:** 1–54.

Effects of Electroconvulsive Shock and Serotonin Axon Lesions on Beta-Adrenergic and Serotonin-2 Receptors in Rat Brain

KENNETH J. KELLAR AND CRAIG A. STOCKMEIER

Department of Pharmacology
Georgetown University Schools of Medicine and Dentistry
3900 Reservoir Road, N.W.
Washington, D.C. 20007

Information derived from animal studies in many laboratories has formed a base for a better understanding of the mechanisms of action of antidepressant treatments. This information can point to new directions for the development of future antidepressant treatments, and it might provide important clues to the pathophysiological mechanisms underlying depression.

There is a high degree of concordance with respect to certain molecular changes induced in rat brain by repeated administration of a large number of antidepressant drugs. This concordance extends across different chemical classes of antidepressants with different acute neurochemical effects. Furthermore, electroconvulsive shock (ECS) induces molecular changes in rat brain that in at least one case are very similar to those induced by antidepressant drugs, but in at least one other case are actually opposite to those of drugs. The similarities in the molecular changes induced by drugs and ECS help to reinforce the concept that these effects are relevant to antidepressant mechanisms, while the differences accentuate the gaps in our fundamental knowledge about depression. Optimistically, the differences may be related to the greater efficacy of ECS in some patients or to differences in side effects of the treatments.

Two of the most consistent neurochemical changes that have been found following repeated administration of antidepressant drugs are reductions in the numbers of beta-adrenergic receptors[1–4] and serotonin-2 (5-HT-2) receptors[5,6] in brain. The decrease in beta-adrenergic receptors leads to a decrease in the receptor-mediated production of cyclic adenosine monophosphate (cAMP).[7,8] The functional consequences of the decrease in 5-HT-2 receptors are less clear at this time. It may be linked to decreases in serotonin-mediated behavior, but the high affinity of most of the antidepressants tested for the 5-HT-2 binding site *in vitro* and the possibility that the drugs block 5-HT-2 receptors cloud this issue. Electroconvulsive shock affects both of these receptors. In the case of beta-adrenergic receptors, the effects of ECS are consistent with those of antidepressant drugs.[9,10] In the case of 5-HT-2 receptors, the effects of ECS are opposite to those of antidepressant drugs.[6]

EFFECTS OF ECS ON BETA-ADRENERGIC RECEPTORS IN BRAIN

In our laboratory, ECS is usually administered to unanesthetized rats once a day through saline-moistened corneal electrodes, but the results discussed below are also applicable to experiments in which ECS has been administered three times a week to rats that have been lightly anesthetized.

Repeated administration of ECS decreases binding of [^{3}H]dihydroalprenolol ([^{3}H]DHA) to beta-adrenergic receptors in certain areas of the brain. In the cerebral cortex the decrease in binding is due entirely to a reduction in the number of receptors (down regulation) and appears to be a cellular adaptive mechanism for regulating incoming signals carried by norepinephrine.[9] Time-course studies indicate that the decrease develops gradually; it is evident after 4 days of treatment, and the receptors are maximally decreased to about 60% of control levels after 12–14 days of ECS

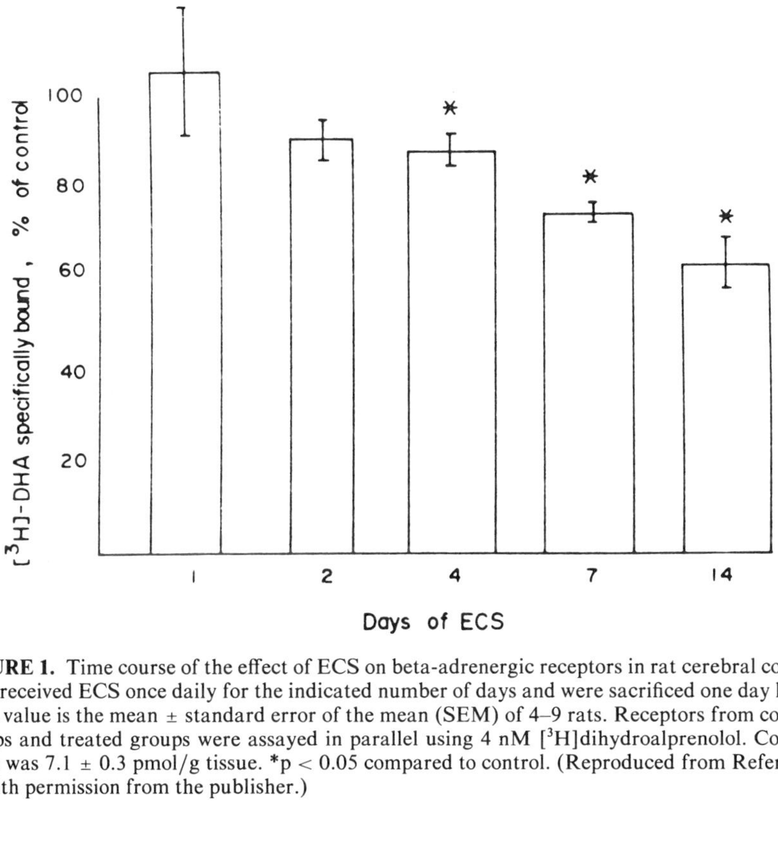

FIGURE 1. Time course of the effect of ECS on beta-adrenergic receptors in rat cerebral cortex. Rats received ECS once daily for the indicated number of days and were sacrificed one day later. Each value is the mean ± standard error of the mean (SEM) of 4–9 rats. Receptors from control groups and treated groups were assayed in parallel using 4 nM [^{3}H]dihydroalprenolol. Control value was 7.1 ± 0.3 pmol/g tissue. *$p < 0.05$ compared to control. (Reproduced from Reference 12 with permission from the publisher.)

(FIGURE 1). The beta-adrenergic receptors are still decreased one week after the last of seven daily ECS (FIGURE 2), but they return to control levels within four weeks.

The decrease in beta-adrenergic receptors is brain-region specific. The receptors are decreased in the cerebral cortex and in the hippocampus, but not in the striatum, cerebellum, or hypothalamus (TABLE 1). [^{3}H]DHA binds to both beta-1 and beta-2 adrenergic receptors, and both subtypes of receptors are found in varying proportions in most areas of brain.[11] However, the brain-region specificity of the decreased binding following ECS suggests that it is only the beta-1 receptors that change, and only those

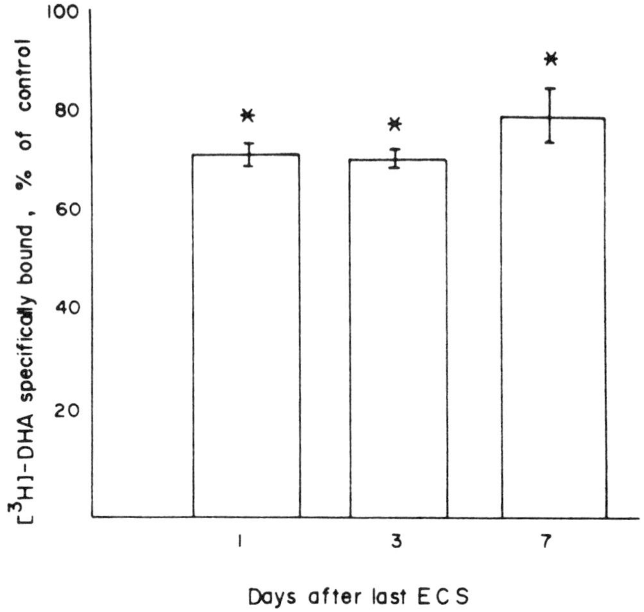

FIGURE 2. Duration of effect of ECS on beta-adrenergic receptors in the cerebral cortex. Rats received ECS once daily for seven days and were then sacrificed on the day indicated after the last ECS. Each value is the mean ± SEM of 4–8 rats assayed using 4 nM [^{3}H]dihydroalprenolol. Control value was 6.5 ± 0.3 pmol/g tissue. *$p < 0.05$ compared to control. (Reproduced from Reference 12 with permission from the publisher.)

in brain areas in which ECS activates norepinephrine axons.[12] In fact, preliminary experiments measuring beta-adrenergic receptors by quantitative autoradiography in the presence of selective antagonists of beta-1 or beta-2 receptors indicate that this is the case (Stockmeier, Rainbow, Wolfe, and Kellar, unpublished observations).

As reported earlier by Vetulani and Sulser,[7] repeated administration of ECS leads

TABLE 1. Effect of Repeated ECS (Once a Day, 12–14 Days) on Beta-Adrenergic Receptors in Different Rat Brain Regions[a]

	[^{3}H]DHA Specifically Bound (pmol/g tissue)	
Brain Region	Control	ECS
Cortex	6.2 ± 0.4	3.9 ± 0.4[b]
Hippocampus	5.9 ± 0.3	4.5 ± 0.3[b]
Striatum	10.1 ± 0.8	9.1 ± 0.1
Hypothalamus	6.2 ± 0.6	5.7 ± 0.6
Cerebellum	5.5 ± 0.4	4.8 ± 0.2

[a]Rats were sacrificed one day after the last ECS. Beta-adrenergic receptor binding sites were measured using 3.5–4.5 nM [^{3}H]dihydroalprenolol ([^{3}H]DHA). Values are mean ± standard error of the mean (SEM) of 5–9 rats. (Reproduced from Reference 12 with permission from the publisher.)

[b]$p < 0.01$ compared to control.

to a decrease in isoproterenol-stimulated production of cAMP. For example, 12 days of ECS decreases cAMP production in the hippocampus by about 35% (FIGURE 3), and this is probably a direct consequence of the reduction in beta-adrenergic receptors.

A corollary of the hypothesis that the down regulation of beta-adrenergic receptors is related to the therapeutic mechanism of action of ECS is that these receptors may be directly involved in the pathophysiology of depression. In fact, reserpine—which can induce depression in humans[13]—increases the number of beta-adrenergic receptors[12,14] and cAMP production[15] in rat brain. Furthermore, recent autoradiographic and

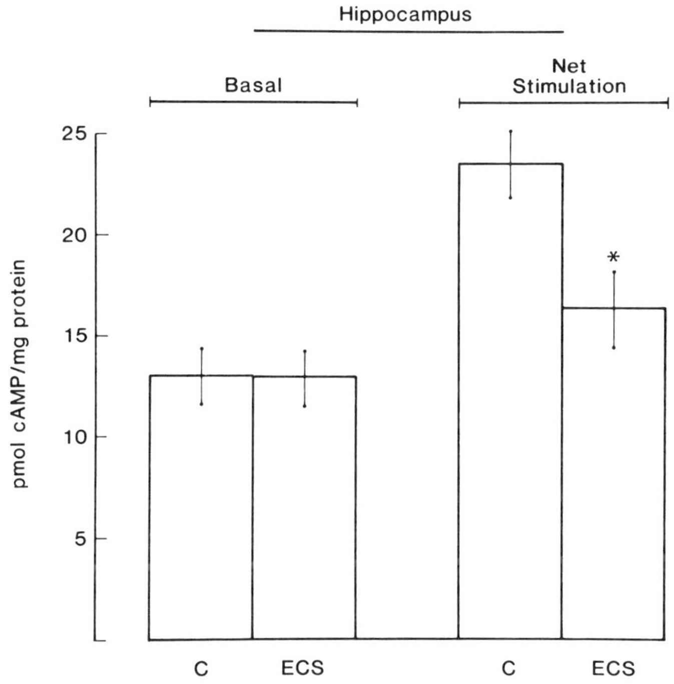

FIGURE 3. Effect of ECS (12 days) on beta-adrenergic receptor–mediated cAMP production in the hippocampus. The basal and the isoproterenol-stimulated production of cAMP was measured in fresh slices of hippocampus from control and ECS-treated rats 1 day after the last treatment. The cAMP was measured by radioimmunoassay[46] after a 10-minute incubation in the absence (basal values) or presence of 10 μM isoproterenol. The net stimulated values are the total cAMP produced in the presence of isoproterenol minus the basal values. Values are the mean ± SEM from nine control (C) and nine ECS treated rats. *$p < 0.01$ compared to control.

homogenate binding studies have found that the number of beta-adrenergic receptors is higher in the brains from suicide victims than in brains from age- and sex-matched controls who died from other causes.[16]

ECS administered concurrently with reserpine prevents the beta-adrenergic receptor–mediated increase in cAMP production in brain slices that is seen in rats treated with reserpine alone.[7] In addition, ECS can still alter the beta-adrenergic receptors when administered *after* a course of reserpine injections.[12] In rats that had received reserpine for 30 days, the beta-adrenergic receptors in the cerebral cortex were still increased 10 days after the last reserpine injection; but in rats that had received ECS for the 10 days following the last injection, the receptors had returned to control values.[12] The capacity of ECS to accelerate the return of beta-adrenergic receptors to normal levels after reserpine is probably a reflection of the actions of ECS on presynaptic processes in norepinephrine neurons, such as increasing the synthesis and turnover of norepinephrine.[17–20]

The selectivity of the effects of ECS on neurotransmitter receptors has been examined by several laboratories. There is widespread agreement that beta-adrenergic receptors are decreased following ECS, but the results of experiments examining the effects of ECS on other receptors are less consistent in some cases. We[9,12] and Deakin *et al.*[21] found no changes among several neurotransmitter receptor binding sites, including alpha-1 and alpha-2-adrenergic, cholinergic, serotonin-1, and tryptamine sites in the cerebral cortex and dopaminergic (D-2) sites in the striatum.[9,21] However, others have reported that alpha-2-adrenergic receptors are decreased[22] and that alpha-1-adrenergic receptors are increased[23] in rat brain following ECS. Further studies are needed in this area.

Although we did not detect a significant change in muscarinic cholinergic receptors following ECS, Lerer and his colleagues have found that ECS induces a small (10–15%) but consistent decrease in these receptors in the cortex and that this decrease appears to parallel the development of anterograde amnesia induced by ECS in the rat[24] (also see Lerer, this volume). All studies to date have employed muscarinic receptor antagonists to quantitate muscarinic receptor changes following ECS. These antagonists do not discriminate among muscarinic receptor subtypes or conformations. In view of the possible relationship between cholinergic neurotransmission and memory, it will be important to examine the effects of ECS on muscarinic receptor subtypes and on the high-affinity agonist conformation using selective ligands, such as [^{3}H]acetylcholine.[25]

EFFECTS OF ECS ON SEROTONIN RECEPTORS

Serotonin-1 (5-HT-1) receptors have high affinity (2–6 nM) for serotonin and can be labeled with [^{3}H]serotonin.[26] Serotonin-2 (5-HT-2) receptors have much lower affinity (1–3 uM) for serotonin and can be labeled with the antagonists [^{3}H]spiperone[27] or [^{3}H]ketanserin.[28] The brain regional distributions, effector coupling mechanisms, and, in all likelihood, the physiological functions of these two receptors are different.

Neither ECS nor most antidepressant drugs cause apparent alterations in 5-HT-1 receptor binding sites.[4,9,21] However, 5-HT-2 receptors are affected by both ECS and antidepressant drugs, though in opposite directions. A wide variety of antidepressant drugs, including "typical and atypical" tricyclic antidepressants and monoamine oxidase inhibitors, decrease 5-HT-2 binding sites labeled by [^{3}H]spiperone in rat brain[5,6,29] (TABLE 2). This effect usually takes several days of repeated administration to be evident,[30] but there may be exceptions to this (e.g., see Reference 29).

In contrast to antidepressant drugs, ECS increases 5-HT-2 receptor binding in the cerebral cortex[6,31] (TABLE 2). The increase in binding becomes statistically significant after 3 days of ECS, and it is maximal after 12–14 days of ECS (FIGURE 4). This increase is due entirely to an increase in the density of 5-HT-2 receptors (FIGURE 4, inset). The increase in receptors is reversible, and binding returns to control values one week after the last ECS (FIGURE 4). We have also used [^{3}H]ketanserin, which may be

TABLE 2. Effects of Chronic Treatment with Antidepressant Drugs (21 Days) or ECS (12 Days) on 5-HT-2 Receptor Binding Sites in Rat Cerebral Cortex[a]

Treatment	[^{3}H]Spiperone Specifically Bound (pmol/g tissue)
Control (vehicle injection)	11.3 ± 1.3
Amitriptyline (10 mg/kg)	7.0 ± 0.9[b]
Iprindole (10 mg/kg)	6.8 ± 1.1[b]
Tranylcypromine (5 mg/kg)	6.2 ± 1.1[b]
Control (handled)	11.2 ± 0.5
ECS (12 days)	15.6 ± 0.2[c]

[a]Rats were sacrificed one day after last treatment, and 5-HT-2 binding sites were measured using 1.0 nM [^{3}H]spiperone. Each value is the mean ± SEM of 5–6 rats. (Reproduced from Reference 6 with permission from the publisher.)

[b]$p < 0.05$ compared to control.

[c]$p < 0.01$ compared to control.

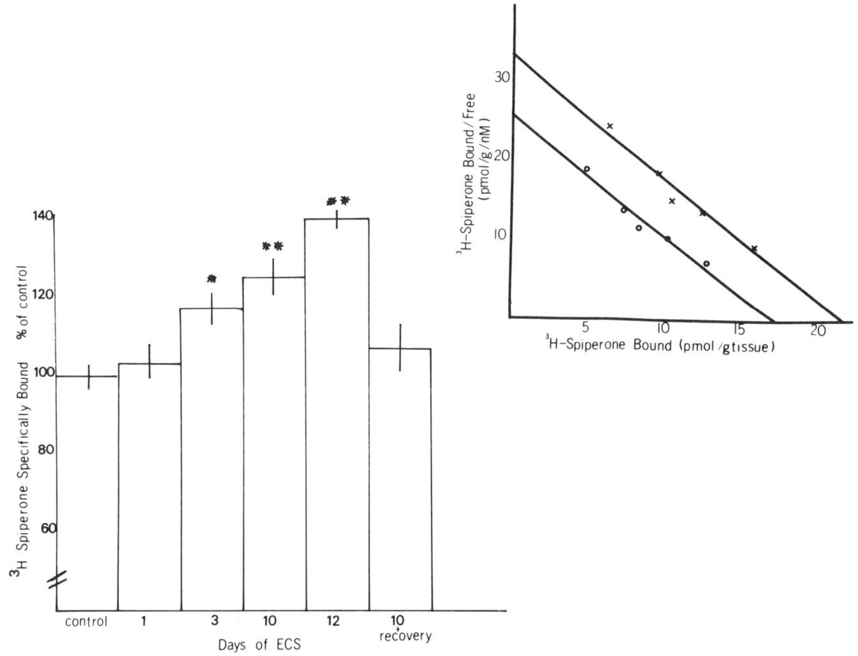

FIGURE 4. Time course of the effects of ECS on [^{3}H]spiperone binding to 5-HT-2 receptors in the cerebral cortex. Rats were given ECS once daily for the indicated number of days and were sacrificed either 1 day later or, in the case of the recovery group, 7 days later. Controls were placed to the electrode, but no current was passed. Each value is the mean ± SEM of 5–10 rats assayed using 1.1 nM [^{3}H]spiperone. The control value was 10.8 ± 0.3 pmol/g tissue. *$p < 0.05$; **$p < 0.01$ compared to control. Inset: Scatchard plots of [^{3}H]spiperone binding in cerebral cortex from control (●) and 10 day ECS treated (×) rats. Points represent the binding over a range of [^{3}H]spiperone concentrations from 0.3 nM to 2 nM. Binding maxima are 16.6 and 21.3 pmol/g tissue for control and ECS-treated rats, respectively ($p < 0.05$). Dissociation constants are not significantly different. This Scatchard plot is representative of eight similar experiments. (Reproduced from Reference 6 with permission from the publisher.)

TABLE 3. Effect of Repeated ECS (13 Days) on Binding Constants of [^{3}H]Ketanserin at Serotonin-2 Receptors in Rat Frontal Cortex[a]

	K_d (nM)	n_H	B_{max} (pmol/g tissue)
Control	0.50 ± 0.07	0.94 ± 0.04	13.4 ± 0.5
ECS	0.66 ± 0.06	0.99 ± 0.02	18.4 ± 1.0[b]

[a]Values are from Scatchard plots from five control and five ECS-treated rats. [^{3}H]Ketanserin concentrations of 0.1–3.0 nM were used, and specific binding was defined as the difference in binding in the absence and presence of 2 μM methysergide.
[b]$p < 0.02$ compared to control.

a more selective ligand for 5-HT-2 receptors,[28] to investigate the effects of ECS on these receptors. As expected, ECS increases the number of [^{3}H]ketanserin binding sites without altering the affinity of the sites or the Hill coefficient (n_H) of the saturation binding curve (TABLE 3). Competition studies between serotonin and [^{3}H]ketanserin indicate that the relative affinity of the 5-HT-2 receptor for serotonin and the Hill coefficient of the competition binding curve are not altered by ECS (FIGURE 5). The absence of effect of ECS on these binding parameters suggests that the increased number of 5-HT-2 receptors retain the properties of native receptors. There is convincing evidence from the studies of Green and Grahame-Smith and their colleagues that certain serotonin-mediated behaviors in rats are enhanced by repeated administration of ECS.[32–34] It is likely that this potentiation of serotonin function is tied to the ECS-induced increase in 5-HT-2 receptors.[6,35]

The underlying mechanisms that lead to the ECS-induced increase in 5-HT-2

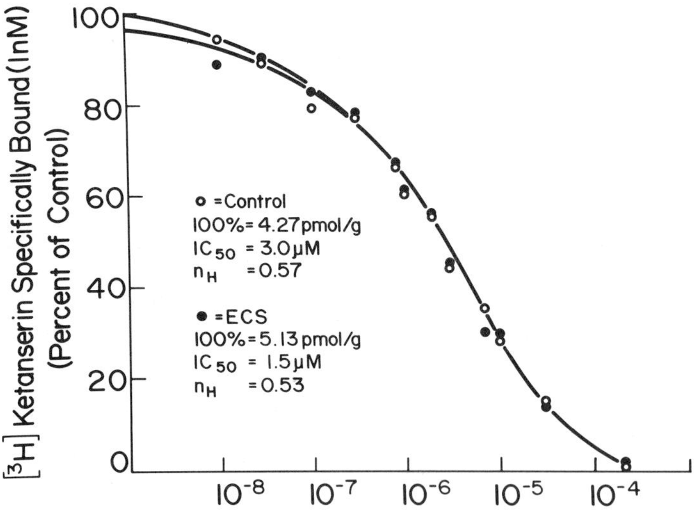

FIGURE 5. Competition between serotonin and [^{3}H]ketanserin (0.4 nM) for 5-HT-2 receptors in frontal cortex from control (O) and ECS-treated (●) rats. These curves are representative of three similar experiments.

TABLE 4. Effect of Lesions with 5,7-Dihydroxytryptamine on ECS-Induced Changes in [^{3}H]Ketanserin Binding in Rat Frontal Cortex[a]

[^{3}H]Ketanserin (1.0 nM) Specifically Bound (fmol/mg protein)			
Nonlesion		5,7-DHT Lesion	
Handled	ECS	Handled	ECS
148.6 ± 8.0	182.8 ± 7.2[b]	159.8 ± 7.8	164.2 ± 14.1

[a]Rats were anesthetized with pentobarbital and pretreated with a single injection of desipramine (25 mg/kg) to prevent uptake of 5,7-DHT into norepinephrine neurons. Lesions were made by injecting 7 μg of 5,7-DHT (free base) in 3 μl vehicle (0.9% saline plus 0.01% ascorbic acid) into the dorsal and median raphe nuclei. In nonlesioned rats, the injection cannula was lowered to just above each of the raphe nuclei, and either no injection or a vehicle injection was made. Beginning 14 days later, half of the rats in each group received ECS once daily for 12 days and were sacrificed 1 day later. The handled rats were placed to the electrodes but not shocked. Values are the mean ± SEM of 6–8 rats.

[b]$p < 0.05$ compared to corresponding control (Duncan's new multiple range test).

receptors are not known; however, the presence of functional serotonin axons appears to be required for this effect of ECS. In rats in which the neurotoxin 5,7-dihydroxytryptamine (5,7-DHT) is injected into the dorsal and median raphe nuclei to eliminate nearly all forebrain serotonin axons, ECS treatment does not increase 5-HT-2 receptors in the frontal cortex (TABLE 4). Similarly, if the synthesis of serotonin is inhibited with *p*-chlorophenylalanine before the start of treatments, ECS does not increase 5-HT-2 receptors.[35] The role of presynaptic mechanisms in the ECS-induced increase in 5-HT-2 receptors was investigated by measuring the effect of ECS on the high-affinity uptake of serotonin and on the binding of [^{3}H]imipramine to presynaptic sites on serotonin axons in the cerebral cortex. Neither the affinity (K_m) nor the maximum velocity (V_{max}, a measure of capacity) of the uptake of serotonin was affected by ECS (TABLE 5); nor was the binding of [^{3}H]imipramine altered (TABLE 5). These results are in contrast to an earlier report that ECS did affect these parameters of serotonin uptake,[36] but there is now agreement that it appears not to (A.R. Green, personal communication).

These effects of ECS on beta-adrenergic receptors and 5-HT-2 receptors are not due to stress alone. Intermittent foot-shock stress for two weeks does not alter these receptors when measured 24 hours after the last stressor (TABLE 6). Furthermore,

TABLE 5. Effect of ECS (10 Days) on [^{3}H]Serotonin Uptake into Rat Cortex Synaptosomes and on [^{3}H]Imipramine Binding in Cortex Homogenates[a]

	[^{3}H]Serotonin Uptake		
	K_m (nM)	V_{max} (pmol/5 mg tissue/4 min)	[^{3}H]Imipramine Binding (pmol/g tissue)
Control	66.6 ± 8.0	2.2 ± 0.14	8.2 ± 0.5
ECS	69.9 ± 7.7	2.2 ± 0.07	7.6 ± 0.5

[a]Rats were sacrificed 24 hours after the last ECS. Uptake was measured over a [^{3}H]5-HT concentration range of 20–400 nM. Kinetic constants were determined by Lineweaver-Burk plots. Values are the mean ± SEM of four control and four ECS-treated rats. [^{3}H]Imipramine binding was measured using a concentration of 4.5 nM. Values are the mean ± SEM of seven control and seven ECS-treated rats.

these ECS-induced changes in receptors are seen in rats that are anesthetized before each ECS and compared to controls that receive anesthesia only.[21,35]

SUMMARY OF EFFECTS OF ECS ON BETA-ADRENERGIC AND 5-HT-2 RECEPTORS

The effects of ECS on neurotransmitter receptors in rat brain appear to be far more selective and specific than might have been predicted. The effects on beta-adrenergic receptors in brain can be summarized as follows:

1. ECS decreases the number of beta-adrenergic receptors. This decrease develops gradually during two weeks of ECS administration, and it lasts at least one week after the last ECS.
2. The reduction in these receptors appears to occur only in those specific brain areas in which the beta-1 subtype of receptor predominates; and, in fact, the effects of ECS on beta-adrenergic receptors may be restricted to the beta-1 subtype of receptor.
3. These effects appear to be dependent on presynaptic activation of norepinephrine axons by ECS.
4. The decrease in beta-adrenergic receptors results in a decrease in receptor-mediated cAMP production, and thus this decrease in receptors is functional at the cellular level. (There is, however, a near vacuum in our understanding of how this cellular change might be translated into effects on behavior or mood.)
5. ECS accelerates the return of beta-adrenergic receptors to normal levels after reserpine treatment.
6. The decrease in beta-adrenergic receptors by ECS is not due to stress alone.
7. The effects of ECS on beta-adrenergic receptors are shared by antidepressant drugs, but not by other types of drugs that have been tested.

The effects of ECS on 5-HT-2 receptors can be summarized as follows:

1. ECS induces a highly selective increase in the density of 5-HT-2 receptors in the cerebral cortex. This increase develops gradually during two weeks of ECS administration, and it is reversible.
2. Neither the affinity of the receptor for serotonin nor the Hill coefficients of the binding of agonists or antagonists to the 5-HT-2 receptor are altered by ECS.

TABLE 6. Effect of Chronic Foot-Shock Stress (14 Days) on Beta-Adrenergic and Serotonin-2 Receptor Binding Sites in Rat Cortex[a]

	Ligand Specifically Bound (pmol/g tissue)	
Receptor Binding Site	Control	Foot Shock
Beta-adrenergic	8.1 ± 0.4	8.0 ± 0.4
5-HT-2	12.9 ± 0.5	13.8 ± 0.3

[a]Rats were given foot-shock stress once a day (four shocks per minute for a 12-minute period) for 14 days and sacrificed 1 day later. Beta-adrenergic receptors were measured using 4.0 nM [^{3}H]dihydroalprenolol. Serotonin-2 receptors were measured using 1.0 nM [^{3}H]spiperone. Values are means ± SEM of five control and six foot-shock rats.

3. The ECS-induced increase in 5-HT-2 receptors is dependent on the presence of serotonin axons, but it does not appear to depend on changes in serotonin uptake or presynaptic imipramine binding sites.
4. The increase in 5-HT-2 receptors by ECS is not due to stress alone.
5. This effect of ECS on 5-HT-2 receptors is opposite to that of presently known antidepressant drugs.

EFFECTS OF SEROTONIN ON NOREPINEPHRINE RECEPTOR REGULATION

For more than 20 years research into depression has looked for telltale signs of aberrations in norepinephrine or serotonin neurotransmission. Much of this work has been guided by the catecholamine and indoleamine hypotheses of affective disorders,[37–39] which were based largely on the known actions of antidepressant drugs at that time. During the last decade, the research emphasis has shifted from the acute presynaptic actions of these drugs to the adaptive postsynaptic changes in receptors that they appear to trigger, and that more closely fit the time course of therapeutic responses.

Regulation of norepinephrine and serotonin receptors has usually been studied independently, but recently the influence of one on the other has been considered. Costa and colleagues[40,41] and Sulser and colleagues[42] have reported that in rats in which the serotonin axons in the forebrain have been lesioned by intraventricular injection of 5,7-DHT, repeated administration of desipramine or imipramine no longer down regulates beta-adrenergic receptors in the cerebral cortex or hippocampus, thus suggesting an important role of serotonin in the regulation of beta-adrenergic receptors by these antidepressant drugs. Interestingly, mianserin and iprindole, two "atypical" antidepressants, still decreased norepinephrine-stimulated cAMP production after these lesions.[41] Thus, the apparent influence of serotonin axons on the regulation of beta-adrenergic receptors by desipramine and imipramine might not extend to all antidepressant drugs. This suggests that antidepressant treatments can induce beta-adrenergic receptor down regulation through different mechanisms—some apparently requiring the presence of serotonin axons and some not. Electroconvulsive shock appears to be in the latter category of treatments. We found that ECS still decreased binding to beta-adrenergic receptors in the cerebral cortex of rats after the serotonin axons had been lesioned by intraventricular injections of 5,7-DHT[43] (FIGURE 6).

The importance of sertonin axons to beta-adrenergic receptor regulatory mechanisms may extend beyond their influence on the down regulation of these receptors by certain antidepressant drugs. Injections of 5,7-DHT directly into the dorsal and median raphe nuclei, which contain the cell bodies of the ascending serotonin axons, result in nearly complete (>90%) elimination of the serotonin axons innervating the frontal cortex and hippocampus without producing any apparent damage to norepinephrine axons in these areas (TABLE 7). (These lesions are more complete and more selective than the lesions that we have been able to produce by intraventricular injection of 5,7-DHT.) Four to six weeks following these lesions of the ascending serotonin neurons, there is a marked increase in the density (B_{max}) of the beta-adrenergic receptors in the frontal cortex and in the hippocampus (TABLE 8). The affinities (K_D) of the receptors are not altered by these lesions (TABLE 8). This effect appears to be selective for beta-adrenergic receptors since the lesions do not alter the binding to alpha-1- or alpha-2-adrenergic receptors (TABLE 9).

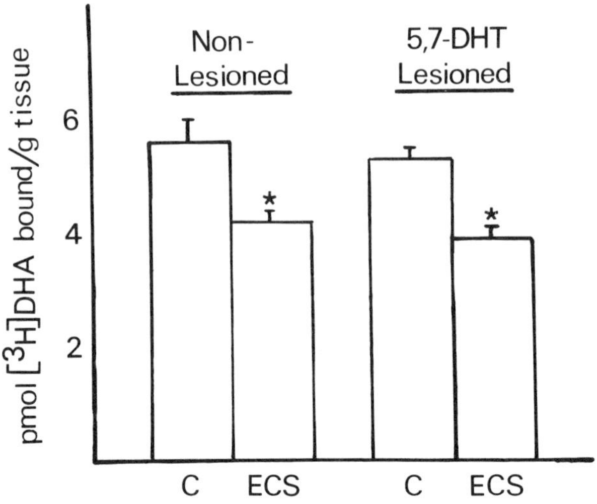

FIGURE 6. Effect of lesions of serotonin axons on ECS-induced decrease in beta-adrenergic receptors in the cerebral cortex. Rats received intraventricular injections of 5,7-dihydroxytryptamine (5,7-DHT; 200 μg) under pentobarbital anesthesia (lesioned group) or anesthesia only (nonlesioned group). Beginning 18 days later, half the rats in each group received ECS once daily for 12 days. The controls were placed to the electrode, but no current was passed. All rats were sacrificed 1 day after the last treatment, and beta-adrenergic receptors were measured using 2.7 nM [^{3}H]dihydroalprenolol. Values are the mean ± SEM of 4–5 rats per group. *$p < 0.05$ compared to corresponding control. (Adapted from Reference 43.)

The mechanism underlying this effect of serotonin axons on beta-adrenergic receptors is presently unknown. But if the regulation of these receptors is important in the pathophysiology and/or the treatment of depression, the influence of serotonin axons on beta-adrenergic receptors may be a critical link between these two neurotransmission systems.

TABLE 7. Effects of Lesions of the Serotonin Cell Bodies in the Dorsal and Median Raphe Nuclei on the Uptake of [^{3}H]Serotonin and [^{3}H]Norepinephrine and the Content of Norepinephrine in the Frontal Cortex and the Hippocampus[a]

	Frontal Cortex		Hippocampus	
	Control	Lesioned	Control	Lesioned
[^{3}H]Serotonin uptake (fmol/mg protein/4 minutes)	2727 ± 129	186 ± 19[b]	3015 ± 218	225 ± 24[b]
[^{3}H]Norepinephrine uptake (fmol/mg protein/4 minutes)	606 ± 50	577 ± 53	989 ± 96	866 ± 60
Norepinephrine content (ng/mg protein)	3.2 ± 0.3	2.7 ± 0.2	3.6 ± 0.3	4.0 ± 0.3

[a]Rats were sacrificed 4–6 weeks after injection of 5,7-DHT or vehicle into the raphe nuclei (see TABLE 4). [^{3}H]Serotonin (25 nM) uptake and [^{3}H]norepinephrine (50 nM) uptake were measured in fresh homogenates. The content of norepinephrine was measured by high-pressure liquid chromatography. Values are the mean ± SEM from 12–24 rats.

[b]$p < 0.001$ compared to control.

TABLE 8. Effect of Lesions of the Serotonin Cell Bodies in the Dorsal and Median Raphe Nuclei on Beta-Adrenergic Receptors in the Frontal Cortex and Hippocampus[a]

	Frontal Cortex		Hippocampus	
	Control	Lesioned	Control	Lesioned
B_{max} (fmol/mg protein)	154.6 ± 7.0	201.6 ± 8.1[b]	154.2 ± 9.9	291.4 ± 25.0[b]
K_d (nM)	1.3 ± 0.1	1.6 ± 0.2	6.0 ± 0.9	6.4 ± 0.3

[a]Rats were sacrificed 4–6 weeks after injections of 5,7-dihydroxytryptamine or vehicle (see TABLE 4). Beta-adrenergic receptors were measured using 0.2–12 nM [^{3}H]dihydroalprenolol. Values are mean ± SEM of 5–9 Scatchard analyses.

[b]$p < 0.001$ compared to control.

CONCLUSIONS

Following ECS, two of the most prominent and consistent changes in neurotransmitter receptors in rat brain are the decrease in beta-adrenergic receptors and the increase in 5-HT-2 receptors. These effects appear to be relatively selective. The reduction in beta-adrenergic receptors by ECS is similar to the effects of antidepressant drugs and is consistent with the concept that these receptors are involved in the treatment of depression and possibly in the pathophysiological process, itself. In contrast, the increase in 5-HT-2 receptors is opposite to the effects of antidepressant drugs. The increase in 5-HT-2 receptors could be important to the therapeutic mechanisms of action of ECS in disorders other than depression, such as manic states or catatonia,[44,45] in which it is an effective treatment; or it might not be important at all.

However, it is also possible that the opposite effects of ECS and antidepressant drugs on 5-HT-2 receptors are related to the therapeutic mechanisms of action in the treatment of different types of depressions with fundamentally different underlying pathologies. For example, increased beta-adrenergic receptors, which could result from a deficit in presynaptic norepinephrine axon function, might be involved in some depressions; and a reduction of these receptors by either antidepressant drugs or ECS, perhaps secondary to effects on presynaptic function, could be beneficial. Other types of depressions might involve hypersensitivity at 5-HT-2 synapses, and a reduction in 5-HT-2 receptors by antidepressant drugs—again, perhaps secondary to presynaptic effects—might be beneficial. Still other types of depression (perhaps the most severe

TABLE 9. Effect of Lesions of the Serotonin Cell Bodies in the Dorsal and Median Raphe Nuclei on Alpha-1- and Alpha-2-Adrenergic Receptors in the Frontal Cortex and Hippocampus[a]

	Binding (fmol/mg protein)			
	Frontal Cortex		Hippocampus	
	Control	Lesioned	Control	Lesioned
[^{3}H]Prazosin	171.9 ± 6.5	168.3 ± 3.0	62.3 ± 4.3	60.9 ± 3.2
[^{3}H]*p*-Aminoclonidine	97.4 ± 7.9	88.8 ± 6.4	—	—

[a]Rats were sacrificed 4–6 weeks after injection of 5,7-DHT or vehicle (see TABLE 4). Alpha-1- and alpha-2-adrenergic receptors were measured using [^{3}H]prazosin (0.5 nM) and [^{3}H]*p*-aminoclonidine (2.0 nM), respectively. Values are mean ± SEM for 6–9 rats.

types) might result from decreases in 5-HT-2 receptor–mediated neurotransmission, possibly due to failure of the receptors to adapt to decreases in presynaptic function. In this case, most tricyclic antidepressant drugs might actually exacerbate the depression by blocking the receptors; but ECS, by increasing the number of 5-HT-2 receptors, could be beneficial. These examples are speculative, of course, and probably simplistic since they do not even begin to take into account the possible interactions between norepinephrine and serotonin neurotransmission systems. Nevertheless, they might serve as simple, working extensions of the original biogenic amine hypotheses[37–39] while waiting to be replaced by more sophisticated and detailed models.

Electroconvulsive shock is a useful tool for identifying cellular and molecular processes possibly related to depression and its treatment. However, it should be kept in mind that most experiments at this level are examining the effects of ECS on essentially normal mechanisms in rodent brain, and the effects on aberrant mechanisms in human brain may be quite different. Nevertheless, the results derived from animal experiments can lead to well-defined hypotheses that can be, and in some cases have been, tested in postmortem human tissue, and that ultimately may be safely examined in patients.

REFERENCES

1. Banerjee, L. P., L. S. Kung, S. T. Riggi & S. K. Chanda. 1977. Development of beta-adrenergic receptor subsensitivity by antidepressants. Nature **268:** 455–456.
2. Wolfe, B. B., T. K. Harden, J. R. Sporn & P. B. Molinoff. 1978. Presynaptic modulation of beta-adrenergic receptors in rat cerebral cortex after treatment with antidepressants. J. Pharmacol. Exp. Ther. **207:** 446–457.
3. Sarai, K., A. Frazer, D. Brunswick & J. Mendels. 1978. Desmethylimipramine-induced decrease in beta-adrenergic receptor binding in rat cerebral cortex. Biochem. Pharmacol. **27:** 2179–2181.
4. Bergstrom, D. A. & K. J. Kellar. 1979. Adrenergic and serotonergic receptor binding in rat brain after chronic desmethylimipramine treatment. J. Pharmacol. Exp. Ther. **290:** 256–261.
5. Peroutka, S. J. & S. H. Snyder. 1980. Long-term antidepressant treatment decreases spiroperidol-labeled serotonin receptor binding. Science **210:** 88–90.
6. Kellar, K. J., C. S. Cascio, J. A. Butler & R. N. Kurtzke. 1981. Differential effects of electroconvulsive shock and antidepressant drugs on serotonin-2 receptors in rat brain. Eur. J. Pharmacol. **69:** 515–518.
7. Vetulani, J. & F. Sulser. 1975. Action of various antidepressant treatments reduces reactivity of noradrenergic cyclic AMP–generating system in limbic forebrain. Nature **257:** 495–496.
8. Vetulani, J., R. J. Stawarz, J. V. Dingell & F. Sulser. 1976. A possible common mechanism of action of antidepressant treatments. Naunyn Schmeideberg's Arch. Pharmacol. **293:** 109–114.
9. Bergstrom, D. A. & K. J. Kellar. 1979. Effect of electroconvulsive shock on monoaminergic receptor binding sites in rat brain. Nature **278:** 464–466.
10. Pandey, G. N., W. J. Heinze, B. D. Brown & J. M. Davis. 1979. Electroconvulsive shock treatment decreases beta-adrenergic receptor sensitivity in rat brain. Nature **280:** 234–235.
11. Rainbow, T. C., B. Parsons & B. B. Wolfe. 1984. Quantitative autoradiography of B_1- and B_2-adrenergic receptors in rat brain. Proc. Nat. Acad. Sci. USA **81:** 1585–1589.
12. Kellar, K. J., C. S. Cascio, D. A. Bergstrom, J. A. Butler & P. Iadarola. 1981. Electroconvulsive shock and reserpine: effects on beta-adrenergic receptors in rat brain. J. Neurochem. **37:** 830–836.
13. Quetsch, R. M., R. W. Achor, E. M. Litin & R. L. Faucett. 1959. Depressive reactions in hypertensive patients. Circulation **19:** 366–375.

14. U'Prichard, D. C. & S. H. Snyder. 1978. [^{3}H]Catecholamine binding to alpha-receptors in rat brain: enhancement by reserpine. Eur. J. Pharmacol. **51:** 145–155.
15. Dismukes, R. J. & J. W. Daly. 1974. Norepinephrine sensitive systems generating adenosine 3′,5′-monophosphate: increased responses in cerebral cortical slices from reserpine-treated rats. Mol. Pharmacol. **10:** 933–940.
16. Zanko, M. T. & A. Biegon. 1983. Increased beta-adrenergic receptor binding in human frontal cortex. Soc. Neurosci. Abstr. **9:** 719.
17. Kety, S. S., F. Javoy, A.-M. Thierry, L. Julou & J. Glowinski. 1967. A sustained effect of electroconvulsive shock on the turnover of norepinephrine in the central nervous system of the rat. Proc. Nat. Acad. Sci. USA **58:** 1249–1254.
18. Modigh, K. 1976. Long-term effects of electroconvulsive shock therapy on synthesis turnover and uptake of brain monoamines. Psychopharmacology **49:** 179–185.
19. Musacchio, J. M., L. Julou, S. S. Kety & J. Glowinski. 1969. Increase in rat brain tyrosine hydroxylase activity produced by electroconvulsive shock. Proc. Nat. Acad. Sci. USA **63:** 1117–1119.
20. Masserano, J. M., G. S. Takimoto & N. Weiner. 1981. Electroconvulsive shock increases tyrosine hydroxylase activity in the brain and adrenal gland of the rat. Science **214:** 662–664.
21. Deakin, J. F. W., F. Owen, A. J. Cross & M. J. Dashwood. 1981. Studies on the possible mechanisms of action of electroconvulsive therapy; effects of repeated electrically induced seizures on rat brain receptors for monoamines and other neurotransmitters. Psychopharmacology **73:** 345–349.
22. Stanford, S. C. & D. J. Nutt. 1982. Comparison of the effects of repeated electroconvulsive shock on alpha-2 and beta-adrenoceptors in different regions of rat brain. Neuroscience **7:** 1753–1757.
23. Vetulani, J., L. Antkiewicz-Michaluk, A. Rokosz-Pelc & A. Pilc. 1983. Chronic electroconvulsive shock treatment enhances the density of [^{3}H]prazosin binding sites in the central nervous system of the rat. Brain Res. **275:** 392–395.
24. Lerer, B., M. Stanley, I. McIntyre & H. Altman. 1984. Electroconvulsive shock and brain muscarinic receptors: relationship to anterograde amnesia. Life Sci. **35:** 2659–2664.
25. Kellar, K. J., A. Martino, D. P. Hall, Jr., R. D. Schwartz & R. L. Taylor. 1985. High affinity binding of [^{3}H]acetylcholine to muscarinic cholinergic receptors. J. Neurosci. **5:** 1577–1582.
26. Bennett, J. P., Jr. & S. H. Snyder. 1976. Serotonin and lysergic acid diethylamide binding in rat brain membranes: relationship to postsynaptic serotonin receptors. Mol. Pharmacol. **12:** 373–389.
27. Peroutka, S. J. & S. H. Snyder. 1979. Multiple serotonin receptors: differential binding of [^{3}H]5-hydroxytryptamine, [^{3}H]lysergic acid diethylamide and [^{3}H]spiroperidol. Mol. Pharmacol. **16:** 687–699.
28. Leysen, J. E., C. J. E. Niemegeers, J. M. Van Nueten & P. Laduron. 1982. [^{3}H]Ketanserin, a selective ligand for serotonin-2 receptor binding sites. Binding properties, brain distribution and functional role. Mol. Pharmacol. **212:** 301–314.
29. Blackshear, M. A. & E. Sanders-Bush. 1982. Serotonin receptor sensitivity after acute and chronic treatment with mianserin. J. Pharmacol. Exp. Ther. **221:** 303–308.
30. Peroutka, S. J. & S. H. Snyder. 1980. Regulation of serotonin-2 (5-HT_2) receptors labeled with [^{3}H]spiroperidol by chronic treatment with the antidepressant amitriptyline. J. Pharmacol. Exp. Ther. **215:** 582–587.
31. Vetulani, J., U. Lebrecht & A. Pilc. 1981. Enhancement of responsiveness of the central serotonergic system and serotonin-2 receptor density in rat frontal cortex by electroconvulsive treatment. Eur. J. Pharmacol. **76:** 81–85.
32. Evans, J. P. M., D. G. Grahame-Smith, A. R. Green & A. F. C. Tordoff. 1976. Electroconvulsive shock increases the behavioral responses of rats to brain 5-hydroxytryptamine accumulation and central nervous system stimulant drugs. Br. J. Pharmacol. **56:** 193–199.
33. Green, A. R., D. J. Heal & D. G. Grahame-Smith. 1977. Further observations on the effect of repeated electroconvulsive shock on the behavioral responses of rats produced by

increases in the functional activity of brain 5-hydroxytryptamine and dopamine. Psychopharmacology **52:** 195–200.

34. Green, A. R. & J. F. W. Deakin. 1980. Depletion of brain noradrenaline prevents electroconvulsive shock induced enhancement of 5-hydroxytryptamine and dopamine mediated behavior. Nature **285:** 232–233.
35. Green, A. R., P. Johnson & V. Nimgaonkar. 1983. Increased 5-HT-2 receptor number in brain as a probable explanation for the enhanced 5-hydroxytryptamine mediated behavior following repeated electroconvulsive shock administration to rats. Br. J. Pharmacol. **80:** 173–177.
36. Minchin, M. C. W., J. Williams, J. M. Bowdler & A. R. Green. 1983. Effect of electroconvulsive shock on the uptake and release of noradrenalin and 5-hydroxytryptamine in rat brain slices. J. Neurochem. **40:** 765–768.
37. Bunney, W. E., Jr. & J. M. Davis. 1965. Norepinephrine in depressive reactions. Arch. Gen. Psychiatry **13:** 483–494.
38. Schildkraut, J. J. 1965. The catecholamine hypothesis of affective disorders: a review of supporting evidence. Am. J. Psychiatry **122:** 509–522.
39. Coppen, A. 1967. The biochemistry of affective disorders. Br. J. Psychiatry **113:** 1237–1264.
40. Brunello, N., M. L. Barbaccia, D.-M. Chuang & E. Costa. 1982. Down-regulation of beta-adrenergic receptors following repeated injections of desmethylimipramine: permissive role of serotonergic axons. Neuropharmacology **21:** 1145–1149.
41. Gandolfi, O., M. L. Barbaccia & E. Costa. 1984. Comparison of iprindole, imipramine and mianserin action on brain serotonergic and beta-adrenergic receptors. J. Pharmacol. Exp. Ther. **229:** 782-786.
42. Janowsky, A., F. Okada, D. H. Manier, C. D. Applegate & F. Sulser. 1982. Role of serotonergic input in the regulation of the beta-adrenergic receptor-coupled adenylate cyclase system. Science **218:** 900–901.
43. Kellar, K. J., C. A. Stockmeier & J. M. Gomez. 1985. Regulation of serotonin neurotransmission by antidepressant drugs and electroconvulsive shock: the fall and rise of serotonin receptors. Acta Pharmacol. Toxicol. **56**(Suppl. 1)**:** 138–145.
44. Fink, M. 1979. Convulsive Therapy: Theory and Practice: 172–183. Raven Press. New York, N.Y.
45. Freedman, A. M., H. I. Kaplan & B. J. Sadock. 1976. Comprehensive Textbook of Psychiatry. 2nd edit.: 992–993. Williams and Wilkens Co. Baltimore, Md.
46. Harper, J. F. & G. Brooker. 1975. Femtomole sensitive radioimmunoassay for cAMP and cGMP after 2′0 acetylation by acetic anhydride in aqueous solution. J. Cyclic Nucleotide Res. **1:** 207–218.

An Animal Model of Electroconvulsive-Therapy-Induced Amnesia

Possible Neurochemical Correlates

BERNARD LERER,[a,b] MICHAEL STANLEY,[b]
HARVEY ALTMAN,[b] AND MICHAEL KEEGAN[b]

[a]*Jerusalem Mental Health Center*
Post Office Box 140
Jerusalem 91001, Israel

[b]*Department of Psychiatry*
Wayne State University and
Lafayette Clinic
Detroit, Michigan 48207

Although modifications in electrode placement and stimulus parameters may considerably reduce the severity of electroconvulsive therapy (ECT)-induced memory impairment,[1] cognitive deficits remain an important drawback of the treatment. Little is known regarding the biological basis underlying such deficits, and pharmacological interventions that might prevent or alleviate them are still unavailable. Experimental efforts aimed at addressing these issues are considerably hampered by the absence of an appropriate animal model. Although the proactive and retroactive effects of a single electroconvulsive shock (ECS) on memory function have been extensively investigated,[2,3] such studies have primarily dealt with acute effects of a single ECS and have not systematically examined the cumulative sequellae of a series of ECS administrations. Cumulative effects are more relevant to clinical ECT, which invariably involves the administration of a series of treatments. Moreover, since the acute cognitive sequellae of ECT are generally transient, delayed rather than acute effects on memory function are of considerably greater clinical relevance.

This paper summarizes a series of studies aimed at developing an animal model of ECT-induced memory impairment and preliminary experiments that have examined possible neurochemical correlates.

CRITERIA FOR AN ANIMAL MODEL OF ECT-INDUCED AMNESIA

Memory impairment induced by bilateral ECT administration has been qualitatively defined in an extensive series of studies, some of which are reported in the present volume (Cf. Squire, Weiner). The central characteristics of ECT-induced amnesia, which were adopted as guidelines for our studies, may be briefly summarized as follows:

1. The impairment is cumulative and severity increases with increasing numbers of treatments. This conclusion is based on studies that employed serial testing of a variety of memory functions over 5–10 ECT administrations.[4]

2. Anterograde amnestic effects are characterized by a specific deficit in delayed recall of newly learned material while the initial learning of such material is unimpaired.[5] This anterograde amnesia is not permanent and has been reported as no longer demonstrable as early as six weeks after conclusion of the treatment.[6]
3. Retrograde amnestic effects are characterized by a temporal gradient. Memory for events that occurred immediately prior to the ECT course is most prominently impaired while more remote memories appear to be relatively unaffected.[7] A further component of retrograde amnesia relates to memory for personal, autobiographic material which appears to be specifically and possibly permanently impaired by ECT.[8] This latter component is, however, beyond the scope of the rodent models studied.

On the basis of these and other clinical characteristics of ECT-induced memory impairment, our studies were designed so as to assess systematically:

1. Effects of a series of ECS administration versus those of a single treatment.
2. Anterograde effects on immediate and delayed recall of a learned task; the number of treatments required to induce observed effects and the degree of persistence of these effects after the conclusion of the ECS course.
3. Retrograde effects on memory for stimuli to which animals were exposed at increasing intervals prior to the ECS course.

METHODS

The methodological details of these studies have been comprehensively presented in previous publications.[9,10] Male albino rats (200–250 g) were used in all experiments. ECS was administered via earclip electrodes using a Medcraft clinical ECT apparatus (stimulus parameters 130 V for 0.75 second) and was regularly observed to induce a full tonic-clonic seizure lasting 20–25 seconds with recovery within a few minutes. Control animals were subjected to sham ECS—handling and earclips only with no current applied. Memory testing employed a standard passive avoidance procedure. During training, rats were administered an aversive electrical stimulus (0.5 mA for 3.0 seconds) on crossing to the dark side of the chamber. The animals were tested by returning them to the apparatus at varying time intervals following training. Latency to cross (up to a maximum of 600 seconds) was recorded. Animals were used only once for a train-test series.

ANTEROGRADE AMNESIA

Our earlier studies had demonstrated a specific ECS-induced deficit in delayed recall of the aversive stimulus as opposed to intact immediate memory.[9,10] Thus animals trained in the passive avoidance apparatus 24 hours after the last of a series of seven ECS administrations (ECS $\times$ 7) and tested 1 hour later had test latencies that were no different from sham-treated animals. However, animals tested 24 hours after training were grossly amnestic. In a further experiment, summarized in FIGURE 1, we were able to demonstrate a gradual development of amnesia in animals tested at increasing intervals following training and culminating in the complete amnesia observed at 24 hours.

These findings directly parallel those reported by Squire in ECT-treated patients tested for anterograde memory function immediately after training and again 16–19 hours later.[5] They support Squire's conclusion that following ECT, initial learning is intact while delayed recall is significantly impaired.[5] It remains to be established whether erosion of the memory trace occurs over time or whether access to the memory is gradually impeded. Our own preliminary studies suggest that the former may be the case since memory performance could not be improved by pretest administration of cholinergic agents such as oxotremorine or by amphetamine (Lerer *et al.*, unpublished data).

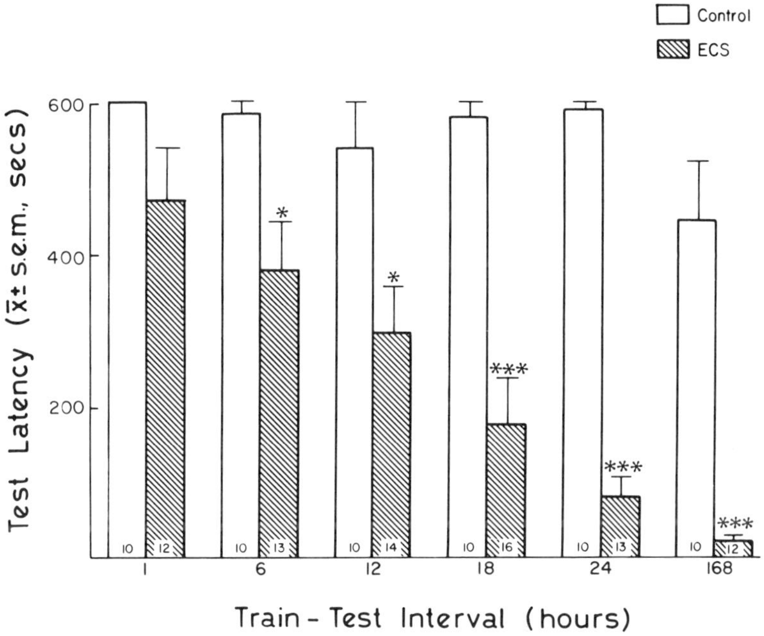

FIGURE 1. Effect of ECS × 7 on passive avoidance retention as a function of train-test interval. Rats were trained 24 hours following the final ECS and tested at varying intervals from 1 hour–168 hours after training. $*p < 0.05$, ECS vs. control. $***\ p < 0.0001$, ECS vs. control. (Mann Whitney U Test.)

As observed in the clinical context, we have found the ECS-induced anterograde amnesia in rats to be cumulatively induced. A single ECS (ECS × 1) did not impair passive avoidance retention in animals trained 24 hours following the treatment and tested 24 hours later.[9,10] Subsequent experiments showed that the memory deficit became evident after the second treatment and was maximal after four ECS administrations (FIGURE 2). The studies reported by Squire in patients were carried out after the fifth ECT,[5] and our findings in this regard are thus analogous.

A gradual recovery from anterograde amnesia was also demonstrated. As shown in FIGURE 3, animals trained 5 days after the last of ECS × 7 were still amnestic when tested 24 hours later. However, by 10 days recovery was evident and at 21 days

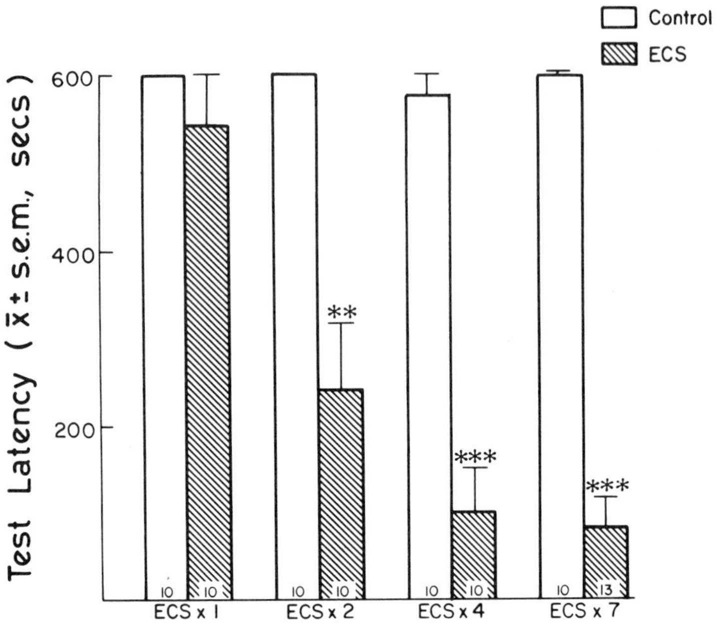

FIGURE 2. Effect of ECS on passive avoidance retention as a function of number of treatments administered. Rats were trained 24 hours after ECS × 1, ECS × 2, ECS × 4, and ECS × 7 and tested 24 hours after training. $^{**}p < 0.01$, ECS vs. control. $^{***}p < 0.0001$, ECS vs. control. (Mann Whitney U Test.)

following ECS × 7, memory performance was intact. Weeks *et al.* have reported intact anterograde memory function in patients by six weeks after a course of ECT.[6]

RETROGRADE AMNESIA

Retrograde memory function was tested by means of the following paradigm. Rats were trained in the passive avoidance apparatus as described above. Twenty-four hours later the animals were divided into three groups and were then subjected to ECS × 7, sham ECS × 6 preceded by ECS × 1, or sham ECS × 7. Testing was conducted 24 hours following the last treatment. An additional group of animals was trained seven days prior to ECS administration, treated in three groups as described above, and tested 24 hours following the last treatment. The results of this study, as summarized in FIGURE 4, showed a significant degree of retrograde amnesia in animals trained 24 hours before a series of ECS × 7 whereas animals subjected to a single ECS were unaffected. However, animals trained seven days prior to ECS showed retention that was no different from sham-treated animals (FIGURE 4).

These findings again closely parallel the results reported in patients administered clinical ECT. Patients tested by Squire *et al.* for retrograde memory function showed a similar temporal gradient, with memory for events occurring close to the ECT course significantly impaired while more distant memories were unaffected.[7]

RECEPTOR BINDING STUDIES

Dashieff *et al.* reported that repeated ECS administration induced a 15–30% decrease in [^{3}H]quinuclidinyl benzilate ([3H]QNB) binding to muscarinic cholinergic receptors in rat hippocampus.[11] An initial report from our laboratory replicated this finding and also demonstrated a small but significant reduction in [3H]QNB binding in the frontal cortex.[12] In a subsequent study we examined [3H]QNB binding at multiple [3H]QNB concentrations and used Scatchard analyses to define receptor number (B_{Max}) and affinity of the radioligand for the muscarinic receptor (K_d).[10] In this study we were again able to demonstrate a small but significant reduction in muscarinic receptor number in the cortex. Receptor affinity for [3H]QNB was unchanged. The B_{Max} and K_d findings for the cortex are shown in FIGURE 5.

We have hypothesized that ECT-induced memory impairment may be related to a reduction in cortical muscarinic receptor number induced by the treatment and resulting in a functional reduction in cholinergic neurotransmission through the affected synapses.[10,12] This hypothesis would imply that other treatments that reduce brain musarinic receptor number (e.g., chronic administration of cholinergic agonists) should likewise impair memory function whereas treatments that increase muscarinic receptor number should enhance memory (e.g., chronic administration of cholinergic antagonists). Preliminary findings in this regard have been reported by Loullis *et al.*[13] Further supporting evidence for this hypothesis and other critical tests are discussed in detail elsewhere.[9]

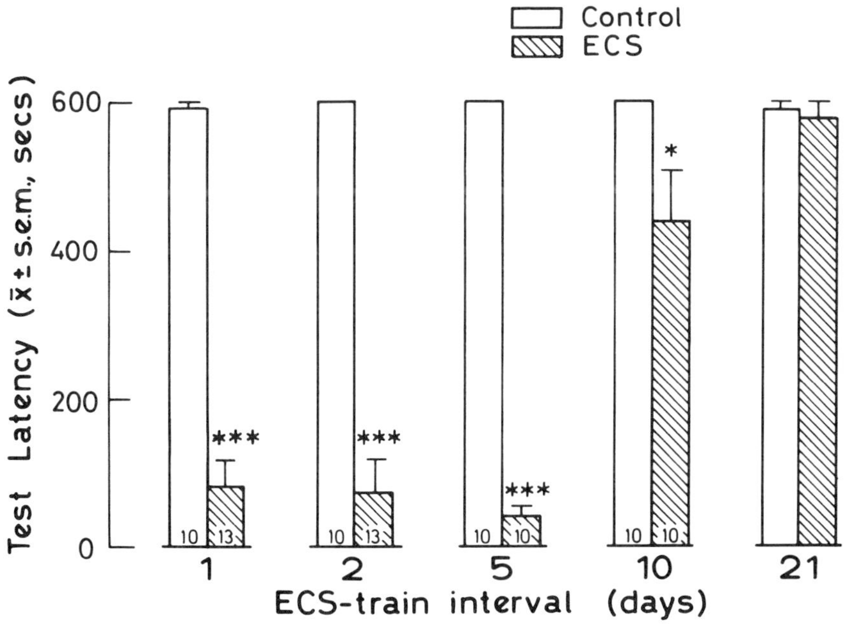

FIGURE 3. Recovery from ECS-induced anterograde amnesia in rats administered ECS × 7, trained on a passive avoidance task at intervals between 24 hours and 21 days after the last treatment, and tested 24 hours after training. *** $p < 0.0001$, ECS vs. control. * $p < 0.05$ ECS vs. control. (Mann Whitney U Test.)

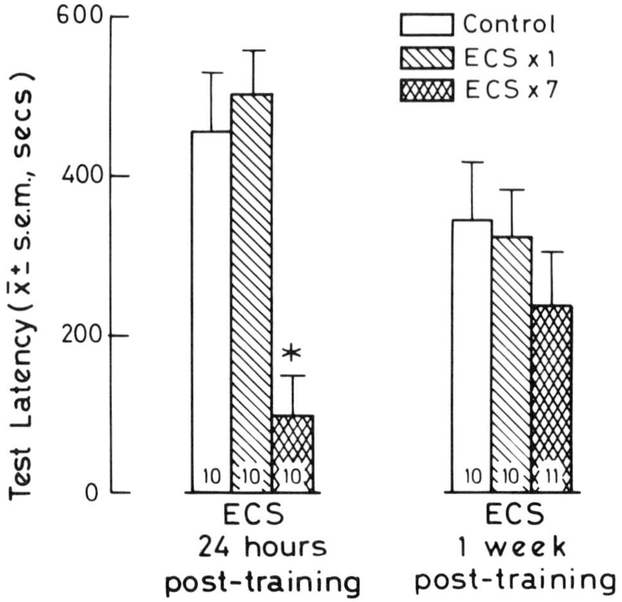

FIGURE 4. Effect of ECS × 1 and ECS × 7 on retrograde memory function in rats trained on a passive avoidance task 24 hours (left) or 7 days (right) before ECS administration. Rats were tested 24 hours following the final ECS in all cases. *$p < 0.001$, ECS × 7 vs. control and ECS × 7 vs. ECS × 1. (Mann Whitney U Test.)

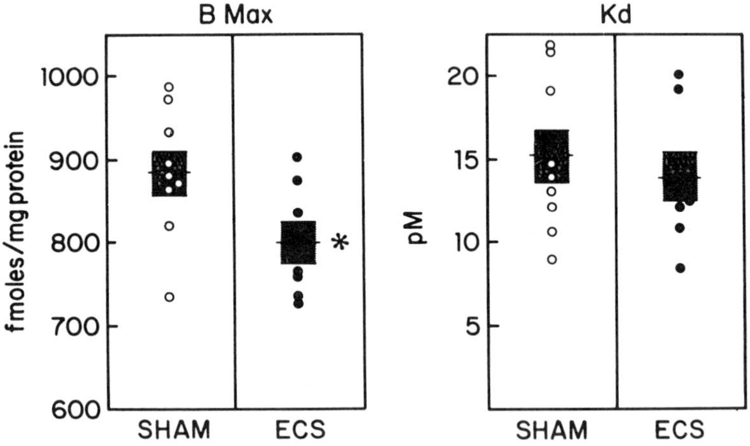

FIGURE 5. Effect of ECS × 7 on [3H]QNB binding parameters (B_{Max} and K_d) in rat cortical membranes. Rats were decapitated 24 hours after the final ECS. The cortex was rapidly dissected and frozen at −80°C until the [3H]QNB binding assays. *$p < 0.05$, ECS vs. control. (Student's t-test.)

CONCLUSIONS

The series of experiments presented here delineates an animal model of ECT-induced memory impairment which closely resembles the clinical syndrome. ECS-induced effects on anterograde memory function have been shown to be cumulative in nature, were characterized by a specific deficit in delayed recall while immediate recall was intact, and gradually dissipated over a period of 21 days following the last ECS administration. Retrograde effects were characterized by gross impairment in recall of an aversive stimulus applied close to the onset of treatment while a more distally applied stimulus was successfully retained. The model described here is more directly relevant to the clinical context than that derived from previous studies based on the acute effects on memory of a single ECS administration.

Further studies are clearly called for in three broad directions:

1. Extension of the methodology to encompass measures of memory function other than the passive avoidance technique used here. Studies currently in progress in our laboratory are utilizing an active avoidance technique which can more accurately assess learning by a series of learning trials rather than on the basis of a single training exposure. Further studies employing positive rather than negative conditioning techniques are also clearly indicated.
2. The hypothesized link between ECS-induced memory impairment and ECS-induced muscarinic receptor subsensitivity is still largely circumstantial. Further studies are needed to examine the relative time courses of the two phenomena and to determine whether in the same animal a correlation exists between severity of memory impairment and degree of muscarinic receptor down regulation.
3. The effect of agents reported to enhance memory function should be studied in the context of the model described here. Potentially memory-active compounds such as vasopressin[14] should be examined for possible prevention or reversal of the memory deficit. Other compounds with reportedly positive effects on memory should be similarly examined. Use of a clinically relevant ECT model is likely to render such results considerably more applicable to the clinical context than the results of previous studies in which acute effects of a single ECS were studied.

ACKNOWLEDGMENTS

The authors thank Samuel Gershon, M.D., for valuable guidance and Sandra Demetriou, Sandra Tait, and Frans Fucek for technical assistance.

REFERENCES

1. WEINER, R. D., H. J. RODGERS, C. A. WELCH, J. R. J. DAVIDSON, R. D. MILLER, D. WEIR & J. F. CAHILL. 1984 ECT stimulus parameters and electrode placement; relevance to therapeutic and adverse mechanisms. *In* ECT: Basic Mechanisms. B. Lerer, R. D. Weiner & R. H. Belmaker, Eds.: 139–147. John Libbey. London, England.
2. MCGAUGH, J. 1974. Electroconvulsive shock: effects on learning and memory in animals. *In* Psychobiology of Convulsive Therapy. M. Fink, S. Kety, J. McGaugh & T. A. Williams, Eds.: 85–97. Winston Sons. Washington, D.C.
3. MILLER, R. & N. MARLIN. 1979. Amnesia following electroconvulsive shock. *In* Functional

Disorders of Memory. J. F. Kihlstrem & F. J. Evans, Eds.: 143–197. Lawrence Erlbaum Associates. Hillsdale, N.J.

4. REICHERT, H., J. BENJAMIN, A. H. NEUFELDT & G. MARGERRISON. 1976. Bilateral and nondominant unilateral ECT. II. Development of prograde effects. Can. Psychiatry Assoc. J. **21:** 79–86.
5. SQUIRE, L. R. 1977. Electroconvulsive therapy and memory loss. Am. J. Psychiatry **134:** 997–1001.
6. WEEKS, D., C. P. L. FREEMAN & R. E. KENDELL. 1978. ECT. III. Enduring cognitive deficits? Br. J. Psychiatry **137:** 26–37.
7. SQUIRE, L. R., P. C. SLATER & P. M. CHACE. 1975. Retrograde amnesia: temporal gradient in very long term memory following electroconvulsive therapy. Science **187:** 77–79.
8. DANIEL, W. F., R. D. WEINER & H. F. CROWITZ. 1983. Autobiographical amnesia with ECT: an analysis of the roles of stimulus waveform, electrode placement, stimulus energy and seizure length. Biol. Psychiatry **18:** 121–126.
9. LERER, B. 1985. Studies on the role of brain cholinergic systems in the therapeutic mechanisms and adverse effects of ECT and lithium. Biol. Psychiatry **20:** 20–40.
10. LERER, B., M. STANLEY, I. MCINTYRE & H. ALTMAN. 1984. Electroconvulsive shock and brain muscarinic receptors: relationship to anterograde amnesia. Life Sci. **35:** 2659–2664.
11. DASHIEFF, R. M., D. D. SAVAGE & J. O. MCNAMARA. 1982. Seizures down-regulate muscarinic cholinergic receptors in hippocampal formation. Brain Res. **235:** 327–334.
12. LERER, B., M. STANLEY, S. DEMETRIOU & S. GERSHON. 1983. Effect of electroconvulsive shock on 3H-QNB binding in rat cerebral cortex and hippocampus. J. Neurochem. **41:** 1680–1683.
13. LOULLIS, C. C., R. L. DEAN, A. S. LIPPA, L. P. MEYERSON, B. BEER & R. T. BARTUS. 1983. Chronic administration of cholinergic agents: effects on behavior and calmodulin. Pharmacol. Biochem. Behav. **18:** 601–604.
14. LERER, B., T. ZABOW, N. EGNAL & R. H. BELMAKER. 1983. Effect of vasopressin on memory following ECT. Biol. Psychiatry **18:** 821–824.

Effect of Electroconvulsive Shock on Serotonin Activity

WALTER B. ESSMAN

Departments of Psychology and Biochemistry
Queens College
City University of New York
65-30 Kissena Boulevard
Flushing, New York 11367

Brain serotonin has been related to electroconvulsive shock (ECS) in a number of ways, involving either a basis for the action of such treatment upon affect or cognitive functions or as a foundation for the clarification of seizure mechanisms. These developments followed the initial observations (1957, 1960) that serotonin concentration is elevated in the rodent brain after ECS. It was further established that a single ECS produced elevation of brain and intestinal serotonin initially after the convulsion and again between 36 and 72 hours following the convulsion.[19] The initial peak elevation of serotonin concentration was comparable for rats given a single ECS or others given a series of 8 ECS treatments. These observations have been confirmed for several species in different laboratories.[3–5,11,12,14,16,28,29,33]

The turnover of serotonin in the rodent brain is decreased after a single ECS.[14] This effect may also relate to the uptake of this biogenic amine, which is lowered by a single ECS[14] in mouse regional tissue and synaptosomes and in rat cerebral cortex slices obtained 30 minutes and 24 hours after a single ECS or after 5 ECS given over 10 days.[31]

It has been suggested that brain serotonin receptors can be altered by ECS,[16] and there have been numerous studies offering a similar suggestion and providing empirical support.[1,6,24–27,30]

The purpose of the present report is to consider the spectrum of serotoninergic changes brought about with ECS, the interactions among these effects, and the cellular and subcellular mechanisms of potential import for ECS, serotonin, and therapeutic effects.

SEROTONIN CONCENTRATION CHANGE FOLLOWING ECS

As previously mentioned, serotonin content is elevated in several brain regions after a single or multiple ECS. This is suggested not only by direct tissue measurement of serotonin, but also by functional studies, the results of which point to an ECS-induced brain serotonin increment. Such evidence has emerged from behavioral and pharmacological studies. For example, massed ECS in rats interrupted escape behavior in an avoidance task: such behavioral disruption was abolished with either *p*-bromo-*N*-methylamphetamine or *p*-chlorophenylalanine, suggesting that the ECS effect is serotonin mediated.[9] Amnesia induced in rats by ECS was protected against by methysergide or bromolysergide, again suggesting that ECS mobilizes serotonin.[32] Multiple ECS produced an enhancement of behavioral function attributable to a serotonin effect,[7] as was similarly observed in developing rats where repeated ECS caused enhancement of behavioral responses to tranylcypromine (TCP) plus L-

TABLE 1. Changes in Serotonin Concentration in Several Regions of the Mouse Brain after a Single ECS. Values Are Given as Mean ($\pm\sigma$) $\mu g/g$

	Condition	
Brain Region	$\overline{\text{ECS}}$	ESS
Cerebral cortex	0.21 (0.04)	0.29 (0.06)
Midbrain	0.82 (0.17)	0.95 (0.15)[a]
Diencephalon	0.76 (0.14)	1.47 (0.38)[b]

[a] $p < 0.02$.
[b] $p < 0.01$.

tryptophan (TPT).[2] A similar result for the enhancement, by a single ECS, of TCP-TPT-induced behavioral change was reported in rats,[8] and has also been shown to depend upon the intact synthesis and release of serotonin by ECS to effect such behaviors.[22] Head twitch induced in rats by 5-hydroxytryptophan is enhanced by repeated ECS;[28,29] similar serotonin-like behavioral enhancement was also observed after multiple ECS treatments.[3] Even though most of these studies suggest that an increased availability of serotonin occurs after ECS, it has been indicated that serotonin concentration increases do not occur, although serotonin release may occur during or just after stimulation.[20]

In our own studies, using mice, ECS was administered by current delivery (20 mA, 400 V, 200 mseconds) through salinized transcorneal electrodes, resulting in a full clonic-tonic convulsion, loss of consciousness for approximately 40 seconds, and a postictal period of about eight minutes.

In TABLE 1 a summary is presented of the regional brain changes in serotonin concentration measured 20 minutes after a single ECS. It is apparent that for those regions sampled, the greatest change in serotonin concentration after a single ECS occurs in the midbrain. Although the change in concentration in the cerebral cortex was small and insignificant, it did occur in the appropriate direction. This raised the question of whether cellular changes might be uniformly effected by a single ECS. Since neurons as well as glia contain serotonin, it is possible that since ECS produces an altered K^+ flux across the cell membranes, that whereas such stimulation depolarizes the neuronal membrane, it affects the glial cell differently.

Following either a single ECS or sham ECS ($\overline{\text{ECS}}$), fractions enriched with either neurons or glia were prepared from the mouse cerebral cortex by differential and density gradient centrifugation and ultrafiltration. Serotonin concentration was measured for each fraction, and these data are summarized in TABLE 2. The data suggest that the major cellular change in cortical serotonin after ECS occurs in glia, where there was a significant elevation by 20 minutes after stimulation.

More detailed studies have shown that a major functionally relevant serotonin-containing site that is modified by ECS is the hippocampus,[15] and more generally

TABLE 2. Mean ($\pm\sigma$) Concentration of Serotonin ($\mu g/g$) in Fractions Enriched with Neurons and Glia from the Mouse Cerebral Cortex: Effect of ECS

	Fraction	
Condition	Neuronal	Glial
$\overline{\text{ECS}}$	1.17 (0.42)	1.22 (0.58)
ECS	0.81 (0.36)	1.72 (0.64)[a]

[a] $p < 0.02$.

TABLE 3. Mean ($\pm\sigma$) Rate of C^{14}-Leucine Incorporation into Hippocampal Protein (mmol/mg protein/hour) at Several Times after a Single ECS

Time after ECS (hour)	Rate of Protein Synthesis	Percent Change
0	32.6 (1.07)	—
1	17.4 (0.90)	−46[a]
12	33.6 (1.30)	+3
24	32.5 (1.10)	−0.3

[a] $p < 0.01$.

several of the structures of the limbic system. These findings will bear upon the functional effects of ECS—relevant to memory processing, affective behaviors, and possibly as model systems for seizure disorders.

One such effect in particular concerns the effect of ECS upon cerebral protein synthesis. It has been previously demonstrated that an inhibition of regional protein synthesis by ECS can be accounted for, and independently mediated by, a change in serotonin.[17] In the following illustration, hippocampi from mice given a single ECS were obtained at several times after the convulsion. The incorporation of C^{14}-leucine into protein was determined; these data are summarized in TABLE 3.

It is apparent that a significant inhibition of protein synthesis follows ECS and is evident in the hippocampus 60 minutes later. A similar effect has been reproduced through the intrahippocampal injection of serotonin in quantities approximating those by which this amine is increased after a single ECS.[13]

Aside from concentration changes and altered turnover (i.e., serotonin synthesis is significantly decreased at 3 and 6 hours after a single ECS given to rats),[21] there are effects of ECS upon serotonin uptake. In rats given a single ECS, the K_m and V_{max} for uptake by slices from the cerebral cortex were lower 24 hours later.[31] The effects of a single ECS upon the regional uptake of C^{14}-serotonin in mouse brain have been summarized in TABLE 4.

Whereas serotonin uptake decreased in the cerebral cortex and midbrain after a single ECS, there was an increased uptake by the cerebellar cortex. These findings suggest that there is regional specificity for the changes in uptake produced by ECS and that such changes may not necessarily depend upon regional differences in endogenous serotonin content.

Perhaps one of the more exciting aspects of the brain serotoninergic system lies in the receptor sites for this amine and how such sites are modified by ECS. Repeated ECS did not alter the specific binding of serotonin 24 hours after the last of 10 treatments.[1] The tissue sampled consisted mainly of striatum. Using whole cerebral cortex, 5-HT_2 receptors, labeled with H^3-spiperone, were shown to increase (approximately 38%) after a series of 12 ECS.[27] Similar findings have been reported for

TABLE 4. Serotonin Uptake (μm/mg) in Several Regions of the Mouse Brain 45 Minutes after a Single ECS. Uptake Measurement was 15 Minutes

Brain Region	$\overline{ECS}$	ECS
Cerebral cortex	1.48 (0.07)	1.13 (0.05)[a]
Midbrain	1.50 (0.12)	1.06 (0.04)[a]
Limbic structure	0.63 (0.01)	0.55 (0.01)
Cerebellar cortex	0.16 (0.01)	0.59 (0.05)[a]

[a] $p < 0.02$.

serotonin–type 2 receptor sites in rat frontal cortex after repeated ECS,[24,25] as well as for cerebral cortex more generally.[26] It may be observed that all of these studies have confined their receptor locus to postsynaptic sites and in the main have limited the observations to specific binding in the cerebrum.[23] Recent autoradiographic localization of specific serotonin binding sites in the rat brain has included the participation of the frontal and prefrontal cortex, septal region, and hippocampus.[10]

Serotonin receptors have been identified on presynaptic membranes from several regions of the mouse brain.[18] It is reasonable, therefore, that specific serotonin receptors both presynaptically as well as postsynaptically are influenced by ECS. In our studies synaptosomes were prepared from the cerebral cortex, hippocampus, and cerebellar cortex of mice, 45 minutes following a single ECS. Differential and density gradient methods previously described[17] with morphological confirmation of fraction homogeneity were employed. The synaptosomes were then osmotically ruptured and the fractional organelles were dispersed on a sucrose density gradient (0.2 M to 1.2 M), from which a population of presynaptic membranes were isolated at a density of approximately 5.2 M. These membranes were washed, recentrifuged, pelleted, and resuspended in sucrose, with the protein concentration of 0.1 ml aliquots determined.

TABLE 5. Mean ($\pm\sigma$) Specific Serotonin Binding and Affinity for Purified Presynaptic Membranes from Several Brain Regions: Effects of ECS

	Serotonin Receptor Binding							
	Serotonin-1				Serotonin-2			
	n (fmol/mg protein)		k_D (nM)		n (fmol/mg protein)		k_D (nM)	
Brain Region	$\overline{\text{ECS}}$	ECS			$\overline{\text{ECS}}$	ECS		
Cerebral cortex	21.26 (2.87)	49.26[a] (3.97)	0.89	0.91	91.34 (6.11)	92.23 (8.40)	0.85	0.88
Hippocampus	31.38 (4.60)	44.18 (2.86)	0.78	0.75	282.42 (17.30)	290.20 (11.65)	0.76	0.78
Cerebellar cortex	20.63 (3.84)	41.83 (4.11)	0.86	0.84	185.67 (10.69)	194.27 (12.03)	0.88	0.86

[a] $p < 0.01$.

Receptor binding for serotonin-1 and serotonin-2 sites was determined by (a) determining the total number of specific, high-affinity serotonin binding sites through the displacement of ^{3}H-serotonin by differing concentrations of unlabeled serotonin; (b) determining the specific, high-affinity serotonin-2 binding sites by determining ^{3}H-spiperone binding to membranes, with lysergic acid diethylamide as the displacing agent; and (c) subtraction of b from a for matched aliquots from each sample, to provide a measure of serotonin-1 binding sites. All data were analyzed by Scatchard plots with a linear regression analysis to yield n, the number of binding sites, and k, the affinity constant.

These data have been summarized in TABLE 5, where for presynaptic membranes from each region sampled after ECS, both classes of serotonin receptor have been identified.

It is apparent that a single ECS increases the density of presynaptic serotonin-1 receptor sites and does not change presynaptic serotonin-2 binding sites. This effect contrasts with those reports of postsynaptic serotonin binding, where 5-HT_2 sites were increased by ECS and 5-HT_1 sites were unchanged. The changes in presynaptic serotonin-1 receptors produced by a single ECS are consistent with ECS-induced concentration increases in serotonin, reduced regional uptake, decreased turnover, and alterations in the availability of serotonin for other events.

In this paper the effects of a single ECS upon the disposition and function of serotonin in the mouse brain have been examined. The consequences of such treatment include (1) an increase in regional and cellular concentration; (2) a decreased turnover; (3) a decreased regional uptake; and (4) an increase in the density of type 1 presynaptic receptors. These changes, along with a serotonin-related, ECS-induced inhibition of protein synthesis, and a focus of serotonin-related effects in the hippocampus, point toward areas of functional significance; such import lies in the effects of ECS upon memory and affective behaviors as well as for ECS-induced seizures as a model for seizure disorders.

REFERENCES

1. ATTERWILL, C. K. 1980. Lack of effect of repeated electroconvulsive shock on [^{3}H]spiroperidol and [^{3}H]5-hydroxytryptamine binding and cholinergic parameters in rat brain. J. Neurochem. **35:** 729–734.
2. ATTERWILL, C. K. & A. R. GREEN. 1980. Responses of developing rats to L-tryptophan plus an MAOI. II. Effects of repeated electroconvulsive shock. Neuropharmacology **19:** 337–341.
3. BHAVSAR, V. H., V. R. DHUMAL & V. V. KELKAR. 1983. The effect of estradiol on the alterations in monoamine-mediated behavioural responses induced by administration of electroconvulsive shocks or imipramine to female rats. Neuropharmacology **22:** 751–756.
4. BREITNER, C., A. PICCHIONI, L. CHIN & L. E. BURTON. 1961. The effect of electrostimulation on brain 5-hydroxytryptamine concentration. Dis. Nerv. Syst. **22:** 93–96.
5. BREITNER, C., A. PICCHIONI & L. CHIN. 1964. Neurohormone levels in brain after CNS stimulation including electrotherapy. J. Neuropsychiatry **5:** 153–158.
6. CHNEIWEISS, H., A. PROCHIANTZ, J. GLOWINSKI & J. PREMONT. 1984. Biogenic amine-sensitive adenylate cyclases in primary culture of neuronal or glial cells from mesencephalon. Brain Res. **302:** 363–370.
7. COSTAIN, D. W., A. R. GREEN & D. G. GRAHAME-SMITH. 1979. Enhanced 5-hydroxytryptamine-mediated behavioural responses in rats following repeated electroconvulsive shock: relevance to the mechanism of the antidepressive effect of electroconvulsive therapy. Psychopharmacology **61:** 167–170.
8. COWEN, P. J., D. J. NUTT & A. R. GREEN. 1980. Enhanced 5-hydroxytryptamine and dopamine-mediated behavioural responses following convulsions. II. The effects of anaesthesia and current conditions on the appearance of enhanced responses following electroconvulsive shock. Neuropharmacology **19:** 901–906.
9. DALLÓ, J. 1979. Possible role of the serotonergic system in the behavioural effect of massed electroconvulsive shock in rat. Pol. J. Pharmacol. Pharm. **31:** 271–276.
10. DESHMUKH, P. P., H. I. YAMAMURA, L. WOODS & D. L. NELSON. 1983. Computer assisted autoradiographic localization of subtypes of $serotonin_1$ receptors in rat brain. Brain Res. **288:** 338–343.
11. ESSMAN, W. B. 1968. Electroshock induced retrograde amnesia and brain serotonin metabolism: effect of several antidepressant compounds. Psychopharmacologia **13:** 258–266.
12. ESSMAN, W. B. 1970. The role of biogenic amines in memory consolidation. *In* The Biology of Memory. G. Adam, Ed.: 213–238. Akademiai Kiado Publishing. Budapest, Hungary.
13. ESSMAN, W. B. 1972. Neurochemical changes in ECS and ECT. Semin. Psychiatry **4:** 67–79.
14. ESSMAN, W. B. 1973. Neurochemistry of Cerebral Electroshock. Spectrum Publishing. New York, N.Y.

15. ESSMAN, W. B. 1973. Neuromolecular modulation of experimentally induced retrograde amnesia. Confinia Neurol. **35:** 1–22.
16. ESSMAN, W. B. 1980. Functional properties of brain serotonin receptors. *In* Neurotransmitters, Receptors and Drug Action. W. B. Essman, Ed.: 105–142. Spectrum Publishing. New York, N.Y.
17. ESSMAN, W. B. & S. G. ESSMAN. 1977. Amine regulation of protein synthesis in retrograde amnesia. *In* Behavioral Neurochemistry. J. M. R. Delgado & F. DeFeudis, Eds.: 25–61. Spectrum Publishing. New York, N.Y.
18. ESSMAN, E. J. & L. VALZELLI. 1984. Regional brain serotonin receptor sites: effects of amphetamine in aggressive mice. Pharmacol Res. Commun. **16:** 401–408.
19. GARATTINI, S. & L. VALZELLI. 1956. Effect of some substances on serotonin activity. Commun. XX Int. Physiol. Congress, Brussels, Belgium.
20. GRAHAME-SMITH, D. G. 1984. The neuropharmacological effects of electroconvulsive shock and their relationship to the therapeutic effect of electroconvulsive therapy in depression. *In* Frontiers in Biochemical and Pharmacological Research in Depression. E. Usden *et al.*, Eds.: 327–343. Raven Press. New York, N.Y.
21. GRAHAME-SMITH, D. G., A. R. GREEN & D. W. COSTAIN. 1978. Mechanism of the antidepressant action of electroconvulsive therapy. Lancet **1:** 245–256.
22. GREEN, A. R., D. W. COSTAIN & J. F. W. DEAKIN. 1980. Enhanced 5-hydroxytryptamine and dopamine-mediated behavioural responses following convulsions. III. The effects of monoamine antagonists and synthesis inhibitors on the ability of electroconvulsive shock to enhance responses. Neuropharmacology **19:** 907–914.
23. GREEN, A. R., A. P. GUY & C. R. GARDNER. 1984. The behavioural effects of RU 24969, a suggested 5-HT_1 receptor agonist in rodents and the effect on the behaviour of treatment with antidepressants. Neuropharmacology **23:** 655–661.
24. GREEN, A. R., D. J. HEAL, P. JOHNSON, B. E. LAURENCE & V. L. NIMGAONKAR. 1983. Antidepressant treatments: effects in rodents on dose-responsive curves of 5-hydroxytryptamine- and dopamine-mediated behaviours and 5-HT_2 receptor number in frontal cortex. Br. J. Pharmacol. **80:** 377–385.
25. GREEN, A. R., P. JOHNSON & V. L. NIMGAONKAR. 1983. Increased 5-HT_2 receptor number in brain as a probable explanation for the enhanced 5-hydroxytryptamine-mediated behaviour following repeated electroconvulsive shock administration to rats. Br. J. Pharmacol. **80:** 173–177.
26. KELLAR, K. J. & D. A. BERGSTROM. 1983. Electroconvulsive shock: effects on biochemical correlates of neurotransmitter receptors in rat brain. Neuropharmacology **22:** 401–406.
27. KELLAR, K. J., C. S. CASCIO, J. A. BUTLER & R. N. KURTZKE. 1981. Differential effects of electroconvulsive shock and antidepressant drugs on serotonin- 2 receptors in rat brain. Eur. J. Pharmacol. **69:** 515–518.
28. LEBRECHT, U. & J. Z. NOWAK. 1980. Effect of single and repeated electroconvulsive shock on serotonergic system in rat brain. I. Metabolic studies. Neuropharmacology **19:** 1049–1053.
29. LEBRECHT, U. & J. Z. NOWAK. 1980. Effect of single and repeated electroconvulsive shock on serotonergic system in rat brain. II. Behavioural studies. Neuropharmacology **19:** 1055–1061.
30. LERER, B. & N. SITARAM. 1983. Clinical strategies for evaluating ECT mechanisms—pharmacological, biochemical and psychophysiological approaches. Prog. Neuro-Psychopharmacol. Biol. Psychiatry **7:** 309–333.
31. MINCHIN, M. C. W., J. WILLIAMS, J. M. BOWDLER & A. R. GREEN. 1983. Effect of electroconvulsive shock on the uptake and release of noradrenaline and 5-hydroxytryptamine in rat brain slices. J. Neurochem. **40:** 765–768.
32. MONTANARO, N., R. DALL'OLIO & O. GANDOLFI. 1979. Bromolysergide and methysergide protection against ECS-induced retrograde amnesia. Neuropsychobiology **5:** 174–180.
33. WIELOSZ, M. 1983. Effects of electroconvulsive shock on monoaminergic systems in the rat brain. Pol. J. Pharmacol. Pharm. **35:**127–130.

Changes in γ-Aminobutyric Acid Biochemistry and Seizure Threshold

A. RICHARD GREEN

MRC Clinical Pharmacology Unit
Radcliffe Infirmary
Oxford OX2 6HE, England

INTRODUCTION

Successful treatment with electroconvulsive therapy (ECT) demands a series of electroconvulsive shock (ECS) administrations spread out over two to three weeks. Both the repeated ECS administration and the passage of time appear to be vital, several ECS being given in one day having no therapeutic benefit (see the review by Fink).[1] Nevertheless, changes must be occurring after even a single ECS which initiate the changes that produce the therapeutic benefit and which are presumably enhanced and sustained by further treatments.

It was this consideration that led to our approach of examining some of the immediate biochemical and behavioral consequences of ECS in rodents. In particular, this paper will concentrate on the changes in the biochemistry and function of the neurotransmitter γ-aminobutyric acid (GABA).

MATERIALS AND METHODS

Animals

Both rats and mice have been used in the studies. Rats were adult male Sprague-Dawley derived (Charles River, Ramsgate, United Kingdom) weighing 120–180 g. Mice were C57/BL6/Ola strain (Olac, Bicester, United Kingdom) weighing 20–25 g. All animals were kept in conditions of controlled heat (20°C) and light (dark period: 19 h 00 min–07 h 00 min) and fed an *ad libitum* diet of 41B pellets and tap water.

Measurement of Seizure Threshold

Seizure threshold in rats was measured by the method of Nutt and colleagues.[2,3] Basically this involves constant infusion via a tail vein of a known concentration of convulsant drug. Measurement of the time from onset of infusion to the appearance of the first myoclonic jerk allows calculation of the dose of drug required to elicit a seizure.[2,3]

Electrically induced seizures were produced by administration of a single ECS (125 V, 50 Hz sinusoidal for 1 second) through ear-clip electrodes; control animals had electrodes placed but no current passed. ECS produced a full tonic-clonic seizure lasting for about 20 seconds.

Flurothyl-induced seizures were produced by exposing the rats to flurothyl vapor (0.3 ml was vaporized in a desiccator jar). After approximately 20 seconds the rats displayed myoclonic jerks followed immediately by a tonic-clonic seizure. At this time the animals were rapidly removed and allowed to recover in their home cage, convulsions normally lasting about 15 seconds after removal from the jar.

Measurement of GABA, GABA Synthesis, and GABA Release

For measurement of brain GABA concentration rats were killed by exposure of the head to a focused high-intensity (70 W cm^2) microwave beam for four seconds,[4] the brain dissected, and GABA concentration measured by an enzymatic-fluorimetric assay as detailed elsewhere.[5]

GABA synthesis was measured by determining the rate of GABA accumulation in specific brain regions following administration of the GABA transaminase inhibitor aminooxyacetic acid (AOAA; 10 mg/kg) as described by others.[6]

Release of endogenous GABA was measured in slices of brain as follows. Brain regions were dissected out and chopped on a McIlwain tissue chopper in two directions at 45°C at 0.2 mm intervals. The slices were rinsed three times in oxygenated Krebs solution. Approximately 200 mg of tissue was then incubated for 10 minutes in oxygenated Krebs solution at 37°C, the supernatant withdrawn and replaced with a Krebs solution containing high K^+ (40 mM) for 10 minutes. Both supernatants were acidified with 50 μl HCl (1 M) and placed on a Dowex H^+ column. GABA was eluted with NH_4OH (1 M), the eluate dried under N_2, and the residue dissolved in HCl (0.002 M) for fluorimetric analysis of GABA.[5]

For experiments on [^{3}H]-GABA release, tissue samples were prepared as outlined above (except that the slices were 0.1 mm thick), preincubated with 2 μCi [^{3}H]-GABA for 30 minutes at 37°C, and filtered. Tissue was placed in a superfusion system, and the fractional rate constant determined prior to and during K^+-evoked release.

Radioligand-Receptor Binding

5-HT_2 receptor binding studies were performed essentially by the method of Rosenfeld and Makman[7] using [^{3}H]-spiperone. β-Adrenoceptor number was measured as described by Green *et al.*[8] using [^{3}H]-dihydroalprenolol. Saturation binding curves were examined with subsequent Scatchard analysis performed using linear regression analysis. Full details are given elsewhere.[8]

Behavioral Studies

5-Hydroxytryptamine (5-HT)-mediated behavioral responses in mice were examined by administration of carbidopa (25 mg/kg intraperitoneally) followed 30 minutes later by L-5-hydroxytryptophan (5-HTP) at various doses. The resultant head twitches induced were counted over a 2-minute period 30 minutes after the 5-HTP (see Reference 9). Dopamine-mediated behavior was examined by measuring the locomotor response on LKB Animex meters of pairs of mice following administration of apomorphine (1.0 mg/kg).[9] The clonidine-induced sedation response was determined by the rating of a group of behavioral changes at 10-minute intervals in the 60 minutes following injection of clonidine at low dose (see Results) as described by Heal *et al.*[10,11] In all cases, where practical, the observer or rater was unaware of the previous treatment of the animals. Studies on the effect of any particular treatment on a

TABLE 1. Effect of a Bicuculline-Induced Seizure on the Seizure Threshold to Pentylenetetrazole (PTZ) 30 Minutes Later[a]

Treatment	Dose of PTZ to Produce Seizure (mg/kg)
Saline	35 ± 3 (5)
Bicuculline	66 ± 8 (11)

[a]Dose of bicuculline was 0.35 mg kg^{-1} (intravenously). Results show mean ± standard deviation (SD) with number of observations in brackets. Bicuculline-treated group different from control $p < 0.001$.

behavioral measure were always performed in parallel with the appropriate control since behavioral scores do change slightly from experiment to experiment.

RESULTS

Seizure Threshold following a Convulsion

Following the administration to rats of a single electroconvulsive shock there is a marked rise in seizure threshold, as demonstrated by the increase in the dose of bicuculline necessary to elicit a further convulsion (FIGURE 1). The change was seen within five minutes of the convulsion and lasted for at least three hours. The increase in threshold was seen after a drug-induced seizure (TABLE 1) and could be demonstrated to occur by infusion with any convulsant drug that antagonized GABA function (TABLE 2) but not those that produced seizures through a non-GABAergic mechanism, such as strychnine (glycine antagonist) or quipazine (5-HT agonist). This suggested an increase in GABA function in animals that had experienced a convulsion. The specificity of the change was further emphasized by the fact that the increase in threshold still occurred in rats given *p*-chlorophenylalanine or α-methyl-*p*-tyrosine to deplete respectively 5-HT and catecholamines (TABLE 3) or drugs such as atropine and naloxone which interfere with the function of other central neurotransmitters.[3]

Rat Brain GABA Concentration following a Seizure

Following a seizure the concentration of GABA rose in various brain regions (FIGURE 2).[5] The change occurred at different rates in the brain regions studied but

TABLE 2. Effect of ECS on the Dose of Isopropylbicyclophosphate (IPTBO), Pentylenetetrazole (PTZ), Strychnine, and Quipazine Required to Elicit a Seizure 30 Minutes Later[a]

Convulsant Drug	Dose of Drug to Elicit Seizure (mg/kg)	
	Control	ECS
IPTBO	0.40 ± 0.03	0.49 ± 0.03 (5)[b]
PTZ	35 ± 3 (16)	49 ± 47 (7)[c]
Strychnine	2.36 ± 0.12 (6)	2.37 ± 0.19 (6)
Quipazine	122 ± 6 (6)	119 ± 11 (7)

[a]Results show mean ± SD with observations in brackets.
[b]Different from handled control group: $p < 0.05$.
[c]Different from handled control group: $p < 0.001$.

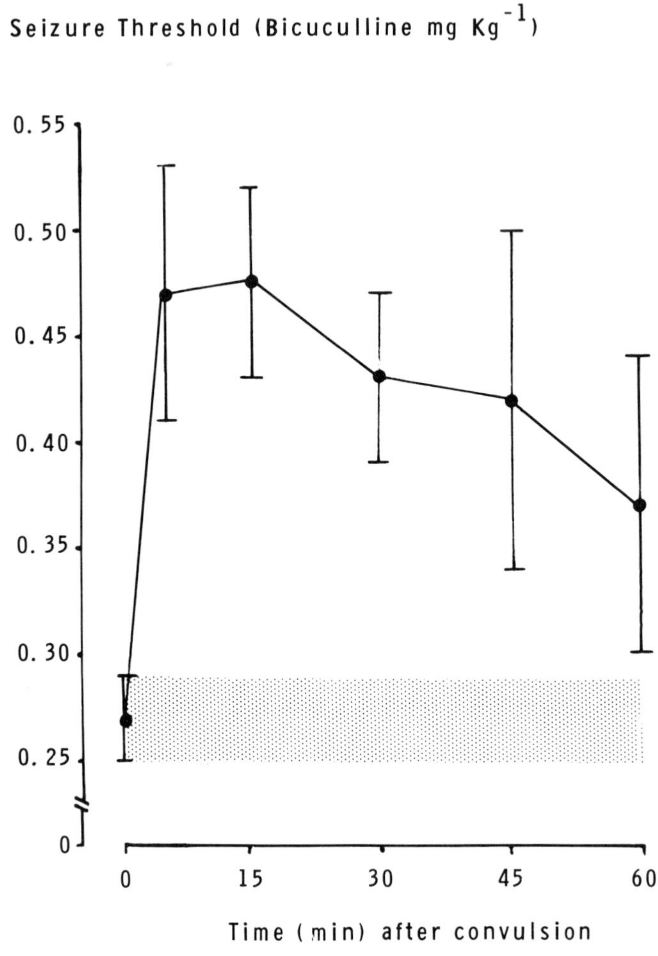

FIGURE 1. The dose of bicuculline necessary to elicit a seizure at various times following an electroconvulsive shock. Rats were either handled or given an ECS. Results shown as mean dose with standard deviation (SD) shown by vertical bars. Six or more determinations, each on a separate rat, were made for each value. Handled control values (mean ± SD) shown as stippled area. All values 5–45 minutes of experimental group different from controls $p < 0.001$, 60-minute value different from control $p < 0.01$, and 60-minute value lower than 15-minute value $p < 0.05$. Ordinate: seizure threshold (bicuculline mg/kg). (Reproduced from Reference 3 with permission from Elsevier-North Holland.)

occurred most rapidly in the hippocampus (FIGURE 2). This change also occurred in rats given a bicuculline-induced seizure but not a flurothyl-induced seizure.[5] Since both of the latter procedures increased seizure threshold,[5] these data suggest that the rise in seizure threshold is not simply the consequence of an increase in GABA concentration.

Rate of GABA Synthesis following a Seizure

The rate of GABA synthesis was determined in various brain regions following a convulsion by measuring the rate of accumulation of GABA following administration of AOAA (see Methods).

Following the administration of AOAA to control rats the concentration of GABA rose linearly in striatum, hippocampus, and cortex (FIGURE 3). In rats given a single ECS there was a rise in GABA concentration, confirming the earlier finding.[5] However, in the rats given ECS there was essentially no further rise following AOAA (FIGURE 3) in any of the three brain regions studied.[12] This suggests that GABA synthesis is almost totally inhibited immediately following a seizure. Two hours later the rate of GABA synthesis had returned to normal.[12]

Rate of GABA Release following a Seizure

Rats were given a single ECS, and K^+-evoked release of endogenous GABA was measured in slices of rat brain prepared 30 minutes later (see Methods). Potassium-evoked GABA release was inhibited in all three regions studied—hippocampus (32%), cortex (30%), and striatum (51%)—while spontaneous release was unaltered (TABLE 4).[13]

Interestingly, K^+-evoked release in slices preloaded with $[^3H]$-GABA was unaltered (TABLE 4) in brain tissue prepared from ECS-pretreated rats.[13]

Effects of Repeated ECS on Monoamine Biochemistry and Function

Following repeated ECS, various changes in monoamine biochemistry and function occur and these are now outlined as a preliminary to presenting data suggesting that some of the changes might result from the alteration in GABA function that follows a seizure.

With regard to 5-HT biochemistry and function, it was first shown in 1976 that following repeated ECS there was an enhancement of behavioral response to 5-HT and 5-HT agonists.[14] These findings have been confirmed[15] and extended to show that there

TABLE 3. Effect of Pretreatment with Various Drugs on the Raised Seizure Threshold following an Electroconvulsive Shock. Rats Were Infused with Bicuculline following Pretreatment with *p*-Chlorophenylalanine (PCPA, 200 mg/kg) or α-Methyl-*p*-tyrosine (α-MPT, 200 mg/kg)[a]

Treatment	Pretreatment	Time of Pretreatment before ECS	Dose of Bicuculline to Produce Seizure (mg/kg)
Handled	—	—	0.27 ± 0.02 (10)
ECS × 1	—	—	0.44 ± 0.03 (9)[b]
Handled	PCPA	24 hours	0.27 ± 0.05 (6)
ECS × 1	PCPA	24 hours	0.18 ± 0.08 (6)[b]
Handled	αMPT	18 hours	0.31 ± 0.03 (6)
ECS × 1	αMPT	18 hours	0.64 ± 0.07 (5)[b]

[a]Results show mean ± SD of the dose required to elicit a seizure 30 minutes after handling or a single ECS, with number of observations in brackets.

[b]Different from the appropriate handled control value: $p < 0.001$.

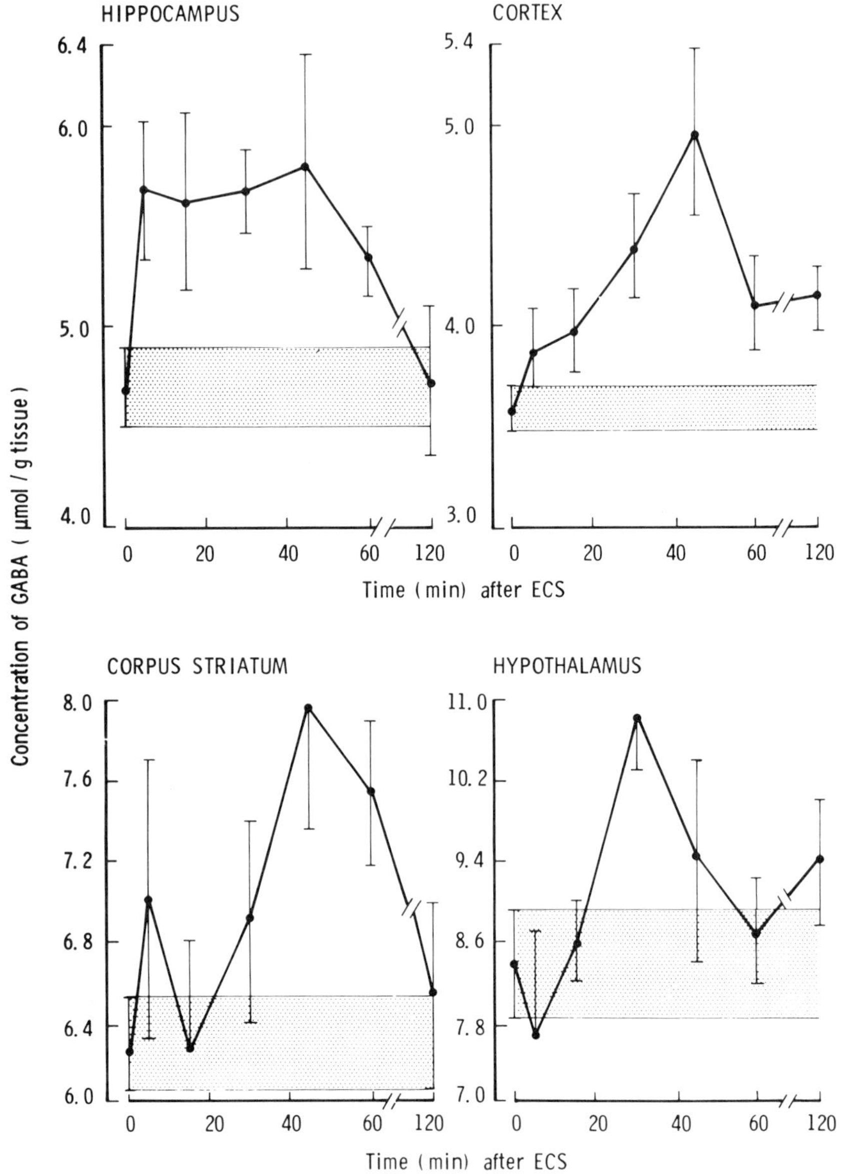

FIGURE 2. γ-Aminobutyric acid (GABA) concentration in (a) hyppocampus, (b) cortex, (c) corpus striatum, and (d) hypothalamus in the 120 minutes after an electroconvulsive shock (ECS). Shaded area shows projection of the mean ± standard error of the mean (SEM) of GABA concentration in the control (handled only) group. Statistically significant increases ($p < 0.05$ or better): hippocampus (5–45 minutes), cortex (30–120 minutes), striatum (45–60 minutes), and hypothalamus (30 minutes). (Reproduced from Reference 5 with permission from Macmillan Press.)

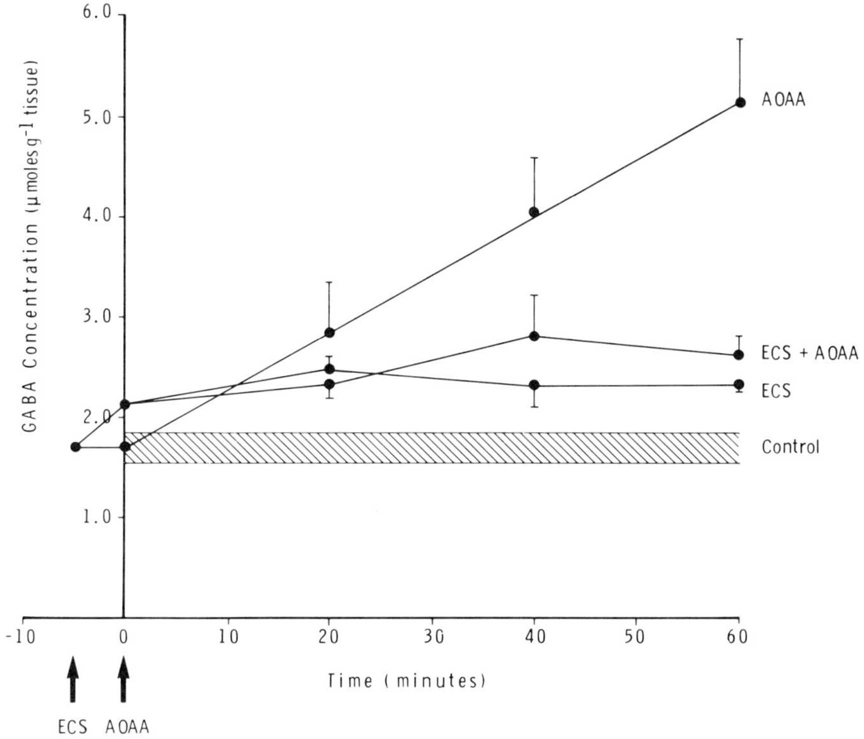

FIGURE 3. Effect of aminooxyacetic acid (AOAA) on accumulation of GABA following a seizure. Rats were given either no seizure (control) or no seizure followed five minutes later by AOAA (10 mg/kg), or single electroconvulsive shock (ECS), or ECS followed five minutes later by AOAA (10 mg/kg) (ECS + AOAA). Shaded area shows mean ± SD of control group. All other points show mean ± SD ($n = 6$).

is also an enhanced 5-HT-induced head-twitch response in mice following repeated ECS[9,16] (FIGURE 4), a response thought to be 5-HT_2 receptor mediated.[17,18] In support of this contention it has been found that 5-HT_2 receptor number is increased after repeated ECS in the brain of both rats[19–21] and mice[22] and that this change in receptor number seems to be responsible for the enhanced 5-HT-mediated behavior seen after

TABLE 4. Release of GABA in Slices of Cortex from Rats Given a Single ECS[a]

	Endogenous GABA Release (μmol/g/hour)		[^{3}H]-GABA Release Fractional Rate Constant ($min^{-1} \times 10^{-3}$)	
	Spontaneous	K^+ (40 mM)	Spontaneous	K^+ (40 mM)
Control	2.51 ± 0.36 (5)	7.72 ± 0.45 (5)	5.4 ± 0.4 (7)	14.9 ± 2.2 (7)
ECS	2.57 ± 0.61 (6)	5.43 ± 0.51 (6)[b]	5.6 ± 0.6 (7)	14.9 ± 2.8 (7)

[a]Values are mean ± SD with the number of experiments in brackets.
[b]Different from control K^+-induced release: $p < 0.001$ two-tailed t-test.

repeated ECS.[21] In contrast, most other antidepressants appear to decrease 5-HT_2 receptor number and 5-HT-induced head-twitch behavior in mice.[22]

Dopamine-mediated behavior has also been shown in several studies to be enhanced by repeated ECS.[15]

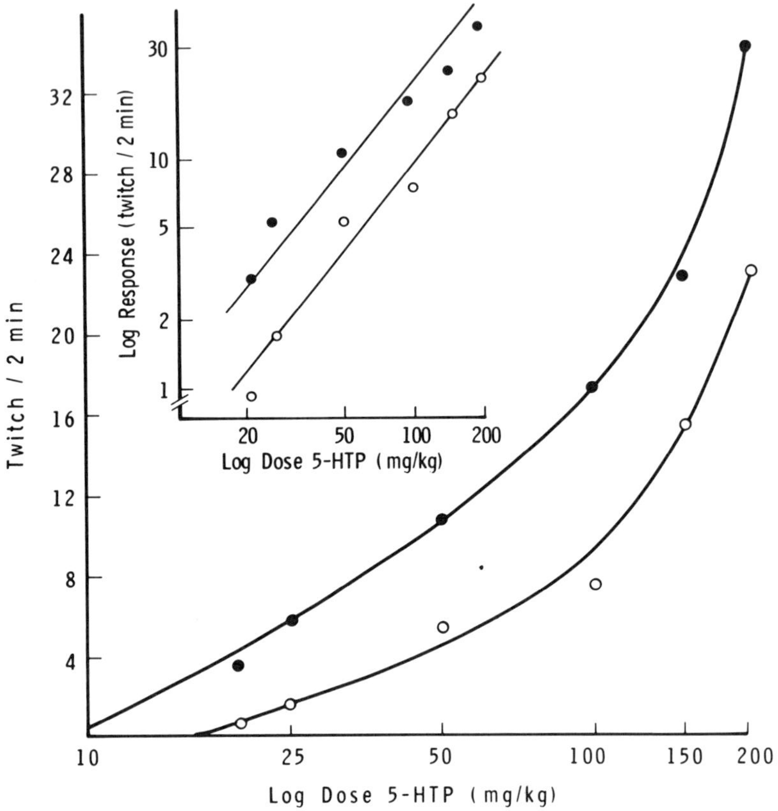

FIGURE 4. Effect of repeated ECS on the behavioral response to carbidopa and 5-hydroxytryptophan. Mice were given either 5 ECS spread over 10 days (●) or 5 anesthetic exposures only (○). Twenty-four hours after the last treatment both groups were given carbidopa (25 mg/kg) followed by various doses of 5-hydroxytryptophan. Main graph shows the log dose of 5-HTP versus total number of head twitches in 2 minutes, 30 minutes after the 5-HTP. Small graph shows the log-dose-log response curve. Experimental group significantly different from control group ($p < 0.05$ or better) at every dose. Eight animals used at each dose point.

With regard to changes in noradrenaline biochemistry and function, β-adrenoceptor number has been shown to decrease after ECS and most other antidepressant treatments.[23] Clonidine-induced sedation responses, a possible measure of α_2-adrenoceptor function,[10,11] are decreased in both mice and rats after both ECS[10] (FIGURE 5) and several other antidepressant drugs.[11]

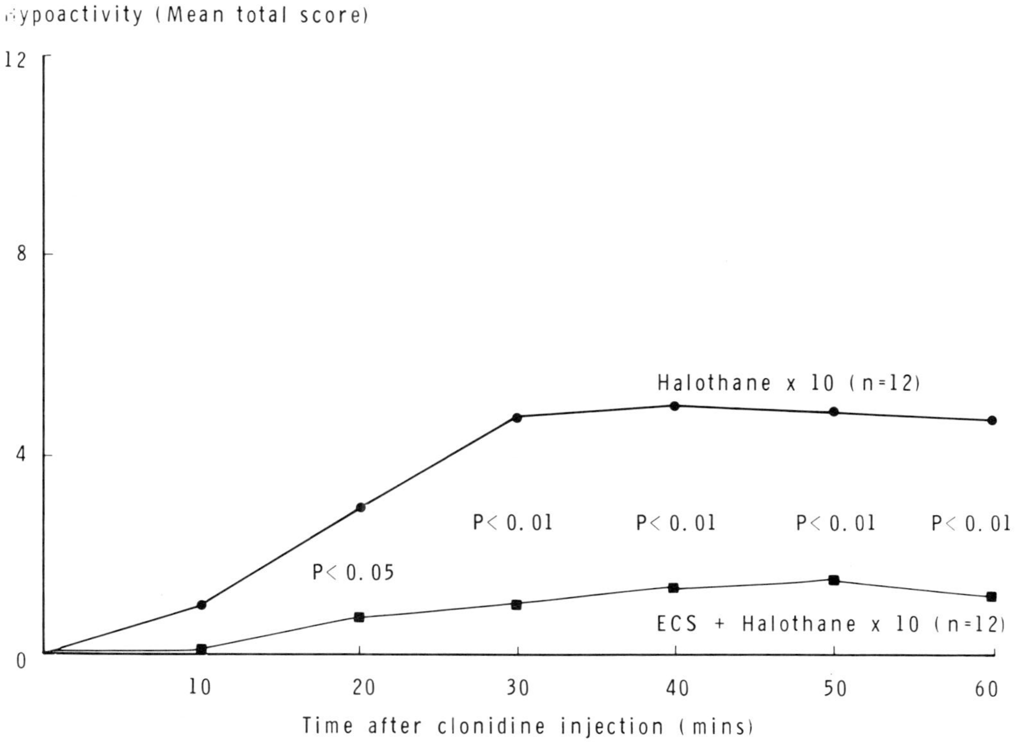

FIGURE 5. Effect of repeated ECS on clonidine-induced hypoactivity in rats. Rats were given either a single ECS while under halothane anesthesia (■) or halothane anesthesia alone (●) once daily for 10 days. Both groups were injected with clonidine (0.1 mg/kg) 24 hours after the final treatment. Hypoactivity, shown as mean total score, is plotted against time after clonidine injection. Results were analyzed using Wilcoxon's rank order test and where results are significantly different, the significance levels are shown. Twelve rats were used in each group. (Reproduced from Reference 10 with permission from Elsevier-North Holland.)

Are the Monoamine-Mediated Changes Induced by ECS Induced by Changes in GABA Function?

If the changes in monoamine-mediated behavior following repeated ECS are induced by changes in GABA function, then it is reasonable to suggest that it should be possible to mimic the action of ECS with drugs altering GABA function. Recently we attempted to do this by using the drug progabide. This drug is a specific GABA-mimetic drug. It is metabolized to the acid and both progabide and the acid are metabolized to form GABA in the brain.[24] The acid has GABA receptor agonist properties.[25] Progabide injection therefore increases GABA concentration and function in the brain and raises seizure threshold,[24] and, as reviewed earlier, both these changes occur after administration of a single ECS.

In initial experiments mice were injected with progabide (400 mg/kg ip) twice daily for 14 days and the 5-HTP-induced head-twitch response measured at various periods thereafter. The number of head twitches was markedly enhanced in the progabide-injected mice for at least 8 days after the last injection.[8] The probable reason for this increased behavioral response is the increase in 5-HT_2 receptor number also seen at this time (TABLE 5). Administration of progabide at the same dose twice daily or once daily for 10 days also markedly increased the 5-HT-mediated behavior (FIGURE 6), and enhancement was seen even when the progabide was given in a manner very similar to repeated ECS, that is, five injections over 10 days (FIGURE 6). Recent work has found that progabide given five times over 10 days at the much lower dose of 100 mg/kg produces the same effect (Gray and Green, unpublished).

Unlike ECS, repeated progabide injection did not result in enhanced dopamine-mediated behavior,[8] but it did lead to a marked attenuation of the clonidine-induced sedation response (FIGURE 7), suggesting a change in α_2-adrenoceptor function. In contrast to ECS, β-adrenoceptor number was unaltered following chronic progabide administration (TABLE 5).

DISCUSSION

The data reviewed above outline part of our research program designed to elucidate the possible therapeutic mechanism of action of ECT. Space constraints have precluded full review of both the work on monoamine-mediated behavior and the

TABLE 5. Characteristics of 5-Hydroxytryptamine (5-HT_2) Receptor in Frontal Cortex and β-Adrenoceptor in the Rest of the Cerebral Cortex following Repeated Administration of Progabide[a]

	5-HT_2 Receptor			β-Adrenoceptor		
	B_{max}	K_D	n	B_{max}	K_D	n
Control	188 ± 8	2.40 ± 0.32	4	64.7 ± 1.0	0.78 ± 0.09	4
Progabide	253 ± 9[b]	1.47 ± 0.34	4	57.2 ± 6.0	0.97 ± 0.20	4

[a]β-Adrenoceptor characteristics were measured using [^{3}H]-dihydroalprenolol binding and 5-HT_2 receptor characteristics using [^{3}H]-spiperone. Mice were treated twice daily with progabide (400 mg kg^{-1}) or vehicle for 14 days. Twenty-four hours after the last dose binding was performed on frontal cortex. Results are expressed as mean ± standard error of the mean with number of Scatchard analysis determinations shown (n). B_{max} expressed in fmol mg^{-1} protein and K_D in nM.

[b]Different from appropriate control: $p < 0.01$.

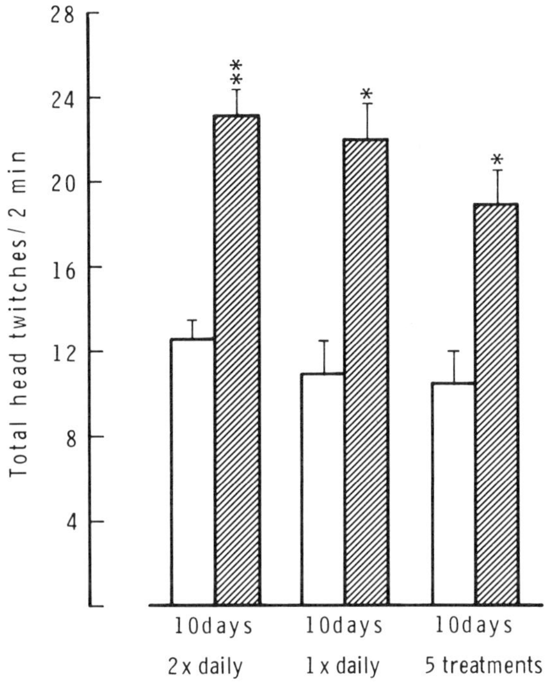

FIGURE 6. Effect of progabide administration on 5-hydroxytryptophan (5-HTP) induced head twitch. Mice were treated for 10 days with progabide (400 mg/kg intraperitoneally) either twice daily, once daily, or five times over the 10 days, and the head-twitch behavior assessed 24 hours after the last dose. Results show median head twitch and bars show the interquartile ranges in vehicle (open columns) and progabide (stippled columns) treated groups of at least eight animals per group. Different from control: $*p < 0.05$; $**p < 0.01$. (Reproduced from Reference 8 with permission from Macmillan Press.)

involvement of GABA in the changes seen, but these findings have recently been discussed elsewhere.[15,26]

A single ECS clearly produces profound changes in GABA function. Our initial view was that there was a marked increase in GABA function following a seizure and indeed the seizure threshold data would support this. However it is hard to equate this view with the observation that there is an almost total inhibition of GABA synthesis and a marked inhibition of GABA release following a convulsion. Both these changes, one would suggest, might in fact decrease GABA function. One is therefore left with an apparent paradox between the biochemistry and functional measure, suggesting that we are either interpreting the biochemistry wrongly or, perhaps, that the functional change is not crucially dependent on a change in GABA biochemistry.

At any rate, perhaps by serendipity, the data on seizure threshold led us to investigate the effects of progabide, and, as has been shown, this drug will produce at least some of the changes associated with repeated ECS. At present we cannot explain why progabide attenuates clonidine-induced sedation. There are however clues to the mechanism of the change in 5-HT biochemistry and function. Recently, Schlicker and colleagues demonstrated that $GABA_B$ receptors mediated an inhibition of 5-HT

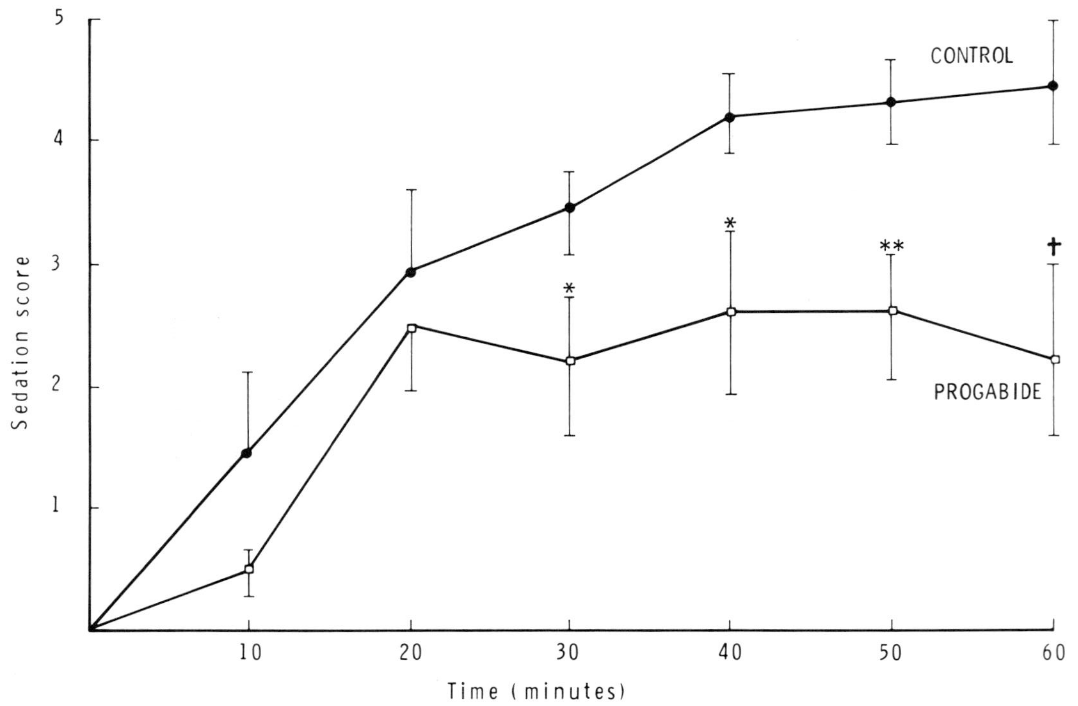

FIGURE 7. Effect of progabide (400 mg/kg intraperitoneally) twice daily for 14 days (O) or vehicle (●) on the sedation response to clonidine (0.15 mg/kg ip) in mice. The sedation response was measured as described in the Methods section. Points show median sedation response and bars the interquartile ranges. Different from the vehicle-treated mice at the same time point: *$p < 0.05$; †$p < 0.01$, with at least eight mice in each group. (Reproduced from Reference 8 with permission from Macmillan Press.)

release in rat brain.[27] Progabide is very potent at that receptor.[27] It seems reasonable to suggest therefore that chronic inhibition of 5-HT release by progabide acting at that receptor leads to a supersensitivity of the postsynaptic 5-HT_2 receptor. In support of this contention we have recently observed that chronic administration of another potent $GABA_B$-receptor agonist, baclofen, also increases both 5-HT_2 receptor number and the head-twitch response (Metz, Goodwin, and Green, unpublished). Furthermore, chronic benzodiazepine administration, which also decreases 5-HT synthesis and release,[28] also increases both the 5-HT_2 receptor number and the 5-HT-induced head-twitch response.[8]

The importance of the biochemical changes seen in rodent brain after repeated ECS to the antidepressant action of ECT in humans is uncertain. However we have shown that we can mimic some of the changes induced by ECS by administration of progabide and it is interesting therefore that there is some evidence for this drug having an antidepressant activity.

ACKNOWLEDGMENTS

The work presented here reflects many years fruitful collaboration with my colleagues. In particular I thank Drs. D. J. Heal, P. J. Cowen, D. J. Nutt, G. M. Goodwin, V. L. Nimgaonkar, and N. D. Vincent and Professor D. G. Grahame-Smith.

REFERENCES

1. FINK, M. 1979. Convulsive Therapy: Theory and Practice. Raven Press. New York, N.Y.
2. NUTT, D. J., P. J. COWEN & A. R. GREEN. 1980. On the measurement in rats of the convulsant effect of drugs and the changes which follow electroconvulsive shock. Neuropharmacology **19:** 1017–1023.
3. NUTT, D. J., P. J. COWEN & A. R. GREEN. 1981. Studies on the post-ictal rise in seizure threshold. Eur. J. Pharmacol. **71:** 287–295.
4. GUIDOTTI, A., D. L. CHENEY, M. TRABUCCI, M. DOTEUCHI, C. WANG & R. A. HAWKINS. 1974. Focussed microwave irradiation: a technique to minimise post-mortem changes in cyclic nucleotides, dopa and choline and to preserve brain morphology. Neuropharmacology **13:** 1114–1121.
5. BOWDLER, J. M. & A. R. GREEN. 1982. Regional rat brain benzodiazepine receptor number and γ-aminobutyric acid concentration following a convulsion. Br. J. Pharmacol. **76:** 291–298.
6. BERNASCONI, R., L. MAITRE, P. MARTIN & F. RASCHDORF. 1982. The use of inhibitors of GABA-transaminase for the determination of GABA turnover in mouse brain regions: an evaluation of aminooxyacetic acid and gabuculline. J. Neurochem. **38:** 57–66.
7. ROSENFELD, M. R. & M. H. MAKMAN. 1981. The interaction of lisuride an ergot derivative with serotonergic and dopaminergic receptors in rabbit brain. J. Pharmacol. Exp. Ther. **216:** 526–531.
8. GREEN, A. R., P. JOHNSON, J. M. MOUNTFORD & V. L. NIMGAONKAR. 1985. Some anticonvulsant drugs alter monoamine mediated behaviour in mice in ways similar to electroconvulsive shock: implications for antidepressant therapy. Br. J. Pharmacol. **84:** 337–346.
9. GREEN, A. R., D. J. HEAL, P. JOHNSON, B. E. LAURENCE & V. L. NIMGAONKAR. 1983. Antidepressant treatments: effects in rodents on dose response curves of 5-hydroxytryptamine and dopamine mediated behaviour and 5-HT receptor number in frontal cortex. Br. J. Pharmacol. **80:** 377–385.
10. HEAL, D. J., H. AKAGI, J. M. BOWDLER & A. R. GREEN. 1981. Repeated electroconvulsive

shock attenuates clonidine-induced hypoactivity in rodents. Eur. J. Pharmacol. **75:** 231–237.

11. HEAL, D. J., S. LISTER, S. L. SMITH, C. L. DAVIES, S. G. MOLYNEUX & A. R. GREEN. 1983. The effects of acute and repeated administration of various antidepressants on clonidine-induced hypoactivity in mice and rats. Neuropharmacology **22:** 983–992.
12. GREEN, A. R., C. HAYES, A. METZ, M. C. W. MINCHIN, H. WILLIAMS & N. D. VINCENT. 1985. Decreased GABA synthesis in regions of rat brain following a convulsion. Br. J. Pharmacol. **84:** 88P.
13. GREEN, A. R., M. C. W. MINCHIN & N. D. VINCENT. 1985. GABA release in rat brain following a seizure. Br. J. Pharmacol. **84:** 89P.
14. EVANS, J. P. M., D. G. GRAHAME-SMITH, A. R. GREEN & A. F. C. TORDOFF. 1976. Electroconvulsive shock increases the behavioural responses of rats to brain 5-hydroxytryptamine accumulation and central nervous system stimulant drugs. Br. J. Pharmacol. **56:** 193–199.
15. GREEN, A. R. 1984. Alterations in monoamine-mediated behaviour and biochemical changes after repeated ECS: studies in their possible association. *In* ECT: Basic Mechanisms. B. Lerer, R. D. Weiner & R. H. Belmaker, Eds. John Libbey & Co. London, England.
16. LEBRECHT, V. & J. Z. NOWAK. 1980. Effect of single and repeated electroconvulsive shock on serotonergic system in rat brain. II. Behavioural studies. Neuropharmacology **19:** 1055–1061.
17. GREEN, A. R., K. M. O'SHAUGHNESSY, M. HAMMOND, M. SCHACHTER & D. G. GRAHAME-SMITH. 1983. Inhibition of 5-hydroxytryptamine-mediated behaviour by the putative 5-HT antagonist pirenperone. Neuropharmacology **22:** 573–578.
18. GOODWIN, G. M. & A. R. GREEN. 1985. A behavioural and biochemical study in mice and rats of putative selective agonists and antagonists for 5-HT_1 and 5-HT_2 receptors. Br. J. Pharmacol. **84:** 743–753.
19. VETULANI, J., V. LEBRECHT & A. PILC. 1981. Enhancement of responsiveness of the central serotonergic system and serotonin-receptor density in rat frontal cortex by electroconvulsive treatment. Eur. J. Pharmacol. **76:** 81–85.
20. KELLAR, K. J., C. S. CASCIO, J. A. BUTLER & R. N. KULTZKE. 1981. Differential effects of electroconvulsive shock and antidepressant drugs on serotonin-2 receptors in rat brain. Eur. J. Pharmacol. **69:** 515–518.
21. GREEN, A. R., P. JOHNSON & V. L. NIMGAONKAR. 1983. Increased 5-HT_2 receptor number in brain as a probable explanation for the enhanced 5-hydroxytryptamine-mediated behaviour following repeated electroconvulsive shock administration to rats. Br. J. Pharmacol. **80:** 173–177.
22. GOODWIN, G. M., A. R. GREEN & P. JOHNSON. 1984. 5-HT_2 receptor mediated head-twitch behaviour following antidepressant treatment to mice. Br. J. Pharmacol. **83:** 235–242.
23. SULSER, F. & P. L. MOBLEY. 1981. Regulation of central noradrenergic receptor function: new vistas on the mode of action of antidepressant treatments. *In* Neuroregulators: Basic and Clinical Aspects. E. Usdin, J. M. Davis & W. E. Bunney, Eds.: 55–83. John Wiley & Sons. Chichester, England.
24. WORMS, P., H. DEPOORTERE, A. DURAND, P. L. MORSELLI, K. G. LLOYD & G. BARTHOLINI. 1982. γ-Aminobutyric acid (GABA) receptor stimulation. I. Neuropharmacological profiles of progabide (SL 76002) and SL 75102 with emphasis on their anticonvulsant spectra. J. Pharmacol. Exp. Ther. **220:** 660–671.
25. LLOYD, K. G., S. ARBILLA, K. BEAUMONT, M. BRILEY, G. DEMONTIS, B. SCATTON, S. Z. LANGER & G. BARTHOLINI. 1982. γ-Aminobutyric acid (GABA) receptor stimulation. II. Specificity of progabide (SL 76002) and SL 75102 for the GABA receptor. J. Pharmacol. Exp. Ther. **220:** 672–677.
26. GREEN, A. R. Electroconvulsive therapy: a GABAergic mechanism? *In* GABA and Mood Disorders: Animal and Clinical Studies. K. G. Lloyd, G. Bartholini & P. L. Morselli, Eds. Raven Press. New York, N.Y. (In press.)
27. SCHLICKER, E., K. CLASSEN & M. GOTHERT. 1984. GABA_B receptor-mediated inhibition of serotonin release in the rat brain. Naunyn-Schmiedeberg's Arch. Pharmacol. **326:** 99–105.

28. SANER, A. & A. PLETSCHER. 1979. Effect of diazepam on 5-hydroxytryptamine synthesis. Eur. J. Pharmacol. **55:** 315–318.
29. LLOYD, K. G., P. L. MORSELLI, H. DEPOORTERE, V. FOURNIER, B. ZIVKOVIC, B. SCATTON, C. BROEKKAMP, P. WORMS & G. BARTHOLINI. 1983. The potential use of GABA agonists in psychiatric disorders; evidence from studies with progabide on animal models and clinical trials. Pharmacol. Biochem. Behav. **18:** 957–966.

Biochemical and Neuroendocrinological Effects of Electroconvulsive Therapy

Discussion of Part II

AMIRAM I. BARKAI

Department of Psychiatry
College of Physicians and Surgeons
Columbia University
722 West 168 Street
New York, New York 10032

This first session on biochemical and neuroendocrinological effects includes four presentations. Two papers (by Kellar and Stockmeier and by Lerer *et al.*) describe changes in neurotransmitter-receptor binding following repeated administration of electroconvulsive shock (ECS) whereas the other two papers (by Essman and by Green) deal with neurochemical changes occurring after a single ECS. Essman's studies were carried out with mice; Green utilized both mice and rats; studies described in the other two presentations were conducted with rats.

The results presented by Kellar and Stockmeier reinforce previous observations that repeated ECS down regulates β-adrenergic receptors and up regulates serotonin-2 (5HT-2) receptors in the cerebral cortex and hippocampus of the rat brain. The down regulation of β-adrenergic receptors by repeated ECS as well as by various antidepressants, taken together with the observation that a course of reserpine injections had resulted in a substantial increase in the density of β-adrenergic receptors, may indicate that β-adrenergic receptors are involved in pathophysiological processes underlying depression (reserpine-treated animals have been used by several investigators as an animal model for depression). Further support for this notion is provided by the finding that concurrent administration of ECS with reserpine prevented the up regulation of β-adrenergic receptors seen after reserpine alone.

The authors have also attempted to relate the increase in 5HT-2 receptors, after repeated ECS, to the therapeutic effect of this treatment in depression. In contrast to ECS, treatment with antidepressant drugs has been shown to result in down regulation of 5HT-2 receptors. Kellar and Stockmeier have speculated that the opposite effects of ECS and antidepressant drugs on 5HT-2 receptors might be related to therapeutic mechanisms of action in the treatment of certain depressions which have different underlying pathologies. Treatment of such depressions with antidepressant drugs would probably be ineffective or would even exacerbate the illness, whereas ECT could be therapeutically beneficial.

The influence of serotonin axons on β-adrenergic receptors has also been investigated by Kellar and Stockmeier. They have demonstrated that down regulation of adrenergic receptors by repeated ECS could be obtained even after destruction of the serotonergic system by the serotonin neurotoxin 5,7 dihydroxytriptamine (5,7 DHT). In this respect the action of ECS resembles that of "atypical" antidepressants (mianserin or iprindole) which do not require an intact 5HT system to induce β-adrenergic down regulation. In contrast repeated administration of imipramine or desipramine to rats with lesioned 5HT axons did not down regulate β-adrenergic receptors, indicating that an intact 5HT system is required for β-adrenergic down regulation by these "typical" antidepressants. Selective lesions of the 5HT system by direct injections of 5,7 DHT into the raphe nuclei resulted in a marked increase in the density of β-adrenergic receptors without alterations in the binding properties of α-adrenergic binding sites. These observations are important for the understanding of the intricate relationships between noradrenergic and serotonergic systems in the brain. Further studies are clearly needed to investigate whether noradrenergic axons play a role in the regulation of 5HT receptors. It has been shown recently that the presence of an intact noradrenergic system is required to induce changes in dopamine receptor functions by neuroleptics or by repeated ECS.

Lerer and his colleagues have studied the possibility that ECS-induced memory impairment is related to a functional reduction in cholinergic neurotransmission in the cerebral cortex. They were able to demonstrate a small, but significant, reduction in the density of muscarinic receptors in rat cortex following repeated administration of ECS. However, as pointed out by the authors, the hypothesized link between ECS-induced memory impairment and the ECS-induced reduction in muscarinic receptor density is still largely circumstantial. Most of the studies described by Lerer *et al.* were aimed at developing an animal model of ECT-induced memory impairment. They have directed their efforts mainly to develop a useful animal model for examining cumulative effects which are more relevant to clinical ECT. The experiments that examined the relationship between memory impairment and muscarinic receptors are considered by the authors as preliminary ones. They provide guidelines for future studies which are clearly needed in order to understand the biological basis underlying ECT-induced cognitive deficits. Such studies, although not directly related to mechanisms involved in the therapeutic effects of ECT, are important, since they may lead to the development of pharmacological interventions aimed at preventing or alleviating the ECT-induced cognitive deficits.

The paper by Essman describes a series of studies on the effects of a single ECS on serotonin activity in the mouse brain. A significant increase in serotonin has been observed in several areas of the mouse brain following ECS. According to Essman the ECS-induced increases in cerebral 5HT concentration are responsible for the reduction in the rate of protein synthesis seen in selected brain areas after ECS. A similar effect has been reproduced through the injection of 5HT into the mouse hippocampus. Interestingly, the data presented suggest that the higher 5HT concentration seen after a single ECS reflects a substantial increase in glia while the concentration of 5HT in neurons tends to be lower at 20 minutes after the stimulation. In addition to the increase in regional 5HT concentration, Essman has reported a decreased 5HT turnover accompanied by a reduction in 5HT uptake, and an increase in the density of 5HT-1 binding sites, on presynaptic membranes. However, a single ECS did not modify 5HT-2 presynaptic binding sites. The apparent discrepency between this latter finding and the findings by others that 5HT-2 binding sites were increased by ECS, while 5HT-1 binding sites were unchanged, was explained by a different cellular localization of binding sites; the results presented by Essman represent only presynaptic 5HT binding sites.

The paper by A. R. Green focused on the biochemical and functional changes of γ-aminobutyric acid (GABA) following a single ECS. One of the immediate changes induced by a single ECS is a marked increase in seizure threshold. Similar increases in seizure threshold could be obtained by various convulsant drugs that are known to antagonize GABA functions (but not by seizure-producing drugs that act as glycine or 5HT antagonists). However, the finding that not all treatments that induced elevations of seizure threshold were associated with changes in cerebral GABA suggests that the rise in seizure threshold is not simply the consequence of an increase in GABA concentrations. In addition, the ECS-induced seizure was associated with a marked inhibition of GABA release and the cerebral synthesis of GABA was almost totally inhibited.

According to Green, the initial changes in GABA functions following each ECS administration would eventually influence monoamine-mediated functions which are known to be modified by repeated ECS. Recent studies by other investigators demonstrated that GABA-ergic receptors may participate in the regulation of 5HT release in rat brain. It was assumed therefore that such GABA-ergic receptors could also influence the density of 5HT receptors. Thus, Green has addressed the question as to whether it might be possible to mimic the action of ECS with drugs that alter GABA function. The GABA-mimetic drug progabide was used since it has been shown to increase cerebral GABA concentration; its metabolite has GABA-receptor agonist properties, and its injection brings about a rise in seizure threshold. The results presented by Green indicate that repeated administration of progabide to mice increased the density of 5HT-2 binding sites in frontal cortex and also enhanced 5HT-mediated behavior. Thus, the action of repeated progabide on the 5HT system resembles that of repeated ECS. However, unlike repeated ECS there was no enhancement of dopamine-mediated behavior and the density of β-adrenergic receptors was not altered following chronic progabide administration.

The studies presented in this session apply research strategies that appear to be based on the assumption that ECT exerts its therapeutic action on the same neurochemical mechanisms that underlie the therapeutic efficacy of psychopharmacological treatments. The literature dealing with psychopharmacological therapy of affective disorders includes ample evidence to support the notion that antidepressive effects involve the modification of noradrenergic or serotonergic functions. Therefore, it is not surprising that these neurotransmitter systems were investigated quite extensively in search of a mode of action of ECT.

While the bulk of the studies presented in this session were aimed at establishing a scientific basis for therapeutic action of ECT, the study by Lerer *et al.* was primarily directed to investigate biological mechanisms of adverse effects. These investigators have presented a clinically relevant animal model of ECS-induced amnesia which is based on repeated exposure to ECS. Clearly, the experiments designed to examine the relationship between muscarinic receptors and memory impairment should be repeated. It is critically important to verify the results obtained by Lerer *et al.*, since there are published reports by several investigators who were unable to demonstrate a significant change in muscarinic receptor binding in rodent brain after repeated ECS. In addition, it might be useful to utilize the animal model presented by Lerer *et al.* to examine possible relationships between memory impairment and receptor binding in other neurotransmitter systems. The observation by Essman that 5HT may influence protein synthesis in the hippocampus provides a clue to a possible relationship between 5HT receptors and memory functions.

The research on the mechanisms of action of ECS has reached a stage of extensive data accumulation and verification. Most animal studies published so far were subjected to clinically oriented adjustments in experimental design and were directed at seeking a "proven" mechanism of action of ECT in clinical situations. However, the available data are not yet adequate to explain how ECT works. They might indicate, perhaps, that inasmuch as the clinical implications of animal studies are important, the questions addressed by basic researchers should not focus exclusively on issues related to the clinical efficacy of ECT. The use of ECS as a tool for the study of intricate relationships among different neurotransmitter systems in the brain may be equally important. Thus, the study of Kellar and Stockmeier and that of A. R. Green represent a noticeable progress since they have explored interactions between different neurotransmitter systems in relation to ECS. A close interaction between basic and clinically oriented researchers should clearly generate studies that could answer questions of clinical importance. However, the design of studies that have no immediate clinical implications should not be discouraged, since such studies are more likely to enhance our understanding of the nature of the underlying disorders in which ECT is effective.

Endogenous Opioids and Their Receptors[a]

Evidence for Involvement in the Postictal Effects of Electroconvulsive Shock

JOHN W. HOLADAY, FRANK C. TORTELLA, JOSEPH B. LONG, G. L. BELENKY,[b] AND ROBERT J. HITZEMANN[c]

Neuropharmacology Branch
Department of Medical Neurosciences
Division of Neuropsychiatry
Walter Reed Army Institute of Research
Washington, D.C. 20307-5100

BRIEF OVERVIEW OF ENDOGENOUS OPIOID SYSTEMS

The endogenous opioids are a family of different peptide ligands that may function as neurotransmitters, neuromodulators, or hormones. Specifically, three primary families of endogenous opioid peptides have been demonstrated, including the enkephalins, dynorphins, and endorphins (see References 1 and 2 for review). Although all share a common amino acid sequence homology at the *N*-terminus of the peptide, they are each derived from distinctly different precursor molecules, and their unique characteristics are imparted by the sequences of amino acids found at the *C*-terminus. These ligands exert their selective opioid actions through multiple opiate receptors which recognize structural differences among the various opioid molecules.

The pentapeptides methionine enkephalin (Met-enk) and leucine enkephalin (Leu-enk), as well as extended versions of these enkephalins, derive from the precursor molecule termed pro-enkephalin A. This precursor peptide contains a total of six Met-enk molecules (some in extended forms) and one Leu-enk molecule.[2] Dynorphin-related substances derive from a precursor peptide (pro-dynorphin) that contains three copies of Leu-enk extended by several basic amino acid molecules which distinguish these peptides as either neo-endorphins or dynorphins. Lastly, β-endorphin (β-EP) is a cleavage product of β-lipotropic hormone (β-LPH) which, in turn, is derived from pro-opiomelanocortin (POMC). In addition to β-EP and β-LPH, POMC serves as the precursor molecule for adrenocorticotropic hormone (ACTH) and various melanocyte-stimulating hormones (MSH).[1,2]

These different opioid peptides are released from nerve cells in the brain and periphery as well as from endocrine glands, implying their respective roles as neurotransmitters or hormones. Enkephalins are contained in over 30 distinct brain

[a] The views of the authors do not purport to reflect the positions of the Department of the Army or the Department of Defense. (Para. 4-3, AR 360-365).

[b] Department of Behavioral Biology.

[c] Department of Psychiatry, University of Cincinnati School of Medicine, Cincinnati, Ohio 45267.

regions, and they are also localized peripherally in the autonomic ganglia and adrenal medulla in high concentrations.[2] Likewise, dynorphin-related molecules are found in 20–30 different brain regions as well as the spinal cord; the most well-defined source for circulating dynorphins is the posterior pituitary gland. Lastly, β-EP-containing nerve cells are concentrated in only two brain nuclei located in the hypothalamus and brain stem, with long axonal projections to numerous other brain regions. The anterior and intermediate lobes of the pituitary gland are rich sources of circulating β-EP. In the anterior lobe of the pituitary, the release of β-EP is concomitantly regulated with ACTH through corticotropin releasing factor (CRF) and negative feedback inhibition by adrenal glucocorticoids.[1]

Endogenously mediated opioid effects (as opposed to pharmacological responses) are not usually revealed in the resting, homeostatic organism. Physiological or behavioral stressors are required to activate these systems. Once activated, investigations into possible physiological or behavioral functions of endogenous opioid systems require a consideration of the potential origins and types of opioid peptides as well as their sites of action and receptor subtype involvements.

At least five different types of opiate receptors have been described in the brain and periphery, largely through the combined use of different natural and synthetic alkaloid and peptide congeners of opioids. These include μ, δ, κ, ϵ, and σ receptors. Although this nomenclature has become widely accepted, perhaps it would be more physiologically pertinent to define these various opiate receptors on a basis of the endogenous ligands for which they demonstrate relative selectivity.[3] Mu receptors, first described using morphine, may exist in high- or low-affinity binding states that serve distinctly different biological functions.[4,5] Among the endogenous opioids, only β-EP (and to a lesser extent Met-enk) appears to serve as a ligand for the μ receptor.[5,6] Delta receptors, initially defined by the selective actions of Leu-enk on the mouse vas deferens preparation, are preferentially responsive to Leu-enk, although Met-enk and β-EP may also act on this receptor subtype.[6] Kappa receptors, first defined by the use of the alkaloid ketocyclazocine,[5] are preferentially affected by dynorphin peptides.[7] The ϵ and σ receptors are less well defined. The ϵ receptor may be a different recognition site for β-EP distinct from μ and δ binding sites. Lastly, the σ receptor may not even be an "opiate" receptor in the classic sense; although the synthetic alkaloid *N*-allylnormetazocine (SKF 10,047) binds to the σ receptor, the hallucinogenic compound phencyclidine also binds avidly to this site.[8] It is important to note that these various receptor subtypes are only *relatively* selective. Thus, if adequate concentrations of almost any of these "selective" opioid ligands are achieved, regardless of their structure, it is very possible that they will bind to several of the various receptor subtypes.

INTRODUCTION

The biological mechanisms responsible for the therapeutic effects of electroconvulsive therapy (ECT) remain to be defined. In experimental animals as well as humans, it has been demonstrated that many neurotransmitter and neuroendocrine substances are profoundly affected by electroconvulsive shock (ECS). Among the classic neurotransmitters, ECS has been shown to affect such ligands as serotonin (Kellar and Stockmeier and Essman, this volume), γ-aminobutyric acid (GABA) (Green *et al.*, this volume), as well as catecholamines (Kellar and Stockmeier, this volume). Circulating concentrations of pituitary peptides and target gland hormones are also affected by ECS (References 9 and 10 and Fink, this volume). Likewise, many of the receptors with which these substances interact are modified following acute or repeated ECS (see below and this volume). Ultimately, the therapeutic effects of ECT are probably a result of interactions among these many endogenous ligands and their altered receptors. Is it possible that any one endogenous system plays a primary role in ECT?

Since their discovery almost a decade ago, endogenous opioid peptides have been implicated as being either causative or curative in a variety of mental disorders (for review, see References 11 and 31). Historically, morphine has been shown to have antidepressant effects. Consequently, we initially wondered whether the therapeutic effects of ECT were in part mediated via the release of endogenous opioid peptides.[12] Indeed, over the past several years, evidence has accumulated to support the hypothesis that endogenous opioids and their receptors play a functional role in a multitude of the postictal events following ECS.[12–27]

The following review emphasizes our own results identifying opioid-like behavioral, electroencephalographic, and autonomic effects of acute and repeated ECS in rats. Evidence as to the source of opioid peptides involved in postictal responses as well as the effects of ECS on opiate receptors will also be reviewed. Finally, the role of opioids as endogenous anticonvulsants released by ECS-induced seizures will be presented.

BEHAVIORAL EFFECTS OF ECS

Immediately following the tonic-clonic seizure produced by a single transauricular ECS (150 V, 60 Hz, 2 seconds duration), rats become rigid with a loss of righting reflex.[12,15,17,18] Based upon the distinguishing characteristics of lost righting reflexes and an inability to cling to an inclined wire screen, this effect of ECS resembles an opioid (as opposed to neuroleptic) form of catalepsy.[17] During this postictal interval, rats are also significantly less responsive to nociceptive stimuli produced by hot-plate and tail-flick exposure.[12,15,17,18,24,27] These cataleptic and antinociceptive effects of ECS are significantly blocked by pretreatment with the opioid antagonist naloxone. Thus, evidence indicates that a single ECS results in the functional activation of endogenous opioid systems.

Therapeutic responses to ECT routinely require its repeated administration over several days. In order to extrapolate basic science observations to this clinical requirement, the effects of repeated daily ECS were studied in rats. Repeated ECS, delivered for nine consecutive days, resulted in a progressive exaggeration of antinociceptive responses[19] and a more protracted duration of the postictal behavioral stupor (catalepsy).[18] This reverse tolerance (sensitization) produced by repeated ECS was unexpected since repeated activation of opioid systems should result in the development of a tolerant (desensitized) state similar to that produced by chronic morphine administration. Additionally, although these opioid-like effects of ECS (antinociception and stupor) were enhanced by repeated ECS, high doses of naloxone were no longer able to completely reverse these behaviors.[18] The opposite is true in morphine-tolerant animals, e.g., it is well known that as the degree of tolerance increases, *less* naloxone is required to precipitate withdrawal and to reverse opioid effects.[28]

Additional studies were performed to assess the potential development of cross tolerance between repeated ECS and morphine challenge and, conversely, chronic morphine and single ECS challenge.[19] Once again, we were surprised to find that instead of cross tolerance, cross sensitization occurred. Repeated daily ECS enhanced the acute effects of morphine, and chronic morphine enhanced the acute opioid-like effects of ECS. Furthermore, chronic heat exposure, a condition also associated with augmented opioid responses,[25] similarly produced an enhanced opioid-like response to ECS challenge.[26] In an attempt to define a molecular explanation for cross sensitization, we found that both repeated ECS and morphine tolerance resulted in a significant *increase* in the number of opioid binding sites in whole brain, suggesting that the cross sensitization between these two experimental conditions may be consequential to an increased availability of opiate receptors[23] (see below).

Urca and colleagues have also investigated the relationships between repeated ECS and chronic morphine.[27] In contrast to our results reviewed above, they observed that repeated daily ECS resulted in a gradual tolerance to ECS-induced antinociceptive responses. Additionally, they observed cross tolerance between chronic morphine treatment and the acute opioid-like effects of ECS. In agreement with our results, however, they reported that the acute effects of morphine were enhanced in rats receiving repeated daily ECS for nine days.

Experimental differences may account for these opposing findings. Urca and colleagues used tail-flick latencies in restrained rats to assess nociceptive responses,[27] whereas our studies used hot-plate escape latencies in freely moving rats.[30] These two nociceptive tests are known to involve different opioid systems, with tail-flick latencies predominantly involving a spinal reflex and hot-plate escape involving an integration of sensory and somatic responses in the brain.[29] In our hands, the increases in tail-flick latencies produced by a single ECS were not reliably antagonized by naloxone.[17] Additionally, Urca *et al.* used chronically restrained rats for tail-flick determinations.[27] Restraint alone is known to be a potent activator of endogenous opioid responses,[30] which may complicate interpretations when ECS and restraint are combined. Owing to these methodological differences, it is difficult to directly compare results between these two studies.

Several experiments were conducted to evaluate the source and identity of the endogenous opioids involved in acute and chronic ECS responses. Lewis and colleagues reported that, although hypophysectomy did not prevent the antinociceptive effect of a single ECS, naloxone's reversal of this opioid-like response was blocked by removal of the pituitary.[24] Our results using hypophysectomized rats also revealed that removal of the pituitary blocked naloxone's ability to reverse ECS-induced behaviors.[22] However, in our experiments, hypophysectomy itself decreased the intensity and duration of the antinociception as well as the postictal depression produced by ECS (FIGURE 1). In other studies measuring tissue concentrations of opioid peptides, Green *et al.* and Hong *et al.* demonstrated that a single ECS failed to alter brain or pituitary concentrations of enkephalins or β-EP.[13,14] However, in humans, a single ECT produced significant increases in circulating β-EP.[31]

Considering these results described above, it is possible that circulating pituitary opioids (e.g., β-EP or dynorphin) may be involved in the manifestation of *acute* ECS responses.[22,24] However, the behavioral consequences of *repeated* daily ECS probably involve brain opioid peptides and their receptors since, unlike single ECS, repeated ECS-induced seizures produced significant increases in Met-enk immunoreactivity in the nucleus caudatus, hypothalamus, and limbic areas.[13,14] Przewlocki and colleagues have also reported selective increases in hippocampal dynorphin immunoreactivity following repeated ECS in rats.[32] Thus, single ECS appears to activate primarily opioid peptides derived from endocrine sources, whereas repeated ECS may activate opioid ligands (and their receptors—see below) in selected brain regions.

Further experiments were conducted to determine the specific central opioid receptor subtype(s) involved in acute ECS responses.[33] We used the selective, long-lasting μ-antagonist, β-funaltrexamine (β-FNA) and the δ-antagonist ICI 154,129 (ICI) at doses previously demonstrated to block μ and δ responses, respectively.[34,35] Using the increase in hot-plate escape latency produced by ECS as our end point, β-FNA pretreatment was without effect upon the antinociceptive response to ECS, whereas ICI significantly antagonized ECS antinociception[33] (FIGURE 2). As expected, these selective antagonists had the opposite effect upon antinociceptive responses produced by the prototype μ agonist, morphine.[35] From these results, we concluded that opioid peptides, activated by a single ECS, act upon δ receptors to exert their postictal antinociceptive effects.

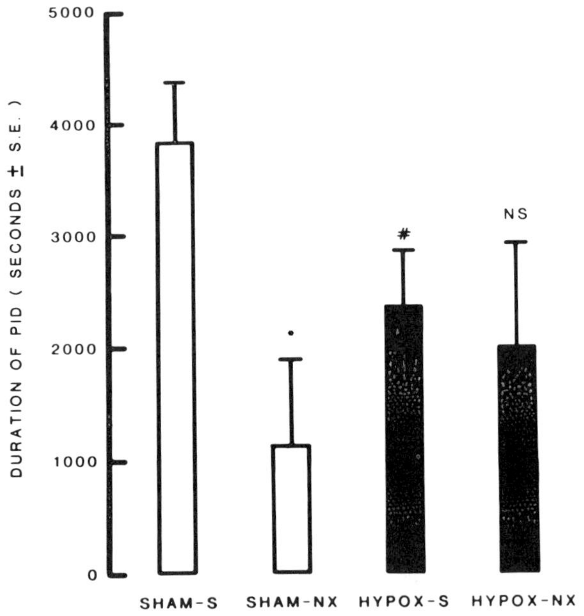

FIGURE 1. The effects of hypophysectomy (HYPOX) (solid bars) or sham hypophysectomy (SHAM) (open bars) on the duration of postictal depression (PID) following ECS in rats pretreated with naloxone (NX) (3 mg/kg) or saline (S). Vertical bars are mean + standard error of the mean (SEM), n = 5–6 rats/group. *p < 0.05, compared to corresponding saline group; #p < 0.05 compared to corresponding sham group; NS, not significantly different compared to corresponding sham group (Student's t-test) (see Reference 22).

ELECTROENCEPHALOGRAPHIC EFFECTS OF ECS

Tortella and colleagues have demonstrated that opioid peptides, injected intracerebroventricularly (icv), produce a distinctive pattern of electroencephalographic (EEG) responses.[36,37] Initially, a transient polyspike epileptiform discharge occurs without any overt behavioral convulsion. Subsequently, after the first five minutes a pattern of slow-wave, synchronous EEG develops and persists up to an hour after peptide injection. ECS produces a remarkably similar pattern of EEG responses, including a polyspike EEG seizure and a postictal isoelectric period, followed by a protracted interval of slow-wave synchronous EEG.[18,20] The behavioral stupor (catalepsy) that follows ECS is temporally associated with the duration of the slow-wave EEG pattern as well as a significant reduction of electromyographic (EMG) activity, indicating a possible cause-effect relationship between this EEG pattern and the associated EMG

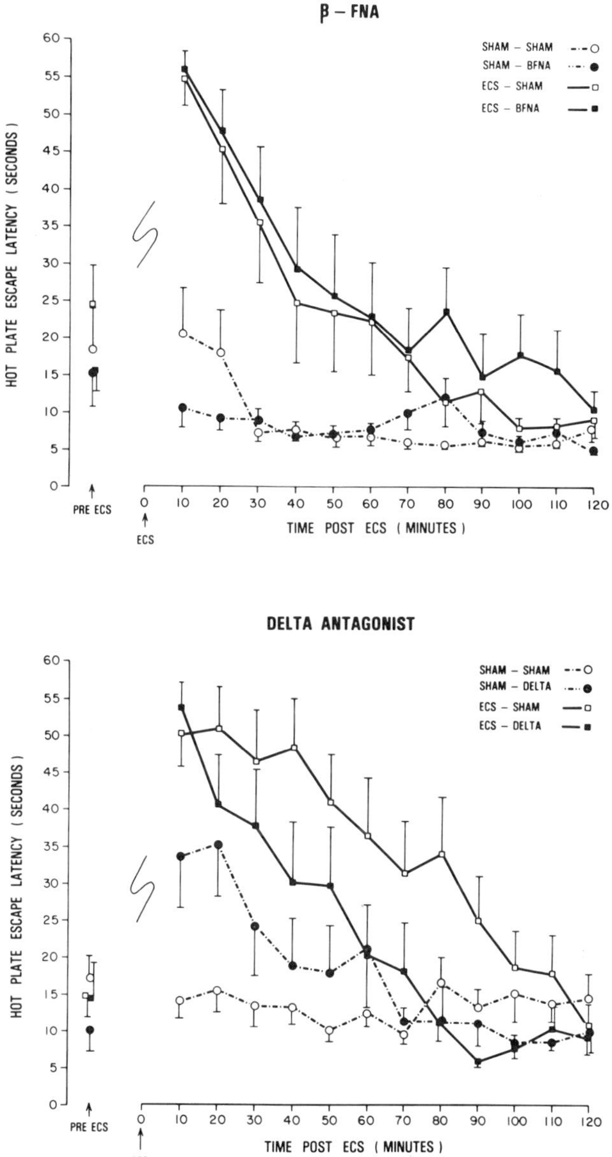

FIGURE 2. Top: Effects of pretreatment with the long-lasting μ-antagonist β-funaltrexamine (β-FNA, 20 nM icv) or saline on hot-plate escape latencies following ECS or sham ECS. Vertical bars are mean ± SEM, n = 8–10 rats/group. β-FNA, in doses that completely blocked the antinociceptive effects of morphine (10 mg/kg), was without effect upon ECS-induced antinociception (ANOVA with repeated measures, p = NS) (see Reference 33). **Bottom:** Effects of the δ-antagonist ICI 154,129 (DELTA) (200 μg icv) or saline on the hot-plate escape latencies following ECS or sham ECS as above. The δ-antagonist had mild antinocicpetive effects of its own; however, this compound also significantly decreased the antinociceptive effects of ECS (ANOVA with repeated measures, $p < 0.05$).

and behavioral responses.[18] Additionally, the possible involvement of pituitary-derived opioids in these acute EEG effects of ECS was demonstrated;[22] hypophysectomy significantly reduced the postictal increase in voltage output, and naloxone failed to further antagonize this EEG response in these animals (FIGURE 3).

The relationships between ECS, opioids, and other behavioral end points were further clarified by Tortella and Cowan.[21] Since β-EP injections were shown to attenuate the excessive grooming and wet-dog shaking produced by dihydrocodeinone (RX 336-M) in a naloxone-reversible manner,[38] the opioid-like effects of ECS were

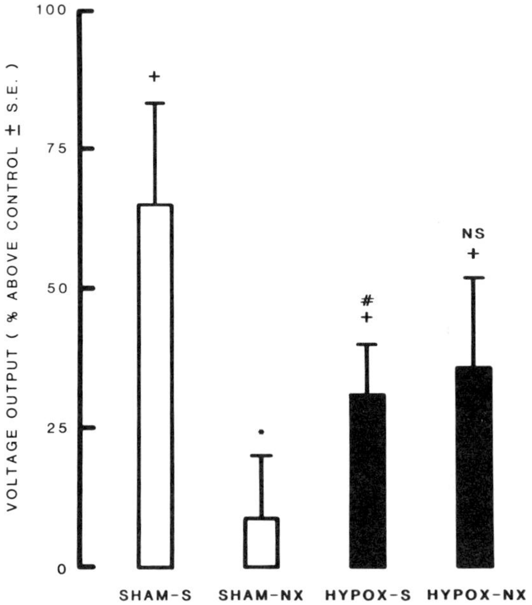

FIGURE 3. The effects of hypophysectomy (HYPOX) (solid bars) or sham hypophysectomy (SHAM) (open bars) on the EEG voltage output following ECS in rats pretreated with naloxone (NX) (3 mg/kg) or saline (S) as described for FIGURE 1. These data were obtained simultaneously with data in FIGURE 1, and the duration of the elevated voltage output correlated with the duration of postictal depression described in FIGURE 1. $^{+}p < 0.05$ compared to pre-ECS baseline (paired t-test); $^{*}p < 0.05$, compared to corresponding saline group; $^{\#}p < 0.05$ compared to corresponding sham group; NS, not significantly different compared to corresponding sham group (Student's t-test) (see Reference 22).

evaluated in conjunction with RX 336-M administration. It was found that ECS produced the same attenuation of the behavioral responses to RX 336-M as did β-EP injections. Moreover, the cortical activating properties of RX 336-M were absent following ECS. Naloxone pretreatment significantly reversed this effect of ECS on the RX 336-M–induced responses. These findings further substantiate the opioid-like effects of ECS and their relationships to postictal EEG and behavioral end points.

Repeated daily ECS results in a progressive increase in the duration and voltage output of the slow, synchronous cortical EEG pattern.[18] As reviewed above, the duration of the EEG response was parallel to the duration of the postictal behavioral depression in acute and chronic ECS studies.[18] Although naloxone antagonized the EEG and behavioral responses produced by a single ECS, naloxone pretreatment failed to antagonize the enhanced EEG and behavioral responses after nine days of ECS. Since naloxone is less effective in opposing δ-mediated effects than μ-mediated responses, this reverse-tolerant state produced by repeated ECS may relate to the increased number of δ binding sites following repeated ECS (see below).

ANTICONVULSANT EFFECTS OF ENDOGENOUS OPIOIDS RELEASED BY ECS

The occurrence of experimentally induced seizures is known to offer temporary protection against subsequent seizures.[39] Several studies have demonstrated that opioid peptides are potent anticonvulsants (for review, see Reference 40). Since ECS activates endogenous opioid systems, Tortella and colleagues have proposed that the endogenous opioid peptides, following activation by seizures, may be endogenous anticonvulsant substances.[18,41–43]

In their initial investigations, Tortella and Cowan measured the effects of ECS on seizure thresholds in rats exposed to the volatile convulsant flurothyl.[42] Following ECS seizures, rats exposed to flurothyl vapors required significantly longer exposures before convulsions occurred. This ECS-induced increase in flurothyl seizure thresholds was significantly antagonized by naloxone, which itself did not affect seizure thresholds.

These findings were recently reinforced by studies examining the effects of intermittent ECS on seizure severity.[43] It should be noted that effects of intermittent ECS delivered at 10-minute intervals for one hour are quite different from the effects of repeated daily ECS administered for nine days as described earlier. Similar to the anticonvulsant effects of ECS on flurothyl-induced seizures, repeated intermittent ECS resulted in a progressive decrease in the severity of seizures over time (FIGURE 4). Naloxone reversed and morphine tolerance prevented this anticonvulsant effect of intermittent ECS, providing further evidence of an endogenous opioid involvement in limiting seizure recurrence or severity.

The anticonvulsant effects of opioids activated by intermittment ECS are similar to the EEG and behavioral effects of opioids activated by a single ECS. For example, hypophysectomy, but not adrenalectomy, attenuated the normal anticonvulsant response to intermittent ECS.[44] Similarly, hypophysectomy attenuated the EEG and behavioral responses to ECS and blocked naloxone's antagonism of these end points (Reference 22, see above). From these findings, it appears that pituitary-derived opioid peptides may play a prominent role in the EEG and behavioral responses to a single ECS or intermittent ECS delivered at 10-minute intervals.

Importantly, repeated *daily* ECS may alter different endogenous opioid systems than are affected by acute *intermittent* ECS administered over one hour. As reviewed above, repeated daily ECS results in an increased duration of postictal responses that become progressively more resistant to naloxone antagonism and exhibit cross sensitization to acute morphine challenge. Additionally, the actual duration (or intensity) of the ECS-induced tonic-clonic convulsions is unaffected by the repeated daily ECS or naloxone treatment. By contrast, Tortella *et al.* have recently shown that repeated intermittent ECS, delivered at 10-minute intervals, results in a progressive *decrease* in seizure severity and duration which is stereospecifically antagonized by naloxone and diminished by morphine tolerance[43] (TABLE 1).

AUTONOMIC EFFECTS OF ECS

The clinical administration of ECT is accompanied by pronounced changes in autonomic function, including an acute elevation of arterial pressure resulting from the seizure, and a postictal depression of respiration. Since endogenous opioids may play a functional autonomic role in altering cardiovascular, respiratory, temperature, and other vegetative functions,[11,45] we investigated the effects of naloxone pretreatment on the magnitude and duration of autonomic responses following ECS in rats.[16]

In conscious, unrestrained rats, ECS resulted in an immediate 250% increase in mean arterial pressure which returned to normal values within 20 seconds in

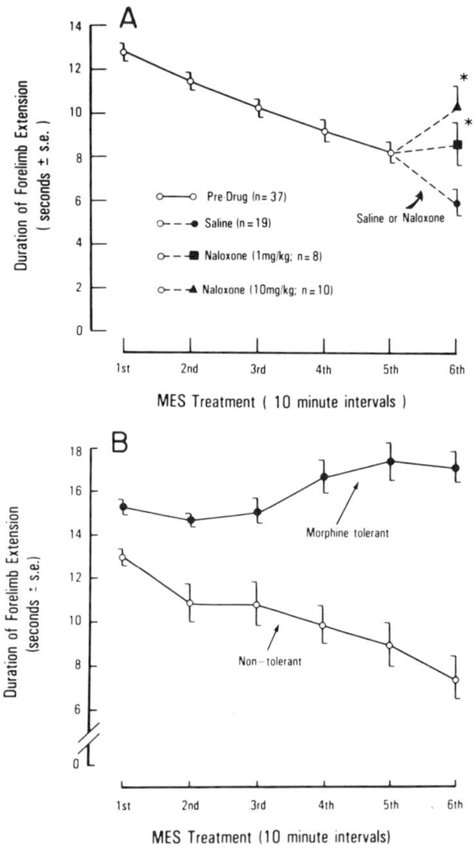

FIGURE 4. Effects of repeated intermittent ECS delivered at 10-minute intervals on the severity of seizures as measured by the duration of forelimb extension. (A) The decrease in the duration of forelimb extension associated with intermittent ECS; naloxone (1.0 and 10.0 mg/kg) significantly reversed the declining seizure severity, resulting in a more intense seizure in response to the last ECS. $^*p < 0.01$ compared to saline group (ANOVA), vertical bars represent ± SEM. (B) The effects of morphine tolerance on the duration of forelimb extension. Morphine-tolerant animals (filled circles) failed to demonstrate the progressive decline in seizure severity seen in nontolerant rates (open circles) (see Reference 43).

TABLE 1. Seizure Severity in Naloxone-Treated or Morphine-Tolerant Rats Subjected to a Single MES Seisure[a]

Treatment (dose)	Duration of TFE (seconds)	Motor Pattern Score (0 to 3 rating scale)
Saline (1 ml/kg)	12.3 ± 0.4	3.0 ± 0.0
Naloxone (1 mg/kg)	11.7 ± 0.6	3.0 ± 0.0
Saline (1 ml/kg)	13.6 ± 0.6	2.9 ± 0.1
Naloxone (10 mg/kg)	14.5 ± 0.5	2.7 ± 0.2
Sham pellets	13.0 ± 0.4	2.0 ± 0.3[b]
Morphine pellets	16.3 ± 0.4[c]	2.7 ± 0.2

[a]Saline and naloxone were administered subcutaneously 10 minutes prior to MES. The values are means ± standard errors for 6 to 10 rats per group.

[b]As many as 10–30% of naive rats fail to respond to a single MES with complete hind limb extension (motor pattern score of 3.0). Because of the variability of this measure (unlike TFE), it is necessary to include separate control groups with each experimental manipulation.

[c]Significantly different from sham-pelleted controls ($p < 0.05$; student's t-test).

saline-pretreated animals.[16] During this interval, heart rate became erratic and characterized by prolonged periods of asystole. Naloxone pretreatment, at doses between 1.0 and 10 mg/kg, was without effect on arterial pressure or heart rate *before* ECS. However, these doses of naloxone resulted in a significant overshoot of both arterial pressure and heart rate below control values seen at 30–40 seconds following ECS. These observations provided the first evidence that the activation of endogenously derived opioids plays a role in blunting baroreceptor reflexes. This opioid inhibition of baroreceptor responses has since been confirmed by the use of many other experimental models.[45]

In behaviorally alert rats, ECS produced a marked reduction of respiratory rates, persisting up to one hour, which was significantly attenuated by naloxone pretreatment.[15] In rats that appeared to be asleep before remote ECS administration, there was no apparent change in postictal respiratory rates.[16] In these rats, naloxone pretreatment increased post-ECS respiratory rates in a dose-related manner. Thus, under two different experimental conditions, naloxone increased postictal respiratory rates at doses that were without effect on this measure in normal rats. These data provided initial evidence that endogenous opioids, like morphine, inhibit respiratory function after their release by stressors such as ECS.

Similar to the effects of low doses of morphine, acute ECS also results in a slight, transient hyperthermia.[17] This effect may be a consequence of the motor activity resulting from the behavioral seizure. Although over a one-hour interval following ECS there was a trend for naloxone-treated rats to have lower body temperatures, this effect did not reach significance.

The autonomic effects of repeated ECS were compared to the effects of acute ECS in morphine-tolerant rats.[19] Unlike single ECS, repeated daily ECS resulted in a sustained hyperthermia that persisted at least 24 hours following the last of nine daily treatments. Additionally, body weight gain was significantly less in rats receiving repeated ECS. These effects were mimicked in rats receiving chronic morphine treatments, providing a further indication of similar effects of repeated ECS and morphine tolerance.

As with behavioral studies, cross sensitization, instead of cross tolerance, was observed when repeated ECS rats were injected with morphine and chronic morphine-treated rats were given a single ECS. For example, the hyperthermic response to a single ECS was enhanced in morphine-tolerant animals. Likewise, the respiratory depressant effects of ECS were magnified in morphine-tolerant rats. Collectively, there are many similar effects of chronic morphine treatment and repeated ECS, including decreased weight gain, sustained hyperthermia, and cross sensitization between these two treatments. However, there are also pronounced differences between repeated ECS and morphine tolerance. For example, it is difficult to reconcile our findings that repeated ECS results in sensitization to the acute opioid-like behavioral, EEG, and autonomic end points, whereas chronic morphine treatment results in a progressive desensitization (tolerance) to morphine's effects.

OPIATE RECEPTORS: EFFECTS OF REPEATED ECS AND MORPHINE TOLERANCE

As reviewed above, both repeated ECS administered daily for nine consecutive days and chronic morphine treatment result in pharmacological cross sensitization.[19] In an initial attempt to define a molecular explanation for the cross sensitization, we observed that repeated ECS and morphine tolerance resulted in a significant increase in the number of ^{3}H-D-Ala^2-D-Leu^5-enkephalin (^{3}H-DADLE) binding sites in rat brain membranes.[23] These increases in binding sites provided one explanation for the pharmacological cross sensitization we observed between these two treatments.

Recently, we repeated these studies using five groups of rats including rats given repeated daily ECS for nine days, sham ECS for nine days, single ECS, six morphine pellets (75 mg; two pellets at 0 hours, four pellets at 36 hours, sacrifice at 72 hours), or six placebo pellets (according to the same schedule). The day after the last ECS or immediately following sacrifice of pelleted rats, rat brains were frozen for binding assays using three different opioid ligands [^{3}H-diprenophine (^{3}H-DP; a putative δ and μ-antagonist which also binds to κ sites), ^{3}H-DADLE (a δ agonist with lesser μ properties), and ^{3}H-morphine (^{3}H-MOR; a μ agonist)]. Binding assays were conducted on synaptic membranes prepared from individual rat brains as described previously.[23]

Apparent K_D values (affinities) did not significantly differ among the five experimental and control groups (TABLE 2). By contrast, repeated ECS and chronic morphine administration resulted in significant increases in B_{max} values (receptor numbers) for all three ligands when compared to respective control groups (TABLE 3). Using ^{3}H-MOR, a single ECS also resulted in significantly higher B_{max} values. An additional observation was that ^{3}H-DADLE binding was more elevated (higher B_{max}

TABLE 2. Computer Log Transformation Fit of "Klotz" Plots Using ^{3}H-DP as a Ligand in the Presence (+) or Absence (−) of 100 mM NaCl[a]

	K_D (× 10^{-10}M)		B_{max} (pmol/mg protein)	
	−NaCl	+NaCl	−NaCl	+NaCl
Sham ECS	2.2 ± 0.4	3.6 ± 0.4	0.31 ± 0.03	0.54 ± 0.06
Single ECS	2.8 ± 0.4	3.2 ± 0.5	0.33 ± 0.04	0.51 ± 0.06
Repeated ECS	1.9 ± 0.2	2.4 ± 0.4	0.72 ± 0.08[b]	0.58 ± 0.09
Placebo pellets	2.9 ± 0.5	5.0 ± 0.6	0.42 ± 0.05	0.84 ± 0.09
Morphine pellets	2.3 ± 0.6	4.4 ± 0.4	0.71 ± 0.06[b]	0.81 ± 0.10

[a] The values are means ± standard errors for nine or more rats per group.

[b] $p < 0.01$ against respective control groups.

TABLE 3. B_{max} Values at 1/3× and at 3× K_D as a Percentage of Control Groups[a]

	Diprenorphine		DADLE		Morphine	
	0.1 nM	0.9 nM	1.0 nM	9.0 nM	15 nM	135 nM
Sham ECS	100	100	100	100	100	100
Single ECS	93 ± 6	95 ± 7	102 ± 5	97 ± 9	131 ± 7[b]	122 ± 6[b]
Repeated ECS	182 ± 13[b]	167 ± 10[b]	143 ± 7[b]	131 ± 10[b]	138 ± 12[b]	130 ± 9[b]
Placebo pellets	100	100	100	100	100	100
Morphine pellets	173 ± 15[b]	191 ± 9[b]	114 ± 7[b]	122 ± 9[b]	155 ± 13[b]	142 ± 9[b]

[a] B_{max} values described at these two concentrations (in nM) of ligands were chosen since they bracket the average K_D, providing added confidence in B_{max} estimations. Values are means ± standard error with populations of nine or more rats per group.

[b] $p < 0.01$ against respective control groups.

values) in repeated ECS rats than in chronic morphine-treated rats, whereas ^{3}H-MOR binding was more elevated in chronic morphine-treated rats than repeated ECS rats (TABLE 3).

Further experiments using ^{3}H-DP were conducted. The ^{3}H-DP ligand appears to bind to a single, high-affinity site and is best suited to establishing saturation kinetics. In addition, ^{3}H-DP binding assays were performed both with and without 100 mM NaCl to examine binding variables in assays respectively selective for the antagonist and agonist conformations of the opioid receptor. As with prior studies,[23] only the repeated ECS and chronic morphine groups had elevated B_{max} values when binding was conducted in the absence of 100 mM NaCl (−NaCl, TABLE 2). However, in the presence of 100 mM NaCl (+NaCl, TABLE 2), B_{max} values were equally elevated and there were no longer any differences among experimental and control groups within respective treatments (ECS or chronic pellets).

Since the presence of NaCl is generally accepted to favor opioid antagonist binding, one interpretation of our results is that these experimental procedures may functionally lock opioid receptors in the antagonist (Na^+) conformation. This may be due to an intracelluar effect of Na^+ since it has been demonstrated that the Na^+ binding site, which decreases α_2-receptor binding in platelets, is located intracellularly.[46] By analogy, changes in intracellular Na^+ at the plasma membrane–cytoplasm boundary during depolarization-repolarization cycles of nerve cells following repeated ECS or chronic morphine may also influence the Na^+ pool(s) involved in the regulation of opioid receptor binding. However, these explanations may be overly simplistic in view of the numerous actions of repeated ECS and chronic morphine exposure.

Recent investigations have provided preliminary information indicating that the enhanced opioid binding is distributed in selective brain regions (in preparation). In descending order, binding sites were significantly elevated in the following regions: olfactory buld > striatum > nucleus accumbens > hypothalamus = pyriform cortex > septum (no significant changes in the cortex or brainstem). These increases show remarkable parallelism with the regional increases in enkephalin concentrations demonstrated by Hong and colleagues:[13] hypothalamus > septum = amygdala > nucleus accumbens > nucleus caudatus (no changes were observed in the cortex, hippocampus, brainstem, or pituitary or in circulating opioids). Thus, there is an excellent apparent correlation between regional increases in enkephalin concentrations and regional changes in opioid receptors.

Based upon many studies with numerous biologically active agonists, it may have been expected that the chronic presence of agonists from endogenous or exogenous sources would result in down regulation (decreased B_{max}) of receptor numbers.

Conversely, antagonists may increase (up regulate) receptor numbers.[47] Since repeated ECS may evoke the release of numerous ligands, a number of investigators have evaluated the effects of this procedure on various receptor systems. For example, Lerer *et al.* (see these proceedings) have demonstrated small but significant decreases in muscarinic cholinergic receptors. Kellar and Stockmeier (see these proceedings) have demonstrated that repeated ECS decreases β-adrenergic receptors yet increases serotonin$_2$ receptors, a finding also observed by Essman (see these proceedings). Pilc *et al.* have demonstrated slight increases in α_1 binding sites with repeated ECS.[48] Single ECS is also known to increase the number of benzodiazepine receptors.[49]

Thus, there is extensive evidence that ECS evokes significant changes in the numbers, but not affinities, of numerous receptor systems. In view of the observations that serotonin and opioid responses are often in parallel, the down regulation of both of these receptor systems by repeated ECS provides further evidence for the mutual association of these two systems. These changes may account in part for the altered pharmacological responses evoked by repeated ECS or drug treatments and may contribute to the spectrum of neurochemical changes responsible for therapeutic effects of ECT.

TABLE 4. Summary of ECS Findings

	Effects of Naloxone	Effects of Hypophysectomy	Effects of Morphine Tolerance
Acute ECS			
Behavior & EEG	blocked	attenuated	enhanced
Seizure severity	no change	less severe	more severe
Intermittent ECS (10 minutes)			
Seizure protection	reversed	blocked	blocked
Repeated daily ECS			
Behavior & EEG	resistant	?	?
Seizure severity	no change	?	?

OPIOIDS AND ECT: PERSPECTIVES AND CLINICAL IMPLICATIONS

From the results summarized above, there is little doubt that endogenous opioids and their receptors are activated by ECS in experimental animals. The supporting evidence includes information gained from behavioral, electroencephalographic, autonomic, and biochemical experiments (TABLE 4). Not only are the effects of single and repeated ECS in many ways similar to those evoked by opioid injections, but the administration of opioid antagonists significantly alters the ictal and postical effects of ECS. Perhaps the information gleaned from these studies is at present more relevant to fundamental mechanisms defining the role of endogenous opioid systems in analgesia, EEG responses, autonomic regulation, seizures, and receptor dynamics. Future work will attempt to correlate opioid responses with antidepressant efficacy in various animal models of "depression." Nonetheless, it remains an important issue that endogenous opioids, working in concert along with many other neurotransmitters and hormones, may play an important role in the therapeutic outcome of ECT.

There are several important clinical implications from these studies; however, some of these pose serious ethical questions. For example, if the antidepressant effects of ECT depend in part upon the actions of endogenous opioids, would naloxone block the therapeutic effects of repeated ECT? Such a study would directly address the hypothesis, but few patients would likely consent to enrollment in such a protocol.

However, we have also demonstrated that the opioid agonist morphine augments the opioid-like effects of ECS. From these results, one would predict that injections of opioids such as morphine simultaneously with ECT may decrease the number of required treatments and improve clinical outcome if care is given to maintain ventilation during the procedure.

Amnesia is a well known clinical complication of ECT.[9,50] Messing and colleagues have demonstrated that naloxone can reverse the retrograde amnesia produced by ECS in rats.[51] From these results, it may be possible that specific doses of naloxone would decrease the retrograde (and possibly anterograde) amnesia resulting from ECT.

Importantly, a therapeutic "window" for naloxone was shown to be necessary for its antiamnestic effects in rats. Doses markedly less than or greater than 0.5 mg/kg had no effect on improving retention in a one-trial avoidance following a single ECS treatment.[51] Likewise, Urca and colleagues observed that reversal of the antinociceptive effects of ECS with naloxone required lower doses, whereas higher doses were ineffective.[52] Thus, any clinical trials using naloxone or other opioid antagonists must be carefully designed to evaluate a number of doses since too much or too little antagonist may be ineffective.

The effects of ECT on arterial pressure and respiration have long been known as complications of this procedure. For this reason, we investigated these responses to ECS in a rat model, with particular emphasis on evaluating the potential endogenous opioid involvement in autonomic regulation.[19] Although evidence was obtained that naloxone modified several autonomic effects of ECS, none of these were worsened by this opioid antagonist. In fact, the respiratory depression produced by ECS was significantly improved.

From the work of Tortella *et al.*, it was shown that repeated intermittent ECS results in the release of endogenous opioids, resulting in a decreased probability of seizure recurrence as well as decreased seizure severity.[43] Naloxone reversed and morphine tolerance prevented this protective, anticonvulsant effect of endogenous opioids. Very recently, Tortella and Long have reported that cerebrospinal fluid obtained following seizures from donor rats decreased seizure severity in recipient rats, and this response was also blocked by naloxone.[53] From these results, they have provided convincing evidence that endogenous opioid systems may play a physiological role in the self-regulation of seizures, thereby decreasing the probability of status epilepticus. Of clinical importance, it may be likely that the use of naloxone or chronic morphine treatment in epileptic patients may increase the probability of seizures. This potential adverse effect must be taken into account in considering clinical trials with naloxone.

There are severe limitations in using animal models to extrapolate to the clinical domain, particularly in behavioral experiments. Until clinical trials are designed to address these questions, using appropriate doses of agonists and antagonists, the question as to how pivotal endogenous opioids are to the cause or treatment of depression and other behavioral disorders remains unresolved. It is hoped that continued experimentation in this area will not only provide new insights into the etiology of depression, but also novel therapeutic strategies for its treatment.

REFERENCES

1. HOLADAY, J. W. 1984. *In* Neuroendocrine Perspectives. E. Muller & R. Macleod, Eds. **3:** 161–199. Elsevier. Amsterdam, Holland.
2. AKIL, H., S. J. WATSON, E. YOUNG, M. E. LEWIS, H. KHACHATURIAN & J. M. WALKER. 1984. Annu. Rev. Neurosci.: 223–255.

3. LEE, N. M. & A. P. SMITH. 1984. Trends Pharmacol. Sci. **3:** 108–110.
4. GOODMAN, R. R. & G. W. PASTERNAK. 1984. *In* Analgesics: Neurochemical, Behavioral, and Clinical Perspectives. M. Kuhar & G. Pasternak, Eds.: 69–96. Raven Press, New York, N.Y.
5. MARTIN, W. R. 1984. Pharmacol. Rev.: 283–323.
6. PATERSON, S. J., L. E. ROBSON & H. W. KOSTERLITZ. 1983. Br. Med. Bull. **39:** 31–36.
7. HUIDOBRO-TORO, J. P., K. YOSHIMURA, N. M. LEE, H. H. LOH & E. L. WAY. 1981. Eur. J. Pharmacol. **72:** 265–266.
8. ZUKIN, R. S. & S. R. ZUKIN. 1981. Life Sci. **29:** 2681–2690.
9. FINK, M. & J. O. OTTOSON. 1980. Psychiatry Res. **2:** 49–61.
10. ALLEN, J. P., D. DENNY, J. W. KENDWALL & P. H. BLACHLY. 1974. Am. J. Psychiatry **131:** 1225.
11. HOLADAY, J. W. & H. H. LOH. 1981. *In* Hormonal Proteins and Peptides: β-Endorphin. C. H. Li, Ed.: 202–291. Academic Press. New York, N.Y.
12. HOLADAY, J. W., G. L. BELENKY, H. H. LOH & J. L. MEYERHOFF. Soc. Neurosci. Abstr. **4:** 409.
13. HONG, J. S., J. C. GILLIN, H.-Y. T. YANG & E. COSTA. 1979. Brain Res. **177:** 273.
14. GREEN, A. R., E. PERALTA, J. S. HONG, C. C. MAO, C. K. ATTERWILL & E. COSTA. 1978. J. Neurochem. **31:** 607.
15. BELENKY, G. L. & J. W. HOLADAY. 1979. *In* Endogenous and Exogenous Opiate Agonists and Antagonists. E. L. Way, Ed. Pergamon Press. New York, N.Y.
16. BELENKY, G. L. & J. W. HOLADAY. 1979. Brain Res. **177:** 414–417.
17. HOLADAY, J. W. & G. L. BELENKY. 1980. Life Sci. **27:** 1929–1938.
18. TORTELLA, F. C., A. COWAN, G. L. BELENKY & J. W. HOLADAY. 1981. Eur. J. Pharmacol. **76:** 121–128.
19. BELENKY, G. L. & J. W. HOLADAY. 1981. Life Sci. **29:** 553–563.
20. HOLADAY, J. W., F. C. TORTELLA & G. L. BELENKY. 1981. *In* The Role of Endorphins in Neuropsychiatry. H. Emrich, Ed.: 142–157. Karger. Basel, Switzerland.
21. TORTELLA, F. C. & A. COWAN. 1982. Life Sci. **31:** 881–888.
22. TORTELLA, F. C., A. COWAN & J. W. HOLADAY. 1984. Peptides **5:** 115–118.
23. HOLADAY, J. W., R. J. HITZEMANN, J. CURELL, F. C. TORTELLA & G. L. BELENKY. 1982. Life Sci. **31:** 2209–2212.
24. LEWIS, J. W., J. T. CANNON, E. H. CHUDLER & J. C. LIEBESKIND. 1981. Brain Res. **208:** 230–233.
25. HOLADAY, J. W., E. WEI., H. H. LOH & C. H. LI. 1978. Proc. Nat. Acad. Sci. USA **75:** 2923–2927.
26. BELENKY, G. L., V. E. BATES & J. W. HOLADAY. 1980. Soc. Neurosci. Abstr. **6:** 318.
27. URCA, G., A. NOF, B. A. WEISSMAN & Y. SARNE. 1983. Brain Res. **260:** 271–277.
28. WAY, E. L., H. H. LOH & F. H. SHEN. 1969. J. Pharmacol. Exp. Ther. **167:** 1–8.
29. YAKSH, T. L. & T. A. RUDY. 1978. Pain **4:** 299–359.
30. AMIR, S. & Z. AMIT. 1978. Life Sci. **23:** 1143–1152.
31. EMRICH, H. M., V. HOLLT, H. LASPE, M. FISCHLER, H. HEINEMANN, W. KISSLING, D. ZERSSEN & A. HERZ. 1979. *In* Neruo-psychopharmacology. Saletu, Berner & Hollister, Eds.: 527–534. Pergamon Press. Oxford, England.
32. PRZEWLOCKI, R., W. LASON, R. STACH, D. KACZ, L. STALA & B. PRZEWLOCKA. 1981. *In* Advances in Endogenous and Exogenous Opioids. H. Takagi, Ed.: 238–240. Kodansha Ltd. Tokyo, Japan.
33. BELENKY, G. L., D. GELINAS-SORELL, J. R. KENNER & J. W. HOLADAY. 1983. Life Sci. **33:** 585–586.
34. WARD, S. J. & J. W. HOLADAY. 1982. Soc. Neurosci. Abstr. **8:** 388.
35. HOLADAY, J. W. & F. C. TORTELLA. 1984. *In* Central and Peripheral Endorphins: Basic and Clinical Aspects. E. E. Miller & A. R. Genazzani, Eds.: 237–250. Raven Press, New York, N.Y.
36. TORTELLA, F. C., J. E. MORETON & N. KHAZAN. 1978. J. Pharmacol. Exp. Ther. **206:** 636–642.
37. ADLER, M. W. & F. C. TORTELLA. 1983. Pharmacologist **25:** 152.
38. COWAN, A., & F. C. TORTELLA. 1982. Life Sci. **30:** 171–176.

39. Nutt, D. J., P. J. Cowan & A. R. Green. 1981. Eur. J. Pharmacol. **71:** 287–295.
40. Tortella, F. C., A. Cowan & M. W. Adler. 1984. Neuropharmacology **23**(7A): 749–754.
41. Tortella, F. C., A. Cowan & M. W. Adler. 1980. Life Sci. **29:** 1039–1045.
42. Tortella, F. C. & A. Cowan. 1982. Life Sci. **31:** 2225–2228.
43. Tortella, F. C., J. B. Long & J. W. Holaday. Brain Res. (In press.)
44. Long, J. B., J. W. Holaday & F. C. Tortella. 1984. IUPHAR 9th International Congress of Pharmacology Abstracts, No. 1460.
45. Holaday, J. W. 1983. Annu. Rev. Pharmacol. Toxicol. **23:** 541–594.
46. Motulsky, H. J. & P. A. Insel. 1983. J. Biol. Chem. **285:** 3913–3919.
47. Tempel, A., R. S. Zukin & E. L. Gardner. 1982. Life Sci. **31:** 1401–1404.
48. Pilc, A., A. Rokosz-Pelc & J. Vetulani. 1984. Eur. J. Pharmacol. **98:** 429–431.
49. Paul, S. M. & P. Skolnick. 1978. Science **202:** 892–894.
50. d'Elia, G. 1974. *In* Psychobiology of Convulsive Therapy. M. Fink, Ed.: 21–34. V. H. Winston & Sons. Washington, D.C.
51. Messing, R. B., R. A. Jensen, J. L. Martinez, Jr., V. R. Spieler, B. J. Vasquez, B. Soumireu-Mourat, K. C. Liang & J. L. McGaugh. 1979. Behav. Neural Biol. **27:** 266–275.
52. Urca, G., A. Harouni & Y. Sarne. 1982. Eur. J. Pharmacol. **81:** 237–243.
53. Tortella, F. C. & J. B. Long. 1985. Science **228:** 1106–1107.

Electroconvulsive Therapy Effects on Synaptic Proteins

T. G. BOLWIG AND O. S. JØRGENSEN

Department of Psychiatry and
Psychochemistry Institute
Rigshospitalet
University of Copenhagen
9 Blegdamsvej
DK-2100 Copenhagen O, Denmark

The working action of electroconvulsive therapy (ECT) is so far still unknown in spite of the great number of studies concerning this highly efficacious antidepressant treatment modality. Both from clinical findings and from experimental studies it seems clear that seizure activity generated from upper brainstem centers is a prerequisite for therapeutic effects.[1] Hypotheses on the mode of action of ECT should be based mainly on the effects still demonstrable after a period of time following the last seizure, since the introduction of seizure itself leads to a multitude of immediate physiological and biochemical effects which rapidly wear off. Therefore, the immediate effects may represent phenomena that have no relation to the sustained clinical effect, which comprises both the positive influence on the symptomatology of depression and the negative influence on the cognitive functions. However, short-lasting events such as functionally determined increase of cerebrovascular permeability to small and large molecules which occur during ECT[2–5] may contribute to the changes by way of an accumulated effect, and they should therefore not be completely disregarded.

Among the many theories put forward, that of the involvement of the diencephalon in the therapeutic process[1,6–8] seems to gain an even stronger position due to the development in our understanding of neuroendocrine functions in affective disorders (for a thorough review, see Fink and Ottosson).[9] Clinical support is lent to the theory by the fact that ECT has the highest rate of efficacy in patients in whom "hypothalamic" symptoms such as decreased libido, anorexia, loss of weight, and sleep disturbances are predominant.[7] The demonstration that lidocaine modifies the ECT-induced seizures into a spike-and-wave pattern on the electroencephalogram (EEG) and that the duration of this type of upper brain stem–originated activity is positively related to the antidepressant effect is likewise a strong indicator of the importance of the diencephalon. Also the observation by Roth *et al.* that the probability of relapse is inversely proportional to the amount of postseizure slow-wave activity[10] points to centrencephalic seizures playing a crucial role in the antidepressant action of ECT.

At the level of the neuron it must be assumed that some chemical processes operating at the synapses are changed during antidepressant therapy, whether this be ECT or drug administration. So far, however, the common denominators demonstrated have been too few for the formulation of a unitary hypothesis for antidepressant action. The release of hypothalamic hormones is assumed to be regulated via monoaminergic nerve transmission. Such mechanisms seem influenced by ECT, as illustrated in animal experiments in which an increased sensitivity of dopamine and norepinephrine receptors[11,12] was found as well as an increase in the sensitivity of serotonin receptors.[13] However, studies of monoamine metabolites in the cerebrospinal fluid of patients undergoing ECT have not shown changes to support involvement of monoamines in the working action of ECT.[14]

On this basis we studied synaptic proteins after electroconvulsive stimulation in the rat.[15] This study was designed with the purpose of demonstrating a direct effect of repeated electroconvulsions on the brain synapses, using the rat brain synaptic proteins synaptin, D1, D2, D3, and 14-3-2 as markers. The method used was immunoelectrophoresis. Subcellular fractions of both synaptic vesicles and synaptosomal plasma membranes are found enriched with synaptin.[16,17] This protein is located on the outside of the vesicles and on the inside of the plasma membranes. The synaptin is assumed to play a functional role in the exo-endocytotic process of synaptic nerve transmission[18] and may be an indicator of the amount of synaptic vesicles. D1, D2, and D3 are enriched in the synaptosomal membrane fractions but are absent from synaptic vesicles and cultured astroglial cells.[15,16,19] D2 is closely related to the well-described neuronal cell adhesion molecule N-CAM,[20,21] and is hypothesized to be involved in intercellular adhesion during neuronal migration, neuritic fasciculation, and synaptogenesis.[22,23] In contrast to D2, which can be used as a marker for synaptic turnover in adult brain, D3 is localized in mature synapses[22] and can be used as marker of synaptic density.[22,23] The 14-3-2 protein isolated from brain has been localized to the neuronal cytoplasm.[24,25] It is composed of two electrophoretically different forms, 14-3-2 ac and 14-3-2 cc, which are identical with the neuronspecific isoenzymes $\gamma\gamma$-enolase and $\alpha\gamma$-enolase, respectively.[26,27]

Our studies so far have comprised two investigations, one in which the effects of a single series of electroconvulsive stimulations (ECS) were given followed by a similar period of recovery, and one in which the first study was replicated and the reversibility and regional differences of findings were studied following a recovery period of four weeks.[14,28]

MATERIAL AND METHODS

Wistar rats, 35 days old at the start of the study, were given electroconvulsive stimulation (50 mA for 0.9 second), a stimulus comparable to electroconvulsive therapy in patients. In the first investigation the following situations were studied: (1) ECS three times weekly for 4 weeks; (2) ECS three times weekly for 8 weeks; and (3) ECS three times weekly for 4 weeks followed by 4 weeks of sham treatment. All experimental animals were compared to their sham-treated littermates. In the second part of the study we again gave ECS three times weekly for 4 weeks and this time we let a similar group have a period of recovery of 12 weeks whereupon they were studied. In the second part of the study glutamine synthetase was also investigated. In the brain this protein has only been found in astrocytes[29,30] and may therefore be considered an indicator of astroglial cytoplasm.

Calculations

The amounts of D1, D2, D3, and synaptin in the various regions of the brains were quantitated using planimetry of the corresponding areas of the immunoplates, that of 14-3-2 by the height of the rockets. The samples from normal controls and from the littermate experimental animals were always analyzed together on the immunoplates. The mean values and standard errors of the mean (SEM) of the percentage deviation

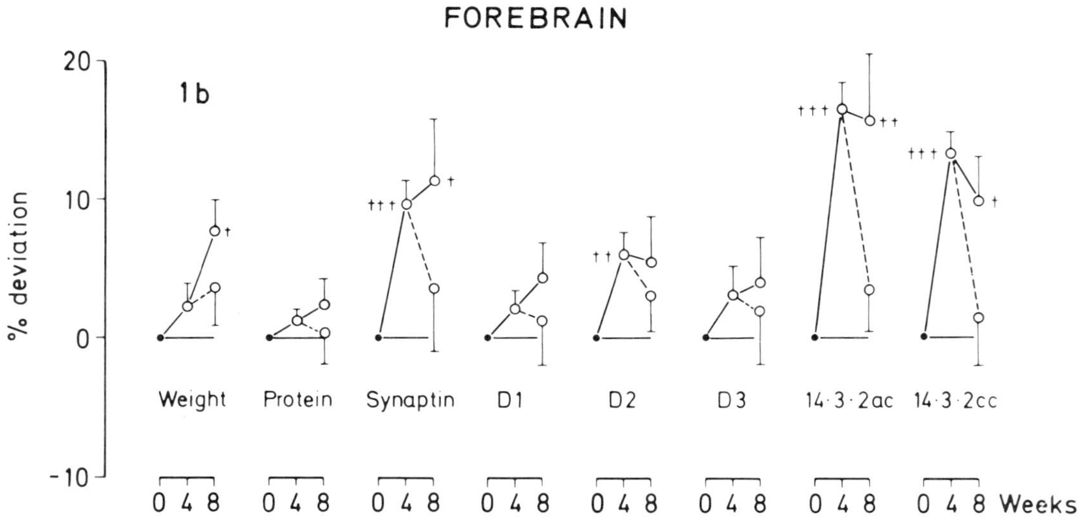

FIGURE 1. Rats were given ECS for four weeks [$n = 10$, solid line from (●) to four-week (○) point], for eight weeks [$n = 10$, solid line from four-week (○) point to eight-week (○) point], or for four weeks followed by four weeks of sham treatment ($n = 10$, dashed line). The results indicate percentage deviations between the littermate controls of the same age and the ECS rats. Means and standard errors are given. Significance levels: †$p < 0.05$, ††$p < 0.01$, and †††$p < 0.001$.

between the experimental animals and littermate controls are used. The values for whole forebrain given in the Results section were calculated by combining the values for the occipital cortex, hypothalamus, and residual forebrain using the tissue weight as an adjusting factor. Statistical analysis was made using two-tailed Student's paired t-test.

RESULTS

The results for the first part of the study appear in FIGURE 1, which gives the data for forebrain only. In this region there was a significant increase of synaptin, D2, and the 14-3-2 enolase isoenzymes. The increase was still present after another 4 weeks of stimulation. However, in the group having a period of 4 weeks sham ECS after the 4 weeks of ECS the values dropped to insignificant levels.[14] For the second part of the study the results obtained are given in TABLE 1. The previous forebrain findings were replicated. Hypothalamus was in this study analyzed separately, and it appeared that in this region the increase of synaptic markers was more pronounced than in the whole forebrain, pointing to a stronger involvement of hypothalamus in the effects of the seizures. After 12 weeks of recovery a high degree of normalization had taken place both for forebrain and hypothalamus.[28]

TABLE 1. Electroconvulsive Stimulation of Rats[a]

	Four Weeks ECS		Four Weeks ECS + 12 Weeks Recovery	
	Whole Forebrain	Hypothalamus	Whole Forebrain	Hypothalamus
Weight	0.8 ± 1.2	15.6 ± 5.5^{b}	-0.3 ± 1.5	-0.2 ± 6.2
Protein	1.2 ± 2.2	15.2 ± 5.9^{b}	3.7 ± 2.0	-6.5 ± 5.0
Synaptin	8.5 ± 2.3^{c}	7.5 ± 4.8	5.2 ± 3.0	-9.8 ± 4.9
D1	1.8 ± 2.1	16.1 ± 5.6^{b}	1.7 ± 2.2	-6.5 ± 6.5
D2	5.2 ± 2.3^{b}	9.5 ± 4.6	1.4 ± 1.5	-8.0 ± 4.4
D3	1.0 ± 2.9	20.2 ± 7.2^{b}	4.9 ± 3.4	-10.6 ± 7.7
14-3-2	9.7 ± 1.5^{d}	15.8 ± 3.5^{d}	0.3 ± 1.6	-2.3 ± 4.5

[a]Rats were given ECS for 4 weeks or for 4 weeks followed by 12 weeks recovery. The results indicate percentage deviations between the littermate controls of the same age and ECS rats. Means and standard errors are given.

[b]Significance level: $p < 0.05$.

[c]Significance level: $p < 0.01$.

[d]Significance level: $p < 0.001$.

DISCUSSION

The study shows that electroconvulsion produces changes in specific brain proteins related to synapses. In the first part of our studies the increases of synaptin, D2, and 14-3-2 were interpreted as being indicative of an increase in the number of synaptic vesicles, an increased synaptic remodeling, and an increase in the preparedness to glycolytic demands, respectively. All the changes in specific proteins were normalized following four weeks of recovery. The second part of the study seems to indicate that the region mostly influenced is the hypothalamus. Thus, considerable and sustained, though not permanent, changes indicative of a stimulatory effect at the synaptic level are found after a series of ECS in the rat. This is in good accordance with the results from studies of animals showing an increased effect of receptor agonists after electroconvulsion. Those studies point to a sustained increase in postsynaptic nerve transmission.[10,12,31] The fact that seizure activity does not exert identical effects on synaptic proteins in different regions of the brain is interesting, and may help to explain the phenomenon of simultaneous stimulatory and inhibitory effects as a result of generalized seizure activity: alleviation of depressive inhibition—mnemic dysfunction. This dual action might also be explained in the light of the variety of functions linked to the various regions of the brain (e.g., "vegetative" functions and the hypothalamus, memory function and the hippocampus). A homogeneous synaptic response to seizure activity therefore may have grossly different effects on the complex interplay between facilitating and inhibiting neuronal systems.

In the discussion of these phenomena it is important to look at the few studies of depressed patients in which some of these brain-specific proteins have been investigated. The study by Jørgensen *et al.*[32] pointing to an increase in the cerebrospinal fluid (CSF) concentration of the soluble form of D2 in depressed patients after successful antidepressant therapy seems probably to be the result of an increased dilution of brain extracellular fluid by choroid plexus-produced CSF.[33] However, the increased level of D2-like protein in plasma from depressed patients compared to nonpsychotic controls may indicate a higher rate of synaptic turnover.[33] Postmortem samples of brain tissue from patients with endogenous depression, with Parkinson's disease, and from controls without known neurological or psychiatric disorders were also studied.[34] Compared to controls as well as to Parkinson's disease patients, both D2 and D3 proteins were significantly increased in the hippocampus of depressed patients whereas no significant change could be observed in the frontal cortex. The above-mentioned increased levels in plasma D2 protein and the described tissue findings both point to an increased synaptic turnover during endogenous depression in at least certain brain regions. Therefore it may be important for the therapeutic efficacy of ECT that one of its effects may be an increased turnover of synapses, especially in hypothalamus.

REFERENCES

1. Ottosson, J.-O. 1962. Seizure characteristics and therapeutic efficiency in electroconvulsive therapy: an analysis of the antidepressive efficiency of grand mal and lidocaine-modified seizures. J. Nerv. Ment. Dis. **135:** 239–251.
2. Bolwig, T. G., M. M. Hertz, O. B. Paulson, H. Spotoft & O. J. Rafaelsen. 1977. The permeability of the blood-brain barrier during electrically induced seizures in man. Eur. J. Clin. Invest. **7:** 87–93.
3. Bolwig, T. G., M. M. Hertz & J. Holm-Jensen. 1977. The permeability of the blood-brain barrier during electroshock siezures in the rat. Eur. J. Clin. Invest. **7:** 95–100.
4. Bolwig, T. G., M. M. Hertz & E. Westergaard. 1977. Acute hypertension causing blood-brain barrier breakdown during epileptic seizures. Acta Neurol. Scand. **56:** 335–342.
5. Petito, C. K., J. A. Schaefer & F. Plum. 1977. Ultrastructural characteristics of the brain and blood-brain barrier in experimental seizures. Brain Res. **127:** 251–267.
6. Roth, M. 1951. Changes in the EEG under barbiturate anaesthesia produced by electroconvulsion treatment and their significance for the theory of ECT-action. Electroencephalograph. Clin. Neurophysiol. **3:** 261–280.

7. POLLITT, J. 1965. Suggestions for a physiological classification of depression. Br. J. Psychiatry **111:** 489–495.
8. FINK, M. 1979. Convulsive Therapy: Theory and Practice: 238. Raven Press. New York, N.Y.
9. FINK, M., & J.-O. OTTOSSON. 1980. A theory of convulsive therapy in endogenous depression: significance of hypothalamic functions. Psychiatr. Res. **2:** 49–55.
10. ROTH, M., D. W. K. KAY, J. SHAW & J. GREEN. 1957. Prognosis and pentotal induced electroencephalographic changes in electroconvulsive treatment. Electroencephalogr. Clin. Neurophysiol. **9:** 225–237.
11. MODIGH, K. 1975. Electroconvulsive shock and postsynaptic catecholamine effects: increased psychomotor stimulant action of apomorphine and clonidine in reserpine pretreated mice by repeated ECS. J. Neural Transm. **36:** 1932.
12. EDEN, S. & K. MODIGH. 1977. Effects of cypomorphine on rat plasma growth hormone after treatment with reserpine and electroconvulsive shocks. Brain Res. **179:** 379–384.
13. EVANS, P. P. M., D. G. GRAHAME-SMITH, A. R. GREEN & A. F. C. TORDORFF. 1977. Electroconvulsive shock increases the behavioural responses of rats to 5-HT accumulation and central nervous system stimulant drugs. J. Pharmacol. **56:** 193–199.
14. NORDIN, G., J.-O. OTTOSSON & B.-E. ROSS. 1971. Influence of convulsive therapy on 5-hydroxy-indole-acetic acid and homovanilic acid in cerebrospinal fluid in endogenous depression. Psychopharmacologia **20:** 315–320.
15. JØRGENSEN, O. S. & T. G. BOLWIG. 1979. Synaptic proteins after electroconvulsive stimulation. Science **205:** 705–707.
16. BOCK, E. & O. S. JØRGENSEN. 1975. Rat brain synaptic vesicles and synaptic plasma membranes compared by crossed immunoelectrophoresis. FEBS Lett. **52:** 37–39.
17. BOCK, E., O. S. JØRGENSEN, L. DITTMANN & L. F. ENG. 1975. Determination of brain-specific antigens in short term cultivated rat astroglial cells and in rat synaptosomes. J. Neurochem. **25:** 867–870.
18. BOCK, E. 1978. Nervous system specific proteins. J. Neurochem. **30:** 4–14.
19. JØRGENSEN, O. S. & E. BOCK. 1974. Brain specific synaptosomal membrane proteins demonstrated by crossed immunoelectrophoresis. J. Neurochem. **23:** 879–880.
20. JØRGENSEN, O. S., A. DELOUVEE, J.-P. THIERY & G. M. EDELMANN. 1980. The nervous system specific protein D2 is involved in adhesion among neurites from cultured rat ganglia. FEBS Lett. **111:** 39–42.
21. EDELMANN, G. M. 1984. Modulation of cell adhesion during induction, histogenesis, and perinatal development of the nervous system. Annu. Rev. Neurosci. **7:** 339–377.
22. JØRGENSEN, O. S. 1981. Neuronal membrane D2-protein during rat brain ontogeny. J. Neurochem. **37:** 939–946.
23. JØRGENSEN, O. S. 1983. D2-protein and D3-protein as markers for synaptic turnover and concentration. J. Neural Transm. Suppl. **18:** 245–255.
24. MOORE, B. W. & V. J. PEREZ. 1968. Specific acidic proteins of the nervous systems. *In* Physiological and Biochemical Aspects of Nervous Integration. F. D. Carlsson, Ed.: 343–359. Prentice Hall. Englewood Cliffs, N.J.
25. PICKEL, V. M., D. J. REIS, P. J. MARANGOS & C. ZOMZELY-NEURATH. 1976. Immunocytochemical localization of nervous system specific proteins (NSP-R) in rat brain. Brain Res. **105:** 184–187.
26. BOCK, E. & J. DISSING. 1975. Demonstration of enolase activity connected to the brain-specific protein 14-3-2. Scand. J. Immunol. **4:**(Suppl. 2): 31–36.
27. JØRGENSEN, O. S. & G. CENTERVALL. 1982. $\alpha\gamma$-Enolase in the rat: ontogeny and tissue distribution. J. Neurochem. **39:** 537–542.
28. BOLWIG, T. G. & O. S. JØRGENSEN. 1980. Synaptic proteins after electroconvulsive stimulation: reversibility and regional differences in the brain. Acta Psychiatr. Scand. **62:** 486–493.
29. MARTINEZ-HERNANDEZ, A., K. P. BELL & M. D. NORENBERG. 1977. Glutamine synthetase: glial localization in brain. Science **195:** 1356–1358.
30. NORENBERG, M. D. & A. MARTINEZ-HERNANDEZ. 1979. Fine structural localization of glutamine synthetase in astrocytes of rat brain. Brain Res. **161:** 303–310.
31. GREEN, A. R., D. J. HEAL & D. G. GRAHAME-SMITH. 1977. Further observations on the

effect of repeated electroconvulsive shock on the behavioural responses of rats produced by increases in the functional activity of brain 5-HT and dopamine. Psychopharmacology **52:** 195–200.
32. JØRGENSEN, O. S., E. BOCK, P. BECH & O. J. RAFAELSEN. 1977. Synaptic membrane protein D2 in the cerebrospinal fluid of manic-melancholic patients. Acta Psychiatr. Scand. **56:** 50–56.
33. JØRGENSEN, O. S., A GJERRIS & O. J. RAFAELSEN. 1984. Increased dilution of brain extracellular fluid in CSF of depressed and schizophrenic patients marked by neuronal D2-like protein concentration. Clin. Neuropharmacol. 7(Suppl. 1): 296–297.
34. JØRGENSEN, O. S. & P. RIEDERER. 1985. Increased synaptic markers in hippocampus of depressed patients. J. Neural Transm. **64:** 55–66.

Interactions of Drugs and Electroshock Treatment on Cerebral Monoaminergic Systems[a]

AMIRAM I. BARKAI

New York State Psychiatric Institute and
Department of Psychiatry
College of Physicians and Surgeons
Columbia University
722 West 168 Street
New York, New York, 10032

INTRODUCTION

The bulk of research on biochemical and physiological mechanisms that may be linked to the therapeutic effects of electroshock treatment (EST) in psychiatry has been reviewed comprehensively.[1–5] Many studies on EST-induced changes have focused on the central nervous system (CNS) and involve cerebral monoamines. The findings of most of those studies reflect modified activities in serotonergic or catecholaminergic synapses and are thus consistent with observations that implicate dysfunction of these systems in affective disorders or schizophrenia. The recent findings that long-term treatment with antidepressants, neuroleptics, or EST may be associated with changes in the responsiveness of certain monoamine receptors, and that such changes parallel fairly well the time course for clinical effects, represent a new approach to studying neurochemical correlates of behavioral changes following the administration of EST or psychoactive drugs.

The number of studies on the biological mechanisms involved in the therapeutic effects of EST is small compared to the large quantity of studies on psychopharmacological effects; the number of studies bearing directly on physiological or biochemical changes following a combined application of EST and drugs is even smaller. Although clinical studies on the efficacy of combined EST and drug therapy have been carried out,[6] the majority of animal research on drug-EST interaction was directed in the field of anticonvulsants and only little attention was given to psychoactive drugs.[7] Studies on the interaction of EST and drugs are of critical importance for establishing a scientific basis for combined EST and drug treatment. It is possible for example that drugs that act synergistically with EST to produce certain neurochemical changes would also act synergistically to produce therapeutic effects. In addition, the study of EST-drug interaction should yield valuable information for the understanding of the nature of the underlying disorders in which a certain drug or EST might be effective.

The first series of experiments described here had been carried out to study EST-drug interaction on the metabolism of catecholamines and serotonin in the intact brain. Additional studies to explore possible relationships between observed metabolic changes and the modification of synaptic receptors are also described. Finally, the

[a]This research was supported by National Institute of Mental Health Grant No. 33690.

results are discussed in terms of a model which might contribute to the understanding of synaptic processes that may function improperly in certain psychiatric disorders.

INTERACTION OF EST AND DRUGS ON THE CEREBROSPINAL FLUID LEVELS OF MONOAMINE METABOLITES

Four drugs that have clinical use in psychiatry were selected for the study of EST-drug interaction on cerebral monoamine metabolism. These include lithium, carbamazepine (CBZ), imipramine (IMI), and haloperidol (HLDL). The interaction of each of these drugs on the cerebral metabolism of dopamine (DA), norepinephrine (NE), and serotonin (5HT) was assessed by studying long-term changes in the concentrations of their respective metabolites in the cerebrospinal fluid (CSF).

Experiments were carried out with male Sprague-Dawley rats (200–300 g). Food and water were supplied *ad libitum*. For the study with each drug animals were divided into four groups and treated daily for seven days as follows: (a) control, 0.2 ml saline; (b) drug; (c) EST; and (d) EST plus drug. The animals were allowed a washout period of one, four, or eight days after the last treatment and then anesthesized with urethane (1g/kg) for CSF withdrawal. Methods for the administration of EST and for CSF withdrawal are described in detail elsewhere.[8] Drugs were administered as follows: Li was provided in the diet (purina chow + 0.2% Li); CBZ was injected subcutaneously (sc) (20 mg/kg); IMI (10 mg/kg) was given sc as a solution of IMI-HCl in saline; HLDL was injected sc (2 mg/kg) as injectable Haldol (McNeil Pharm., Springhouse, Pa.). CSF samples were analyzed for the DA metabolites DOPAC and HVA, the 5HT metabolite 5HIAA, and the NE metabolite MHPG (free). These metabolites were determined in the same CSF sample (25 μl) by a high-pressure liquid chromatography–electrochemical detection procedure (HPLC-EC) (FIGURE 1).

The results are presented in FIGURE 2. Administration of EST alone resulted in changes in the CSF levels of DOPAC and HVA but had no apparent effect on free MHPG or 5HIAA. The CSF levels of DOPAC decreased during the four-day period following the last EST; it then increased significantly and reached a level of 168% of the mean control value at eight days after the last EST. Similar decreases were seen in the HVA levels one and four days following EST but no rebound was apparent; HVA levels returned to the control value at eight days after the last EST. Administration of Li had no apparent effect on DA metabolites but resulted in a significant decrease of MHPG which remained lower than control levels even eight days after Li withdrawal. A significant increase in 5HIAA levels was seen one day after Li withdrawal. Separate experiments with labeled 5HIAA indicated however that this increase in the level of 5HIAA was due to a slower 5HIAA removal from the CSF compartment. Concurrent administration of EST and Li resulted in the disappearance of the EST-induced changes in the levels of DA metabolites. In addition, the decrease in free MHPG seen one day after Li alone was no longer apparent, but no similar interaction on MHPG levels was seen on the eighth day. The combined EST-Li treatment had no apparent interaction on 5HIAA levels. Carbamazepine had no apparent effect on the levels of the studied metabolites, but its concurrent administration with EST resulted in the disappearance of the decrease in HVA levels seen one day after the last EST in animals receiving EST alone. Chronic administration of IMI had an effect similar to that of EST on the levels of DA metabolites, but in addition brought about a significant decrease in the levels of both MHPG and 5HIAA. This decrease was detectable one day after the last IMI treatment but disappeared when EST was administered in combination with IMI. However, there were no apparent EST-IMI interactions on the levels of DA metabolites. Chronic HLDL treatment resulted in marked changes of DOPAC, HVA, and 5HIAA levels but had no apparent effect on MHPG. Higher levels than control were seen in both DA and 5HT metabolites one day after the last HLDL injection. However, after four days the levels of the two DA metabolites decreased significantly whereas 5HIAA remained elevated. No changes were seen eight days after the last injection of HLDL. The most significant EST-HLDL interaction observed was on the HLDL-induced increase of 5HIAA levels which was markedly attenuated in animals subjected to a combined EST-HLDL administration.

One limitation of the approach taken in this EST-drug interaction survey is the

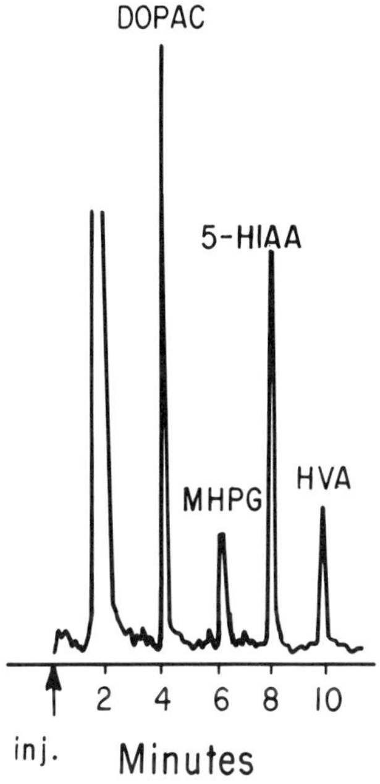

FIGURE 1. HPLC-EC separation of DOPAC, MHPG, 5HIAA, and HVA after injection of 25 μl artificial CSF containing 160 ng/ml of each metabolite. The HPLC system consisted of a model 6000A solvent delivery system (Waters, Milford, Mass.) equipped with a reverse phase column (Whatman Partisil 5 ccs/c8 25) and a guard column. The mobile phase was 0.12 M Na_2HPO_4, 0.05 M citric acid, and 5% methanol containing 0.05 M EDTA at pH 5. The flow rate was set at 2 ml/minute. The concentration of each metabolite was determined from standard curves which were linear at the range from 20 to at least 640 ng/ml.

inability to determine whether an observed change in the level of a given metabolite is a result of a change in the turnover of the parent monoamine or of a change in the rate at which the metabolite is removed from the CSF. Separate experiments were carried out to investigate this question in relation to the increase of 5HIAA levels following treatment with Li or HLDL. These studies employed a ventricularcisternal perfusion technique combined with isotope dilution of ^{14}C-5HIAA. These experiments were designed to estimate the rates of appearance and disappearance of 5HIAA in the CSF compartment.[9] The results indicated that the increase in 5HIAA levels after chronic Li was due to slower removal of 5HIAA from the CSF and did not represent enhanced

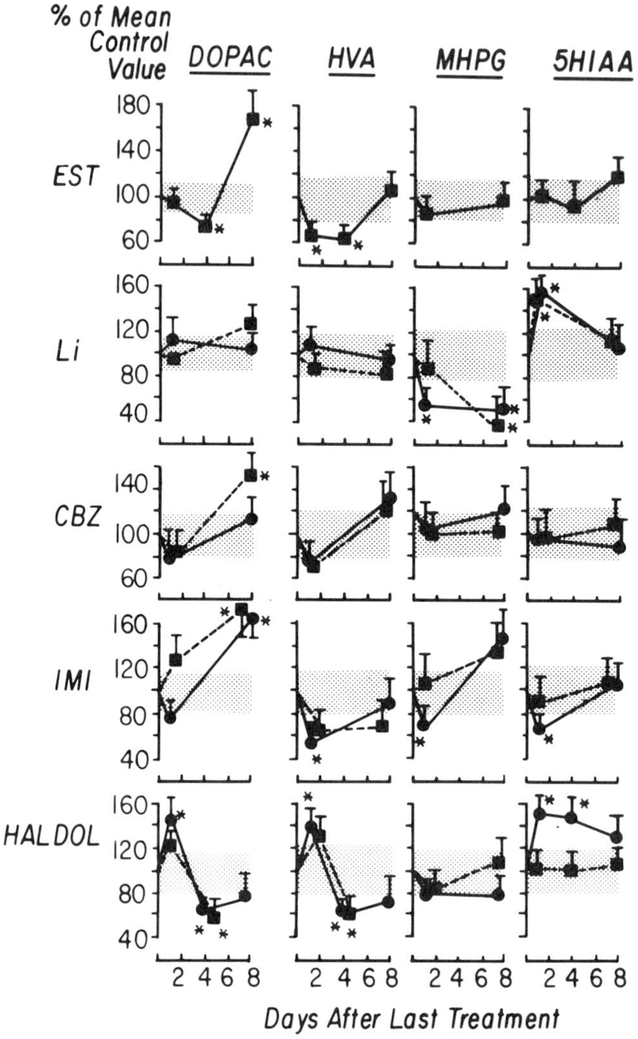

FIGURE 2. Effects of EST, psychoactive drugs, and a combined treatment of EST and drug on the CSF levels of monoamine metabolites in rats. Animals were treated daily for seven days with EST, drug, or a combination of EST plus drug, and the level of the metabolite in the CSF was determined 1–8 days following the last treatment. The effect is expressed as percent change of control level. Circles represent data from 7–9 animals treated with the indicated drug. Squares represent data obtained from 7–9 animals after repeated EST or repeated EST plus drug. Vertical bars represent 1 standard deviation (SD). Shaded areas represent ±1 SD of the mean control value (presented as 100%) obtained from 11 rats treated with 0.2 ml saline. The mean values for the concentrations of the metabolites in the CSF of control rats were: DOPAC 250 ± 28 nM; HVA, 360 ± 60 nM; MHPG, 121 ± 22 nM, and 5HIAA, 1230 ± 250 nM. *$p < 0.02$ compared to the corresponding control value (Student's t-test).

5HT turnover. In fact, the rate of appearance of 5HIAA in the CSF—a parameter representing turnover of 5HT in the intact brain—was found to be inversely related to the plasma Li concentrations. The increase in 5HIAA levels in the HLDL-treated rats reflected, however, an increased rate of appearance of 5HIAA, indicating enhanced 5HT turnover in the HLDL-treated animals. Similar experiments with ^{3}H-HVA indicated that the changes in this DA metabolite seen following HLDL or EST correspond to changes in the rate of appearance of endogenous HVA and thus reflect changes in DA turnover rate.

Thus the described survey revealed that EST-drug interactions on cerebral monoamines were detectable with each of the four drugs studied. The most significant interaction was the attenuation by EST of the HLDL-induced rise in 5HIAA levels. Other interactions involved one or more monoaminergic systems and all were antagonistic in nature; either EST attenuated the drug effect or the drug attenuated the EST effect. It is interesting to note that synergistic interactions were not observed in these studies.

THE DOPAMINERGIC SYNAPSE: EFFECTS OF EST AND HALOPERIDOL

The decrease in the CSF levels of DA metabolites four days after the withdrawal of either chronic HLDL or repeated EST indicated that DA turnover had decreased during the withdrawal period. The subsequent increase in DOPAC at eight days after the last EST may reflect a rebound effect on DA turnover. The decrease in DA turnover following chronic HLDL was probably mediated by increased sensitivity of both pre- and postsynaptic DA receptors during the initial period of withdrawal (four days). After longer periods (eight days), "down regulation" of DA receptors might have taken place, resulting in a rebound increase in DA turnover. Apparent evidence for modified sensitivity of DA receptors following chronic HLDL has been obtained in behavioral studies. It has been demonstrated that certain behavioral responses to DA agonists may be enhanced following chronic HLDL treatment.[10] These observations correspond fairly well with the finding of increased ^{3}H-spiroperidol binding in the striatum following chronic HLDL.[11] Repeated EST has also been shown to increase the responsiveness of DA receptors to DA agonists in behavioral studies,[12–14] but attempts to demonstrate EST-induced alterations in DA receptors by changes of ^{3}H-spiroperidol binding were unsuccessful.[15–16] The observations that repeated EST may increase the responsiveness of DA receptors to DA agonists in behavioral paradigms without a demonstrable effect on ^{3}H-spiroperidol binding may be due to the fact that such binding studies were conducted exclusively with striatal tissue. It is possible that the enhanced behavioral response to DA agonists could be reflected in a change of ^{3}H-spiroperidol binding in brain areas other than the striatum, such as the n. accumbens. In addition, it is not clear yet to what extent changes in DA receptors occur in presynaptic membranes following repeated EST. The question as to whether there are interactions between chronic HLDL treatment and repeated EST on the development of changes in DA receptors is also of considerable interest. These questions were addressed in a recent study in which tissue of n. accumbens was studied in addition to striatal tissue, and presynaptic DA receptors were assessed biochemically by the inhibitory effect of apomorphine on DA synthesis.[17] The experiments were conducted with four groups of rats which were treated with saline, HLDL, EST, and a combination of HLDL and EST. HLDL (2 mg/kg) was given daily whereas EST was applied three times a week for a four-week period. Rats were sacrificed five days after the last treatment, their brains removed rapidly, and both the striatum and the n.

TABLE 1. Effects of Chronic HLDL and EST on Presynaptic DA Receptors[a]

Treatment Group	Striatum	N. Accumbens
Control	3.8 ± 0.3	2.2 ± 0.2
Haldol	2.3 ± 0.3[b]	1.7 ± 0.1[b]
EST	2.0 ± 0.2[b]	1.7 ± 0.1[b]
Haldol plus EST	1.7 ± 0.2[b]	1.2 ± 0.2[b]

[a]The table is based on Reches *et al.*[17] Numbers denote mean ± standard error of the mean (SEM) of DOPA concentrations (ng/mg tissue). The responsiveness of presynaptic DA receptors was assessed by the inhibitory effect of apomorphine (0.5 mg/kg) on DA synthesis in the presence of GBL (750 mg/kg) and the DOPA decarboxylase inhibitor NSD-1015. Animals were sacrificed five days after the last EST or HLDL treatment. One-way ANOVA revealed significant effects of the treatment schedules on DOPA concentrations in both the striatum and n. accumbens ($p < 0.001$). *Post hoc* Duncan's multiple range tests showed that either HLDL or EST induced significant increases in apomorphine-induced inhibition of DOPA accumulation. The cumulative effects of both HLDL and EST were additive but did not reach significant levels compared to each treatment alone.

[b]Significantly different from the corresponding control ($p < 0.05$).

accumbens dissected out and used for the receptor assays. The responsiveness of presynaptic DA receptors was assessed biochemically by the apomorphine-induced effect on the accumulation of DOPA,[18] whereas assays for specific binding of ^{3}H-spiroperidol were performed according to Reches *et al.*[19]

The results of these experiments showed that chronic HLDL or repeated EST both enhanced apomorphine-induced inhibition of DA synthesis. Levels of DOPA obtained after combined HLDL-EST administration were not significantly different than levels obtained with either treatment separately, indicating a lack of interaction between the two treatments (TABLE 1). Specific binding of ^{3}H-spiroperidol to membranes of either striatal or n. accumbens origin was increased significantly by chronic HLDL but not by repeated EST. Concomitant administration of EST and HLDL had no effect on the neuroleptic-induced increase in the density of ^{3}H-spiroperidol binding sites, indicating a lack of interaction on postsynaptic DA receptors (TABLE 2). The effects of repeated

TABLE 2. Effects of Chronic HLDL and EST on ^{3}H-Spiroperidol Binding in Rat Striatum and N. Accumbens[a]

Treatment Group	Striatum[b]			N. Accumbens		
	Binding at 0.2 nM	B_{max}	K_d	Binding at 0.2 nM	B_{max}	K_d
Control	266 ± 19	391	0.19	176 ± 23	266	0.21
HLDL	408 ± 24[c]	692	0.19	258 ± 34[c]	384	0.19
EST	306 ± 26	329	0.16	198 ± 41	292	0.20
EST + HLDL	364 ± 28[c]	640	0.17	282 ± 32[c]	398	0.23

[a]Membranes from individual animals were assayed in triplicates at a single ligand concentration of 0.2 nM. For Scatchard analysis, membranes from individual animals were pooled and binding was assayed at various ligand concentrations (0.02–0.4 nM). Binding values including B_{max} are expressed as fmol/mg protein. K_d is expressed as nM. One-way analysis of variance showed significant effects ($p < 0.01$) of treatment on binding sites. Concurrent administration of EST did not affect the HLDL-induced increase in binding.

[b]Based on Reches *et al.*[17]

[c]*Post hoc* Duncan's multiple range analysis indicated that HLDL induced a significant ($p < 0.001$) increase in binding relative to control.

EST or chronic HLDL are depicted in FIGURE 3. It is seen that either repeated EST or chronic HLDL induced hypersensitivity of putative presynaptic receptors in both the nigrostriatal and mesolimbic DA pathways. The effects of combined administration of EST and HLDL on presynaptic DA receptors did not appear to be additive. Chronic HLDL induced a significant increase in the density of ^{3}H-spiroperidol binding sites which largely represent D2-type postsynaptic DA receptors. Repeated EST did not modify ^{3}H-spiroperidol binding and had no apparent effect on the HLDL-induced increase in the density of D2-type receptors.

While it should be kept in mind that unaltered binding of antagonists such as ^{3}H-spiroperidol to DA receptor sites does not necessarily reflect a lack of change in agonist-receptor interactions, the observed hypersensitivity of presynaptic DA receptors following repeated EST might explain the decrease in the levels of DA metabolites in the CSF following the withdrawal from EST (FIGURE 2).

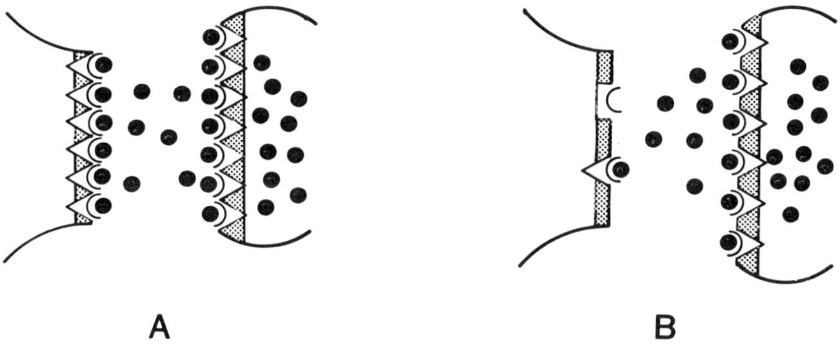

FIGURE 3. A graphic representation of changes in pre- and postsynaptic DA receptors following withdrawal of chronic HLDL (A) or repeated EST (B). Chronic HLDL induced hypersensitivity of presynaptic DA receptors (as indicated by increased apomorphine inhibition of DOPA accumulation) and increased the density of ^{3}H-spiroperidol binding sites which largely represent D2-type postsynaptic receptors. A combined EST-HLDL treatment produced changes similar to those obtained after HLDL alone.

THE SEROTONERGIC SYNAPSE: EST-HLDL INTERACTION

The observation that chronic HLDL treatment resulted in a long-term elevation of 5HIAA levels in the CSF is consistent with previous findings from our laboratory suggesting that HLDL may act on 5HT receptors to initiate feedback processes that enhance 5HT turnover.[9] The regulation of cerebral 5HT turnover is mediated, in part, by neuronal mechanisms that control 5HT uptake. It is possible therefore that HLDL-induced changes in 5HT turnover are induced by the action of the drug on presynaptic processes that are responsible for the uptake and release of 5HT. In addition, HLDL may influence 5HT turnover by its action on cerebral 5HT2 receptors which bind butyrophenone neuroleptics with high affinity.[20] It has been shown recently that repeated EST induced a significant increase in the density of such 5HT2 receptors in the cerebral cortex,[21,22] but it is not clear whether this increase in density occurs on pre- or postsynaptic membranes.

The present study was conducted to investigate whether HLDL or EST has demonstrable effects on presynaptic components of the 5HT system, and whether the apparent interaction between HLDL and EST on the 5HIAA levels in the CSF could be reflected at the presynaptic level in 5HT neurons. Presynaptic mechanisms that participate in the regulation of 5HT metabolism were assessed by high-affinity binding of ^{3}H-imipramine (^{3}H-IMI). Studies on the binding of this ligand to cerebral membranes have established a close relationship between 5HT uptake and ^{3}H-IMI binding sites.[23] It was assumed, therefore, that modification of processes that regulate 5HT uptake would be associated with changes in ^{3}H-IMI binding. The experimental design was similar to that described previously,[17] but rats were sacrificed either one hour or five days after the last treatment. The preparation of cerebral cortex

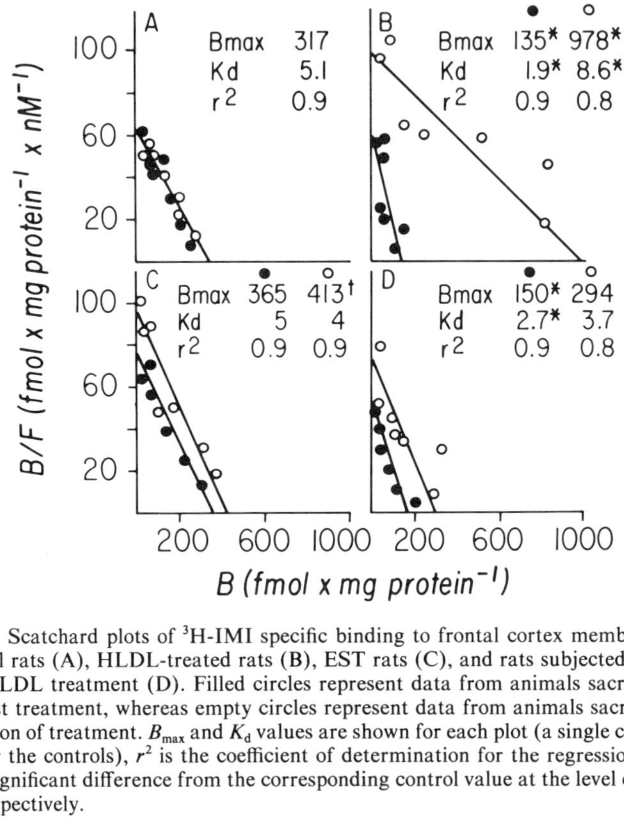

FIGURE 4. Scatchard plots of ^{3}H-IMI specific binding to frontal cortex membranes obtained from control rats (A), HLDL-treated rats (B), EST rats (C), and rats subjected to a combined EST and HLDL treatment (D). Filled circles represent data from animals sacrificed one hour after the last treatment, whereas empty circles represent data from animals sacrificed five days after cessation of treatment. B_{max} and K_d values are shown for each plot (a single combined plot is depicted for the controls), r^2 is the coefficient of determination for the regression line; * and † indicate a significant difference from the corresponding control value at the level of $p < 0.01$ and $p < 0.05$ respectively.

membranes and the ^{3}H-IMI binding assay were carried out essentially according to Raisman *et al.*[24] Values for B_{max} and K_d were obtained by Scatchard analyses. Statistical tests for equality of slope and intercept were performed using the SAS General Linear Models Procedures (SAS Institute; 1982 edition).

The results are summarized in FIGURES 4 and 5. Chronic HLDL resulted in a significant decrease in the density of ^{3}H-IMI binding sites in animals sacrificed one hour after the last treatment but binding was markedly increased after a "washout" period of five days. With regard to EST alone, there were no apparent changes in binding when the animals were sacrificed one hour after the last treatment, but when

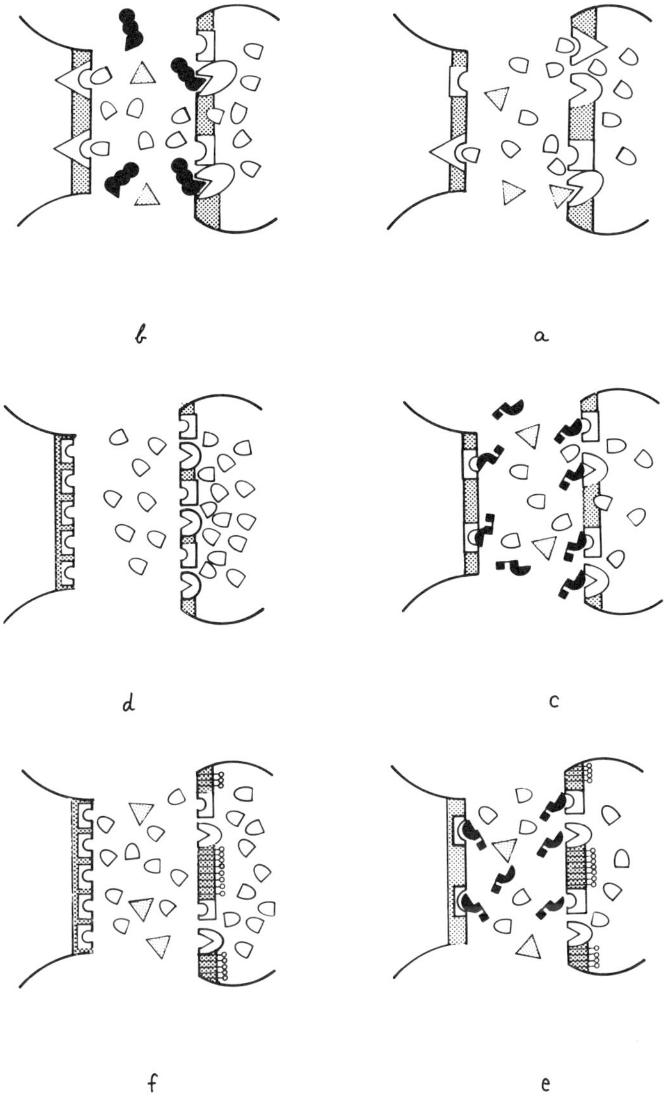

FIGURE 5. The ^{3}H-IMI binding site and its modification by HLDL or EST: a possible mode of action. (**a**) The ^{3}H-IMI binding site is located on presynaptic membranes of 5HT neurons and probably represents a receptor for an endogenous modulator (triangles) that affects 5HT uptake; when this modulator interacts with its receptor, the transport of 5HT molecules (semiellipsoids) from the synaptic cleft into the presynaptic neuron is blocked. (**b**) IMI molecules (tricyclic) interact with this binding site and produce a similar effect on 5HT reuptake. (**c**) HLDL molecules (spoon shaped) block both 5HT receptors and the ^{3}H-IMI binding sites that are closely associated with them, but the interaction of this antagonist drug with the presynaptic receptors does not block 5HT transport. (**d**) Withdrawal of chronic HLDL treatment results in up regulation of both 5HT receptors and ^{3}H-IMI binding sites. (**e**) When EST is administered with HLDL it "stabilizes" 5HT presynaptic membranes and prevents HLDL-induced up regulation of ^{3}H-IMI binding sites. (**f**) Following withdrawal of the combined EST-HLDL treatment, the HLDL-induced up regulation of ^{3}H-IMI binding sites is no longer apparent. The possible HLDL-induced up regulation of 5HT postsynaptic receptors is not necessarily reduced by the concurrent EST administration.

animals were allowed a recovery period of five days there appeared to be a slight increase in binding. When animals were treated concurrently with HLDL and EST, the marked increase in ^{3}H-IMI binding seen after HLDL alone was no longer apparent, indicating that EST attenuated the increase in ^{3}H-IMI binding seen after withdrawal of chronic HLDL.

Thus, this study has demonstrated that chronic administration of HLDL to rats modifies ^{3}H-IMI binding in membranes prepared from their cerebral hemispheres. Binding was lower during the treatment period but was markedly elevated five days after withdrawal of the drug. The apparent "down regulation" of ^{3}H-IMI binding sites during HLDL treatment may be a result of increased 5HT turnover due to the blocking of 5HT receptors by HLDL, or may be due to the occupancy of binding sites by the administered HLDL. The level of HLDL in the brain following daily injections of 2 mg/kg doses (about 6 μM) may be adequate to significantly inhibit ^{3}H-IMI binding in cerebral membranes.[25] The apparent "up regulation" after HLDL withdrawal may be due to the development of hypersensitivity in presynaptic (and possibly postsynaptic) 5HT receptors. This explanation, however, encounters some difficulties since the apparent turnover of 5HT, which is expected to be lower when such hypersensitivity is developed, remained elevated during the period of HLDL withdrawal. Alternatively, it is possible that HLDL acted on ^{3}H-IMI binding sites independently of its action on 5HT receptors.

An important finding was the attenuation by EST of the enhanced ^{3}H-IMI binding seen after HLDL withdrawal. This EST-HLDL interaction resembles previously described drug-EST interactions involving DA,[26] NE,[27] or histamine[28] receptors. However, in those studies the drug-EST interaction presumably modified postsynaptic receptors whereas in the present study presynaptic receptors were influenced. It appears that EST affects certain neuronal receptors in a manner similar to that of Li, which has a "stabilizing" effect on receptor functions of NE,[29] acetylcholine,[30] or DA[31] systems. Further research is clearly needed to investigate whether the changes in ^{3}H-IMI binding following HLDL treatment are directly related to the changes in 5HT metabolism, and to study the possible role of other neuronal receptors in mediating the combined effects of EST and HLDL on ^{3}H-IMI binding and 5HT metabolism.

NEUROTRANSMITTER TURNOVER AND RECEPTOR REGULATION: A PROPOSED MODEL

The studies described above demonstrated that changes in DA or 5HT turnover, resulting from either repeated EST or long-term treatment with HLDL, were associated with alterations in presynaptic receptor binding in DA or 5HT systems respectively. Furthermore, the interaction of EST and HLDL on the 5HIAA level in the CSF was associated with EST-HLDL interaction on ^{3}H-IMI binding sites that specifically label the presynaptic 5HT transporter in brain.[23] The relationship between changes in the turnover of a neurotransmitter and changes in the function of its receptors may be discussed in terms of system variables which include the concentration of the neurotransmitter in the synaptic cleft, the density of occupied pre- and postsynaptic receptors, the density of the total pre- and postsynaptic receptors available, and the turnover rate determinants that are involved in the production, release, uptake, and breakdown of the neurotransmitter. A proposed model for this system is presented in FIGURE 6. This model might be useful for simulation of the system behavior under various conditions that result from a change in the value of one or more of the system variables.

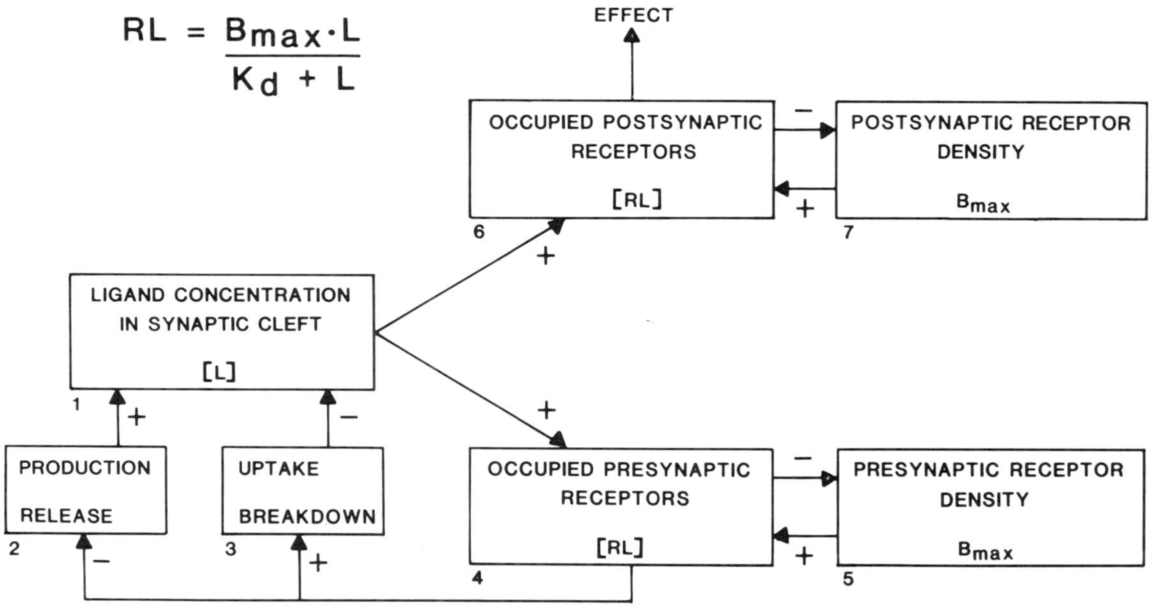

FIGURE 6. A proposed model of possible relationships among pre- and postsynaptic variables that regulate the formation of the receptor-ligand (RL) complex in the postsynaptic membrane. Postsynaptic RL is the variable that determines the postsynaptic response. Variables 2–5 represent presynaptic components, while variables 6 and 7 represent postsynaptic elements. (See text for a more detailed description of this model.)

A variable change, particularly if induced in a variable of the presynaptic components, is expected to initiate a series of changes in other system variables and may ultimately result in a change of the number of occupied postsynaptic receptors; the variable that determines the magnitude of the postsynaptic response. Thus, when a change occurs in one or more of the presynaptic processes that determine production, release, uptake, or breakdown of the neurotransmitter, its immediate effect would be on the concentration of neurotransmitter in the synaptic cleft, which in turn would influence the pre- or postsynaptic number of occupied receptors. A change in the number of occupied receptors may also occur when the receptor density is altered. The relationship between the number of occupied receptors, the concentration of available neurotransmitter, and the receptor density (pre- or postsynaptic) may be described according to the Clark occupancy principle by the following equation which is commonly used in receptor-binding studies:

$$\mathrm{RL} = \frac{B_{max} \times L}{K_d + L} \qquad \textbf{(1)}$$

where RL is the density of occupied receptors, B_{max} is the density of total receptors available; L is the concentration of the ligand neurotransmitter, and K_d is a constant representing affinity. According to this equation a change in the value of RL may result from a change in B_{max} or in L (or in both). Since in the present model the value of B_{max} is a function of L and similarly L is a function of presynaptic B_{max}, the value for RL at any given time depends on the relationship between L and B_{max} at that time. The model implies that these variables are inversely related, i.e., an increase in L is followed by a decrease in B_{max} and vice versa.

It is possible to describe changes in both L and B_{max} as functions of time (for example, monotonic exponential functions) and to examine the resulting changes in RL with time. An example is given in FIGURE 7. In this particular case the increase of B_{max} proceeded according to an exponential function of time with a rate constant $k = -0.1$ while the exponential decrease of L with time was assigned three different rate constants: -0.1, -0.2, and -0.4 per unit time. When values for RL are calculated at different points in time (between 0 and 24 time units; K_d kept constant) according to Equation 1, it becomes apparent that the pattern of change of RL with time may show an increase, a decrease, or an increase followed by a decrease, compared to the original RL value (FIGURE 7). The pattern of change in RL is apparently dependent on the rate constants that determine the changes in L and B_{max}. It appears that when the decrease in L with time proceeds at a rate slower than or equal to the rate of increase in presynaptic B_{max}, the values for RL during the period of the change are higher, but when L decreases at a much faster rate than B_{max} increases, the values representing RL are lower in comparison to the original RL values; the RL values may fluctuate when the rate of decrease in L slightly exceeds the rate of increase in B_{max}.

Thus it might be assumed that when a change occurs initially in the production, release, uptake, or breakdown of the neurotransmitter, and if the immediate effect of this change is a decrease in L with time, the decrease in L would proceed at a rate faster than the subsequent increase in B_{max} and consequently the value of RL would decrease. The decrease in RL might result in a "depressed" output (smaller postsynaptic effect). Alternatively, if the initial change occurs in mechanisms responsible for receptor synthesis and availability, and if the effect of this change is an increase in B_{max} with time, the increase in B_{max} would probably proceed at a rate faster than the subsequent decrease in L and consequently RL may either fluctuate or increase. This might result in an "augmented" output (enhanced postsynaptic effect). These examples demonstrate that a decrease in L that is associated with an increase in B_{max} may result in either a "depressed" or "augmented" output. The direction of the response depends largely on the ratio between the rate of change of L to that of B_{max}.

A change may also occur initially in RL. For example, treatment with receptor-blocker drugs would lower the number of receptors occupied by the endogenous neurotransmitter ligand and would result in activation of processes that increase both L and B_{max}. Withdrawal of the receptor antagonist should result in a higher value of RL compared to the pretreatment value, and the result would be a decrease in both L and B_{max}. The changes observed in the DA system following chronic administration of HLDL are consistent with a system behavior of this kind. The decrease in occupied DA receptors by HLDL caused an increase in both DA turnover and B_{max}. Following

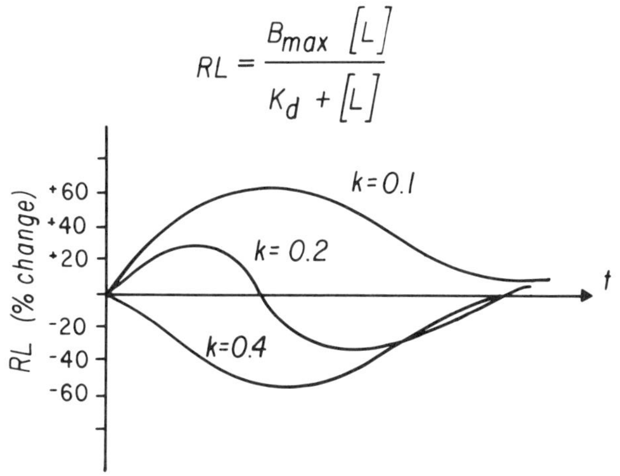

FIGURE 7. An example for possible changes in RL under three different conditions of a decrease in L with time. According to the model in FIGURE 6, a decrease in L is accompanied by an increase in B_{max}. The function for a twofold increase in B_{max} with time was assigned arbitrarily as the following monotonic function: $B_{max}(t) = 100 + 100\,(1 - e^{-0.1t})$. The decrease in L with time was assumed to be exponential according to the function $L(t) = L_o\,e^{-kt}$. When values for $B_{max}(t)$ and $L(t)$ are substituted in Equation 1 in the text (and values for L_o and K_d are kept constant at 20 and 10 respectively), the resulting change in RL with time appears to depend on the rate constant k in the equation describing the exponential decrease of L with time. The change in RL is shown here for three different values of k: 0.1, 0.2, and 0.4. Note that RL may increase, decrease, or fluctuate depending on the ratio between the rate constants of the changes in B_{max} and L with time. (See text for further detail.)

HLDL withdrawal there was a substantial increase in RL which in turn activated feed-back processes aimed at lowering both L and B_{max}. This resulted in a biphasic effect: an increase in DA turnover and B_{max} during or immediately after chronic HLDL treatment followed by a decrease in these variables after HLDL withdrawal. The experimental results showed a biphasic effect on the turnover of DA (FIGURE 2), but a decrease in B_{max} was not apparent at least five days after HLDL withdrawal. This observation suggests that the change in receptor density is regulated by slower processes compared to those regulating the neurotransmitter turnover.

Repeated EST, on the other hand, was associated with an increase in the responsiveness of presynaptic DA receptors but also with a decrease in DA turnover.

Since the change in DA turnover was apparent only after long-term EST, when presynaptic DA receptors were hypersensitive, it is possible that EST had initially modified the presynaptic (but not postsynaptic) DA receptors. At the present time it is not possible to assess presynaptic DA receptors separately in receptor-binding studies and therefore it is not known whether the EST-induced increase in DA receptor responsiveness was due to changes in density or affinity. Nevertheless, the change in presynaptic DA receptors by EST is probably mediated by the same processes that regulate DA presynaptic receptors following chronic HLDL, since no additive effects were seen when both treatments were given concurrently.

The action of HLDL on the 5HT system is apparently more complicated. If HLDL acts in a similar manner to its action on the DA system and brings about a decrease in the number of occupied 5HT receptors, one might expect an increase in both L and B_{max}. Withdrawal of HLDL would then result in a decrease in these variables. However, a decrease in 5HT turnover was not observed experimentally after HLDL withdrawal. It is possible that HLDL interferes with mechanisms that "up regulate" the density of 5HT presynaptic receptors, or perhaps even "down regulates" these receptors similarly to its "down regulation" of ^{3}H-IMI binding sites. If such is the case, the rebound of 5HT turnover would not be as noticeable as the rebound observed in DA turnover after HLDL. EST may antagonize such HLDL-induced effects, and thus a combined EST-HLDL treatment could result in attenuation of the HLDL-induced increase in 5HT turnover. This explanation implies that presynaptic 5HT receptors are not regulated by the same mechanisms that regulate ^{3}H-IMI binding sites, since EST prevents the "up regulation" of ^{3}H-IMI binding sites but presumably facilitates "up regulation" of 5HT presynaptic receptors following HLDL withdrawal. Presynaptic 5HT receptors may consist of 5HT2-type receptors which are known to be "up regulated" by repeated EST.

SUMMARY

The interaction of EST and drugs on the CSF levels of several monoamine metabolites was studied with four drugs that have been used in the treatment of psychiatric disorders, namely, lithium, carbamazepine, imipramine, and haloperidol. EST-drug interactions were observed with each of these drugs on one or more monoaminergic systems. All interactions were antagonistic in nature. Changes in the CSF levels of monoamine metabolites did not always reflect corresponding changes in the monoamine turnover; the increase in 5HIAA seen after chronic Li was due to slower removal of this metabolite from the CSF. However, the changes in the CSF levels of DA and 5HT metabolites following chronic HLDL reflected changes in the turnover of the parent amine in the brain. The effects of both HLDL and EST on DA metabolism in the intact brain could be related to alterations by these treatments of the responsiveness of DA presynaptic receptors. Similarly, the effect of HLDL on 5HT turnover and the antagonistic interaction of EST on this HLDL-induced effect were associated with changes in ^{3}H-IMI binding sites that label the 5HT transporter in serotonergic presynaptic terminals. The results are discussed with the aid of a model that depicts possible relationships between pre- and postsynaptic variables and their influence on each other. According to this model an increase in the neurotransmitter turnover is associated with "down regulation" of both pre- and postsynaptic receptors whereas a decrease in turnover is associated with receptor "up regulation." However, "up regulation" of receptors is not necessarily associated with augmented postsynaptic response. Analysis of the model variables by the "binding equation" which obeys the Clark occupancy principle revealed that receptor "up regulation" which is associated with decreased turnover may result in either an augmented or a depressed postsynaptic response (related to the number of occupied receptors). The direction of the response depends on the ratio between the rate of receptor "up regulation" and the rate of decrease in neurotransmitter turnover.

ACKNOWLEDGMENTS

Part of the DA receptor data is based on a collaborative study with Drs. A. Reches, H. R. Wagner, and S. Fahn of the Neurological Institute, Columbia University College of Physicians and Surgeons. Mr. T. B. Cooper assisted in the analysis of the ^{3}H-IMI binding data. The technical assistance of Ms. S. Kowalik, Mr. N. Rienzi, and Mr. H. Nelson is gratefully acknowledged.

REFERENCES

1. ESSMAN, W. B. 1973. Neurochemistry of Cerebral Electroshock. Spectrum Inc. Flushing, N.Y.
2. FINK, M., S. KETY, J. MCGOUGH & T. A. WILLIAMS, Eds. 1974. Psychobiology of Convulsive Therapy. Winston & Sons. Washington, D.C.
3. FINK, M. 1979. Convulsive Therapy: Theory & Practice. Raven Press. New York, N.Y.
4. ABRAMS, R. & W. B. ESSMAN, Eds. 1982. Electroconvulsive Therapy: Biological Foundations and Clinical Applications. Spectrum Inc. Jamaica, N.Y.
5. LERER, B., R. D. WEINER & R. H. BELMAKER, Eds. 1984. ECT: Basic Mechanisms. John Libby & Co. London, England.
6. SIRIS, S. G., A. H. GLASSMAN & F. STATNER. 1982. *In* Electroconvulsive Therapy. R. A. Abrams & W. B. Essman, Eds.: 91–112. Spectrum Inc. Jamaica, N.Y.
7. SQUIRES, R. F. 1978. *In* Handbook of Psychopharmacology. K. R. Iversen, S. D. Iversen & S. H. Snyder, Eds. **14:** 1–58. Plenum Press. New York, N.Y.
8. BARKAI, A. I., S. KOWALIK & A. RECHES. 1984. Psychopharmacology **84:** 352–355.
9. BARKAI, A. I. 1979. J. Pharmacol. Exp. Ther. **208:** 44–48.
10. HEAL, D. J., A. R. GREEN, D. L. BOULLIN & D. G. GRAHAME-SMITH. 1976. Psychopharmacology **49:** 287–291.
11. BURT, D. R., I. CREESE & S. H. SNYDER. 1977. Science **196:** 326–328.
12. MODIGH, K. 1975. J. Neural Transm. **36:** 19–32.
13. GREEN, A. R., D. J. HEAL & D. G. GRAHAME-SMITH. 1977. Psychopharmacology **52:** 195–200.
14. GREEN, A. R. & J. F. W. DEAKIN. 1980. Nature **285:** 232–233.
15. BERGSTROM, D. A. & K. J. KELLAR. 1979. Nature **278:** 464–466.
16. ATTERWILL, C. K. 1980. J. Neurochem. **35:** 729–734.
17. RECHES, A., H. R. WAGNER, A. I. BARKAI, V. JACKSON, E. Y. ALTER & S. FAHN. 1984. Psychopharmacology **83:** 155–158.
18. RECHES, A., H. R. WAGNER, D. JIANG, V. JACKSON & S. FAHN. 1982. Life Sci. **31:** 37–44.
19. RECHES, A., H. R. WAGNER, V. JACKSON & S. FAHN. 1982. Brain Res. **246:** 172–177.
20. PEROUTKA, S. J., R. M. LEBOVITZ & S. H. SNYDER. 1981. Science **212:** 827–829.
21. KELLAR, K. J., C. S. CASCIO, J. A. BUTLER & R. N. KURTZKI. 1981. Eur. J. Pharmacol. **69:** 515–518.
22. VETULANI, J., U. LEBRECHT & A. PILC. 1981. Eur. J. Pharmacol. **76:** 81–85.
23. LANGER, S. Z. & R. RAISMAN. 1983. Neuropharmacology **22:** 407–413.
24. RAISMAN, R., M. S. BRILEY & S. Z. LANGER. 1980. Eur. J. Pharmacol. **61:** 373–380.

25. REHAVI, M., S. PAUL, P. SKOLNIK & F. GOODWIN. 1980. Life Sci. **26:** 2273–2279.
26. LERER, B., K. JABOTINSKY-RUBIN, K. BANNET, R. B. EBSTEIN & R. H. BELMAKER. 1982. Eur. J. Pharmacol. **80:** 131–134.
27. KELLAR, K. J., C. S. CASCIO, D. A. BERGSTROM, J. A. BUTLER & P. IADOROLA. 1981. J. Neurochem. **37:** 830–836.
28. PILC, A. & A. ROKOSZ-PELC. 1983. Eur. J. Pharmacol. **88:** 255–257.
29. TREISER, S. & K. J. KELLAR. 1979. Eur. J. Pharmacol. **58:** 85–86.
30. PESTRONEK, A. & D. B. DRACHMAN. 1980. Science **210:** 342—343.
31. PERT, A., J. ROSENBLATT, C. SIVIT, C. B. PERT & W. E. BUNNEY, JR. 1978. Science **201:** 171–173.

Neuroendocrine Responses as a Probe into the Mechanisms of Action of Electroconvulsive Therapy[a]

P. J. COWEN

MRC Unit of Clinical Pharmacology
and University Department of Psychiatry
Research Unit
Littlemore Hospital
Littlemore
Oxford OX4 4XN, United Kingdom

INTRODUCTION

There is much evidence from animal studies that repeated electroconvulsive shock (ECS) results in functional changes in brain monoamine pathways.[1] It would clearly be desirable to know whether electroconvulsive therapy (ECT) produces similar changes in man, but direct investigation is extremely difficult.

In recent years it has been demonstrated that the secretion of many anterior pituitary hormones is under the control of brain monoamine pathways.[2] Drugs that alter brain monoamine function produce changes in plasma levels of certain hormones, and the size of the hormonal response depends on the functional activity of the monoamine pathway with which the drug interacts. Thus drugs with selective pharmacological properties may be used to probe the function of a specific monoamine pathway involved in the release of the hormone that is being measured. This "neuroendocrine strategy" has proved an acceptable, albeit indirect, method of assessing brain monoamine function in depressive illness.[2] While it may be argued that the hormonal responses are mediated by hypothalamic and pituitary mechanisms that might not be relevant to the phenomenon of depressed mood, depressed patients frequently show abnormalities in endocrine function,[2] which implies that investigation of these brain regions may well be of value. In addition, drugs used in neuroendocrine tests often produce other specific changes such as sedation that may also be mediated by changes in monoamine function. Therefore assessment of both behavioral and endocrine effects produced by drug challenge can provide information about monoamine-mediated responses in a number of brain regions.

The difficulties common to all neuroendocrine studies have been well reviewed by Checkley.[2] While it can be shown that the stimulation of monoamine pathways will alter plasma levels of various hormones, there are, of course, a large number of steps between administration of the drug and measurement of the hormone response in plasma.[2-4] At the simplest level, for example the suppression of plasma prolactin by the dopamine agonist apomorphine, the response involves the direct interaction of a drug with pituitary receptors.[2] Other neuroendocrine responses are more complex. For example, the stimulation of growth hormone release by clonidine is probably mediated

[a]The support of the Wellcome Trust is gratefully acknowledged.

via growth hormone releasing factor in the hypothalamus.[2,4] Thus, many factors other than changes in monoamine function can alter neuroendocrine responses.

A particular difficulty with ECT concerns the administration of concurrent psychotropic medication. Antidepressant drugs, for example, have marked effects on brain monoamine pathways, and if patients receive ECT combined with antidepressant drug therapy, interpretation of the resulting changes may be difficult, even where the effect of the drug concerned on neuroendocrine function is known and the dose held constant throughout the course of ECT. A related problem with ECT studies is the effect of repeated anesthesia on neuroendocrine responses,[5] which has not been investigated in man.

A further problem in the assessment of the effect of ECT on neuroendocrine function is that depressed patients frequently exhibit abnormal responses prior to treatment. If, after a course of ECT, these responses are altered, it may not be clear whether the changes are attributable to ECT itself or rather clinical recovery.

The following sections discuss the findings of some neuroendocrine investigations into the effects of ECT using three relatively specific drug challenges (TABLES 1 and 2). Animal studies are quoted where they aid interpretation of the results in man (TABLE 2).

CLONIDINE

The α-adrenoceptor agonist clonidine has been shown in both receptor binding and functional studies to be a relatively specific ligand for α_2-adrenoceptors.[6] The administration of clonidine to both animals and man results in an increase in plasma growth hormone levels,[4,7] which is probably due to the stimulation of postsynaptic α_2-adrenoceptors in the forebrain.[8] Other changes produced by clonidine include a reduction in blood pressure,[6] behavioral sedation,[9] and a decrease in brain noradrenaline turnover,[10] which can be measured in man as a decline in plasma levels of the noradrenaline metabolite 3-methoxy-4-hydroxyphenylglycol (MHPG).[11] The latter two actions of clonidine have been attributed to the stimulation of the presynaptic α_2-adrenoceptors in the brain.[11]

Studies in Animals

In the rat repeated ECS appears to reduce the sensitivity of presynaptic α_2-adrenoceptors. Thus both the sedative effect of clonidine and the reduction in brain MHPG were attenuated by ECS.[12] While in the rat the growth response to clonidine was not altered by ECS,[13] an enhanced response was found in the baboon.[8] However, this was not apparent 24 hours after the last ECS but was seen only after a seven-day lag period. Since, after a course of photic convulsions without anesthetic, baboons showed enhanced growth hormone responses to clonidine 24 hours after the final convulsion,[8] the authors proposed that the anesthetic given with the ECS may have retarded the appearance of the enhanced growth hormone responses. It is not clear if any other responses to clonidine were rated in these studies.

Similarly to ECS, repeated administration of tricyclic antidepressants (TCAs) antagonizes the behavioral sedation caused by clonidine in the rat.[14] A minority of TCAs also attenuate the reduction in brain MHPG produced by clonidine.[10] In the rat TCA treatment reduced the growth hormone response to clonidine[15] and both ECS[16] and TCA treatment[17] may reduce brain α_2-adrenoceptor binding, which is thought to be predominantly to postsynaptic receptor sites.

TABLE 1. Neuroendocrine Effects of Clonidine, Amphetamine, and Apomorphine in Man

Drug	Neuroendocrine Effect	Receptor Involved
Clonidine	↑ Growth hormone[4,7]	α_2-Adrenoceptor
	↓ Plasma MHPG[11]	α_2-Adrenoceptor
	↓ Blood pressure[18]	α_2-Adrenoceptor
	Sedation[18]	α_2-Adrenoceptor
Amphetamine	↑ ACTH and cortisol[22]	α_1-Adrenoceptor
	↑ Growth hormone[22]	?α_2-Adrenoceptor
Apomorphine	↑ Growth hormone[3,28]	Dopamine receptor
	↓ Prolactin[28]	Dopamine receptor

Thus both ECS and TCA treatment appear to produce changes consistent with a reduction in α_2-adrenoceptor sensitivity. The increased growth hormone response to clonidine in the baboon following both electrically and chemically induced convulsions is at odds with another animal data, suggesting a decrease in α_2-adrenoceptor sensitivity following ECS. However, the finding is of interest since changes found in this species might be more relevant to man.

Studies in Man

There has been one study in depressed patients on the effect of ECT on the growth hormone and other responses to clonidine.[18] In six subjects there was no change in the growth hormone response to clonidine when pretreatment values were compared with those following ECT. In addition, there was no change in the sedative or blood pressure changes produced by clonidine following ECT.[18]

TABLE 2. Effect of Repeated Electroconvulsive Shock in Animals and Electroconvulsive Therapy in Depressed Patients on Neuroendocrine Responses to Clonidine, Apomorphine, and Methylamphetamine

Drug	Effect of ECS	Effect of ECT
Clonidine	No change in growth hormone response in rats;[13] increase in baboons[8]	No change in growth hormone response[18]
	Attenuated reduction in brain MHPG[12]	Not tested
	Attenuation of sedation[12]	No change in sedative response[18]
Amphetamine	Not tested	Increase in cortisol response[18]
	Not tested	No change in growth hormone response[18]
Apomorphine	Increased growth hormone response[13]	Increased growth hormone response;[29] increased prolactin suppression;[30] no change in growth hormone or prolactin response[31]

Interpretation of these results, however, is difficult. Depressed patients have reduced growth hormone responses to clonidine prior to treatment,[19,20] and it is unclear whether the responses return to normal following clinical recovery.[21] Two of the patients studied were taking TCAs, which may themselves suppress clonidine-induced growth hormone release.[21] TCAs also have been reported to attenuate the sedative and blood pressure responses to clonidine.[21] Finally, there is the complication of the effect of repeated anesthesia, which was shown to mask an enhanced growth hormone response, in the baboon study.[8]

At present, therefore, the effect of ECT on α_2-adrenoceptor-mediated responses in man requires further study.

AMPHETAMINE

Amphetamine releases and blocks the uptake of noradrenaline, dopamine, and 5-hydroxytryptamine. Because of its lack of pharmacological specificity it has not been widely used in animal studies of the effects of ECT. However, it is discussed here because the endocrine responses to amphetamine administration have been studied in depressed patients receiving ECT.

Amphetamine elevates plasma cortisol, via the release of ACTH from the pituitary.[22] There is evidence that this response is mediated by α-adrenoceptors,[22] and the lack of effect of clonidine on plasma cortisol[7] would suggest that the receptor concerned is of the α_1 subtype. In addition, amphetamine causes an increase in plasma growth hormone. This is also thought to be mediated by a noradrenergic mechanism[23] that might involve α_2-adrenoceptors, since these have been implicated in growth hormone release. In depressed patients the cortisol response to methylamphetamine is blunted.[24] The same may be true of the growth hormone response but there is some inconsistency between the various studies.[24,25]

Following a course of ECT in depressed patients the cortisol response to methylamphetamine was increased but there was no change in the growth hormone response.[18] On the face of it, this might be consistent with an enhancement of α_1-adrenoceptor-mediated responses following ECT. However, the changes cannot be interpreted simply. The major difficulty is that the blunted cortisol responses to methylamphetamine in depression probably normalize following clinical recovery,[26] and indeed this was the explanation favored by the authors for the cortisol changes following ECT. However, a number of the patients who did not recover also showed an enhanced cortisol response after ECT.[24]

APOMORPHINE

The dopamine agonist apomorphine has been used to investigate the effects of ECS and ECT in several studies.

Animal Studies

In the rat, administration of apomorphine produces characteristic dopamine-mediated responses including locomotor activity and behavioral stereotypy. It is well established that repeated ECS leads to enhancement of these behavioral responses.[1] ECS does not apparently cause changes in dopamine receptor binding[27] and it has been

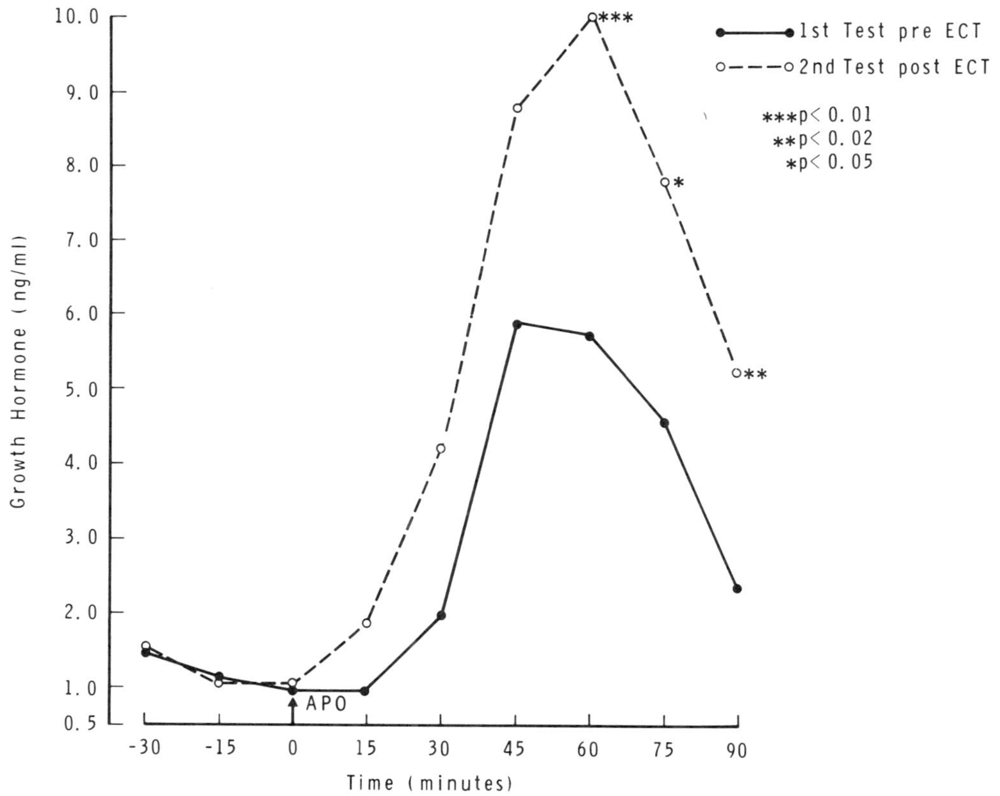

FIGURE 1. The curves represent the mean GH responses over 90 minutes of the 15 ECT patients following apomorphine (APO) 0.005 mg/kg subcutaneously. Patients were tested at the beginning of their ECT course (solid line) and after its conclusion (broken line). The responses at 60, 75, and 90 minutes are significantly greater after ECT. (Reproduced from Reference 29 with permission from the publisher.)

proposed that the enhancement of dopamine-mediated responses is caused by changes beyond the dopamine receptor, perhaps in a postsynaptic modulatory system.[1]

While apomorphine does not increase plasma growth hormone levels in the rat, it does potentiate the growth hormone increase seen following clonidine.[13] The growth hormone response to the combined administration of clonidine and apomorphine was increased in the rat following a course of ECS,[13] while the growth hormone response to

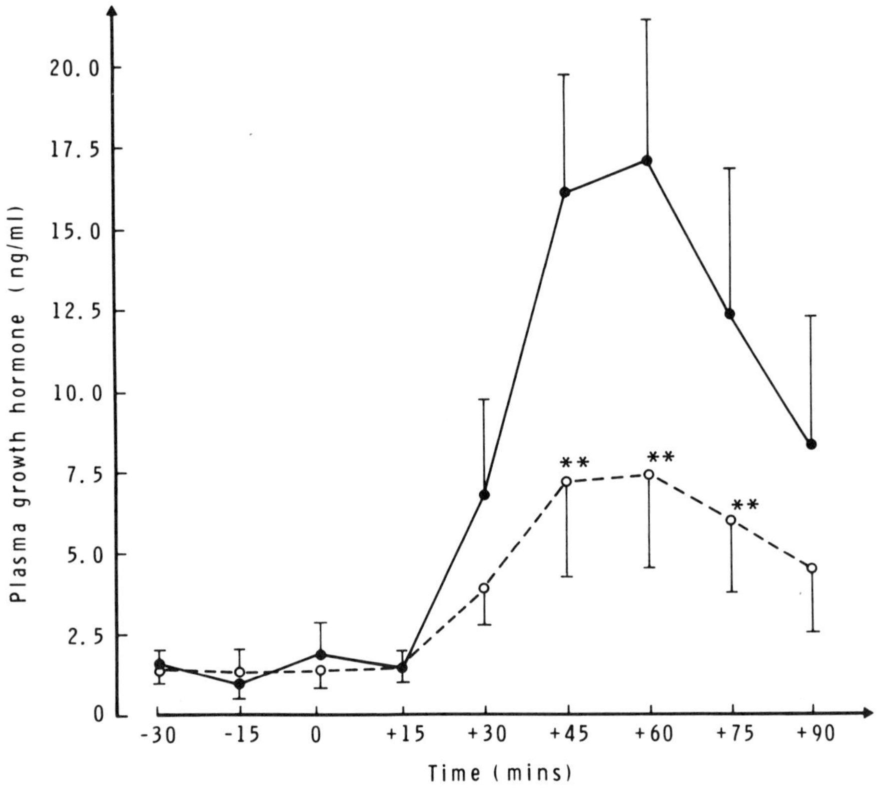

FIGURE 2. Mean (± standard error of the mean) GH response to apomorphine (administered at time 0) in six normal subjects tested on two occasions: (a) prior to amitriptyline treatment (solid line), and (b) at the end of amitriptyline treatment (broken line). $^{**}p < 0.01$ (paired t-test). (Reproduced from Reference 32 with permission from the publisher.)

clonidine alone was not altered.[13] It was concluded that ECS increases the responsiveness of postsynaptic dopamine pathways involved in growth hormone release.

Studies in Man

In man administration of apomorphine causes an increase in plasma growth hormone (GH)[3,28] and a decrease in plasma prolactin.[28] The former response is probably due to stimulation of postsynaptic dopamine receptors in the hypothalamus,[28] while the latter is caused by direct stimulation of dopamine receptors in the pituitary.[3]

A number of studies have investigated the effects of ECT on these effects of apomorphine. Our own investigation in 15 depressed patients revealed a significant increase in the growth hormone response to apomorphine following a course of ECT (FIGURE 1).[29] In the study by Balldin *et al.*, while the growth hormone response to apomorphine was not altered by ECT, the suppression of prolactin was enhanced,[30] again suggesting an increase in certain dopamine-mediated endocrine responses. However, Christie *et al.* found no effects of ECT on either the growth hormone or prolactin response to apomorphine.[31]

There are a number of methodological differences between the various studies that might account for these discrepant findings. In our own investigation some of the patients were treated with TCAs but the enhanced response to apomorphine following ECT was still seen when these subjects were excluded.[29] In addition, we have shown in parallel studies that treatment with amitriptyline, in fact, reduces the growth hormone response to apomorphine[29,32] (FIGURE 2).

The growth hormone response to apomorphine is apparently normal in depression.[2] Therefore, if there is an increase in growth hormone response to apomorphine following ECT, it may well be due to an enhancement caused by the treatment and cannot be attributed to clinical recovery alone, especially since recovery with TCA treatment is associated with a decreased growth hormone response.[29,32] However, because of the inconsistency of the findings it is premature to conclude that ECT does increase the growth hormone or prolactin responses to apomorphine, and further investigations are needed that take account of the methodological differences between the studies already published.

CONCLUSIONS

Neuroendocrine studies can be used to investigate monoamine function in man. However, so far such studies have not enabled us to draw firm conclusions about the effects of ECT on brain monoamine pathways. In recent years there has been an improvement in the technique of neuroendocrine studies, so that more specific drug challenges are available and the mechanisms by which the hormone and other responses occur are better understood. We may hope that better designed studies in the future will enable us to learn more about the neuropharmacological mechanisms that underlie the effectiveness of ECT.

REFERENCES

1. GRAHAME-SMITH, D. G., A. R. GREEN & D. W. COSTAIN. 1978. Mechanism of the antidepressant action of electroconvulsive therapy. Lancet **i:** 254–256.
2. CHECKLEY, S. A. 1980. Neuroendocrine tests of monoamine function in man: a review of basic theory and its application to the study of depressive illness. Psychol. Med. **10:** 35–53.
3. LAL, S., C. E. DE LA VEGA, T. L. SOURKES & H. G. FRIESEN. 1972. Effect of apomorphine on human growth hormone secretion. Lancet **ii:** 661.
4. TERRY, L. C. & J. B. MARTIN. 1971. Evidence for alpha-adrenergic regulation of episodic growth hormone and prolactin secretion in the undisturbed male rat. Endocrinology **108:** 1869–1873.

5. STEINER, J. A. & D. G. GRAHAME-SMITH. 1980. The effect of repeated electroconvulsive shock on corticosterone responses to centrally acting pharmacological stimuli in the male rat. Psychopharmacology **71:** 205–212.
6. SCHMITT, H. 1977. The pharmacology of clonidine and related products. *In* Hanbuch der experimenteller Pharmakologie. F. Gross, Ed.: 299–396. Springer. Berlin, FRG.
7. LAL, S., G. TOLLU, J. B. MARTIN, G. M. BROWN & M. GUYDA. 1975. Effect of clonidine on growth hormone, prolactin, lutenizing hormone, follicle stimulating hormone and thyroid stimulating hormone in the serum of normal men. J. Clin. Endocrinol. Metab. **41:** 823–832.
8. MCWILLIAM, J. R., B. S. MELDRUM & S. A. CHECKLEY. 1982. Changes in noradrenergic neuroendocrine responses following repeated seizures and the mechanism of action of ECT. Psychopharmacology **77:** 53–57.
9. DREW, G. M., H. J. GOWER & A. S. MARRIOTT. 1979. Alpha-2-adrenoceptors mediate clonidine-induced sedation in the rat. Br. J. Clin. Pharmacol. **67:** 133.
10. SUGRUE, M. F. 1981. Effects of acutely and chronically administered antidepressants on the clonidine-induced decrease in rat brain 3-methoxy-4-hydroxyphenylethylene glycol sulphate content. Life Sci. **28:** 377–384.
11. CHARNEY, D. S., G. R. HENINGER & D. E. STERNBERG. 1983. Alpha-2 adrenergic sensitivity and the mechanism of action of antidepressant therapy: the effect of long-term amitriptyline treatment. Br. J. Psychiatry **142:** 265–275.
12. HEAL, D. J., H. AKAGI, J. M. BOWDLER & A. R. GREEN. 1981. Repeated electroconvulsive shock attenuates clonidine-induced hypoactivity in rats. Eur. J. Pharmacol. **75:** 231–237.
13. EDEN, S. & K. MODIGH. 1977. Effect of apomorphine and clonidine on rat plasma growth hormone after pretreatment with reserpine and electroconvulsive shocks. Brain Res. **129:** 379–384.
14. HEAL, D. J., S. LISTER, S. L. SMITH, C. L. DAVIES, S. G. MOLYNEUX & A. R. GREEN. 1981. The effects of acute and repeated administration of various antidepressant drugs on clonidine-induced hypoactivity in mice and rats. Neuropharmacology **22:** 983–992.
15. ERIKSSON, E., S. EDEN & K. MODIGH. 1982. Up-and-down regulation of central postsynaptic α_2 receptors reflected in the growth hormone response to clonidine in reserpine-pretreated rats. Psychopharmacology **77:** 327–331.
16. STANFORD, C. & D. J. NUTT. 1982. Comparison of the effect of repeated electroconvulsive shock on α_2 and β-adrenoceptors in different regions of rat brain. Neuroscience **7:** 1753–1757.
17. SMITH, C. B., J. A. GARCIA-SEVILLA & P. J. HOLLINGSWORTH. 1981. α_2-Adrenoceptors in rat brain are decreased after long-term tricyclic antidepressant drug treatment. Brain Res. **210:** 413–418.
18. SLADE, A. P. & S. A. CHECKLEY. 1980. A neuroendocrine study of the mechanism of action of ECT. Br. J. Psychiatry **137:** 217–221.
19. MATUSSEK, N., M. ACKENHAIL, H. HIPPIUS, F. MULLER, H. SCHRODER, H. SCHULTES & B. WASILEWSKI. 1980. Effect of clonidine on growth hormone release in psychiatric patients and controls. Psychiatr. Res. **2:** 25–36.
20. CHECKLEY, S. A., A. P. SLADE & E. SHUR. 1981. Growth hormone and other responses to clonidine in patients with endogenous depression. Br. J. Psychiatry **138:** 51–55.
21. GLASS, I. B., S. A. CHECKLEY, E. SHUR & S. DAWLING. 1982. The effect of desipramine upon central adrenergic function in depressed patients. Br. J. Psychiatry **141:** 372–376.
22. REES, L., P. W. P. BULLER, C. GOSLING & G. M. BESSER. 1970. Adrenergic blockade and the corticosteroid and growth hormone responses to methylamphetamine. Nature **228:** 565–566.
23. JOHNSTONE, E. C. & W. FERRIER. 1980. Neuroendocrine markers of CNS drug effects. Br. J. Clin. Pharmacol. **10:** 5–21.
24. CHECKLEY, S. A. 1979. Corticosteroid and growth hormone responses to methylamphetamine in depressive illness. Psychol. Med. **9:** 107–115.
25. LANGER, G., C. HEINZE, B. REIM & N. MATUSSEK. 1976. Reduced growth hormone responses to amphetamine in "endogenous" depressive patients. Arch. Gen. Psychiatry **33:** 1471–1475.

26. CHECKLEY, S. A. & J. L. CRAMMER. 1977. Hormone responses to methylamphetamine in depression: a new approach to the noradrenaline depletion hypothesis. Br. J. Psychiatry **131:** 582–586.
27. DEAKIN, J. W. F., F. OWEN, A. J. CROSS. & M. J. DASHWOOD. 1981. Studies on possible mechanisms of electroconvulsive therapy and effects of repeated induced seizures on rat brain receptors for monoamine and other neurotransmitters. Psychopharmacology **73:** 345–349.
28. LAL, S., C. E. DE LA VEGA, T. L. SOURKES & H. G. FRIESEN. 1973. Effect of apomorphine on growth hormone, prolactin, luteinising hormone and follicle-stimulating hormone levels in human serum. J. Clin. Endocrinol. Metab. **37:** 719–724.
29. COSTAIN, D. W., P. J. COWEN, M. G. GELDER & D. G. GRAHAME-SMITH. 1982. Electroconvulsive therapy and the brain: evidence for increased dopamine-mediated responses. Lancet **ii:** 400–404.
30. BALLDIN, J., A-K. GRANERUS, G. LINDSTEDT, K. MODIGH & J. WALLINDER. 1982. Neuroendocrine evidence for increased responsiveness of dopamine receptors in humans following electroconvulsive therapy. Psychopharmacology **76:** 371–376.
31. CHRISTIE, J. E., L. J. WHALLEY, N. S. BROWN & H. DICK. 1982. Effect of ECT on the neuroendocrine response to apomorphine in severely depressed patients. Br. J. Psychiatry **140:** 268–273.
32. COWEN, P. J., L. E. BRADDOCK & B. GOSDEN. 1984. The effect of amitriptyline treatment on the growth hormone response to apomorphine. Psychopharmacology **83:** 378–379.

The Biochemistry of Electroconvulsive Therapy[a]

Discussion of Part III

PAOLO DECINA

Department of Biological Psychiatry
New York State Psychiatric Institute
and
Department of Psychiatry
College of Physicians and Surgeons
Columbia University
722 West 168 Street
New York, New York 10032

A major area of research on the mechanisms of action of electroconvulsive therapy (ECT) centers around the acute and chronic effects of treatment on the synaptic junctions of various central neurotransmitter systems. Because of the inherent difficulties in conducting this research directly *in situ,* investigators have attempted to extrapolate data mostly derived from experimental animals and, less frequently, from neuroendocrine studies in humans. The four papers presented here are illustrative of this line of research.

The authors—Drs. Barkai, Bolwig and Jørgensen, Cowen, and Holaday and colleagues—present their research in the context of a review of other relevant findings already published in the literature. The result is a comprehensive and up-to-date overview of the topics discussed. While the information gleaned from these studies is still inconclusive, it indicates that ECT, like psychotropic drugs, results in marked alterations of synaptic systems that are thought to be implicated in psychiatric phenomena.

Chronic administration of ECT results in general synaptic remodeling as suggested by Bolwig's work. This author demonstrates how in rats ECT produces changes in specific brain proteins particularly related to hypothalamic synapses. Overall, these changes are interpreted as indicating that during and for a period after ECT treatment there is a central nervous system (CNS) increase in the number of synaptic vesicles and in the preparedness of glycolitic demands accompanying seizure. Holaday and colleagues present biochemical experiments indicative of an activation of endogenous opioids and their receptors by electroconvulsive shock (ECS) in rats. This acute effect of ECT may play a role in various clinical phenomena observed after ECS like increase in seizure threshold, amnestic side effects, and postictal euphoric states.

The focus of interest in the last two papers is the monoaminergic system. In rats, Barkai has investigated ECT interactions with the commonest drugs used in the treatment of affective disorders, i.e., lithium, imipramine, carbamazepine, and haloperidol. Interestingly, synergistic interactions were not observed although the haloperidol-induced changes in 5-hydroxytryptamine presynaptic receptors were prevented by

[a]The preparation of this paper was supported in part by National Institute of Mental Health Grant Number MH 35636.

ECT. Thus, it would appear that ECT affects certain neuronal receptors in a way similar to lithium, which has been previously shown to "stabilize" some receptor functions. This effect may be of relevance in accounting for both the antidepressant and antimanic action of ECT. Finally, Cowen's study is concerned with pharmacologic probes to assess the effects on the monoamine pathways involved in the regulation of pituitary hormone release. Still in their infancy, these studies have generated contradictory findings, the least controversial of which appears to be the enhancement by ECT of the cortisol response to amphetamines thought to be mediated by α_2 adrenoceptors.

Stimulus Parameters and Electroconvulsive Therapy

LELON A. WEAVER, JR.[a] AND RONALD W. WILLIAMS[b]

[a]*Department of Psychiatry*
[b]*Department of Electrical Engineering*
University of Vermont
Burlington, Vermont 05401

The purpose of this paper is to outline what we do and do not know about the electroconvulsive therapy (ECT) stimulus; the latter will require somewhat more time than the former. Papers that deal in any systematic way with the ECT stimulus comprise only a minute percentage of the literature. It ranges from difficult to impossible to say very much of a definitive nature based on our present fund of knowledge. We have many fragments of information but nothing approaching a systematic whole.

Historically there are several roots to this problem. First, simple ordinary basic research was omitted. Essentially, the profession took whatever instruments manufacturers chose to provide—seldom based on clinical expertise and almost never on scientific data—and proceeded with treatment and clinical research on this basis. There were usually a few articles published each time a new machine was introduced, but we are unaware of any follow-up evaluative papers concerned with the design, utility, and shortcomings of the instrument. It took nearly 20 years before Davies *et al,* published an article critical of the MOLAC II, pointing out that the three voltage settings were essentially equal.[1] Curiosity about performance characteristics ought to have a shorter gestational period than that.

This brings us to the second root: failure to do traditional dose-response investigations. There is almost a total lack of studies investigating the clinical and electrical results of the various stimulus parameter combinations available on any commercially produced instrument. This is as true for the Medcraft and MECTA instruments as it was for the Reiter CW, the MOLAC II, and their predecessors. During the past five years, it has become more common for authors to mention the range of stimulus parameters employed, a practice that is a distinct improvement over those studies that compared ECT with antidepressant drugs and dismissed the stimulus with a succinct "ECT was given."

A third root has been failure to bring under experimental scrutiny and control basic physical factors relating to the ECT process. It has been known for many years that the resistance or impedance between the stimulating electrodes is inversely related to the energy actually reaching the brain. It was also known that measuring the resistance between electrodes with an ordinary ohmmeter gave no useful information regarding impedance as actually measured during treatment. Maxwell presented evidence that impedance diminished as voltage increased and that impedance could be considered constant above 135 volts.[2] No study has been published that deals with variations in impedance within patient or between patients or the factors that produce these variations; nor has any study confirmed or taken issue with Maxwell's findings.

Regrettably, then, what we shall have to say regarding stimulus parameters must be regarded as tentative, pending the availability of more systematic research data. The quality of the published data is usually adequate; the deficiencies lie in the quantity and a suitable framework within which to place and evaluate such studies.

One basic parameter of the ECT stimulus is the amplitude of the signal, either in terms of voltage or current. Technically, we can achieve satisfactory control of either voltage or current but, because of the uncontrolled factor of patient impedance, never both. It is possible to measure both but to specify only one. Because of the relative ease with which voltage-tapped transformers can be constructed, voltage control has been the most usual method.

In the case of the alternating current (AC) instruments, voltage will remain constant at the set level. Current will vary inversely with the momentary resistance of the patient, at least up to the capacity of the transformer. Thus, for example, using the Medcraft with a setting of 170 volts, a patient with 200 ohms impedance would receive a current of 850 mA while one with 400 ohms would get 425 mA. Unless special provision is made for measurements, none of these changes would be known to the operator. In this design, then, the amplitude of the voltage would remain constant; the amplitude of the current would vary inversely with the impedance load.

In the constant current design, e.g., the MECTA, current remains relatively fixed and the voltage varies with the impedance load, presumably up to some predetermined limit. This approach has the advantage of keeping both current and voltage within controlled limits, although in the case of the MECTA other design decisions appear to have affected these parameter limits. Specifically, using the cycles-per-second approach to determining the interval between pulses and limiting the overall pulse train duration to two seconds means that the current must be high enough to introduce sufficient energy to elicit a convulsion in a comparatively brief period of time. It is known that the MECTA can produce up to 500 volts in the event of high patient impedance. Even a relatively modest impedance of 300 ohms will require 240 volts to produce the current of 800 mA. It is noteworthy that this voltage is quite comparable to the highest voltage available on the Medcraft. Given the respective design decisions, both machines must be time limited to avoid applying excessive stimulus energy to the patient. This fact does not necessarily constitute evidence that these decisions were correct. There was little if any published evidence that lower amplitudes and longer times were compared to higher amplitudes and shorter times prior to making these decisions.

The following data were collected during the period of waiting for completion of a new model pulse machine. While not a formal study, it was designed to duplicate the experience of a clinician using the Medcraft B-24 and investigating various combinations of time and voltage settings. A total of 15 patients were given 246 treatments: 167 initial treatments and 79 retreatments. The results are presented in TABLE 1, classified in terms of voltage, stimulus duration, and outcome. Cell entries are the number of treatments. Most patients were begun at the 150 volt level. All subsequent initial treatments were oriented towards determining the minimal voltage and time setting that would produce an adequate convulsive response. A conscious effort was made to obtain data on as many stimulus combinations as possible, consonant with avoiding an excessive number of failures. An unsuccessful treatment was always followed by a retreatment, almost always at a higher level.

Despite the complications introduced by the clinical treatment situation, TABLE 1 shows two clear trends: (1) there are significantly more trials at the longest time interval, and (2) a significantly greater number of trials in the 170-V × 1.0-second cell. Also noteworthy is the fact that 69% of the retreatments occurred in this cell and that the overall success rate was only 74%. This rate would have been lower if we had included the data from four patients who required double stimulations in rapid succession in order to obtain a satisfactory convulsion.

These data informally demonstrate what most clinicians know: that the higher settings of the Medcraft are required more frequently and that the lower voltage and shorter times are less successful. The few studies that give information on the Medcraft settings used seldom mention the lower range of settings. Weiner mentions only starting values of 140 V and 0.6 seconds.[3] Of six other studies published since 1980,[4–9] all equal or exceed this level with two mentioning only the 170-V × 1.0-second setting.

Turning now to the amplitude of brief-pulse stimuli, the data are even more scanty. Much of the published research is based on the use of the MECTA which produces only a constant current of 800 mA. Since the impedance during treatment is available from the chart record, the voltage can be obtained by calculation. To date, no one has published such data.

In our laboratory we record the voltage and current of each treatment on a storage oscilloscope. FIGURES 1 and 2 contain the distributions of these data. Almost all of these data were collected under various research protocols, of which only one varied

TABLE 1. Convulsion Production as a Function of the Time and Voltage Settings of the Medcraft B-24 Instrument[a]

		Time in Seconds				
Voltage	Outcome	1.0	0.75	0.6	0.5	Totals
170	Success	43	2	0	—	45
	Fail	25	4	1	—	30
160	Success	16	4	5	3	28
	Fail	2	6	2	3	13
150	Success	29	3	3	11	46
	Fail	13	6	2	6	27
140	Success	10	2	3	3	18
	Fail	2	1	0	1	4
130	Success	13	2	0	0	15
	Fail	3	3	3	2	11
120	Success	0	—	—	—	0
	Fail	9	—	—	—	9
Totals	Success	111	13	11	17	152
	Fail	54	20	8	12	94
	Column	165	33	19	29	246

[a]Cell entries are the number of treatments or retreatments. $n = 15$ patients.

voltage and none current. Since the instrument was of the constant-voltage design, current was the parameter most influenced by resistance.

FIGURE 1 shows that 75% of the trials were at 200 volts, reflecting primarily the value associated with our standard stimulus. Of the 8.6% of the trials below 200 volts, 6% were from the voltage threshold study. Of the 18% above 200 volts, 7% were from this study. All stimuli above 200 volts were in response to persistent failure; none were programmed by a protocol. The mean was 202.91 volts with a standard deviation (SD) of 18.51.

FIGURE 2 shows that the current is distributed approximately normally from 300 to 900+ mA with a mean of 587 and an SD of 127.53. About 62% of the observations fall between 500 and 700 mA.

Taken together, these voltage and current data constitute substantial evidence that moderate parameter values can achieve positive results. Of the 2003 trials represented, 1650 (82%) were successful treatments or retreatments. Since two of the six protocols involved threshold determinations for the number of pulses and interpulse interval

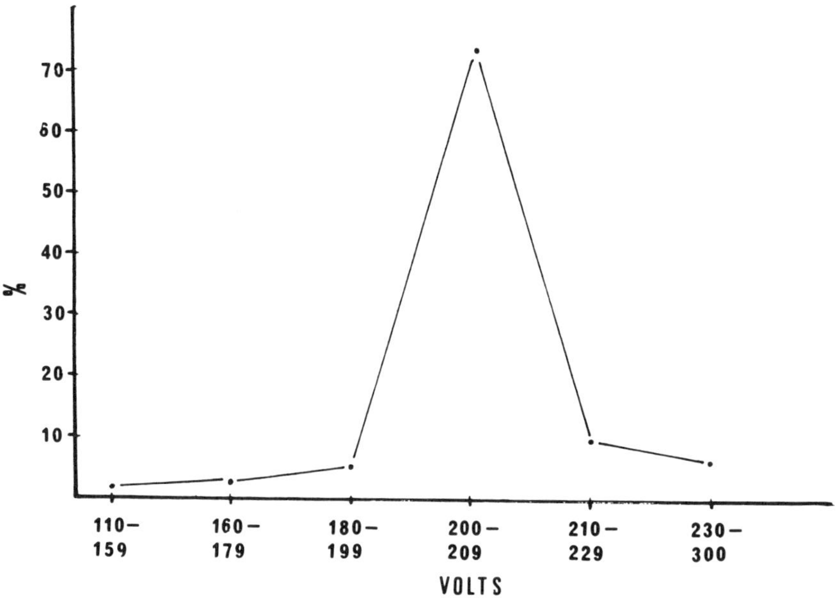

FIGURE 1. The distribution of voltages from 2003 treatments. The ordinate is the percent of the treatments given at each voltage interval. Mean value was 203 volts.

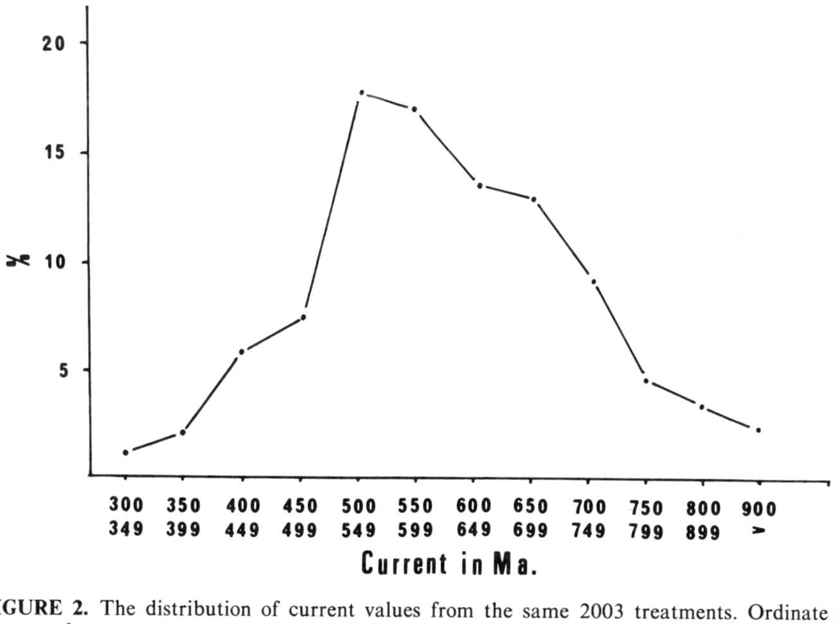

FIGURE 2. The distribution of current values from the same 2003 treatments. Ordinate is percent of treatments at each current interval. Mean value was 587 milliamperes.

parameters, some failures were encountered that were not determined by voltage or current values; the above estimates of success are quite conservative.

The second parameter of the stimulus is pulse width. For the 60-cycle AC waveform, this width is always fixed at 8.33 mseconds zero-to-zero amplitude. Since it cannot be varied, it has not been used as an independent variable. There seems to be general agreement that the pulse is unnecessarily wide, particularly in view of the widespread successful use of pulses of 1 msecond or less. Significant amounts of energy are being transmitted for about 6 of the 8 mseconds.

In Europe, the AC stimulus has been more varied. With the 50 cycle AC waveform, the zero-to-zero time is 10 mseconds. In the case of the Siemens KV series instruments, the leading half of the positive deflection of the sine wave is suppressed so that the stimulus waveform is the falling half. The negative phase is suppressed entirely so that the stimulus is "on" for 5 mseconds with an interpulse interval of 15 mseconds. The rationale for continuing the stimulus for 5 mseconds rather than terminating it after 1 msecond is obscure.

In Great Britain, the Ectron Duopulse instrument produces either a bidirectional sine wave or a unidirectional half-wave rectified signal. Frequency apparently varies from 40–60 cycles per second (cps) according to the mains input. Since the rectified signal also consists of the falling half of the deflection, at 50 cps input the waveform in this mode would be quite comparable to the output of the Siemens instrument. The Ectron Duopulse in the brief-pulse mode produces brief pulses of unknown width. The information sheet from the manufacturer does not specify width.

Valentine *et al.*, using an "Ectonus Mark 3" instrument, specified a pulse width of 1/2000 second (0.5 msecond) in the text.[10] Their oscillographic tracings specified 200 microseconds (0.2 msecond). Whatever the pulse width, it was apparently fixed, so that comparative studies are not available.

Experience with rectangular pulses has not settled the question of the optimum pulse width. European research on pulse width has been somewhat limited by the equipment available. Cronholm and Ottoson investigated the use of ultrabrief pulses with the Elther ES instrument.[11] This produced a stimulus pulse 0.1 msecond wide and a 67-msecond interpulse interval. Peak current was 2.1 amps which, through 200 ohms resistance, would require about 420 volts. Stimulation time ranged from 4–10 seconds with an average total energy of 11.4 joules. They concluded that there was no significant advantage to using ultrabrief pulses. Retrospectively, it is clear that this conclusion was valid for only the particular combination of parameters. The pulse width and spacing are now known to be marginal values while the pulse current was 2–4 times higher than that of other brief-pulse instruments. This well-conducted and influential study probably had an inhibiting effect on brief-pulse research for some time.

In the United States there has been more opportunity for research on this factor. The MECTA provides six pulse widths (0.15, 0.2, 0.3, 0.5, 0.75, and 1.5 mseconds). A sample of seven studies[7,12–17] published since 1979 reported the use of pulse widths from 0.75–1.5 mseconds in six instances and one cited 0.3–0.5-msecond widths. We have not located any comparative study of pulse width using this instrument.

Our own work on pulse width has been limited. In almost all of our previous work 1 msecond has been standard, in part because it was the shortest width available with our first instrument. In a few instances where a high-threshold patient was being treated, doubling the pulse width (and energy) did not result in a satisfactory response. Increasing other stimulus parameters, notably the number of pulses (and stimulus duration), was much more successful and at lower energy values.

Having recently acquired a more adequate instrument, we have been investigating the utility of pulse widths below 1 msecond. The design involves starting at 1 msecond and decreasing width in 0.25-msecond steps until 0.25 msecond or a threshold is reached. Our preliminary results are presented in TABLE 2 which shows convulsive response as a function of pulse width. From inspection, the data clearly show that successful treatments were given at all pulse widths in sufficient numbers to demonstrate that these short widths can be successfully used. This observation is valid, but other comparisons must be made with caution. Since the methodology involved threshold determinations, the number of trials at the different widths was unequal. Comparisons involving the percent successes are not valid; low-threshold patients are overrepresented as successes and high-threshold patients underrepresented as failures. Hence, the percent successful data may give a false impression. Had an equal number of trials at all widths been given, the results would have been quite different.

The basic purpose of the study from which these data were drawn was twofold: (1) to see if seizures could be elicited at these shorter widths, and (2) to investigate the role of total energy in the situation. If all other parameters are held constant and the pulse width decreased, there is a concurrent decrease in the total energy administered. At some point, this energy may become insufficient to produce a seizure, no matter what combination of parameters is used in the treatment. Ascribing this failure to the pulse width parameter alone would be unjustified, particularly in the absence of an adequate control. Our approach has been to reduce pulse width until a failure occurs. The energy

TABLE 2. Convulsive Outcome as a Function of Pulse Width[a]

		Pulse Width (mseconds)				
Outcome	Measure	1.0	0.75	0.50	0.25	Totals
Success	*n*	83	39	35	43	200
	%	87	87	81	88	
Fail	*n*	12	5	8	6	31
	%	13	13	19	12	
	Totals	95	44	43	49	231

[a]Cell entries are the number of trials, initial and retreatment, and percent within column.

level for the last successful treatment is now taken as the reference level and the stimulus parameters adjusted to approximate this level on the next initial treatment. This is usually done by increasing the current level.

To date, the incomplete results have been encouraging: increasing the energy has resulted in successful treatments at pulse widths that previously resulted in failure. Because of the complexity of the possible interactions among individual threshold variation, current levels, and pulse widths, much additional data will be required for reliable findings. If these are obtained, investigation into the amplitude and spacing of these ultrabrief pulses will be needed to establish the efficient combinations.

The third parameter, the interpulse interval (IPI), likewise has not been thoroughly investigated. While there seems to be a concensus that the AC stimulus lacks sufficient intervals, there is no experimental evidence on what these intervals ought to be. In large part, it seems to be the case of taking whatever the manufacturers choose to provide. The Siemens KV instrument provides two interpulse interval options. In the "steady" mode there is an interval of 15 mseconds between each 5 msecond pulse. In the "interrupted" state, after a series of four such pulses, there is an interval of 95 mseconds before the next series ensues. So far as can be determined, this pattern was not based on published research findings; at least, the first publication dealing with the instrument makes no mention of it.[18]

Essentially the same thing seems to be true of the instruments based on the capacitor-discharge principle. The provision for equal on-off intervals apparently was not based on experimental data. In reality, the choice was counterproductive. Since the capacitors were not recharged in the same length of time it took to discharge them, the design resulted in a steady decline in signal amplitude. This necessitated both an unnecessarily high initial level as well as the continuation of a stimulus fallen below the effective level. A more realistic choice of the interpulse interval might have resulted in a much better instrument. As it is, the 5 msecond pulse is far too wide and the interpulse interval much too short.

The advent of a commercially available rectangular pulse instrument in the United States was accompanied by the use of cycles per second as the stimulus parameter determining the interpulse interval. To some extent, this was a curious choice since there was no preceding instrument to establish the practice; all previous instruments were not equipped to alter frequency. It was also needlessly complicated. To understand the stimulus, it was necessary to multiply the frequency by 2 to obtain the number of pulses per second and divide this figure into 1 second to obtain the

TABLE 3. The Interpulse Interval and Number of Pulses Parameters[a]

	Interpulse Interval (mseconds)				
Number of Pulses	20	30	40	50	Totals
200		2			2
150	2	3	2	6	13
140				3	3
130				0	0
120				1	1
110				2	2
100				3	3
90				5	5
80				0	0
70				1	1
Totals	2	5	2	21	30

[a]Cell entries are the number of patients reaching threshold at the various combinations.

stimulus-plus-IPI time. Subtracting the pulse width from this gives the IPI. The superiority of this method over the direct specification of the IPI is not obvious. Disregarding pulse widths, the MECTA has options of 25, 17, 12, 10, 8, and 7-msecond IPIs. It is doubtful that this close grouping, four options in a space of 5 mseconds, serves any clinical purpose.

In the sample of publications cited above, a range of cps settings was mentioned: 30–50 (1), 40–60 (1), 50–70 (1), 50 (1), 60 (2), and 60–70 (1). We have been unable to locate studies using cps as the independent variable.

One study used the IPI as the independent variable.[19] The method entailed holding a nominal stimulus (200 V, 600 mA, 150 1-msecond pulses) constant and successively increasing the IPI from 20 to 50 mseconds in 10-msecond steps. The data are summarized in TABLE 3. Of 30 patients, all except 2 reached threshold at the standard stimulus and some increased interpulse interval. Twenty-one reached the 50-msecond interval. Since most of these patients reached this point early in the series of 10 treatments, during the remainder the number of pulses was decreased daily in steps of 10 until threshold was reached.

It seems quite clear that, for the treatment parameters mentioned above, intervals of up to 50 mseconds are quite useable for treatment. While we cannot document it, it was our clinical impression that the 50-msecond IPI was a bit too slow; the muscle reaction to each pulse was clearly visible and the stimulus train duration of 7.6 seconds unnecessarily long. We have subsequently used 30 mseconds as standard with satisfactory results.

It is not clear whether these data are applicable to the MECTA instrument. Only two of the MECTA settings (20, 30 cps; 25, 17-msecond IPI) overlap in part with the range of IPI values. A further limitation may be imposed by the length of the stimulus train available; the MECTA terminates at 2.0 seconds while our standard stimulus ran for 4.5 seconds at an IPI of 30 mseconds. It may be noted that, of the range of cps settings in the sample of studies mentioned above, six of the seven used shorter IPIs, some of them substantially shorter. This may be related to the necessity for introducing sufficient energy in the shorter stimulus train time.

The fourth parameter, stimulus train duration, is difficult to establish as an independent variable. The objective is clear: to introduce the smallest amount of energy sufficient to elicit a convulsion at the slowest possible effective rate. This rather basic approach is usually complicated by decisions about other parameters that directly influence duration. In the case of the AC waveform, significant amounts of current flow for about 75% of the stimulus duration. This places a limit on the duration of the stimulus in the interests of avoiding the excessive application of energy. A stimulus with peak values of 240 volts, 850 mA and a current flow time of 75% obviously requires a short time limit. Whether an AC stimulus of more modest proportions needs to be as severely restricted is an open question, although there is some information available. With the brief AC stimulus, it is not unusual for the onset of the tonic phase to be delayed 2–4 seconds after stimulus offset. Studies involving the MOLAC-II instrument mention continuing the (untimed) stimulus for up to five seconds or until convulsive activity was observed. Since this instrument could produce only 110–120 volts through a normal impedance load,[1] the energy was about 50 joules per second, or about half the Medcraft rate.

Studies involving the Siemens instrument used stimulus durations equal to the patient's age in decades, or 2–7 seconds, to administer 35–40 joules.[11] The peak current values, 0.7–0.8 amp, are similar to those of the Medcraft, but the "interrupted" mode of the stimulus produced a much slower rate of application. It may well be that the higher voltage settings of the Medcraft are necessitated by the short stimulus time and that the same or perhaps less energy, distributed over a longer time, would be effective.

The optimal duration for the rectangular brief-pulse stimulus is likewise indeterminate. There have been no direct studies of the matter for reasons already mentioned. The MECTA provides six duration options from 0.5 to 2.0 seconds. In our sample of studies, the durations mentioned tend toward the longer values: 0.75–1.25 seconds (1), 1.0–2.0 (2), 1.25 (3), and 1.5–2.0 (1). From this it might be concluded that durations below 1.0 second have been found less useful. Since at maximum the MECTA produces 40 joules per second for 2 seconds, such a limitation on stimulus duration is a conservative approach. This does not, however, rule out the possible effects of design decisions on parameter values. It will be recalled that no study in the sample cited a frequency of 20 cps (IPI = 25 mseconds) and only one included 30 cps (IPI = 17 mseconds) in the range of settings used; all other rates were higher. This contrasts strongly with our finding that 28 of 30 patients were successful with IPIs of 30–50 mseconds which are equal to 16 and 10 cps respectively. Since there is little difference between the mean threshold energies cited by Weiner[3] (22 joules) and our usual values of 15–20 joules, it seems clear that the shorter IPIs are required in order to introduce sufficient energy in the time available. It is probable that a longer duration limit would have made the lower cps settings useable.

A fair question may be posed, "Is this a difference that makes a difference?" There is no unequivocal answer at this time. Yet the Weiner data cited above mentioned initial values of 150 pulses in 1.25 seconds with an IPI of 8 mseconds and 17.5 joules total energy. The rate was 14 joules per second. Had the IPI been 30 mseconds for the same number of pulses, the time would have been 4.6 seconds and the rate 3.8 joules per second for a 368% reduction in rate with no decrease in reliability. While presently there is no way to decide if this difference has any practical significance, the conservative approach would favor the slower rate.

The final parameter, impedance, is, strictly speaking, not a parameter of the ECT stimulus. It is discussed here since it greatly influences the effects of some of the parameters, depending in large part on the design of the machine. If the instrument is a constant-current design, e.g., MECTA, voltage increases with impedance up to the design limits of the instrument. If it is a selected voltage design such as the Medcraft, a high impedance may decrease the current, depending upon the adequacy of the transformer design. In some instances, the indicated voltage may not be reached. In existing capacitor-discharge designs, impedance above the manufacturer's reference level causes a decrement in the voltage, current, and energy below the purported levels.

It was determined early on that there was no correlation between resistance as measured across the electrodes with an ordinary ohmmeter and the resistance obtained from measures made during the course of actual treatment. Maxwell investigated the relationship between stimulus voltage and impedance during treatment, using electrodes 6 cm in diameter.[2] His results indicated that at 80 volts, impedance was just under 200 ohms and that it leveled off at about 150 ohms with a stimulus of 150 volts or higher. This work has been cited repeatedly, but it seems to be at considerable variance with subsequent experience. Weiner cites a mean value of 220 ohms for 50 patients treated with the MECTA.[3] Based in part on a literature survey, he estimated a resistance of 250 ohms for the Medcraft AC stimulus. Based on these data, the MECTA was producing 175 volts while the Medcraft was producing 140 volts root mean square (RMS) or 198 volts peak. Neither of these voltages or impedances were close to Maxwell's.

Gordon published a table of 240 observed resistances, ranging from 194 to 1000 ohms, with a mean of 453 ohms.[20] The instrument apparently used, the "City University instrument," has 12 values of current from 80 to 1100 mA. Assuming a nominal value of 600 mA current and 450 ohms resistance, the voltage would be 272 volts. No information was included on the voltage capabilities of the instrument although an 1100-mA current at 450 ohms would require 500 volts, a value comparable to the upper limit of the MECTA. Again, these data are not very close to Maxwell's.

In our own research, we have data on the resistance for over 2000 treatments, both initial and retreatments. The distribution of these data is presented in FIGURE 3. The mean was 359 ohms with an SD of 76 and a range of 167 to 667 ohms. It is clear that these data are not close to Maxwell's either.

The reasons for these observed differences are not at all clear, although there are several observable differences in technique that may contribute. The first lies in the choice of the medium used to couple the electrode to the epidermis. Gordon mentions the use of "cotton wool and lint soaked in sodium chloride,"[20] presumably in the form of a pad over a metal electrode of unspecified size. It is not known whether variability is introduced by the degree of saturation, the concentration of the solution, or the pressure with which the electrodes are applied. In the case of a saturated pad, firm pressure would expel some of the solution and effectively increase the area of electrode contact. In the early days of unilateral treatment, some workers cautioned against the possibility of a short path across the scalp occurring in this manner. However, if this effect were at work here, it would tend to reduce the impedance while Gordon's differences lie in the opposite direction. Other factors must be operative.

It is tempting to ascribe the observed differences to electrode size. Maxwell used an electrode of 2827 mm^2, Weiner 2027, and Weaver 507. If these values are plotted against mean resistance, all three points fall on a straight line. Unfortunately, Gordon's data do not conform for any possible electrode size. Whether the linearity is due to coincidence or whether the Gordon data are idiosyncratic is impossible to determine.

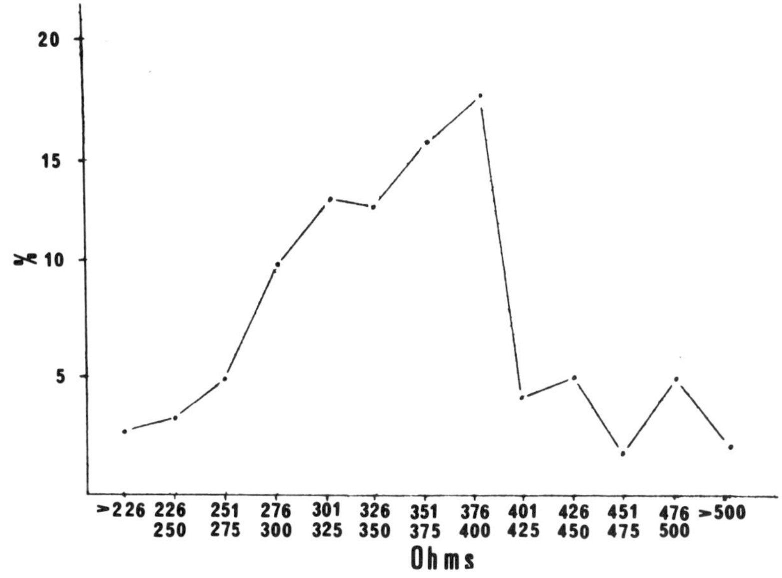

FIGURE 3. The distribution of observed patient resistance values for 2003 treatments. Mean value was 359 ohms.

The problem of electrode size and resistance has other practical implications. Weiner reports the use of the standard two-inch diameter MECTA stainless steel electrodes, coupled to the scalp with an abrasive gel following cleaning of the site with alcohol.[3] These data were gathered in a hospital populated largely by middle-aged or elderly males, presumably with a high incidence of male-pattern baldness. To this is added the practice of clipping the hair at the site of the parietal electrode in order to improve contact. While this doubtless produces excellent results, it is not a practice likely to be popular with the predominantly female population of most general hospital psychiatric units. A smaller electrode which can be placed in close contact with a well-coupled electrode site may actually give lower impedances in such a population. In theory, the effective area of an electrode may be increased by using an area of electrode gel greater than the electrode area, thus reducing the impedance. The matter should be worked out experimentally on a male population where precise control is easier, although the clinical application would be more germane to female patients.

It is appropriate to summarize what we know and need to know about the various aspects of the ECT stimulus. With respect to the AC stimulus, we know:

1. That the sine wave, half-wave, and full-wave rectified stimuli have been used successfully.
2. That the full-width deflection is too wide and that stimuli consisting only of the falling half of the deflection are successful.
3. That a continuous stimulus is not required; interrupted stimuli with wider spacing work equally well.
4. That higher voltages necessitate shorter stimulus durations and conversely.

We need to know whether stimulus combinations involving lower voltages and longer durations can be successfully used.

With respect to the brief-pulse stimuli, we know:

1. That pulse widths ranging from 1 msecond to 0.1 msecond have been used successfully.
2. That interpulse intervals can vary at least from 10 to 50 mseconds.
3. That pulse currents and voltages in the vicinity of 600 mA and 200 volts can be used successfully.
4. That the pulse train durations may vary widely with the stimulus characteristics and that durations from 4–8 seconds provide satisfactory reliability and reduced rate of energy application.
5. That short-duration stimulus trains require shorter IPIs in order to apply sufficient energy.
6. That high energy levels are not required for most patients; 10–25 joules properly distributed over time will be successful with the majority of patients.

We need to know:

1. The threshold values for current.
2. The role of total energy and rate of application. While these measures are not complete descriptors for the stimulus, they are the only ones applicable to all stimuli of whatever parameters.
3. The dimensions of the area of equipotentiality, i.e., the limits for the several parameters within which variations do not materially affect reliability. The most efficient stimulus combinations will almost certainly occur in this area.

Without reference to stimulus waveform, we need to know:

1. The results of systematic investigations into the effects of varying single parameters around a reference combination of stimulus parameter values.
2. The results of systematic investigation of the optimal parameter values as determined in the single-parameter investigations with a view towards specifying the optimal values for a reference standard stimulus.
3. The interaction between electrode placement and stimulus parameters. If the optimal values for AC and brief-pulse stimuli are different with unilateral and bilateral placement, this needs to be established before definitive research on the clinical efficacy of electrode placement can be undertaken.

In addition, there are several more general research needs:

1. To complete basic research on the stimulus as rapidly as possible. A framework within which to evaluate stimuli used in clinical research is essential.

2. To avoid premature closure and overgeneralization from limited results. There is a tendency to select some aspect of a study, i.e., electrode placement or stimulus waveform, and to ascribe all observed differences to this selected aspect. In the absence of a solid background of basic physical research, such procedure cannot be justified and thus the research does less than it might to advance our knowledge. Without system and order, progress is bound to be uncertain.

REFERENCES

1. Davies, R., T. Detre, M. Egger, G. Tucker & R. Wyman. 1971. Electroconvulsive therapy instruments. Arch. Gen. Psychiatry **25:** 97–99.
2. Maxwell, R. 1968. Electrical factors in electroconvulsive therapy. Acta Psychiatr. Scand. **44:** 436–448.
3. Weiner R. 1980. ECT and seizure threshold: effects of stimulus wave form and electrode placement. Biol. Psychiatry **15:** 225–241.
4. Squire, L., P. Slater & P. Miller. 1980. Retrograde amnesia and bilateral electroconvulsive therapy: long-term follow-up. Arch. Gen. Psychiatry **38:** 89–95.
5. Miller, M., I. Small, V. Milstein, F. Malloy & J. Stout. 1981. Electrode placement and cognitive change with ECT: male and female response. Am. J. Psychiatry **138:** 384–386.
6. Staton, D., P. Hass & R. Brumback. 1981. Electroencephalographic recording during bitemporal and unilateral non-dominant hemisphere (Lancaster position) electroconvulsive therapy. J. Clin. Psychiatry **42:** 264–269.
7. Weiner, R. 1982. The role of stimulus waveform in therapeutic and adverse effects of ECT. Psychopharmacol. Bull. **18:** 71–72.
8. Abrams, R., M. Taylor, R. Faber, T. Ts'o, R. Williams & G. Almy. 1983. Bilateral versus unilateral electroconvulsive therapy: efficacy in melancholia. Am. J. Psychiatry **140:** 463–465.
9. Daniel, W., R. Weiner, H. Crovitz, G. Strong & M. Christenbury. 1983. ECT-induced delirium and further ECT: a case report. Am. J. Psychiatry **140:** 922–924.
10. Valentine, M., K. Keddie & D. Dunne. 1968. A comparison of techniques in electroconvulsive therapy. Br. J. Psychiatry **114:** 989–996.
11. Cronholm, B. & J.-O. Ottosson. 1963. Ultra-brief stimulus technique in electroconvulsive therapy. J. Nerv. Ment. Dis. **137:** 117–123.
12. Weiner, R. 1979. The psychiatric use of electrically induced seizures. Am. J. Psychiatry **136:** 1507–1517.
13. Erman, M., C. Welch & M. Mandel. 1979. A comparison of two unilateral electrode placements: efficacy and electrical energy considerations. Am. J. Psychiatry **136:** 1317–1319.
14. Christensen, P. & E. Hedemand. 1983. EEG and EMG monitored electroconvulsive therapy. Psychopharmacol. Bull. **19:** 20–22.
15. Daniel, W., R. Weiner & H. Crovitz. 1983. Autobiographical amnesia with ECT: an analysis of the roles of stimulus wave form, electrode placement, stimulus energy and seizure length. Biol. Psychiatry **18:**121–126.
16. Martin, B., S. Strigler, K. Bezchlibnyk & G. Harris-Brandts. 1983. Electroconvulsive therapy and the seizure threshold. Can. J. Psychiatry **28:** 445–448.
17. Kramer, B. 1983. Seizure parameters in depressed patients receiving electroconvulsive therapy: a pilot study. Compr. Psychiatry **24:** 259–261.
18. von Braunmuhl, A. 1951. Ein neues gerat fur die Hilfkrampfbehandlung mittels elektrischen stranes. Fortschr. Neurol. Psychiatr. Ihrer Grenzgerifte **19:** 325–332.
19. Weaver, L., J. Ives & R. Williams. 1982. Studies in brief-pulse electroconvulsive therapy: the voltage threshold, interpulse interval and pulse polarity parameters. Biol. Psychiatry **17:** 1131–1137.
20. Gordon, D. 1982. Electroconvulsive therapy with minimum hazard. Br. J. Psychiatry **141:** 12–18.

Neuropathological Consequences of Chemically and Electrically Induced Seizures

BRIAN S. MELDRUM

Department of Neurology
Institute of Psychiatry
De Crespigny Park
London SE5 8AF, United Kingdom

This presentation reviews the evidence for brain damage occurring as a sequel to electrically or chemically induced seizures in man and in experimental animals. *Status epilepticus* when severe and prolonged can be followed by a characteristic pattern of selective brain damage involving neuronal loss and glial proliferation in the hippocampus, neocortex, cerebellum, and, to a lesser extent, in the thalamus and basal ganglia.[1] The mechanisms leading to such damage have been reviewed previously.[2,3]

ELECTROCONVULSIVE THERAPY IN MAN

The neuropathological consequences of electroconvulsive shock in man have been the subject of numerous reviews,[1,4–7] the most recent and comprehensive being by Weiner.[8] Published reports tend to concern autopsy material in which preexisting neurological or cardiovascular disease, or some complication of unmodified electroconvulsive therapy (ECT) apparently contributed to the pathology observed. The pattern of neuronal loss that could be ascribed to seizure activity (i.e., hippocampal and cerebellar necrosis) was described by Zeman,[9] but the patients concerned had severe cardiorespiratory problems (endocarditis and pneumonia). Meyer did not find any hippocampal sclerosis or lobular cerebellar atrophy in the brains of patients having previously experienced a course of ECT and dying subsequently from intercurrent disease.[7]

A retrospective study in 41 elderly depressives found a correlation between frontal atrophy, as assessed by computed tomography, and a history of ECT.[10] However, it is possible that the correlation arises because ECT is more likely to be used in drug-resistant depressive disorders associated with a degenerative disorder. In a ventriculographic study in 66 psychiatric patients, ventricular enlargement was found in 3 out of 8 patients over 60 years of age with schizoaffective illness.[11] In the group as a whole there was no correlation between ventricular enlargement and history of ECT.

ELECTROCONVULSIVE SHOCK IN EXPERIMENTAL ANIMALS

A great many experimental studies have been published since the original report of Cerletti and Bini in 1940.[12] They are reviewed by Wiener.[8] TABLE 1 illustrates the wide range of species and the varied protocols used. Nevertheless the results can be summarized fairly succinctly. The majority of studies have found no significant neuropathological changes even though the seizures were unmodified and their frequency or number exceeded that customary in clinical practice.

The only consistent specific finding in the early studies (reviewed by Hartelius)[5] is petechial hemorrhages, often subpial. These are a consequence of the increase in arterial and central venous pressure associated with unmodified seizures.[20]

A carefully controlled quantitative study on cell loss has been performed by Agnete Dam and her colleagues.[17,18] In this rats received three unmodified electroshock seizures daily for 50 days and the brains were perfusion fixed 2 or 12 weeks after the last seizure. Pyramidal cell counts in the hippocampal fields (H_1, H_2, H_3, and H_4) showed no differences between control and experimental animals. Using similar quantitative histological techniques Dam did find quantitative evidence for neuronal loss in patients with epilepsy and in gerbils with a genetically determined type of reflex epilepsy.[18,21]

Neonatal rats exposed to 10 daily electroshock seizures do not show specific cerebral pathology but the brain weight and total DNA content are reduced.[19] However this phenomenon would appear to be a consequence of the severe systemic

TABLE 1. Animal Studies of Cerebral Pathology following Electroconvulsive Shock

Species		Survival (days)	Pathology	Reference
Monkeys	13–19 Unmodified	1–2	Nil	13
Monkeys	4–18 Unmodified	1–2	Perivascular (glial and neuronal)	14
Cats	4–16 Unmodified	1–8	Vessel wall dilatations Neurons—chromophobia	5
Cats	10 Unmodified	1–84	Nil	15
Rats	12 Unmodified	60	No change (nuclei shrink by 3%)	16
Rats	140 Unmodified	14	No change in hippocampal cell counts	17, 18
Rats (neonatal)	10 Unmodified	19	Reduced brain weight and DNA content	19

disturbances and local alterations in protein synthesis disrupting ontogeny at a critical phase.

CHEMICALLY INDUCED SEIZURES IN EXPERIMENTAL ANIMALS

Convulsant drugs may be administered systemically or focally into the brain. Most systemic convulsants give rise to generalized seizure activity involving the cerebral hemispheres.[22] However strychnine and related alkaloids that block inhibition due to glycine produce predominantly spinal seizures. Certain drugs (including kainic acid, lidocaine, and pilocarpine) produce seizures that are predominantly limbic.[23] Sustained limbic seizures can also be induced by the focal injection of convulsants into the amygdala or hippocampus.[24,25]

We shall consider here the characteristics of seizures that give rise to brain damage, as assessed by conventional histological techniques, noting primarily studies in primates as these provide the closest parallel to man.

GENERALIZED SEIZURES

Convulsant drugs used include pentylenetetrazol, picrotoxin, bicuculline, methoxypyridoxine, and allylglycine, (see TABLE 2). Our own studies in adolescent baboons and in rats have utilized bicuculline which blocks the postsynaptic inhibitory action of γ-aminobutyric acid (GABA), inducing sustained generalized seizure activity, and allylglycine which blocks the synthesis of GABA and at just-convulsive doses induces multiple brief generalized seizures, but at higher doses induces status epilepticus.

Physiological changes during unmodified siezures induced by bicuculline in adolescent baboons fall into two phases. In the first 30 minutes there is an initial arterial hypertension and an increase in plasma glucose concentration. In the later phase (0.5–5 hours) there is arterial hypotension, hyperpyrexia, and hypoglycemia.[20] Perfusion fixation of the brain a few hours after the seizure reveals ischemic cell change in vulnerable neurons in the hippocampus, neocortex, and cerebellum of animals having experienced sustained seizure activity lasting more than 1.5 hours.[26]

Seizures modified by curarization (with mechanical ventilation) show less marked late metabolic and systemic physiological changes (hyperpyrexia and arterial hypotension are absent or slight). Cerebellar damage is not seen but ischemic cell change occurs in the hippocampus and cortex after three to seven hours of seizure activity.[27]

These studies in baboons are closely matched by observations of the neurological sequelae of status epilepticus in man.[30] Thus brain damage is a sequel only to seizures lasting more than two hours.

LIMBIC SEIZURES

Limbic seizures induced in baboons or marmosets by focal injection of kainic acid into one amygdala[3,24] are followed by nerve cell loss and gliosis in the hippocampus when the limbic seizure has been sustained for at least three to five hours. Such seizures in primates are commonly associated with minimal motor signs (arrest of motor activity, facial clonus).

Limbic seizures induced in rodents by systemic kainic acid or pilocarpine can

TABLE 2. Selected Animal Studies Demonstrating Cerebral Pathology after Chemically Induced Seizures

Convulsant	Animal	Seizures	Pathology	Reference
Bicuculline	Adolescent baboons	Sustained myoclonus 1.5–5 hours	Hippocampus, cortex, cerebellum	26
		Modified (curare) 3–7 hours	Hippocampus, cortex	27
Allylglycine	Adolescent baboons	Recurrent, brief	Hippocampus, 26–64 in 2–11 hours	28
Focal (limbic)				
Kainate	Baboons	Limbic status 2.5–150 hours	Hippocampus, amygdala	24
Kainate	Rats	Limbic status 2–3 hours +	Hippocampus, amygdala, thalamus	25
Pilocarpine	Rats	Limbic status	Hippocampus, amygdala, thalamus, s. nigra.	29

TABLE 3. Reversible Metabolic and Cytological Changes during Electroshock and Chemical Seizures

	References
Ribosomal disaggregation	32
Inhibition of protein synthesis	33
Inhibition of DNA synthesis	34
Increase in cAMP	35
Increase in cGMP	35
Decrease in creatine phosphate	36
Decrease in ATP	36
Enhanced calcium entry into neurons	37, 38
Mitochondrial swelling	39
Mitochondrial calcium accumulation	40, 41
Phospholipase A activation	42, 43
Free fatty acid increase	42, 43
Proteinase activation	44

produce more widespread lesions involving hippocampus, entorhinal cortex, anterior thalamus, basal ganglia, etc.[25,29]

Sustained electrical stimulation (20 Hz for two hours) of the perforant path (the principal excitatory input to the hippocampus) leads to a typical "epileptic" pattern of damage, involving hilar interneurons and pyramidal cells in CA_1 and CA_3.[31]

REVERSIBLE AND IRREVERSIBLE METABOLIC AND CYTOLOGICAL CHANGES

The cellular mechanisms determining the irreversibility of cellular pathology and hence neuronal loss during and after seizures are not understood (see Reference 3 and Siesjö, this volume). However, most of the metabolic and cytological changes listed in TABLE 3 have at one time or another been considered as playing a role in the sequence of events leading to irreversible cell damage.

To illustrate the problems relating to studies of the critical irreversible step, we will consider calcium accumulation in vulnerable neurons during prolonged seizures.

There is a very steep electrochemical gradient for Ca^{2+} across the neuronal membrane; extracellular $[Ca^{2+}]$ is 1.3 mM, and intracellular $[Ca^{2+}]$ is in the range of 20–170 nM.[45] Some membrane Ca^{2+} channels are receptor operated but the majority are voltage sensitive, opening during depolarizations associated with spikes or a paroxysmal depolarizing shift with burst firing. Thus calcium-sensitive microelectrodes reveal a marked drop in extracellular $[Ca^{2+}]$ at the onset of seizure activity in the hippocampus or cortex.[38] This calcium entry is balanced or buffered by active transport across the cell membrane (requiring adenosine triphosphate), by buffering with cytoplasmic proteins (calmodulin, etc.), by uptake into synaptic vesicles or endoplasmic reticulum (requiring ATP), and by uptake into mitochondria (also requiring ATP, and activation of mitochondrial metabolism). Mitochondrial calcium influx and efflux are independently regulated and thus provide an upper set point for cytosolic $[Ca^{2+}]$. This mitochondrial Ca^{2+} buffer system has a very high capacity, as the calcium can be stored as $Ca_3(PO_4)_2$ in the mitochondrial matrix. It is possible to visualize intracellular Ca^{2+} at the electron microscopic level by precipitating it as oxalate during perfusion fixation with glutaraldehyde and subsequently conjugating it with pyroantimonate.[46,47] In control material the most prominent calcium deposits visualized by this method are in synaptic vesicles.[40,47] However after 30–60 minutes of sustained seizure activity, dense deposits of calcium pyroantimonate become visible in mitochondria in dendrites and soma of vulnerable neurons in hippocampal CA_1 and CA_3 subfields.[47,41] After 60–120 minutes of sustained seizure activity, these are associated with gross distension of mitochondria. However, if seizure activity is arrested by administration of diazepam, these changes are rapidly reversible—hardly any swollen mitochondria with calcium deposits are visible after a 60-minute recovery period.[41,48] However a small number of cells (principally interneurons) show "ischemic cell change" ("dark cell change") with multiple small vacuoles containing calcium.

It has been suggested that the selective vulnerability to status epilepticus and ischemia of neurons in hippocampus and cortex is related to their tendency to show burst firing and the associated massive calcium entry leading to calcium overload of mitochondria.[2,3] However, it is clear that the supposed cascade of lethal events—activation of phospholipase A, release of arachidonic acid, and formation of superoxide radicals—can be initiated (as shown during seizures by the early increase in free fatty acids and arachidonic acid)[43] and yet not lead to any irreversible pathology. Mitochondria provide the most important protection against any excessive increase in cytosolic $[Ca^{2+}]$, and restitution of normal calcium distribution is dependent on ATP. Thus if there is no energy substrate available or oxidative phosphorylation is blocked, recovery may not be possible. Such a combination of calcium overload and failure of energy metabolism may occur after two hours of continuous seizure activity.

PRESENT UNCERTAINTIES AND PROPOSALS FOR FUTURE STUDIES

From the available postmortem and experimental data we must conclude that there is no evidence that ECT administered in current clinical practice causes structural brain lesions. Indeed the hazards would appear to be less than those of other minor procedures employing general anesthesia (such as dental extractions), probably because of close medical and nursing supervision. Thus hypotensive accidents (due to cardiac arrhythmias, etc.) seem to be very rare.

However there are two possibilities that it is hard to exclude absolutely. It is possible that multiple electroshock causes an acceleration of the neuronal dropout associated with aging. Mouritzen Dam, in her quantitative cell counts in normal adult hippocampus and epileptic hippocampus, found an enhanced neuronal loss in pyramidal and granule cells that was most marked in patients having had epilepsy for more than 30 years in whom seizures occurred more than twice a month.[18,21] This neuronal dropout had some characteristics suggesting that it was an acceleration of the normal cell loss associated with aging. As depression is a common feature of mild dementing syndromes, any study intended to evaluate this hypothesis would have to be designed with great care.

The second possibility is that in a susceptible patient (probably with existing limbic system pathology), it might be possible to trigger a period of limbic status that would be clinically manifest as a prolonged period of postictal confusion and might give rise to further limbic pathology. However the absence of clinically documented cases of this kind, and experimental data such as those presented by Richard Green (this volume), indicate that the usual effect of ECT is to suppress other seizure activity. Indeed this anticonvulsant effect of ECT has been used clinically by Sackeim and colleagues.[49]

Could further animal studies help resolve these uncertainties? Relevant experiments would involve large primates (monkeys or baboons) receiving ECT with protocols exactly matching those in current clinical use, followed after a moderate survival period by perfusion fixation of the brain and rigorous cells counts of selected blocks of hippocampus. However the probability that the results would be entirely negative is in my view so high that the costs of the experiment (in animals and research time) would not be justified. However it might be possible to justify such an experiment if it formed part of a more complex study concerned with the mechanisms of action of ECT, involving for example changes in receptor function assessed both functionally in life and by autoradiography or immunocytochemistry postmortem.

CONCLUSIONS

Experimental studies show that selective brain damage involving neuronal loss and gliosis in the hippocampus can follow sustained generalized seizure activity lasting more than 90 minutes, multiple brief recurrent seizures (more than 26 in eight hours), or sustained continuous limbic seizure (lasting longer than three to five hours). Modified or unmodified ECT, given singly at intervals up to three times daily, over several weeks does not produce selective neuronal loss.

There is no evidence that ECT produces brain damage in man (other than as a very rare complication following impaired cerebral circulation due to peripheral accidents).

ACKNOWLEDGMENTS

I thank my colleagues Dr. A. G. Chapman, Dr. M. C. Evans, and Dr. T. Griffiths for their collaboration and the Wellcome Trust, the Medical Research Council, and the Chest, Heart, and Stroke Association for financial support.

REFERENCES

1. Meldrum, B. S. & J. A. N. Corsellis. 1984. Epilepsy. *In* Greenfield's Neuropathology. J. H. Adams, J. A. N. Corsellis & L. W. Duchen, Eds.: 921–950. E. Arnold. London, England.
2. Meldrum, B. 1981. Metabolic effects of prolonged epileptic seizures and the causation of epileptic brain damage. *In* Metabolic Disorders of the Nervous System. F. C. Rose, Ed.: 175–187. Pitman Medical. London, England.
3. Meldrum, B. S. 1983. Metabolic factors during prolonged seizures and their relation to nerve cell death. Adv. Neurol. **34:** 261–275.
4. Corsellis, J. A. N. & A. Meyer. 1954. Histological changes in the brain after uncomplicated ECT. J. Ment. Sci. **100:** 375–383.
5. Hartelius, U. 1952. Cerebral changes following electrically induced convulsions. An experimental study on cats. Acta Psychiatr. Neurol. Scand. (Suppl. 77): 1–128.
6. Madow, L. 1956. Brain changes in electro-shock therapy. Am. J. Psychiatry **113:** 337–347.
7. Meyer, A. 1963. Epilepsy. *In* Greenfield's Neuropathology. 2nd edit.: 602–620. Edward Arnold. London, England.
8. Weiner, R. D. 1984. Does electroconvulsive therapy cause brain damage? Behav. Brain Sci. **7:** 1–54.
9. Zeman, W. 1950. Zur Frage der Hirngewebeschädigung durch Heilkrampf behandlung. Arch. Psychiatr. Nervenkr. **184:** 440–457.

10. Calloway, S. P., R. J. Dolan, R. J. Jacoby & R. Levy. 1981. ECT and cerebral atrophy: a computed tomographic study. Acta Psychiatr. Scand. **64:** 442–445.
11. Van Boxel, P., P. K. Bridges, J. R. Bartlett & T. Trauer. 1978. Size of cerebral ventricles in 66 psychiatric patients. Br. J. Psychiatry **133:** 500–506.
12. Cerletti, Y. & L. Bini. 1940. Le alterazioni istopatologische del sistema nervoso nell'elettroshock. Riv. Sper. Freniatr. Med. Leg. Alienazioni Ment. **64:** 2.
13. Siekert, R. G., S. C. Williams & W. F. Windle. 1950. Histologic study of brains of monkeys after experimental electroshock. Arch. Neurol. Psychiatry **63:** 79–86.
14. Ferraro, A., L. Roizin & M. Helfand. 1946. Morphologic changes in the brain of monkeys following convulsions electrically induced. J. Neuropathol. Exp. Neurol. **5:** 285–308.
15. Masserman, J. H. & M. G. Jacques. 1947. Effects of cerebral electroshock on experimental neuroses in cats. Am. J. Psychiatry **104:** 92–99.
16. Colon, E. J. & S. L. H. Notermans. 1975. A long term study of the effects of electroconvulsions on the structure of the cerebral cortex. Acta Neuropathol. **32:** 21–25.
17. Dam, M., M. Hertz, T. Bolwig & A. M. Dam. 1981. The number of hippocampal neurons and Purkinje cells in rats after electrically-induced seizures. *In* Advances in Epileptology XII Epilepsy International Symposium. M. Dam, L. Gram & J. K. Penry, Eds.: 395–401. Raven Press. New York, N.Y.
18. Dam, A. M. 1982. Hippocampal neuron loss in epilepsy and after experimental seizures. Acta Neurol. Scand. **66:** 601–642.
19. Wasterlain, C. G. & F. Plum. 1973. Vulnerability of developing rat brain to electroconvulsive seizures. Arch. Neurol. **29:** 38–45.
20. Meldrum, B. S. & R. W. Horton. 1973. Physiology of status epilepticus in primates. Arch. Neurol. **28:** 1–9.
21. Dam, A. M. 1980. Epilepsy and neuron loss in the hippocampus. Epilepsia **21:** 617–629.
22. Meldrum, B. 1983. Convulsant and anticonvulsant drug mechanism. *In* Cerebral Blood Flow, Metabolism and Epilepsy. M. Baldy-Moulinier, D. H. Ingvar & B. S. Meldrum, Eds.: 324–335. John Libbey. London, England.
23. Meldrum, B. 1984. Anticonvulsants and the limbic system. *In* Psychopharmacology of the Limbic System. M. R. Trimble & Z. Zarifian, Eds.: 89–109. Oxford University Press. Oxford, England.
24. Menini, C., B. S. Meldrum, D. Riche, C. Silva-Comte & J. M. Stutzmann. 1980. Sustained limbic seizures induced by intraamygdaloid kainic acid in the baboon: symptomatology and neuropathological consequences. Ann. Neurol. **8:** 501–509.
25. Ben-Ari, Y., E. Tremblay, O. P. Ottersen & B. S. Meldrum. 1980. The role of epileptic activity in hippocampal and 'remote' cerebral lesions induced by kainic acid. Brain Res. **191:** 79–97.
26. Meldrum, B. S. & J. B. Brierley. 1973. Prolonged epileptic seizures in primates: ischaemic cell change and its relation to ictal physiological events. Arch. Neurol. **28:** 10–17.
27. Meldrum, B. S., R. A. Vigoroux & J. B. Brierley. 1973. Systemic factors and epileptic brain damage. Prolonged seizures in paralysed artificially ventilated baboons. Arch. Neurol. **29:** 82–87.
28. Meldrum, B. S., R. W. Horton & J. B. Brierley. 1974. Epileptic brain damage in adolescent baboons following seizures induced by allylglycine. Brain **97:** 417–428.
29. Turski, W. A., E. A. Cavalheiro, M. Schwarz, S. J. Czuczwar, Z. Kleinrok & L. Turski. 1983. Limbic seizures produced by pilocarpine in rats: behavioural, electroencephalographic and neuropathological study. Behav. Brain Res. **9:** 315–335.
30. Aminoff, M. J. & R. O. Simon. 1980. Status epilepticus. Causes, clinical features and consequences in 98 patients. Am. J. Med. **69:** 657–666.
31. Sloviter, R. S. 1983. 'Epileptic' brain damage in rats induced by sustained electrical stimulation of the perforant path. I. Acute electrophysiological and light microscopic studies. Brain Res. Bull. **10:** 675–697.
32. Popoli, M. & A. Giuditta. 1980. Effect of electroconvulsive shock on polysomes of rabbit brain, liver and kidney. J. Neurochem. **35:** 1319–1322.

33. DUNN, A., A. GIUDITTA & N. PAGLIUCA. 1971. The effect of electroconvulsive shock on protein synthesis in mouse brian. J. Neurochem. **18:** 2093–2099.
34. GIUDITTA, A., P. ABRESCIA & B. TUTIGLIANO. 1978. Effect of electroshock on thymidine incorporation into rat brain DNA. J. Neurochem. **31:** 983–987.
35. FERENDELLI, J. A., A. C. BLANK & R. A. CROSS. 1980. Relationships between seizure activity and cyclic nucleotide levels in brain. Brain Res. **200:** 93–103.
36. CHAPMAN, A. G., B. S. MELDRUM & B. K. SIESJÖ. 1977. Cerebral metabolic changes during prolonged epileptic seizures in rats. J. Neurochem. **28:** 1025–1035.
37. DELGADO-ESCUETA, A. V., S. VICTOR & D. DAVIDSON. 1980. The effects of electroshock convulsions on calcium transport within synaptic terminals. J. Neurochem. **34:** 1140–1148.
38. HEINEMANN, U. & H. D. LUX. 1983. Ionic changes during experimentally induced epilepsies. *In* Research Progress in Epilepsy. F. C. Rose, Ed.: 87–102. Pitman Medical. London, England.
39. EVANS, M., T. GRIFFITHS & B. S. MELDRUM. 1983. Early changes in the rat hippocampus following seizures induced by bicuculline or L-allylglycine: a light and electron microscope study. Neuropathol. Appl. Neurobiol. **9:** 39–52.
40. GRIFFITHS, T., M. C. EVANS & B. S. MELDRUM. 1982. Intracellular sites of early calcium accumulation in the rat hippocampus during status epilepticus. Neurosci. Lett. **30:** 329–334.
41. GRIFFITHS, T., M. C. EVANS & B. S. MELDRUM. 1984. Status epilepticus: the reversibility of calcium loading and acute neuronal pathological changes in the rat hippocampus. Neuroscience **12:** 557–567.
42. BAZAN, N. G. 1971. Changes in free fatty acids of brain by drug-induced convulsions, electroshock and anaesthesia. J. Neurochem. **18:** 1379–1385.
43. CHAPMAN, A. G. 1981. Free fatty acid release and metabolism of adenosine and cyclic nucleotides during prolonged seizures. *In* Neurotransmitters, Seizures and Epilepsy. P. L. Morselli, K. G. Lloyd, W. Löscher, B. Meldrum & E. Reynolds, Eds.: 165–173. Raven Press. New York, N.Y.
44. SCHLAEPFER, W. W. & L. A. FREEMAN. 1980. Calcium-dependent degradation of mammalian neurofilaments by soluble tissue factor(s) from rat spinal cord. Neuroscience **5:** 2305–2314.
45. MELDRUM, B. S. 1984. Calcium entry blockers and cerebral function: introduction *In* Calcium Entry Blockers in Cardiovascular and Cerebral Dysfunctions. T. Godfraind, A. Hermann & D. Wellens, Eds.: 207–219. Martinus Nijhoff Publishers. The Hague, Holland.
46. BORGERS, M., F. THONE, & J. M. NEUTEN. 1981. The subcellular distribution of calcium and the effects of calcium-antagonists as evaluated with a combined oxalate-pyroantimonate technique. Acta Histochem. Suppl. **24:** 327–332.
47. GRIFFITHS, T., M. C. EVANS & B. S. MELDRUM. 1983. Intracellular calcium accumulation in rat hippocampus during seizures induced by bicuculline or L-allylglycine. Neuroscience **10:** 385–395.
48. EVANS, M. C., T. GRIFFITHS & B. S. MELDRUM. 1984. Kainic acid seizures and the reversibility of calcium loading in vulnerable neurons in the hippocampus. Neuropathol. Appl. Neurobiol. **10:** 285–302.
49. SACKEIM, H. A., I. PROHOVNICK, P. DECINA, S. MALITZ & S. RESOR. 1983. Anticonvulsant properties of electroconvulsive therapy: theory and case report. *In* Cerebral Blood Flow, Metabolism and Epilepsy. M. Baldy-Moulinier, D. H. Ingvar & B. S. Meldrum, Eds.: 370–377. John Libbey. London, England.

Cerebral Blood Flow and Metabolic Rate during Seizures[a]

Relationship to Epileptic Brain Damage

MARTIN INGVAR

Laboratory for Experimental Brain Research
University Hospital
University of Lund
S-22185 Lund, Sweden

INTRODUCTION

Seizures, when recurrent or prolonged, represent a condition in which neuronal damage may be incurred. Neuropathological observations on human material have displayed damage in the regions classically denoted "selectively vulnerable," i.e., neocortex, hippocampus, and cerebellum.[1,2] The damage incurred in the human material may at least in part be due to complicating hypoxia-ischemia. This has prompted several investigators over the years to try and elucidate the pathophysiology of epileptic neuronal damage in animal models. The object of this paper is to summarize some of the present knowledge of the cerebral blood flow (CBF) and cerebral metabolic rate (CMR) during induced generalized seizure activity, and to relate this to seizure-induced neuronal damage.

HISTOLOGICAL DAMAGE DUE TO EXPERIMENTAL STATUS EPILEPTICUS

Many models have been used by investigators over the years in the effort of trying to emulate the human epilepsies in the laboratory.[3] The γ-aminobutyric acid (GABA) blocker bicuculline has been used to induce grand mal status epilepticus in both monkeys and rats.[4–6] These studies reported histopathological changes in many areas of the brain, even if the physiological parameters were controlled.[6–9] Among the affected areas were the cerebral cortex, the hippocampus, and the thalamus. The perfusion fixation in these studies was done in direct conjunction to the end of the seizure activity, precluding an analysis of the final histological outcome, as many of the changes reported were reversible.[10]

In order to study the final histological sequelae after experimental status epilepticus, it was necessary to develop a long-term recovery model, which allows reversible alterations to disappear. Fluorothyl (hexafluorodiethylether), a gas previously used as an alternative for electroconvulsive therapy (ECT) in man,[11] was suitable for this purpose. The gas has been used to induce experimental seizures of both short and long

[a]This study was supported by grants from the Swedish Medical Research Council (No. 14X-263 and K85-14P-6954-02), the U.S. Public Health Service (National Institutes of Health Grant No. 5 RO1 NS-07838), the ERCO foundation for epilepsy research, and the Margaretahemmet Foundation.

duration.[12] An advantage of this gas to drugs like bicuculline and pentylenetetrazol is that the seizure activity stops spontaneously if the administration is terminated within 25 minutes after the start of the status epilepticus. After this period the seizures can be terminated by, e.g., a small dose of sodium pentothal. The cortical metabolic changes and the electroencephalograph (EEG) pattern are essentially the same during this type of seizure as with status epilepticus induced by either bicuculline or pentylentetrazol,[13–16] in spite of the presumably different mechanisms of action for the drugs.[3]

We modified the use of fluorothyl to allow recovery of the animals after extended periods of status epilepticus.[17,18] In short, we used intubated and ventilated rats that were exposed to fluorothyl on a rebreathing system. Catheters in the tail artery and vein allowed monitoring of blood gases and sampling of blood. The EEG and body temperature were also monitored. With this technique, it was possible to maintain status epilepticus in well-oxygenated rats for up to two hours and then study the final outcome by later histological analysis. The brains were subserially sectioned and then stained with cresyl violet/acid fuchsin. If some time is allowed to pass before the perfusion fixation is performed then the necrotic cells are clearly discernible from the nonaffected by their acidophilic properties.

The pattern of cell damage resulting from 15–120 minutes of status epilepticus has been described previously.[18] We found that there was a selective neuronal necrosis in the cerebral cortex, mainly layer 3-4, that affected a few neurons in some of the 45-minute animals and increased in frequency with longer seizure periods. This was also seen in the thalamus (ventroposterior lateral and medial nuclei), in the hippocampus (CA1 and CA4), and to some extent in the purkinje cells in the cerebellum. This selective necrosis was in contrast with the findings in the substantia nigra pars reticulata (SNPR) (FIGURE 1a) and the globus pallidus (GP) (FIGURE 1b). In the SNPR a necrosis of all cellular elements (pan-necrosis) involving large parts of the nucleus had occurred in all but one animal with a seizure period longer than 30 minutes. The GP also had pan-necrosis, but here it was a less regular finding and only in some instances in the 120-minute animals did it comprise a major part of the nucleus. A third pattern of neuronal necrosis, which was designated "periventricular pattern," was also evident in the 120-minute animals. These cells were few and all close to the ventricles in areas where no white matter is seen between gray matter and the cerebrospinal fluid. FIGURE 2 depicts the areas with either necrotic cells or pan-necrosis, at the level of the mesencephalon, in the animals subjected to 120 minutes of seizure activity.

The major finding that cell death occurred in the central nervous system (CNS) after limited periods of status epilepticus in well-oxygenated animals[17,18] was at variance with some previous studies. The study by Mouritzen-Dam *et al.*, where repeated electroshocks were administered to rats (three daily for 50 days), did not yield any neuronal loss in the hippocampus.[19] These authors later provided data supporting the conclusion that the paroxysmal activity must go on uninterrupted for an extended time if seizure damage is to develop.[20] Our findings indicate that the minimum time needed to induce neuronal necrosis by seizures in well-oxygenated animals is 25–30 minutes.[17,18]

METABOLIC RATE DURING SEIZURE ACTIVITY

Generalized seizures represent the most intense cellular work possible in the brain.[21] The synchronized activity in the neurons forces the cells to repump large amounts of ions in order to maintain equilibrium. Whole brain measurements of the

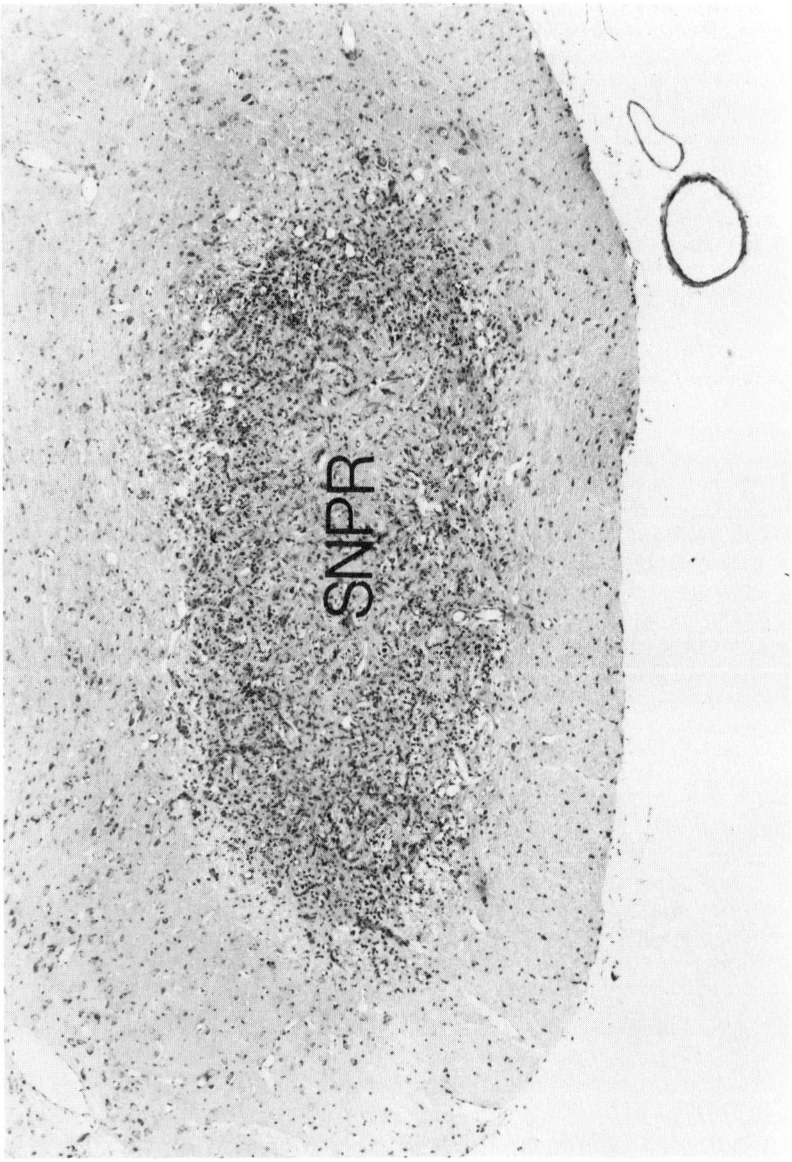

FIGURE 1a. The substantia nigra pars reticulata (SNPR) one week after a period of 120 minutes of status epilepticus in the rat. The whole of the SNPR is necrotic and invaded by macrophages. Stained with acid fuchsin/cresyl violet.

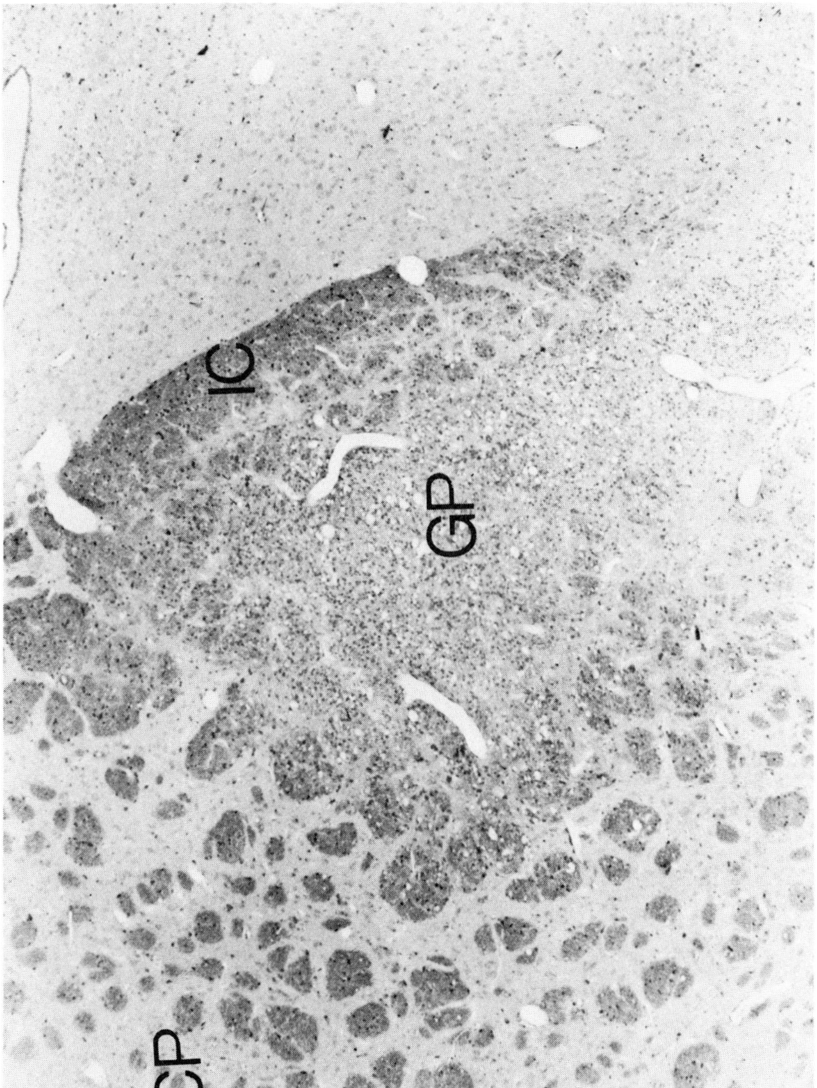

FIGURE 1b. The globus pallidus (GP) in the same animal is also infarcted and the caudoputamen is not affected by the seizure period. IC = internal capsule.

metabolic rate for oxygen during seizures have indicated an increase to between 200% and 300% of control.[5] The rate in the glycolytic pathway can increase more than the oxidative metabolism.[14,22] In the beginning of the seizure activity, there are estimates of up to four times the control rate for the glycolysis in the cerebral cortex.[23] In sustained seizures these authors reported increases in the metabolic rate for oxygen in the forebrain.[5]

The first semiquantitative measurements of the local cerebral metabolic rate for glucose during generalized seizure activity led to the proposal that the increased

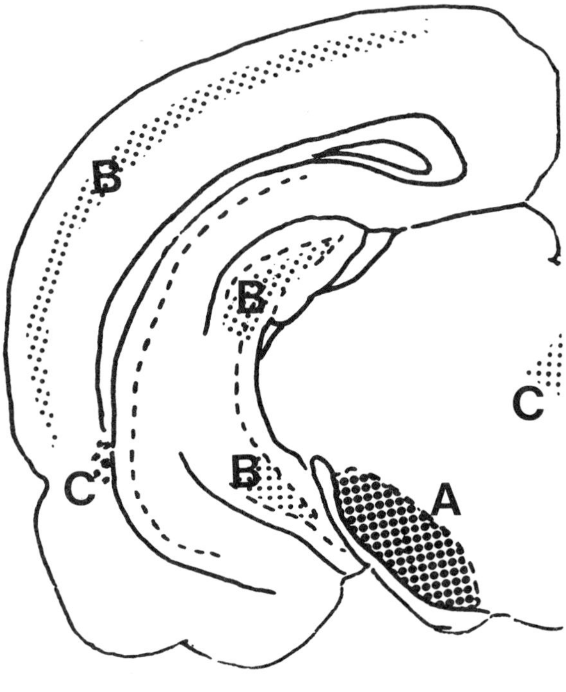

FIGURE 2. Schematic drawing of a coronal section at the level of the mesencephalon in the rat. The three different types of damage incurred by status epilepticus in well-ventilated rats is indicated. (A) The SNPR is subjected to pan-necrosis, whereas (B) layers 3-4 of the cortex and CA1 and CA4 of the hippocampus show selective neuronal necrosis (neuroanatomical pattern). (C) The periventricular damage is indicated at the aqueduct and in layer 6 of the cortex where no white matter is in between the CSF and the gray matter. (Data from Reference 18.)

metabolic rate, per se, was responsible for the development of neuronal damage.[24] Many later studies have supported this proposal. When quantitative data were published for the CMRgl during ventilated bicuculline-induced status epilepticus, it was shown that the regions with a very marked increase in metabolic rate during the whole period of status epilepticus in large part coincided with the regions susceptible to neuronal damage.[25] Other regions, with no or only minor increase in the metabolic rate for glucose, were among the resistant. The question arose if this pattern of glucose metabolism was specific for the bicuculline seizures or whether the pattern provoked was common to other models of status epilepticus. Later it has been shown that at least three different models for generalized seizures (bicuculline, pentylenetetrazol, fluorothyl) have almost identical regional distribution of the metabolic rate for glucose during seizures (References 25, 26, and Ingvar and Nevander, unpublished results). The acute morphological tissue changes are also identical,[9,15,18] and at least in the case of the substantia nigra pars reticulata, the final pan-necrosis is apparent in all three models (References 13, 18, and Auer *et al.*, unpublished results). In the substantia nigra pars reticulata and the globus pallidus there is a dynamic change in the metabolic rate during the status epilepticus period if it lasts for more than 30 minutes. In the beginning of the ictal phase the metabolic rate is increased 6–10 times control,[b,13] later to fall to almost zero in spite of ongoing status epilepticus[13,25] (FIGURE 3). This decrease in metabolic rate in the substantia nigra pars reticulata is probably due to the neuronal necrosis that starts within 30 minutes from the start of the seizure activity (Auer *et al.*, unpublished results).

The damage incurred by the excitotoxin kainic acid is preceded by a period of sustained increased metabolic rate.[29,30] The localization of the damaged neurons seems to correspond to the distribution of kainate receptors, a subset of the glutamate receptors.[30,31] Kainic acid causes distant damage, i.e., damage not directly related to the deposition of the compound, when applied locally, e.g., in the hippocampus. If the animals are treated with diazepam this transsynaptic spread of the damage is inhibited, as is the increase in the metabolic rate at the distant location.[32] This suggests that the increase in metabolic rate is necessary for the development of damage due to increased neuronal activity. The development of "distant damage" in response to sustained seizure activity has very elegantly been shown in the thalamus if a focus is created in the sensorimotor area of the rat cortex using folic acid or bicuculline.[33] These results emphasize that "distant damage" as a phenomenon is not restricted to excitotoxin models (kainic acid, ibotenic acid, etc.); rather it is a general response to pathologically sustained and increased neuronal firing.

HAS THE REGIONAL CEREBRAL METABOLIC RATE ANY BEARING ON THE DISTRIBUTION OF DAMAGE?

Only regions where the metabolic rate is increased during status epilepticus develop neuronal necrosis. However, the regions with the highest increase in metabolic rate during status epilepticus as determined by ^{14}C-deoxyglucose autoradiography[27] do not correspond directly to the areas that have the highest rate of necrotic neurons. The autoradiogram in FIGURE 4 indicates that the metabolic rate is higher in the CA3 and dentate gyrus than in the CA1 and CA4.

The two former regions never develop necrotic neurons in the model employed, whereas damaged neurons are visible in the two latter regions. Two very likely reasons emerge for this "lack" of correlation between neuronal damage and increased metabolic rate during seizures. The metabolic rate is more increased in the synaptic areas of the neurons during increased functional activity. This will be especially evident in the hippocampus due to its layered architecture.[34] Also, as both excitatory and inhibitory neuronal work expends energy,[35] simple explanations are not always at hand for the deoxyglucose autoradiograms obtained with the 2-deoxy-*d*-glucose

[b]This value was calculated using a lumped constant of 0.48.[27] Even if an increase of the lumped constant is assumed to be 1.0,[28] the metabolic rate in the substantia nigra pars reticulata is more enhanced than in other areas of the brain like, e.g., the neocortex.

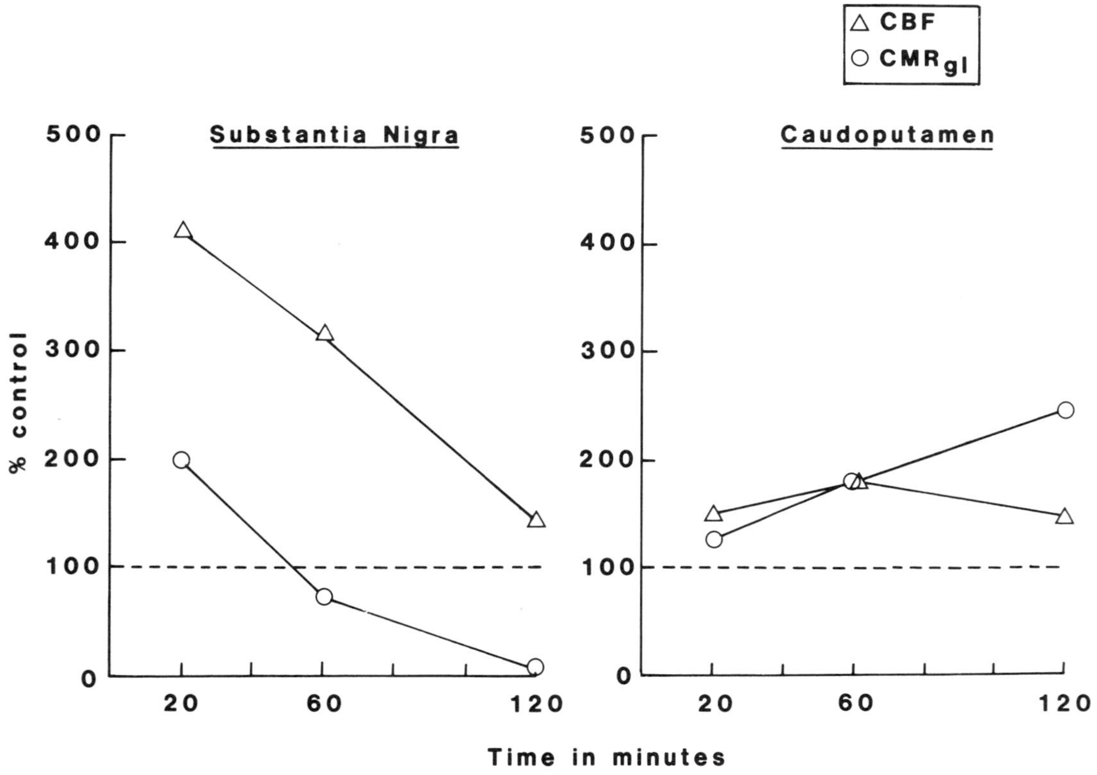

FIGURE 3. The local blood flow and glucose consumption in the rat substantia nigra (SN) and in the caudoputamen (CP) at different times after induction of status epilepticus with bicuculline. Note the initial increase in the glucose consumption in the SN which later falls to very low values and that the blood flow is maintained augmented above control even at 120 minutes of seizure activity. Also note that the CP does not markedly increase its metabolic rate in the beginning of the seizure period. (Data are from Reference 25.)

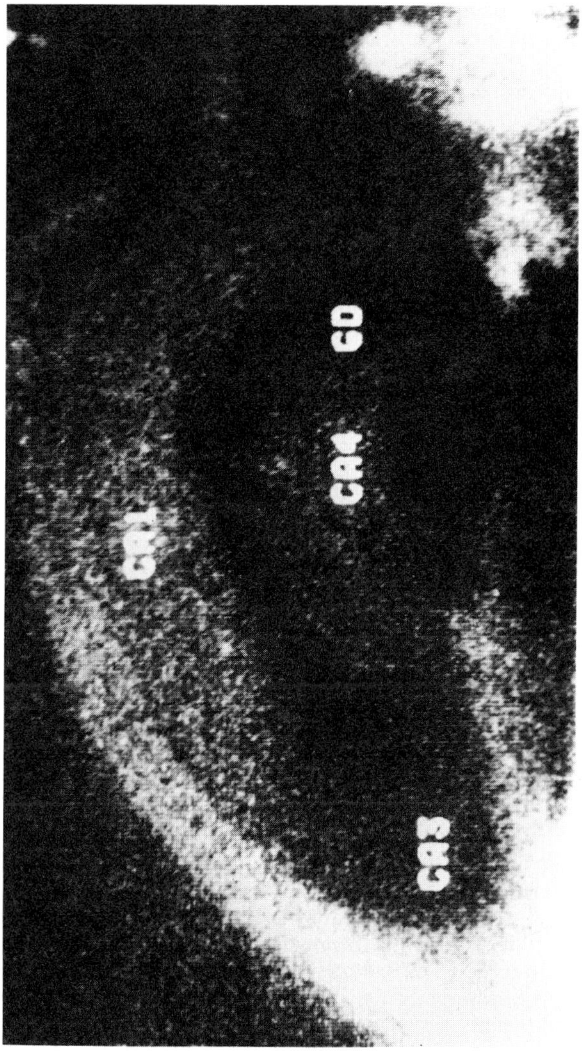

FIGURE 4. Deoxyglucose autoradiogram from the hippocampus of the rat subjected to fluorothyl seizures. The CA4 and CA1 have a lower deoxyglucose uptake than does the CA3 (see text).

technique. In ischemia, activation of the perforant path seems to be at least partly responsible for neuronal damage in the hippocampus in the same regions as during status epilepticus.[36] As seen in FIGURE 4 the synaptic zones of the perforant path coincide with the area with the most intense activation.

The suggestion that the excitation caused by the putative transmitters glutamate and aspartate is especially deleterious for the neurons[33,37,38] is supported by the data presented here. The SNPR has excitatory input pathways both from the prefrontal cortex and from the limbic system via the preoptic area in the hypothalamus which probably is glutamatergic.[39,40] Activation of the SNPR is seen with the deoxyglucose technique during seizures with several models. Thus both focal cortical as well as focal limbic seizures lead to an increase in metabolic rate during the seizure activity.[34,41,42] Since the regions that contain the dendrites for the glutamatergic neurons have a very marked increase of metabolic rate (neocortex and hippocampus), it is possible that the activation of the SNPR is due to the glutamatergic input. So far, however, only generalized status epilepticus of at least 30 minutes duration has been reported to yield activation intense enough to damage the SNPR. From the caudoputamen, a substance P pathway has been identified,[43,44] which is proposed to be an excitatory transmittor.[45] Further studies will reveal whether interaction between glutamate and substance P in the SNPR may be responsible for the extraordinary rapid cell destruction encountered in this region during status epilepticus.

Another region that receives glutamatergic input from the cerebral cortex is the caudoputamen.[46] The explanation for the lack of damage in the caudoputamen during experimental status epilepticus is evident from the metabolic profile of this region.[25] At the start of the seizure activity, the metabolic rate has a very limited increase and the caudoputamen does not become metabolically active until late in the seizure period. We note that the development is contrary to that of the substantia nigra pars reticulata[25] and conclude that the late rise in the metabolic rate in the caudoputamen is possibly a result of the damage developing in the substantia nigra pars reticulata, releasing inhibitory influence of the caudoputamen from this structure (via the compacta).[39] This reasoning supports the concept that a minimum time of excitation due to seizure activity is necessary before any seizure-induced neuronal damage develops.

CEREBRAL BLOOD FLOW DURING SEIZURE ACTIVITY

Penfield *et al.* reported that blood flow was increased during the ictal phase of induced seizures.[47] These authors concluded that the change in blood flow probably did not initiate the seizure activity; rather it was a consequence of increased neuronal work. Later, together with a confirmation of the increase of the cerebral blood flow during the ictal activity in patients, Penfield and Jasper reported that postictally a pial blanching was seen in patients undergoing craniotomy.[48] Before the EEG had come into clinical practice, this blanching had erroneously been assumed to represent an active vasoconstriction possibly playing a role in the initiation of the seizure activity as well as in the development of seizure damage.[49]

Since the first quantitative measurement of the increased cerebral blood flow during seizures,[50] many authors have confirmed the intraictal increase of cerebral blood flow in both animals and man (e.g., Reference 51). The increase in cerebral blood flow is very rapid and detectable within seconds after the onset of a generalized epileptic seizure.[5,52] The magnitude of the ictal increase has been under some debate, as the range of the increase in CBF during seizures has been so disperse. Thus, during generalized seizures increases have been reported from 141% of control up to 900% of control.[5,53] The explanation of the differences in the results published is partly that the abolishment of the autoregulation during seizures[54] makes the CBF very dependent on the systemic blood pressure. Thus, the high extreme published (900% of control CBF) was recorded in rats with a mean arterial blood pressure exceeding 175 mmHg.[5]

During the ictal phase of generalized seizure activity, the augmentation is not homogenous in the brain. Local CBF has been measured during generalized seizures induced with the GABA blocker bicuculline.[25,55,56] These studies showed that the increase in regional CBF is inhomogenous both in absolute numbers and when calculated as percent of control. The most striking finding was that there was a total loss of the close coupling of metabolic rate and blood flow during the generalized seizures. This was due to the fact that in the regions with a marked increase in metabolic rate the increase in blood flow was of similar magnitude when calculated as percent of control, whereas in the regions with no or only small augmentations in metabolic rate the blood flow was markedly increased. Generalized seizures induced with other agents like pentylentrazol and fluorothyl display the same regional pattern and magnitude in the increase during the seizure activity (Reference 15 and Nevander and Ingvar, in preparation). These results indicate, together with the results on energy metabolite determinations during seizures (Siesjö *et al.*, this volume), that even the regions with a marked and prolonged seizure-induced augmentation of the metabolic rate are not subjected to relative hypoxia. Notably, the pallidoreticularis maintained the blood flow augmented above control value even late during the seizure activity although the region revealed a very low functional activity judging from the ^{14}C-2-deoxy-*d*-glucose autoradiograms (FIGURE 3).[25] This underlines that insufficient blood flow is not the primary cause of the cell damage.

A question remains whether the cerebral blood flow during the postictal vasoconstriction would be so low as to compromise the delivery of glucose and/or oxygen. Data on the CBF during the immediate postictal phase are much more sparse. Recently, we measured the CBF regionally in rats 5 and 45 minutes after a 20-minute period of status epilepticus induced by fluorothyl (Nevander and Ingvar, in preparation). Measurements of the cerebral tissue glucose content in the same periods[16] indicate that the postictal reduction in the cerebral blood flow (down to 30% of control in the neocortex) is secondary to the postictal depression of metabolic rate as the tissue-to-plasma ratio for glucose increased in the cortex. It is thus unlikely that the cerebral blood flow either during or after sustained seizures as such determines what areas are to be damaged. Rather it is likely that it may play a secondary role in the development of neuronal damage, at least as long as the blood pressure is maintained at normal levels.

CONCLUSIONS

During seizure activity the metabolic rate is increased due to the increased neuronal work. There is an intense vasodilation resulting in a concomitant increase in cerebral blood flow if the systemic blood pressure is maintained.

Neuronal necrosis does not occur after single seizures, even if repeated. Rather the minimum time of intense status epilepticus required experimentally to yield neuronal necrosis is 25–30 minutes.

Increased metabolic rate is not the sole factor responsible for the development of the neuronal damage. Rather it seems that other factors, like, e.g., the excitatory amino acids, play a role in the transsynaptic killing of cells.

SUMMARY

After long periods of status epilepticus, selective neuronal necrosis is incurred in the neocortex (layer III–IV), in the hippocampus (CA1 and CA4), and in the thalamus (VPL-VPM). In these areas the cerebral metabolic rate for glucose is increased to between 200–300% of control, indicating a correlation between neuronal damage and enhanced neuronal activity. Measurements of local cerebral blood flow indicate that the damage is not due to insufficient supply of oxygen. In most rats with status epilepticus lasting longer than 30 minutes, an infarction develops in the substantia nigra pars reticulata. In this region the metabolic rate is first increased but later during the seizure activity falls to very low values indicating cell necrosis. Conclusion: prolonged neuronal hyperactivity with a concomitant increase in the metabolic rate for glucose is a prerequisite for the development of neuronal damage. However, the necrosis of the SNPR demonstrates that other factors determine the vulnerability of neurons to hyperexcitation, e.g., the type of agonist acting on the neuron.

REFERENCES

1. NORMAN, R. M. 1964. The neuropathology of status epilepticus. Med. Sci. Law **4:** 46–51.
2. CORSELLIS, J. A. N. & B. S. MELDRUM. 1976. The pathology of epilepsy. *In* Greenfields Neuropathology. 3rd edit. W. Blackwood & J. A. N. Corsellis, Eds.: 771–795. Edward Arnold. London, England.
3. WOODBURY, D. M. 1983. Experimental models of status epilepticus and mechanisms of drug action. Adv. Neurol. **34:** 149–160.
4. MELDRUM, B. S. & J. B. BRIERLEY. 1973. Prolonged epileptic seizures in primates: ischemic cell change and its relation to ictal physiological events. Arch. Neurol. Chicago **28:** 10–17.
5. MELDRUM, B. S. & B. NILSSON. 1976. Cerebral blood flow and metabolic rate early and late in prolonged epileptic seizures induced in rats by bicuculline. Brain **99:** 523–542.
6. BLENNOW, G., B. NILSSON & B. K. SIESJÖ. 1977. Sustained epileptic seizures complicated by hypoxia, arterial hypotension and hyperthermia: effects on cerebral energy state. Acta Physiol. Scand. **100:** 126–128.
7. MELDRUM, B. S., R. A. VIGOROUX & J. B. BRIERLEY. 1973. Systemic factors and epileptic brain damage. Prolonged seizures in paralysed, artificially ventilated baboons. Arch. Neurol. **29:** 82–87.
8. BLENNOW, G., J. B. BRIERLY, B. S. MELDRUM & B. K. SIESJÖ. 1978. Epileptic brain damage. The role of systemic factors that modify cerebral energy metabolism. Brain **101:** 687–700.
9. SÖDERFELDT, B., H. KALIMO, Y. OLSSON & B. K. SIESJÖ. 1981. Pathogenesis of brain lesions caused by experimental epilepsy. Light- and electron-microscopic changes in the rat cerebral cortex following bicuculline-induced status epilepticus. Acta Neuropathol. Berlin **54:** 219–231.
10. SÖDERFELDT, B., H. KALIMO, Y. OLSSON & B. K. SIESJÖ. 1983. Bicuculline induced brain injury: transient and persistent changes in rat cerebral cortex in the early recovery period. Acta Neuropathol. **62:** 87–95.
11. KRANTZ, J. C., JR. 1963. Volatile anesthetics and indoklon. J. Neuropsychiatry **4:** 157–161.
12. DUFFY, T. E., D. C. HOWSE & F. PLUM. 1975. Cerebral energy metabolism during experimental status epilepticus. J. Neurochem. **24:** 925–934.
13. HOWSE, D. C., J. J. CARONNA, T. E. DUFFY & F. PLUM. 1974. Cerebral energy metabolism, pH, and blood flow during seizures in the cat. Am. J. Physiol. **227:** 1444–1451.
14. CHAPMAN, A. G., B. S. MELDRUM & B. K. SIESJÖ. 1977. Cerebral metabolic changes during prolonged epileptic seizures in rats. J. Neurochem. **28:** 1025–1035.

15. INGVAR, M., B. SÖDERFELDT, J. FOLBERGROVA, H. KALIMO, Y. OLSSON & B. K. SIESJÖ. 1984. Metabolic, circulatory, and structural alterations in the rat brain induced by sustained pentylenetetrazol seizures. Epilepsia **25:** 191–204.
16. FOLBERGROVA, J., M. INGVAR, G. NEVANDER & B. K. SIESJÖ. Cerebral metabolic changes during and following fluorothyl-induced seizures in ventilated rats. J. Neurochem. (In press.)
17. NEVANDER, G., M. INGVAR, R. AUER & B. K. SIESJÖ. 1984. Irreversible brain cell damage after short periods of status epilepticus. Acta Physiol. Scand. **120:** 155–157.
18. NEVANDER, G., M. INGVAR, R. AUER & B. K. SIESJÖ. Status epilepticus in well oxygenated rats causes neuronal necrosis. Ann. Neurol. (In press.)
19. MOURITZEN-DAM, A., M. HERTZ & T. G. BOLWIG. 1980. The number of hippocampal neurons in rats after electrically induced generalized seizures. Brain Res. **193:** 268–272.
20. MOURITZEN DAM, A., J. BAJORECK & P. LOMAX. 1981. Hippocampal neuronal density and seizures in mongolian gerbil. Epilepsia **22:** 268–277.
21. BALAZS, R. 1970. Carbohydrate metabolism. *In* Handbook of Neurochemistry. A. Lahjta, Ed. **3:** 1–36. Plenum Press. New York, N.Y.
22. KING, L. J., O. H. LOWRY, J. V. PASSONEAU & V. VENSON. 1967. Effects of convulsants on energy reserves in the cerebral cortex. J. Neurochem. **14:** 599–611.
23. BORGSTRÖM, L., A. G. CHAPMAN & B. K. SIESJÖ. 1976. Glucose consumption in the cerebral cortex of the rat during bicuculline induced status epilepticus. J. Neurochem. **27:** 971–973.
24. SIESJÖ, B. K. & A. ABDUL-RAHMAN. 1979. A metabolic basis for the selective vulnerability of neurons in status epilepticus. Acta Physiol. Scand. **106:** 377–378.
25. INGVAR, M. & B. K. SIESJÖ. 1983. Local blood flow and glucose consumption in the rat brain during sustained bicuculline-induced seizures. Acta Neurol. Scand. **68:** 129–144.
26. HOWSE, D. 1983. Cerebral energy metabolism during experimental status epilepticus. Adv. Neurol. **34:** 209–216.
27. SOKOLOFF, L., M. REIVICH, C. KENNEDY, M. H. DES ROSIERS, C. S. PATLACK, K. D. PETTIGREW, O. SAKURADA & M. SHINOHARA. 1977. The 14-C-Deoxyglucose method for the measurement of local cerebral glucose utilization: theory, procedure, and normal values in the conscious and anesthetized albino rat. J. Neurochem. **28:** 897–916.
28. PARDRIDGE, W. M., P. D. CRANE, L. J. MIETUS & W. H. OLDENDORF. 1982. Kinetics of regional blood brain barrier transport and brain phosphorylation of glucose and 2-deoxyglucose in the barbiturate-anesthetized rat. J. Neurochem. **38:** 560–568.
29. LOTHMAN, E. W. & R. C. COLLINS. 1981. Kainic acid induced limbic seizures: metabolic, behavioural, electroencephalographic, and neuropathological correlates. Brain Res. **218:** 299–318.
30. BEN-ARI, Y., E. TREMBLAY, E. RICHE, G. GHILINI & R. NAQUET. 1981. Electrographical, clinical, and pathological alterations following systemic administration of kainic acid, bicuculline, or pentetrazole: metabolic mapping using the deoxyglucose method with special reference to the pathology of epilepsy. Neuroscience **6:** 1361–1391.
31. MONAGHAN, D. T., V. R. HOLETS, D. W. TOY & C. W. COTMAN. 1983. Anatomical distributions of four pharmacologically distinct 3H-L-glutamate binding sites. Nature **306:** 176–179.
32. BEN-ARI, Y., E. TREMBLAY, O. P. OTTERSEN & B. S. MELDRUM. 1980. The role of epileptic activity in hippocampal and remote cerebral lesions induced by kainic acid. Brain Res. **191:** 79–97.
33. COLLINS, R. C. & J. OLNEY. 1983. Focal cortical seizures cause distant thalamic lesions. Science **218:** 177–179.
34. COLLINS, R. C., E. W. LOTHMAN & J. W. OLNEY. 1983. Status epilepticus in the limbic system: biochemical and pathological changes. Adv. Neurol. **34:** 277–288.
35. ACKERMANN, R. F., D. M. FINCH, T. L. BABB & J. ENGEL, JR. 1983. Increased glucose metabolism during long-duration recurrent inhibition of hippocampal pyramidal cells. J. Neurosci.
36. WIELOCH, T., O. LINDVALL, P. BLOMQVIST & F. GAGE. Evidence for ameloration of ischemic neuronal damage in the hippocampal formation by lesions of the perforant path. Neurol. Res. (In press.)

37. CROUCHER, M. J., J. F. COLLINS & B. S. MELDRUM. 1982. Anticonvulsant action of excitatory amino acid antagonists. Science **216:** 899–901.
38. WIELOCH, T. Neurochemical correlates to regional selective neuronal vulnerability. Prog. Brain Res. (In press.)
39. NAUTA, W. J. H. & V. B. DOMESICK. 1980. Afferent and efferent relationships of the basal ganglia. Ciba Foundation Symp.: 3–29.
40. KORNHUBER, J., J-S. KIM, M. E. KORNHUBER & H. H. KORNHUBER. 1984. The cortico nigral projection—reduced glutamate content in the substantia nigra following frontal cortex ablation in the rat. Brain Res. **322:** 124–126.
41. KATO, M., B. L. MALAMUT, W. F. CAVENESS, S. HOSOKAWA, S. WAKISAKA & R. R. O'NEILL. 1980. Local cerebral glucose utilization in newborn and pubescent monkeys during focal motor seizures. Ann. Neurol. **7:** 204–212.
42. HOSOKAWA, S., T. IGUCHI, W. F. CAVENESS, M. KATO, R. R. O'NEILL, S. WAKISAKA & B. L. MALAMUT. 1980. Effects of manipulation of the sensorimotor system on focal motor seizures in the monkey. Ann. Neurol. **7:** 222–229.
43. KANAZAWA, I., P. C. EMSON & A. C. CUELLO. 1977. Evidence for the existence of substance P–containing fibers in strionigral and pallidonigral pathways in rat brain. Brain Res. **119:** 447–453.
44. GRAYBIEL, A. M. & C. W. RAGSDALE. 1983. Biochemical anatomy of the striatum. *In* Chemical Neuroanatomy, P. C. Emson, Ed.: 427–504. Raven Press. New York, N.Y.
45. GAINER, H. & M. J. BROWNSTEIN. 1981. Neuropeptides. *In* Basic Neurochemistry. G. J. Siegel, R. W. Albers, B. W. Agranoff & R. Katzman, Eds.: 269–296. Little, Brown and Co. Boston, Mass.
46. FONNUM, F. 1984. Glutamate: a neurotransmitter in mammalian brain. J. Neurochem. **42:** 1–11.
47. PENFIELD, W., K. VON SANTHA & A. CAPRIANI. 1939. Cerebral blood flow during induced epileptorm seizures in animals and man. J. Neurophysiol. **2:** 257–267.
48. PENFIELD, W. & H. JASPER, Eds. 1954. Epilepsy and the Functional Anatomy of the Human Brain. Little, Brown and Co. Boston, Mass.
49. SPIELMEYER, W. 1927. Die pathogenese des epileptischen krampfes. Zeitschr. Neurol. Psychiatr. **109:** 515–520.
50. DUMKE, P. R. & C. F. SCHMIDT. 1943. Quantitative measurements of the cerebral blood flow in the maquaque monkey. Am. J. Physiol. **138:** 421–431.
51. HOUGARD, K., T. OIKAWA, E. SVEINSDOTTIR, E. SKINHOJ, D. H. INGVAR & N. A. LASSEN. 1976. Regional blood flow in focal cortical epilepsy. Arch. Neurol. **33:** 527–535.
52. WHITE, P. T., P. GRANT & J. MOSIER. 1961. Changes in cerebral dynamics associated with seizures. Neurology Minneapolis **11:** 354–361.
53. SCHMIDT, C. F., S. S. KETY & H. H. PENNES. 1945. The gaseous metabolism of the brain of the monkey. Am. J. Physiol. **143:** 33–52.
54. PLUM, F., J. B. POSNER & B. TROY. 1968. Cerebral metabolic and circulatory responses to induced convulsions in animals. Arch. Neurol. **18:** 1–13.
55. HORTON, R. W., B. S. MELDRUM, T. A. PEDLEY & J. R. MCWILLIAM. 1980. Regional cerebral blood flow in the rat during prolonged seizure activity. Brain Res. **192:** 399–412.
56. INGVAR, M., B. NILSSON & B. K. SIESJÖ. 1981. Local cerebral blood flow during bicuculline induced seizures and the modulating influence of inhibition of prostaglandin synthesis. Acta Physiol. Scand. **111:** 202–212.

Cellular and Molecular Events Underlying Epileptic Brain Damage[a]

BO K. SIESJÖ, MARTIN INGVAR, AND
TADEUSZ WIELOCH

Laboratory for Experimental Brain Research
University Hospital
University of Lund
S-22185 Lund, Sweden

It has been known for more than 150 years that many patients with epilepsy can have unequivocal brain damage, usually localized to the hippocampus (for literature, see Reference 1). Such findings led to several important questions. The first was whether the brain damage was secondary to the seizures, or their cause. Since it subsequently emerged that repeated seizures and/or status epilepticus can in fact cause brain damage, the next important question arose: Is the damage due to the seizure discharge per se, or to systemic complications which encroach upon the oxygenation of brain cells? A related and equally pertinent question concerns the minimal period of seizure activity that carries the risk of inducing irreversible structural and functional lesions. We must ask, Can short electroconvulsive seizures, when administered singly or repetitively, cause such lesions? Many experimental protocols have been designed to provide appropriate answers to these questions (see Reference 2). Such experiments, as well as those designed to unravel the pathophysiology of ischemic or hypoglycemic brain damage, have yielded much useful information. As a result, we can now define in some detail pathophysiological conditions under which damage is incurred, and speculate about the mechanisms involved. It is the objective of this paper to discuss the neurochemical pathology of such damage.

NEUROCHEMICAL EVENTS DURING SUSTAINED SEIZURES

We begin discussing perturbation of cerebral metabolism in epilepsy by considering the transition from a normal state to a condition of sustained, generalized seizures. When induced in ventilated and well-oxygenated experimental animals, such seizures are accompanied by sustained, two- to threefold increases of oxygen and glucose consumption in neocortex and hippocampus.[3] Our initial discussion will be centered on these structures.

Cellular Energy Metabolism

Detailed information exists on changes in labile metabolites during seizures.[4–7] FIGURE 1 illustrates changes in compounds involved in energy transduction. At seizure

[a]This study was supported by grants from the Swedish Medical Research Council (Project No. 14X-263), and from the U.S. Public Health Service (National Institutes of Health Grant No. 2 R01 NS 07838).

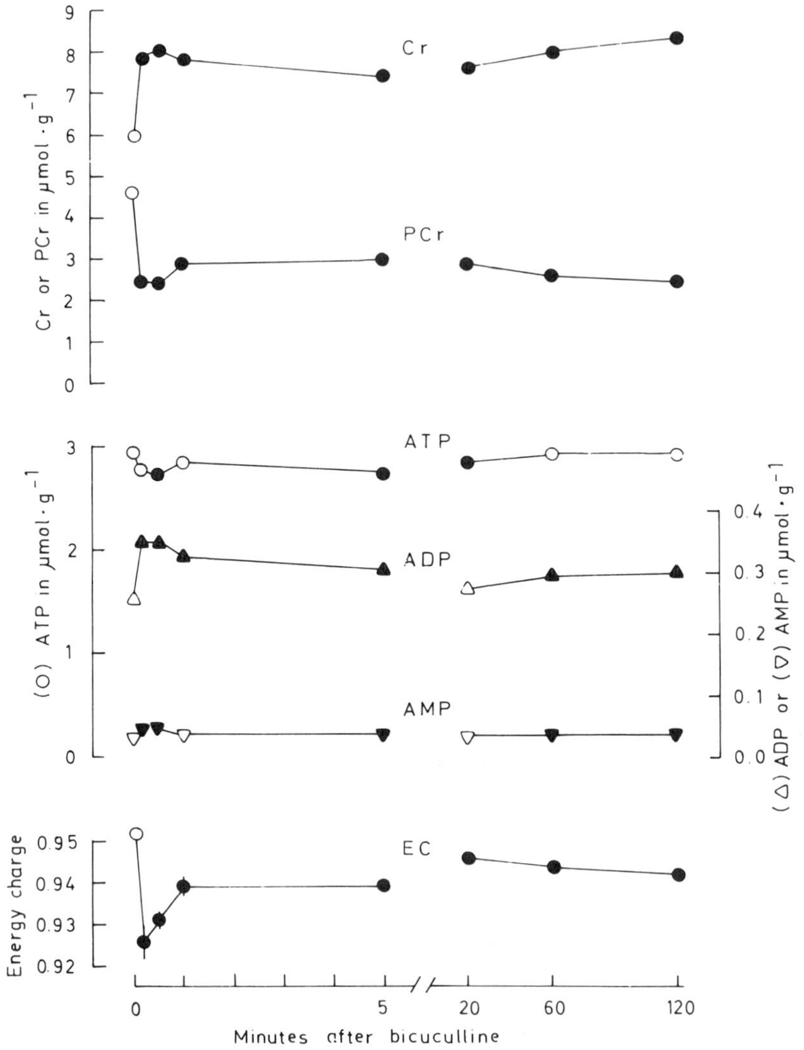

FIGURE 1. Changes in labile metabolites reflecting cerebral cortical energy state following induction of generalized epileptic seizures with intravenous bicuculline. Cr = creatine; PCr = phosphocreatine; EC = adenylate energy charge, calculated as ([ATP] + 0.5 [ADP])/([ATP] + [ADP] + [AMP]). Filled symbols denote values significantly different from control ($p < 0.05$). (Modified after Reference 6.)

onset, a clear perturbation is observed in cellular energy state, with decreases in phosphocreatine (PCr) and ATP concentrations, and increases in creatine, ADP, and AMP. However, this perturbation is modest, and a new steady state is soon reached in which concentrations of labile phosphates are close to normal; for example, the calculated adenylate energy charge is maintained at about 98% of control.

If tissue oxygenation remains adequate, little change occurs in the sum of adenine nucleotides ([ATP] + [ADP] + [AMP]).[5,6] However, since AMP concentration initially rises some degradation of this nucleotide occurs by deamination and dephosphorylation, leading to enhanced levels of ammonia, as well as of purine nucleosides and bases.[6,8,9] More comprehensive data on this have been collected in electroshock experiments (see below).

Changes also occur in cyclic nucleotides. Seizures invariably increase tissue concentrations of cAMP and cGMP; however, whereas cAMP concentrations return towards control during continued seizures, cGMP levels remain elevated.[7,10] Probably, the rise in cAMP reflects the release of adrenoceptor agonists such as noradrenaline and adenosine (see References 8, 9, and 11). This conclusion is corroborated by results showing that lesions of the noradrenergic innervation to the forebrain attenuate the rise in cAMP.[12] The mechanisms leading to an elevation of cGMP are less well defined but circumstantial evidence indicates a coupling to enhanced activity in cholinergic neurons.[13]

Changes in labile phosphates are accompanied by alterations in glycolytic metabolites, reflecting increased aerobic formation of pyruvate and lactate.[4-6] FIGURE 2 shows that tissue lactate concentrations increase to 8–10 μmol $\times$ g^{-1} during the first five minutes of seizures, with an associated elevation of the lactate/pyruvate ratio. Coupled to these alterations are changes in citric acid cycle intermediates and associated amino acids, reflecting shifts of the equilibrium position of reactions with common reactants.[5,6]

Cerebral metabolic changes during seizures reflect an increased metabolic demand rather than a deficient oxygen supply (see below, and Reference 2). However, alterations in labile phosphates and in glycolytic metabolites are modulated by the oxygen and the substrate supplies. A restriction of oxygen supply by moderate hypotension (blood pressure about 70 mmHg) or moderate hypoxia (arterial PO_2 about 50 mmHg) only marginally affects adenine nucleotides but clearly raises tissue lactic acid concentrations.[14] Complicating hypoglycemia has a similar effect on the energy state but an opposite effect on tissue lactate concentrations.[7,15] There are reasons to believe, therefore, that restriction of oxygen and glucose supply has widely different effects on intra- and extracellular pH. It is not known if hypoxia, when complicating seizures, ameliorates or aggravates cell damage.[14,16] This issue cannot be settled until experiments with long-term recovery have been performed. The following discussion is confined to seizures occurring in the absence of hypotension, hypoxia, or hypoglycemia.

The maintenance of near-normal adenine nucleotide concentrations during seizures demonstrates that respiratory functions can keep pace with the enhanced ATP hydrolysis. This conclusion is corroborated by data on venous and tissue oxygen tensions, and on the redox state of mitochondrial respiratory carriers.[5,17-19] Thus, at least in the beginning of a series of seizures, tissue oxygen tensions rise. Later, this rise may be attenuated or transformed into a decrease.[17,18] However, since cerebral energy state is maintained there is no reason to suspect that oxygen supply becomes limiting for cerebral metabolism. The adequacy of energy-linked cellular functions is also evident from the fact that both glycogen (which is broken down in the initial phase) and glutamine are synthesized during ongoing seizures.[6]

Conservative and Dissipative Ion Fluxes

The cardinal feature of seizures is enhanced excitation which entails massive agonist-receptor interaction. The resulting depolarization is associated with efflux of

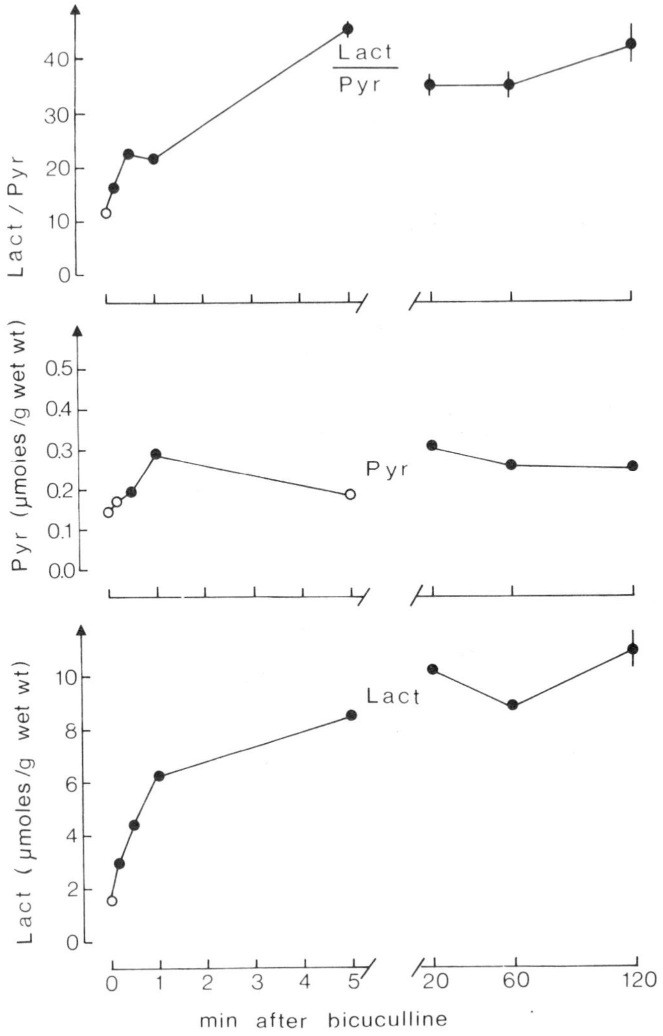

FIGURE 2. Changes in lactate and pyruvate concentrations, as well as in the lactate/pyruvate ratio, of cerebral cortex during sustained bicuculline-induced seizures. Filled symbols denote values significantly different from control ($p < 0.05$). (Data from Reference 6.)

K^+ and influx of Na^+, events that will activate membrane-bound Na^+-K^+-ATPases and increase oxygen and glucose consumption. Even though dissipative ion fluxes are high, ATP-dependent conservative fluxes ("repumping") can almost keep pace; thus extracellular K^+ concentrations (K^+_e) do not exceed 10 μmol $\times$ ml^{-1}.[20,21] Another energy-linked transport function that is well preserved is that leading to regulation of intracellular pH (pH_i). Lactic acid production during seizure onset is sufficient to lower pH_i by about 0.20 unit.[22,23] However, in spite of continuing seizures and maintained lactate concentrations, pH_i rises towards control and, if seizures are terminated, pH_i overshoots the control value and becomes alkaline.[23] This is probably the result of H^+ extrusion via an enhanced Na^+/H^+ exchange, the energy source of which is the Na^+ gradient generated by the Na^+, K^+-ATPase (see References 24 and 25).

In view of these well-maintained conservative functions, it is somewhat surprising that seizures are accompanied by relatively pronounced decreases in extracellular Ca^{2+} concentrations (Ca^{2+}_e), suggesting partial failure of Ca^{2+} extrusion[20] (see also References 26 and 27). It is interesting to compare calcium influx into cells in ischemia, hypoglycemia, and epileptic seizures. In the first two conditions, calcium influx occurs first when K^+_e concentrations rise above 15 μmol $\times$ ml^{-1},[28–30] but during seizures, relatively marked reduction in $[Ca^{2+}]_e$ is observed although $[K^+]_e$ remains well below 10 μmol $\times$ ml^{-1}.[20] This suggests a large dissipative flux of calcium through agonist-dependent channels.

Phospholipids and Free Fatty Acids

Early results reported by Bazan[31,32] (see also Reference 33) demonstrated that electroshock and chemically induced seizures in animals with unsupported ventilation were accompanied by increases in cerebral free fatty acid concentrations (FFAs). It could later be shown that increased FFA concentrations are observed also if animals are ventilated and well oxygenated.[34–36] Since seizures lead to the release not only of FFAs but also of diglycerides one has to invoke activation of both phospholipase A_2 and C.[35] Perturbation of lipid metabolism is maximal initially; however, although FFA concentrations gradually return towards normal, raised concentration of arachidonic (20:4) and docosahexanoic (22:6) acid persist even after two hours of sustained seizures (FIGURE 3).

As observed in FIGURE 3 arachidonic acid shows the largest relative increase in concentration. Since oxygen supply is maintained one would expect an increased flux along reaction sequences for which arachidonic acid is a substrate, e.g., the cyclooxygenase and the lipoxygenase pathways. This has also been shown to occur since increased tissue prostaglandin concentrations have been reported in experimentally induced seizures (for literature, see References 35 and 37).

Protein Metabolism

Seizures lead to several potentially important alterations of protein metabolism, encompassing changes in protein synthesis, protein phosphorylation, and proteinase activity. In this context, our concern is protein synthesis, while protein phosphorylation and proteinase activity will be discussed in relationship to calcium homeostasis. We have referred to the fact that seizures allow some synthetic tasks to continue unabated. It is therefore somewhat surprising that seizures, even when instituted in ventilated and well-oxygenated animals, markedly depress protein synthesis. This has been observed both with chemical measurements of incorporation of ^{14}C-labeled amino acids into proteins,[38–40] and by visualization of ^{3}H-tyrosine incorporation with stripping film autoradiography.[41,42] The latter technique has nicely illustrated a marked reduction in ^{3}H incorporation into proteins in cerebral structures of the rat which by ^{14}C-deoxyglucose autoradiography emerge as intensely hypermetabolic ones.[43,3] Although the association between increased oxidative metabolism and decreased protein synthesis is obvious, the factors mediating the effect on protein synthesis, which seems to operate at the initiation step, have not been defined. It has been suggested that a minor alteration in the GDP/GTP ratio, secondary to a corresponding change in ADP/ATP ratio, is responsible.[44]

Regional Differences in Metabolic Response

Most, if not all, of the metabolic alterations discussed are qualitatively and quantitatively similar in neocortex and hippocampus, two structures with grossly

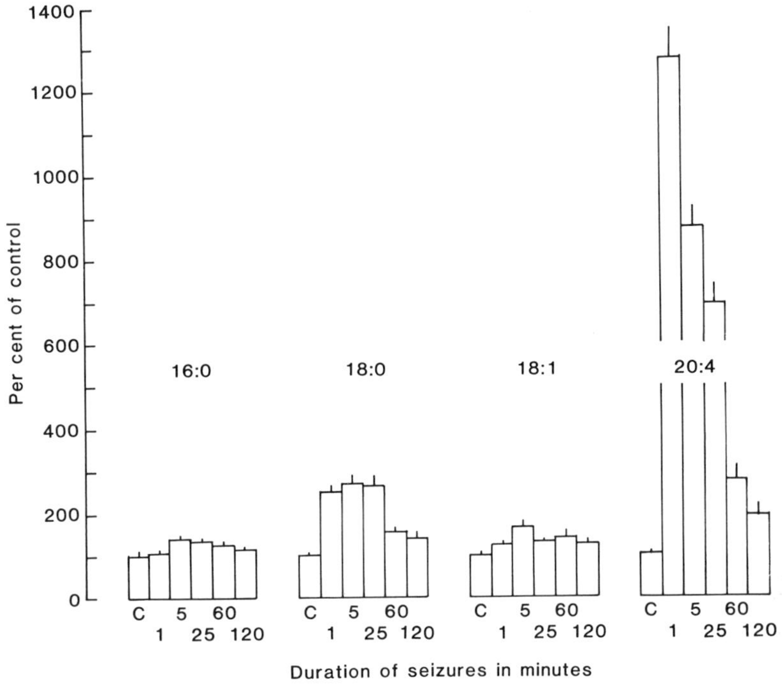

FIGURE 3. Changes in individual free fatty acids of cerebral cortex in bicuculline-induced seizures of 1–120 minutes duration. The values are means ± standard error of the mean in percent of control. Palmitic acid = 16:0; stearic acid = 18:0; linoleic acid = 18:1; arachidonic acid = 20:4. (Reproduced from Reference 36 with permission.)

enhanced metabolic rate.[7,36,42] In contrast, the cerebellum, which does not participate in the intense functional and metabolic activation, shows moderate and transient signs of metabolic perturbation. In general, the metabolic perturbation should correlate to the enhancement in local metabolic rate. Extensive measurements of metabolic rates have been performed both in generalized[3] and in limbic[45] seizures (for further references, see Reference 60).

The finding of bilateral infarction of the substantia nigra pars reticulata (SNPR) after seizure periods of 30–45 minutes[46,47] prompted a study of metabolic alterations in this structure.[48] The results showed that a more marked deterioration of cellular energy state developed within the first 60 minutes with energy charge values decreasing by close to 10% and lactate values reaching 25 μmol $\times$ g^{-1}. SNPR thus represents a special case, one in which early mitochondrial failure develops. The histological appearance[47] makes us believe that similar changes occur in parts of the globus pallidus.

NEUROCHEMICAL EVENTS DURING SHORT-LASTING SEIZURES

Much information exists on the perturbation of cerebral metabolic state caused by single or repeated electroshocks, delivered to rats or mice, or on seizures of equivalent duration, induced by convulsants such as fluorothyl (indoklon) and 3-mercaptopro-prionic acid. Following the pioneering work of Minard and Davies,[49] several workers studied changes in labile phosphates, in glycolytic metabolites, in citric acid cycle intermediates, and in related amino acids.[5,50–54] In summary, such results have shown a relatively pronounced perturbation of cerebral energy state, with ATP concentrations approaching 50% of control and lactate values reaching 300% of control, or more. However, these alterations have been relatively short lasting, and normal values have been obtained a few minutes following a single electroshock or a brief drug-induced seizure.

Results on electroshcok seizures clearly demonstrated accumulation of breakdown products of AMP, including ammonia, IMP, and hypoxanthine.[54] It is also of interest that single electroshocks lead to release of FFAs, particularly of arachidonic acid,[31] and to a short-lasting inhibition of protein synthesis.[55,56] Essentially, therefore, short-lasting seizures lead to qualitatively similar metabolic changes as sustained seizures, but the metabolic perturbation is transient, leaving functional alterations as the only detectable residue.

With few exceptions, results obtained in short-lasting seizures have been obtained in animals with unsupported ventilation, and without an extra oxygen supply. Under such conditions, arterial oxygenation can decrease drastically (see Reference 40). However, although complicating hypoxia may exaggerate the metabolic perturbation, part of it is related to the intense neuronal discharge per se, as experiments on ventilated animals demonstrate.[5,6]

MECHANISMS OF BRAIN DAMAGE

The metabolic alterations discussed above all have a bearing on the cellular and molecular events that may be responsible for epileptic brain damage. It seems justified to discuss separately mechanisms responsible for selective neuronal necrosis and for infarction, respectively. Since the mechanisms have not been definitively characterized, those discussed are at present speculative. There is no doubt that one prerequisite for cell damage to be incurred is sustained overactivation of certain neuronal systems, with incessant synaptic bombardment of the vulnerable neurons. Thus, those areas that contain necrotic neurons are those that show enhanced metabolic rate.[43,57] and experiments with stimulation of the afferent input to selectively vulnerable regions demonstrate that activation must be sustained for certain minimal periods for damage to occur[58,59] (see also Reference 60). However, since different cell populations vary in their sensitivity to the epileptic insult there is no simple, general relationship between time and intensity of metabolic activation and neuronal damage. Differences of this kind have led to the hypothesis that selectively vulnerable cells have certain neurochemical features that make them prone to incur damage. Such a feature is a high density of postsynaptic calcium channels, one basis for the calcium hypothesis of cell death.[2,61–63]

However, neurons considered to contain a high density of calcium channels are not equally sensitive to epileptic and other insults. This has led to the alternative hypothesis that, although loss of intracellular calcium homeostasis may be involved, yet another thing is required: a special type of agonist-receptor interaction. Work on the neurotoxicity of excitatory amino acids (glutamate and aspartate) and their analogues like kainic acid focused interest on agonist-receptor interactions at glutamate receptors.[64,65] It subsequently turned out that in dissociated neuronal cultures cell death in response to anoxia required an intact synaptic function, and that the effects of anoxia could be

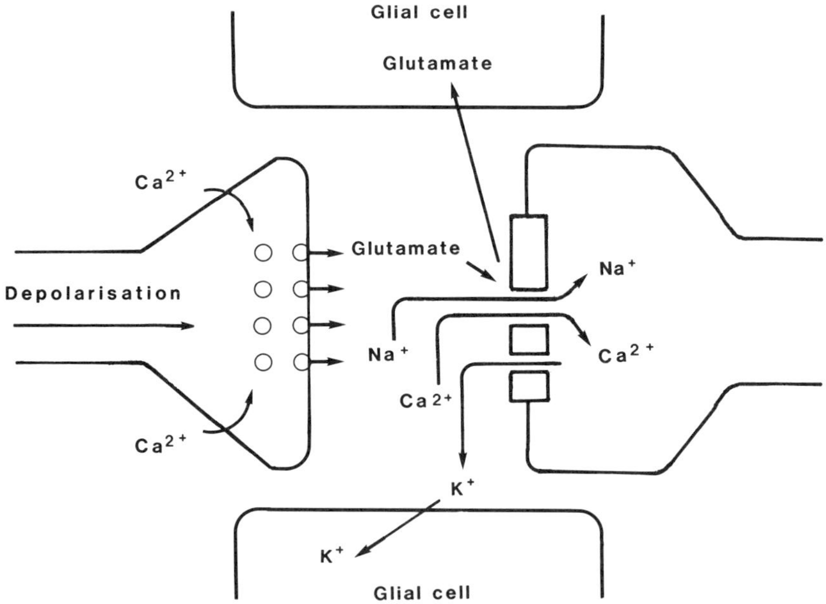

FIGURE 4. Schematic diagram demonstrating ionic events during release of transmitter at an excitatory synapse. The calcium-induced release of glutamate from presynaptic endings is shown to induce postsynaptic flux of Na^+ and Ca^{2+}. (Slightly modified after Reference 96.)

reproduced by glutamate addition to the cultures.[66,67] Recent results also indicate that locally injected glutamate antagonists ameliorate ischemic damage to the hippocampus,[68] and demonstrate such amelioraton following interruption of the (presumably glutamatergic) input to CA1 pyramidal cells.[69] Such results have led to the general hypothesis that excitatory amino acids mediate neuronal necrosis in several different conditions which share in common perturbation of cerebral energy metabolism, and enhanced transmitter release at glutamatergic and/or aspartergic nerve endings.[70]

According to prevailing views, excitatory amino acids exert their effects by increasing Na^+ conductances of postsynaptic membranes, thereby causing depolarization (FIGURE 4). This depolarization would then open voltage-dependent Ca^{2+} channels, and allow Ca^{2+} influx. In view of this, it is tempting to conclude that the chief adverse effect of excitatory amino acids is to cause such influx. However, the results reported by Rothman[67] suggest that glutamate is toxic to cells in culture even in the absence of added calcium (see also Reference 71). Two possible explanations emerge. One is that depolarization releases membrane-bound calcium in sufficient amounts to trigger a cascade of calcium-related reactions. Alternatively calcium pathology is not involved but cell necrosis is initiated by influx of Na^+, perhaps also of Cl^- (see below).

Although excitatory amino acids could be responsible for necrosis of pyramidal cells in the hippocampus, and in the neocortex, perhaps also for the corresponding lesion of the pallidoreticularis, they may not be involved in the concomitant destruction of glial cells and vascular tissue in the latter structure. After having discussed calcium-related pathology, we will, therefore, bring up yet another type of mechanism of damage, viz., that related to loss of intracellular H^+ and Na^+ homeostasis.

Calcium and Cell Death

Calcium, being a first or a second messenger, exerts a multitude of functions in the cell. In order to proceed at orderly rates these functions require that the free cytosolic Ca^{2+} activity is maintained at levels of 10^{-7} to 10^{-8} mol × l^{-1} (see References 72–76). Since the external concentration is 10^4–10^5 times higher, and since the interior of the cell is negative with respect to extracellular fluid (ECF), metabolic energy is required to extrude calcium from cytosol to ECF. Influx and efflux pathways, as well as intracellular sites of calcium sequestration, are schematically shown in FIGURE 5. We will assume that long-term regulation of $Ca^{2+}{}_i$ activity is due to plasma membrane transport, and that short-term regulation in response to large loads occurs by binding to calcium-binding protein (CaBP) and other macromolecular structures, as well as by sequestrating of Ca^{2+} in mitochondria, perhaps also in endoplasmic reticulum. It is of importance that calcium export has a finite capacity, and that even a small increase in cytosolic Ca^{2+} activity will lead to gradual calcium sequestration in mitochondria (see Reference 76).

It has been assumed for some time that uncontrolled influx of calcium into skeletal,[77] cardiac,[78] and liver cells[79] causes cell necrosis. One likely mechanism is calcium overload of mitochondria which then lose their capacity to synthesize ATP. Indirect evidence supports this hypothesis since mitochondria with high-amplitude swelling have been found to contain dense calcium deposits.[80,81] It should be emphasized, though, that mitochondrial calcium accumulation also occurs in cells subjected to reversible insults (e.g., Reference 80), also that it has been questioned whether death of hepatic cells *in vitro* is mediated by calcium influx.[71]

Central to the calcium hypothesis of cell death is that the calcium leak, i.e., the influx along agonist- and voltage-dependent channels, exceeds the energy-dependent efflux. One can envisage that repetitive stimulation, with sustained release of, e.g., glutamate from presynaptic terminals, maintains calcium influx into postsynaptic terminals. However it is also possible that the metabolic effects of the initial perturbation of calcium homeostasis contribute to increase calcium influx so altering membrane permeability that gradual, net calcium influx occurs. In order to discuss this we have to consider the cascades of reactions set in motion by influx/release of calcium.

FIGURE 6 demonstrates that loss of calcium homeostasis perturbs lipid and protein metabolism (for further discussion, and original references, see References 2 and 63). The major effect on lipid metabolism is activation of phospholipases C and A_2, with an ensuing release of fatty acids, particularly of arachidonic acid, and of diglycerides. In

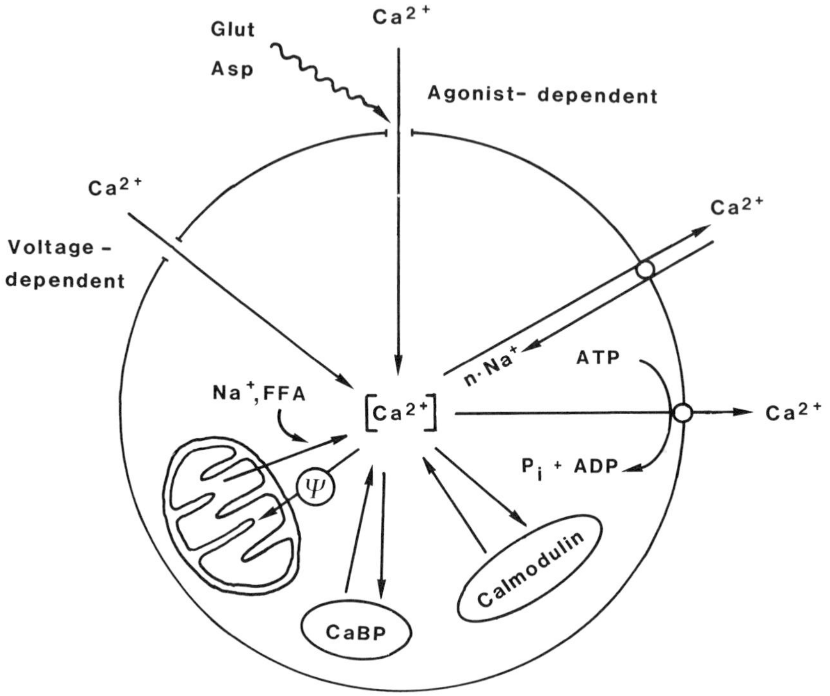

FIGURE 5. Schematic diagram illustrating transport, binding, and sequestration of calcium. Calcium entry is shown to occur via voltage- and agonist-dependent gates, and exit by Na^+/Ca^{2+} exchange and ATP-driven transport. Binding to calmodulin and calcium-binding protein (CaBP), and sequestration by mitochondria are indicated. (Modified after Reference 72.)

the presence of oxygen, arachidonic acid will trigger a cascade of reactions along the cyclooxygenase and lipoxygenase pathways, with the production of classical prostaglandins, thromboxanes, and hydroxy fatty acids. Many of these compounds, and the FFAs themselves, have ionophoretic effects and could, therefore, cause an unspecific increase in calcium permeability. If formed in increased amounts, free radical compounds and 5-lipoxygenase products of the leucotriene type have the potential of inducing membrane damage. It should also be recalled that lysophospholipids formed as a result of phospholipase A_2 activity are toxic, and such compounds have been incriminated in the pathogenesis of high-amplitude mitochondrial swelling caused by a large increase in the permeability of the inner mitochondrial membrane.[82] As a speculative possibility, therefore, it seems likely that sustained lipolysis and oxidative conversion of polyenoic FFAs so alter plasma membrane function that $[Ca^{2+}]_i$ is moderately increased. If this increase is sufficient to sustain mitochondrial uptake of Ca^{2+}, the end result may be mitochondrial overload and respiratory failure.

Calcium-triggered events include enhanced protein phosphorylation, proteinase activity, and disassembly of microtubuli (for overview, see References 2 and 63). It has been postulated that pre- and postsynaptic phosphorylation of proteins must influence ionic permeabilities of membranes, and thereby synaptic efficacy (see References 83 and 84). Activation of calcium-dependent proteases has two potentially important

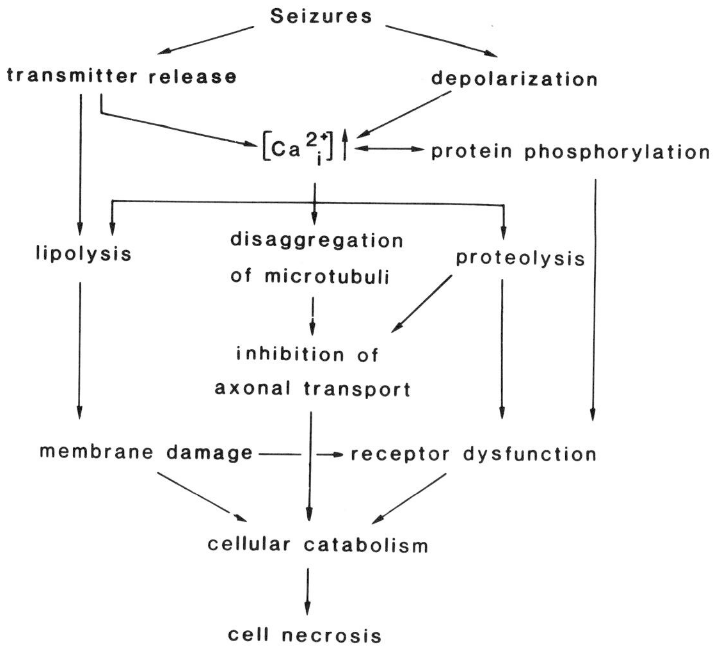

FIGURE 6. Tentative scheme illustrating cascade of potentially harmful reactions elicited by seizure activity. Central to this scheme is the fact that seizures give rise to massive transmitter release and to depolarization, thereby promoting influx/release of calcium. (Modified after Reference 63.)

effects: degradation of neurofilaments,[85] and increased density of glutamate receptors.[86,87] The degradation of neurofilaments, together with a calcium-dependent disassembly of microtubuli,[88] could interfere with intracellular communication by disrupting the cytoskeleton, while uncovering of more glutamate receptors has been proposed to underlie both the increased synaptic efficacy associated with long-term potentiation (LTP) of synaptic transmission in the hippocampus, following brief tetanic stimulation, and memory formation.[87] Other results hint that LTP has a presynaptic origin, involving enhanced release of transmitter for a given presynaptic stimulus, possibly due to phosphorylation of mitochondrial pyruvate dehydrogenase.[89–91] What seems clear is that LTP and increased synaptic efficacy result from enhanced influx of calcium.[90] It is of interest that transient ischemia, another condition leading to calcium influx, is followed by enhanced neuronal activity in CA1 pyramidal cells, and delayed neuronal death.[92]

Acidosis and Tissue Infarction

There is a growing body of evidence showing that excessive tissue acidosis aggravates brain damage due to ischemia/hypoxia, and that the aggravation chiefly involves massive astrocytic edema, with a resulting infarction (for documentation and original references, see References 61, 93, 94, and 95). Under ischemic/hypoxic conditions excessive acidosis develops provided that tissue hypoxia is severe enough to release aerobic control of glycolysis, and that some glucose supply persists.

It is not known why excessive acidosis leads to uncontrolled glial swelling, and to infarction. However, it seems likely that acidosis disrupts cell volume control by causing Na^+ influx via an Na^+/H^+ exchange mechanism, with coupled Cl^- influx via a Cl^-/HCO_3^- antiporter.[94,25]

In view of the infarction of SNPR, it was of interest to study whether excessive acidosis developed in that structure. Four experiments were conducted with fluorothyl-induced seizures in ventilated rats. In two of them ^{14}C-DMO, a weak acid pH

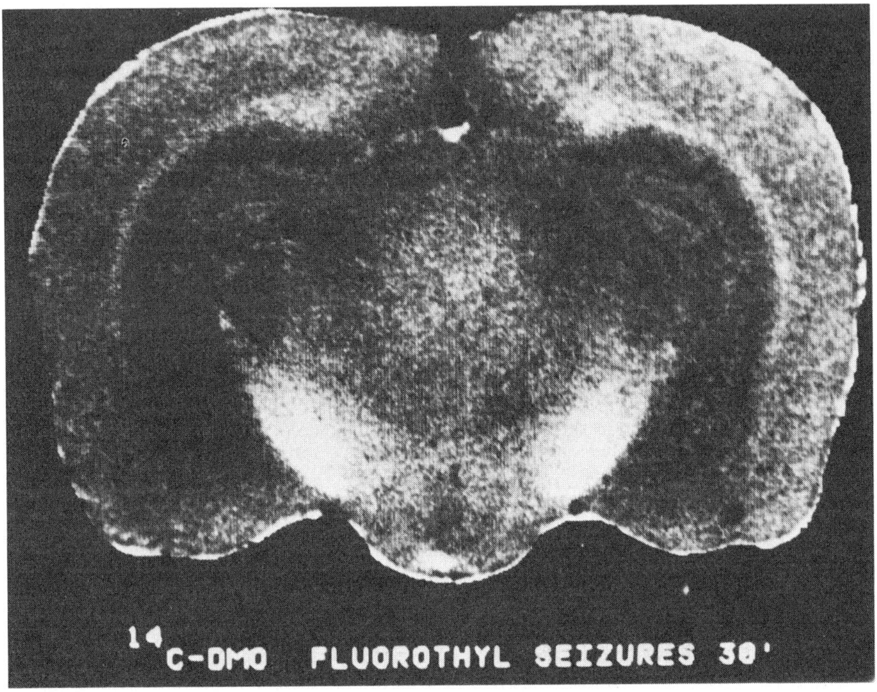

FIGURE 7. Autoradiogram showing tissue concentration of ^{14}C-DMO during fluorothyl-induced seizures. The tracer was injected intravenously after 30 minutes of seizures and allowed to equilibrate for another 30-minute period. Note low concentration in substantia nigra, demonstrating marked cellular acidosis.

indicator, was injected after 5 or 30 minutes of seizures and tissue was sampled for quantitative autoradiography after an additional 30-minute period. In the other two, ^{14}C-DMO was allowed to equilibrate for 45 minutes before seizures were started, and allowed to continue for 20 or 60 minutes. The results were comparable and showed very faint uptake of the label in the substantia nigra (and globus pallidus), indicating marked tissue acidosis (FIGURE 7). These results were corroborated by direct analyses of tissue lactate content which showed values of about 15 $\mu mol \times g^{-1}$ after 20 minutes and about 25 $\mu mol \times g^{-1}$ after 60 minutes of seizures.

These results, which confirm the hypothesis of an association of massive acidosis and infarction, raise the question of how the acidosis arises. Possibly, early mitochondrial damage releases aerobic control of glycolysis. However, we lack information on why mitochondria in this location should be more vulnerable than others.

CONCLUDING REMARKS—RELATIONSHIP TO ELECTROCONVULSIVE THERAPY

The results discussed in preceding paragraphs suggest that one requirement for cell damage to be incurred in seizure states is sustained activation of target neurons, another requirement being agonist-receptor interactions of a type that trigger dissipative fluxes of Na^+ and/or Ca^{2+} across postsynaptic membranes. It seems highly unlikely that both these requirements are fulfilled in electroconvulsive therapy. Thus, the brevity of the seizure discharge, and the long interseizure periods allowed, probably prevent membrane changes of a type that triggers irreversible neuronal changes.

REFERENCES

1. CORSELLIS, J. A. N. & B. S. MELDRUM. 1976. Epilepsy. *In* Greenfield's Neuropatholgy. W. Blackwood & J. A. N. Corsellis, Eds.: 771–795. Edward Arnold. London, England.
2. SIESJÖ, B. K. & T. WIELOCH. Epileptic brain damage: pathophysiology and neurochemical pathology. *In* Basic Mechanisms of the Epilepsies. A. Delgado-Escueta, A. Ward & D. Woodbury, Eds. Raven Press. New York, N.Y. (In press.)
3. INGVAR, M. & B. K. SIESJÖ. 1983. Local blood flow and glucose consumption in the rat brain during sustained bicuculline-induced seizures. Acta. Neurol. Scand. **68:** 129–144.
4. SACKTOR, B., J. E. WILSON & C. G. TIEKERT. 1966. Regulation of glycolysis in brain, in situ, during convulsions. J. Biol. Chem. **241:** 5071–5075.
5. DUFFY, T. E., D. C. HOWSE & F. PLUM. 1975. Cerebral energy metabolism during experimental status epilepticus. J. Neurochem. **24:** 925–934.
6. CHAPMAN, A. G., B. S. MELDRUM & B. K. SIESJÖ. 1977. Cerebral metabolic changes during prolonged epileptic seizures in rats. J. Neurochem. **28:** 1025–1035.
7. FOLBERGROVÁ, J., M. INGVAR & B. K. SIESJÖ. 1981. Metabolic changes in cerebral cortex, hippocampus, and cerebellum during sustained bicuculline induced seizures. J. Neurochem. **37:** 1228–1238.
8. SCHRADER, J., M. WAHL, W. KUSCHINSKY & G. W. KREUTZBERG. 1980. Increase of adenosine content in cerebral cortex of the cat during bicuculline-induced seizure. Pflügers Arch. **387:** 245–251.
9. WINN, H. R., J. E. WELSH, R. RUBIO & R. M. BERNE. 1980. Changes in brain adenosine during bicuculline-induced seizures in rats. Circ. Res. **47:** 568–577.
10. FERRENDELLI, J. A., A. C. BLANK & R. A. GROSS. 1980. Relationships between seizure activity and cyclic nucleotide levels in brain. Brain Res. **200:** 93–103.
11. CALDERINI, G., A. CARLSSON & C. -H. NORDSTRÖM. 1978. Monoamine metabolism during bicucilline-induced epileptic seizures in the rat. Brain Res. **157:** 295–302.
12. INGVAR, M., O. LINDVALL, J. FOLBERGROVÁ & B. K. SIESJÖ. 1983. Influence of lesions of the noradrenergic locus coeruleus system on the cerebral metabolic response to bicuculline-induced seizures. Brain Res. **264:** 225–231.
13. BLOOM, F. E. 1975. The role of cyclic nucleotides in central synaptic function. Rev. Physiol. Biochem. Pharmacol. **74:** 1–103.
14. BLENNOW, G., J. B. BRIERLEY, B. S. MELDRUM & B. K. SIESJÖ. 1978. Epileptic brain damage. The role of systemic factors that modify cerebral energy metabolism. Brain **101:** 687–700.
15. BLENNOW, G., J. FOLBERGROVÁ, B. NILSSON & B. K. SIESJÖ. 1979. Effects of bicuculline-induced seizures on cerebral metabolism and circulation of rats rendered hypoglycemic by starvation. Ann. Neurol. **5:** 139–151.

16. SÖDERFELDT, B., H. KALIMO, Y. OLSSON & B. K. SIESJÖ. 1983. Bicuculline-induced epileptic brain injury. Acta Neuropathol. Berlin **62:** 87–95.
17. CASPERS, H. & E. -J. SPECKMANN. 1972. Cerebral pO_2, pCO_2 and pH: changes during convulsive activity and their significance for spontaneous arrest of seizures. Epilepsia **13:** 699–725.
18. KREISMAN, N. R., M. ROSENTHAL, T. J. SICK & J. C. LAMANNA. 1983. Oxidative metabolic responses during recurrent seizures are independent of convulsant, anesthetic, or species. Neurology **33:** 861–867.
19. MERRIL, D. K. & R. W. GUYNN. 1982. The calculation of the mitochondrial free [NAD^+] / [NADH] [H^+] ratio in brain: effect of electroconvulsive seizure. Brain Res. **239:** 71–80.
20. HEINEMANN, U., H. D. LUX & M. J. GUTNICK. 1977. Extracellular free calcium and potassium during paroxysmal activity in the cerebral cortex of the cat. Exp. Brain Res. **27:** 237–243.
21. ASTRUP, J., G. BLENNOW & B. NILSSON. 1979. Effects of reduced cerebral blood flow upon EEG pattern, cerebral extracellular potassium, and energy metabolism in the rat cortex during bicuculline-induced seizures. Brain Res. **177:** 115–126.
22. HOWSE, D. C., J. J. CARONNA, T. E. DUFFY & F. PLUM. 1974. Cerebral energy metabolism, pH and blood flow during seizures in the cat. Am. J. Physiol. **227:** 1444–1451.
23. SIESJÖ, B. K., R. VON HANWEHR, G. NERGELIUS, G. NEVANDER & M. INGVAR. 1985. Extra- and intracellular pH in the brain during seizures and in the recovery period following arrest of seizure activity. J. Cereb. Blood Flow Metab. **5:** 47–57.
24. ROOS, A. & W. F. BORON. 1981. Intracellular pH. Physiol. Rev. **61:** 296–434.
25. SIESJÖ, B. K. Acid-base homeostasis in the brain: physiology, chemistry, and neurochemical pathology. Prog. Brain Res. **63.** (In press.)
26. NICHOLSON, C., G. TEN BRUGGENCATE, R. STEINBERG & H. STÖCKLE. 1977. Calcium modulation in brain extracellular microenvironment demonstrated with ion-selective micropipette. Proc. Nat. Acad. Sci. USA **74:** 1287–1290.
27. HEINEMANN, U. & R. PUMAIN. 1980. Extracellular calcium activity changes in cat sensorimotor cortex induced by iontophoretic application of aminoacids. Exp. Brain Res. **40:** 247–250.
28. HANSEN, A. J. & T. ZEUTHEN. 1981. Extracellular ion concentrations during spreading depression and ischemia in the rat brain cortex. Acta Physiol. Scand. **113:** 437–445.
29. HARRIS, R. J., L. SYMON, N. M. BRANSTON & M. BAYHAN. 1981. Changes in extracellular calcium activity in cerebral ischemia. J. Cereb. Blood Flow Metab. **1:** 203–210.
30. HARRIS, R. J., T. WIELOCH, L. SYMON & B. K. SIESJÖ. 1984. Cerebral extracellular calcium activity in severe hypoglycemia: relation to extracellular potassium and energy state. J. Cereb. Blood Flow Metab. **4:** 187–193.
31. BAZÁN, N. G., JR. 1971. Changes in free fatty acids of brain by drug-induced convulsions, electroshock and anaesthesia. J. Neurochem. **18:** 1379–1385.
32. BAZÁN, N. G., JR. 1976. Free arachidonic acid and other lipids in the nervous system during early ischemia and after electroshock. *In* Function and Metabolism of Phospholipids in the Central and Peripheral Nervous Systems. G. Porcellati, L. Amaducci, C. Galli, Eds.: 317–356. Plenum Press. New York, N.Y.
33. MARION, J. & L. S. WOLFE. 1978. Increase in vivo of unesterified fatty acids, prostaglandin $F_{2\alpha}$ but not thromboxane B_2 in rat brain during drug induced convulsions. Prostaglandins **16**(1): 99–109.
34. CHAPMAN, A., M. INGVAR & B. K. SIESJÖ. 1980. Free fatty acids in the brain in bicuculline-induced status epilepticus. Acta Physiol. Scand. **110:** 335–336.
35. BAZÁN, N. G., S. A. MORELLI DE LIBERTI & E. B. RODRIGUEZ DE TURCO. 1982. Arachidonic acid and arachidonyldiglycerols increase in rat cerebrum during bicuculline-induced status epilepticus. Neurochem. Res. **7**(7): 839–843.
36. SIESJÖ, B. K., M. INGVAR & E. WESTERBERG. 1982. The influence of bicuculline-induced seizures on free fatty acid concentrations in cerebral cortex, hippocampus, and cerebellum. J. Neurochem. **39:** 796–902.
37. WOLFE, L. S. 1982. Short review. Eicosanoids: prostaglandins, thromboxanes, leukotrienes, and other derivates of carbon-20 unsaturated fatty acids. J. Neurochem. **38:** 1–14.

38. WASTERLAIN, C. G. 1974. Inhibition of cerebral protein synthesis by epileptic seizures without motor manifestations. Neurology **175:** 175–180.
39. WASTERLAIN, C. G. 1977. Effects of epileptic seizures on brain ribosomes: mechanism and relationship to cerebral energy metabolism. J. Neurochem. **29:** 707–716.
40. FANDO, J. L., M. CONN & C. G. WASTERLAIN. 1979. Brain protein synthesis during neonatal seizures: an experimental study. Exp. Neurol. **63:** 220–228.
41. KIESSLING, M. & P. KLEIHUES. 1981. Regional protein synthesis in the rat brain during bicuculline-induced epileptic seizures. Acta Neuropathol. Berlin **55:** 157–162.
42. KIESSLING, M., Y. XIE & P. KLEIHUES. 1984. Regional impairment of protein synthesis in the rat brain during biculline-induced seizures. Brain. Res. **296:** 1–13.
43. SIESJÖ, B. K. & A. ABDUL-RAHMAN. 1979. A metabolic basis for the selective vulnerability of neurons in status epilepticus. Acta Physiol. Scand. **106:** 377–378.
44. DWYER, B. & C. G. WASTERLAIN. 1980. Regulation of the first step of the initiation of brain protein synthesis by guanosine diphosphate. J. Neurochem. **34**(6): 1639–1647.
45. LOTHMAN, E. W. & R. C. COLLINS. 1981. Kainic acid induced limbic seizures: metabolic, behavioural, electroencephalographic, and neuropathological correlates. Brain Res. **218:** 299–318.
46. NEVANDER, G., M. INGVAR, R. AUER & B. K. SIESJÖ. 1984. Irreversible brain cell damage after short periods of status epilepticus. Acta Physiol. Scand. **120:** 155–157.
47. NEVANDER, G., M. INGVAR, R. AUER & B. K. SIESJÖ. Status epilepticus in well oxygenated rats causes neuronal necrosis. Ann. Neurol. **18.** (In press.)
48. INGVAR, M., J. FOLBERGROVÁ, G. NEVANDER, R. N. AUER & B. K. SIESJÖ. 1985. Epileptic neuronal damage: selective neuronal necrosis versus hypermetabolic infarction. J. Cereb. Blood Flow Metab. **5**(Suppl. 1): S353–S354.
49. MINARD, F .N. & R. V. DAVIS. 1962. The effects of electroshock on the acid-soluble phosphates of rat brain. J. Biol. Chem. **237:** 1283–1289.
50. SACKTOR, B., J. E. WILSON & C. G. TIEKERT. 1967. Regulation of glycolysis in brain, in situ, during convulsions. J. Biol. Chem. **241**(21): 5071–5075.
51. KING, L. J., O. H. LOWRY, J. V. PASSONNEAU & V. VENSON. 1967. Effects of convulsants on energy reserves in the cerebral cortex. J. Neurochem. **14:** 599–611.
52. FERRENDELLI, J. A. & D. B. MCDOUGAL, JR. 1971. The effect of electroshock on regional CNS energy reserves in mice. J. Neurochem. **18:** 1197–1205.
53. FOLBERGROVÁ, J. 1977. Changes in cyclic AMP and phosphorylase a in mouse cerebral cortex during seizures induced by 3-mercaptopropionic acid. Brain Res. **135:** 337–341.
54. SCHULTZ, V. & J. M. LOWENSTEIN. 1978. The purine nucleotide cycle. Studies of ammonia production and interconversions of adenine and hypoxanthine nucleotides and nucleosides by rat brain in situ. J. Biol. Chem. **253:** 1938–1943.
55. DUNN, A., A. GIUDITTA & N. PAGLIUCA. 1971. The effect of electroconvulsive shock on protein synthesis in mouse brain. J. Neurochem. **18:** 2093–2099.
56. METAFORA, S., M. PERSICO, A. FELSANI, R. FERRAIUOLO & A. GIUDITTA. 1977. On the mechanism of electroshock-induced inhibition of protein synthesis in rabbit cerebral cortex. J. Neurochem. **28:** 1335–1346.
57. COLLINS, R. C., E. W. LOTHMAN & J. W. OLNEY. 1983. Status epilepticus in the limbic system: biochemical and pathological changes. Adv. Neurol. **34:** 277–288.
58. COLLINS, R. C. & J. W. OLNEY. 1983. Focal cortical seizures cause distant thalamic lesions. Science **218:** 177–179.
59. MCINTYRE, D. C., D. NATHANSON & N. EDSON. 1982. A new model of partial status epilepticus based on kindling. Brain Res. **250:** 53–63.
60. INGVAR, M. 1986. Cerebral blood flow and metabolic rate during seizures: relationship to epileptic brain damage. Proc. N.Y. Acad. Sci. (This volume.)
61. SIESJÖ, B. K. 1981. Cell damage in the brain: a speculative synthesis. J. Cereb. Blood Flow Metab. **1:** 155–185.
62. MELDRUM, B. S. 1983. Metabolic factors during prolonged seizures and their relation to nerve cell death. Adv. Neurol. **34:** 261–276.
63. SIESJÖ, B. K. & T. WIELOCH. 1985. Brain injury: neurochemical aspects. *In* Central

Nervous System Trauma—Status Report. D. P. Becker & J. T. Povlishock, Eds.: 513–532. William Byrd Press Inc. Richmond, Va.
64. NADLER, J. V. 1981. Minireview. Kainic acid as a tool for the study of temporal lobe epilepsy. Life Sci. **29:** 2031–2042.
65. COYLE, J. T. 1983. Short review. Neurotoxic action of kainic acid. J. Neurochem. **41**(1): 1–11.
66. ROTHMAN, S. M. 1983. Synaptic activity mediates death of hypoxic neurons. Science **220:** 536–537.
67. ROTHMAN, S. 1984. Synaptic release of excitatory amino acid neurotransmitter mediates anoxic neuronal death. J. Neurosci. **4**(7): 1884–1891.
68. SIMON, R. P., J. H. SWAN, T. GRIFFITHS & B. S. MELDRUM. 1984. Blockade of *N*-methyl-D-aspartate receptors may protect against ischemic damage in the brain. Science **226:** 850–852.
69. WIELOCH, T., O. LINDVALL, P. BLOMQVIST & F. H. GAGE. 1985. Evidence for amelioration of ischemic neuronal damage in the hippocampal formation by lesions of the perforant path. Neurol. Res. **7:** 24–26.
70. WEILOCH, T. Neurochemical correlates to regional selective neuronal vulnerability. Prog. Brain Res. **63.** (In press.)
71. SMITH, M-L., H. THOR & S. ORRENIUS. 1980. Toxic injury to isolated hepatocytes is not dependent on extracellular calcium. Science **213:** 1257–1259.
72. BERRIDGE, M. J. 1979. Modulation of nervous activity by cyclic nucleotides and calcium. *In* The Neurosciences: Fourth Study Program. F. O. Schmitt & F. G. Worden, Eds.: 873–889. MIT Press. Cambridge, Mass.
73. BERRIDGE, M. J. 1984. Review article. Inositol triphosphate and diacylglycerol as sound messengers. Biochem. J. **220:** 345–360.
74. CARAFOLI, E. & M. CROMPTON. 1978. The regulation of intracellular calcium. *In* Membrane Properties: Mechanical Aspects, Receptors, Energetics, and Calcium-Dependence of Transport. F. Bronner & A. Kleinzeller, Eds. **10:** 151–216. Academic Press. New York, N.Y.
75. BORLE, A. B. 1981. Control, modulation, and regulation of cell calcium. Rev. Physiol. Biochem. Pharmacol. **90:** 13–164.
76. RASMUSSEN, H. & D. M. WAISMAN. 1983. Modulation of cell function in the calcium messenger system. Rev. Physiol. Biochem. Pharmacol. **95:** 111–145.
77. WROGEMANN, K. & S. D. J. PENA. 1976. Hypothesis. Mitochondrial calcium overload: a general mechanism for cell-necrosis in muscle disease. Lancet (March 17): 672–674.
78. HEARSE, D. J., S. M. HUMPHREY & G. R. BULLOCK. 1978. The oxygen paradox and the calcium paradox: two facets of the same problem? J. Mol. Cell. Cardiol. **10:** 641–668.
79. SCHANNE, F. A. X., A. B. KANE, E. E. YOUNG & J. L. FABER. 1979. Calcium dependence of toxic cell death: a final common pathway. Science **206:** 700–702.
80. GRIFFITHS, T., M. C. EVANS & B. S. MELDRUM. 1983. Intracellular calcium accumulation in rat hippocampus during seizures induced by bicuculline or L-allylglycine. Neuroscience **10**(2): 385–395.
81. VAN REEMPTS, J., M. HASELDONCKX, M. VAN DE VEN & M. BORGERS. 1984. Morphology and ultrastructural calcium distribution in the rat hippocampus after severe transient ischemia. *In* Cerebral Ischemia. A. Bes, P. Braquet, R. Paoletti & B. K. Siesjö, Eds.: 113–118. Elsevier Science Publishers B.V. Amsterdam, Holland.
82. BEATRICE, M. C., J. W. PALMER & R. P. DOUGLAS. 1980. The relationship between mitochondrial membrane permeability, membrane potential, and the retention of Ca^{2+} by mitochondria. J. Biol. Chem. **255**(18): 8663–8671.
83. EHRLICH, Y. H. 1983. Protein phosphorylation, neuronal receptors, and seizures in the central nervous system. Adv. Neurol. **34:** 345–352.
84. DELORENZO, R. J. 1983. Calcium-calmodulin protein phosphorylation in neuronal transmission: a molecular approach to neuronal excitability and anticonvulsant drug action. Adv. Neurol. **34:** 325–337.
85. SCHLAEPFER, W. W., U.-J. P. ZIMMERMAN & S. MICKO. 1981. Neurofilament proteolysis in rat peripheral nerve. Homologies with calcium-activated proteolysis of other tissues. Cell. Calcium **2:** 235–250.

86. BAUDRY, M. & G. LYNCH. 1980. Regulation of hippocampal glutamate receptors: evidence for the involvement of a calcium-activated protease. Proc. Nat. Acad. Sci. USA **77**(4): 2298–2302.
87. LYNCH, G. & M. BAUDRY. 1984. The biochemistry of memory: a new and specific hypothesis. Science **224:** 1057–1063.
88. KAKIUCHI, S. & K. SOBUE. 1981. Ca^{2+}- and calmodulin-dependent flip-flop mechanism in microtubule assembly-disassembly. FEBS Lett. **132**(1): 141–143.
89. BROWNING, M., M. BAUDRY, W. F. BENNET & G. LYNCH. 1981. Phosphorylation-mediated changes in pyruvate dehydrogenase activity influence pyruvate-supported calcium accumulation by brain mitochondria. J. Neurochem. **36:** 1932–1940.
90. TURNER, R. W., K. G. BAIMBRIDGE & J. J. MILLER. 1982. Calcium-induced long-term potentiation in the hippocampus. Neuroscience **7**(6): 1411–1416.
91. BLISS, T. V. P. & A. C. DOLPHIN. 1982. What is the mechanism of long-term potentiation in the hippocampus? Trends Neurosci. (September): 289–290.
92. SUZKUKI, R., T. YAMAGUCHI, C.-L. LI & I. KLATZO. 1983. The effects of 5-minute ischemia in mongolian gerbils. II. Changes of spontaneous neuronal activity in cerebral cortex and CA1 sector of hippocampus. Acta Neuropathol. Berlin **60:** 217–222.
93. MYERS, R. E. 1979. Lactic acid accumulation as a cause of brain edema and cerebral necrosis resulting from oxygen deprivation. *In* Advances in Perinatal Neurology. R. Korobkin & G. Guilleminaulh, Eds.: 85–114. Spectrum Publishers. New York, N.Y.
94. SIESJÖ, B. K. 1984. Review article. Cerebral circulation and metabolism. J. Neurosurg. **60:** 883–908.
95. PLUM, F. 1983. What causes infarction in ischemic brain? The Robert Wartenberg Lecture. Neurology N.Y. **33:** 222–233.
96. SIESJÖ, B. K. & T. WIELOCH. 1985. Molecular mechanisms of ischemic brain damage: calcium-related events. *In* Cerebrovascular Diseases. F. Plum & W. Pulsinelli, Eds.: 187–197. Raven Press. New York, N.Y.

The Role of the Central Adrenergic System in the Regulation of the Cerebromicrocirculation[a]

Basic and Clinical Implications

EUGENE H. RUBIN, SHELDON H. PRESKORN,[b] AND BOYD K. HARTMAN

Department of Psychiatry
Washington University School of Medicine
4940 Audubon Avenue
St. Louis, Missouri 63110

One of the major difficulties in elucidating mechanisms responsible for psychiatric illnesses is the lack of specific anatomic or biochemical markers. There is recent evidence demonstrating functional abnormalities of the neuroendocrine axis in psychiatrically ill patients, although their specificity for particular illnesses is controversial.[1-3] This neuroendocrine approach measures the effect of a drug on the plasma levels of a hormone: for example, the ability of dexamethasone to suppress plasma cortisol levels. Although theoretically interesting, these tests are indirect measures of central nervous system (CNS) activity.

The development of PET (positron emission tomography) scan technology now allows direct investigation of various dynamic aspects of cerebral functioning in man. For example, methods have been recently developed to measure the percentage of radiolabeled water extracted from CNS capillaries into the brain during a single cerebral transit (extraction fraction of water, E_w).[4] This parameter (E_w) has been intensively examined in experimental animals and has been shown to represent a reproducible measure of membrane and microvascular status. In this paper, we will review animal studies that suggest that measuring the magnitude and responsivity of changes in E_w induced by physiological challenges can be used as an *in vivo* bioassay of central adrenergic activity. Since dysfunction of this and other amine systems has been postulated to be etiologically important in the development of a variety of psychiatric illnesses, (e.g., major affective disorder, panic disorder, and dementia of the Alzheimer's type), PET measurement of E_w could provide a direct test of the functional integrity of this system in these disorders.

Until the 1970s, water was thought to have an E_w of 1.0 (i.e., to be freely permeable through CNS capillaries). In 1974, the existence of a barrier to water extraction was demonstrated in monkeys using external positron detection of cyclotron-produced ^{15}O-water.[5] Not only was water shown to exhibit a permeability limitation across the cerebral capillary, but this membrane barrier to water extraction could be altered by changing neural activity. In the monkey, E_w increased when the locus coeruleus was

[a]This work was in part supported by the following grants from NIMH, MH-40553 and NINCDS, NS-22209 and NS-12311.

[b]Present affiliation: Department of Psychiatry, University of Kansas School of Medicine, 1010 North Kansas, Wichita, Kans. 67214.

stimulated electrically[6] or chemically.[7] Conversely, intraventricular injection of phentolamine (an alpha adrenergic agent) decreased E_w in unstimulated animals,[7] and also was able to reverse chemically induced E_w increases.[8] These observations support the idea that water extraction was actively regulated by a central neurogenic mechanism. Since the locus coeruleus is the major adrenergic nucleus projecting to the cortex and phentolamine is an alpha adrenergic antagonist, the central adrenergic system was implicated in the regulation of this fundamental membrane property of the blood-brain barrier.

The above pharmacologic and physiologic investigations of a role for the central adrenergic system in regulating the cerebral vasculature were initiated because of anatomic evidence suggesting that the central adrenergic system influenced this microvasculature. Using immunohistochemical techniques, adrenergic fibers of central origin were shown to be associated with cerebral microvessels.[9–11] At the electron microscope level, monoamine fibers in the paraventricular nucleus were observed to be in direct contact with cerebral microvessels.[12] Paralleling the anatomical relationship between the peripheral adrenergic system and its target capillary end organs, no specialized synaptic contacts between the central adrenergic fibers and cerebral capillaries were observed. The existence of adrenergic receptors on CNS microvessels[13] coupled with the above anatomy strongly suggests that the adrenergic system directly influences some function(s) of the cerebral capillaries.[11]

Anatomical and physiological characteristics of the central adrenergic system suggest that this system is involved with many homeostatic functions.[14–16] In terms of anatomy, the neuronal cell bodies are located in a few brain stem nuclei, but their axons innervate virtually the entire brain and, therefore, might be expected to exert broad influence on brain function. Electrophysiologically, norepinephrine has a major effect on a cell's responsivity to other chemical or electrical signals.[17,18] At the behavioral level, the central adrenergic system is involved in food and water regulation, sleep cycles, fear response to environmental stimuli, temperature regulation, and attentional processes.[17,18] The central adrenergic system may therefore play a role in psychiatric illnesses which involve abnormalities in many of these behaviors.

The initial physiological and pharmacological studies undertaken to test proposed autonomic regulatory function required external positron detection of cyclotron-produced ^{15}O-water in primates. The feasibility of such studies was limited due to the cost of the equipment, animals, and support personnel, making studies in smaller centers impossible. Hence, a small animal model was developed to test this central autonomic concept further and to permit means of dissecting out the relevent neuroanatomic pathways. Pharmacological studies were also designed to provide an indirect test of whether this system might be involved in neuropsychiatric disorders. The latter involved testing whether treatments that ameliorate naturally occurring forms of such illnesses (e.g., tricyclic antidepressants) or treatments that possibly induce such illnesses (e.g., tetrabenazine) have effects on this autonomic and homeostatic function of the central adrenergic system.

In this small animal technique, the extraction of radiolabeled water is compared to that of radiolabeled butanol, a freely permeable tracer.[19,20] If water were to act as a fully permeable compound, E_w would be 1.0. If water were completely impermeable, E_w would equal 0.

Extraction fraction of any substance is influenced by three variables in accordance with the following equation:[21,22]

$$\ln(1 - E_w) = -P \cdot (S/F)$$

in which P is the permeability coefficient of the substance being tested, such as radiolabeled water; S is the surface area of capillaries; and F is cerebral blood flow (CBF). Hence E_w can be increased by increasing P and/or S or by decreasing CBF or by a combination of these factors. Different physiologic mechanisms may well exist for separately influencing P, S, and CBF. Furthermore, techniques have been developed to permit testing effects of experimental manipulations on each of these three variables separately.

One of the major roles of the autonomic system is regulation of blood pressure (BP). If the central adrenergic system is part of a general autonomic system, then changing BP should influence the central adrenergic system. Since E_w responds to changes in central adrenergic activity, it was hypothesized that BP changes would influence E_w. If an adrenergic dependent relationship between E_w and BP exists, by studying this relationship we will better understand the autonomic role of the central adrenergic system. In addition, BP is an easy condition to change in humans. Therefore, characterizing this system in animals will help set the stage for PET studies in man of the responsivity of E_w to physiological challenges mediated through the central adrenergic system. Hence, we can use this approach to determine the functional integrity of this neural system in a variety of neuropsychiatric illnesses.

Increasing blood pressure was shown to cause a rapid decrease in E_w.[23] This E_w response occurred when BP was increased by metaraminol (a peripheral alpha agonist), angiotensin II (a vasoconstrictor), or bilateral vagotomy. Furthermore, this change in E_w is caused by a decrease in $P \cdot S$, since CBF remained essentially unaltered.

Changing BP influences both the peripheral and central nervous system. In order to show that the central nervous system is specifically involved in these E_w effects, the major afferents carrying BP information to the CNS were lesioned. When cranial nerves 9 and 10 were either surgically lesioned[23] or chemically inactivated,[24] changes in blood pressure no longer lowered E_w. The experiment showed that the decrease in E_w was not the result of increased hydrostatic pressure on the cerebral vessel or a direct pharmacologic effect on the capillary, but was neurogenically mediated, requiring afferent BP information to reach the CNS.

In order to test the role of the central adrenergic system in mediating the E_w response to BP, animals with 6-hydroxydopamine (6OHDA) lesions of their central adrenergic system were examined.[25] The 6OHDA treatment blocked BP-induced E_w changes. Furthermore, pretreatment with phenoxybenzamine, an irreversible alpha adrenergic antagonist, also blocked this response.[25]

The E_w response to BP was shown to have many characteristics of an autonomic system designed to maintain cerebral homeostasis in response to acute changes.[26] It occurred rapidly (within one minute) and was sensitive to small fluctuations in BP (20–60 mmHg). If BP was maintained at an elevated level, E_w gradually normalized (i.e., a new set point was achieved). If BP was acutely increased and then rapidly returned to normal, E_w also rapidly returned to baseline (i.e., the response followed acute changes in BP).

The central pathways that mediate E_w changes to blood pressure are not fully known. In order to further characterize the pathways, we have examined the effect of unilateral blockade of the 9th and 10th cranial nerve afferents on BP-induced E_w changes in various regions.[24] Results from this type of experiment coupled with known anatomic circuitry have led to the hypothesis that BP information from the carotid baroreceptors travels to the ipsilateral nucleus tractus solitarius. Information then bilaterally influences the locus coeruleus. The locus coeruleus projects to the ipsilateral cortex, and the released norepinephrine influences the microvasculature. Many aspects of this hypothesis are directly testable. This approach demonstrates the feasibility of studying the functional anatomy of a CNS response that involves the central adrenergic system when the end organ is known and its response easily quantitated. Coupling physiological, anatomical, and biochemical techniques will allow detailed elaboration of this system.

As work proceeds to understand the relevant anatomical pathways mediating the BP-induced changes in E_w, studies have also been conducted to provide some insight into whether dysregulation of this autonomic system may be clinically relevant to neuropsychiatric disorders. These studies have also provided pharmacological data that are compatible with the concept that one function of the central adrenergic system is to regulate E_w. Of the clinically relevant drugs, the most extensively studied have been those that either treat or induce major affective disorder in man.

Tricyclic antidepressants (TCA) block reuptake of norepinephrine, and these drugs, therefore, should increase E_w. This effect has been demonstrated in both rats and primates.[27,28] The rank order of the different commercially available antidepressants for increasing E_w correlated with their binding affinity for alpha adrenergic receptor, suggesting the importance of the central adrenergic system in mediating this finding.[29] This suggestion was further supported by the finding that E_w was not changed by tricyclics if the animals' adrenergic system had been previously destroyed by 6OHDA.[30] Pretreatment with phenoxybenzamine, an irreversible alpha adrenergic antagonist, also blocked the tricyclic effect.[30] The blockade of TCA-induced changes in E_w by either 6OHDA or phenoxybenzamine pretreatment parallels the effect of these two treatments on the previously described BP-induced changes in E_w. These findings are particulary interesting since TCA increased E_w whereas elevated BP decreased E_w. This suggests that the central adrenergic system is tonically involved in regulating E_w and can regulate it in either direction.

The plasma tricyclic level required to produce these effects was similar to levels seen in patients being treated for affective disorder, suggesting the relevance to humans.[29,31] Unlike their clinical antidepressant effect which requires prolonged exposure (on the order of several weeks), TCA changed E_w within minutes of acute administration. However, this acute effect was short-lived. With chronic administration patterned after the clinical use of the drugs, the effect on E_w became sustained and enhanced. This time course is more compatible with the clinical setting. This phenomenon of chronic treatment producing an enhanced and sustained effect is also consistent with an adrenergic mechanism of action. Antidepressants administered chronically have different CNS effects than when administered one time only.[32,33] Beta and alpha-two adrenergic receptor subsensitivity occurs following chronic, but not acute, treatment. Hence, the much larger changes in E_w that occur in chronically treated animals given an acute challenge may be mediated by these adaptive changes in receptor function or related adaptive changes in other systems.

The chronic experiments described demonstrate an enhanced response with time, an effect consistent with the delayed effectiveness these agents have when used to treat depression. Other treatments for depression were also examined in our model. Mianserin, an antidepressant that may have different mechanisms of action than tricyclics, also increased E_w.[34] Electroconvulsive therapy (ECT), one of the most effective treatments for depression, increased E_w, but only under conditions where blood flow was slow.[35] At higher CBF, ECT actually lowers E_w compared to nontreated controls. (CBF was altered in these experiments by changing the CO_2 content of the inspired air.) Lithium is also an effective antidepressant, especially in patients with bipolar affective disorder. This agent, similar to ECT, increased E_w at low CBF while decreasing it at high flows.[35] In contrast to lithium or ECT, TCA increased E_w throughout the P_aCO_2 range studied (20–80 mmHg). Interestingly, both lithium and ECT are effective treatments for manic episodes, whereas tricyclics are contraindicated during such episodes. Though highly speculative, the E_w effect at low CBF may be related to antidepressant efficacy whereas the blunted E_w at higher flows with ECT and lithium may relate to their efficacy in mania.

Evidence in favor of a relationship between the effect of antidepressants on E_w and antidepressant efficacy includes the results of the chronic treatment study, and the fact that different types of antidepressant treatments share this effect. In addition, all the antidepressant treatments examined increase E_w by increasing $P \cdot S$ as opposed to lowering blood flow. Many other types of treatments for depression exist. Trazodone, buproprion, monoamine oxidase inhibitors, and alprazolam may have different antidepressant mechanisms, and we need to examine these drugs in this system.

In addition to the above antidepressant treatments, other classes of agents have been examined for their effects on E_w and $P \cdot S$. Atropine, phenoxybenzamine, hydroxyzine, and *p*-chloroamphetamine did not change E_w.[29] Interestingly, neuroleptics and benzodiazepines were capable of increasing E_w, but the mechanism involved decreasing CBF; $P \cdot S$ was not influenced.[34]

If antidepressant effects on E_w have some relationship to mechanisms of action of these agents on affective disorder, a relationship between the effect of these drugs on E_w and the effect of these drugs on various animal models of depression should exist. The reversal of various physiological effects of tetrabenazine is a commonly used rodent model for screening various antidepressants. Tetrabenazine decreased E_w especially at higher blood flows.[36] This effect on E_w was reversed by amitriptyline, again consistent with the hypothesis of a relationship between E_w changes and antidepressant efficacy.[36]

OVERVIEW

E_w is a fundamental parameter that reflects several important aspects of cerebral microvascular function. E_w can be precisely measured in experimental animals and can now be measured in humans using PET technology. Anatomical, physiological, and pharmacological evidence strongly suggests that the central adrenergic system plays a major role in mediating changes in E_w. Compelling experimental evidence also indicates that E_w changes reflect changes in central adrenergic activity in response to both physiological and pharmacological variables.

Studies of E_w are just beginning and many questions remain to be addressed. The above working hypothesis concerning the anatomic relationship between the central adrenergic system and E_w needs to be tested further. One approach to this question involves lesioning the locus coeruleus. Lesion studies coupled with quantitative autoradiographic receptor studies will help determine the site(s) of action of the various drug treatments as well as help in clarifying mechanisms of supersensitivity.

The broader question of why E_w is regulated also needs to be addressed. One hypothesis is that this system represents a mechanism for rapid control of fluid fluxes that might otherwise occur with changes in BP. Water is only one of several important compounds whose entry into the CNS probably requires finely tuned neurogenic regulation.

Recent PET scan technology allows measurement of E_w in humans.[4] The work reviewed here suggests that E_w may reflect a central adrenergic activity directly. We, therefore, have the potential to use this approach to safely examine central adrenergic activity in humans with specific CNS illnesses. We also have a small animal technique to measure experimentally induced changes in E_w. This technique can be used to dissect out the possible mechanisms of abnormalities that might be found.

Certain CNS illnesses may involve degeneration of central adrenergic function and, therefore, baseline E_w values may be affected. Senile dementia of the Alzheimer's type would be an example of an illness where a substantial number of patients have degenerating adrenergic and cholinergic systems.[37] Other illnesses such as affective disorder and panic disorder may involve reversible abnormalities in central adrenergic functioning.[38,39] In these illnesses, we may find either reversible changes in baseline E_w or reversible abnormalities in the responsivity of the central adrenergic system to physiological or pharmacological challenges. The responsivity can be examined by challenging the patients with stimuli known to affect E_w such as mild changes in BP or CO_2. Obviously, at this time, many of these proposals are speculative. The purpose of this communication is to familiarize the reader with the clinical potential of a basic, neurobiologic discovery involving extraction of water into the CNS.

ACKNOWLEDGMENTS

The authors gratefully acknowledge Ms. Sylvia Sirkin for manuscript preparation.

REFERENCES

1. CARROL, B. J., M. FEINBERG, J. F. GREDEN, J. TARIKA, A. A. ALBALA, R. F. HASKETT, N. M. JAMES, Z. KRONFOL, N. LOHR, M. STEINER, J. F. DE VIGNE & F. YOUNG. 1981. A specific laboratory test for the diagnosis of melancholia. Arch. Gen. Psychiatry **38:** 15–22.
2. PEPPER, G. M., & D. T. KRIEGER. 1984. Hypothalamic-pituitary-adrenal abnormalities in depression: their possible relation to central mechanisms regulating ACTH release. *In* Neurobiology of Mood Disorders. R. Post & J. Ballenger, Eds.: 539–553. Williams and Wilkins. Baltimore, Md.
3. UHDE, T., L. SIEVER, & R. POST. 1984. Clonidine: acute challenge and clinical trial paradigms for the investigation and treatment of anxiety disorders, affective illness, and pain syndromes. *In* Neurobiology of Mood Disorders. R. Post & J. Ballenger, Eds.: 554–571. Williams and Wilkins. Baltimore, Md.
4. HERSCOVITCH, P., M. RAICHLE, M. KILBOURN & M. WELCH. 1984. Positron emission tomography measurement of cerebral blood flow and water permeability with O-15 water, and C-11 butanol. Soc. Neurosci. Abstr. **10**(Part 2): 792.
5. EICHLING, J. O., M. E. RAICHLE, R. L. GRUBB & M. M. TER POGOSSIAN. 1974. Evidence of the limitations of water as a freely diffusable tracer in brain of the rhesus monkey. Circ. Res. **35:** 358–364.
6. RAICHLE, M. E., J. O. EICHLING, R. L. GRUBB & B. K. HARTMAN. 1976. Central noradrenergic regulation of brain microcirculation. *In* Dynamics of Brain Edema. M. Hanna, H. Papius & W. Feindel, Eds.: 11–17. Springer-Verlag. New York, N.Y.
7. RAICHLE, M. E., B. K. HARTMAN, J. O. EICHLING & L. G. SHARPE. 1975. Central noradrenergic regulation of cerebral blood flow and vascular permeability. Proc. Nat. Acad. Sci. USA **72**(9): 3726–3730.
8. HARTMAN, B. K., L. W. SWANSON, M. E. RAICHLE, H. B. CLARK & S. H. PRESKORN. 1979. Evidence for central adrenergic regulation of cerebral vascular permeability and blood flow. *In* Catecholamines: Basic and Clinical Frontiers. **1:** 450–452. Pergamon Press. New York, N.Y.
9. HARTMAN, B. K. & S. UDENFRIEND. 1972. The application of immunological techniques to the study of enzymes regulating catecholamine synthesis and degradation. Pharmacol. Rev. **24:** 311.
10. HARTMAN, B. K., D. ZIDE & S. UDENFRIEND. 1972. The use of dopamine-β-hydroxylase as a marker for the central noradrenergic nervous system in the rat brain. Proc. Nat. Acad. Sci. USA **69:** 2722–2727.

11. Hartman, B. K. 1973. The innervation of cerebral blood vessels by central noradrenergic neurons. *In* Frontiers in Catecholamine Research. E. Usden & S. H. Snyder, Eds.: 91–96. Pergamon Press. New York, N.Y.
12. Swanson, L. W., M. A. Connelly & B. K. Hartman. 1977. Ultrastructural evidence for central monoaminergic innervation of blood vessels of paraventricular nucleus of the hypothalamus. Brain Res. **136:** 166–173.
13. Harik, S., V. Sharma, J. Wetherbee, R. Warren & S. Banerjee. 1981. Adrenergic and colinergic receptors of cerebral microvessels. J. Cereb. Blood Flow Metab. **1:** 329–338.
14. Hartman, B. K. 1980. Effect of tricyclic antidepressants on cerebral capillary permeability: an action on a fundamental cerebral homeostatic mechanism. *In* The Psychobiology of Affective Disorders. Pfizer Symposium on Depression: 111–129. Karger. Basel, Switzerland.
15. Hartman, B. K., L. W. Swanson, M. E. Raichle, S. H. Preskorn & H. B. Clark. 1980. Central adrenergic regulation of cerebral microvascular permeability and blood flow: anatomic and physiologic evidence. *In* The Cerebral Microvasculature. H. Eisenberg & R. Suddith, Eds.: 113–126. Plenum Press. New York, N.Y.
16. Preskorn, S. H., B. K. Hartman, M. E. Raichle, L. E. Swanson & H. B. Clark. 1981. Central adrenergic regulation of cerebral microvascular permeability and blood flow: pharmacologic evidence. *In* The Cerebral Microvasculature. H. Eisenberg & R. Suddith, Eds.: 127–138. Plenum Press. New York, N.Y.
17. McNaughton, N. & S. Mason. 1980. The neuropsychology and neuropharmacology of the dorsal ascending noradrenergic bundle—a review. Prog. Neurobiol. **14:** 157–219.
18. Van Dongen, P. 1981. The central noradrenergic transmission and the locus coerulus. A review of the data and their implications for neurotransmission and neuromodulation. Prog. Neurobiol. **16:** 117–143.
19. Clark, H. B., B. K. Hartman, M. E. Raichle, S. H. Preskorn & K. B. Larson. 1981. Measurement of cerebral vascular extraction fraction in the rat using intracarotid injection techniques. Brain Res. **208:** 322–323.
20. Clark, H. B., B. K. Hartman, M. E. Raichle, S. H. Preskorn & K. B. Larson. 1982. An intravenous technique for the measurement of cerebral vascular extraction fraction in the rat. J. Cereb. Blood Flow Metab. **2**(2): 187–196.
21. Crone, C. 1963. The permeability of capillaries in various organs as determined by use of the "indicator diffusion" method. Acta Physiol. Scand. **58:** 292–305.
22. Renkin, E. M. 1959. Transport of potassium-42 from blood to tissue in isolated mammalian skeletal muscles. Am. J. Physiol. **197:** 1205–1210.
23. Ling, R. T. K., B. K. Hartman & H. B. Clark. 1984. Hypertension induced changes in cerebral capillary permeability to water are mediated by afferent neuronal connections from the carotid sinus to the brain. Brain Res. **308:** 301–308.
24. Rubin, E. H. & B. K. Hartman. 1984. Right and left sided baroreceptor afferents each convey blood pressure information to both sides of cortex. Soc. Neurosci. Abstr. **10**(Part 2): 832.
25. Ling, R. T. K., B. K. Hartman, R. E. Schmidt, E. H. Rubin & H. B. Clark. Hypertension induced changes in cerebral capillary permeability to water are mediated by a central adrenergic mechanism. (In preparation.)
26. Ling, R. T. K., B. K. Hartman & H. B. Clark. Characterizations of the changes in cerebral capillary permeability of water induced by hypertension. Brain Res. (Submitted.)
27. Preskorn, S. & B. K. Hartman. 1979. The effect of tricyclic antidepressants on cerebral fluid mechanics. Biol. Psychiatry **14:** 235–250.
28. Preskorn, S. H., M. E. Raichle & B. K. Hartman. 1982. Antidepressants alter cerebrovascular permeability and metabolic rate in primates. Science **217:** 250–252.
29. Preskorn, S. H., B. K. Hartman, M. E. Raichle & H. B. Clark. 1980. The effects of dibenzapines (tricyclic antidepressants) on cerebral capillary permeability in the rat *in vivo.* J. Pharmacol. Exp. Ther. **213**(2): 313–320.
30. Preskorn, S. H., B. K. Hartman, G. H. Irwin & C. W. Hughes. 1982. Role of the central adrenergic system in mediating amitriptyline-induced alteration in the mammalian blood-brain barrier *in vivo.* J. Pharmacol. Exp. Ther. **223**(2): 388–395.

31. PRESKORN, S., B. K. HARTMAN & H. B. CLARK. 1980. Long-term antidepressant treatment. Alterations in cerebral capillary permeability. Psychopharmacology **70:** 1–4.
32. SUGRUE, M. 1981. Current concepts of the mechanism of action of antidepressant drugs. Pharmacol. Ther. **13:** 219–247.
33. SULSER, F. 1982. Antidepressant drug research: its impact on neurobiology and psychobiology. *In* Typical and Atypical Antidepressants: Molecular Mechanism. E. Costa & G. Racagni, Eds.: 1–20, Raven Press. New York, N.Y.
34. SCHWARTZMAN, J., S. PRESKORN, T. KENT, S. GOLDBERG & R. GLOTZBACH. 1983. Effects of different classes of psychopharmaceuticals on cerebral capillary permeability and blood flow. Soc. Neurosci. Abstr. **9:** 157.
35. PRESKORN, S. H., G. H. IRWIN, S. SIMPSON, D. FORESEN, J. RINNE & G. JERKOVICH. 1981. Medical therapies for mood disorders alter blood-brain barrier. Science **223:** 469–471.
36. PRESKORN, S. H., T. A. KENT, R. K. GLOTZBACH, G. H. IRWIN & J. V. SOLNICK. 1984. Cerebromicrocirculatory defects in animal model of depression. Psychopharmacology **84:** 196–199.
37. BONDAREFF, W., C. Q. MOUNTJOY & M. ROTH. 1982. Loss of neurons of origin of the adrenergic projection to cerebral cortex (nucleus locus ceruleus) in senile dementia. Neurology **32:** 164–168.
38. SCHILDKRAUT, J. 1965. The catecholamine hypothesis of affective disorders: a review of the supporting evidence. Am. J. Psychiatry **122:** 509–522.
39. REDMOND, D. E. & Y. H. HUANG. 1979. New evidence for a locus-coeruleus-norepinephrine connection with anxiety. Life Sci. **25:** 2149–2162.

Neurophysiology of Electroconvulsive Therapy[a]

Discussion of Part IV

ISAK PROHOVNIK

Department of Biological Psychiatry
New York State Psychiatric Institute
and
Department of Psychiatry
College of Physicians and Surgeons
Columbia University
722 West 168 Street
New York, New York 10032

The five papers in this session are concerned with diverse issues. The first deals with electrical stimulus parameters, the second with adrenergic regulation of the blood-brain barrier and related effects, and the third describes acute changes of cerebral metabolism and blood flow in relation to neuropathological sequelae of status epilepticus. The last two papers address the mechanisms and extent of permanent brain damage following prolonged seizures. Hence, these papers represent a progression from an examination of the treatment/organism interface, through a substantial part of the treatment effects on brain function and environment and to the possibility of iatrogenic damage.

Weaver and Williams discuss the nature of the electrical ECT (electroconvulsive therapy) stimulus. Their emphasis on the scarcity of available information is noteworthy: few other somatic treatment modalities have been successfully employed for 50 years with so little attention to the equivalents of dose-response curves and kinetics studies. Superficially, the problem appears simple: compared to the complexity and flexibility of biochemical systems, electrical systems are fully described by a small number of variables and a small set of completely understood equations. Yet little progress has been made in the understanding of the electrical properties of different forms of ECT, their interactions with tissue, and the resulting implications for the design and administration of ECT. The difficulty is associated precisely with the fact that we are dealing with a biological electrical system: it is the interaction between the treatment stimulus and the tissue, and the ultimate clinical response of the patient, that introduce complexities beyond those usually encountered in electrical circuit design.

Weaver and Willams discuss various instruments, and the influence of electrical parameters such as voltage, current, and pulse width on the probability of eliciting a generalized seizure. They also provide data on the effectiveness of certain parameter combinations, assuming that an effective stimulus will elicit a seizure at the lowest energy level. The authors conclude with a list of proposed known facts and necessary questions, and caution against premature closure and overgeneralization.

The work conducted and reviewed by these authors represents a substantial

[a]This work was partially supported by National Institute of Mental Health Grant MH 35636.

fraction of what is currently believed about the electrical properties of ECT. For purposes of integration with this session and with the other parts of the volume, several other aspects need to be raised. Perhaps the major one refers to the need to inspect electrical theory with greater emphasis on clinical aims. For instance, most of the work reported here by Weaver and Williams is based on the elicitation of a seizure as the criterion for stimulus effectiveness. This reflects a widely held conjecture: the elicitation of a generalized seizure is a necessary and sufficient condition for the clinical efficacy of ECT, whereas higher supraliminal electrical energy levels increase the undesirable side effects without contributing to clinical response. Thus, the ideal ECT would elicit a generalized seizure with minimal electrical energy, and all other parameters are means to this end. This conjecture is now challenged by recent findings. As detailed elsewhere in this volume, elicitation of generalized seizure does not ensure clinical response, nor are side effects solely determined by electrical energy. Although a generalized seizure does appear necessary for clinical response, its elicitation is insufficient for the definition of successful treatment. Clinical efficacy and severity of side effects must be considered.

Weaver and Williams do not distinguish between simulation experiments, animal studies, and clinical research in the area of ECT parameters. An examination of the literature reveals, however, an extreme paucity of the first two types of the work, and the little that has been done is not recent. It is unclear why most recent research on electrical parameters has been attempted in a clinical setting. This is understandable if ultimate clinical response is used as a criterion, but not if seizure elicitation is the goal. Another distinction that may be useful is related to the anatomical and conceptual locus of effect. As mentioned above, electrical theory is explicitly understood and easily applied to the stumulus-generating apparatus; the complications are introduced by interactions with biological tissue. Even before the current reaches tissue, however, it is conducted by the electrode paste and modified by its interface with the skin. The current then heavily interacts with scalp, muscle, and bone before reaching the brain. Many of the relevant parameters can be manipulated and investigated much more effectively by simulations and animal studies, and systematic study of the possible effects at each stage of the current path appears indicated. Yet there have been very few pertinent studies. Basic processes, such as the decrease of impedance with increasing voltage, are poorly understood, as are the contributions of treatment techniques (electrode size, nature of coupling medium, etc.). Moreover, it is well established that human depression responds to a series of ECTs, and that there are gradual electrical changes during a course of treatment, such as an increase of seizure threshold. These processes have not been adequately addressed in either simulation or animal studies. One is, thus, inclined to agree with Weaver and Williams' call for further research, but I am inclined to propose that such research be extended in two directions: more clinically relevant human studies on the one hand (e.g., the papers by Malitz *et al.* and Weiner *et al.* in this volume) and more basic animal studies on the other hand. Such basic studies should consider the properties of the human head in greater detail than so far achieved, and examine individual components of the circuit formed during ECT.

Whereas Weaver and Williams write specifically about ECT technology without reference to the therapeutic effects, the paper by Rubin *et al.* presents almost an opposite perspective. These authors are not concerned with the specific properties and techniques of ECT. Rather, they include ECT in a long list of manipulations that share the ability to modify both affective disorders and central adrenergic tone, as reflected in the extraction fraction of water, E_w. These authors have examined a large number of pharmacological, physiological, and clinical interventions that were thought to exert some influence on the central adrenergic system, and found effects on E_w. This empirical relationship between affective properties and E_w effects supports the common assumption of adrenergic involvement in affective disorders and their treatment, and provides another possible biological indicator for adrenergic tone, and perhaps of neural mechanisms related to affective disorders.

It is unfortunate that ECT actually yields results less clear than tricyclic antidepressants (TCA) from this viewpoint. Rubin *et al.* report that ECT increased E_w at hypocapnia, but reduced E_w during hypercapnia. The authors relate this difference to different cerebral blood flow levels, rather than the P_aCO_2 levels, and offer the speculation that the two effects may somehow be related to the effectiveness of ECT in mania. Support for this suggestion is offered from the similar effects of lithium. ECT is not further examined here, thus leaving a few questions unanswered. Most obviously, ECT apparently changed the slope of the E_w/CO_2 correlation. Does this really represent two opposite effects, dichotomously organized, as the authors seem to suggest, or is this the result of a continuous readjustment of another variable? Their description of the results appears consistent with a single effect, i.e., an increased sensitivity of E_w to P_aCO_2 following ECT. A discussion of the other cerebrovascular consequences of ECT, relevant for this point, is provided in other papers of this volume. The authors discuss the different effects of acute and chronic TCA administration, but do not examine this relationship for ECT. Furthermore, as the authors indicate, the relevance of most of this work to human clinical conditions is still obscure: the work has been performed on animal models, and we must await results in human patients.

The next three papers in this session constitute an examination of the possibility of tissue damage due to ECT. Since seizures are known to represent hypermetabolic and hyperemic states, it is not surprising that a consideration of possible causes of damage should start with investigations of cerebral blood flow (CBF) and metabolism in epilepsy. Additionally, it is sensible to examine a condition representing the highest likelihood of damage, and then look for similar effects in the relatively benign conditions of ECT.

Ingvar reviews a series of experiments on local cerebral blood flow and metabolism during and after prolonged seizures, and pathological examinations of neuronal loss. Several major conclusions emerge from this work. First, there appears to be a threshold of duration for damage to occur: in well-oxygenated rats, status epilepticus of at least 25–30 minutes is required for any neuronal necrosis to be detectible, and more prolonged seizures are necessary for widespread neuronal cell loss. Second, the intense ictal increases of metabolism are heterogenously represented in the brain, whereas blood flow increases in this preparation appear more diffuse. Thus, rather than a state of relative ischemia, luxury perfusion is more likely. The increases of blood flow are at least matched to the metabolic increases, and often exceed them. Ischemia cannot be invoked to explain tissue damage, nor can hypoxia in well-oxygenated animals. Third, substantial increases of metabolism appear a necessary, but not sufficient, condition for tissue damage. Assuming that these results can be generalized to the clinical human ECT, they imply that permanent tissue damage cannot occur from modern ECT, in which seizures typically last 30–150 seconds in well-oxygenated patients. Finally, Ingvar reviews some evidence that the postictal flow reductions are coupled to a similar postictal metabolic suppression; this evidence is important for interpretation of the human regional CBF results reported in another section of this volume. The neurochemical mechanisms of cell damage due to status epilepticus are discussed in detail by Siesjö *et al.* Three mechanisms are proposed, involving calcium influx, interaction with excitatory amino acids (chiefly glutamate), and acidosis.

Meldrum reviews the literature on neuropathological sequelae of induced seizures, and concludes that there is no evidence that modern ECT could cause structural brain lesions. He does not provide numerical estimates of mortality and morbidity, but states that hazards appear less than those of other minor procedures with general anesthesia.

The last three papers, taken together, demonstrate the extremely low probability that structural brain damage can be found after modern ECT administration. The treatment is not completely devoid of undesirable side effects: other papers in this volume suggest that there is a disruption of memory processes following a course of ECT, which may be reversible, and that such side effects may be related to electrical ECT parameters as described by Weaver and Williams. These side effects may be related to ECT effects on protein synthesis, mentioned both by Siesjö and Meldrum, and such transient and subtle effects would not be revealed by routine neuropathological studies.

This reviewer would conclude that the search for permanent structural brain alterations following modern ECT should now be terminated. There is an important distinction between gross structural damage, as revealed by routine neuropathology or *in vivo* computed tomography (CT) scans, and functional changes of a more subtle nature. Traditionally, the search for brain damage following ECT was concerned with gross morphological tissue necrosis. Since there is no empirical evidence of such effects in human patients, as reviewed by Meldrum, and since our current data from animal studies strongly suggest that modern ECT is far from approaching conditions that cause structural brain damage in rodents, the price of such investigations and their very low likelihood of positive results suggest that they are inefficient, as mentioned by Meldrum. Future investigations would appear to have a greater productivity if directed at the more functional effects of ECT. Thus, the possibility of neurochemical and neurophysiological changes of brain function may better correlate with the suggested cognitive side effects than the structural brain damage that has failed to be documented.

We are still far from understanding the origin and propagation of ECT-induced seizures as a function of their electrical properties and electrode placement. Furthermore, these seizures exert local influence on cellular processes; those should be investigated. Finally, the processes that terminate the seizures, and the immediate postictal period, may offer vital insights into the mechanisms of action and the side effects of ECT. Perhaps the primary insight to be gained from this session involves the emerging emphasis on the interaction of ECT with the functioning brain, and the numerous physiological systems affected by this treatment. A convergence of research techniques and conceptual directions will hopefully lead to a coherent theoretical framework in the future.

Acute and Late Effects of Electroconvulsive Therapy[a]

Clinical Outcome, Regional Cerebral Blood Flow, and Electroencephalogram

PETER SILFVERSKIÖLD,[b] LARS GUSTAFSON,[b]
JARL RISBERG,[b] AND INGMAR ROSÉN[c]

[b]*Department of Psychiatry*
[c]*Department of Clinical Neurophysiology*
University Hospital
University of Lund
S-221 85 Lund, Sweden

INTRODUCTION

Electroconvulsive therapy (ECT) is generally accepted as the superior treatment in severe depression. In spite of little evidence of persistent negative effects it is mainly the transitory acute side effects and fear of possible brain damage that are of concern among professionals and laymen.

The degree of generalization of electrically induced seizures is likely to be an important factor in the understanding of the positive and negative effects related to electrode placement and current characteristics.[1] Thus bilateral (BL) ECT is known to cause more posttreatment confusion and amnesia than the nondominant (ND) unilateral (UL) technique.[2] As to possible differences in therapeutic effect of right ND UL and BL ECT there are equivocal opinions. There is empirical support in favor of BL treatment,[3] at least in the beginning of a series, but in other reports the two techniques have been found to be therapeutically equivalent.[4–6]

One method in the study of acute and late effects of ECT on the brain is measurement of cerebral blood flow (CBF). During seizures Brodersen *et al.* found a twofold increase of CBF and cerebral oxygen consumption,[7] while Kety *et al.* found a marked (35%) decrease postictally within 15 minutes after treatment.[8] Wilson *et al.* found a small, nonsignificant CBF decrease from before to after an ECT series.[9] Before treatment, depressed patients have been found to have a normal flow level and distribution,[10–12] in contrast to the findings of Mathew *et al.*, who reported a decreased flow.[13,14]

Fink and Weiner have reviewed the effects of ECT on the electroencephalogram (EEG).[15,16] One of the main findings is an increase in amplitude and a building up of slow waves during the treatment series generally reversible within one month.[17,18]

[a]This investigation was supported by grants from "Förenade Liv," Mutual Group Life Insurance Company, Stockholm, Sweden, Svenska Läkaresällskapet, the Swedish Society of Medical Sciences, Svenska Livförsäkringsbolags Nämnd för Medicinsk Forskning, the Medical Research Council of the Swedish Life Insurance Companies, the Sjöbring Foundation, Lund University Funds, and the Swedish Medical Research Council (projects No. 3950, 4939, and 4803).

A main purpose of this investigation was to study the immediate as well as the long-term effects of single and serial BL or right ND UL ECT on cerebral functions as measured by clinical evaluation, psychometric testing (not reported here), regional cerebral blood flow (rCBF), and EEG.

MATERIAL

Thirty-two inpatients (15 men, 17 women, mean age 60 ± 14 years) referred for ECT were studied. ND UL ECT is the standard mode of treatment at our psychiatric clinic, but it was decided to give BL ECT during a limited period of time to enable a comparison between the two techniques. The diagnoses according to DSM III[19] are shown in TABLE 1.

Most patients belonged to the category of major depression and bipolar disorder. The patients had not received ECT within 12 months prior to the investigation except for one case who relapsed and was treated again with BL ECT after 6 months. All patients reported right-handedness. Patients with neurological deficits, chronic psychosis, or addiction were excluded from the study. Two patients with bipolar disorder were on prophylactic lithium medication during the trial, and two more bipolar patients were put on lithium after completion of the ECT series. Tricyclic antidepressants, barbiturates, and benzodiazepines were not used during the ECT series. When needed, lower doses of other tranquilizers such as Dixyrazine and/or hypnotics were given.

TABLE 1. DSM III Diagnosis in Patients Treated with Unilateral or Bilateral ECT

	Unilateral ECT Group	Bilateral ECT Group
Bipolar disorder—depressed	3	1
Atypical bipolar disorder (bipolar II)	6 (3)[a]	2
Major depression		
Single episode	3 (2)	1
Recurrent	10 (7)	4
Dysthymic disorder		1
Atypical depression	2 (1)	
Atypical somatoform disorder	1	
Atypical psychosis		1
	25 (13)	10

[a]Numbers in parentheses are patients including results from EEG.

Results will be presented from two parts of the material.

Material I

The total material ($n = 36$). Based on type of ECT the sample was divided in two groups:

1. UL ECT group: 25 patients (13 men, 12 women), 25 ECT series, age 57.6 ± 13.9 years (range 33–83).

2. BL ECT group: 10 patients (4 men, 6 women), 11 ECT series, age 64.7 ± 13.2 years (range 37–78). One woman was treated twice with a six-month interval. This woman and 2 of the men in the BL ECT group had been treated with UL ECT during an earlier depressive episode and are therefore present in both groups. The data are thus based on 25 series of UL and 11 series of BL ECT in 32 patients.

Material II

A subgroup of patients from the total ECT group in which EEG recordings were made. The group included the total BL ECT group and 13 patients (4 men, 9 women) of the UL ECT group. The mean age of this latter group was 63.6 ± 11.6 years (range 44–83).

Results including EEG will be presented from these two groups put together, thus 24 ECT series in 23 patients.

METHODS

The patients were examined immediately before and one to two hours after ECT on three different occasions during the ECT series; ECT 1, ECT 3 or 4 (ECT 3–4), and ECT 5, 6, or 7 (ECT 5–7) and at follow-up within three months and four to nine months after the ECT series.

A conventional *ECT* apparatus (Siemens Convulsator 622) and procedure were used. The electrode placement was either bifrontotemporal (BL ECT) or right ND UL as described by d'Elia.[4] Atropine, methohexital, and a muscle relaxant were used during brief narcosis.

The *clinical psychiatric evaluation* was made by one of the authors (P.S.) during a semistructured interview using specially designed rating scales. The rating scales contained 38 reported and 28 observed symptoms. These were described in two dimensions: frequency (seven steps) and intensity (four steps). A factor analysis was made on ratings from 117 psychiatric inpatients suffering from depression, mania, or anxiety neurosis. Factor analysis of observed variables presented seven factors with eigenvalues above 1.0 explaining 74% of the variance. The seven factors and the items with a factor loading above 0.35 are presented in TABLE 2.

The factors, *depression-retardation* and *self-depreciation,* describe two important aspects of the melancholic syndrome—the mental and motoric retardation and self-depreciation including symptoms of ambivalence and introverted aggression such as worthlessness and suicidal thoughts. Two factors, *anxiety-agitation* and *vegetative anxiety,* describe different expressions of emotional and vegetative anxiety. The *confusion* factor focused on symptoms of cognitive impairment. The *manic* factor included elated mood, lack of judgment, and motoric expressions of the manic state. The *aggression-restlessness* factor contained symptoms of extraverted aggression and restlessness.

Based on factor scores from the 117 patients mentioned above, a standardized normal distribution scale could be estimated (FIGURE 2). The factor scores were used for clinical description and for correlations with rCBF values. In this presentation, four factors (*depression-retardation, self-depreciation, anxiety-agitation,* and *confusion*) were used for this purpose.

rCBF was measured during rest in 16 regions of each hemisphere by the ^{133}Xe inhalation technique.[20,21] A detailed description of the measurement system (NDSinhalation-cerebrograph) and the methods of curve analysis are presented elsewhere.[22] In the present study the initial slope index (ISI)[21] will be used. This index of mainly grey matter blood flow was selected due to its high reliability. The ISI flow values are presented as absolute values or as relative distribution values (regional values in percent of the mean of all regions). Arterial CO_2 pressure (pCO_2) was estimated from end-tidal values of expired CO_2 concentrations.

Routine EEG recordings were carried out with a Siemens-Elema electroencephalograph. A quantitative frequency analysis of the EEG from four channels was made on each occasion using a fast Fourier transform (FFT) aligorithm. From the FFT spectra, the total EEG power (PW) within the frequency range of 0.5–25 Hz was automatically calculated as well as the proportions of power within the delta (0.5–4 Hz), theta (4.1–8 Hz), alpha (8.1–13 Hz), and beta (13.1–25 Hz) bands (%). From these values the power within each frequency band was calculated. The effects of ECT on spectrum analysis EEG in one depressed patient are shown in FIGURE 1.

TABLE 2. Factor Analysis of Psychiatric Symptoms

1. *Depression-Retardation.* Reduced motor tempo Decreased motor activity Depressed facial expression Reduced speech tempo Raters' estimation of depression	3. *Manic.* Raters' estimation of mania Lack of judgement Reduced insight Manic glance Increased speech tempo Increased motor tempo	5. *Aggression-Restlessness.* Extraverted aggression Increased motor tempo Restlessness
2. *Self-Depreciation.* Introverted aggression Self-depreciation Raters' estimation of depression	4. *Anxiety-Agitation.* Anxious facial expression Tense, jerky movements Raters' estimation of anxiety Anxious, roving glance Anxious speech Anxious posture Restlessness Vegetative symptoms	6. *Vegetative Anxiety.* Vegetative symptoms Increased speech tempo
		7. *Confusion.* Spatial disorientation Temporal disorientation Reduced ability to understand questions Amnesia for names (well-known persons) Incoherence Inability to give adequate answers

A low-frequency power index (LFPI, 0.5–8 Hz) and a high-frequency power index (HFPI, 8.1–25 Hz) were used with the EEG before ECT 1 taken as a baseline. In this report the sums of the EEG power from each of the four EEG channels have been used in the analysis. Also the frequency of EEG activity within each frequency band having the highest power values was automatically calculated. The peak frequency of the dominant EEG activity (DF) was calculated as an average of the four recorded EEG channels.

RESULTS

Clinical Outcome

The general impression was that ECT had a satisfactory antidepressant effect in this patient group. In only one patient the depressive symptoms did not respond to ECT

(14 BL treatments) and permanent hospitalization was required. Complete recovery was not achieved in seven patients but a major improvement had occurred permitting discharge from the hospital. FIGURE 2 illustrates the mean clinical course of the patients during ECT as described by the scores of four psychiatric factors.

A progressive recovery is illustrated by the decrease of mean factor scores during the ECT series. The decrease in factor score from pre-ECT 1 to pre-ECT 3–4 was significant ($p < 0.05$) for the self-depreciation factor and close to significant for the depression-retardation factor but nonsignificant for the two remaining factors. From pre-ECT 1 to the first follow-up (usually within the first week after completed ECT

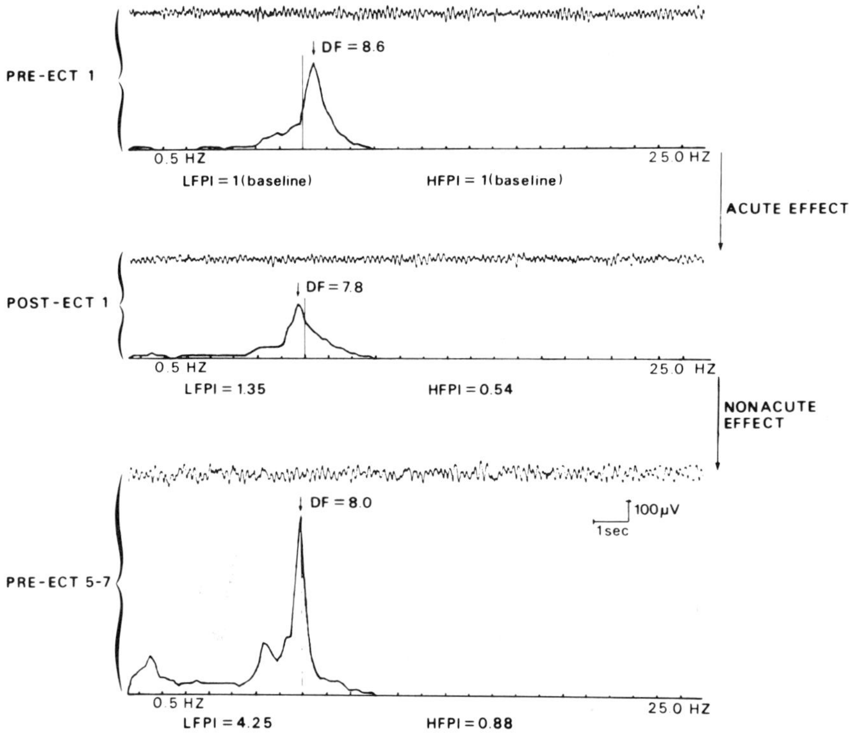

FIGURE 1. ECT effects on spectrum analysis EEG in one depressed patient. Original EEG and FFT analysis records (C3-P3) from one patient pre- and post-ECT 1 and pre-ECT 5–7. Note acute leftward shift of the peak frequency (DF) following ECT 1 and increase of LFPI pre-ECT 5–7 as compared to pre- and post-ECT 1.

series) all four factors had decreased significantly (*depression-retardation* $p < 0.001$; *self-depreciation* $p < 0.001$; *anxiety-agitation* $p < 0.01$; *confusion* $p < 0.05$).

rCBF

The mean hemispheric flow level and distribution in the depressed patients before treatment and in a healthy male reference group[23] are presented in FIGURE 3.

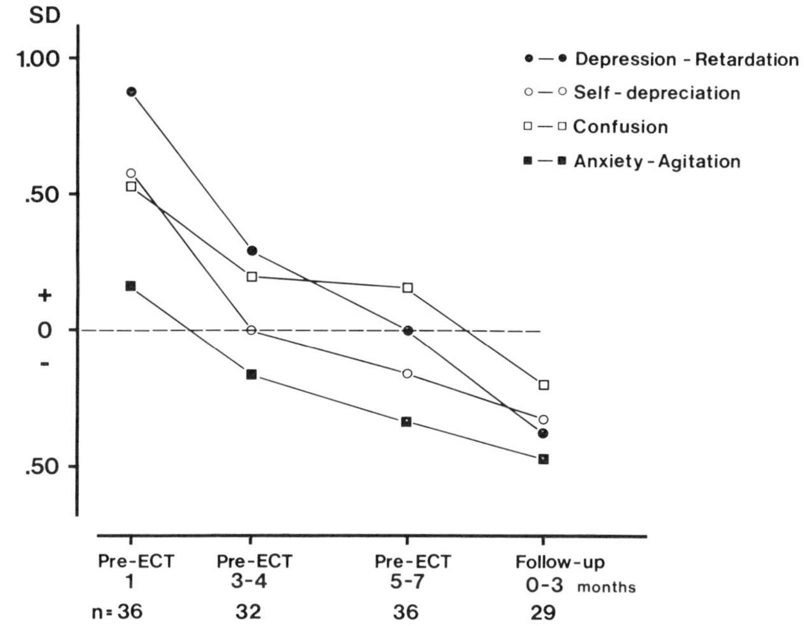

FIGURE 2. Changes in factor scores during ECT in depression (standardized normal distribution).

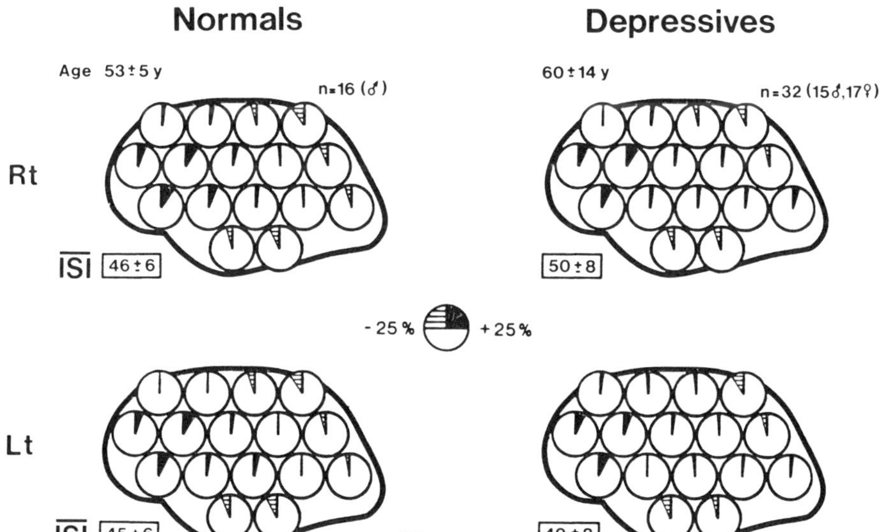

FIGURE 3. rCBF values (ISI) of the right (Rt) and left (Lt) hemispheres in male normals ($n = 16$) and depressives ($n = 32$). The mean hemispheric flow values are shown in the squares. The clock symbols indicate the regional variation from the mean hemispheric flow values. Black means above, hatched means below the mean hemispheric flow value; 90° indicates a 25% deviation from the mean hemispheric value.

TABLE 3. rCBF in 15 Male Patients with Depression and in a Reference Group Matched for Age and Sex

	Age	rCBF (mean)
Depressives	53.9 ± 13.6	48.4 ± 4.5
Reference group	53.1 ± 12.5	45.1 ± 5.0
t-Test one-tailed	NS	$p < 0.05$
pCO_2 correlation		

The flow level of the depressed group was higher than that of the reference group. The differences were close to significant (right $p = 0.09$; left $p = 0.06$). To further control for effects of age and sex, 15 male patients from the depressed group were compared to an age- and sex-matched reference group.

As shown in TABLE 3, the flow level was significantly higher in the depressed group ($p < 0.05$).

Before treatment, the depressed group showed a normal rCBF distribution (FIGURE 3) similar to that of the reference group.

The acute and prolonged effects of UL and BL ECT on the hemispheric mean rCBF are illustrated in FIGURE 4.

UL ECT

ECT 1 and ECT 3–4 were accompanied by a significant flow decrease of about 6%, which was more pronounced in the right than in the left hemisphere (ECT 1: right $p < 0.01$, left $p < 0.05$; ECT 3–4: right $p < 0.001$, left $p < 0.01$). A smaller but similar

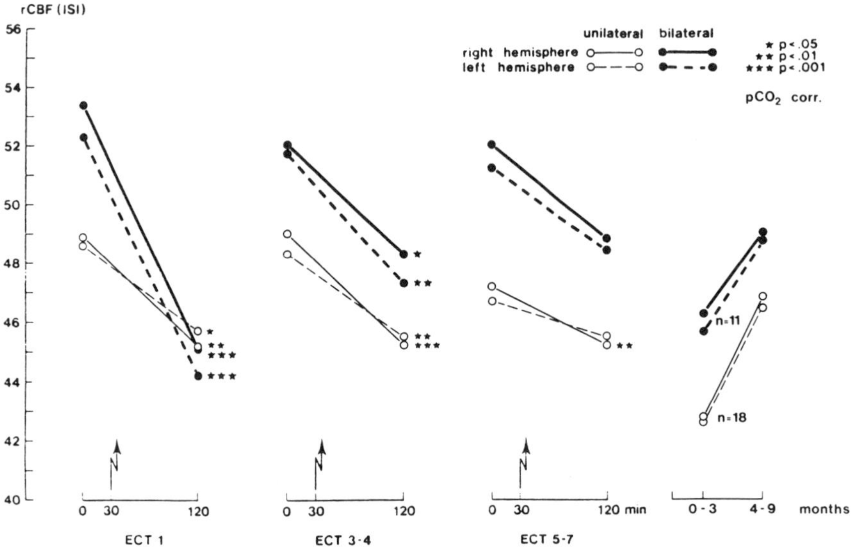

FIGURE 4. Changes of mean rCBF (ISI) following unilateral ($n = 25$) and bilateral ($n = 11$) ECT and at follow-up.

change was seen following ECT 5–7 [right $p < 0.01$, left not significant (NS)]. Before ECT 3–4 and ECT 5–7 the flow level tended to return to the pretreatment level. The patients ($n = 18$) at the first follow-up (0–3 months) showed a significantly lower flow level (86%, both hemispheres $p < 0.001$) than pre-ECT. Four to nine months after the ECT series, the flow level of the 13 patients studied was about 96% (NS) of the pretreatment level. CO_2 pressure showed a small but consistent increase from pre- to post-ECT on all three ECT occasions, being significant ($p < 0.01$) on the third occasion.

The pretreatment regional flow distribution showed the normal hyperfrontal pattern (FIGURE 2). FIGURE 5 shows the acute effects of ECT on the flow distribution values.

The flow decreases following UL ECT were most marked and significant in frontal areas and on the right side. These acute regional changes became less marked towards the end of the ECT series.

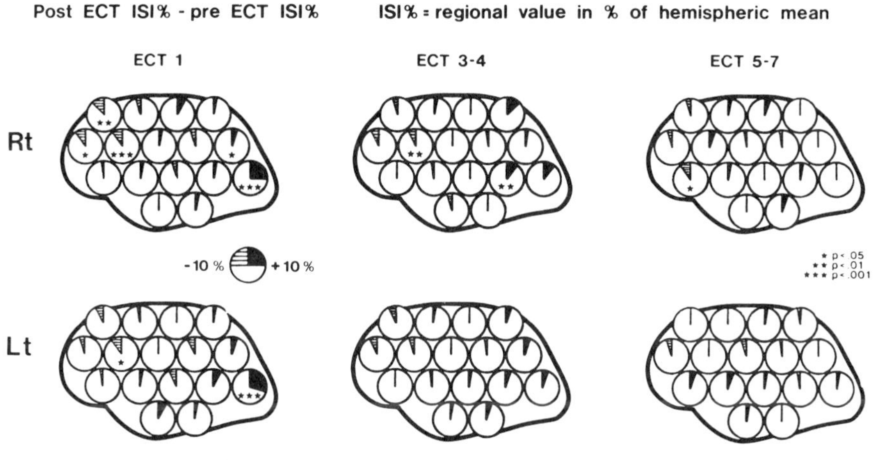

FIGURE 5. Changes of rCBF distribution during unilateral ECT ($n = 25$). The clock symbols indicate the regional values in percent (ISI%) of the hemispheric mean. Post-ECT minus pre-ECT (ISI%); 90° indicates a 10% deviation from the hemispheric mean value.

BL ECT

The pretreatment flow level of the BL group (FIGURE 4) was somewhat higher (ISI: right 4.5 NS; left 3.7 NS) than that of the UL. The flow reduction post-ECT 1 was symmetrical and about twice the size of that of the UL group (both hemispheres $p < 0.01$). The tendency of the flow level to return to the pretreatment level before ECT 3–4 and ECT 5–7 was similar to the findings in the UL group. At the posttreatment follow-up within three months, the mean hemispheric rCBF was about 88% of the pretreatment level (both hemispheres $p < 0.01$). Ten of the patients were examined also 4–9 months after the ECT series, and by then the flow level was about 94% (NS) of the pretreatment level.

The changes of the regional flow distribution following BL ECT are shown in FIGURE 6.

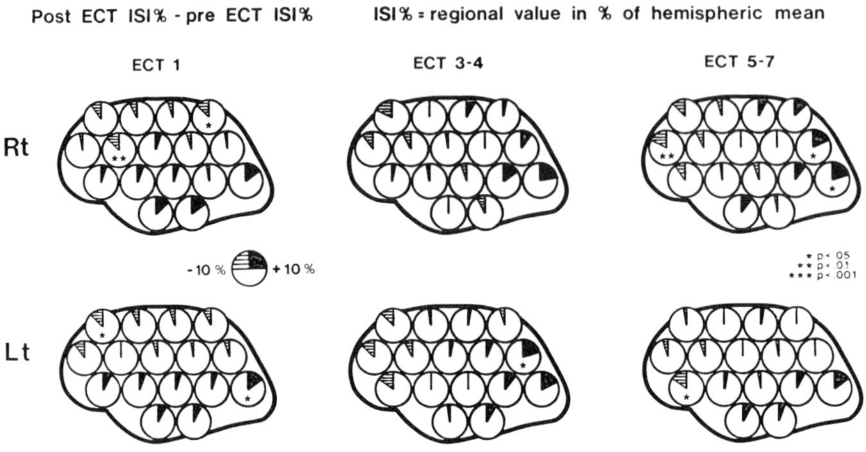

FIGURE 6. Changes of rCBF distribution during bilateral ECT (n = 11). Symbols as in FIGURE 5.

The rCBF changes following BL ECT were similar to those following UL ECT. The most marked flow decreases were found in the upper frontal areas with a tendency to be more marked on the right side following ECT 5–7.

Psychiatric Factors and rCBF

The correlations between the standardized factor scores in four psychiatric factors (*depression-retardation, self-depreciation, anxiety-agitation,* and *confusion*) and rCBF before treatment are presented in TABLE 4.

There were positive correlations between all four factors and the mean rCBF of both hemispheres reaching a significant level for all but the *anxiety-agitation* factor.

EEG

Before treatment the patients by and large had a normal EEG. With increasing number of treatments there was a progressive slowing of the EEG. The changes of EEG and CBF following single electroconvulsive treatments were considered more acute effects whereas the pretreatment EEG and CBF from one ECT occasion to the other were interpreted as prolonged, nonacute effects. These acute and nonacute

TABLE 4. Correlation Coefficients between Psychiatric Factor Scores and rCBF in Depression before Treatment (n = 36)

rCBF	Depression-Retardation	Self-depreciation	Anxiety-Agitation	Confusion
Rt mean	0.369[a]	0.448[b]	0.271	0.365[a]
Lt mean	0.359[a]	0.456[b]	0.284	0.357[a]

[a] $p < 0.05$.
[b] $p < 0.01$.

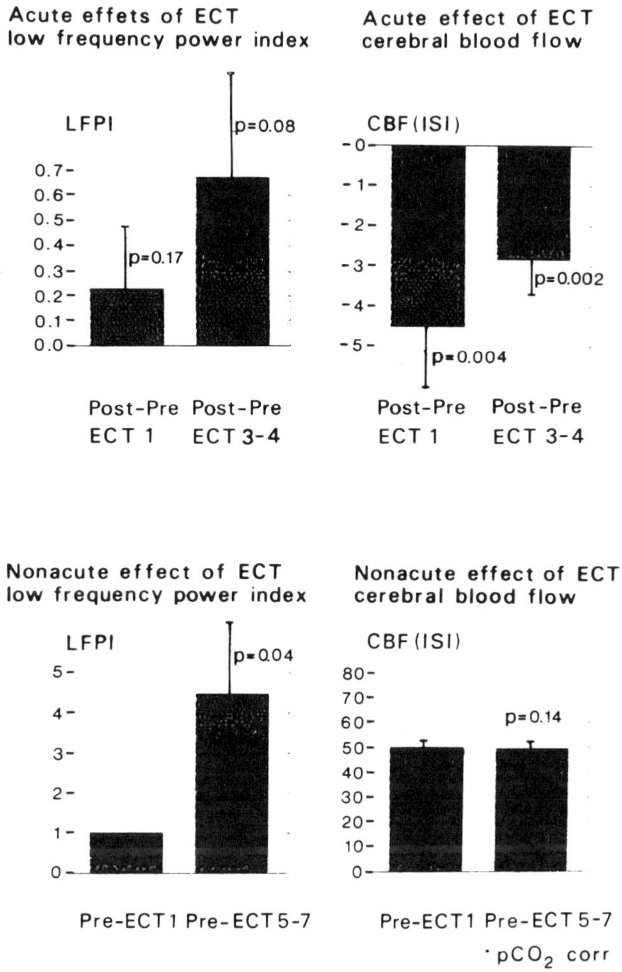

FIGURE 7. ECT effects on EEG and CBF in depression ($n = 24$). Diagrams in the upper half of the figure show acute changes of LFPI and CBF following ECT 1 and ECT 3–4. Diagrams below show EEG and CBF pre-ECT 1 and 5–7. Means and standard errors of the mean are given as well as p values (paired t-test).

effects on EEG (LFPI) and rCBF (mean of both hemispheres) following ECT 1 and ECT 3–4 are shown in FIGURE 7.

Compared to the pre-ECT levels, there was a nonsignificant increase of LFPI following the two treatments. The increase was about three times higher on the second occasion where the difference from pre- to post-ECT was almost significant ($p = 0.06$). At these instances the general flow level decreased significantly and this flow decrease was more marked following the first ECT ($p = 0.004$) than following ECT 3–4 ($p = 0.002$).

The nonacute effects of ECT on EEG and rCBF are shown in the lower part of

FIGURE 6. There was a significant increase of LFPI at this interval ($p = 0.04$) while at the same time there was a small, nonsignificant decrease of the mean rCBF ($p = 0.14$).

Baseline EEG was judged as normal in all cases. FIGURE 1 illustrates the analysis of the recordings from one patient on three occasions during the ECT series (pre- and post-ECT 1 and pre-ECT 5–7). The dominant frequency (DF) was within the normal range (8.6 Hz) before treatment. The acute effects of the first ECT are seen as an increase of the LFPI and a decrease of both HFPI and DF.

The nonacute effects are illustrated by the pre-ECT 5–7 values showing a marked increase of the LFPI quotient (4.25) while the values for HFPI and DF are in between the pre- and postvalues of the first ECT (HPFI 0.88, DF 8.0).

DISCUSSION

Concerning age and degree of illness, the patients included in this material constitute a representative sample well suited for ECT. This is indicated by the clinical outcome. The distribution of diagnosis and the pre-ECT EEG point to similarities between the two ECT groups. However, the BL group showed a higher mean age (7 years, NS) and a tendency of higher (NS) mean flow level and a somewhat more severe depression than the UL group. To our knowledge no systematic errors of sampling can explain these differences between the UL and the BL group and they thus seem to be an effect of chance. Because of these differences it may be difficult to interpret divergent results in the two ECT groups. Accordingly the results sometimes are presented from the two groups separated and sometimes put together.

The finding that all four of the psychiatric factors used in the present analysis correlated positively with mean rCBF indicates a relation between productive symptoms and an increased neuronal functional level as reflected by rCBF. A similar finding has been reported in schizophrenics showing a positive correlation between degree of psychotic symptoms and elevated rCBF.[24–26] This is in contrast to Mathew *et al.* who found a negative correlation between severity of depressive symptoms and hemispheric flow level.[13]

The mean rCBF level of the untreated depressed patients in this study seems to be somewhat higher ($p < 0.05$) than that found in our reference group. This could not be explained by differences in pCO_2, age, or sex. The higher flow in the untreated depressed patient group may indicate a higher cortical activity related to the underlying disorder. This is supported by the positive correlations between the presented psychiatric factors and mean rCBF. Our findings are not in agreement with those of Mathew *et al.* who reported a decreased flow level in depressed patients.[13] They reported a flow level seemingly within normal range while the control group showed surprisingly high flow values. Mathew *et al.* later confirmed their finding of a higher rCBF level in an age- and sex-matched control group compared to depressed patients. The normal rCBF level reported by Gur *et al.* in medicated depressed patients[27] strongly supports our finding. Possibly the somewhat lower flow level at follow-up (4–9 months) expresses the patients' habitual flow level.

The consistent decrease of mean rCBF in connection with single UL or BL electroconvulsive treatments followed a similar pattern during the ECT series. Similar flow decreases following ECT have been reported by Kety *et al.*[8] and Bolwig *et al.*[10] These flow decreases can neither be explained by differences in pCO_2 nor by medication. Nor can they be explained by effects of narcosis, as the mean rCBF following sham ECT showed a tendency to rise.[12] There is thus reason to believe that the flow decreases occurring after single treatments are related to the seizure. The flow decreases being somewhat more marked on the right stimulated side in UL ECT could be either an effect of the current passing mainly through this hemisphere and/or indicate greater seizure involvement on the stimulated side. The latter explanation is supported by a preliminary report from Prohovnik *et al.*[28] They have found much more marked flow decreases in the stimulated hemisphere when using a threshold stimulation technique in UL ECT.

The twofold flow decrease following BL ECT 1 compared to the UL ECT could be related to the relatively higher pretreatment flow level of the BL group or it may indicate a more powerful seizure with this stimulation technique. This difference between the techniques disappeared later during the ECT series. A possibly more powerful rCBF effect early in the BL ECT series may be related to a superior therapeutic effect of BL ECT at least in the short perspective. Sometimes a few extra treatments have to be given with the UL technique.

During both BL and UL ECT series only a slight flow decrease occurred as measured from pretreatment to pre-ECT 5–7. At the first follow-up (0–4 months), however, a marked flow decrease was found which could not be explained by differences in pCO_2. Pretreatment, the UL group ($n = 18$) had even a somewhat higher flow level than the mean of the total UL ECT group. Eight patients in the UL and five in the BL group were put on a low to moderate dose of tricyclic antidepressants. The mean level of total medication did not change, however, and therefore medication probably is of minor importance to this finding.

The results confirm earlier findings of increased slowing of EEG during serial ECT. The comparisons between the effects of ECT on CBF and EEG show markedly divergent patterns of these two physiological variables suggesting that they reflect partly independent postictal pathophysiological events.

At this stage of data analysis the acute CBF decrease following single treatments does not seem to be related to the psychiatric condition but rather seems to be an unspecific postictal effect. The absence of correlation between major changes of EEG and CBF probably reflects different effects of ECT where the underlying mechanism is still unknown.

ACKNOWLEDGMENTS

The authors are indebted to Mrs. Helena Fernö for excellent technical assistance and to Mrs. Maria Regnér for efficient secretarial aid.

REFERENCES

1. Robin, A. & S. de Tissera. 1982. A double-blind controlled comparison of the therapeutic effects of low and high energy electroconvulsive therapies. Br. J. Psychiatry **141:** 357–366.
2. Valentine, M., K. M. G. Keddie & D. Funne. 1968. A comparison of techniques in electroconvulsive therapy. Br. J. Psychiatry **114:** 989–996.
3. Abrams, R., M. A. Taylor, R. Faber, T. O. T. Ts's, R. A. Williams & G. Almy. 1983. Bilateral versus unilateral electroconvulsive therapy: efficacy in melancholia. Am. J. Psychiatry **140**(4): 463–465.
4. d'Elia, G. 1970. Unilateral electroconvulsive therapy. Acta Psychiatr. Scand. (Suppl. 215).
5. d'Elia, G. & H. Raotma. 1975. Is unilateral ECT less effective than bilateral ECT? Br. J. Phychiatry **126:** 83–89.

6. Strömgren, L. S. 1973. Unilateral versus bilateral ECT. Acta Psychiatr. Scand. (Suppl. 240).
7. Brodersen, P., O. B. Paulson, T. G. Bolwig, Z. E. Rogon, O. J. Rafelsen & N. A. Lassen. 1973. Cerebral hyperemia in electrically induced epileptic seizures. Arch. Neurol. **28:** 334–338.
8. Kety, S. S., R. B. Woodford, M. H. Harmel, F. A. Freyhan, K. E. Appel & C. F. Schmidt. 1948. Cerebral blood flow and metabolism in schizophrenia. Am. J. Psychiatry **104:** 765–770.
9. Wilson, W. P., J. F. Schieve, N. C. Durham & P. Scheinberg. 1952. Effect of series of electric shock treatments on cerebral blood flow and metabolism. Arch. Neurol. Psychiatry **68:** 651–654.
10. Bolwig, T. G., M. M. Hertz, O. B. Paulson, H. Spotoft & O. J. Rafaelsen. 1977. The permeability of the blood-brain barrier during electrically induced seizures in man. Eur. J. Clin. Invest. **7:** 87–93.
11. Silfverskiöld, P., L. Gustafson, M. Johanson & J. Risberg. 1979. Regional cerebral blood flow related to the effect of electroconvulsive therapy in depression. *In* Biological Psychiatry Today. J. Obiols, C. Ballús, E. Gonzalez, G. Monclús & J. Pujol, Eds.: 1178–1183. Elsevier/North Holland Biomedical Press. Amsterdam, Holland.
12. Silfverskiöld, P., L. Gustafson & J. Risberg. 1984. Changes in regional cerebral blood flow during ECT. *In* ECT: Basic Mechanisms. Biological Psychiatry—New prospects. B. Lehrer, R. D. Weiner & R. H. Belmaker, Eds.: **1:** 124–130. John Libbey. London, England.
13. Mathew, R. J., J. S. Meyer, D. J. Francis, K. M. Semchuk, K. Mortel & J. L. Claghorn. 1980. Cerebral blood flow in depression. Am. J. Psychiatry **137**(11): 1449–1450.
14. Mathew, R. J., J. S. Meyer, K. M. Semchuk, D. J. Francis, K. Mortel & J. L. Claghorn. 1980. Cerebral blood flow in depression. Lancet.: 1308.
15. Fink, M. 1979. Convulsive Therapy: Theory and Practice. Raven Press. New York, N.Y.
16. Weiner, R. D. 1980. Persistence of ECT-induced EEG changes. J. Nerv. Ment. Dis. **168:** 224–228.
17. Klotz, M. 1955. Serial electroencephalographic changes due to electrotherapy. Dis. Nerv. Syst. **16:** 120–121.
18. Nilsson, L. & G. J. W. Smith. 1965. Optical analysis of EEG changes during ECT and imipramine treatment. Acta Psychiatr. Scand. **41:** 141–156.
19. APA. 1980. Diagnostic and Statistical Manual of Mental Disorders. 3rd edit. American Psychiatric Association. Washington, D.C.
20. Obrist, W. D., H. K. Thompson, H. S. Wang & W. E. Wilkinson. 1975. Regional blood flow estimated by ^{133}xenon inhalation. Stroke **6:** 245–256.
21. Risberg, J., Z. Ali, E. M. Wilson, E. L. Wills & J. H. Halsey. 1975. Regional cerebral blood flow by ^{133}xenon inhalation. Preliminary evaluation of an initial slope index in patients with unstable flow compartments. Stroke **6:** 142–148.
22. Risberg, J. 1980. Regional cerebral blood flow measurements by ^{133}xenon inhalation: methodology and applications in neuropsychology and psychiatry. Brain Lang. **9:** 9–34.
23. Hagstadius, S. & J. Risberg. 1983. The effects of normal aging on rCBF during resting and functional activation. rCBF Bull **6:** 116–120.
24. Ingvar, D. H. & G. Franzen. 1974. Abnormalities of cerebral blood flow distribution in patients with chronic schizophrenia. Acta Psychiatr. Scand. **50:** 425–462.
25. Franzen, G. & D. H. Ingvar. 1975. Abnormal distribution of cerebral activity in chronic schizophrenia. J. Psychiatr. Res. **12:** 199–214.
26. Hoyer, S. & K. Oesterreich. 1975. Blood flow and oxidative metabolism of the brain in patients with schizophrenia. Psychiatr. Clin. **8:** 304–313.
27. Gur, R. E., B. E. Skolnick, R. C. Gur, S. Caroff, W. Rieger, W. D. Obrist, D. Younkin & M. Reivich. 1984. Brain function in psychiatric disorders. II. Regional cerebral blood flow in medicated unipolar depressives. Arch. Gen. Psychiatry **41:** 695–699.
28. Prohovnik, I., H. A. Sackeim, P. Decina & S. Malitz. 1986. Acute reductions of regional cerebral blood flow following electroconvulsive therapy: interactions with modality and time. Ann. N.Y. Acad. Sci. (This volume.)

Acute Reductions of Regional Cerebral Blood Flow following Electroconvulsive Therapy[a]

Interactions with Modality and Time

ISAK PROHOVNIK, HAROLD A. SACKEIM,[b]
PAOLO DECINA, AND SIDNEY MALITZ

Department of Biological Psychiatry
New York State Psychiatric Institute
and
Department of Psychiatry
College of Physicians and Surgeons
Columbia University
722 West 168 Street
New York, New York 10032

Neurophysiological effects of electroconvulsive therapy (ECT) have traditionally been investigated by electrophysiological[1-3] or biochemical techniques.[4-6] Recently, a new method was introduced to this area, the noninvasive measurement of regional cerebral blood flow (rCBF).[7] This method is safe and repeatable, and thus suitable for following patients through a course of treatment. Due to the tight coupling between local flow and metabolism in the brain, flow maps may be interpreted as indicating regional metabolic activity levels.[8] The first such study reported symmetric frontal flow decreases following unilateral ECT.[7] The same group recently reported "somewhat asymmetric flow decrease in frontal areas"[9] following unilateral ECT. In contrast, we have recently suggested that there are marked lateralized and regional differences between the effects of bilateral and unilateral treatments.[10] The present report is an extension of these findings, and includes preliminary data on cumulative temporal trends and relations with eventual clinical response to treatment.

METHODS

Patients

Most of the patients included here were also included in other papers from our group, where the inclusion/exclusion criteria are specified (Malitz *et al.*, Sackeim *et al.*, this volume). To maximize the sample sizes, three different groups were assembled and used to study three issues. The largest sample contained 17 patients, each of whom had at least one ECT treatment with two rCBF studies (before and after the seizure); this sample was used to define the average flow response to ECT. Two other samples,

[a]This work was supported in part by National Institute of Mental Health Grant No. MH 35636.

[b]Also affiliated with the Department of Psychology, New York University.

with 11 patients each, were used to examine cumulative trends throughout a course of ECT (each patient having had at least three ECT treatments with the same modality, with at least six rCBF studies) and the relationship of initial flows to eventual clinical response. The patients will be described separately for each sample.

rCBF Procedure

A standard commercial system (Novo Cerebrograph 32c) was used to measure rCBF by the 133-xenon inhalation technique. The procedures were always performed about 25 minutes before and 50 minutes after the induced seizure. Each hemisphere was covered by 16 scintillation detectors, fixed in a helmet that was designed to enhance the sensitivity to asymmetries.[11] Clearance curves were analyzed by two physiological models: M1, a simple bicompartmental model,[12] and M2, a more complex six-unknown model with included artifact correction.[13] Five indices were derived from each model, and all analyses were performed separately for the 10 resulting parameters. Only 1 parameter will be presented here in detail, the M2-derived initial slope index (ISI). This parameter is superior on theoretical grounds, and we have verified that all phenomena found with this parameter were also detectable with the others, although with less magnitude, more noise, or weaker significance. The ISI was computed as originally proposed by Risberg *et al.*[14] and modified by Prohovnik *et al.*[15]

Due to the large variation of end-tidal CO_2 pressure (P_eCO_2) within and between subjects and its interaction with independent variables such as treatment mode and response, and because we were primarily interested in flow as a metabolic index, we employed a CO_2 pressure (PCO_2) correction. All ISI values were corrected to $P_eCO_2 =$ 40 mmHg by a factor of 0.75/mmHg.[16]

ECT Procedure

Our low-dosage ECT procedure is described in detail elsewhere (Malitz *et al.*, this volume). Briefly, patients were randomly assigned to either bilateral (standard bifrontotemporal placement) or right unilateral (d'Elia placement) treatment modes. All treatments were administered by the MECTA brief-pulse instrument, with electrical dosage titrated to each patient's seizure threshold. In all instances, the patients had a generalized seizure, verified by cuff and EEG, lasting over 25 seconds; there was no difference in average seizure duration in our total material between bilateral and unilateral modes. rCBF measurements were conducted about 25 minutes before and 50 minutes after the first, fourth, seventh, and last ECT.

RESULTS

Mean ECT Effects

Seventeen depressed inpatients were used for this comparison of average effects of bilateral and unilateral treatments. Fifteen met Research Diagnostic Criteria (RDC) for primary major depressive disorder (one complicated by small infarcts in the left hemisphere), and two fulfilled criteria for secondary major depression. At least five days prior to treatment, patients were withdrawn from all psychotropic medication except lorazepam (1 mg PO Q12H) with the exception of one patient who received phenothiazines during treatment. Seven patients had additional medical conditions: three presented with moderate tardive dyskinesia, two with diabetes mellitus, one with Parkinson's disease, and one was on thyroid replacement therapy and one on diuretics for hypertension. Overall, the mean serial position of ECT session compared here was about the fifth (mean total treatments = 9). Other descriptive data are presented in TABLE 1.

An analysis of variance was performed on the mean hemispheric values of the M2 ISI, using treatment mode (bilateral/unilateral) as a between-subject factor and hemisphere (right/left) and treatment status (pre-/post-ECT) as within-subject repeated measures. There was a significant reduction of flow acutely following ECT ($F = 24.67$, $p < 0.001$). There were also significant interactions of mode by hemisphere ($F = 5.75$, $p = 0.03$), status by hemisphere ($F = 14.55$, $p = 0.002$), and mode by status by hemisphere ($F = 22.63$, $p < 0.001$). FIGURE 1 depicts these effects. Both treatment modes resulted in flow reductions. These flow reductions were symmetric with bilateral ECT but lateralized to the right hemisphere with right unilateral ECT.

As depicted in FIGURES 2 and 3, not only did the unilateral treatment result in lateralized hemispheric effects, but the regional distribution of flow decreases was

TABLE 1. Patient Data, Sample 1 (Mean ECT Effect)

Treatment Mode	Bilateral	Right Unilateral
n	9	8
Age	58.33 (11.09)	68.88 (7.31)
Male:female	5:4	1:7
Handedness (rt:lt)	7:2	6:2
Response (yes:no)	4:3	1:5
Average ECT number (treatment session)	5.51 (2.13)	4.27 (1.51)
BP pre-ECT[a]	124/82	142/88
BP post-ECT	128/85	144/88
P_eCO_2 pre-ECT	38.97 (4.33)	37.32 (2.80)
P_eCO_2 post-ECT	41.62 (4.03)	37.94 (3.10)

[a]BP is blood pressure.

markedly different from that of bilateral treatment. Bilateral ECT resulted in symmetric frontal flow reductions (13–17%), which gradually diminished caudally so that only about 5% reductions were found occipitally. Following unilateral ECT, the contralateral, nonstimulated hemisphere showed the same weak 5% reductions in most areas, with the exception of the temporal pole and three vertex regions. In contrast, the stimulated right hemisphere demonstrated frontal reductions equal to those obtained with bilateral treatment, but also marked flow decreases centrally around the lateral sulcus and extending into the parietal lobe.

Cumulative Trends

Eleven patients, who had rCBF studies before and after the first, third to fifth, and sixth to eighth treatment, were used in this analysis. Their data are detailed in TABLE 2. Mean treatment numbers were first, fourth, and seventh ECT.

An analysis of variance was performed on mean hemispheric values of M2 ISI, using treatment mode (bilateral/unilateral) as a between-subject factor and time

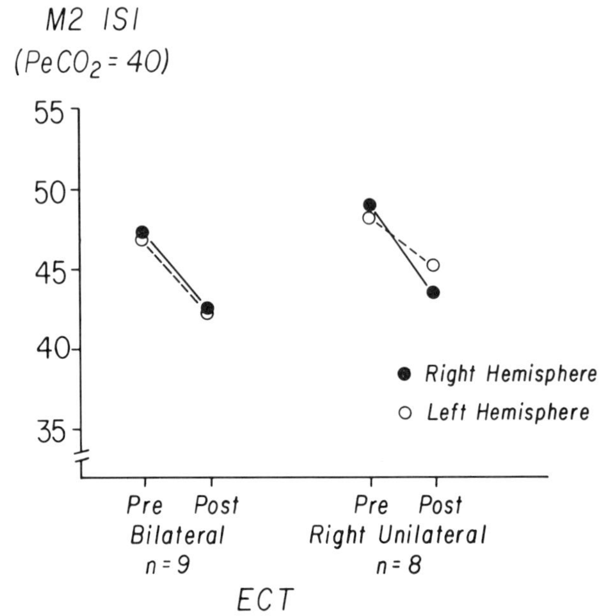

FIGURE 1. Mean hemispheric CBF before and after bilateral and unilateral ECT. All treatment sessions of each patient were averaged for this analysis.

(three treatments), status (pre-/post-ECT), and hemisphere as within-subject repeated measures. As expected, there was a significant main effect of status ($F = 9.09$, $p = 0.015$). There were also significant interactions of status by hemisphere ($F = 11.32$, $p = 0.009$) and mode by status by hemisphere ($F = 8.38$, $p = 0.018$). These results are presented in FIGURE 4, and confirm that this subsample demonstrates phenomena identical to the larger previous sample.

Time was found to yield a significant effect ($F = 5.96$, $p = 0.001$). Overall, flow was 42.83 on the first ECT, and increased to 47.96 and 47.24 on fourth and seventh ECT, respectively. There was also a significant interaction of time by hemisphere ($F = 10.26$, $p = 0.002$) and time by mode by status ($F = 7.70$, $p = 0.004$). These results are illustrated in FIGURES 5 and 6, and indicate that the flow-reducing effect of bilateral ECT is greatly attenuated after the first treatment, whereas it is maintained at the fourth unilateral treatment and disappears at the seventh.

Relations of Flow to Clinical Response

Eleven patients, who had full rCBF data at first treatment and a rigorously documented response after last treatment, were used (TABLE 3). Clinical response was defined (Sackeim *et al.*, this volume) as at least a 60% drop in the Hamilton depression score, to below 16. Response was evaluated for this purpose on the day of the last treatment.

An analysis of variance was performed on mean hemispheric M2 ISI, using response (yes/no) as a between-subject classification and status and hemisphere as within subject factors. Status again showed a significant main effect ($F = 11.25$, $p = 0.009$), with post-ECT flows being lower than pre-ECT. The effect of response was also significant ($F = 9.54$, $p = 0.013$). The four patients who eventually responded favorably to treatment had overall flows of 38.78 (standard deviation 1.57), whereas the seven patients who did not fulfill our strict response criteria had overall flows of 43.74 (SD 2.94). There were no significant interactions, and the flow reduction due to first ECT was about 18% for the responders (all bilateral) and about 10% for the nonresponders (5/7 unilateral); this difference was not significant. None of the 10

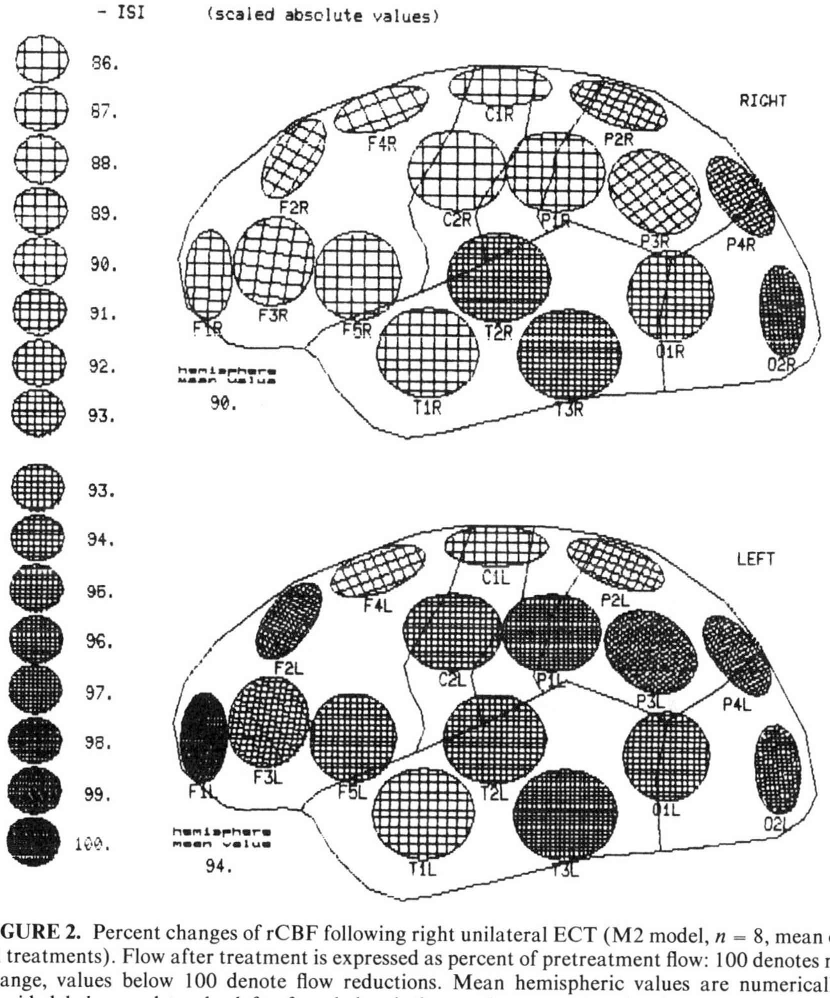

FIGURE 2. Percent changes of rCBF following right unilateral ECT (M2 model, $n = 8$, mean of all treatments). Flow after treatment is expressed as percent of pretreatment flow: 100 denotes no change, values below 100 denote flow reductions. Mean hemispheric values are numerically provided below and to the left of each hemisphere, whereas regional values are graphically presented by the grey scale, as defined on the left side. Note that most of the left hemisphere, and the right occipital lobe, show no changes of flow, whereas most of the right hemisphere demonstrates significant decreases. All treatment sessions of each patient were averaged for this analysis.

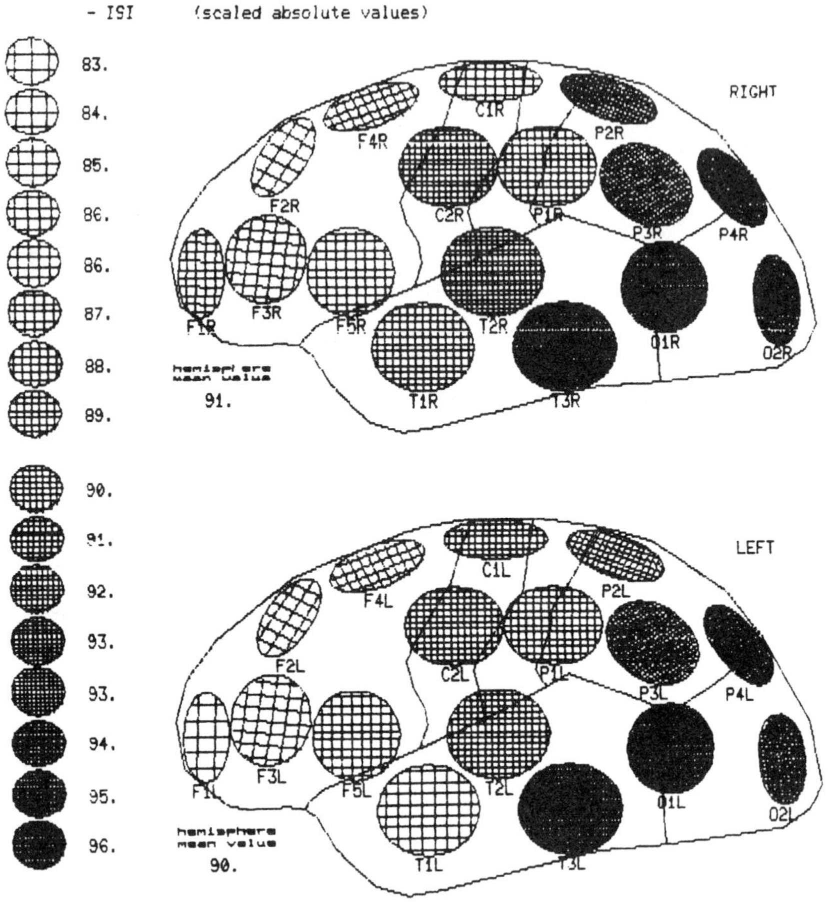

FIGURE 3. Percent changes of rCBF following bilateral ECT (M2 model, $n = 9$, mean of all treatments). Symbols as in FIGURE 2. Note the bilateral frontal reduction of flow, with minimal effects in the occipital lobes (dark shades denote small changes, light shades denote large decreases).

parameters examined showed a significant interaction of response with either status or hemisphere, but the main effect of response was consistent (FIGURE 7).

DISCUSSION

Our results demonstrate, for the first time to our knowledge, a clear difference in the regional cerebral distribution of the acute effects of right unilateral and bilateral ECT. Global reductions of cerebral blood flow following ECT have been known since 1948,[17] but noninvasive, bilateral, quantitative regional techniques have not been available until recently. Using such techniques, Silfverskiöld *et al.* have not found effects similar to ours following unilateral ECT.[7,8] Our data demonstrated a clear and highly significant effect. Bilateral ECT resulted in bilateral frontal flow reductions. Right unilateral ECT resulted in negligible effects in the left hemisphere, and greater effects of different regional patterns in the right hemisphere.

The reasons for this disparity may include several factors. Technically, Silfverskiöld *et al.* have been using a parallel-bank detector array, whereas our studies were conducted with a helmetlike device, containing detectors largely perpendicular to the skull. This helmet was developed, among other reasons, to maximize sensitivity to asymmetries by minimizing "crosstalk."[11] Indeed, the regions of maximal asymmetry in our data include parietal and frontal midline detectors which were specifically designed to have no crosstalk. In addition, Silfverskiöld *et al.* have been using the M1 model, mentioned in the Methods section. In our comparisons, this model was found to be less sensitive than the M2 model. The difference may be especially relevant under low-flow conditions, such as acutely follow ECT, where the M1 model is prone to physiological noise.[13] Furthermore, the ISI parameter used by Silfverskiöld *et al.* is the original version, described by Risberg *et al.*,[14] whereas we use a modified version which was designed for higher sensitivity to grey-matter flow.[15]

There are other possible reasons for the absence of clear lateral and regional differences following unilateral ECT in the Silfverskiöld *et al.* data. Their post-ECT studies were performed at 60–120 minutes after the seizure, and possibly after a sleep period; both the longer time interval and the intervening sleep may have modified cerebral activity in the direction of reduced laterality. Electrophysiological asymmetries following unilateral ECT are well known;[2] there is evidence, however, that their time course is rapid and transient. Small and Small found no significant asymmetries

TABLE 2. Patient Data, Sample 2 (Temporal Trends)

Treatment Mode	Bilateral	Right Unilateral
n	5	6
Age	56.00 (7.18)	70.17 (8.03)
Male:female	2:3	1:5
Handedness (rt:lt)	5:0	4:2
Response (yes:no)	3:2	0:5
ECT number		
First	1.00 (0.0)	1.00 (0.0)
Second	4.00 (0.63)	4.33 (0.47)
Third	6.80 (0.98)	7.17 (0.37)
BP pre-ECT		
First	116/70	138/92
Fourth	124/84	147/86
Seventh	122/82	141/86
BP post-ECT		
First	124/80	142/90
Fourth	119/80	140/88
Seventh	126/89	155/90
P_eCO_2 pre-ECT		
First	39.48 (6.08)	37.82 (4.24)
Fourth	38.96 (5.01)	36.93 (2.78)
Seventh	41.86 (4.80)	36.75 (2.28)
P_eCO_2 post-ECT		
First	42.54 (5.18)	37.47 (5.21)
Fourth	40.92 (4.78)	37.90 (2.77)
Seventh	43.44 (3.35)	38.35 (2.98)

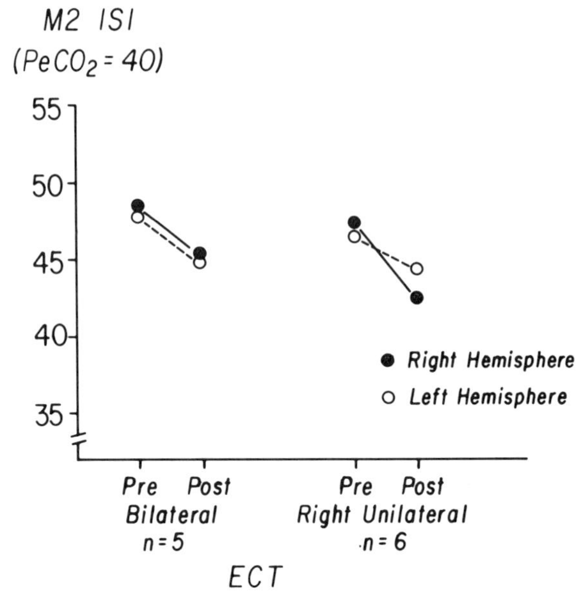

FIGURE 4. Mean hemispheric CBF before and after bilateral and unilateral ECT in a subsample of patients. Note the similarity of flow values to those of the full sample, depicted in FIGURE 1.

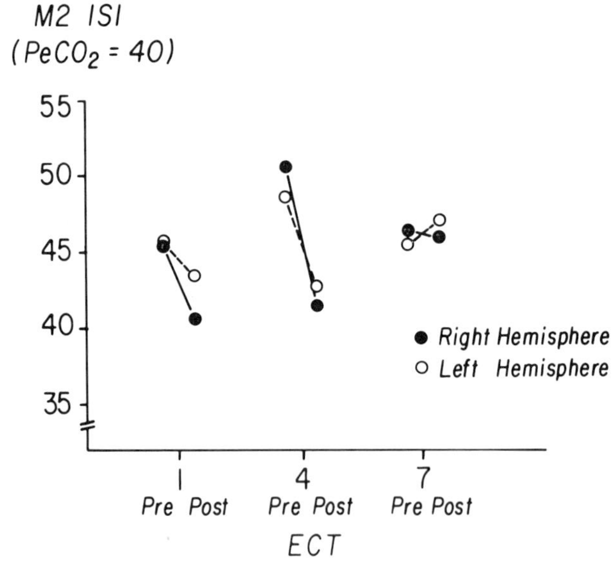

FIGURE 5. Serial temporal trends throughout a course of right unilateral ECT ($n = 6$); symbols as in FIGURE 4. Note the disappearance of ECT-induced flow reduction after the fourth treatment.

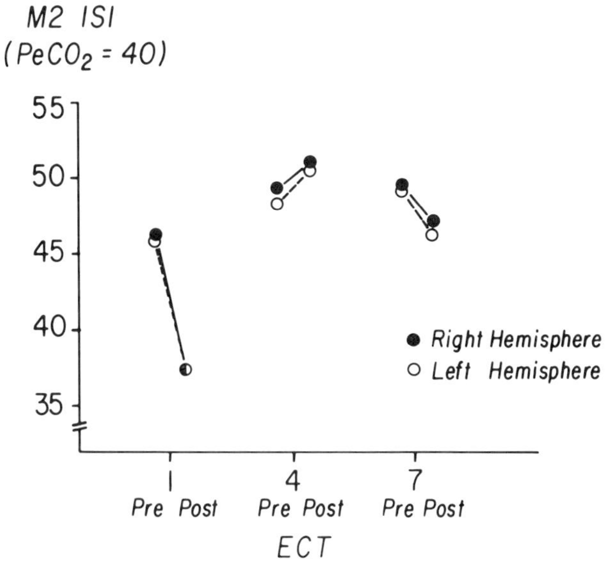

FIGURE 6. Serial temporal trends throughout a course of bilateral ECT ($n = 5$). Note the disappearance or substantial diminution of ECT effect after the first treatment.

in either a visual or auditory evoked potential one hour after unilateral ECT.[18] Kriss *et al.*, however, demonstrated significant asymmetries of the EEG immediately following the treatment which were still evident, although attenuated, 30 minutes after seizure.[1] These authors also demonstrated asymmetries in the visual evoked potential immediately after unilateral ECT, which disappeared after 9–15 minutes. Transient neurological deficits were also asymmetrically present, and disappeared within a few minutes. The rCBF effects of unilateral ECT may follow a similar time course, and their magnitude may be a function of the elapsed time since seizure. Finally, the electrical dosage used by Silfverskiöld *et al.*, although unspecified, was not titrated and was most probably considerably higher than the dosage employed by us. Conceivably, higher electrical dosage may diminish the unique regional pattern elicited by our low-dosage technique.

The specific patterns elicited by bilateral and unilateral ECT deserve further

TABLE 3. Patient Data, Sample 3

	Responders	Nonresponders
n	4	7
Age	57.75 (10.21)	66.57 (8.53)
Male:female	1:3	2:5
Handedness (rt:1t)	2:2	5:2
Mode (Bilateral:unilateral)	4:0	2:5
BP pre-ECT no. 1	126/73	129/87
BP post-ECT no. 1	130/78	132/86
P_eCO_2 pre-ECT no. 1	41.55 (4.18)	37.34 (4.65)
P_eCO_2 post-ECT no. 1	45.30 (2.61)	38.06 (4.91)

comment. There were no differences in medication and diagnosis between the groups that could be associated with these effects. The nature and duration of seizures were equal in our material, and the nonsignificant age differences between the bilateral and unilateral sample cannot easily be evoked for this purpose. An examination of the processes leading to seizure elicitation, propagation, and termination appears necessary for formulation of hypotheses.

The induction of general anesthesia has profound and complex effects on cerebral metabolism and blood flow,[19] but there were no differences in type or dosage of anesthetic between our two treatment groups, nor is it likely that the brief-acting anesthetics used were still exerting significant influence after 50 minutes, when patients were fully oriented. The seizure itself is little understood on the cellular level,[20] but its macroscopic metabolic and circulatory correlates are known, and consist of

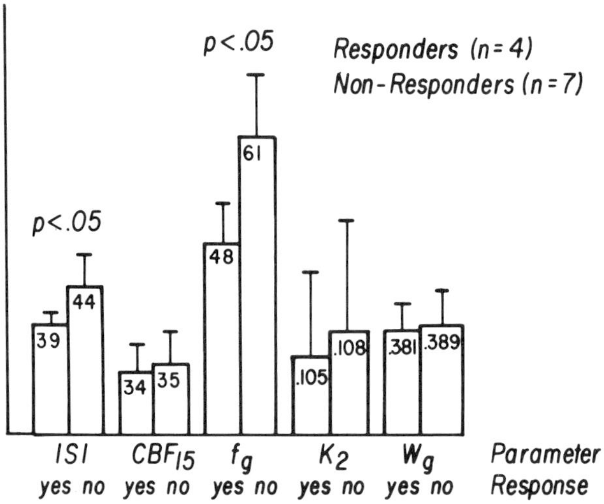

FIGURE 7. Comparison of several parameters between patients who eventually responded to ECT and patients who did not. First treatment (averaged pre and post); M2 model. Responders appeared to have significantly lower grey-matter blood flow at first treatment than nonresponders, but the effect is confounded with treatment modality.

concomitant and coupled increases of metabolism and blood flow with no detectable hypoxia.[20,21]

Biochemically, ECT results in a plethora of changes that are only beginning to be listed. ECT-induced effects have been demonstrated to involve endorphins,[22] noradrenaline,[23] acetylcholine,[24] and many other substances and chemical systems.[5,25] We have proposed that the therapeutic efficacy of ECT may be partially explained by its effects on γ-aminobutyric acid (GABA) systems.[26] All of the substances mentioned have profound effects on cerebral function, and interact in many ways. GABA, for instance, is a metabolic inhibitor but also a vasodilator.[27] In addition, GABA is a ventilatory inhibitor,[28] which tends to increase arterial PCO_2 and may thus raise CBF even further. Indeed, the significantly greater post-ECT increase of P_eCO_2 observed here following bilateral ECT may be related to a greater GABAergic enhancement, which would also be related to the greater therapeutic efficacy observed with this modality.

We have not found, however, a biochemical effect of ECT that would easily explain the observed regional flow effects.

Two other possible mechanisms should be briefly mentioned. First, there are some similarities between the global effects of ECT and those caused by "spreading depression," which also demonstrates a marked metabolic and flow enhancement followed acutely by a depressed state.[29] Secondly, induced seizures can open the blood-brain barrier, possibly by the combination of acute hypertension and vasodilation.[30] Such disruption, although fully reversible, may induce increased glucose utilization, decreased blood flow, and decoupling between them, in addition to vasogenic edema and other effects.[31] Although the mechanisms of action are unknown, an open blood-brain barrier may allow entry of potassium from blood into the brain, thus precipitating a phenomenon akin to spreading depression, which may also be elicited by local application of KCl.[32] Indeed, a disruption of the blood-brain barrier through acute hypertension has been suggested to be correlated to cognitive deficits following ECT.[33] Moreover, both ECT and antidepressant medications may produce similar changes in cerebral metabolism, blood flow, and the permeability of the blood-brain barrier.[34,35] Again, although we recognize these effects, we cannot easily relate them to the rCBF patterns we observed.

We suggest that the regional patterns of flow reduction observed acutely following ECT can best be explained as a correlate of the cerebral distribution of maximal current density associated with our electrode placement. Such patterns of current density arise due to the peculiar nature of the human head as an electrical conductor. The electrical resistance of scalp and brain is very low, compared to the skull. During the passage of the currents employed in ECT, skin resistance drops even further and becomes virtually negligible, compared to the skull.[36–39] Under these conditions, currents do not flow directly between the two electrodes. Instead, the scalp serves as a large virtual electrode of negligible impedance, and a large proportion of the induced current is shunted through it and never reaches the brain. Hayes suggested that with bilateral temporal electrodes, maximum current density will occur anteriorly to the electrode locations, mostly in the frontal lobe.[40] This observation was derived by application of current to the head of a spider monkey; if the current was applied directly to the brain with the skull removed, maximal current density did peak on the line connecting the two electrodes. Different results were obtained by Lorimer *et al.* in experiments on a cadaver,[41] but extensive recent work essentially confirmed Hayes' observations. Weaver *et al.* concluded that bilateral ECT results in maximal current densities "along the surface of the brain over the frontal lobes."[42] Unilateral ECT, on the other hand, results in maximum current density "along the interelectrode axis and lying on the surface of the cortex."[42] Moreover, Weaver *et al.* concluded that unilateral ECT would result in a largely ipsilateral current distribution. We believe that our data are in agreement with their calculations. Bilateral ECT resulted in bilateral frontal flow reductions, whereas unilateral ECT caused lateralized flow reduction over central and frontal areas, corresponding to the path between the electrodes in the d'Elia placement we use.

We thus suggest that maximal regional flow reductions occur acutely after ECT in the cortical areas that sustain the maximal current density during the seizure-inducing stimulation. This does not imply, however, that the flow reductions 50 minutes after the seizure are a direct result of current passage. We would propose, instead, that local biochemical effects, probably associated with initiation or termination of the seizure, are responsible for reduced metabolic activity, reflected in regional flow decreases. That such local processes occur, and that they are associated with seizure mechanisms, is illustrated by the different rCBF response elicited by bilateral ECT in a case of focal epilepsy.[43] In that case, with an EEG-documented left frontal focus, bilateral ECT resulted in a right frontal flow reduction but no changes in the left frontal area. Further implications are discussed by Sackeim *et al.* (this volume).

Regarding temporal trends of CBF through the treatment course, we found that flows generally increased between the first and fourth session, and that the flow-reducing effect of ECT was maximal after the first session and diminished with time. The second effect was also reported by Silfverskiöld *et al.*[9] and may have contributed to the first effect in our material. The significance of these findings is unclear at the moment. We are analyzing the flow data as a function of clinical status (Hamilton ratings) and seizure parameters (such as electrical dosage) to explore possible correlations. Finally, we found that patients who eventually responded to the treatment had lower flows at the first session. Although they also showed stronger flow reductions following the first session than the nonresponders, this interaction was not significant, and is confounded by the interaction with treatment modality. The lower flow in the responding patients is in contradiction with the findings of Silfverskiöld *et al.*,[7] and its significance is unclear.

In conclusion, we found strong evidence for differential acute rCBF effects of unilateral and bilateral low-dose ECT. The patterns of flow reduction are consistent with the known paths of maximal current density in the brain, and may reflect local biochemical processes associated with elicitation or termination of the seizures. Such findings may contribute to the understanding of ECT mechanisms of action, and may be the basis for the design of more effective treatment.

ACKNOWLEDGMENTS

Unflagging technical assistance was contributed by Irwin Weiss, B.A., and Seth Apter, B.A.

REFERENCES

1. Kriss, A., A. M. Halliday & R. T. C. Pratt. 1981. Transitory electrophysiological and neurological asymmetries following unilateral ECT. *In* Electroconvulsive Therapy: An Appraisal. R. L. Palmer, Ed.: 236–252. Oxford University Press. New York, N.Y.
2. Weiner, R. D. 1980. The persistence of electroconvulsive therapy–induced changes in the electroencephalogram. J. Nerv. Ment. Dis. **168**(4): 224–228.
3. Abrams, R. & W. B. Essman, Eds. 1982. Electroconvulsive Therapy: Biological Foundations and Clinical Applications. Spectrum Publications, Inc. New York, N.Y.
4. Green, A. R., E. Peralta, J. S. Hong, C. C. Mao, C. K. Atterwill & E. Costa. 1978. Alterations in GABA metabolism and met-enkephalin content in rat brain following repeated electroconvulsive shocks. J. Neurochem. **31:** 607–611.
5. Ferrendelli, J. A. 1984. Roles of biogenic amines and cyclic nucleotides in seizure mechanisms. Ann. Neurol. **16:** 98–103.
6. Lerer, B. 1984. Electroconvulsive shock and neurotransmitter receptors: implications for mechanism of action and adverse effects of electroconvulsive therapy. Biol. Psychiatry **19**(3): 361–383.
7. Silfverskiöld, P., L. Gustafson, M. Johanson & J. Risberg. 1979. Regional cerebral blood flow related to the effect of electroconvulsive therapy in depression. *In* Biological Psychiatry Today. J. Obiols, C. Ballus, E. Gonzalez Monclus & J. Pujol, Eds.: 1178–1183. Elsevier. Amsterdam, Holland.
8. Lebrun-Grandie, P., J. C. Baron, R. Soussaline, C. Loch'h, J. Sastre & M. G. Bousser. 1983. Coupling between regional blood flow and oxygen utilization in the normal human brain. Arch. Neurol. **40:** 230–236.

9. SILFVERSKIÖLD, P., L. GUSTAFSON & J. RISBERG. 1984. Changes in regional cerebral blood flow during ECT. *In* ECT: Basic Mechanisms. B. Lehrer, R. D. Weiner & R. H. Belmaker, Eds.: 124–130. John Libbey. London, England.
10. PROHOVNIK, I., H. A. SACKEIM, P. DECINA, D. KAHN & S. MALITZ. 1984. Acute effects of ECT on regional cerebral blood flow as a function of treatment modality. Paper presented at the 39th Annual Meeting of the Society of Biological Psychiatry, May 2–6, Los Angeles, Calif.
11. PROHOVNIK, I., J. O. ESPERSEN & F. K. CHRISTENSEN. 1983. Development and initial evaluation of a helmet for rCBF measurements. *In* rCBF Bull. **6:** 107–115.
12. ORBIST, W. D., H. K. THOMPSON, H. S. WANG & W. E. WILKINSON. 1975. Regional cerebral blood flow estimated by 133xenon inhalation. Stroke **6:** 245–256.
13. PROHOVNIK, I., E. KNUDSEN & J. RISBERG. 1983. Accuracy of models and algorithms for determination of fast-compartment flow by noninvasive 133Xe clearance. *In* Functional Radionuclide Imaging of the Brain. P. L. Magistretti, Ed.: 87–115. Raven Press. New York, N.Y.
14. RISBERG, J., S. ALI, E. M. WILSON, W. L. WILLS & J. H. HALSEY. 1975. Regional cerebral blood flow by 133xenon inhalation. Stroke **6:** 142–147.
15. PROHOVNIK, I., E. KNUDSEN & J. RISBERG. 1985. Theoretical evaluation and simulation test of the initial slope index for noninvasive rCBF. *In* Cerebral Blood Flow and Metabolism Measurement. A. Hartmann & S. Hoyer, Eds.: 56–60. Springer-Verlag. Berlin, FRG.
16. MAXIMILIAN, V. A., I. PROHOVNIK & J. RISBERG. 1980. Cerebral hemodynamic response to mental activation of normo- and hypercapnia. Stroke **11:** 342–347.
17. KETY, S. S., R. B. WOODFORD, M. H. HARMEL, F. A. FREYHAND, K. E. APPEL & C. F. SCHMIDT. 1948. Cerebral blood flow and metabolism in schizophrenia: the effects of barbiturate semi-narcosis, insulin coma and electroshock. Am. J. Psychiatry **104:** 765–770.
18. SMALL, I. F. & J. G. SMALL. 1971. Electroencephalographic, evoked potential, and direct current responses with unilateral electroconvulsive treatment. J. Nerv. Ment. Dis. **152:** 396–404.
19. CUCCHIARA, R. F., J. H. TINKER & P. A. STEEN. 1980. Anesthesia and the central nervous system: pharmacological, toxic and protective effects. Int. Anesthesiol. Clin. **18**(3): 123–138.
20. COLLINS, R. C., J. W. OLNEY & E. W. LOTHMAN. 1983. Metabolic and pathological consequences of focal seizures. *In* Epilepsy. A. A. Ward, J. K. Penry & D. Purpura, Eds.: 87–107. Raven Press. New York, N.Y.
21. POSNER, J. B., F. PLUM & A. VAN POZNAK. 1969. Cerebral metabolism during electrically induced seizures in man. Arch. Neurol. **20:** 388–395.
22. BELENKY, G. L. & J. W. HOLADAY. 1979. The opiate antagonist naloxone modifies the effects of electroconvulsive shock (ECS) on respiration, blood pressure and heart rate. Brain Res. **177:** 414–417.
23. DEAKIN, J. F. W., F. OWEN, A. J. CROSS & M. J. DASHWOOD. 1981. Studies on possible mechanisms of action of electroconvulsive therapy: effects of repeated electrically induced seizures on rat brain receptors for monoamines and other neurotransmitters. Psychopharmacology **73:** 345–349.
24. LERER, B. 1985. Studies on the role of brain cholinergic systems in the therapeutic mechanisms and adverse effects of ECT and lithium. Biol. Psychiatry **20:** 20–40.
25. ESSMAN, W. B. 1982. Electroconvulsive shock and cerebral chemistry: changes and sequelae. *In* Electroconvulsive Therapy: Biological Foundations and Clinical Applications. R. Abrams & W. B. Essman, Eds.: 199–244. Spectrum Publications, Inc. New York, N.Y.
26. SACKEIM, H. S., P. DECINA, I. PROHOVNIK, S. MALITZ & S. R. RESOR. 1983. Anticonvulsant and antidepressant properties of electroconvulsive therapy: a proposed mechanism of action. Biol. Psychiatry **18**(11): 1301–1310.
27. MCCULLOCH, J., P. KELLY & J. J. GROME. 1981. GABAergic influence upon cerebral metabolism and perfusion. *In* Cerebral Microcirculation and Metabolism. J. Cervos-Navarro & E. Fritschka, Eds.: 189–193. Raven Press. New York, N.Y.

28. HEDNER, J., T. HEDNER, P. WESSBERG & J. JONASON. 1984. An analysis of the mechanism by which gamma-aminobutyric acid depresses ventilation in the rat. J. Appl. Physiol. **56**(4): 849–856.
29. LAURITZEN, M., M. B. JORGENSEN, N. H. DIEMER, A. GJEDDE & A. J. HANSEN. 1982. Persistent oligemia of rat cerebral cortex in the wake of spreading depression. Ann. Neurol. **12:** 469–474.
30. JOHANSSON, B. & B. NILSSON. 1977. The pathophysiology of the blood-brain barrier dysfunction induced by severe hypercapnia and by epileptic brain activity. Acta Neuropathol. **38:** 153–158.
31. PAPPIUS, H. M., H. E. SAVAKI, C. FIESCHI, S. I. RAPOPORT & L. SOKOLOFF. 1979. Osomotic opening of the blood-brain barrier and local cerebral glucose utilization. Ann. Neurol. **5:** 211–219.
32. RAPOPORT, S. I. 1980. Structure and function of the blood-brain barrier. *In* Cerebral Metabolism and Neural Function. J. V. Passonneau, R. A. Hawkins, W. D. Lust & F. A. Welsh, Eds.: 96–105. Williams & Williams. Baltimore, Md.
33. STOKER, M. J., C. M. SPENCER & M. HAMILTON. 1981. Blood-pressure elevation during ECT and associated cognitive deficit. *In* Electroconvulsive Therapy: An Appraisal. R. L. Palmer, Ed.: 106–123. Oxford University Press. New York, N.Y.
34. PRESKORN, S. H., G. H. IRWIN, S. SIMPSON, D. FRIESEN, J. RINNE & G. JERKOVICH. 1981. Medical therapies for mood disorders alter the blood-brain barrier. Science **213:** 469–471.
35. PRESKORN, S. H., M. E. RAICHLE & B. K. HARTMAN. 1982. Antidepressants alter cerebrovascular permeability and metabolic rate in primates. Science **217:** 250–252.
36. SPIEGEL, E., M. SPIEGEL-ADOLF & G. HENNY. 1942. Physiochemical changes in the brain accompanying electrically induced convulsive discharges. Trans. Am. Neurol. Assoc.:174. (Presented at the 68th Annual Meeting, Chicago, Ill., June 4–6.)
37. OFFNER, G. 1946. Electrical properties of tissues in shock therapy. Proc. Soc. Exp. Biol. **49:** 571–575.
38. LOWENBACK, H. & J. E. MORGAN. 1943. The human skin as a conductor of 60 cycle alternating current of high intensity, studied on "electroshock" patients. J. Lab. Clin. Med. **28:** 1103–1106.
39. MAXWELL, R. D. H. 1968. Electrical factors in electroconvulsive therapy. Acta Psychiatr. Scand. **44:** 436–448.
40. HAYES, K. J. 1950. The current path on electric convulsion shock. Arch. Neurol. Psychiatry **63:** 102–109.
41. LORIMER, F. M., M. M. SEGAL & S. N. STEIN. 1949. Path of current distribution in brain during electro-convulsive therapy. EEG Clin. Neurophysiol. **1:** 343–348.
42. WEAVER, L., R. WILLIAMS & S. RUSH. 1976. Current density in bilateral and unilateral ECT. Biol. Psychiatry **11**(3): 303–312.
43. SACKEIM, H. A., I. PROHOVNIK, P. DECINA, S. MALITZ & S. RESOR. 1983. Anticonvulsant properties of electroconvulsive therapy: theory and case report. *In* Cerebral Blood Flow, Metabolism and Epilepsy. M. Baldy-Moulinier *et al.* Eds.: 370–377. John Libbey. London, England.

Positron Emission Tomography and Autoradiographic Studies of Glucose Utilization following Electroconvulsive Seizures in Humans and Rats[a]

ROBERT F. ACKERMANN,[b,c,f,g] JEROME ENGEL, JR.,[c,d,f]
AND LEWIS BAXTER[e]

[b]Department of Radiological Sciences,
Division of Nuclear Medicine and Biophysics
[c]Department of Neurology
[d]Department of Anatomy
[e]Department of Psychiatry
[f]Brain Research Institute
[g]Laboratory of Biomedical and Environmental Sciences
UCLA School of Medicine
Los Angeles, California 90024

Positron emission tomography (PET) has been used in conjunction with modifications of the 2-deoxyglucose (2DG) method[1,2] to study local brain glucose metabolism in a variety of human seizure syndromes.[3,4] It would seem that seizures induced by electroconvulsive therapy (ECT) are ideal for PET studies in that they are more uniform from patient to patient than many other types of seizures, and in that their occurrence is controlled. However, ECT seizures have not been studied in detail, perhaps because these advantages bring with them some methodological disadvantages that are not easily overcome.

2DG METHOD

The 2DG method[1] exploits several facts concerning brain glucose metabolism to allow visualization of any brain regions that may be unusually active or inactive during a given physiological state. First, the adult brain normally utilizes glucose almost exclusively as its metabolic substrate for ATP production. Second, in brain a major demand for ATP comes from the various physiological processes associated with neuronal firing; the principal demand is for ion pumping.[5] Third, 2DG is sufficiently similar in structure to glucose to be taken up into brain by hexose carrier and then phosphorylated by hexokinase, but it is not sufficiently similar to proceed further in glucose metabolic pathways. Consequently, 2DG accumulates in brain cells in proportion to their glucose metabolic activity. If radioactive 2DG is administered, its accumulation in brain regions can be measured by localizing and counting the particles emitted as the isotope decays. For human studies 2DG is labeled with [^{18}F] to make [^{18}F]-fluorodeoxyglucose (FDG) which is localized and quantified within the brain by

[a]Supported by Department of Energy Contract No. DE-AC03-76-SF00012 and National Institutes of Health Grants No. NS-15654 and MH-037916

means of PET (see Reference 2 for theory and technical details). The most commonly used labeling isotope in animal studies is [^{14}C]; it is localized and quantified by means of contact autoradiography.[1]

SEIZURES AND THE 2DG METHOD

Seizure phenomena are well suited for analysis by the deoxyglucose method in that they are characterized by increased neuronal activity during ictus, and decreased activity during postictus. Thus seizure-mediating structures can in principle be identified by their increased ictal glucose utilization and decreased postictal utilization. A minor methodological complication can occur if seizures are sufficiently severe and prolonged to increase glucose metabolism to the point of depleting intracellular glucose pools; if this occurs, the precise extent to which ictal metabolism has increased may be overestimated.[6] However, this potential methodological limitation is not serious unless seizure-induced hypoglycemia is both severe and uncompensated for by increased glucose delivery,[7] e.g., by increased blood flow. Since there is considerable residual physiological capacity for increasing glucose delivery, this limitation becomes significant only under extreme conditions (much more extreme than are induced by a single ECT seizure). Even when present, this overestimation may in fact be useful to epileptologists since it makes more evident those structures that are most profoundly involved in mediating the seizures under study.

A methodological issue more relevant to quantitative 2DG analysis of ECT is the necessary assumption of a steady metabolic state lasting at least 30 minutes.[1] However, ECT seizures are episodic events rarely lasting more than 2 minutes. Therefore, all "ictal" 2DG measurements necessarily include postical as well as ictal glucose utilization. Since the relatively brief epochs of increased metabolism (ictus) are invariably paired with substantially longer epochs of decreased metabolism (postictus), the apparent metabolic rate for any structure involved in the ECT seizure will tend to be a weighted average of ictal hypermetabolism and postictal hypometabolism. Thus, ictal hypermetabolism may be underestimated, or possibly even undetected, if it is counterbalanced by subsequent postictal hypometabolism occurring in the same structure. This issue is of present interest because the preliminary results ($n = 6$) from our studies at the University of California, Los Angeles have thus far detected only global cerebral metabolic changes associated with ECT.

HUMAN STUDIES

All the patients in the present series were studied during a sequence of ECT treatments for depression. Four of the six patients were unipolar depressives; the other two were bipolar. Three of the six patients received bilateral ECT as treatment; the other three received unilateral ECT. All the patients received bilateral ECT on the day of PET scanning, regardless of their usual treatment, except one who received unilateral ECT. PET occurred randomly within a particular patient's treatment series, which consisted of 8–15 stimulations. All ECT were administered with a MECTA device; stimulation parameters were 70 Hz pulsed stimulation, 0.75 msecond pulse width, 1–2 second train duration, 100 V (<0.8 amp, 22 WS). All ECT were administered under methohexital anesthesia and mild succinyl choline paralysis. The usual practice of placing a tourniquet on one arm to confirm that a seizure had in fact been induced was not possible due to the need for bilateral intravenous lines to infuse

FDG and to obtain blood samples for quantitative metabolic analysis; seizure occurrence was confirmed, therefore, by EEG alone using gold disc electrodes placed according to the international 10–20 system and an 18-channel electroencephalograph (EEG) machine. PET scans were obtained under three conditions: baseline (fully conscious, no ECT); ictal (ECT seizure induced 1–3 minutes following an FDG bolus infusion); and postictal (an FDG bolus infusion administered 10–60 seconds following termination of an ECT seizure). In each condition, PET scans were obtained 45 minutes following FDG administration. For each patient, data were collected from 8–12 cortical and subcortical regions of interest on four separate image planes, comparable for all patients. The mean estimated metabolic rate of all the regions of interest on all four image planes was taken as an estimate of global metabolic rate. Technically satisfactory data were obtained from all three conditions (baseline, ictal,

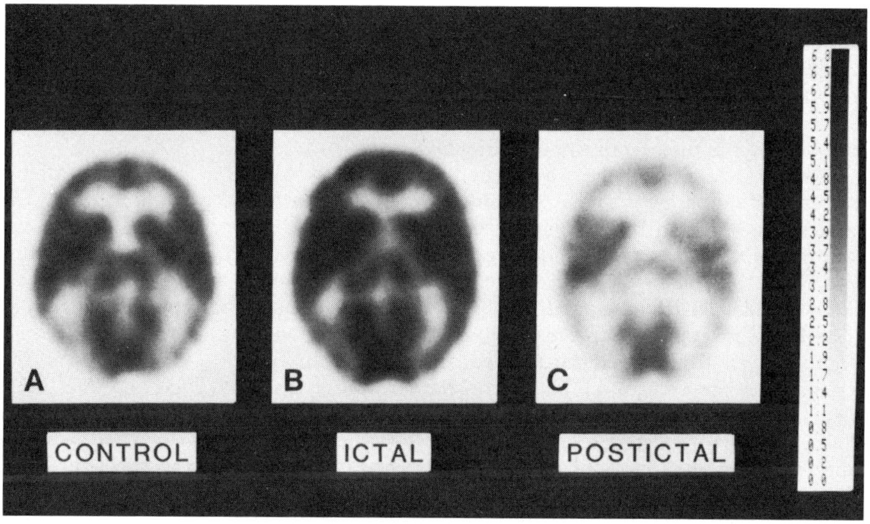

FIGURE 1. Control (A), ictal (B), and postictal (C) FDG scans of a patient undergoing ECT. Note the global ictal hypermetabolism and postictal hypometabolism. (Reproduced from Reference 8 with permission. © 1982 by the AAAS.)

and postictal) in two of the six patients; in two other patients, only ictal and postictal data were obtained; the remaining two patients had unsatisfactory quantitative data, and thus their scans were analyzed qualitatively by inspection.

Results from the first patient of this series were previously reported.[8] These data indicated that ictal glucose utilization increased globally from baseline levels, then dropped sharply during the ensuing postictal depression (FIGURE 1) (cf. Reference 9). These results were expected given that ECT induces increased neuronal activity during seizures, which is followed immediately by profound postictal depression. The reported results for ECT seizures contrast with those from petit mal seizures, which were associated with much greater increases in global metabolism ictally.[10] This latter observation does not necessarily suggest that petit mal seizures require more energy than do ECT seizures. Rather, it may reflect the absence of a hypometabolic postical depression following petit mal seizures. Neither ECT nor petit mal seizures showed discernable changes in glucose utilization pattern. With these generalized seizures, only global changes were observed.

The subsequent five patients have confirmed this latter finding that glucose utilization pattern does not change across seizure conditions. However, data from these patients have not confirmed the quantitative findings from the first. Rather, these patients have failed to show a reliable relationship between seizure condition and estimated global metabolic rate.

Both the nature of electroconvulsive seizures and the procedures employed for human ECT make it difficult to obtain valid and reliable quantitative glucose utilization data. For example, one virtually insurmountable procedural problem with ECT studies is that ethical considerations require induction of seizures under general anesthesia to prevent bone fractures and other injuries. However, since a finite risk accompanies general anesthesia, it cannot be induced to obtain comparable baseline data. Moreover, since short-acting barbiturates are used, postictal data are necessarily generated while the patient is emerging from anesthesia. Anesthesia complicates estimation of metabolic rate because it depresses brain metabolism by as much as 50% in both animals[1,11–17] and humans.[18,19] Therefore, baseline, ictal, and postictal metabolic data are not comparable unless the ictal and postictal "signals" are large enough to override the "noise" introduced by the differing anesthetic states. Apparently, this occurred only in the first of the six patients.

Moreover, some of the above-cited studies show also that anesthesia affects structures differentially; that is, not only is the global metabolic rate reduced, but the pattern of glucose utilization changes under anesthesia. However, as stated above, the pattern of glucose utilization did not appear to change during either ictus or postictus, even though blood flow studies have shown pattern changes with ECT[20] (see also Silfverskiöld, and Prohovnik, this volume). A possible reason for this discrepancy is that FDG scans represent the accumulated metabolic activity over the entire procedure (45 minutes), while both the seizure and the anesthetic state occur only at the beginning of the procedure. This opens the possibility that both ictal and anesthetic effects can be normalized by subsequent countervailing postictal and postanesthetic effects. On the other hand, ictal PET studies with the FDG method have been shown to reliably detect focal zones of hyper- and hypometabolism during partial seizures.[21,22] Therefore, the method is clearly capable of detecting local ictal metabolic changes in seizure phenomena known to be focal.

A third procedural problem has been that the ECT seizures have been difficult to define and quantify from EEG. They have been variable from patient to patient, and from seizure to seizure in the same patient, in both duration and characteristic EEG pattern; and the end of a seizure has not always been represented by a clear change in EEG pattern ("fit switch"). Moreover, the precise duration of postictal depression cannot be definitively determined from the EEG data.

ANIMAL STUDIES

In order to clarify some of the issues raised by our human ECT studies, we have begun a parallel 2DG study of electroconvulsive shock (ECS) in rats. To date, we have glucose utilization data from nine rats distributed among the same three conditions as the human study: baseline ($n = 3$), ictal ($n = 2$), and postictal ($n = 4$). However, in the rat study all data have been collected from unanesthetized subjects. The ECS consists of 60 Hz sinusoidal electrical stimulation delivered across the ear pinnae. In all the present animals stimulation parameters were 45–50 mamp, 2 seconds duration. This stimulation induced tonic-clonic seizures that lasted approximately 45 seconds.

"Baseline" animals were treated the same as "ictal" and "postictal" animals up to the point of stimulation. In ictal experiments, the ECS seizure was induced 80–120 seconds after infusion of [^{14}C]-2DG. In postictal experiments, the 2DG was infused 120 seconds after the ECS stimulation, i.e., approximately 75 seconds after termination of the seizure.

Global and regional quantitative estimates of glucose metabolic rate were obtained by Sokoloff's contact autoradiographic method.[1]

The animal data thus far corroborate those of the original published patient[8] in that ictal global metabolic rate is substantially increased (177% of baseline), while postictal global metabolism is profoundly depressed (only 32% of baseline). Importantly, inspection of the animal autoradiograms reveals that there is regional differentiation in both ictal and postictal utilization patterns which, as described above, is not evident thus far in the human FDG scans. However, as would be expected, these patterns are not as apparent as those associated with "generalized" seizures induced by amygdaloid kindling.[23,24]

CONCLUSIONS

The present results illustrate the utility of performing autoradiographic studies on animal models in conjunction with human tomographic studies. Obtaining reliable quantitative human data from ECT seizures is a difficult enterprise because experimental design must be compromised for the sake of patient welfare, and because the induced seizures are much more variable in humans than in rats. Were it not for the corresponding animal data one might have presumed that the results obtained from the first patient were spurious; but the animal data suggest that the first patient's results were probably correct, and those of the other patients probably incorrect, due to technical and methodological difficulties.

PET images have significantly less structural resolution than do autoradiographic images, even when the difference in size between human and rat brains is taken into account. For example, one can easily differentiate the amygdaloid nuclei on 2DG autoradiograms, but cannot do so on FDG scans.[25,26] However, with the continuing advance of PET technology[27] we can now realistically anticipate the ability to detect and measure metabolic alterations in small cortical regions of interest and in subcortical nuclei. Even so, autoradiography will probably always be necessary for maximal resolution. On the other hand, animal autoradiographic studies have the disadvantage of being a static (one subject per datum) method, while PET allows repeated studies of the same subject.

Clearly then, human PET and animal autoradiographic methods are complementary, and data from both methodologies are needed to gain an anatomically and temporally detailed understanding of the effects of ECT on brain glucose utilization. At UCLA, human and animal metabolic ECT studies are continuing with the goal of identifying those structures that are either activated or suppressed during ictal and postictal states. This information will then allow investigation of the relationship between alterations of metabolism in specific cerebral structures both ictally and postictally, and the relative efficacy of ECT.

REFERENCES

1. SOKOLOFF, L., M. REIVICH, C. KENNEDY, M. H. DES ROSIERS, C. S. PATLAK, K. D. PETTIGREW, O. SAKURADA & M. SHINOHARA. 1977. The [^{14}C]deoxyglucose method for

the measurement of local cerebral glucose utilization: theory, procedure, and normal values in the conscious and anesthetized albino rat. J. Neurochem. **28:** 897–916.
2. PHELPS, M. E., J. C. MAZZIOTTA & S.-C. HUANG. 1982. Study of cerebral function with positron computed tomography. J. Cereb. Blood Flow Metab. **2:** 113–162.
3. ENGEL, J., JR. 1984. The use of positron emission tomographic scanning in epilepsy. Ann. Neurol. **15**(suppl.): S180–S191.
4. ACKERMAN, R. F., J. ENGEL, JR. & M. E. PHELPS. Identification of seizure-mediating brain structures with the deoxyglucose method: studies of human epilepsy with positron emission tomography, and animal seizure models with contact autoradiography. *In* Basic Mechanisms of the Epilepsies. A. V. Delgado-Escueta, A. A. Ward & D. M. Woodbury, Eds. Raven Press. New York, N.Y. (In press.)
5. MATA, M., D. J. FINK, H. GAINER, C. B. SMITH, L. DAVIDSEN, H. SAVAKI, W. J. SCHWARTZ & L. SOKOLOFF. 1980. Activity-dependent energy metabolism in rat posterior pituitary primarily reflects sodium pump activity. J. Neurochem. **34:** 213–215.
6. PARDRIDGE, W. M., P. D. CRANE, L. J. MIETUS & W. H. OLDENDORF. 1982. Nomogram for 2-deoxyglucose lumped constant for rat brain cortex. J. Cereb. Blood Flow Metab. **2:** 197–202.
7. INGVAR, M. & B. K. SIESJÖ. 1983. Local blood flow and glucose consumption in the rat brain during sustained bicuculline-induced seizures. Acta Neurol. Scand. **68:** 129–144.
8. ENGEL, J., JR., D. E. KUHL & M. E. PHELPS. 1982. Patterns of human local cerebral glucose metabolism during epileptic seizures. Science **218:** 64–66.
9. KETY, S. S., R. B. WOODFORD, M. H. HARMEL, F. A. FREYHAN, K. E. APPEL & C. F. SCHMIDT. 1947–48. Cerebral blood flow and metabolism in schizophrenia: the effects of barbiturate semi-narcosis, insulin coma and electroshock. Am. J. Psychiatry **104:** 765–770.
10. ENGEL, J., JR., P. LUBENS, D. E. KUHL & M. E. PHELPS. 1985. Local cerebral metabolic rate for glucose during petit mal absences. Ann. Neurol. **17:** 121–128.
11. HAWKINS, R. A., A. L. MILLER, J. E. CREMER & R. L. VEECH. 1974. Measurement of the rate of glucose utilization by rat brain *in vivo*. J. Neurochem. **23:** 917–923.
12. CRANE, P. D., L. D. BRAUN, E. M. CORNFORD, J. E. CREMER, J. M. GLASS & W. H. OLDENDORF. 1978. Dose dependent reduction of glucose utilization by pentobarbital in rat brain. Stroke **9:** 12–18.
13. HERKENHAM, M. 1978. Demonstration of the habenulo-interpeduncular fiber system by [^{14}C]-2-deoxy-glucose. Neurosci. Abstr. **4:** 222.
14. SHAPIRO, H. M., J. H. GREENBERG, M. REIVICH, G. ASHMEAD & L. SOKOLOFF. 1978. Local cerebral glucose uptake in awake and halothane-anesthetized primates. Anesthesiology **48:** 97–103.
15. MYERS, R. R. & H. M. SHAPIRO. 1979. Local cerebral metabolism during enflurane anesthesia: identification of epileptogenic foci. Electroencephalogr. Clin. Neurophys. **47:** 153–162.
16. ABDUL-RAHMAN, A., N. DAHLGREN, M. INGVAR, S. REHNCRONA & B. K. SIESJÖ. 1979. Local versus regional cerebral blood flow in the rat at high (hypoxia) and low (phenobarbital anesthesia) flow rates. Acta Physiol. Scand. **106:** 52–60.
17. CILLUFO, J. M., R. E. ANDERSON, F. W. SHARBROUGH & T. M. SUNDT, JR. 1981. Correlation of brain blood flow, intracellular pH and metabolism in hypoglycemic cats under halothane and barbiturate anesthesia. Brain Res. **216:** 125–143.
18. PIERCE, E. C., JR., C. J. LAMBERTSEN, S. DEUTSCH, P. E. CHASE, H. W. LINDE, R. D. DRIPPS & H. L. PRICE. 1962. Cerebral circulation and metabolism during thiopental anesthesia and hyperventilation in man. J. Clin. Invest. **41:** 1664–1671.
19. HIMWICH, W. A., E. HOMBURGER, R. MARESCA & H. E. HIMWICH. 1946–1947. Brain metabolism in man: unanesthetized and in pentothal narcosis. Am. J. Psychiatry **103:** 689–696.
20. SILFVERSKIÖLD, P., L. GUSTAFSON & J. RISBERG. 1983. Changes in regional cerebral blood flow during ECT. Proceedings of 13th C.I.N.P. Congress. *In* ECT: Basic Mechanisms. R. H. Belmaker, B. Lerer & R. D. Weiner, Eds.: 124–131. John Libbey. London, England.
21. ENGEL, J., JR., D. E. KUHL, M. E. PHELPS & J. C. MAZZIOTTA. 1982. Interictal cerebral

glucose metabolism in partial epilepsy and its relation to EEG changes. Ann. Neurol. **12:** 510–517.
22. THEODORE, W. H., M. E. NEWMARK, S. SATO, R. BROOKS, N. PATRONAS, R. DE LA PAZ, G. DI CHIRO, R. M. KESSLER, R. MARGOLIN, R. G. MANNING, M. CHANNING & R. J. PORTER. 1983. [^{18}F] Fluorodeoxyglucose positron emission tomography in refractory complex partial seizures. Ann. Neurol. **14:** 429–437.
23. ENGEL, J., JR., L. WOLFSON & L. BROWN. 1978. Anatomical correlates of electrical and behavioral events related to amgydaloid kindling. Ann. Neurol. **3:** 538–544.
24. ACKERMANN, R. F., H. CHUGANI, S. CALDECOTT-HAZARD & J. ENGEL, JR. 1984. Postictal cerebral metabolism–blood flow mismatches observed in hippocampus and substantia nigra of amygdala-kindled rats. Neurosci. Abstr. **10:** 3.
25. GOOCHEE, C., W. RASBAND & L. SOKOLOFF. 1980. Computerized densitometry and color coding of [^{14}C] deoxyglucose autoradiographs. Ann. Neurol. **7:** 359–370.
26. MAZZIOTTA, J. C., M. E. PHELPS, D. PLUMMER & D. E. KUHL. 1981. Quantitation in positron emission computed tomography. 5. Physical-anatomical effects. J. Comput. Assisted Tomography **5:** 734–743.
27. HOFFMAN, E. J., M. VAN DER STEE, A. R. RICCI & M. E. PHELPS. 1984. Prospects for both precision and accuracy in positron emission tomography. Ann. Neurol. **15**(suppl): S25–S34.

Effects of Electroconvulsive Therapy upon Brain Electrical Activity[a]

RICHARD D. WEINER,[b,c,e] HELEN J. ROGERS,[b]
JONATHAN R. T. DAVIDSON,[b,c] AND
E. MICHAEL KAHN[d]

[b]*Department of Psychiatry*
Duke University Medical Center
Durham, North Carolina 27710

[c]*Psychiatry Service*
Durham Veterans Administration Medical Center
508 Fulton Street
Durham, North Carolina 27705

[d]*Western Psychiatric Institute*
3811 O'Hara Street
Pittsburgh, Pennsylvania 15213

INTRODUCTION

Electroconvulsive therapy (ECT) acts through the elicitation of a series of brief paroxysmal electrophysiologic events involving neurons throughout the brain. The mechanisms by which seizure activity produces both therapeutic and adverse effects are a major focus of this conference. The data presented here, however, will center both upon the characteristics of the seizures themselves and upon the interictal neurophysiologic changes that are produced as a result of such seizure activity. It is felt that attention to the electrophysiologic domain, particularly with respect to the effects of variations in ECT technique, may provide useful information not only clinically, but in the understanding of mechanisms as well.

METHODS

The data to be presented are part of a larger study, for which some preliminary results have already been reported.[1-3] Other findings relating to cognitive effects are presented elsewhere in this volume.[4] With respect to electrophysiologic variables, data were collected from a total of 74 subjects before, during, and after a course of ECT to which they were referred for clinical indications, independent of the research protocol. A reference group consisted of 21 depressed psychiatric inpatients not referred for ECT.

Experimental subjects were randomly assigned to receive their ECT treatments using either bilateral or right unilateral electrode placement, and either brief pulse or

[a]Supported by the National Institutes of Mental Health, the Veterans Administration, and the Department of Psychiatry, Duke University Medical Center.

[e]Address correspondence to Dr. Weiner at the Durham VA Medical Center.

sine wave stimulus. This resulted in four experimental groups: pulse unilateral (PUL), sine unilateral (SUL), pulse bilateral (PBL), and sine bilateral (SBL) (TABLE 1). In the rare case where a subject's behavioral dominance was equivocal on a performance battery,[5] assignment to bilateral electrode placement was made. In order to maximize efficacy for unilateral placement, a high centroparietal location was used in conjunction with a standard frontotemporal location. The pulse stimulus was generated by a Mecta Corporation MECTA ECT device, with typical starting parameters of 60 pulse pairs per second, 0.75 msecond pulse width, and 1.25 seconds duration. The sine wave stimulus was generated by a Medcraft Corporation B-24 Mark III ECT device with typical starting parameters of 140 volts rms for 0.6 second. Stimulus intensity was titrated so as to produce seizures greater than 25 seconds by electroencephalographic (EEG) criteria. Seizures more than 60 seconds in duration were followed by a decrease in stimulus intensity at the next treatment session unless such settings had already proven ineffective in eliciting an adequate seizure. In all cases, ECT was given three times weekly, with the end point of the ECT course determined by the subject's attending psychiatrist.

Single-channel EEG monitoring of the seizure was obtained using the MECTA ECT device, which has such capability built in. A custom switch (Mecta Corp.) allowed the seizure monitoring also to be carried out in conjunction with the Medcraft apparatus. EEG electrodes were placed in a headband, with bifrontopolar placement for bilateral ECT and left frontopolar to left anterior temporal locations for right unilateral ECT. The latter configuration was chosen so as to ensure the presence of bilaterally generalized seizures with the unilateral technique. The seizure recordings were later rated, blind to subject group, with regard to duration of paroxysmal activity, degree of postictal suppression, and the presence or absence of various ictal stages, as outlined in FIGURE 1.

TABLE 1. Number of Subjects Receiving EEG Testing

	C[a]	PUL	SUL	PBL	SBL
Ictal and Acute interictal effects	21	14	18	24	18
Six-month follow-up	12	11	11	13	11

[a]C is control.

Prior to ECT and both two to three days and six months following completion of the ECT course, eight-channel EEG recordings were made, using standard referential and bipolar montages and incorporating runs during photic stimulation and hyperventilation. These EEGs were interpreted, blind to subject group, by one of the investigators (R.D.W.), who is a trained clinical encephalographer. An objective visual rating instrument was designed for this purpose, in order to allow an assessment of various EEG features thought to be affected by ECT (TABLE 2). Using a series of five-point ratings, ranging from "absent" to "severe," measures were determined for both overall abnormality and frequency of the dominant posterior rhythm, along with composite indices for extent and symmetry of slowing and for hyperventilation-induced changes.

During these EEG recording sessions, several minutes of EEG data were also transferred on-line into a digital computer present in our laboratory. A special montage was used for this purpose, which also included an eye movement channel and a marker channel which was controlled by the computer to denote the beginning of each contiguous four-second epoch of digitized data. This information was then used to

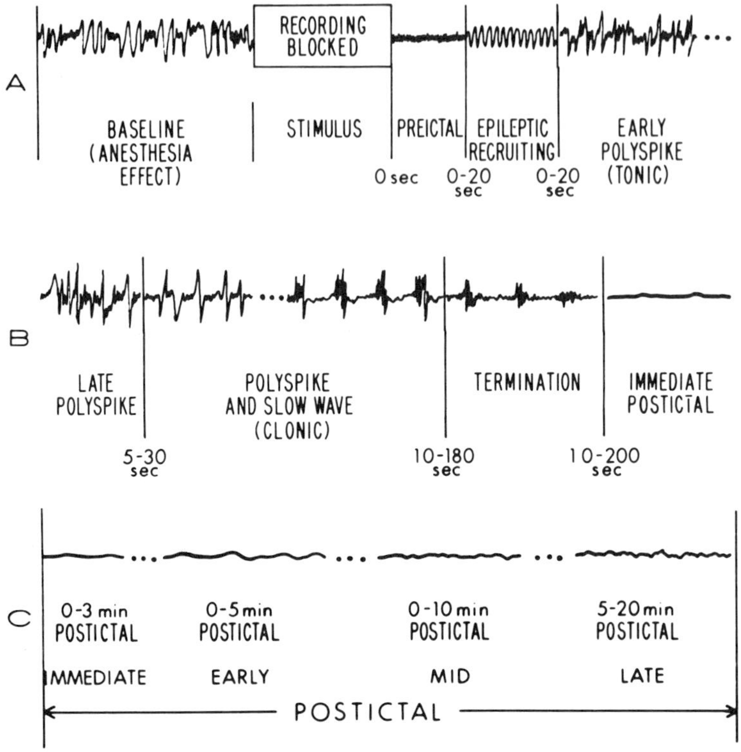

FIGURE 1. Ictal and postictal EEG stages with ECT. (From Reference 6.)

allow manual rejection of data contaminated by artifact or drowsiness. For the purposes of the present investigation, only two channels of computerized data were subjected to further analysis. These consisted of homologous left and right frontocentral derivations (F3-C3 and F4-C4). Unrejected segments of EEG were analyzed off-line by fast Fourier transform. The results of the spectral analysis were then used to determine a slowing index, defined as mean of delta plus theta activity (1 to 7.75 Hz) for left and right frontocentral channels added together. In addition, a slowing symmetry index, defined as left minus right slowing, was also calculated. The choice of

TABLE 2. EEG–Visual Rating Method

A. Types of slowing—rated as absent, borderline, mild, moderate, or severe by objective criteria
   1. Spontaneous slowing
   2. Frontal intermittent slowing
   3. Other rhythmic slowing
   4. Asymmetry of slowing
   5. Hyperventilation-induced slowing
B. Frequency of posterior rhythm
C. Overall level of abnormality—rated absent to severe as above

the specific frequency bands utilized was based upon a general acceptance of delta and theta band rhythms as pathologic manifestations of most encephalopathic entities, including ECT.[7]

RESULTS AND DISCUSSION

No significant intergroup differences were found on the basis of subject age, number of ECT treatments received, number of missed seizures, and presence of psychotropic medication during the week prior to baseline testing. Likewise, an equivalency was demonstrated among the experimental groups with regard to both mean and cumulative adequate seizure duration (57.2 seconds, 509 seconds).

In view of claims that cumulative seizure duration might represent an objective means of "dosing" ECT,[8] the extent of correlation between this parameter and therapeutic response was determined, using the mean improvement in Hamilton Depression Rating Scale[9] scores for this purpose. Interestingly, no significant relationship was found, suggesting that when the presence of adequate seizures and a sufficient number of treatments are assured, the actual total amount of time spent seizing is of little therapeutic import.

In a related analysis, neither mean nor cumulative seizure duration was observed to have a significant effect upon degree of either memory impairment[4] or EEG slowing (which will be discussed below). Accordingly, both of these findings appear to demonstrate that the mechanism by which induced seizures produce both beneficial and adverse effects with ECT has to do with factors other than the mere duration of the paroxysmal activity.

The seizures produced with ECT have been described as quite similar, not only to those produced by pharmacoconvulsive agents, but also to those occurring spontaneously in individuals with major motor epilepsy.[10,11] While preictal and epileptic recruiting activity are frequently not observed, both polyspike and polyspike and slow wave stages, which are electrophysiologic concomitants of tonic and clonic behavioral stages respectively, are almost invariably present with a well-generalized ictal response (FIGURE 1). The polyspike and slow wave phase may either terminate abruptly or may dissipate over a period of time. Postictally, some degree of transient suppression, or flattening, of EEG activity may be present.

With only a single EEG recording channel in the present study, the symmetry of the ictal response, which has been reported as more intense over the stimulated hemisphere with unilateral ECT,[12] could not be investigated. An analysis of ictal and postictal stages for the single channel of available data was, however, carried out. This revealed that while the presence of ictal stages was independent of ECT modality, the extent of postictal suppression, already established to be less with unilateral ECT, particularly over the cerebral hemisphere contralateral to stimulation, was found to be particularly intense with sine wave bilateral ECT (p [SBL > PBL, PUL, SUL] = 0.007, 0.002, 0.002).

This finding suggests that sine wave bilateral ECT, drawing upon its combination of bilateral stimulation with the presence of a long duration for each phase of the stimulus cycle, may be characterized by particularly intense seizures. Empirical data reported during the preanesthetic/relaxant era appear to substantiate this effect, with notations that patients receiving sine wave bilateral treatments were less responsive during the seizure, showed more intense convulsive movements, and took longer to arouse postictally.[13,14] Other more recent findings, presented elsewhere in this volume,[15] dealing with the recovery of orientation post-ECT, are also supportive of the concept of a specificity of ECT modality on the basis of generalization and/or intensity of the ictal discharge. Finally, the acute postictal and interictal hypometabolic effects which have been reported by others to take place in association with ECT, and which have also been discussed elsewhere in this volume,[16,17] are additionally quite compatible with this sort of hypothesis.

Over a course of ECT, some degree of EEG slowing often occurs. This slowing tends to be generalized, frontally predominant, and both regular and irregular in morphology. Electroencephalographically, such a pattern is considered nonspecific and is observed in a variety of conditions, including postictal delirium in epileptics.[7] In addition to a considerable interindividual variability in extent of ECT-induced slowing, some investigations have reported that number of treatments and electrode placement also play a significant role.[11,18]

In terms of the present study, both visual ratings and computer analysis revealed that over a course of ECT, subjects receiving either bilateral electrode placement or sine wave stimuli demonstrated greater EEG slowing increases than subjects receiving unilateral, brief pulse, or no ECT (TABLE 3). The mean spectral slowing indices, which were found to be more sensitive than visual ratings for subtle differences (e.g., PUL vs. C), are shown in FIGURE 2. These data represent the first time that increased ECT-induced EEG slowing has been shown to occur on the basis of stimulus waveform.

TABLE 3. Acute EEG Slowing Increases (2–3 Days Post-ECT vs. Baseline)

	p Values (2 × 2 + 1 ANOVAS)		
	BL > UL	BL > C	UL > C
Visually rated	0.03	0.0001	0.0001
Computer analyzed	0.02	0.0001	0.05
	S > P	S > C	P > C
Visually rated	0.03	0.0001	0.0001
Computer analyzed	(0.07)	0.002	0.02

Based upon the postictal suppression findings described above, it is tempting to postulate that, again, something more "intense" about the seizures produced by bilateral electrode placement and sine wave stimuli may be responsible for these differences. In fact, postictal suppression and EEG slowing were indeed found to be highly correlated. Another related result was the extent of hyperventilatory response, an effect that is known to be sensitive to encephalopathic changes, particularly those involving the diencephalon.[7] In the present sample, subjects receiving sine wave ECT were found to have a greater hyperventilatory response than those receiving pulse ECT ($p = 0.05$), despite the fact that no electrode-placement-specific effect was observed. Together, these data provide evidence to support the hypothesis that different types of ECT exert differential effects upon the brain substance.

Although, as noted earlier, some researchers have presented evidence for greater EEG slowing ipsilateral to the side of stimulation with unilateral ECT, this was not observed in the present study, at least in terms of intergroup differences. This, perhaps, is not surprising, given the tendency of encephalopathic changes involving deep midline structures to reveal themselves in a symmetrical fashion.[7] It may also reflect the use of a centroparietal electrode located close to the cerebral midline, as opposed to a more lateral position. Still, analysis of symmetry relationships was productive of a tendency

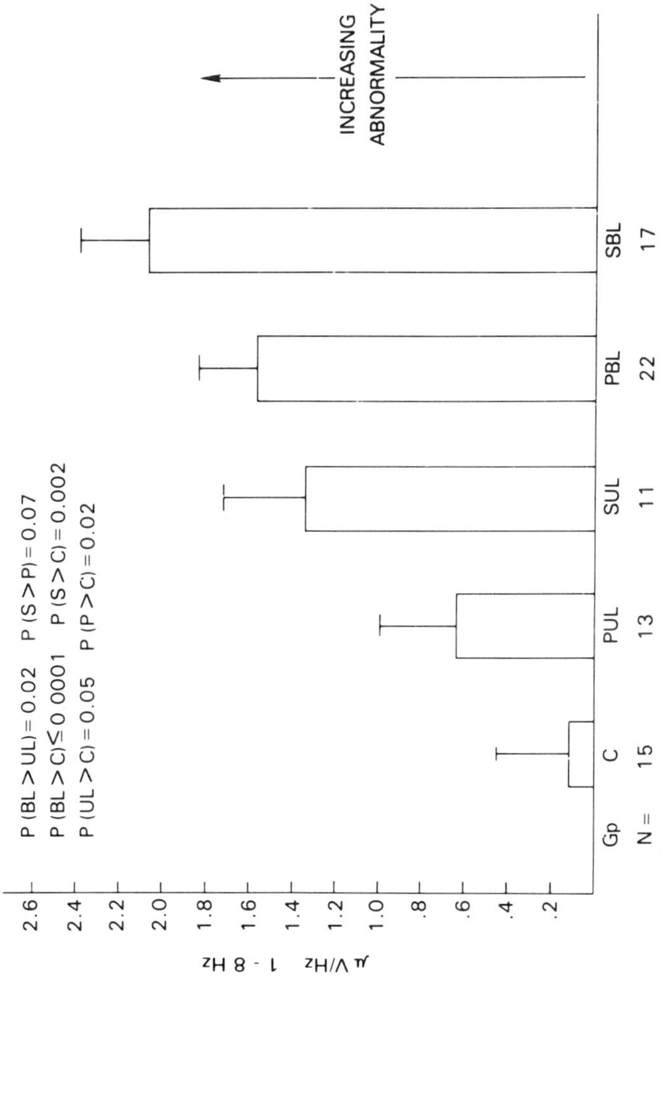

FIGURE 2. Acute bifrontocentral computer-analyzed slowing change with ECT (delta through theta bands). Difference between 2–3 days post-ECT and baseline; means (standard error, SE).

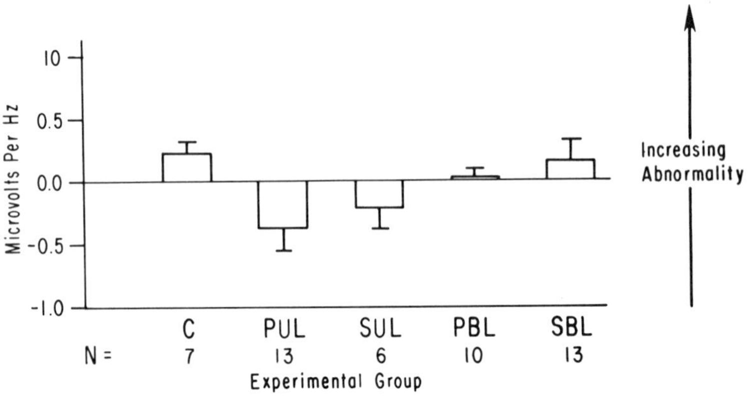

FIGURE 3. Long-term bifrontocentral computer-analyzed slowing change with ECT (delta through theta bands). Six months post-ECT minus baseline score (+SE).

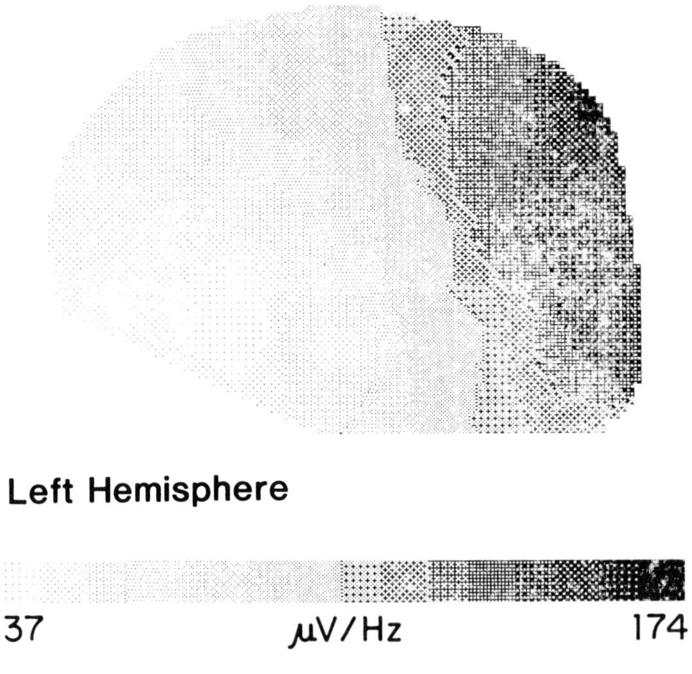

FIGURE 4. Topographic map of left hemispheric alpha activity during the resting state with eyes closed (control subject). Scale in microvolts per Hertz. Nineteen standard scalp leads placed per International 10-20 format, with linked ear electrodes used as a reference.

for sine wave bilateral stimuli to produce slightly greater left- than right-sided slowing ($p < 0.02$ for visual rating, $p < 0.03$ for computer analysis). This latter finding, which is compatible with some earlier studies,[11,19] may be secondary to an underlying predisposition for the left hemisphere to manifest signs of impairment, assuming an insult of sufficient magnitude.

Given the presence of acute adverse central nervous system (CNS) changes with ECT, it is important to establish the extent of their persistence, especially with the widespread concern that exists regarding the possibility of irreversible brain damage with this treatment modality.[20] While previous investigators have reported that ECT-induced EEG slowing has a duration of weeks rather than months or years,[21] such work tended to be unsystematic in its approach and did not incorporate quantitative

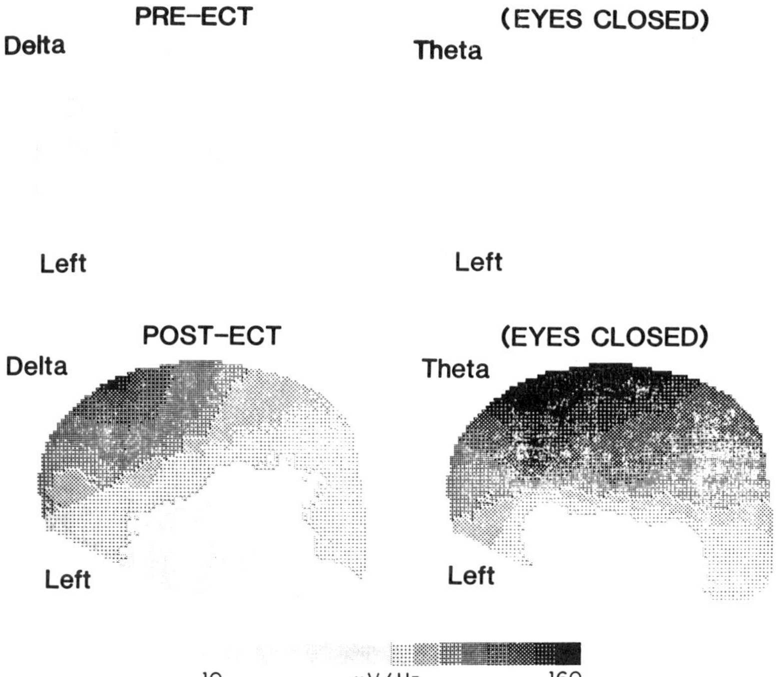

FIGURE 5. Left hemispheric delta and theta activity before (upper) and two days after (lower) a course of pulse unilateral ECT. Scale, lead locations, and reference as in FIGURE 4.

analytic techniques. In an attempt to compensate for these deficiencies, we looked at differences in both visually rated and computer-analyzed EEG parameters between pre-ECT baseline testing and six months following completion of the ECT course. The computer-analyzed data for long-term slowing changes are shown in FIGURE 3.

Overall, in terms of intergroup effects, it appeared that acute slowing had dissipated by the time of the six-month follow-up test session. Still, when the results of individual cases were considered, it was found that the three individuals with the greatest amount of residual slowing all received sine wave bilateral ECT. While such a finding is not necessarily statistically meaningful, it may serve to illustrate the manner in which intergroup comparisons can wash out effects characterized by a low incidence of occurrence. In any event, it leaves open the issue of persistent CNS deficits, something that will be discussed elsewhere in this volume, with regard to alterations in memory function.[4]

CONCLUSIONS AND FUTURE DIRECTIONS

The results presented above, combined with the related work of others, provide support for the hypothesis that variations in ECT technique produce seizures that differ from one another in some fundamental, though not well-understood, fashion.

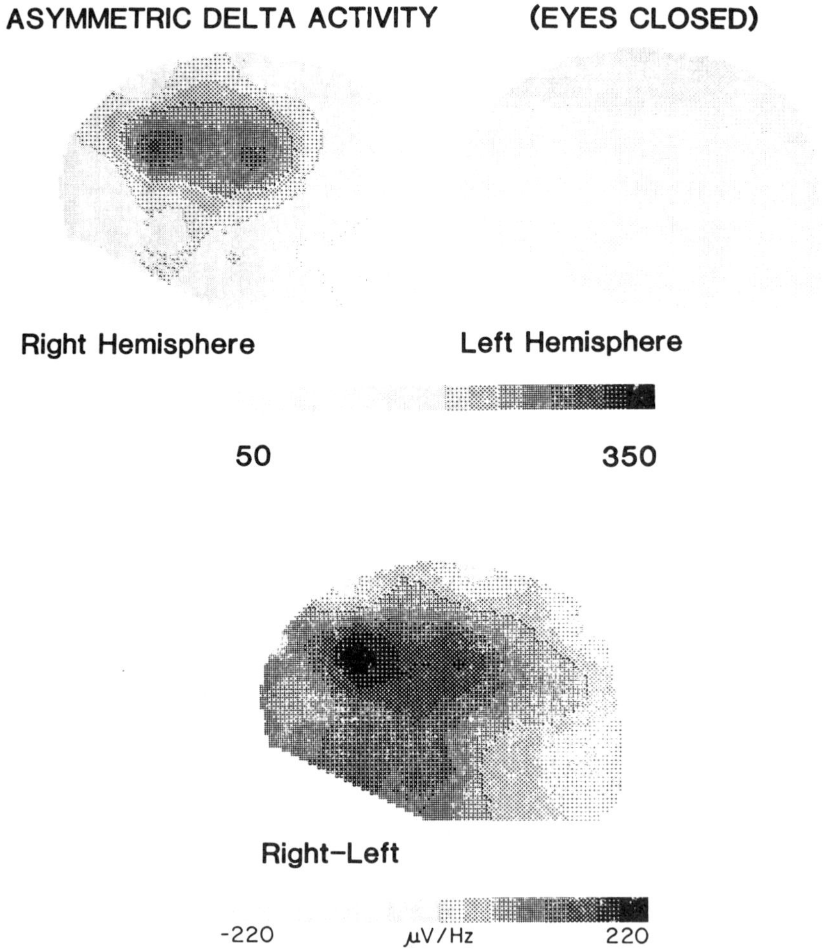

FIGURE 6. Upper: left and right delta activity during burst of asymmetrical slowing two days after a course of six pulse unilateral and two pulse bilateral ECT. Lower: hemispheric difference map (right-left) for the above. Scale, lead locations, and references as in FIGURE 4.

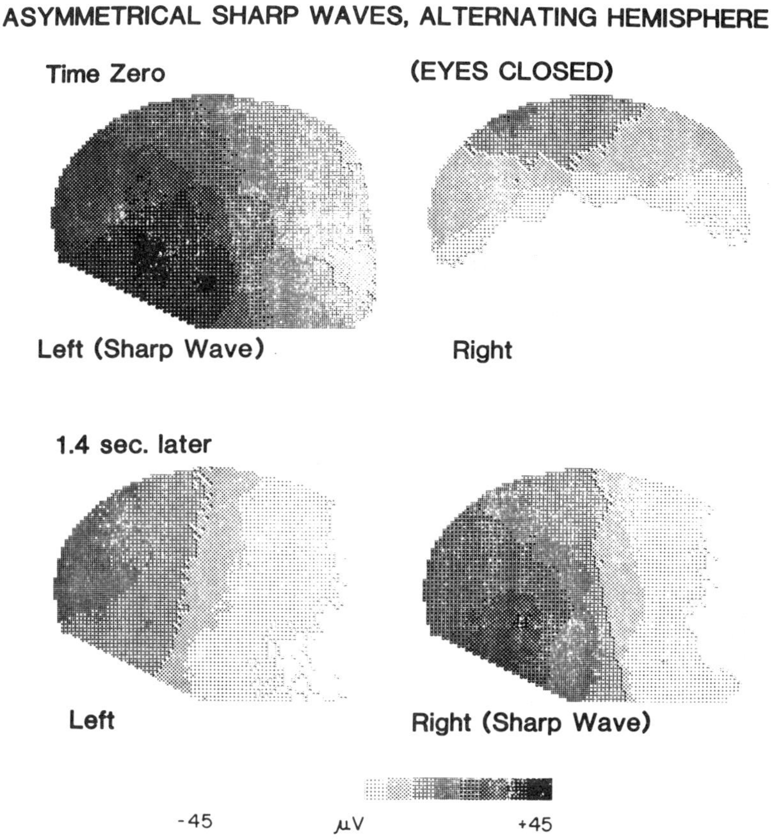

FIGURE 7. Left and right hemispheric voltage field maps for peaks of shifting asymmetrical sharp transients occuring two days following a course of pulse bilateral ECT. Scale, lead locations, and reference as in FIGURE 4.

Furthermore, such differences may well underlie the degree of CNS dysfunction produced by this treatment modality, irrespective of therapeutic effects. In particular, unilateral nondominant electrode placement and low-energy stimuli both appear to offer the opportunity to lower neurophysiologic morbidity with ECT, at least in terms of acute effects.

Presently, our laboratory is embarking upon a replication and extension of these findings. With respect to baseline and follow-up EEG data collection, we have, in order to gain better spatial resolution, now begun to utilize 19, as opposed to 2, channels of EEG. In addition to this expansion of acquisition capability, we are also carrying out topographic mapping of spectral EEG indices, based upon methods developed at the National Institutes of Mental Health and elsewhere.[22] This new technique provides two-dimensional color-coded or grey-scale displays of any scalp-recorded electrophysiologic parameter in a format that is both easy to interpret and anatomically relevant.

FIGURE 4 demonstrates a left hemispheric display of alpha activity in the resting state with eyes closed for a control subject. One can easily appreciate the classical frontal-occipital gradient of the resting alpha pattern, with darker patterns signifying greater alpha intensity (publication costs precluded the use of the considerably more striking color display). An example of left hemispheric slowing before and after a course of ECT is depicted in FIGURE 5. In this instance, both a diffuse, but frontally predominant, delta increase and a diffuse, centrally maximal theta increase post-ECT can be easily appreciated. Potential asymmetries in spectral indices are particularly easy to visualize with this technique. FIGURE 6 portrays left, right, and hemispheric difference maps for a period of asymmetrical delta activity in an individual who, two days post-ECT, had intermittent runs of such slowing.

Aside from the mapping of time-averaged spectral parameters associated with EEG background activity, our system can also map out the spatial electrical fields of transient electrophysiologic events, such as spikes or sharp waves. FIGURE 7 shows the left and right hemispheric fields associated with the peaks of two asymmetric sharp transients in a patient two days following completion of an ECT course. One could, of course, easily adapt this latter process to the investigation of ictal phenomena with ECT. In addition to the primary use of these types of EEG mapping, it can also be used to provide an electrophysiologic correlate to other imaging techniques, such as regional cerebral blood flow, positron emission tomography, or nuclear magnetic resonance. This can be accomplished by using, where appropriate, specialized analytic techniques designed to extract cortical information from whole brain scans.

In summary, it is hoped that with refinements in methodology such as these, a more definitive understanding of the electrophysiology of ECT can be established. The increase in knowledge gained should help to carry us closer to a characterization of the mechanisms underlying ECT, which is, of course, itself electrophysiologic in nature.

REFERENCES

1. WEINER. R. D., H. J. ROGERS, J. DAVIDSON & R. D. MILLER. 1982. Evaluation of the central nervous system risks of ECT. Psychopharmacol. Bull. **18:** 29–31.
2. WELCH, C. A., R. D. WEINER, D. WEIR, J. F. CAHILL, H. J. ROGERS, J. DAVIDSON, R. D. MILLER & M. R. MANDEL. 1982. Efficacy of ECT in the treatment of depression: wave form and electrode placement considerations. Psychopharmacol. Bull. **18:** 31–34.
3. WEINER, R. D., H. J. ROGERS, C. A. WELCH, J. R. T. DAVIDSON, R. D. MILLER, D. WEIR, J. F. CAHILL & L. R. SQUIRE. 1984. ECT stimulus parameters and electrode placement: relevance to therapeutic and adverse effects. *In* ECT: Basic Mechanisms. B. Lerer, R. D. Weiner & R. H. Belmaker, Eds.: 139–147. John Libbey and Co. London, England.
4. WEINER, R. D., H. J. ROGERS, J. R. T. DAVIDSON & L. R. SQUIRE. 1986. Effects of stimulus parameters on cognitive side effects. Ann. N.Y. Acad. Sci. (This volume.)
5. D'ELIA, G. 1970. Unilateral ECT. Acta Psychiatr. Scand. Suppl. **215:** 5–98.
6. WEINER, R. D. 1982. Electroencephalographic correlates of ECT. Psychopharmacol. Bull. **18:** 78–79.
7. KILOH, L. G., A. J. MCCOMAS, J. W. OSSELTON & A. R. M. UPTON. 1982. Clinical Electroencephalography. 4th edit. Butterworths. London, England.
8. MALETZKY, B. M. 1978. Seizure duration and clinical effect in psychiatry. Compr. Psychiatry **19:** 541–550.
9. HAMILTON, M. 1960. A rating scale for depression. J. Neurol. Neurosurg. Psychiatry **23:** 56–62.
10. CHATRIAN, G. E. & M. C. PETERSEN. 1960. The convulsive patterns produced by Indoklon, Metrazol and electroshock: some depth electrographic observations in human patients. Electroencephalogr. Clin. Neurophysiol. **12:** 715–725.
11. WEINER, R. D. 1983. EEG related to electroconvulsive therapy. *In* EEG and Evoked

Potentials in Psychiatry and Behavioral Neurology. J. R. Hughes & W. P. Wilson, Eds.: 101–126. Butterworth Publishers. Boston, Mass.
12. STATON, R. D., P. J. HASS & R. A. BRUMBACK. 1981. Electroencephalographic recording during bitemporal and unilateral nondominant hemisphere (Lancaster position) electroconvulsive therapy. J. Clin. Psychiatry **42:** 264–269.
13. LIBERSON, W. T. 1948. Brief stimulus therapy: physiological and clinical observations. Am. J. Psychiatry **105:** 28–39.
14. MARSHALL, T. J. & D. DOBBS. 1959. Treatment technique and apnea in electroshock. Dis. Nerv. Syst. **20:** 582–583.
15. DANIEL, W. F. & H. F. CROVITZ. 1986. Disorientation during electroconvulsive therapy. Ann. N.Y. Acad. Sci. (This volume.)
16. SILFVERSKIÖLD, P., *et al.* 1986. Acute and late effects of electroconvulsive therapy. Ann. N.Y. Acad. Sci. (This volume.)
17. PROHOVNIK, I., *et al.* 1986. Acute reduction of regional cerebral blood flow following electroconvulsive therapy. Ann. N.Y. Acad. Sci. (This volume.)
18. FINK, M. 1979. Convulsive Therapy—Theory and Practice. Raven Press. New York, N.Y.
19. VOLAVKA, J. 1974. Is EEG slowing related to therapeutic effect of convulsive therapy? *In* Psychobiology of Convulsive Therapy. M. Fink, S. Kety, J. McGaugh, & T. A. Williams, Eds.: 35–40. V. H. Winston and Sons. Washington, D.C.
20. WEINER, R. D. 1984. Does ECT cause brain damage? Behav. Brain Sci. **7:** 1–53.
21. WEINER, R. D. 1980. The persistence of ECT-induced changes in the electroencephalogram. J. Nerv. Ment. Dis. **168:** 224–228.
22. COPPOLA, R., M. S. BUCHSBAUM & F. RIGAL. 1982. Computer generation of surface distribution maps of measures of brain activity. Comput. Biol. Med. **12:** 191–199.

Neurophysiological Effects

Discussion of Part V

VICTOR MILSTEIN

Larue D. Carter Memorial Hospital and
Indiana University School of Medicine
1315 West Tenth Street
Indianapolis, Indiana 46202

Although the therapeutic effectiveness of electroconvulsive therapy (ECT) is generally accepted, a major criticism is that those giving the treatment have little idea of how it works. While this can be said also of a number of very effective treatments in medicine (digitalis, for example), it does not diminish the need to understand and explain ECT's mode of action, especially since ECT affects the brain, a fact to which many respond emotionally. Drug therapy in psychiatry, much of which developed empirically (the MAOIs and lithium) or serendipitously (the tricyclic antidepressants), has stimulated the development of the "catecholamine hypothesis" with regard to depression and the "dopamine hypothesis" with respect to schizophrenia. Although ECT is a commonly used treatment, it has by no means had comparable theoretical significance.

However, papers in this volume indicate that this may no longer be the case. The papers in this section provide a hope that the techniques employed, namely, regional cerebral blood flow (rCBF) and quantitative electroencephalography (EEG), will help answer such critical questions as: (1) How are side effects produced and how may they be reduced or eliminated; are any so-called side effects necessary for the clinical effectiveness of ECT? (2) Does ECT have a different mode or focus of action when used to treat patients with different diagnoses; if so how may these be differentiated? (3) What is the effect of ECT on sleep? (4) What is the effect of repeated electrical stimuli on the functioning of neurotransmitter systems? (5) What is the relationship between the effects of antidepressant drugs and the effects of ECT; are they different qualitatively? (6) Is it possible to answer these questions before a reliable and valid measure of depression is devised? (7) What measure or combination of measures predicts the outcome of treatment with ECT?

The three reports in this section address some of these issues. Prohovnik *et al.* found differences in the acute effects of right unilateral vs. bilateral ECT in the distribution of rCBF changes. They also report the important finding that patients who eventually respond to a course of ECT have lower rCBFs at their first recording session than those who do not. Unfortunately, previous work from Silfverskiöld's group does not support this finding. These authors report that although the group of depressed patients had somewhat higher flow levels than a normal comparison group, the pattern of rCBF was normal prior to ECT. As did Prohovnik's group, they found differences between nondominant unilateral and bilateral ECT in rCBF. Prior to ECT there were significant correlations between mean left and right CBF and three of four items of the depression tetrad. Silfverskiöld *et al.* also report a normal EEG in their patients before ECT and, along with many others, a progressive increase in slowing during the course of treatment. Weiner *et al.* found that variations in the specific procedures employed in ECT produce different seizures as reflected by qualitative and quantitative analyses of the EEG.

The use of such relatively precise techniques as rCBF and quantitative analysis of the EEG should reduce the uncertainty associated with giving ECT by delineating both the acute and long-term changes. However, the difficulties associated with any study of ECT must be considered, namely, selection of appropriate subjects and comparison groups and control of possibly confounding variables. These probably account for the differences in the results of the two cerebral blood flow studies as there were differences in age, in ratio of males to females, and in type of ECT employed. Along with experimental design problems that are not unique to these studies, there are technical problems associated with decisions concerning which of the possible measures obtained in rCBF studies to employ and the time needed to acquire the data. Although these are formidable problems, they are not insurmountable and the neurophysiological techniques described provide a hope that soon we will be able to explain "how ECT works."

Neuropsychological and Behavioral Sequelae of Spontaneous Seizures

MICHAEL R. TRIMBLE

Psychological Medicine
The National Hospitals for Nervous Diseases
Queen Square
London, WC1N 3BG, England
and
Behavioral Neurology
The Institute of Neurology—London University
Queen Square
London, WC1N 3BG, England

PAMELA J. THOMPSON

Department of Neuropsychiatry
The Institute of Neurology—London University
Queen Square
London, WC1N 3BG, England
and
The Chalfont Center for Epilepsy
Chalfont St. Peter
Buckinghamshire
England

Spontaneous seizures are not infrequent events clinically, and it is estimated that some 5% of us will undergo a spontaneous seizure some time during our life. The causes for such seizures are multiple, but one of the commonest is epilepsy. Epilepsy by definition is a liability to recurrent seizures, but at the outset it should be made clear that one seizure is not sufficient to diagnose epilepsy, the latter being a clinical diagnosis based on a history of recurrent seizures backed up if possible by electroencephalographic (EEG) evidence of abnormal brain activity during the seizure.

The International League Against Epilepsy has for a number of years been attempting to arrive at a satisfactory classification of both seizures and epilepsy, greater success being achieved with the former. Improved diagnostic accuracy of spontaneous seizures has occurred by the introduction of videotelemetry, a procedure in which patients may be viewed on a television monitor while their electroencephalogram is also displayed, using a split screen design. The latest edition of the International Classification of Seizures is shown in TABLE 1.[1] The initial definition is between generalized and partial seizures. Generalized seizures are those that affect the body bilaterally, and do not show any evidence from the clinical, electrophysiological, or other data of a focal onset. The paradigm of the generalized seizure is the tonic-clonic convulsion (grand mal) in which consciousness is lost and the patient makes bilateral neuromuscular convulsive movements. Other forms include myoclonic seizures, atonic seizures, and generalized absence seizures (petit mal).

Partial seizures may originate in any area of the brain and are broadly divided into simple and complex. Simple partial seizures are those accompanied by motor or sensory events during which consciousness is preserved. These seizures are much rarer than partial seizures with alteration of consciousness, the latter being referred to as complex partial seizures. During complex partial seizures, alterations of higher cognitive function and the experiencing of emotional and cognitive events referred to as aurae are frequent. The commonest location of abnormality for complex partial seizures is the temporal lobes, and this term therefore embraces many of the seizures earlier referred to as psychomotor seizures or temporal lobe seizures. Partial seizures may secondarily generalize, and a common clinical sequence of events is for the patient to experience a complex aura followed by loss of consciousness and rapid progression to a generalized tonic-clonic seizure.

In contrast to the classification of seizures, the classification of epilepsy has been far less successful. Nonetheless, at the present time, an international commission has been working on an update of an international classification of epilepsies and this is due to present its data in 1985.

Classification of seizures has importance, not only clinically in the sense that anticonvulsant drug prescription is in many cases dependent upon the type of seizures from which the patient is suffering, but also in the context of this presentation because of the differing effects of partial and generalized seizures on neuropsychological performance and behavior.

TABLE 1. An Abbreviated Classification of Seizures[a]

Partial (begins locally)
Elementary symptoms (simple partial)
Complex symptoms[b] (complex partial)
Generalized (bilateral from outset, without local features) includes:
Absence (petit mal)
Myoclonic
Clonic
Tonic
Tonic-clonic (grand mal)
Unilateral
Unclassified

[a] As recommended by the International League Against Epilepsy.
[b] Complex refers to alteration of consciousness.

NEUROPSYCHOLOGICAL SEQUELAE OF SPONTANEOUS SEIZURES

There is no evidence that a single isolated seizure has any long-lasting consequence on cognitive function. Immediately following such a seizure the patient will show a typical organic brain syndrome with loss of awareness for reality, lack of orientation to the surroundings, and on formal cognitive testing would show disorientation and inability to perform higher cognitive activity. In some cases, following either a partial or a generalized seizure, an automatism may occur and this last anything up to 15 or 30 minutes. Automatisms following partial seizures tend to be of longer duration than those following generalized seizures, and during them the patient may undertake a series of apparently coordinated and complex behavioral manipulations subsequently being amnesic for this. Again, during this period, confusion and disorientation will be displayed if the patient is clinically examined.

In contrast, there is a considerable literature on the cognitive impairments associated with epilepsy, a problem that has been recognized for several centuries. Willis, for example, in his 17th century Oxford lecture, stated, "It often happens that epileptic patients, during their paroxysm and afterwards, suffer a loss of memory, intellect and phantasy."[2] This feature of epilepsy received prominent attention from 19th century physicians who, invoking a genetic theory, influenced by the ideas of degeneracy introduced by Morel and others, implied that intellectual and moral deterioration was an inevitable part of the epileptic progress.

Since that time, and especially since the 1950s, there has been an extensive discussion of intellectual changes in epilepsy although there have been few systematic investigations of this problem. Earlier attempts to assess cognitive function in epilepsy used either clinical judgments or overall IQ measurements, but more recently specific tests have been designed to assess differing aspects of cognition.

One of the earliest reports of standardized tests was that of Fox, who gave a mean IQ of 150 institutionalized children to be 71 for males and 65 for females.[3] Although several other reports confirmed such findings of low IQs in patients with epilepsy, they mainly come from institutionalized settings and when other groups were examined, lack of deterioration became stressed.[4] Lennox provided data on nearly 2000 epileptic patients and came to the conclusion that two-thirds were to be regarded as mentally normal, and only one-seventh as unmistakably subnormal.[5]

A summary of the data using simple IQ tests would suggest that, in an unselected group of epileptic patients, the mean IQ is probably within or just below the normal range unless epilepsy is associated with overt neurological disease or brain damage, although there is a tendency for the lower ranges of IQ to be overrepresented.

Of the specific deficits in cognitive function examined in epilepsy, memory, perceptuomotor skills, speed of mental processing, and attention are of particular importance, since many patients with epilepsy will complain of problems in these areas.

Deficits in memory in association with epilepsy have been reported for more than a hundred years. In the last century, clinicians variously described the memory of epileptic patients as "defective," "more or less treacherous," and "impoverished." Lennox, considering the nature of these difficulties wrote, "The patient finds it hard to recall events and names particularly those learned recently."[5] Deutsch assessed the memory skills of 30 patients with epilepsy and brain damage, 30 with epilepsy and no brain damage, and 30 with brain damage and no epilepsy.[6] Both groups with epilepsy showed a similar pattern of deficits on tests of learning and memory including impairments in tactile learning and auditory perceptual tests, which was different from that observed in the brain damaged group. That author claimed that the results were attributable to some specific epileptic factor, although she did not go on to elaborate what that might be. Mohan *et al.* administered the Boston memory scale to 50 patients with generalized epilepsy and 50 nonepileptic controls matched for age and level of education.[7] The average performance of the epileptic group was inferior to that of the controls but this was not significant. Loiseau reported a study in which he evaluated the memory skills of 100 epileptic patients and 100 controls matched for age, sex, education, and social status.[8] Retention of both verbal and nonverbal material was assessed. Memory was found to be impaired in the epileptic group, in particular the ability to remember lists of words and simple geometric designs.

The evidence for memory deficits in epilepsy is stronger when patients with temporal lobe abnormalities are examined. Many studies, however, have been based on patients with intractable epilepsy undergoing temporal lobectomy. In these studies, considerable agreement exists that the side of the excision determines the kind of material that will be more difficult for the individual to remember, left-sided lesions yielding memory defects for verbal material and right-sided ones for nonverbal material.[9,10] Much less attention has been paid to patients with temporal lobe epilepsy who do not require surgical intervention, and the findings from these studies have not been entirely consistent. Glowinski compared the performance of 30 patients with chronic generalized epilepsy with 30 who had chronic unilateral temporal lobe epilepsy, and he found the latter to display greater deficits on the Wechsler memory scale.[11] Other studies have reported similar findings for both children and adults.[12,13] On the other hand Mirsky *et al.* failed to differentiate between patients with focal and generalized epilepsy on the Wechsler memory scale.[14] Their design was somewhat different, however, including patients with other focal epilepsies in addition to those with temporal lobe foci in their focal group.

Laterality effects have also been examined. Fedio and Mirsky found that children with left temporal lobe foci displayed memory deficits for verbal material while having retention of nonverbal material.[12] The converse was true for children with right temporal foci. Similarly, Ladavas *et al.* reported a differential effect according to the side of the focus, their left temporal group being impaired on verbal recognition tasks whereas the right-sided group were more impaired on a spatial memory task.[15] Delaney *et al.* compared the test performance of right and left temporal lobe epileptic patients matched for age of onset, duration of epilepsy, and seizure frequency.[16] Tests used included logical memory and visual reproduction of the Wechsler memory scale and word list learning. Results revealed significant impairments of verbal memory in the left temporal epileptic subjects and significant impairments of nonverbal, visual memory in those with right-sided abnormalities.

Although these investigations show a degree of conformity of results, other data are less clear. Agnetti *et al.* were able to demonstrate verbal learning deficits in patients with left-sided foci, but no significant differences between right and left temporal lobe patients on nonverbal retention tasks.[17] Others have also failed to find impairments of nonverbal memory in those with a right temporal lobe focus,[18] and some investigators have been unable to clearly demonstrate laterality effects at all.[11]

An interesting interpretation of these findings comes from the work of Mayeaux *et al.*, who postulate that the interictal memory impairment may be an anomia. They examined 29 patients with epilepsy and gave them a variety of cognitive tasks including tests for aphasia and anomia.[19] No differences on memory tests were noted between groups with left-sided and those with right-sided temporal lobe epilepsy, but the left temporal lobe patients performed much more poorly on the confrontation naming tasks. Further, several measures of verbal intelligence, learning, and memory were highly correlated with the naming test performance. Their conclusion was that "the relative anomia demonstrated in temporal lobe epilepsy patients may have been interpreted by these patients and their relatives as poor memory."[19]

In contrast to memory, impairments of attention in the absence of overt clinical seizures have been described by several writers. Holdsworth and Whitmore found 42% of their sample of epileptic children were rated by teachers as markedly inattentive.[20] In another study, Stores *et al.* compared the performance of 71 children with epilepsy and 35 nonepileptic controls on a series of specially designed tests of attention.[21] Epileptic boys were found to be significantly less attentive than nonepileptic boys, although no comparable differences were found with the girls.

Some researchers have suggested that the attentional deficits of epilepsy are related to seizure type, being more common with generalized seizures.[12,14]

Perceptuomotor skills are commonly noted in patients with epilepsy including clumsiness, difficulty with visual perception, and impairment on performance of such psychological tests as the Bender Gestalt task.[22] In contrast to the above studies, no clear picture emerges as to which seizure type is most likely to impair such skills.

Speed of mental processing is often reported impaired in patients with epilepsy, and many investigators use such terms as "slow," "sticky," "viscous," when referring to epileptic cerebration. Studies of this component of cognitive function have mainly involved reaction time tasks in epileptic patients, and they are usually shown to be impaired when compared to matched controls.[23]

ROLE OF SEIZURES IN COGNITIVE IMPAIRMENT

From the above it would seem that two outstanding problems of cognitive functioning that patients with recurrent spontaneous seizures suffer from are memory deficits, which seem more linked to temporal lobe dysfunction and partial seizures, and attentional deficits, which relate to generalized epilepsy. The number of variables in addition to seizures that could be involved in these problems include the more generalized phenomenon of brain damage, anticonvulsant drug prescription, and social and psychological factors that impair learning ability in patients with epilepsy including more time off school, overdependent parental attitudes, and problems with peers and teachers. Preexisting brain damage, although a factor, does not provide a complete explanation for the neuropsychological deficits observed in epilepsy since some investigations have controlled for this,[24] indicating that the performance of patients with epilepsy and brain damage is inferior to those with epilepsy and no brain damage although normal subjects are still superior in their performance to epileptic groups without brain damage.

With regard to epileptic variables one should consider, in addition to the type of seizure, age of onset of seizure and seizure frequency.

The majority of investigators suggest an early onset of seizures carries a poor prognosis with regard to neuropsychological function although most studies do not make a distinction between the age of onset and duration of epilepsy. Dikmen *et al.* compared the performance of two groups of patients on the WAIS and the Halstead Reitan test battery, matched for the duration and frequency of tonic-clonic seizures but differing with regard to age and onset.[25] Patients with epilepsy starting before the age of 5 were more impaired on the majority of tasks than those with an age of onset between 10 and 15. Similar data have been reported by others.[26]

Although some investigators report that frequent seizures are associated with more marked impairment of cognitive abilities,[27] this has not been demonstrated consistently.[8,16] In a recent study, Seidenberg *et al.* attempted to explore the influence of seizure frequency using the longitudinal design.[28] They compared the test retest performance on the WAIS of two groups of adult epileptic patients. For one group, seizure frequency had improved during the test retest interval, and in the other it had worsened or remained unchanged. The former group showed significant improvement on several more psychological tests than the latter. Taken together these data suggest that seizure frequency may be an important factor associated with fluctuations of test performance in epileptic patients, although its impact on more permanent deficits of cognition is as yet unclear.

EEG PATTERNS

Another variable explored has been the relationship between neuropsychological function and various EEG patterns. Most work in this field has centered around the classical three-per-second spike and wave activity that accompanies generalized absence seizures. The prevailing view is that such activity impairs test performance, and that this is most marked on measures of reaction time and vigilance particularly if the task is experimenter paced.[29] Some authors have demonstrated that alterations in the frequency of spike wave bursts seem dependent on the meaning of the task for the individual, with reduction in this abnormal activity during periods of increased alertness.[30] Interestingly, in some studies, the observed changes of cognitive function precede spike wave bursts by 1 to 1½ seconds, and their amelioration likewise precedes the cessation of the burst by a similar time period (for review see Reference 31). This has led to some speculation as to the mechanism of these changes, which at the present time is not clear.

Other forms of epileptic activity on the EEG have also been associated with neuropsychological dysfunctioning. In one study, patients with frequent epileptiform activity were found to be more impaired on a series of neuropsychological tasks than those for whom such activity was either infrequent or absent,[32] although not all investigators have detected impairments that relate so clearly to changes of scalp EEG activity. This may be related to the insensitivity of such recordings, but studies involving depth electrode recordings, although infrequent, do seem to support the view that subclinical epileptic discharges may interfere with cognitive processes.[33]

BEHAVIORAL CONSEQUENCES OF RECURRENT SPONTANEOUS SEIZURES

That epilepsy may be associated with alterations of behavior has been written about for many years. Of particular interest has been the potential for interictal behavior changes, and much of the discussion has involved the development of interictal personality change and psychoses in these patients (for review see Reference 34). An approximate summary of the situation at present would be as follows. It is now accepted that some patients with epilepsy undergo personality change or develop complicated psychiatric presentations such as psychosis. The majority of investigations at the present time are concentrating on the issue as to whether patients with temporal lobe epilepsy, on account of recurrent seizures in limbic system structures, and possible continuous interictal disruption of electrical activity in this system, are more prone to the development of psychopathology than those with, for example, only generalized seizures. No clear consensus view has been derived, although there is a growing awareness that temporal lobe epilepsy forms a heterogeneous group and more recently an attempt has been made to isolate those with allocortical (limbic) dysfunction, who may well be more prone to behavior disturbances, from those with primarily neocortical sites of abnormality. It is not clear, however, from the literature that the presenting pattern of the behavior disturbance in temporal lobe epilepsy is necessarily different from that found in psychiatric patients without epilepsy, a feature that leads to the suggestion that the development of psychiatric disturbances in patients with temporal lobe epilepsy who have complex partial seizures may well represent a good model for investigation of the development of psychopathology in patients without epilepsy.

With particular regard to electroconvulsive therapy (ECT), the most interesting aspects of the link between spontaneous seizures and behavior are those that relate to observations that periods of psychosis in epileptic patients may be resolved by spontaneous seizures, the presentation of Landolt of the concept of forced normalization,[35] and the recording of a declining incidence of seizure frequency in many patients with epilepsy who tend to develop psychosis (for review see Reference 36). Landolt described a group of patients with epilepsy and psychosis, the latter was short-lived, during which the electroencephalogram tended to lose its abnormalities, and with resolution of the psychosis, the epileptiform discharges reappeared on the electroencephalogram. Landolt referred to this phenomenon as forced normalization, and noted that it could be precipitated by the prescription of anticonvulsant drugs to patients, or that the psychosis could resolve with a spontaneous seizure. Although in Landolt's earlier writings he was discussing mainly temporal lobe seizures, he later extended his observations to generalized seizures. It is now recognized that forced normalization may be an accompaniment of generalized absence seizures when treated with ethosuccimide.[37] Although primarily an EEG phenomenon, the clinical counterpart, referred to as alternating psychosis, is also described, in which the intensity of the patient's psychosis and the seizure frequency vary in intensity in alternating phases of the patient's history.

These electroencephalographic and clinical phenomena would appear to be important with regard to the theoretical underpinning of the use of the ECT in psychiatric practice, especially for the treatment of psychosis. The history of this is reviewed elsewhere, but it is suggested that von Meduna introduced convulsive therapy on account of observations of a similar nature,[37] and these phenomena should be taken into account in any theoretical model of the therapeutic action of the convulsive process. It has been argued elsewhere that a number of possible candidates at, for example, a biochemical level could be invoked to explain these phenomena, including a link with dopamine or γ-aminobutyric acid (GABA).[38] Another phenomenon, which may be related in terms of basic underlying biological processes, is the observation that patients with epilepsy who tend to become psychotic in a more chronic course do so as the tendency to seizure frequency declines. Several authors have described these events (see Reference 36), and the figure of approximately one-third of epileptic patients with psychosis who undergo such a clinical course is derived. It is important to recognize this subgroup, not only because they may require ECT in treatment, but further because it again emphasizes that there is a group of patients in whom psychotic and seizure events are antithetical, although these are different from the more acute short-lived clinical episodes described by Landolt. Again the precise mechanism underlying these changes is a matter of speculation, although the concept of kindling, based on an experimental model of epilepsy, which would suggest that over time kindling of limbic system structures distant from the site of origin of a focus in the amygdala may occur, is one possibility. Thus, such kindling (with an as yet unknown biochemical and neurophysiological base) may provoke a change in the central nervous system that is psychotogenic, but also increases the seizure threshold.[36]

CONCLUSIONS

From this review it is concluded that the study of spontaneous convulsions, in particular in the form of epilepsy, has much importance for psychiatry. Not only are some seizure disorders, in particular temporal lobe epilepsy with a limbic system focus, a good natural model for trying to understand the development of psychopathology in nonepileptic patients, but further the links between seizures and changes of cognitive function and behavior clearly have relevance for ECT as a form of therapy in man. With regard to cognitive disabilities, it is suggested that patients with epilepsy often suffer from these although they are often not recognized. Some of the cognitive deficits may well be related to seizure phenomena, and disturbances of memory in patients with temporal lobe epilepsy are especially prominent. Attentional deficits may well be seen in those with generalized seizures, and again this may well reflect the underlying neuroanatomy of attentional processes. Other cognitive disturbances, for example slowing, perceptuomotor difficulties, and disturbances of higher cognitive function, particularly in the absence of overt brain damage, may be related to other variables and anticonvulsant prescription is important here.[39] It should be emphasized however that the seizure-related cognitive disturbances are more likely to occur in those with long-standing epilepsy, starting earlier in life, and are not discernible after recovery from single seizures.

With regard to the behavioral changes, the antagonistic link between psychosis and epilepsy is observed in two separate forms, namely, acutely, clearly described by Landolt, and the more chronic form. The biological mechanisms of these may be similar or dissimilar, but their existence and description clearly have importance for an understanding of the mechanisms of action of electroconvulsive therapy.

REFERENCES

1. GASTAUT, H. 1969. Epilepsia **10:** s2–s21.
2. DEWHURST, K. 1980. Thomas Willis's Oxford Lectures. Sanford. Oxford, England.
3. FOX, J. T. 1924. Br. J. Med. Psychol. **4:** 235–248.
4. KEATING, L. E. 1960. J. Ment. Sci. **106:** 1042–1059.
5. LENNOX, W. G. 1942. Am. J. Psychiatry **99:** 174–180.
6. DEUTSCH, C. P. 1953. Arch. Neurol. Psychiatry **70:** 474–482.
7. MOHAN, V., V. K. VARMA & B. B. SANHNEY. 1976. India Neurol. **24:** 110.
8. LOISSEAU, P., E. STUBE, D. BROUSTET, S. BATTELLEOCHI, C. GOMENI & P. D. MORSELLI. 1980. Acta Neurol. Scand. **62**(Suppl.80): 58–61.
9. MILNER, B. 1975. Adv. Neurol. **8:** 299–321.
10. IVERSEN, S. 1977. Temporal lobe amnesia. *In* Amnesia. C. W. M. Whitty & O. L. Zangwill, Eds. Butterworths. London, England.
11. GLOWINSKI, H. 1973. J. Nerv. Ment. Dis. **157:** 129–137.
12. FEDIO, P. & A. F. MIRSKY. 1969. Neuropsychologica **7:** 287–300.
13. QUADFASAL, A. F. & P. W. PRUYSER. 1955. Epilepsia **4:** 80–90.
14. MIRSKY, A. F., D. W. PRIMAC, C. A. MARSAN, H. E. ROSVOLD & J. R. STEVENS. 1960. Exp. Neurol. **2:** 75–89.
15. LADAVAS, E., C. UMILTA & L. PROVINCIALI. 1979. Epilepsia **20:** 493–502.
16. DELANEY, R. C., A. J. ROSEN, R. H. J. H. MATTSON & R. A. NOVELLY. 1980. Cortex **16:** 103–117.
17. AGNETTI, V., M. GANGA, M. MURRIGAILE, M. R. PIRAS & A. TICCA. 1979. Paper presented at the 11th Epilepsy International Symposium, Florence, Italy.
18. BERENT, S., T. J. BOLL & B. GIORDANA. 1980. Adv. Epilept. **12:** 185–190.
19. MAYEUX, J., J. BRANDT, J. ROSEN & F. BENSON. 1980. Neurology **30:** 120–125.
20. HOLDSWORTH, L. & K. WHITMORE. 1974. Dev. Med. Child Neurol. **16:** 746–748.
21. STORES, G., J. HART & N. PIRAN. 1978. Epilepsia **19:** 169–175.
22. SCHWARTZ, M. L. & R. D. DENNERLL. 1970. Percept. Motor Skills **30:** 111–121.
23. ARENA, R., G. MENCHETTI, G. TASSINARI & M. TOGNETTI. 1979. Paper presented at the 11th Epilepsy International Symposium, Florence, Italy.
24. KLOVE, H. & C. G. MATTHEWS. 1966. Epilepsia **7:** 330–338.
25. DIKMEN, S., C. G. MATTHEWS & J. P. HARLEY. 1975. Epilepsia **16:** 73–81.
26. O'LEARY, D. S., M. SEIDENBERG, S. BERENT & T. J. BOLL. 1981. Epilepsia **22:** 197–204.
27. RODIN, E. A. 1968. The Prognosis of Patients with Epilepsy. Charles C. Thomas. Chicago, Ill.
28. SEIDENBERG, M., D. S. O'LEARY, S. BERENT & T. J. BOLL. 1981. Epilepsia **22:** 75–83.
29. BROWNE, T. R., J. K. PENRY, R. J. PORTER & F. E. DREIFUSS. 1974. Neurology **24:** 659–665.
30. GUEY, T., C. CHARLES, C. COQUILERY, J. ROGER & R. SOULAYROL. 1967. Epilepsia **8:** 129–144.
31. FENWICK, P. 1982. EEG Studies in Epilepsy and Psychiatry. E. H. Reynolds & M. R. Trimble, Eds.: 242–263. Churchill Livingstone. Edinburgh, Scotland.

32. WILKUS, R. J. & C. B. DODRILL. 1976. Epilepsia **17:** 89–100.
33. RAUSCH, R., J. P. LIEB & P. H. CRANDALL. 1978. Arch. Neurol. **35:** 699–705.
34. TRIMBLE, M. R. 1983. *In* Recent Advances in Epilepsy. T. Pedley & B. S. Meldrum, Eds. **1:** 211–229. Churchill Livingstone. Edinburgh, Scotland.
35. LANDOLT, H. 1953. *In* Lectures on Epilepsy. A. M. Lorentz de Haas, Ed.: 91–133. Elsevier. London, England.
36. TRIMBLE, M. R. 1983. *In* Advances in Epilepsy: 14th Epilepsy International Symposium. M. Parsonage *et al.,* Eds.: 165–171. Raven Press. New York, N.Y.
37. WOLF, P. & M. R. TRIMBLE. 1985. Br. J. Psychiatry **146:** 272–276.
38. TRIMBLE, M. R. 1977. Biol. Psychiatry **12**(2): 299–304.
39. THOMPSON, P. J. & M. R. TRIMBLE. 1982. Epilepsia **23:** 531–544.

Disorientation during Electroconvulsive Therapy[a]

Technical, Theoretical, and Neuropsychological Issues

WALTER F. DANIEL[b] AND HERBERT F. CROVITZ[b,c]

[b]*Medical Research Service*
Veterans Administration Medical Center
508 Fulton Street
Durham, North Carolina 27705

[c]*Department of Psychiatry*
Duke University Medical Center
Durham, North Carolina 27710

The purpose of the present paper is to discuss disorientation occurring during electroconvulsive therapy (ECT). The present report will summarize *preliminary* findings from a study that is still being statistically analyzed. In this regard, findings presented in this report should not be considered definitive, because of statistical problems (see Results) we are still working on. Nevertheless, this preliminary report was felt to be justified in order to expedite research into an easily studied, and too often overlooked, area of ECT-induced central nervous system (CNS) dysfunction that is of clinical importance. The final results will be presented elsewhere; further information on the results until that time can be obtained by writing the authors.

A recent review of the ECT-induced disorientation literature[1] revealed a number of technical, theoretical, and neuropsychological issues that deserve clarification in future studies.

With respect to ECT technical issues, the following questions need to be answered:

1. Does sinusoidal high-energy electrical stimulation produce more disorientation than brief-pulse low-energy electrical stimulation, as has been demonstrated in only one study to date?[2]
2. Does postictal disorientation increase across treatment number, as has been statistically demonstrated to date in only one study?[3]
3. If disorientation does increase across treatment number, what causes it? (It has been hypothesized that increased CNS disturbance occurring with increasing treatments may be related to the typically increased electricity administered across treatments rather than, or in addition to, more endogenous CNS alterations occurring across treatments.)[4]
4. Does ECT produce *interictal* (the period between seizures after the postictal period has cleared)[4] disorientation in addition to postictal disorientation? If so, what type of organic brain syndrome does this imply that ECT produces?
5. How are seizure and/or electrical variables related to ECT-induced disorientation?
6. What produces the disorientation differences resulting from variations in

[a]This work was supported by the Medical Research Service of the Veterans Administration.

electrode placement (right unilateral versus bilateral) and electrical stimulus waveform (brief-pulse versus sinusoidal)?

With respect to neuropsychological issues, the following questions need to be answered:

1. Does age have a bearing on ECT-induced disorientation?
2. Does orientation for "person" return before "place" orientation, with "time" orientation returning last,[1,5] or is some other model of orientation recovery more appropriate (see References 6–8)?
3. Why do various orientation items (e.g., year versus month versus day of the week) return at different times? Can differences in repetition or remoteness of the orientation item account for these differences?
4. Is delirium (as manifested in disorientation occurring in the ECT-induced "postictal state" of delirium) a random or chaotic phenomenon, or does an orderly march of reorientation occur, thereby indicating the converse?

With respect to ECT and neuropsychological *theoretical* issues, the following questions need to be answered:

1. Can disorientation be understood as a memory disorder, and, if so, what are the limits to such a model?
2. Does the return of orientation for time (age and current year) "shrink" following ECT, and, if so, how is this phenomenon related to the shrinkage of retrograde amnesia following closed-head injury?[9]
3. What are the relationships between ECT-induced delirium (indexed by disorientation) and more persistent ECT-induced CNS disturbance (e.g., amnesia, EEG slowing)?

METHOD

Subjects

Thirty male and one female depressed inpatients were studied. Selection criteria for these patients are the same as in our previous investigations into ECT-induced amnesia,[10–13] and will not be discussed in detail in the present report. For the purpose of keeping the patient sample more totally homogenous, only preliminary results pertaining to the 30 male subjects will be discussed.

ECT Technique

Patients were randomly assigned to one of four ECT groups: brief-pulse right unilateral ($n = 8$), sinusoidal right unilateral ($n = 6$), brief-pulse bilateral ($n = 8$), or sinusoidal bilateral ECT ($n = 8$). Further ECT details will be presented in a future report, and are comparable to those described in our earlier reports.[10–13]

As in other studies,[1,4,12–15] we hypothesized that variations in seizure generalization (i.e., the number of cerebral neurons participating in the seizure)[12,13] may underlie CNS disturbance resulting from modifications of electrode placement and stimulus waveform.

One hypothetical index of seizure generalization we found in a previous study[13] to be related to ECT-induced *amnesia* was postictal EEG suppression (see FIGURE 1). Presumably, a more generalized seizure should result in greater numbers of neurons being refractory postictally, leading to greater suppression of the postictal EEG.[13] In the present experiment, we hypothesized that seizure generalization, as indexed by postictal EEG suppression, was more important than electrical variables (i.e., current) in determining the amount of ECT-induced disorientation.

Orientation Testing

Patients were tested with respect to orientation before and after their third and eighth ECT. Testing was conducted 15 minutes, 30 minutes, 45 minutes, 1 hour, 2

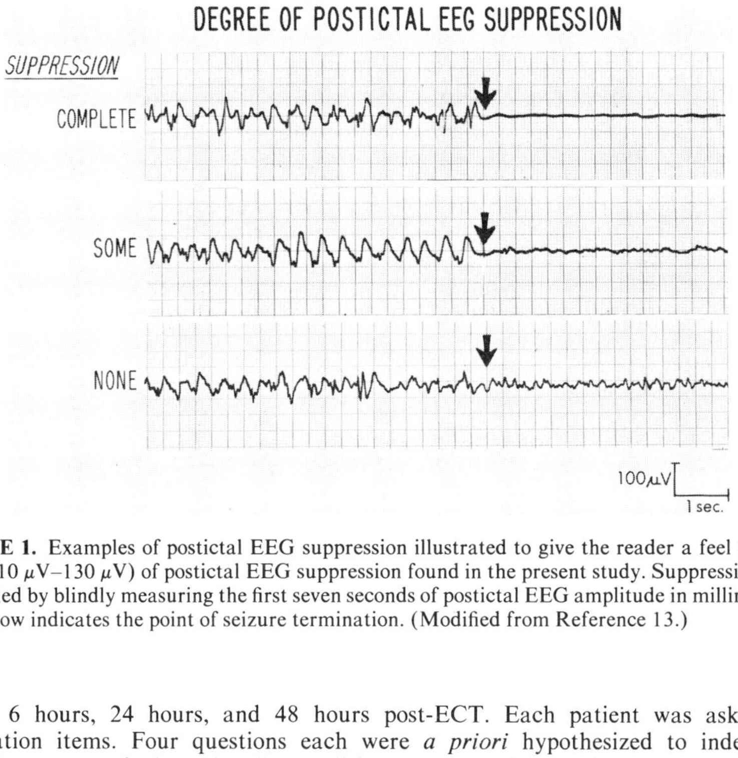

FIGURE 1. Examples of postictal EEG suppression illustrated to give the reader a feel for the range (10 μV–130 μV) of postictal EEG suppression found in the present study. Suppression was quantified by blindly measuring the first seven seconds of postictal EEG amplitude in millimeters. The arrow indicates the point of seizure termination. (Modified from Reference 13.)

hours, 6 hours, 24 hours, and 48 hours post-ECT. Each patient was asked 12 orientation items. Four questions each were *a priori* hypothesized to index the following aspects of orientation: "person" (name, age, social security number, and year of birth), "place" (country, city, name of the building, and floor of the hospital), and "time" (year, official season of the year, month, and day of the week).

In some cases, we either noticed or the treating psychiatrist asked for advice concerning unusually severe and prolonged "confusional states" (DSM-III: delirium) occurring in some of the ECT patients. We consequently followed and measured disorientation and other features of delirium in such patients until it cleared to make sure that no irreversible ECT-induced CNS effects had occurred. These cases will be discussed later.

RESULTS AND DISCUSSION: ECT TECHNICAL ISSUES

Statistics

It is clear that the orientation testing times we used do not constitute an equal interval scale of time measurement. We chose these time intervals because most other ECT investigations, reviewed elsewhere,[1] found that ECT-induced disorientation clears within two hours or less post-ECT. Furthermore, many epileptologists (e.g., McNamara)[16] have suggested that disorientation clears within two hours or less following spontaneously occurring tonic-clonic seizures in epileptics. However, our clinical impressions from this hospital suggested that some patients are disoriented several *days* post-ECT. Consequently, we chose the aforementioned time intervals in an attempt to gain some handle on the time course of ECT-induced disorientation occurring in this hospital's patient population.

For the purpose of statistics in this prelminary communication, the session number when orientation was fully regained will be utilized, although this utilization carries with it certain problems. For example, session number omits meaningful information concerning reorientation in relation to real time (e.g., minutes, hours, days). Nevertheless, session number will suffice for this preliminary communication.

Another statistical problem in the present preliminary report is that subject testing at treatments three and eight constitutes a repeated measures design. The conventional repeated measures analysis of variance requires stringent assumptions regarding the variance-covariance (i.e., correlations among repeated measures structure of the data, violations of which result in too many rejections of the null hypothesis for the stated significance level).[17,18] Sensitivity to this issue is rarely found in the literature. Consequently, until these assumptions are checked with respect to the present data, and ruled out, certain repeated measures results should be regarded only as preliminary at best.

Given these disclaimers, we now proceed to discuss preliminary results we have to date found with respect to ECT-induced disorientation.

ECT-Induced Disorientation

Postictal Disorientation

Full reorientation was regained later following sinusoidal than brief-pulse ECT ($p = 0.007$), and full reorientation was regained later following bilateral than right unilateral ECT ($p = 0.0001$). There is an interaction effect between stimulus waveform and electrode placement as to when full reorientation returned ($p = 0.01$) (see TABLE 1). This interaction effect appears to be the result of sinusoidal unilateral ECT patients regaining full orientation later than did brief-pulse bilateral ECT patients.

Furthermore, the session at which full reorientation returned increased from treatment three to treatment eight ($p = 0.005$). Taken collectively, these findings support the results obtained by Valentine *et al.*[2] with respect to the four ECT groups, and the results obtained by Wilson and Gottlieb with respect to a cumulative increase in ECT-induced disorientation across treatments.[3]

Interictal and Posttreatment Disorientation

Some subjects ($n = 11$) missed more orientation items before treatment eight than before treatment three. This decline indicates *interictal* disorientation, and the trend across treatment groups parallels the postictal findings. A greater increase in incorrect answers from treatment three to treatment eight occurred with bilateral than with right unilateral ECT ($p = 0.02$), and with sinusoidal than with brief-pulse ECT ($p = 0.04$). FIGURE 2 illustrates this result. To date, no study has addressed interictal disorientation. The present finding may parallel the differential build-up in EEG slowing that occurs with electrode placement and stimulus waveform variations.[19–21]

As previously mentioned, we on occasion either noticed or the treating psychiatrist asked for advice concerning unusually severe and prolonged confusional states (DSM-III: delirium) occurring in some of the patients undergoing ECT. We consequently followed and measured disorientation and other features of delirium[d] in such patients until it cleared to make sure that no irreversible ECT-induced CNS effects had occurred. TABLES 2 and 3 illustrate orientation and neuropsychological test results in two patients who developed severe delirium after receiving sinusoidal bilateral and sinusoidal unilateral ECT, respectively.

TABLE 1. Postictal Disorientation in Relation to ECT Group[a]

ECT Group	Treatment Three Mean	Treatment Three SD[b]	Treatment Eight Mean	Treatment Eight SD
Brief-pulse unilateral	1.0	0	1.1	0.4
Sinusoidal unilateral	5.0	2.2	6.0	1.7
Brief-pulse bilateral	3.0	1.4	4.9	1.2
Sinusoidal bilateral	5.2	2.5	6.0	2.0
All brief-pulse patients	2.0	1.4	3.0	2.1
All sinusoidal patients	5.1	2.3	6.0	1.8
All unilateral patients	2.7	2.5	3.2	2.7
All bilateral patients	4.1	2.3	5.4	1.7
All patients	3.4	2.4	4.4	2.5

[a]Mean session when reoriented.
[b]SD is standard deviation.

Of the patients we saw who developed a severe prolonged delirium, all received sinusoidal ECT, with electrode placement being bilateral or right unilateral. Thus the sinusoidal stimulus alone may in some way be responsible for the development of these states. It must be realized, however, that the referral of patients to us was not conducted randomly. Nevertheless, this finding may be of clinical importance, and further investigation into the possible etiologies of these confusional states is under way.[23]

ECT-Induced CNS Dysfunction: Delirium, Amnestic Syndrome, or Dementia?

The occurrence of these severe "confusional states" (DSM-III: delirium) in the present and other studies, juxtaposed with the fact that bilaterally generalized

[d]A case report of one such patient, who was not studied in the present investigation because of preexisting neurological abnormalities, is reported in detail elsewhere.[22] It is interesting to note that this patient developed a severe delirium after sinusoidal bilateral ECT, but did not redevelop a severe delirium after brief-pulse unilateral ECT, findings that are consistent with results presented in this preliminary report.

(nonspecific) EEG slowing frequently occurs during and after ECT,[19-21] leads us to formulate the following *simple* hypothesis concerning ECT-induced cognitive disturbance that has to date been overlooked: ECT simply produces *delirium,* which varies in length and severity, depending on variables such as electrode placement and stimulus waveform.[4] To date, many investigators have assumed that ECT produces an *amnestic syndrome* in which memory is selectively impaired. Yet, according to DSM-III (page 112), the essential feature of an amnestic syndrome is impaired memory "occurring in a normal state of consciousness (i.e., not clouded). . . . Amnestic Syndrome is not diagnosed if memory impairment exists in the context of clouded consciousness

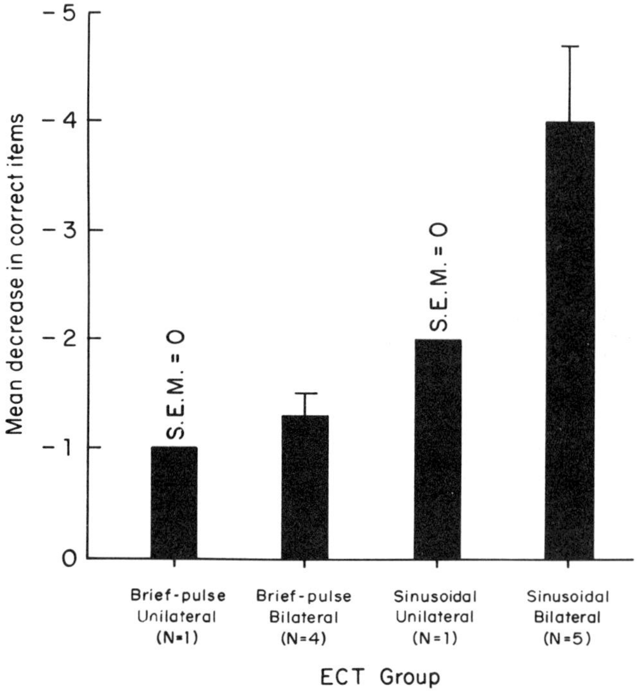

FIGURE 2. Interictal disorientation in relation to ECT group. The mean decrease in correct items on the y axis indicates that there was an increase in errors from pretreatment three to pretreatment eight.

(Delirium)."[42] The occurrence of generalized EEG slowing, disorientation, attentional deficits, memory impairment, and other neuropsychological deficits with ECT (see FIGURE 3) is more consistent with the diagnosis of delirium than amnestic syndrome, in our opinion.

Another hypothesis frequently put forth by anti-ECT activists (e.g., Breggin)[24] is that ECT produces dementia. However, there are very few, if any, research data that suggest that *modern* ECT produces anything but a transient organic brain syndrome.

This discussion may seem to be a trivial semantic argument. However, there is an important reason to be clear on classifying ECT-induced CNS dysfunction. If all ECT

TABLE 2. Orientation Testing in a Patient Who Developed Severe Delirium with Sinusoidal Bilateral ECT

Testing Time	Number of Correct Orientation Items ($n = 12$)
Pre-ECT (baseline)	12
Pre–treatment three	12
15 Minutes post treatment three	3
30 Minutes post treatment three	3
45 Minutes post treatment three	4
60 Minutes post treatment three	4
2 Hours post treatment three	5
6 Hours post treatment three	8
1 Day post treatment three	9
2 Days post treatment three	12
Pre–treatment eight	6
15 Minutes post treatment eight	0
30 Minutes post treatment eight	1
45 Minutes post treatment eight	4
60 Minutes post treatment eight	4
2 Hours post treatment eight	5
6 Hours post treatment eight	5
1 Day post treatment eight	5
2 Days post treatment eight	6
4 Days after last (ninth) treatment	6
10 Days after last (ninth) treatment	8
12 Days after last (ninth) treatment (patient discharged)	10

does is to induce *delirium,* then eventual biochemical cures for memory impairment occurring in the more specific *amnestic syndrome* (e.g., herpes simplex encephalitis) may not work for the memory impairment occurring during delirium, because the underlying neurophysiological and neurochemical mechanisms may be entirely different.

TABLE 3. Neuropsychological Testing in a Patient with Severe Delirium

Neuropsychological Function	Post-ECT Time[a]	
	2–3 Days	8 Days
Orientation (12 items)	75% ●●	100% ●
Perseveratory behavior 1. reciprocal inhibition	36% ●●●	100% ●
Perseveratory behavior 2. alternate letters	7% ●●●	100% ●
Verbal fluency	9 ●●●	25 ●
Immediate memory (digits forward)	3 ●●	5 ●
Attention/concentration	23 ●●	28 ●
Right-left and visuospatial orientation	50% ●●●	75% ●●
Visuographic single tracking (trails A)	99 seconds ●●●	73 seconds ●●
Visuographic double tracking (trails B)	817 seconds ●●●	253 seconds ●●

[a]● = normal; ●● = impaired; ●●● = grossly impaired. (Note: this patient received 10 sinusoidal right unilateral ECTs.)

Do Seizure or Electrical Variables Cause ECT-Induced Disorientation?

Correlational analyses indicate that duration of postictal disorientation was greater with increased electricity at treatments three and eight (e.g., milliamperes of current: $r = +0.670, +0.575$, respectively; $p = 0.0001, 0.0027$, respectively). To our knowledge, this is the first Pearson correlational analysis showing a relationship between electricity and ECT-induced CNS dysfunction. However, correlational analyses also

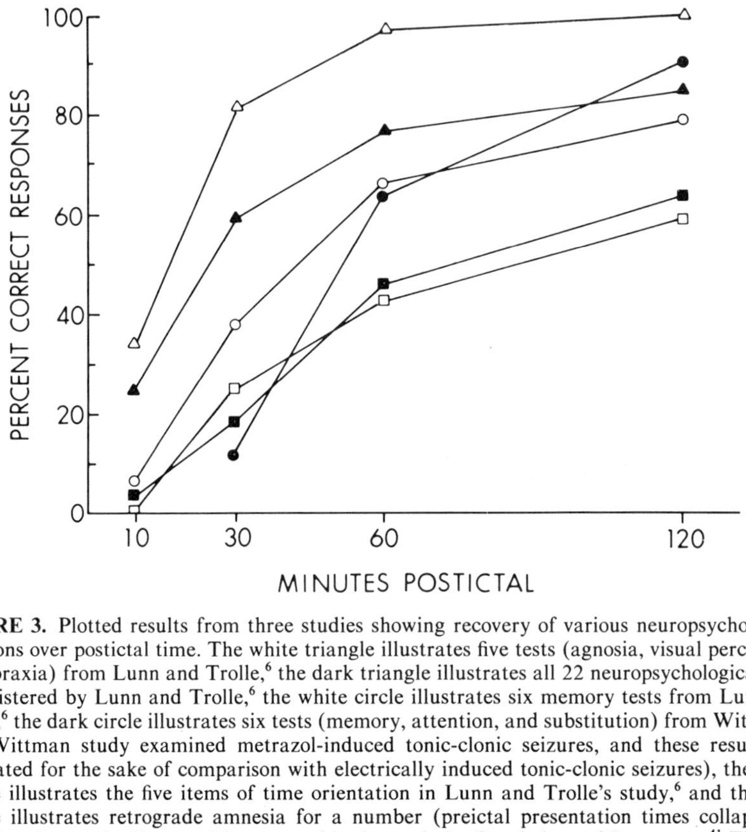

FIGURE 3. Plotted results from three studies showing recovery of various neuropsychological functions over postictal time. The white triangle illustrates five tests (agnosia, visual perception, and apraxia) from Lunn and Trolle,[6] the dark triangle illustrates all 22 neuropsychological tests administered by Lunn and Trolle,[6] the white circle illustrates six memory tests from Lunn and Trolle,[6] the dark circle illustrates six tests (memory, attention, and substitution) from Wittman[40] (the Wittman study examined metrazol-induced tonic-clonic seizures, and these results are illustrated for the sake of comparison with electrically induced tonic-clonic seizures), the white square illustrates the five items of time orientation in Lunn and Trolle's study,[6] and the dark square illustrates retrograde amnesia for a number (preictal presentation times collapsed: 5 seconds, 15 seconds, 60 seconds) presented in the study by Cronholm and Lagergren.[41] The very similar recovery of the five time orientation items (white square) in Lunn and Trolle's study[6] and the resolution of retrograde amnesia in Cronholm and Lagergren's study[41] is important perhaps with respect to the very last section of this paper.

indicated that postictal EEG suppression is somehow related to ECT-induced disorientation at treatments three and eight ($r = -0.535, -0.449$, respectively; $p = 0.002, 0.02$, respectively). These correlations indicate that the picture is complex.

As in our previous investigations,[4,11–14] we hypothesized that electrical variables per se were irrelevant with respect to the production of ECT-induced CNS dysfunction. However, multiple regression analyses revealed that both current and postictal EEG suppression were related to disorientation at treatments three and eight ($p = 0.0001$, 0.0005, respectively) over and beyond the effects of each other. Consequently, electricity and our hypothetical measure of seizure generalization (suppression) are difficult to disentangle. In fact, these two variables are in themselves intercorrelated (treatment three: $r = -0.535$; $p = 0.002$; treatment eight: $r = -0.449$; $p = 0.02$).

With respect to ECT group, we attempted to determine whether seizure generalization (as indexed by postictal EEG suppression) or electricity (i.e., current) was responsible for the ECT-induced disorientation by performing analyses of covariance. However, tests of the heterogeneity of slopes[25] revealed that there was a significant interaction ($p = 0.03$) between postictal EEG suppression and stimulus waveform at treatment three, which indicates that the slopes differed. Consequently, a conventional analysis of covariance cannot be performed, since the basic assumption of homogeneity of slopes cannot be met.[26] Further statistical evaluation[27] of the seizure versus electrical issue is under way, and will be reported elsewhere in the future.

The bottom line on disentangling what actually *causes* ECT-induced CNS dysfunction, however, is that studies need to be conducted, as have been done in the nonhuman literature,[28] in which stimulus intensity within a single electrical stimulus waveform and electrode placement is systematically varied, and the degree of seizure generalization and CNS dysfunction are then measured.[13] Such experiments would result in better experimental control over variables likely to cause ECT-induced CNS disturbance.

Another bottom line on disentangling what causes ECT-induced CNS dysfunction, as discussed elsewhere,[12,13] is that the suggestion that ECT-induced CNS dysfunction results from an exclusively electrical or an exclusively epileptiform influence is probably an oversimplification. Future studies are likely to show that ECT-induced CNS dysfunction is the result of biochemical alterations produced by a complex interaction between electrical and seizure variables.[29,30]

RESULTS AND DISCUSSION: NEUROPSYCHOLOGICAL ISSUES

With respect to ECT technical details, we have utilized a rather crude measure of reorientation: session at which full reorientation was regained. In this next section, we will examine the process of disorientation in a deeper manner, in that the degree of disorientation as indexed by the differential recovery of individual orientation times will be examined.

Age and Postictal Disorientation

Lipowski[5] and others have suggested that the incidence of delirium is greater with increasing age. It might be hypothesized also that the severity and duration of disorientation would be greater with increasing age. As indexed by the session at which full regainment of orientation occurred, however, our results did not reveal any correlations between age and session of regainment of full reorientation that even approached statistical significance at either treatment ($p > 0.40$). Furthermore, a multivariate regression analysis revealed that none of the 12 orientation items at either treatment were significantly related to age ($p > 0.50$).

This lack of an age effect with respect to the severity (i.e., duration) of delirium may be due to the fact that orientation was tested in a predominantly elderly patient sample in the present study; a ceiling effect probably resulted [mean age = 59.9 years; standard deviation (SD) = 6.5; range = 47–74].

TABLE 4. Differential Recovery of 12 Orientation Items[a]

Treatment Three			Treatment Eight		
Item	Mean	SD	Item	Mean	SD
Name	0.13	0.35	Name	0.27	0.46
Year of birth	0.40	0.63	Country	0.87	0.83
Country	0.47	0.92	Year of birth	1.00	1.25
Social Security number	1.00	1.41	Social Security number	1.27	1.67
Building	1.13	1.41	Town	1.33	1.18
Season	1.27	1.98	Age	1.60	1.30
Town	1.40	1.72	Building	1.67	2.19
Age	1.47	1.30	Season	1.67	1.99
Floor of hospital	1.93	1.75	Month	2.93	2.02
Year	2.07	2.34	Day of week	2.93	2.49
Day of week	2.07	2.52	Floor of hospital	3.13	2.70
Month	2.73	2.28	Year	3.20	2.60

[a]Only disoriented subjects' data displayed. Items scored "0" through "8," where "0" indicates that the subject never was disoriented on a particular item at the earliest testing session (15 minutes), and "8" indicates that reorientation never did return on a particular item.

Differential Recovery of Orientation Items

TABLE 4 illustrates when orientation was regained on the 12 orientation items. It is clear from this table that recovery of orientation was stratified across the 12 items ($p < 0.0001$). To test the hypothesis that orientation for "person" returned before "place" orientation, with "time" orientation returning last,[1,5] a composite score for all four items within each of the three categories was formed. TABLE 5 indicates that recovery of orientation was different across these three categories ($p < 0.0001$), thereby supporting this hypothesis.

This differential recovery of orientation in the period of delirium (the "postictal state") following ECT may imply that neuropsychological and neurological impairment comprising delirium does not occur in a totally random or chaotic fashion, but rather that there may be some as yet poorly understood systematization of neurological and neuropsychological processes underlying delirium.[5,6,31–34]

Time Disorientation: Are There Contradictory Responses?

Some investigators have suggested that one way we are able to assess our present age might be through arithmetical reasoning.[7,35] Presumably, if one knew the current

TABLE 5. Person versus Place versus Time[a]

Orientation Aspect	Treatment Three		Treatment Eight	
	Mean	SD	Mean	SD
Person	0.78	0.76	1.16	0.95
Place	1.07	1.12	1.81	1.33
Time	1.91	1.88	3.08	2.13

[a]Individual 12 orientation items were scored just like in TABLE 4. A composite score for "person," "place," and "time" was then formed by using all four items a priori hypothesized (see Methods section) to tap each orientation aspect.

year and one's year of birth, then one should be able to mathematically calculate one's present age. Yet as Mowbray and Zangwill discuss, another hypothesis is that claimed age may be an isolated fact independent of arithmetical reasoning.[7,35]

Our results support this latter hypothesis for two reasons. First, from TABLE 4, it is seen that orientation for "age" returned before orientation for "year" at both treatments. One factor (year) needed to be reasoned arithmetically and therefore tended to be missing in these patients. Second, if one takes the number given for present age and present year seriously, there is almost a total lack of correspondence between a patient's incorrect estimate of his age and his incorrect estimate of the

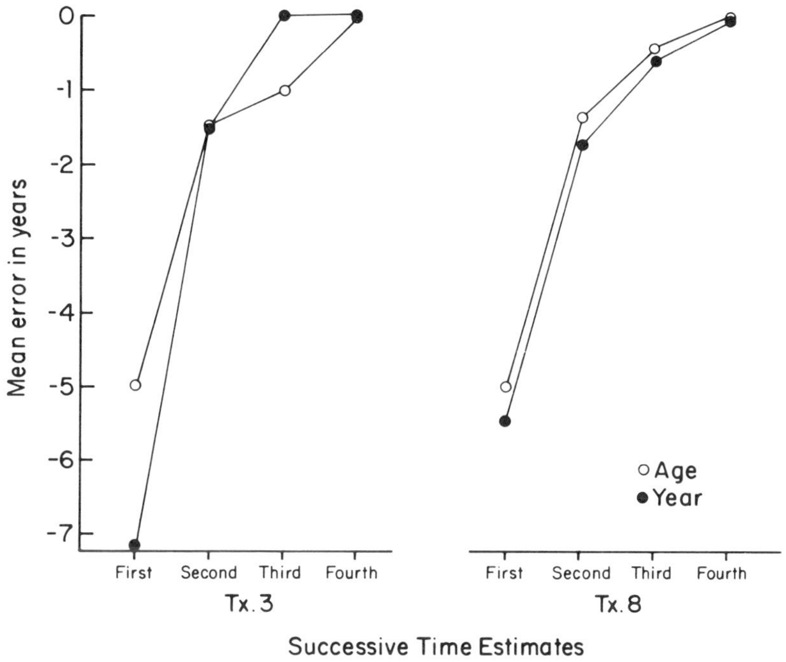

FIGURE 4. Successive quantitatively meaningful time estimates for the orientation questions of age and current year.

current year at any particular test session (e.g., first session where errors were made on both questions at treatments three and eight: $r = -0.03$, -0.06, respectively).

Time Disorientation: It Is Related to "Shrinking Retrograde Amnesia"?

If one does take the numbers given for present age and present year seriously, it may be possible to find some parallels between "shrinking" retrograde amnesia following other etiologies of CNS impairment[9,36–38] and time disorientation following ECT (see FIGURE 3 caption).

FIGURE 4 illustrates successive (the first four) quantitatively meaningful (i.e., excluding perseveratory, mute, and "I don't know") responses to the age and current year orientation questions for all 30 patients. A correct response to either question was considered to differ in "0" years from the correct response, and that particular question was not asked again. We assume that the same correct answer (and resulting "0" score) would have occurred at the remaining successive time estimates illustrated in FIGURE 4 had these questions been reasked.

It is clear from FIGURE 4 that ECT patients had a tendency to give incorrect answers that are at first more remote in years from the correct answer, but that, over postictal time, the incorrect answers tend to be less remote in years from the correct answer. Preliminary statistical analyses of the individual *disoriented* subjects' data indicate that, at treatment three, 12 of 13 regression line slopes for age versus successive time estimates were positive, and 12 of 12 regression line slopes for current year versus successive time estimates were positive. Binomial and sign tests indicate beyond the 0.01 probability level that positive slopes were more common than negative slopes. However, at treatment eight, only 7 of 10 slopes are positive for age and current year; neither of these two trends reaches statistical significance.

These results give us a picture of time reorientation proceeding in a systematic (i.e., nonrandom) quantitatively predictable fashion similar to what is termed "shrinking retrograde amnesia" following other sources of CNS insult, such as closed-head injury.[9,39] One way to interpret this result is to suggest that delirium throws patients into their pasts, and, as they recover, they move closer to the present time. However, the previously mentioned lack of correspondence between age and present year estimates contradicts this hypothesis. Nevertheless, future studies might ask patients questions about the state of the world (e.g., "who is the current president?") along with orientation questions after ECT and other causes of delirium. Such studies might provide more information concerning the actual mechanism(s) with which time reorientation is regained.

REFERENCES

1. DANIEL, W. F. & H. F. CROVITZ. 1982. Recovery of orientation after electroconvulsive therapy. Acta Psychiatr. Scand. **66:** 421–428.
2. VALENTINE, M., M. G. KEDDIE & D. DUNNE. 1968. A comparison of techniques in electroconvulsive therapy. Br. J. Psychiatry **114:** 989–996.
3. WILSON, I. & G. GOTTLIEB. 1967. Unilateral electro-convulsive shock therapy. Dis. Nerv. Syst. **28:** 541–545.
4. DANIEL, W. F. & H. F. CROVITZ. 1983. Acute memory impairment following electroconvulsive therapy. I. Effects of electrical stimulus waveform and number of treatments. Acta Psychiatr. Scand. **67:** 1–7.
5. LIPOWSKI, Z. J. 1980. Delirium: Acute Brain Failure in Man. Charles C. Thomas. Springfield, Ill.
6. LUNN, V. & E. TROLLE. 1949. On the initial impairment of consciousness following electric convulsive therapy: a preliminary communication. Acta Psychiatr. Neurol. Scand. **24:** 33–57.
7. MOWBRAY, R. M. 1954. Disorientation for age. J. Ment. Sci. **100:** 749–752.
8. MOWBRAY, R. M. 1959. Recovery of consciousness after ECT. Acta Psychiatr. Scand. **34:** 330–341.
9. SCHACTER, D. L. & H. F. CROVITZ. 1977. Memory function after closed head injury: a review of the quantitative research. Cortex **13:** 150–176.
10. DANIEL, W. F., H. F. CROVITZ, R. D. WEINER & H. J. ROGERS. 1982. The effects of ECT modifications on autobiographical and verbal memory. Biol. Psychiatry **17:** 919–924.
11. DANIEL, W. F., R. D. WEINER & H. F. CROVITZ. 1983. Autobiographical amnesia with ECT: an analysis of the roles of stimulus wave form, electrode placement, stimulus energy, and seizure length. Biol. Psychiatry **18:** 121–126.
12. DANIEL, W. F., H. F. CROVITZ & R. D. WEINER. 1984. Perceptual learning with right unilateral versus bilateral electroconvulsive therapy. Br. J. Psychiatry **145:** 394–400.

13. DANIEL, W. F., H. F. CROVITZ, R. D. WEINER, H. S. SWARTZWELDER & E. M. KAHN. 1985. ECT-induced amnesia and postictal EEG suppression. Biol. Psychiatry **20:** 329–352.
14. DANIEL, W. F. & H. F. CROVITZ. 1983. Acute memory impairment following electroconvulsive therapy. II. Effects of electrode placement. Acta Psychiatr. Scand. **67:** 57–68.
15. WEINER, R. D. 1984. Does ECT cause brain damage? Behav. Brain Sci. **7:** 1–54.
16. MCNAMARA, J. O. 1979. Human hypoxia and seizures: effects and interactions. Adv. Neurol. **26:** 137–146.
17. MCCALL, R. B. & M. I. APPELBAUM. 1973. Bias in the analysis of repeated-measures designs: some alternative approaches. Child Dev. **44:** 401–415.
18. DAVIDSON, M. L. 1972. Univariate versus multivariate tests in repeated-measures experiments. Psychol. Bull. **77:** 446–452.
19. FINK, M. 1979. Convulsive Therapy: Theory and Practice. Raven Press. New York, N.Y.
20. WEINER, R. D. 1980. Persistence of ECT-induced EEG changes. J. Nerv. Ment. Dis. **168:** 224–228.
21. WEINER, R. D., H. J. ROGERS, J. R. T. DAVIDSON & E. M. KAHN. 1986. Effects of electroconvulsive therapy upon brain electrical activity. Ann. N.Y. Acad. Sci. (This volume.)
22. DANIEL, W. F., R. D. WEINER, H. F. CROVITZ, G. B. STRONG & M. M. CHRISTENBURY. 1983. ECT-induced delirium and further ECT: a case report. Am. J. Psychiatry **140:** 922–924.
23. SUMMERS, W. K., E. ROBINS & T. REICH. 1979. The natural history of acute organic mental syndrome after electroconvulsive therapy. Biol. Psychiatry **14:** 905–912.
24. BREGGIN, P. R. 1979. Electroshock: Its Brain-Disabling Effects. Springer Publishing Company. New York, N.Y.
25. FREUND, R. J. & R. C. LITTELL. 1981. SAS for Linear Models: A Guide to the ANOVA and GLM Procedures. SAS Institute, Inc. Cary, N.C.
26. COHEN, J. & P. COHEN. 1983. Applied Multiple Regression/Correlation Analysis for the Behavioral Sciences. 2nd edit. Lawrence Erlbaum Associates. Hillsdale, N.J.
27. ROGOSA, D. 1980. Comparing nonparallel regression lines. Psychol. Bull. **88:** 307–321.
28. WEISSMAN, A. 1963. Effect of electroconvulsive shock intensity and seizure pattern on retrograde amnesia in rats. J. Comp. Physiol. Psychol. **56:** 806–810.
29. ZORNETZER, S. 1974. Retrograde amnesia and brain seizures in rodents: electrophysiological and neuroanatomical analyses. *In* Psychobiology of Convulsive Therapy. M. Fink, S. Kety, J. McGaugh & T. A. Williams, Eds.: 99–128. V. H. Winston and Sons. Washington, D.C.
30. LERER, B. 1985. Studies on the role of brain cholinergic systems in the therapeutic mechanisms and adverse effects of ECT and lithium. Biol. Psychiatry **20:** 20–40.
31. CHEDRU, F. & N. GESCHWIND. 1972. Disorders of higher cortical functions in acute confusional states. Cortex **8:** 395–411.
32. COHEN, L. 1939. Return of cognitive conscious functions induced with metrazol. Arch. Neurol. Psychiatry **41:** 489–494.
33. KRISS, A., L. D. BLUMHARDT, A. M. HALLIDAY & R. T. C. PRATT. 1978. Neurological asymmetries immediately after unilateral ECT. J. Neurol. Neurosurg. Psychiatry **41:** 1135–1144.
34. LIPOWSKI, Z. J. 1975. Organic brain syndromes: overview and classification. *In* Psychiatric Aspects of Neurologic Disease. D. F. Benson & D. Blumer, Eds.: 11–35. Grune & Stratton. New York, N.Y.
35. ZANGWILL, O. L. 1953. Disorientation for age. J. Ment. Sci. **99:** 698–702.
36. BENSON, D. F. & N. GESCHWIND. 1967. Shrinking retrograde amnesia. J. Neurol. Neurosurg. Psychiatry **30:** 539–544.
37. RUSSELL, W. R. & P. W. NATHAN. 1946. Traumatic amnesia. Brain **69:** 280–300.
38. SISLER, G. & H. PENNER. 1975. Amnesia following severe head injury. Can. Psychiatr. Assoc. J. **20:** 333–336.
39. CROVITZ, H. F. The loss and recovery of autobiographical memory after head injury. *In* Autobiographical Memory. D. Rubin, Ed. Cambridge University Press. Cambridge, England. (In press.)

40. WITTMAN, P. 1939. A psychological study of the mental confusion following metrazol therapy. Pap. Elgin State Hosp. **3:** 67–71.
41. CRONHOLM, B. & A. LAGERGREN. 1959. Memory disturbances after electroconvulsive therapy: an experimental study of retrograde amnesia after electroconvulsive shock. Acta Psychiatr. Scand. **34:** 283–310.
42. American Psychiatric Association. 1980. Diagnostic and Statistical Manual of Mental Disorders. 3rd edit. APA Press. Washington, D.C.

Memory Functions as Affected by Electroconvulsive Therapy[a]

LARRY R. SQUIRE

Psychology Service
Veterans Administration Medical Center
3350 La Jolla Village Drive
San Diego, California 92161
and
Department of Psychiatry
University of California School of Medicine
La Jolla, California 92093

There are some issues that invite continuing disagreement. For example, certain empirical questions about electroconvulsive therapy (ECT) that seem at first glance rather simple to answer by experiment are still widely debated. Does ECT permanently impair memory? Memory impairment is a weighty issue because it is central to all discussions of adverse effects of ECT. From the patient's point of view, memory impairment is the most prominent and troublesome adverse effect of ECT.

The purpose of this chapter is to summarize what has been learned about ECT and memory loss. Specifically, how severe is the memory impairment, and how long does it last? Readers are invited to consult a number of recent reviews that consider these issues in somewhat more detail.[1-4] The discussion here focuses in turn on anterograde amnesia (loss of the ability to accomplish new learning), retrograde amnesia (loss of memory for events that occurred before ECT), and memory complaints. Pertinent information will also be reviewed concerning the difference between bilateral and unilateral treatment. The discussion concerns the effects of a typical course of treatment, i.e., 6–12 treatments, and it is based primarily on studies in which ECT was given with a device delivering sine-wave current. Recently, it has been reported that the cognitive side effects associated with ECT can be reduced by using brief-pulse stimulation instead of sine-wave stimulation (see References 5 and 6). This issue will be touched on at the end of the paper.

MEMORY LOSS FOLLOWING ECT IS A SELECTIVE NEUROPSYCHOLOGICAL IMPAIRMENT

It has been known for a long time that injury in either of two areas of the brain leads to an amnesic syndrome. The medial temporal region, including the hippocampal formation and the amygdala, and the diencephalic midline, including the dorsomedial nucleus of the thalamus and the mammillary bodies, have been most often implicated in the disorder.[7-9] Amnesia is a circumscribed deficit that includes both anterograde and retrograde amnesia, in the absence of other defects of cognitive function. For

[a]Supported by the Medical Research Service of the Veterans Administration and by National Institute of Mental Health Grant MH24600.

example, amnesic patients can have intact intelligence test scores, intact language and praxic functions, and normal premorbid personality.

After the initial confusional period lasting approximately 30 minutes after each seizure, the memory loss associated with ECT resembles this classical picture of amnesia. It can be severe, and it occurs against a background of good performance on many cognitive tests that tap areas of function other than memory. The amnesia is particularly well circumscribed during the first several treatments, because other cognitive impairment can appear later in the treatment course.[3,10] For these reasons, it seems reasonable to think that ECT is having a particularly strong impact on the brain structures that have been linked to amnesia. This same point has been made previously,[11] with emphasis on the medial temporal region and the fact that the hippocampal formation has a very low seizure threshold.

ANTEROGRADE AMNESIA

The anterograde amnesia associated with ECT diminishes between treatments and cumulates across treatments. During the first few hours after each treatment, and particularly after a few treatments have already been given, the anterograde amnesia can be as severe after ECT as in other conditions of amnesia—for example, in the amnesia associated with the alcoholic Korsakoff syndrome.[12] In a test of paired-associate learning, which asks subjects to learn 10 new associations (e.g., army-table), normal control subjects remembered an average of about 5 of the pairs after one presentation of the list and 8 to 10 of the pairs after three presentations. In contrast, amnesic patients, including patients tested two hours after the fourth bilateral ECT, had great difficulty remembering any of the pairs and averaged about 2 pairs correct after three presentations of the list.

It is easy to document the recovery of new learning ability that occurs between each treatment. In one study, lists of 10 words were presented to patients at each of four intervals (45 minutes, 65 minutes, 85 minutes, and nine hours) after the fourth or fifth treatment.[13] Memory was tested 15 minutes after each list presentation by multiple-choice method. Over the intervals tested, performance improved from an initial level that was no better than would have been achieved by chance to a level of about 8 correct words out of 10. This marked initial deficit was observed only for patients receiving bilateral ECT. Patients receiving right unilateral ECT achieved 8 to 9 words correct at all test intervals. A group of depressed patients not receiving ECT averaged 9.5 words correct.

Although the verbal memory impairment associated with right unilateral ECT is considerably less than that associated with bilateral ECT, the advantage of right unilateral ECT is not so great when so-called nonverbal memory tests are used. These tests assess the learning and retention of faces, nonsense shapes, spatial layouts, and other material that is difficult to encode in words. It is known that memory for such material depends on the integrity of the right temporal lobe.[14] Memory for this material is also affected by right unilateral ECT more than verbal material is affected.[6,15]

Once the course of ECT is completed, the capacity for new learning begins to recover. The point at which new learning ability reaches normal levels is difficult to identify exactly, and estimates will vary depending on the sensitivity of the test used to assess memory. One reviewer, considering a large number of studies, found an average return to baseline functions after 72 days.[16] There are two ways to determine baseline. One way is to obtain pre-ECT performance scores. These scores, however, might have been lowered by the depressive illness for which ECT was prescribed, and follow-up scores might therefore have to exceed this baseline by some unknown amount before they can be called normal. Another way to estimate baseline functions is to compare patients who have received ECT to other similar patients who have not received ECT.

In the past several years, studies have used both these methods. Testing instruments have included sensitive delayed-recall tests, whereby subjects are asked to produce, without the help of cues, information that had been presented to them up to two weeks earlier. One test asked subjects to recall information that had been presented to them incidentally two weeks earlier, and which they had not been told would be later tested for.[17] The results from these studies (cf. References 2, 5, 16, and 17) have been quite consistent. Those patients with anterograde amnesia following bilateral ECT seem to have recovered by six months after treatment, and there is no good evidence that new learning ability is still deficient at this time. Presumably, once treatment is completed, recovery occurs gradually in a negatively accelerated fashion over a period of many weeks.

RETROGRADE AMNESIA

Remote memory for events that occurred before ECT can be evaluated either by tests that ask questions about public events, which are verifiable because the events were in the news, or by tests that ask about past autobiographical events. The latter are often difficult to verify, but the method has the advantage that a large amount of information can be obtained from single subjects. One method for assessing public events that has been useful in evaluating the effects of ECT has been to ask about former television programs that had been broadcast for only one season during the past 15 years.[18] When tested by multiple-choice methods or by sensitive recall methods that asked for details about the programs, patients receiving bilateral ECT initially exhibited a temporally limited gradient of retrograde amnesia. That is, shortly after the fifth treatment memory was lost for programs that had appeared 1 to 3 years previously, but memory was unaffected for programs that had appeared longer ago. This impairment gradually subsided during the weeks after treatment and was not detectable six months later.[19] Right unilateral ECT has considerably less effect than bilateral ECT on remote memory. As measured by the multiple-choice method, memory for past television programs was not affected at all in patients prescribed unilateral ECT, even as early as one hour after the fifth treatment.[20]

Autobiographical memory after ECT was first evaluated systematically by Janis and co-workers in the early 1950s.[21,22] In his studies, patients who received 20 bilateral treatments later seemed to forget autobiographical information that had been reported successfully by the patients before treatment. This retrograde amnesia was present at 4 weeks after the treatment course, and was still present at 10–14 weeks after treatment in a subgroup of five patients who were followed further. In view of the fact that the severity of retrograde amnesia following ECT is related to the recency of the to-be-remembered event, it seemed important to replicate the study by Janis and to include measures of the time period to which the tested material belonged.

In our study patients prescribed bilateral ECT were asked 10 questions about their personal history, which covered the period from elementary school (name the teachers in your first six grades), to the period just prior to hospitalization (tell me everything you can remember about the day you came to the hospital for your present admission).[19] The latter question concerned an event that had occurred from 2 to 36 days before the first ECT (mean = 11 days). These questions were given before ECT, shortly after ECT, and seven months after ECT to 10 patients prescribed bilateral ECT. A group of 7 hospitalized depressed patients not prescribed ECT were also tested at equivalent intervals.

The results were that both the patients prescribed ECT and the control patients reported a large number of autobiographical details on their first testing session (about 58 details for each ECT patient and 62 details for each control patient). Following ECT there was a sharp reduction in the number of facts that could be recalled. At the follow-up period, seven months later, the ECT and control patients once again performed similarly. Thus, when all 10 questions were considered together, there was no indication for a persisting deficit in remote memory.

However, a persisting impairment was present nonetheless, and this became apparent when the results were tallied separately for 3 of the 10 questions that asked about relatively recent events. One of them, the hospital admission question, concerned an event that had occurred 11 days before treatment, another question concerned an event that had occurred 6 to 37 months before ECT, and a third question concerned an event that had occurred 14 to 19 months before ECT. Control subjects recalled an average of about 13 details concerning these three events at the time of the pre-ECT test and recalled almost as much information 7 months later, without intervening ECT. The ECT patients initially recalled a little more information than the control patients about these same three events (about 16 details per person). However, 7 months later they forgot much of what they had previously reported and now recalled only 7 details per person. The great majority of this forgetting applied to the most recent event, i.e., the question about hospital admission.

When patients did not volunteer information that they had recalled before ECT, the omitted detail was given to them and they were asked whether or not it was familiar. This procedure was 71% effective for ECT patients and 100% effective for control patients. The information that was not recognized by ECT patients after the reminding procedure belonged mostly to recent time periods. Thus approximately 3.5 details per person from the hospital admission question were regarded as unfamiliar at the follow-up test, 1.0 detail per person from the other two recent-event questions, and 0.5 detail per person from all the other questions together. These results provide evidence that information about recent events can be lost for a long time, possibly permanently, after bilateral ECT. These data are also compatible with a large literature concerning the effects of electroconvulsive shock (ECS) on memory in rodents, which shows that retorgrade amnesia is temporally graded and that the most recent events are the most vulnerable.[23] Although these retrograde effects have typically extended only to the seconds or minutes preceding a (single) ECS, retrograde amnesia in mice can affect memories acquired one to three weeks previously when four spaced ECS are given.[24]

It is not yet clear how to evaluate the finding that at seven months after treatment persons who had received bilateral ECT occasionally failed to recognize as familiar even remote events that had occurred many years ago. Specifically, 5 of the 10 persons in our sample denied familiarity to a total of 18 remote events that they had reported as facts before ECT, seven months earlier. Unfortunately, it was not possible to verify these pre-ECT reports, so it is not certain that the autobiographical information obtained was always accurate. If it was not accurate before ECT, of course, subsequent failure to recognize the material as familiar cannot be taken as evidence for forgetting. On the other hand, it is not clear why ECT patients would be more likely than control patients to report inaccurate information. There is also another complicating aspect of these data. It is well known that subjects' reports of familiarity about a previously encountered item are determined in part by a subject's "response bias," quite independently of the strength of that item in memory. Perhaps ECT patients were more cautious than control patients. Future studies could use multiple-choice tests and verified material to determine whether long-lasting memory loss can actually occur after ECT for information acquired in the distant past.

MEMORY COMPLAINTS

Many patients who have received ECT continue to report even several months after treatment that their memory is not as good as it used to be, and they attribute their memory problem to the ECT experience.[25–27] When these reports of poor memory were evaluated with a self-rating scale,[25] two important points emerged about the nature of memory complaints. First, memory functions were rated considerably better six months after bilateral ECT than one week after treatment. In this respect, the reports were viridical, because it is known that memory functions do improve during this interval. Second, the quality of the memory complaints seven months after ECT suggested that the patients were interpreting their memory abilities just as they had experienced them shortly after ECT. That is, there could have been continuing doubts that memory had fully recovered and a tendency to refer even normal failures of memory to the ECT. It is also possible that the complaints refer, at least in part, to the lacuna in memory that exists for the time period immediately around the treatment. As patients recover from anterograde amnesia, they do not recover the memories for events that occurred during the period of anterograde amnesia. In addition, persisting memory loss does occur for events that immediately preceded the treatment course.

In a later study, 31 patients who had received bilateral ECT were asked three years later to indicate the portions of past time period that they had trouble remembering.[26] The median response was an anterograde amnesia of two months and a retrograde amnesia of six months. The anterograde amnesia is presumably related to the ECT and appears to be an accurate assessment of missing memories. The retrograde amnesia may also be accurate, but it is not clear how much of it should be related to the ECT and how much to the depression that led up to the ECT. The same patients, three years earlier, had indicated before ECT that it was difficult to remember the previous five months. These results show directly that persisting memory complaints are in part directed toward the lost time period around the treatment.

The difference between bilateral and unilateral ECT, noted in formal tests of anterograde and retrograde amnesia, is also reflected in the self-ratings. In contrast to patients prescribed bilateral ECT, who report markedly reduced memory functions one week after treatment, patients prescribed unilateral ECT do not report that memory is more impaired after treatment than before. However, depressed patients who had not received ECT actually reported significantly improved memory functions during this same interval, so it is possible that unilateral ECT also causes memory complaints. A study involving randomized assignment to ECT and non-ECT groups, where the role of preexisting group differences could be controlled, would be required to settle this issue.

DISCUSSION

The effects of ECT on memory functions can be summarized in the following way. Patients who receive ECT have impaired memory. Eventually, and certainly by six months after treatment, they perform as well on new learning tests and on remote memory tests as they performed before treatment and as well as other patients who have not received ECT. However, information acquired during the days and weeks prior to and following ECT may be permanently lost. Of course, the possibility can really never be ruled out that more sensitive testing methods will some day reveal a greater degree of permanent memory loss than has been detected to date. Bilateral ECT affects memory considerably more than right unilateral ECT, and this difference is reflected as well in patients' own reports of their memory functions.

An important new finding is that the use of brief-pulse stimulation instead of sine-wave stimulation can reduce the memory impairment still further, beyond the reduction achieved by using right unilateral sine wave instead of bilateral ECT sine wave.[5] Brief-pulse stimulation can elicit a seizure with approximately one-third the electrical energy produced by conventional sine-wave current, and this difference in electrical energy (e.g., about 22 joules vs. about 60 joules) probably accounts for its advantage. Interestingly, two previous studies of memory and ECS in animals failed to demonstrate any role for total electrical energy in determining the severity of amnesia.[28,29] As recently as 1982,[3] review articles of ECT could fairly conclude that waveform was probably not an important factor in determining the severity of memory dysfunction.

It is worth emphasizing that reduction of memory impairment by using pulse stimulation may be expected to occur only when the available parameters on the MECTA machine, the most common device in use that delivers brief-pulse stimulation, are set correctly, i.e., so as to optimize seizure induction, but not to exceed seizure threshold by too much. On the one hand, Sackeim and colleagues report that a carefully titrated course of right unilateral, brief-pulse ECT, designed to be as close to seizure threshold as possible, did not achieve good therapeutic efficacy.[6] On the other hand, Weiner and his colleagues report good efficacy with parameters set, on average, as follows: frequency = 60; pulse width = 0.75 msecond; pulse duration = 1.25 seconds for a total of about 22 joules of energy.[5] If maximum dial settings are used to deliver brief-pulse stimulation (2.0 seconds duration and 1.5 mseconds pulse width), the total number of joules increases from 22 to 70, and the energy advantage of pulse stimulation over conventional sine-wave stimulation is lost. Since the parameters must be selected individually for each patient, and since there is considerable variability in seizure threshold among patients, special care may be needed when using the MECTA machine to obtain the full energy advantage without missing seizures or otherwise compromising efficacy.

In any case, it does now seem possible to deliver a therapeutically effective course of right unilateral ECT using brief-pulse stimulation; and to produce less memory impairment than with right unilateral sine wave and markedly less impairment than with bilateral sine wave. It is not yet certain how to characterize the level of memory impairment associated with brief-pulse stimulation. The relative rankings of the four treatment combinations can be given in order of increasing memory impairment: unilateral pulse, unilateral sine wave, bilateral pulse, bilateral sine wave.[5] Moreover, the general conclusions summarized here, i.e., regarding the impairment associated with bilateral sine-wave treatment, presumably apply as well to each of the other treatment combinations, but the severity of the effects on memory and the time needed for recovery are different for each combination.

It is not known whether a similar or different story must be told for patients who have received large numbers of ECT (e.g., more than 50). It is not known whether the persisting report by patients of memory difficulty after ECT refers *entirely* to problems in remembering events that occurred close to the time of treatment. The perception of memory difficulty could in part refer to a subtle compromise of memory functions, but one that would show up only on a test instrument more sensitive than any yet devised. Alternatively, a sense of continuing memory problems might occur because persons who have made a gradual recovery from amnesia tend to doubt that they are fully recovered. We all occasionally have faulty memories. How can we know when memory failures are normal and when they might be attributable to a previous course of ECT? It is not known to what extent persons in this circumstance could be helped by continued consultation or reality testing after ECT, or whether such a perception would be so resistant to change that it must be considered an important cost of ECT. These and other questions remain, but science can address them all.

REFERENCES

1. SQUIRE, L. R. 1984. ECT and memory dysfunction. *In* Basic Mechanisms of ECT. B. Lerer, R. D. Weiner & R. H. Belmaker, Eds.: 156–163. John Libby & Co., Ltd. London, England
2. WEINER, R. D. 1984. Does electroconvulsive therapy cause brain damage? Behav. Brain Sci. **7:** 1–53.
3. PRICE, T. R. P. 1982. Short- and long-term cognitive effects of ECT. I. Effects on memory. Psychopharmacol. Bull. **18:** 81–91.
4. TAYLOR, J. R., R. TOMPKINS, R. DEMERS & D. ANDERSON. 1982. Electroconvulsive therapy and memory dysfunction: is there evidence for prolonged defects? Biol. Psychiatry **17**(10) 1169–1193.
5. WEINER, R. D., H. J. ROGERS, J. R. T. DAVIDSON & L. R. SQUIRE. 1986. Effects of stimulus parameters on cognitive side effects. Ann. N.Y. Acad. Sci. (This volume.)
6. SACKHEIM, H. A., P. NEELEY, B. L. STEIF, P. DECINA, S. PORTNOY & S. MALITZ. 1986. Cognitive consequences of low dosage electroconvulsive therapy. Ann. N.Y. Acad. Sci. (This volume.)
7. BRIERLEY, J. B. 1977. Neuropathology of amnesic states. *In* Amnesia. C. W. M. Whitty & O. L. Zangwill, Eds. 2nd edit.: 199–223. Butterworth. London, England.
8. SQUIRE, L. R. 1982. The neuropsychology of human memory. Annu. Rev. Neurosci. **5:** 241–273.
9. MISHKIN, M. 1982. A memory system in the monkey. Phil. Trans. R. Soc. London **298:** 85–95.
10. FINK, M. 1979. Convulsive Therapy: Theory and Practice. Raven Press. New York, N.Y.
11. INGLIS, J. 1970. Shock, surgery, and cerebral symmetry. Br. J. Psychiatry **117:** 143–148.
12. SQUIRE, L. R. & S. ZOLA-MORGAN. 1983. The neurology of memory: the case for correspondence between the findings for man and non-human primate. *In* Physiological Basis of Memory. J. A. Deutsch, Ed. 2nd edit.: 200–268. Academic Press, Inc. New York, N.Y.
13. SQUIRE, L. R., A. SHIMAMURA & P. GRAF. 1985. Independence of recognition memory and priming effects: a neuropsychological analysis. J. Exp. Psychol. Learning Memory Cognition **11:** 37–44.
14. MILNER, B. 1974. Hemispheric specialization: scope and limits. *In* The Neurosciences Third Study Program. F. O. Schmitt & F. G. Worden, Eds.: 75–89. MIT Press. Cambridge, Mass.
15. SQUIRE, L. R. & P. C. SLATER. 1978. Bilateral and unilateral ECT: effects on verbal and nonverbal memory. Am. J. Psychiatry **11:** 1316–1320.
16. WEEKS, D., C. P. L. FREEMAN & R. E. KENDELL. 1980. ECT. III. Enduring cognitive deficits? Br. J. Psychiatry. **137:** 26–37.
17. SQUIRE, L. R. & P. M. CHACE. 1975. Memory functions six to nine months after electroconvulsive therapy. Arch. Gen. Psychiatry **32:** 1557–1564.
18. SQUIRE, L. R. & M. M. FOX. 1980. Assessment of remote memory: validation of the television test by repeated testing during a seven-year period. Behav. Res. Methods Instrum. **12:** 583–586.
19. SQUIRE, L. R., P. C. SLATER & P. L. MILLER. 1981. Retrograde amnesia and bilateral electroconvulsive therapy: long-term follow-up. Arch. Gen. Psychiatry **38:** 89–95.
20. SQUIRE, L. R., P. C. SLATER & P. M. CHACE. 1975. Retrograde amnesia: temporal gradient in very long-term memory following electroconvulsive therapy. Science **187:** 77–79.

21. JANIS, I. L. 1950. Psychologic effects of electric convulsive treatments. J. Nerv. Ment. Dis. **3:** 359–382.
22. JANIS, I. L. & M. ASTRACHAN. 1951. The effects of electroconvulsive treatments on memory efficiency. J. Abnorm. Soc. Psychol. **46:** 501–511.
23. MCGAUGH, J. L. & M. M. HERZ. 1972. Memory Consolidation. Albion Publishing Co. San Francisco, Calif.
24. SQUIRE, L. R. & C. W. SPANIS. 1984. Long gradient of retrograde amnesia in mice: continuity with the findings in humans. Behav. Neurosci. **98:** 345–348.
25. SQUIRE, L. R., C. D. WETZEL & P. C. SLATER. 1979. Memory complaint after electroconvulsive therapy: assessment with a new self-rating instrument. Biol. Psychiatry **14:** 791–801.
26. SQUIRE, L. R. & P. C. SLATER. 1983. Electroconvulsive therapy and complaints of memory dysfunction: a prospective three-year follow-up study. Br. J. Psychiatry **142:** 1–8.
27. FREEMAN, C. P. L. & R. E. KENDELL. 1980. ECT. I. Patients' experiences and attitudes. Br. J. Psychiatry **137:** 8–16.
28. ZORNETZER, S. & J. L. MCGAUGH. 1971. Retrograde amnesia and brain seizures in mice. Physiol. Behav. **7:** 401–408.
29. SPANIS, C. & L. R. SQUIRE. 1981. Memory and convulsive stimulation: effects of stimulus waveform. Am. J. Psychiatry **138:** 1177–1181.

Effects of Stimulus Parameters on Cognitive Side Effects

RICHARD D. WEINER,[a,b,e] HELEN J. ROGERS,[a]
JONATHAN R. T. DAVIDSON,[a,b] AND
LARRY R. SQUIRE[c,d]

[a]*Department of Psychiatry*
Duke University Medical School
Durham, North Carolina 27710

[b]*Psychiatry Service*
Durham Veterans Administration Medical Center
508 Fulton Street
Durham, North Carolina 27705

[c]*Department of Psychiatry*
University of California School of Medicine
La Jolla, California 92093

[d]*Psychiatry Service*
Veterans Administration Medical Center
3350 La Jolla Village Drive
San Diego, California 92161

INTRODUCTION

This symposium has already focused on recent experimental data directed toward an understanding of the differential effects of electrode placement upon both therapeutic response and adverse cognitive effects with electroconvulsive therapy (ECT). In addition, we have yet to hear a number of further expositions on this subject. The available data, presented both here and elsewhere, suggest that unilateral nondominant (UL) ECT is roughly as effective as bilateral (BL) ECT in producing a remission in severely depressed patients.[1-3] At the same time, it must be pointed out that technical factors such as sufficient interelectrode distance and the assurance of suprathreshold stimuli also appear to play a role in the efficacy of UL treatments. In addition, there is also a possibility that some patients might respond better to the combination of more intense seizures and denser organic interictal changes produced by bilateral stimulation.

The situation with regard to adverse effects, however, is considerably clearer: unilateral nondominant ECT offers a distinct advantage to bilateral treatments with regard to the presence and extent of cognitive disruption, at least with respect to those functions that depend on the dominant hemisphere.[4] Still, the extent of data indicating that such amnestic differences exist longer than a few weeks has been largely limited to reports of self-ratings.[5-6]

Another form of ECT modification, discussed both within this volume as well as elsewhere in the literature, though to a lesser degree than electrode placement, is the

[e]Address correspondence to Dr. Weiner at the Durham VA Medical Center.

stimulus waveform. Over the years, a number of attempts have been made to alter the electrical characteristics of the signal used to generate seizure activity with ECT.[7] Such attempts, while suffering from a variety of methodological inadequancies, have suggested that as long as the duration of the basic stimulus waveform unit does not become too abbreviated, a reasonable degree of therapeutic equivalence appears to exist among the various waveform morphologies.

The role of stimulus waveform in adverse central nervous system (CNS) effects has been a particularly problematic area of investigation. Early studies, which favored low-energy stimuli,[7] were confounded by concomitant differences in electrode placement. Later investigators reported mixed findings, with some claiming less impairment over a course of ECT given by lower energy stimuli,[8–12] and others finding no difference.[13,14] In no case, however, has evidence been presented for persistent deficits on the basis of waveform type.

While a larger number of studies have considered the possible beneficial and/or adverse effects or either electrode placement or stimulus waveform, few have evaluated these effects simultaneously. Valentine *et al.* observed an apparent additive effect of these two modifications on cognitive function during the postictal period.[12] To some degree, Daniel *et al.* found similar additive effects after an individual electrically induced seizure.[15–18] This latter group has also contributed relevant data concerning postictal orientation effects to the present volume.[19]

Still, there has been a notable absence of studies focusing upon differences in effects lasting beyond the postictal period. This is of particular interest, given recent claims that the theoretically most benign ECT combination, consisting of unilateral nondominant electrode placement and brief-pulse stimuli, may be at least relatively ineffective from a therapeutic standpoint.[20,21] In order to investigate more fully the acute and long-term effects of both electrode placement and stimulus waveform on cognitive function, we undertook a prospective study, some of whose results will be presented here. Electrophysiologic findings, suggesting an additive effect for bilateral electrode placement and high-energy sine-wave stimuli in the development of acute adverse cerebral changes with ECT, are presented elsewhere in this volume.[22]

METHODS

Subjects were severely ill psychiatric inpatients referred for ECT independently of the research protocol. All met Research Diagnostic Criteria for major depressive disorder,[23] had no ECT within the past year, and had no present or prior evidence of significant CNS disease. A reference group, consisting of similarly diagnosed inpatients not referred for ECT, was also included in the study design. Experimental subjects were randomly assigned to either bilateral or unilateral nondominant electrode placement and to either sine-wave (S) or brief-pulse (P) stimuli. A widely separated centroparietal to frontotemporal configuration,[24] applied using careful attention to electrode/scalp coupling, was chosen for the unilateral placement, in order to maximize efficiency of seizure induction.[2] MECTA (Mecta Corp.) and Medcraft B-24 Mark III (Medcraft Corp.) ECT devices, representing the most widespread pulse and sine-wave equipment available in the United States during the study period, were used to deliver the electrical stimulus.

Specific initial stimulus parameters for each device were chosen to be relatively equivalent with respect to seizure threshold. Single-channel EEG monitoring allowed iterative adjustment of intensity settings to produce seizures lasting longer than 25 seconds. Digital monitoring of stimulus energy was carried out to facilitate calculation of a variety of electrical parameters. The number of ECT treatments was determined on clinical grounds by the subject's attending psychiatrist. Experimental subjects were tested before ECT, two to three days after the final ECT treatment, and six months following completion of the ECT course. Control subjects were tested at analogous time intervals. A variety of test measures, including those directed toward the assessment of therapeutic outcome, memory function, and EEG, were utilized. Analysis of variance and covariance, along with Pearson-product-moment correlations, formed the basis of statistical determinations.

RESULTS

A total of 53 experimental and 21 control subjects received both baseline and acute post-ECT course testing of clinical and memory parameters (TABLE 1). Thirty-nine of the experimental and 13 of the control subjects also completed the six-month follow-up testing. No differences on the basis of electrode placement or stimulus waveform were found for age ($m = 52.5$), years of education ($m = 11.0$), or socioeconomic status[25] ($m = 4.9$). UL subjects had somewhat lower IQs[26] than did BL subjects (86 vs. 96, $p < 0.01$). No BL vs. UL or S vs. P differences were found on the basis of history of previous ECT (30%), history of drug nonresponse during the present episode (50%), or evidence of psychosis during the present episode (50%).

TABLE 1. Number of Subjects Receiving Clinical and Memory Testing

	C	PUL	SUL	PBL	SBL
Acute effects	21	10	14	14	15
Long-term follow-up	13	8	10	9	12

As noted in a companion paper,[22] no intergroup differences were found on the basis of number of ECT treatments ($m = 9.5$), fraction of treatment sessions resulting in inadequate seizures (less than 25 seconds by single-channel EEG) ($m = 0.08$), or either mean or cumulative adequate seizure duration (57.2 seconds, 509 seconds). Seizure morphology, rated blind to type of ECT, revealed intergroup differences only with regard to postictal suppression.[22] This was particularly prominent for SBL ECT, supporting the hypothesis that this particular ECT combination is characterized by intense seizures.

Measures of stimulus intensity showed highly significant intergroup differences with respect to stimulus waveform ($p < 0.0001$), with sine-wave stimuli associated with 2.6 times the stimulus energy (Joules), 3.1 times the applied charge (coulombs), and 6.9 times the mean current (coulombs per second) as that associated with pulse stimuli. This difference in stimulus energy is similar to that reported elsewhere.[2] Subjects receiving UL ECT tended to receive lower intensity stimuli than those receiving BL treatments (e.g., for energy 36 vs. 44 Joules), though differences just missed statistical significance. In any regard, this ease in producing seizures with the UL technique helps to validate the relatively optimal mode of delivery of UL ECT used in the present investigation.

Therapeutic outcome measures included the Hamilton Depression Rating Scale (HDRS),[27] the Brief Psychiatric Rating Scale (BPRS),[28] the Zung Self-Rating Depression Scale (SDS),[29] and a retrospective four-point global rating based on the discharge summary for the index hospitalization. All ratings were done blind to experimental subgroup. All groups, including controls, were equivalent with regard to baseline HDRS ($m = 23.1$, based on 17-item scale) and degree of acute improvement in HDRS, BPRS, and Zung SDS over the course of treatment ($m = 11.7, 22.5, 15.2$, respectively). A variety of responder criteria, based on combination of HDRS change and cutoff limits, were investigated, without the appearance of significant intergroup differences. Similarly, the retrospective four-point global rating also revealed no variation among subgroups. These findings together suggest an apparent acute therapeutic equivalence on the basis of both electrode placement and stimulus waveform. Finally, no intergroup differences were found in terms of HDRS, BPRS, and Zung SDS change scores between baseline and six-month post-ECT testing, all of which continued to show evidence of improvement ($m = 13.9, 23.9, 11.4$). As described elsewhere,[22] therapeutic response was not related to mean or cumulative seizure duration.

Measures of memory function were subdivided into those assessing newly learned information (anterograde memory performance), information learned prior to the study (retrograde memory performance), and self-perceived, or subjective, memory function. Tasks were specifically chosen to be sensitive to ECT-induced effects, based upon previously reported findings. Specific anterograde memory measures included verbal paired associates,[30] paragraph retention,[31] and complex figure reproduction tasks, along with a newly designed instrument involving the learning and recognition of unfamiliar faces. All of these included 20-minute delayed recall testing. Retrograde memory function was evaluated using newly designed and periodically updated famous events and famous faces recall tasks, in addition to an autobiographical, or personal, memory questionnaire. Subjective memory function was tested using a modified version of Squire's Subjective Memory Questionnaire.[32]

The personal memory questionnaire was developed to cover a number of items relevant to the subject's life experiences, especially the last several years prior to baseline testing. A careful focus upon this difficult area of memory function was chosen because of earlier findings by others,[33] and is consistent with the nature of memory complaints by ECT patients themselves. This questionnaire included material on the following topics: place of residence, neighbors, family members, close friends, last birthday, last New Year's Eve, last overnight trip out of town, favorite television show, last movie seen at a theater, current hospitalization, and recent outstanding experiences. Only questions responded to at baseline were used at post-ECT test sessions.

Acute effects of ECT upon memory function were evaluated by determining the difference between baseline and two to three day post-ECT course scores, except for the personal memory task, where the percentage of items not recalled after ECT was calculated. TABLE 2 presents a listing of significant acute differences in memory function on the basis of electrode placement and stimulus waveform. In terms of acute effects of ECT upon anterograde measures, the verbal paired associate task proved quite sensitive in separating UL from BL subjects and P from S subjects. As in all cases to be discussed here, both BL and S treatments were associated with greater deficits. In addition, S and BL subjects also tended to perform much worse than control subjects. In what proved an extremely common phenomenon throughout these data, the SBL group was clearly the most impaired. The PUL group, on the other hand, in a manner consistent throughout virtually the entire data set, did not differ from the control group. The complex figure reproduction task was quite sensitive in separating S from P subjects ($p < 0.0008$), but was relatively insensitive in separating UL from BL subjects. This is not surprising, given the fact that nonverbally encodable figural information relies heavily upon the nondominant cerebral hemisphere. Control subjects, in this regard, performed much better than both SUL and SBL subjects. The use of baseline HDRS scores as a covariate with regard to acute memory change scores produced no alterations in the above findings. Because of intergroup baseline differences, the IQ score was also used as a covariate, resulting in additional findings favoring UL ECT over BL ECT for both paragraph recall and complex figure reproduction ($p(BL > UL) < 0.03, 0.009$).

In terms of acute effects on retrograde memory measures, the famous events recall task was sensitive in differentiating the acute effects of both UL from BL, and P from S ECT. The SBL group was again more impaired than all others ($p < 0.0001$). The famous faces recall task was somewhat less sensitive in discriminating acute effects of ECT on the basis of electrode placement and waveform. The personal memory recall questionnaire, however, proved to be a very sensitive memory measure (FIGURE 1). All groups except control and PUL showed significant levels of relative impairment in the percent of initial items not recalled at the two to three day post-ECT test session. Main

TABLE 2. Acute Memory Impairment (Two to Three Days Post-ECT vs. Baseline Scores)

	p-Values (2 × 2 + 1 ANOVAS)					
	BL > UL	BL > C	UL > C	S > P	S > C	P > C
Anterograde Deficits (Based on Delayed Recall)						
Verbal paired associates	0.002	0.0001	NS	0.002	0.0001	NS
Paragraph recall	NS	0.01	NS	0.002	0.0008	NS
Unfamiliar faces recognition	NS	NS	NS	NS	NS	NS
Complex figure reproduction	NS	0.0008	0.002	0.0008	0.0001	NS
Retrograde Deficits						
Famous events recall	0.0001	0.0001	NS	0.0001	0.0001	NS
Famous faces recall	0.006	0.0001	NS	0.02	0.0001	NS
Personal memory recall	0.0001	0.0001	NS	0.0001	0.0001	NS
Global self-rating of memory function	NS	NS	NS	NS	NS	NS

effects for UL vs BL and P vs. S differences were present and, in addition, SUL, PBL, and SBL were more impaired than controls ($p < 0.03$, $p < 0.004$, $p < 0.0001$, respectively). In order to evaluate the role of guessing at the time of pre-ECT testing, the percent of baseline items not recalled at the second test session but later recalled at the third test session was determined. This measure showed similar relationships to that described above, suggesting that the results regarding acute effects are in fact valid. Use of baseline HDRS and IQ scores as covariates affected only the famous faces recall findings, for which the differences between UL and BL ECT groups disappeared. This may indicate that our famous faces recall test was not as sensitive as its famous events counterpart.

Overall, the objective data with respect to acute memory changes strongly implicate both bilateral electrode placement and sine-wave stimuli as potent risk factors, as do the EEG results reported elsewhere in this volume.[22] In terms of subjective memory function, however, a rather uniform tendency for self-perceived memory function to improve acutely following ECT was noted. No differences in terms

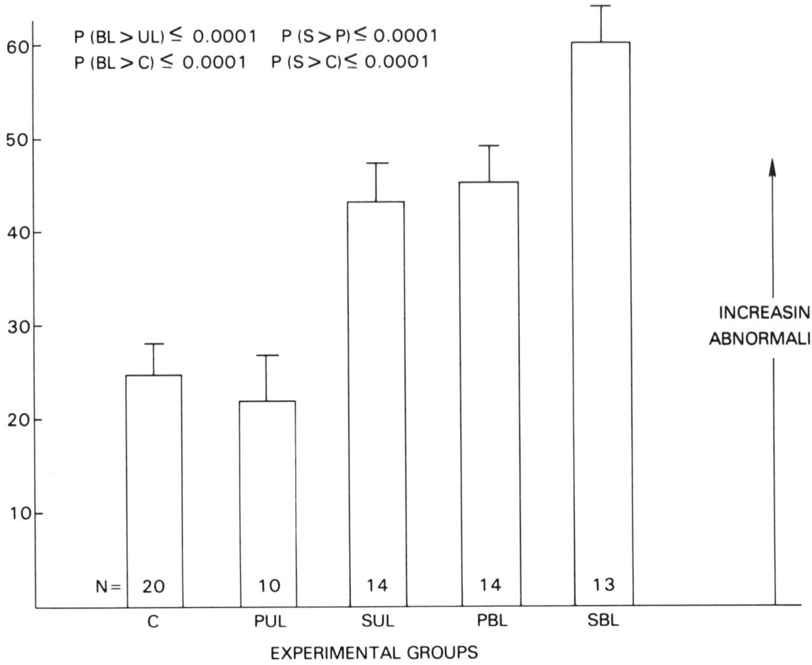

FIGURE 1. Acute personal memory impairment. Ordinate represents percent of baseline items not recalled two to three days post-ECT (+ standard error).

of post-ECT minus pre-ECT change scores, on either a total or an item-by-item basis, were observed as a function of ECT type or between controls and ECT subjects. Also interestingly, no appreciable relationship between subjective and objective memory measures was found, but, instead, acute measures of subjective memory function were significantly correlated with the respective differences in interviewer-rated and self-rated depression scales. While it is possible that the two to three day post-ECT rating time may not have allowed subjects sufficient opportunity to be aware of the extent of their deficits, this latter relationship suggests that self-rated memory changes with regard to a course of ECT may be more a function of the clinical response than of objectively demonstrable changes in memory function. Such a finding is compatible with available data reported by others,[34,35] but represents the first time this has been demonstrated in a systematic fashion.

Persistent ECT-associated effects upon memory function were investigated in a fashion identical to acute effects, except that baseline scores were compared to those obtained at six-month follow-up testing. In general, a return to at least pre-ECT level of function was found, with no evidence of intergroup differences for any of the measures of anterograde memory function. The famous events and famous faces recall tasks were likewise not productive of any long-term intergroup differences, although there was the suggestive finding that the three subjects with the largest long-term losses on the famous events task were all in the SBL group. The personal memory recall task, however, revealed a highly significant persistent intergroup difference favoring UL over BL ECT (FIGURE 2). The percentage of initial items not recalled at both the two to three day post-ECT and six-month post-ECT test sessions revealed a greater impairment for BL subjects than either UL subjects ($p < 0.005$) or control subjects ($p < 0.002$). These differences were significant even when partitioning on the basis of stimulus waveform, and were not affected by the use of baseline HDRS or IQ as covariates. There was also suggestive evidence for a long-term toxicity of S with respect to control subjects ($p < 0.01$) on autobiographic memory, though no P vs. S differences were observed in this regard, and the latter difference disappeared with use of baseline IQ as a covariate. Again, no intergroup differences in long-term subjective memory function, as determined by either total or item-by-item change scores, were found.

The above results represent provocative evidence for what amounts to objective personal memory losses lasting at least six months with BL but *not* with UL ECT, and represents the first time such a differential effect has been reported. While analysis of personal memory data with respect to recency effects has not been completed, a preliminary assessment indicates that items dealing with the year immediately preceding the ECT may have been most affected.[36] At the same time, however, it does appear that the described period of retrograde amnesia is greater than, say, a few weeks.

Unfortunately, the study of autobiographic memory function, as carried out in the present protocol, is confounded by the possibility that some personal memory information given at the time of baseline testing may have been incorrect. In an attempt to partially compensate for such a potential bias all subjects were asked, immediately

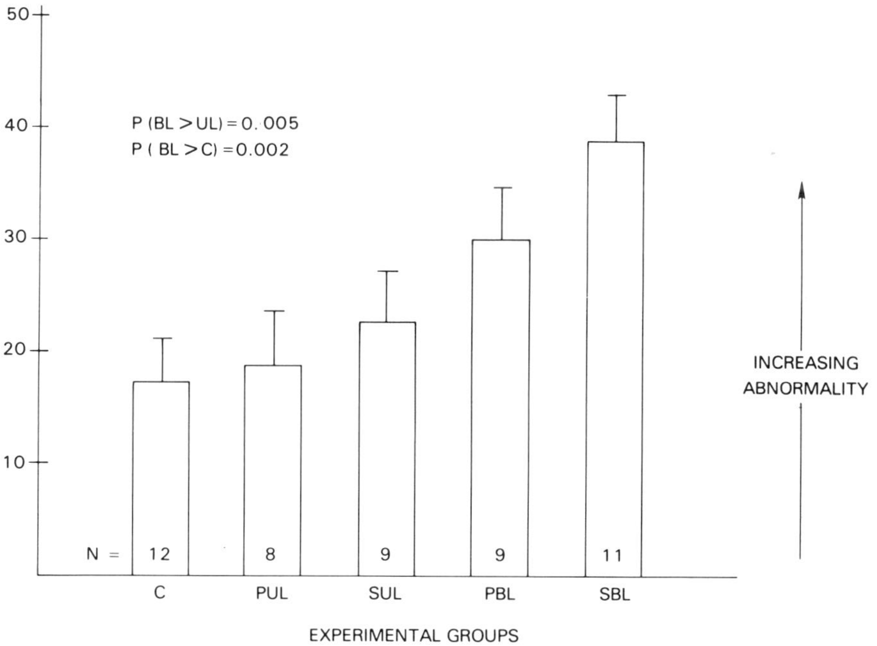

FIGURE 2. Long-term personal memory impairment. Ordinate represents percent of baseline items not recalled at both two to three day and six-month post-ECT test sessions (+ standard error).

following completion of the six-month follow-up personal memory questionnaire, to respond to a series of recognition trials. These consisted of questions based upon all items where both acute and follow-up responses differed from those given at baseline testing. In every case, subjects were given three choices: baseline response correct, six-month follow-up response correct, or unclear which of the two responses was correct. This procedure, in effect, approximated an attempt at "self-corroboration" of baseline items. Choices of the response that was given at baseline would suggest that responses given at the time of six-month follow-up testing may have been based upon incorrect recall, but that recognition of the correct response was still intact. Similarly, choices of the "unclear" alternative would suggest that both recall and recognition might be deficient.

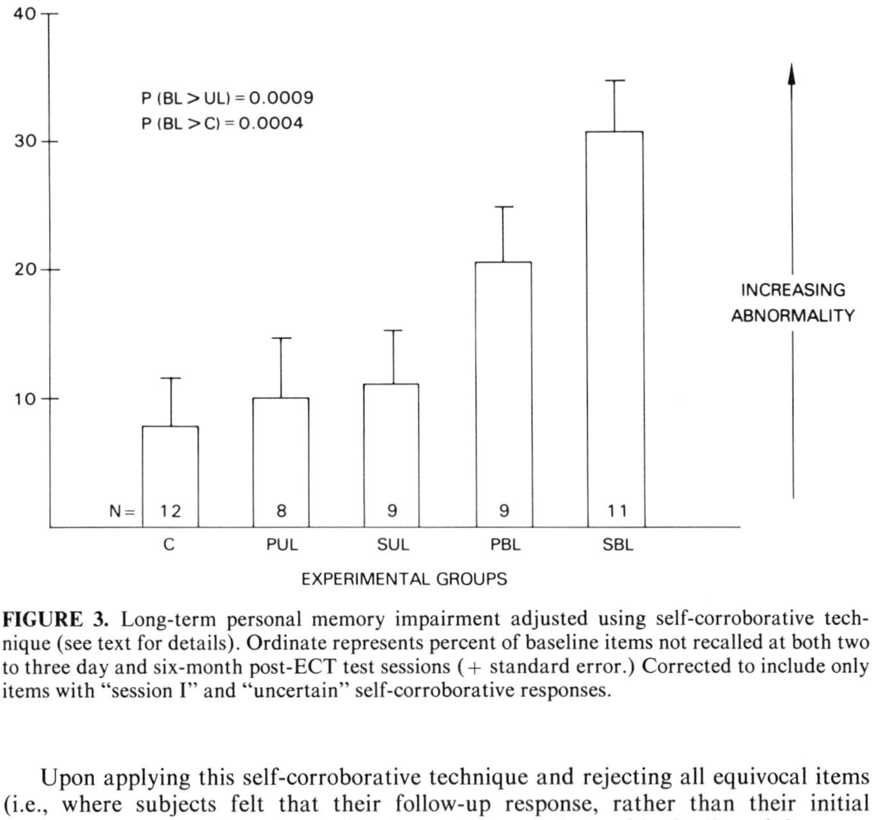

FIGURE 3. Long-term personal memory impairment adjusted using self-corroborative technique (see text for details). Ordinate represents percent of baseline items not recalled at both two to three day and six-month post-ECT test sessions (+ standard error.) Corrected to include only items with "session I" and "uncertain" self-corroborative responses.

Upon applying this self-corroborative technique and rejecting all equivocal items (i.e., where subjects felt that their follow-up response, rather than their initial response, was correct), the level of difference between BL and both UL and C groups was indeed found to increase (FIGURE 3). This strengthens the likelihood that the observed findings represent a true persistent deficit with BL ECT. Still, it must be pointed out that any such self-corroboration would be even more useful when supplemented by external corroboration using significant others or other relevant sources. For this reason, attempts to provide this modification were begun in the latter portion of the study. This allowed a comparison of long-term effects of ECT between C (four subjects) and SBL (three subjects) groups, using externally corroborated items.

It was, in fact, found that corroborated items, which constituted around three-fourths of the entire data set for those subjects, showed at least as much persistent forgetting (35% of baseline items for SBL vs. 13% for C subjects) as was observed based upon analysis without the use of external corroboration.

Given that both acute and persistent memory deficits were present, a further series of points can be made with respect to their possible correlates. First, even though HDRS scores were highly correlated with subjective memory ratings, no such relationship was established between HDRS scores and results on objective memory testing for either acute or long-term effects. This suggests that the findings are in fact organic rather than functional, and is supported by a number of highly significant correlations between acute objective memory test changes and acute EEG abnormalities. Second, the presence and amount of ongoing psychotropic medications presumably could affect memory performance. Analyses of medication effects are pending, though preliminary consideration of these factors indicates that BL subjects, for example, were no more likely to be medicated at the final test session than UL subjects. Next, the possibility that memory changes might be related to number of ECT treatments or EEG seizure parameters was considered. No significant correlations were observed, though the range of available values could have precluded relationships from appearing.

Finally, the effects of stimulus intensity per se (energy, current, and charge) upon objectively assessed memory function were evaluated. Here it was determined that stimulus intensity, especially energy, was correlated significantly with a variety of measures of memory function, particularly both acute and long-term personal memory performance ($p < 0.0002$, $p < 0.0009$, respectively). While at first this was felt to represent perhaps a reflection of S vs. P differences, these relationships were found to be present only with S ECT and *not* with P ECT, despite the existence of wide parameter ranges in each case. This suggests that, as long as stimuli are only slightly suprathreshold, the relatively low-energy stimuli present with the pulse waveform may lie below a cutoff for intensity-related effects upon memory performance with ECT and, furthermore, that only the higher energy sine-wave stimulus is able to exceed this cutoff in an appreciable number of cases.

DISCUSSION AND CONCLUSIONS

This study has provided a number of findings that are both new and potentially pertinent to clinical practice. Evidence presented suggests that unilateral nondominant electrode placement and brief-pulse stimuli may each provide significantly fewer acute CNS adverse effects while remaining equally effective. Given the present widespread clinical reluctance to use such ECT modifications, the finding of long-term personal memory impairment with bilateral electrode placement is particularly important.

The bases for why electrode placement and stimulus waveform should each exert independent and additive differential effects upon memory systems are poorly understood.[6] UL nondominant ECT appears to be associated with less intracerebral current flow, less generalization of the seizure discharge, and less postictal suppression in the dominant, contralateral hemisphere. It has even been proposed that seizures produced by UL and BL ECT differ in their onset, i.e., focal cortical initiation with the former and generalized diencephalic onset with the latter.[37] Certainly, such electrophysiologic differences could well account for the relative sparing of at least verbal memory function with UL nondominant ECT.

The basis of stimulus waveform effects on cognitive performance could be secondary to the direct electrical effects of a higher mean current or charge distribution within the cerebral structures subserving memory function with S ECT. Alternatively, the apparently more intensely generalized seizures produced by the higher energy stimuli, as discussed in a companion paper in this volume,[22] may be involved. The former possibility, when combined with the reported significant relationship between sine wave stimulus intensity and extent of both acute and long-term memory deficits, raises a concern about the use of grossly suprathreshold stimuli,[38] something that was not dealt with in the present study.

At present, we are involved in an attempt to replicate and extend the findings described above. It is felt that such work is crucial, not only to the understanding of how ECT produces both its beneficial and adverse effects, but also in the optimization of a beleaguered and maligned treatment modality which has time and time again proven too clinically valuable to consign to the halls of oblivion.

REFERENCES

1. D'Elia, G. & H. Raotma. 1975. Is unilateral ECT less effective than bilateral? Br. J. Psychiatry **126:** 83–89.
2. Weiner, R. D. 1980. ECT and seizure threshold. Biol. Psychiatry **15:** 225–241.
3. Welch, C. A. 1982. The relative efficacy of unilateral nondominant and bilateral stimulation. Psychopharmacol. Bull. **18:** 68–70
4. Squire, L. R. 1982. Neuropsychological effects of ECT. *In* Electroconvulsive Therapy: Biological Foundations and Clinical Applications. R. Abrams & W. B. Essman, Eds.: 169–186. SP Medical and Scientific Books. New York, N.Y.
5. Squire, L. R. & P. Chace. 1975. Memory functions six to nine months after ECT. Arch. Gen. Psychiatry **32:** 1557–1564.
6. Weiner, R. D. 1984. Does ECT cause brain damage? Behav. Brain Sci. **7:** 1–53.
7. Weaver, L. A., Jr. & R. W. Williams. 1982. The electroconvulsive therapy stimulus. *In* Electroconvulsive Therapy: Biological Foundations and Clinical Applications. R. Abrams & W. B. Essman, Eds.: 129–156. SP Medical and Scientific Books. New York, N.Y.
8. Liberson, W. T. & P. H. Wilcox. 1945. Electric convulsive therapy: comparison of "brief stimuli technique" with Friedman-Wilcox-Reiter technique. Digest Neurol. Psychiatry **13:** 292–302.
9. Kendall, B. S., W. B. Mills & T. Thale. 1956. Comparison of two methods of EST and their effects on cognitive functions. J. Consult. Psychol. **20:** 423–429.
10. Cronholm, B. & J. O. Ottosson. 1963. Ultrabrief stimulus techniques in ECT. I. Influence on retrograde amnesia. J. Nerv. Ment. Dis. **137:** 117–123.
11. Cronholm, B. & J. O. Ottosson. 1963. Ultrabrief stimulus techniques in ECT. II. Comparative studies of therapeutic effects and memory disturbances in treatment of endogenous depression with the Elther ES apparatus and Siemans Konvulsator III. J. Nerv. Ment. Dis. **137:** 268–276.
12. Valentine, M., K. M. G. Keddie & D. Dunne. 1968. A comparison of techniques in electroconvulsive therapy. Br. J. Psychiatry **114:** 989–996.
13. Goldstein, S. G., S. B. Filskov, L. A. Weaver & J. O. Ives. 1977. Neuropsychological effects of electroconvulsive therapy. J. Clin. Psychol. **33:** 798–806.
14. Warren, E. W. & D. H. Groome. 1984. Memory test performance under three different waveforms of ECT for depression. Br. J. Psychiatry **144:** 370–375.
15. Daniel, W. F., H. F. Crovitz, R. D. Weiner & H. J. Rogers. 1982. The effects of ECT modifications on autobiographical and verbal memory. Biol. Psychiatry **17:** 919–924.
16. Daniel, W. F., R. D. Weiner & H. F. Crovitz. 1983. Autobiographical amnesia with ECT: an analysis of the roles of stimulus waveform, electrode placement, stimulus energy, and seizure length. Biol. Psychiatry **18:** 121–126.
17. Daniel, W. F., H. F. Crovitz & R. D. Weiner. 1984. Perceptual learning with right unilateral versus bilateral electroconvulsive therapy. Br. J. Psychiatry **145:** 394–400.
18. Daniel, W. F., H. F. Crovitz, R. D. Weiner, H. S. Swartzwelder & E. M. Kahn.

1985. ECT-induced amnesia and postictal EEG suppression. Biol. Psychiatry **20:** 329–352.
19. DANIEL, W. F. & H. F. CROVITZ. 1986. Disorientation during Electroconvulsive Therapy. Ann. N.Y. Acad. Sci. (This volume.)
20. LAMBOURN, J. & D. GILL. 1978. A controlled comparison of simulated and real ECT. Br. J. Psychiatry **133:** 514–519.
21. PRICE, T. R. P. 1981. Unilateral electroconvulsive therapy for depression. N. Engl. J. Med. **304:** 53.
22. WEINER, R. D., H. J. ROGERS, J. R. T. DAVIDSON & E. M. KAHN. 1986. Effects of electroconvulsive therapy upon brain electrical activity. Ann. N.Y. Acad. Sci. (This volume.)
23. FEIGHNER, J. P., E. ROBINS, S. B. GUZE, R. A. WOODRUFF, A. WINOKUR & R. MUNOZ. 1972. Diagnostic criteria for use in psychiatric research. Arch. Gen. Psychiatry **26:** 57–63.
24. D'ELIA, G. 1970. Unilateral ECT. Acta Psychiatr. Scand. Suppl. **215:** 5–98
25. HOLLINGSHEAD, A. B. & F. C. REDLICH. 1958. Social Class and Mental Illness: A Community Study. John Wiley & Sons. New York, N.Y.
26. SHIPLEY, W. C. 1940. A self-administering scale for measuring intellectual impairment and deterioration. J. Psychol. **9:** 371–377.
27. HAMILTON, M. 1960. A rating scale for depression. J. Neurol. Neurosurg. Psychiatry **23:** 56–62.
28. OVERALL, J. E. & D. R. GORHAM. 1962. The Brief Psychiatric Rating Scale. Psychol. Rep. **10:** 799–812.
29. ZUNK, W. W. K. 1970. A self-rating depression scale. Arch. Gen. Psychiatry **12:** 63–70.
30. SQUIRE, L. R. & P. C. SLATER. 1978. Bilateral and unilateral ECT: effects on verbal and nonverbal memory. Am J Psychiatry **135:** 1316–1320.
31. WECHSLER, D. 1945. A standardized memory scale for clinical use. J. Psychol. **19:** 87–95.
32. SQUIRE, L. R., C. D. WETZEL & P. C. SLATER. 1979. Memory complaint after electroconvulsive therapy: assessment with a new self rating instrument. Biol. Psychiatry **14:** 791–801.
33. JANIS, I. 1950. Psychological effects of electroconvulsive treatments. I. Post-treatment amnesias. J. Nerv. Ment. Dis. **111:** 359–382.
34. CRONHOLM, B. & J. O. OTTOSSON. 1963. The experience of memory function after electroconvulsive therapy. Br. J. Psychiatry **109:** 251–258.
35. STERNBERG, D. E. & M. E. JARVIK. 1976. Memory functions in depression: improvement with antidepressant medication. Arch. Gen. Psychiatry **33:** 219–224.
36. SQUIRE, L. R., P. C. SLATER & P. L. MILLER. 1981. Retrograde amnesia following ECT: long-term follow-up. Arch. Gen. Psychiatry **38:** 89–95.
37. STATON, R. D., P. J. HASS & R. A. BRUMBACK. 1981. Electroencephalographic recording during bitemporal and unilateral nondominant hemisphere (Lancaster position) electroconvulsive therapy. J. Clin. Psychiatry. **42:** 264–269.
38. OTTOSSON, J. O. 1960. Experimental studies on the mode of action of electroconvulsive tharapy. Acta Psychiatr. Neurol. Scand. **36**(Suppl. 145): 1–141.

Cognitive Consequences of Low-Dosage Electroconvulsive Therapy[a]

HAROLD A. SACKEIM,[b,c,d] STEPHANIE PORTNOY,[b,c,d]
PRISCILLA NEELEY,[b] BARBARA L. STEIF,[b,d]
PAOLO DECINA,[b,c,d] AND SIDNEY MALITZ[b,c]

[b]*Department of Biological Psychiatry*
New York State Psychiatric Institute
722 West 168 Street
New York, New York 10032

[c]*Department of Psychiatry*
College of Physicians and Surgeons
Columbia University
722 West 168 Street
New York, New York 10032

[d]*Department of Psychology*
New York University
6 Washington Place
New York, New York 10003

Standard electroconvulsive therapy (ECT) procedures, as a consequence of general anesthesia, muscle relaxation, and the elicitation of generalized seizure, result inevitably in loss of consciousness and of spontaneous respiration. Following the ECT-induced seizure, as with spontaneous generalized seizures and most acute brain injuries and head traumas, there is a variable period of disorientation. The duration of the period of disorientation following ECT appears to be exquisitely sensitive to treatment parameters, including modality or electrode placement (unilateral/bilateral); dosage of electrical stimulation and/or stimulus waveform; cumulative treatment number; and temporal spacing of treatments.[1–3]

With the recovery of orientation during the acute postictal period, patients manifest a variety of neuropsychological deficits. Retrograde memory, usually operationalized as memory for information presented just prior to the treatment, and anterograde memory, usually operationalized as memory for information presented following seizure elicitation, are often grossly disturbed.[4] Postictal deficits have been reported for other aspects of memory functioning, particularly semantic memory.[5] More broadly, there has been relatively little investigation of possible acute postictal effects of ECT on aspects of perceptual-cognitive functioning other than memory. Nonetheless, there is evidence that ECT may temporarily disrupt basic attentional processes, as assessed by simple cancellation procedures,[6] and may alter perceptual thresholds and the localization of sound in space.[7]

It appears that the cognitive deficits induced by ECT are typically most intense during the acute postictal period. Repeated testing at time points further removed from the seizure has demonstrated rapid recovery functions.[8,9] However, with traditional

[a]This research was supported in part by National Institute of Mental Health Grant MH35636.

forms of ECT administration, given at standard intervals of twice or three times a week, recovery from memory deficits is often incomplete by the time of the next treatment. This results in characteristic cumulative deterioration in memory performance with repeated postictal testing over the course of treatment. In line with Daniel and Crovitz's recent review,[8] we identified 16 studies that examined the issue of cumulative effects of treatment number, of which 13 demonstrated cumulative deterioration. Particularly with bilateral electrode placement and verbal memory tasks, a pattern of progressive deficit in postictal testing is to be expected.

While the depth or intensity of postictal deficits may be related to stimulus dosage and/or waveform, number of previous treatments, and the spacing of treatments, the particular areas of deficit are a function in part of electrode placement. Both anterograde and retrograde memory for verbal material are more disrupted by bilateral than right unilateral ECT.[2,4,10,11] This underscores the fact that while generalized seizures are elicited with unilateral placements, marked asymmetries may be observed in acute postictal neuropsychological or neurophysiological measures. The pattern of effects for nonverbal information processing is less clear. Some investigators have claimed that bilateral ECT results across the board in more profound deficits than does right unilateral ECT for tasks principally mediated by either the left or right hemisphere.[4,11] However, postictal testing for nonverbal information processing has rarely been conducted using a retrograde memory testing format.[10] Further, the tasks that have been used to assess the integrity of right hemisphere processing capabilities have often been inappropriate. Frequently, tasks have involved memory for geometric designs or common objects, thereby using stimuli that are readily subject to verbal encoding.[11] Indeed, there is evidence that processing of such material is particularly impaired with posterior left hemisphere lesions.[12] Therefore, it is still an open question, in our view, whether or not the two ECT modalities are equivalent in disruption of right hemisphere processing capabilities.

As noted, there is rapid recovery of function from acute postictal deficits. Further, it appears that as time from last ECT increases, the specificity of effects related to stimulus parameters and electrode placement diminishes. If we consider a subacute period as extending from 12 hours to seven days following the last treatment, a variety of patterns may emerge. For instance, with respect to intelligence, typically no change or a small increase in IQ scores has been observed when posttreatment scores are compared to pretreatment scores.[13] Fromm-Auch has noted that frequently scores on tasks involving nonverbal information processing are improved at posttreatment relative to pretreatment.[14] This has been interpreted as indicating that relief from depression is associated with enhanced right hemisphere processing capabilities. More generally, a variety of studies have suggested that the capacity to acquire new information, that is, immediate memory, is either unchanged or enhanced following ECT. In contrast, the capacity to retain this information once acquired, that is, anterograde delayed memory, is diminished. Currently, the strong claim in the literature is that during the subacute period ECT does not result in deficits in learning but ECT promotes forgetting of what has been newly learned.[4,15]

For a variety of reasons this set of claims requires reconsideration. While it frequently has been shown that following ECT there is a deficit in the delayed reproduction of information relative to immediate reproduction, the interpretation of these findings is problematic. The likelihood of establishing differential deficit is in large part a function of task psychometric properties, which have often not been reported.[16] Tasks in which delayed testing scores have better discriminating power will artifactually result in relatively greater deficits in retention when compared to acquisition. Further, following the classic work of Cronholm and Ottosson,[15] the measure that typically has been used to assess "forgetting" is the difference in accuracy between immediate and delayed test scores. It should be noted, however, that in this classic study, posttreatment immediate test scores, that is, learning, were significantly improved relative to pre-ECT baseline, while there was hardly any movement in delayed scores. Therefore, the difference between immediate and delayed scores increased following ECT and this was interpreted as indicating an ECT-induced deficit in the retention of information. This may be disputed, however. It is an unfortunate aspect of life that the more one learns, the more material is available to be forgotten. If under some circumstances, patients following ECT manifest an increase in how much material they can reproduce immediately after exposure, the fact that the absolute amount of material they forget increases does not necessitate that the rate of forgetting has increased.

The aims of the present study were to examine broadly the effects of ECT on recovery and orientation processes, acute postictal memory functioning, and anterograde immediate and delayed memory in the subacute period. This study was conducted in the context of a double-blind, random assignment trial to bilateral or right unilateral ECT, using a titration procedure designed to minimize convulsive stimulus intensity to just above seizure threshold.[17] This provided an opportunity for initial evaluation of whether a low-dosage technique moderated acute and subacute cognitive side effects. It also permitted comparison of the side effect profiles of bilateral and right unilateral ECT when both were equated for the minimal stimulus intensity necessary to produce generalized seizure, given the waveform being used.

METHODS

Inclusion/exclusion criteria for the efficacy portion of the study are described elsewhere in this volume.[17] Briefly, 52 patients were accepted to the protocol who presented with primary, major depressive disorder (Research Diagnostic Criteria), had pretreatment scores on the 24-item Hamilton Rating Scale for Depression of 18 or greater, and for whom ECT was indicated. No patient had been treated with ECT in the past year, had a history of organic brain syndrome or substance abuse. An additional set of exclusion criteria applied to participation in the neuropsychological portions of the battery reported here. Patients were excluded who were nonfluent in English, who had serious hearing impairment, who did not meet criteria for full orientation prior to their first treatment, who were left-handed and failed at pretreatment testing to manifest a right sensory field advantage on either a dichotic listening fused word task or a split-field tachistoscopic viewing consonant-vowel-consonant (CVC) report task. Data from postictal assessments were excluded if any medication was administered following seizure elicitation. By these criteria, the sample for postictal orientation data comprised 49 patients (25 right unilateral ECT, 24 bilateral ECT).

Patients were randomly assigned to right unilateral and bilateral ECT conditions. The two treatment groups were equivalent in the distributions of age, sex, education, socioeconomic status (SES), full-scale IQ, and handedness, as well as on variables related to the quality of the current depressive episode and psychiatric history. The treatment administration procedures are described elsewhere in this volume.[17] Briefly, ECT stimulus dosage was titrated for each patient to just above seizure threshold, using a method of limits paradigm. At the first treatment session, the frequency of constant current, bidirectional, square wave, brief pulses was set at a level that was rarely convulsive. After a 40-second delay, restimulation was attempted at greater pulse frequency. Each session ended with a convulsive administration. Using this method, seizure threshold was quantified over the course of treatment. In this sample, on average patients received 1.54 [standard deviation (SD) = 0.28] stimulations per treatment session and 43.80% of sessions involved more than one stimulation. This procedure permitted evaluation of the acute neurophysiological and neuropsychological effects of the use of subconvulsive stimulations by contrasting within patients those sessions involving single convulsive administrations with those sessions in which convulsive administrations were preceded by one or more subconvulsive stimulations. The results of these comparisons will be reported in future publications.

With this treatment procedure, seizure length was equivalent in bilateral and right unilateral groups, in terms of average duration per session, the dynamic changes in seizure duration over the course of treatment, and total seizure time. The average seizure duration, as assessed by left frontal EEG, was 61.92 seconds (SD = 20.39) in the bilateral group and 59.55 seconds (SD = 20.91) in the right unilateral group. The two groups received an equivalent number of ECT, with the bilateral group averaging 9.29 treatments (SD = 2.61) and the unilateral group averaging 9.40 treatments (SD = 2.63).

Of relevance here, seizure threshold or the intensity of electrical stimulation required to produce generalized seizures differed as a function of sex and electrode placement.[17] In units of charge (mA-seconds), males required on average 59% greater intensity than did females ($p < 0.001$). The bilateral placement required 68% greater intensity than did the right unilateral placement ($p < 0.001$). The proportional increase in seizure threshold over the course of the treatment was also significantly greater in the bilateral ECT than right unilateral ECT group ($p < 0.001$).

NEUROPSYCHOLOGICAL EVALUATIONS: RECOVERY AND ORIENTATION PROCEDURES

Prior to each treatment session, it was determined whether patients met criteria for full orientation. No patient at any treatment session failed to meet these criteria. After establishing orientation, a set of stimuli were presented and patients were asked to commit them to memory for testing following treatment. These procedures will be detailed below. Following this, patients were administered treatment.

After the elicitation of the generalized seizure, the anesthesiologist reported the first onset of spontaneous respiration. This time point was assessed relative to the end of the seizure, as determined by EEG. The time point of eyes opening on request was then noted by a neuropsychologist. In the data presented here, eyes opening was timed relative to onset of spontaneous respiration. Following eyes opening, the neuropsychologist continuously requested report of the patient's name. Once patients correctly reported their names, requests were made for them to identify where they were, their age, their birth date, and the day of the week. These requests were made continuously until a correct response was given or for 45 minutes postseizure. Timing of orientation questions was relative to eyes opening. The criterion for full orientation was correct response to four of the five questions (name, place, age, birth date, day of the week). Two measures of time to recovery of full orientation were used. The first measure (A) was time taken to reach criterion if orientation was established within 45 minutes of the end of seizure. This measure provides an index of speed of orientation recovery, when recovery is relatively rapid. The second measure (B) arbitrarily gave a score of 60 minutes in those cases in which the orientation criterion was not met. Therefore, the second measure is somewhat more sensitive to the actual time it took patients to orient.

Results

TABLE 1 displays time of return of recovery and orientation subcomponents when each occurred within 45 minutes postseizure, as well as time to reach full orientation. For each measure, including time to spontaneous breathing, eyes opening, and all orientation subcomponents, recovery took significantly longer in the bilateral group. Despite weighting in these data for rapid recovery times, for some subcomponents of orientation there was a threefold difference between the groups. All but two patients, both in the bilateral ECT group, met the full orientation criterion in at least one treatment session prior to the 45-minute cutoff. On average, the right unilateral group

TABLE 1. Time (in Seconds) to Return of Recovery and Orientation Variables as a Function of Electrode Placement

Variable	Bilateral ($n = 24$)	Right Unilateral ($n = 25$)	t-Test	Significance
Spontaneous respiration[a]	77.40 (42.77)	50.72 (48.57)	2.00	0.05
Eyes open[b]	254.65 (138.50)	179.53 (101.05)	2.13	0.04
Name[c]	413.01 (231.09)	197.12 (153.43)	3.79	<0.001
Place[c]	1026.32 (313.30)	295.86 (219.29)	9.09	<0.001
Day[c]	1055.00 (458.85)	315.38 (210.55)	7.03	<0.001
Age[c]	1209.01 (741.40)	341.01 (267.36)	5.38	<0.001
Date of birth[c]	957.28 (470.74)	361.40 (200.21)	5.69	<0.001
Orientation measure A[c]	1173.82 (405.57)	335.23 (227.82)	8.60	<0.001
Orientation measure B[d]	1603.34 (714.21)	514.50 (618.91)	5.59	<0.001

[a]Spontaneous respiration = time from end of seizure assessed by EEG to first spontaneous respiration.
[b]Eyes open = time from first spontaneous respiration to eyes opening upon command.
[c]Orientation subcomponents timed from eyes opening until 45 minutes postseizure. Instances of longer times to recovery not included in data.
[d]Time to full orientation from end of EEG seizure, scoring 60 minutes (3600 seconds) for failures to orient by 45-minute cutoff.

met this condition in 95.8% (SD = 0.11) of treatment sessions, while the bilateral group met this condition in 74.3% (SD = 0.28) of their sessions ($p = 0.002$). Time to full orientation, compensating for lack of orientation at 45 minutes (measure B), averaged 8.58 minutes (SD = 10.32) in the right unilateral group and 26.72 minutes (SD = 11.90) in the bilateral group ($p < 0.001$).

To our knowledge there have not been previous attempts to examine predictors of the duration of disorientation other than with respect to electrode placement and waveform. TABLE 2 presents the product-moment correlations between sex, age, seizure duration, and seizure threshold (average intensity of electrical stimulation) and both measures of orientation time, separately for each modality. Of note, the pattern of

TABLE 2. Correlations between Seizure Duration, Sex, Age, and Intensity of Electrical Stimulation (Seizure Threshold) with Two Measures of Time to Recovery of Full Orientation, as a Function of Electrode Placement

	Orientation Measure A	Orientation Measure B
Right unilateral ECT (n = 25)		
Seizure duration (EEG)	0.42[a]	0.28
Sex (1 = male/2 = female)	−0.49[a]	−0.36
Age	−0.47[a]	−0.43[a]
Seizure threshold (mA-seconds)	−0.19	−0.19
Bilateral ECT (n = 24)		
Seizure duration (EEG)	0.19	0.22
Sex	−0.08	−0.21
Age	0.13	0.21
Seizure threshold (mA-seconds)	0.11	−0.10

[a] $p < 0.05$, two-tailed.

relations was stronger for the measure of rapid orientation rather than the measure compensating for disorientation at 45 minutes postseizure. In line with this, significant associations were obtained only in the right unilateral group. Seizure duration, sex, and age were related to the recovery times. With right unilateral ECT, females, older patients, and patients with short seizures oriented more rapidly than did males, younger patients, or patients with longer seizures. Multiple regression analyses indicated that 49% of the variance in the rapid full orientation measure could be accounted for in the right unilateral group, $F(4,20) = 4.88$, $p = 0.007$, while the predictive ability for the bilateral group was nonsignificant, $F(4,18) = 0.58$, $p > 0.5$, and accounted for only 11% of the variance. Of particular note, even though there was wide variability, seizure threshold, or the absolute dosage of electrical stimulation required to produce seizure, was unrelated to all measures of orientation recovery for both treatment groups.

The cumulative pattern of orientation recovery was examined across treatment sessions. Contrasting the first two treatments with the last two treatments, there was no change in the duration of disorientation in the bilateral group (TABLE 3). In the

TABLE 3. Time (in Minutes) to Recovery of Full Orientation (Measure B) as a Function of Time Point during ECT and Electrode Placement

	Bilateral ECT	Right Unilateral ECT
First two treatments		
Mean	27.10	11.72
Standard deviation (SD)	14.83	12.47
n	24	24
Last two treatments		
Mean	28.10	4.03
SD	14.27	3.30
n	24	24
Change (early–late)		
Mean	−1.01	5.87[a]
SD	15.33	8.45
n	24	24

[a] Paired $t(22) = 3.26$, $p < 0.005$, two-tailed.

right unilateral group, orientation times were significantly shorter late in the ECT course relative to the beginning. More discrete analyses over the first eight treatments confirmed that there was progressive improvement in the orientation times in the right unilateral group as treatment progressed. Whereas it took on average 11.72 minutes for right unilateral patients to orient at the beginning of the ECT course, this was reduced to 4.03 minutes at the end of the course.

Discussion

The recovery of orientation appeared to be notably rapid in both the right unilateral and bilateral groups. Given differences in orientation procedures among various research groups it is difficult to determine the extent to which patients in our sample displayed speedier recovery. Of clinical relevance, however, in no instance in this sample did ECT have to be delayed or interrupted due to development of an organic brain syndrome. We presume that the rapid recovery functions were due largely to the use of a low-dosage, titration procedure.

The pattern of cumulative effects supported this presumption. The typical pattern, particularly with bilateral ECT, is to observe prolongation of recovery as treatment progresses.[1,18,19] In our sample, bilateral ECT patients recovered orientation as quickly at the end of the course as they did at the beginning of the course. The right unilateral group showed substantial cumulative improvement. To our knowledge, the only other study to demonstrate a cumulative improvement in orientation time was conducted by Fraser and Glass.[20] Of note, they also found the improvement in a right unilateral and not a bilateral ECT group and they also used a relatively low-dosage method with an efficient stimulus waveform. We suspect that the cumulative improvement we obtained is related to the fact that seizure duration became progressively shorter as treatment progressed. Epileptologists have long suggested that more prolonged spontaneous generalized seizures are associated with more prolonged periods of disorientation. We confirmed this empirically to the extent that duration of seizure was associated with the period of disorientation in the right unilateral group.

We observed that if orientation occurs before 45 minutes postseizure and the right unilateral placement is used, the duration of disorientation is highly predictable. Bilateral ECT appears to extend the duration sufficiently so that the factors of age, sex, and seizure duration are no longer of consequence. Since time to orientation was longer with bilateral ECT and among the unilateral group longer in males, it might be suspected that electrical dosage is a contributing factor. Seizure threshold was significantly higher with bilateral ECT, and in males generally. However, patients with long seizures and younger patients had relatively lower seizure thresholds and yet more prolonged disorientation in the right unilateral condition. Further, dosage of electrical stimulation was in no instance associated with orientation recovery times, either in product-moment correlations or regression analyses. Therefore, when dosage

TABLE 4. Acute Postictal Neuropsychological Battery: Pretreatment Procedures

A. Orientation testing
B. Stimuli presentation for retrograde memory testing
   1. Words
   2. Geometric shapes
   3. Nonsense shapes
   4. Faces (neutral or affective)
C. Visual analogue mood ratings

TABLE 5. Acute Postictal Neuropsychological Battery

A. Orientation testing
B. Line bisection
C. Cancellation tasks
   1. Geometric shapes
   2. Consonant-vowel-consonant (CVC)
D. Retrograde memory tasks
   1. Word recall
   2. Word recognition
   3. Geometric shape recognition
   4. Nonsense shape recognition
   5. Face recognition (neutral or affective)
E. Anterograde memory tasks
   1. Face recognition (neutral or affective)
F. Semantic memory (dysnomia)
   1. Abstract questions
   2. Concrete questions
G. Line bisection
H. Cancellation tasks
   1. Geometric shapes
   2. CVC
I. Visual analogue mood ratings

is minimized to just above seizure threshold, absolute dosage does not appear to be related to orientation recovery. We suggest that the extent to which dosage exceeds seizure threshold will more critically determine the extent of disorientation than will absolute dosage per se.

POSTICTAL MEMORY PERFORMANCE

Methods

At each treatment session patients were administered a neuropsychological battery. The battery included a variety of tasks assessing attentional processes, retrograde memory, and anterograde memory for deliberate list learning and semantic memory (see TABLES 4 and 5).

Generally, within 15 minutes prior to the administration of ECT, patients were requested to remember a set of materials. They were presented with six words (three concrete, three abstract) that they read and four shapes they traced with the index finger of the left hand. In each set of four shapes, two were geometric designs, readily subject to verbal encoding, and two were nonsense shapes, more resistant to verbal encoding. A subsample of patients was also tested on retrograde and anterograde versions of a neutral face recognition task. In the retrograde version, patients were exposed to a set of eight target faces that they had to commit to memory. The face stimuli were devoid of emotional expression, had no facial hair, and were all taken from college yearbooks in the 1950s. The order of word, shape, and face stimuli presentation was randomized at each treatment session for each patient.

Neuropsychological testing was conducted with patients five minutes after patients met criteria for full orientation. It was decided to titrate time of postictal memory testing to orientation recovery to avoid testing patients while still disoriented. Frequently, in previous work a set time point has been used for both bilateral and right unilateral groups relative to the end of the seizure.[21] With the prolonged disorientation in bilateral ECT, inferior memory performance in this group may have been an artifact of testing patients who were disoriented. Since all but 2 patients met the orientation within 45 minutes at at least one treatment session, the data for retrograde word and shape performance pertain to 47 patients (25 right unilateral, 22 bilateral).

Postictal testing first involved administration of a set of procedures examining attentional processes and, in particular, hemiinattention (see TABLE 5). Retrograde memory testing was conducted next. Patients were asked to recall the six words. For those words not recalled, patients were given a recognition task involving a field array of four words, the target and three buffers. For retrograde testing of shape and face recognition, patients were asked to pick out target stimuli from field arrays also containing four stimuli. Following completion of retrograde tasks, anterograde memory was evaluated. For the anterograde neutral face recognition task, eight target faces were serially exposed to patients. After a 15-second delay, recognition procedures were administered as in retrograde testing. Twelve alternative forms were available for the retrograde word and shape tasks, and nine alternative forms were available for the neutral face tasks.

Results

TABLE 6 presents average performance across treatment sessions for retrograde word and shape memory. On the recall of words, the recall and recognition of words,

TABLE 6. Postictal Performance on Memory Tasks Averaged over the Course of ECT, as a Function of Electrode Placement

Task	Bilateral ECT	Unilateral Right ECT	t-Test	Significance
Retrograde word recall				
Mean[a]	4.72	18.33	3.69	<0.001
SD	6.68	16.67		
n	22	25		
Retrograde word recall and recognition				
Mean	58.80	74.33	3.32	0.002
SD	13.78	17.15		
n	22	25		
Retrograde geometric shape recognition				
Mean	41.30	59.25	2.52	0.02
SD	24.05	23.50		
n	22	25		
Retrograde nonsense shape recognition				
Mean	60.85	73.75	2.69	0.01
SD	18.50	13.65		
n	22	25		
Retrograde neutral face recognition				
Mean	44.40	51.70	1.34	NS[b]
SD	12.20	16.90		
n	16	15		
Anterograde neutral face recognition				
Mean	58.40	51.70	1.03	NS
SD	14.00	21.00		
n	16	17		

[a]All means indicate average percentage correct performance.
[b]NS means not significant.

TABLE 7. Change in Postictal Memory Performance from First Two Treatments to Last Two Treatments, as a Function of Electrode Placement

Task	Bilateral ECT	Right Unilateral ECT
Retrograde word recall		
Mean[a]	1.45	−2.08
SD	8.68	16.43
n	21	23
Retrograde word recall and recognition		
Mean	5.22	−1.68
SD	21.85	18.83
n	21	23
Retrograde geometric shape recognition		
Mean	0.60	2.30
SD	42.40	37.45
n	21	23
Retrograde nonsense shape recognition		
Mean	17.65	0.60
SD	36.50	36.65
n	21	23
Retrograde neutral face recognition		
Mean	0.70	6.65
SD	7.85	8.05
n	9	8
Anterograde neutral face recognition		
Mean	−2.00	−2.50
SD	8.55	11.40
n	11	13

[a]All means indicate change in percentage correct performance, with positive and negative scores reflecting improved and decreased performance at final two relative to first two treatment sessions, respectively.

and the recognition of geometric shapes, performance of the right unilateral group, as expected, was significantly superior to the bilateral group (all p's ≤ 0.02). Likewise, there was a significant advantage for the right unilateral group on nonsense shape recognition ($p = 0.01$). This latter result contradicts earlier findings we obtained in a smaller sample of equivalence between bilateral and right unilateral groups on the nonsense shape task, which is a purer measure of nonverbal information processing.[2] By these data alone it would appear, as had been claimed by Squire[4,11] and others,[22] that bilateral ECT produced greater retrograde memory disturbance for information processing principally mediated by either the left or right hemisphere.

However, as also indicated in TABLE 6, this was not borne out in either retrograde or anterograde neutral face recognition. On these measures, albeit based on a somewhat smaller sample, the two treatment groups had equivalent performance. Further, there is substantial evidence that neutral face recognition is typically a form of cognitive processing particularly sensitive to right hemisphere impairment.[23,24]

The cumulative pattern of effects over the course of treatment was examined for retrograde word and shape tasks and the facial recognition tasks (see TABLE 7). It was noteworthy that for both the right unilateral and the bilateral groups, memory performance at the end of the ECT course (last two treatments) was equivalent to that at the beginning of the course (first two treatments). The only indication of a cumulative effect of ECT was in the bilateral group on nonsense shape recognition. This change over time was in the direction of cumulative improvement. When these same data were analyzed in relation to clinical response, it was found that nonresponders showed no change in performance over the course of treatment, whereas patients with strong therapeutic outcome demonstrated cumulative improvement in nonsense shape recognition. Similar patterns were obtained with the neutral face tasks.

Discussion

In our view, the most compelling findings in these data are the absence of cumulative deterioration in postictal measures over the course of treatment. As noted earlier, with traditional forms of ECT administration, 13 of 16 studies demonstrated deterioration effects.[8] We failed to observe this effect despite testing patients at virtually all treatments and later than typical in the treatment course, using a wider variety of tasks than used previously, and using tasks designed to be specifically sensitive to the range of performance observed during the postictal period. The bulk of patients were administered these tasks during the week prior to the start of ECT, and postictal deficits were significantly evidenced on all tasks. The point here is that the magnitude of deficits did not increase over the course of ECT. This may be attributable to the use of a low-dosage titration procedure.

It should be noted that the only significant cumulative change in these data was improvement for nonsense shape recognition. This improvement pertained for the most part to patients who showed strong clinical response to ECT. This provides some additional support for the suggestion of Fromm-Auch that clinical recovery with ECT is associated with enhanced right hemisphere cognitive processing.[14]

These data were not determinative as to whether or not bilateral ECT produces more intense disruption for cognitive tasks principally mediated by the right hemisphere. Support for this position was obtained with retrograde nonsense shape recognition. Even here the cumulative pattern across treatment suggested that a difference between modalities may obtain early but not late in the treatment course. With respect to retrograde and anterograde neutral face recognition we observed equivalence between the modalities. Therefore, we raise the possibility that statements may be inappropriate concerning differences between the modalities in global effects on right hemisphere cognitive functions. Certainly, the current density patterns of the two modalities[25] and their acute effects on cerebral circulation[26] indicate that bilateral and right unilateral ECT differ not only in dimensions of lateralization of predominant effects but also in regionalization of effects within hemispheres. Therefore, it may be more appropriate to inquire as to the specific types of right hemisphere cognitive functions that are differentially affected by bilateral and right unilateral ECT.

ANTEROGRADE IMMEDIATE AND DELAYED MEMORY

Methods

Patients were administered a memory battery during the two weeks prior to the start of ECT, on the day following the seventh ECT, during the week following termination of ECT, and, in the case of ECT responders, at two-month follow-up. The data presented here concern only the first three testing intervals and only the tasks assessing immediate and delayed recognition memory. A group of 17 patients (10 bilateral, 7 unilateral) were administered these tasks and contrasted with a group of 20 normal controls, matched for age, sex, education, SES, and premorbid estimate of IQ. Normal controls were screened for psychiatric history, were free of all medication, and were tested at intervals corresponding to pretreatment, posttreatment and two-month follow-up in patients.

Two types of recognition memory tasks were used: a paired-word task and a paired-face task. In the paired-word task, subjects were presented serially with a list of 30 word pairs. Twenty-two of these pairs had low association value (e.g., oatmeal and emotion). The data presented here are for the low association or difficult items. Directly following exposure to the list, subjects were tested for immediate recognition performance. They were shown a set of 30 field arrays. Each field contained a target word, which was an element in a previously presented word pair, and four alternatives. One of the alternatives was the other element in the word pair. The paired-face task was similarly structured. Subjects were exposed to a list of 10 pairs of unfamiliar, neutral faces and then tested on immediate recognition performance. A second list of 10 face pairs was then presented followed again by immediate recognition testing. For the face task, the field arrays contained the target face and three alternatives, one of which was the remaining element of the face pair. Immediate and delayed memory for the face task concerned a list of 20 items and a list of 22 items for the word task.

TABLE 8. Immediate and Delayed Anterograde Recognition Performance in Depressed Patients and Normal Controls at First Testing

	Depressed Patients ($n = 17$)	Normal Controls ($n = 20$)	Significance
Combined word and face recognition			
Immediate	0.491 (0.192)	0.763 (0.128)	<0.001
Delayed	0.433 (0.184)	0.777 (0.153)	<0.001
Forgetting rate	0.104 (0.211)	0.143 (0.172)	NS
Paired words			
Immediate	0.435 (0.290)	0.770 (0.219)	<0.001
Delayed	0.368 (0.311)	0.715 (0.214)	<0.001
Forgetting rate	0.262 (0.376)	0.002 (0.390)	NS
Paired faces			
Immediate	0.548 (0.151)	0.749 (0.109)	<0.001
Delayed	0.497 (0.093)	0.585 (0.168)	NS
Forgetting rate	0.043 (0.238)	0.223 (0.189)	0.018

Four hours following initial exposure to each list, recognition memory was tested again. This provided delayed memory scores for both tasks. Subjects were presented with the field arrays in a new random order and simply asked to identify the correct alternative. Four equivalent alternative versions of each task were available and randomly assigned to testing occasion with the constraint of no repetition.

Results

As presented in TABLE 8, at the testing interval corresponding to pretreatment in patients, patients and controls differed markedly in their ability to acquire information, that is, in immediate recognition memory, but not rate of forgetting information over a four-hour delay. This acquisition deficit was observed for both the face and word tasks, although more marked in the latter. Analyses of psychometric properties indicated equivalent internal reliability and appropriate levels of difficulty for the immediate and delayed scores of the word task. Therefore, the claim that depression is associated with a difficulty in the acquisition of information[4,15] was supported and could not be viewed as an artifact of task psychometric properties. Further, the data illustrate some of the problems described earlier in using the absolute difference between immediate and delayed scores as a measure of forgetting. Normal controls clearly had a larger difference than patients did in the face task between immediate and delayed scores. However, controls also acquired more information to begin with.

TABLE 9. Immediate and Delayed Anterograde Recognition Performance in Depressed Patients at Pretreatment, Post–Seventh ECT, and Posttreatment Testing Sessions

	Pretreatment ($n = 17$)	Post–Seventh ECT ($n = 17$)	Posttreatment ($n = 17$)
Combined word and face recognition			
Immediate	0.491 (0.192)	0.439 (0.156)	0.485 (0.165)
Delayed	0.433 (0.184)	0.318 (0.130)	0.343 (0.124)
Forgetting rate	0.104 (0.211)	0.252 (0.308)	0.238 (0.316)
Paired words			
Immediate	0.435 (0.290)	0.343 (0.249)	0.401 (0.229)
Delayed	0.368 (0.311)	0.222 (0.238)	0.243 (0.160)
Forgetting rate	0.262 (0.376)	0.451 (0.326)	0.401 (0.315)
Paired faces			
Immediate	0.548 (0.151)	0.536 (0.187)	0.568 (0.174)
Delayed	0.497 (0.093)	0.414 (0.138)	0.444 (0.163)
Forgetting rate	0.043 (0.238)	0.146 (0.422)	0.160 (0.412)

We would not want to claim that normal controls evidenced a retention deficit relative to depressed patients.

TABLE 9 displays the data for patients at the three testing intervals, combining scores on the face and word tasks. Both tasks yielded the same pattern of effects. One day following the seventh ECT there is a clear-cut reduction in capacity to acquire information, i.e., immediate memory scores were reduced relative to pretreatment. Patients were retested on average four days following the last ECT. Despite additional treatment, the acquisition of information returned to pretreatment baseline. A markedly different pattern was observed for delayed memory scores. These scores were reduced both following the seventh treatment and following the course of treatment. These findings support the classic claim that effects of ECT on the acquisition and retention of information are dissociable.[4,15] Patients displayed a floor effect on posttreatment delayed memory testing, that is, their performance was at chance level. However, patients showed at posttreatment no change in their capacity to acquire information.

GENERAL DISCUSSION

The findings from these three sets of data help to clarify some of the cognitive consequences of titrated, low-dosage ECT. In a variety of acute postictal measures of orientation and memory functioning, we failed to observe cumulative deterioration with advancing treatment number. Indeed, in some cases cumulative improvement was observed. This was the case even though the acute postictal period is typically the most sensitive time for uncovering cumulative patterns. Progressive worsening in memory performance is a robust, highly replicable effect.[8] These findings and the fact that orientation recovery appeared to be unusually speedy suggest that low-dosage titration may indeed lessen some of the adverse effects of ECT. The findings also suggest with respect to orientation recovery that the degree to which electrical dosage exceeds threshold may be more critical than absolute dosage per se in contributing to cognitive side effects.

The modality differences observed in orientation and verbal memory measures were of surprising magnitude. This may be due in part to the psychometric properties of the tasks as well as the procedures for equating the modalities with respect to minimal dosage necessary to elicit seizures. Under standard administration techniques in which all patients receive the same absolute dosage, dosage in excess of threshold is likely to be greater with unilateral than with bilateral ECT.[17] This may artifactually enhance the intensity of side effects associated with right unilateral ECT and diminish modality differences. With respect to modality effects on acute postictal memory for nonverbal material, we must equivocate. A greater deficit was observed in nonsense shape recognition with bilateral ECT and equivalence was observed on two facial recognition tasks. We raise the possibility that modality effects on right hemisphere cognitive processing are specific to particular classes of cognitive function, perhaps reflecting differences in regional neurophysiological effects within the right hemisphere.

Finally, the findings supported the traditional claim that depression is associated with deficits in the acquisition of new information, whereas ECT produces transient disruption of the retention of new information.[4,15] A caveat should be noted that an increased acquisition deficit was observed in testing one day after the seventh ECT. This supports the notion that recovery functions are typically rapid with low-dosage ECT and that time since last treatment may strongly contribute to patterns of deficit. Whether or not a low-dosage technique lessens the intensity of the subacute effects of ECT will be examined in our ongoing research.

REFERENCES

1. DANIEL, W. F. & H. F. CROVITZ. 1982. Recovery of orientation after electroconvulsive therapy. Acta Psychiatr. Scand. **66:** 421–428.
2. MALITZ, S., H. A. SACKEIM, P. DECINA, M. KANZLER, S. PORTNOY, I. PROHOVNIK, N. HOPKINS, B. KERR, C. LEE, S. MUKHERJEE, P. NEELEY & S. C. YUDOFSKY. 1984. Low dosage ECT: electrode placement and acute physiological and cognitive effects. Am. J. Soc. Psychiatry **4:** 47–53.

3. VALENTINE, M., K. M. G. KEDDIE & D. DUNNE. 1968. A comparison of techniques in electroconvulsive therapy. Br. J. Psychiatry **114:** 989–996.
4. SQUIRE, L. 1982. Neuropsychological effects of ECT. *In* Electroconvulsive Therapy: Biological Foundations and Clinical Applications. R. Abrams & W. B. Essman, Eds.: 169–186. S.P. Medical. New York, N.Y.
5. PRATT, R. T. C. & E. K. WARRINGTON. 1972. The assessment of cerebral dominance with unilateral ECT. Br. J. Psychiatry **121:** 327–328.
6. SACKEIM, H. A., S. PORTNOY, P. DECINA, S. MALITZ, V. WARMFLASH, W. VINGIANO & S. YUDOFSKY. 1983. Left-side visual neglect in ECT patients. Psychopharmacol. Bull. **1:** 83–85.
7. ALTMAN, J. A., L. J. BALONOV & V. L. DEGLIN. 1979. Effects of unilateral disorder of the brain hemisphere function in man on directional hearing. Neuropsychologia **17:** 295–301.
8. DANIEL, W. F. & H. F. CROVITZ. 1983. Acute memory impairment following electroconvulsive therapy: a review of the literature. I. The effects of electrical stimulus waveform and number of treatments. Acta Psychiatr. Scand. **67:** 1–7.
9. SQUIRE, L. R. & P. L. MILLER. 1974. Diminution of anterograde amnesia following electroconvulsive therapy. Br. J. Psychiatry **125:** 490–495.
10. DANIEL, W. F. & H. F. CROVITZ. 1983. Acute memory impairment following ECT: a review of the literature. II. The effects of electrode placement. Acta Psychiatr. Scand. **67:** 57–68.
11. SQUIRE, L. R. & P. C. SLATER. 1978. Bilateral and unilateral ECT: effects on verbal and nonverbal memory. Am. J. Psychiatry **135:** 1316–1320.
12. KIMURA, D. 1963. Right temporal lobe damage. Arch. Neurol. **8:** 264–271.
13. MALLOY, F. W., I. F. SMALL, M. J. MILLER, V. MILSTEIN & J. R. STOUT. 1982. Changes in neuropsychological test performance after electroconvulsive therapy. Biol. Psychiatry **17:** 61–67.
14. FROMM-AUCH, D. 1982. Comparison of unilateral and bilateral ECT: evidence for selective memory impairment. Br. J. Psychiatry **141:** 608–613.
15. CRONHOLM, B. & J.-O. OTTOSSON. 1961. Memory functions in endogenous depression before and after electroconvulsive therapy. Arch. Gen. Psychiatry **5:** 193–199.
16. CHAPMAN, L. J. & J. P. CHAPMAN. 1973. Disordered Thought in Schizophrenia. Prentice Hall. Englewood Cliffs, N.J.
17. MALITZ, S., H. A. SACKEIM, P. DECINA, M. KANZLER & B. KERR. 1986. The efficacy of electroconvulsive therapy: dose-response interactions with modality. Ann. N.Y. Acad. Sci. (This volume.)
18. FRASER, R. M. & I. B. GLASS. 1978. Recovery from ECT in elderly patients. Br. J. Psychiatry **133:** 524–528.
19. WILSON, I. C. & G. GOTTLIEB. 1967. Unilateral convulsive shock therapy. Dis. Nerv. Syst. **28:** 541–545.
20. FRASER, R. M. & I. B. GLASS. 1980. Unilateral and bilateral ECT in elderly patients. Acta Psychiatr. Scand. **62:** 13–31.
21. WARRINGTON, E. K. & R. T. C. PRATT. 1973. Language laterality in left-handers assessed by unilateral ECT. Neuropsychologia **11:** 423–428.
22. APA. 1978. Electroconvulsive Therapy: Task Force Report 14. American Psychiatric Association. Washington, D.C.
23. BENTON, A. L. 1980. The neuropsychology of facial recognition. Am. Psychol. **35:** 176–186.
24. MILNER, B. 1968. Visual recognition and recall after right temporal-lobe excision in man. Neuropsychologia **6:** 191–209.
25. WEAVER, L., R. WILLIAMS & S. RUSH. 1976. Current density in bilateral and unilateral ECT. Biol. Psychiatry **11:** 303–312.
26. PROHOVNIK, I., H. A. SACKEIM, P. DECINA & S. MALITZ. 1986. Acute reductions of regional cerebral blood flow following electroconvulsive therapy: interactions with modality and time. Ann. N.Y. Acad. Sci. (This volume.)

Patients' Experiences of and Attitudes to Electroconvulsive Therapy

C. P. L. FREEMAN AND R. E. KENDELL

Department of Psychiatry
University of Edinburgh
Morningside Park
Edinburgh EH10 5HF, Scotland

INTRODUCTION

We would like to present the results of a study that was carried out in Edinburgh, in the late 1970s. At the time it represented the first systematic attempt to assess patients' experiences and views of electroconvulsive therapy (ECT). Gomez (1975) had looked at side effects but confined her questioning to a period 24 hours after the treatment.[3] A large number of other studies had asked systematically about side effects but not about attitudes. Hillard and Folger (1977) compared two wards, one that was a high user and one a low user of ECT.[4] They confined their questioning of patients to side effects and to the use of semantic differentials such as how good, how fast acting, how strong the treatment was.

However, our study had been carried out at a time when there was considerable media interest in ECT. Most of this had been critical, uninformed, and anecdotal. The authors were stimulated to carry out the study following a British Broadcasting Company television program, in which we had both taken part and which had been edited in such a way as to be highly critical of ECT. In particular, it stressed that all of the patients whom the BBC team had interviewed had dreaded ECT and feared it more than anything else they had ever experienced. Bird (1979) attempted to assess the effect this program had on patients' attitudes,[1] in a small study carried out in Bristol, United Kingdom.

METHODS

Sample

We attempted to interview all the patients under the age of 70 who had had ECT during one year (1976) in the Royal Edinburgh Hospital. We tried to interview people approximately one year after their last ECT, but some had had a second course of treatment during the year and were interviewed within 6 months while others, being difficult to contact, were not interviewed until 18 months after their last course. The interviewing took place between February 1977 and October 1978.

Because the study was conducted alongside another investigation concerned with epilepsy following ECT, a number of patients were interviewed who had had ECT in 1971, i.e., six years earlier. No attempt was made to contact everyone who had had ECT in 1971, but it was felt useful to include this group to see if attitudes changed with the passage of time.

Each patient of the sample was sent a letter explaining the nature of the study and asking them to come for an outpatient interview. Those who did not respond were sent a second appointment enclosing a small questionnaire and a stamped, addressed envelope. The few who still did not come were visited at home, where possible with prior telephone contact.

Interview Schedule

Patients were given a semistructured interview based on a questionnaire. They were allowed to talk spontaneously about their views and experiences of ECT for about five minutes and were then asked for specific details about the number and timing of their treatments, why they were given ECT, their psychiatric symptoms at the time, why the treatment was stopped, their experience of the treatment sessions themselves, the side effects that they experienced, whether the treatment helped them, whether they would have it again, and whether they gave consent to the treatment. Finally, they were asked to respond to a number of statements by either agreeing, disagreeing, or saying "don't know." Further details of specific questions are given in the Results section.

Details about number and timing of treatments, psychiatric diagnosis, and type of ECT were also obtained from case notes and ECT records.

At that time the Royal Edinburgh Hospital admitted approximately 2500 patients per annum. In 1976, 714 had a diagnosis of some type of depression or of puerperal psychosis. Almost all fell into 3 ICD-8 categories (296.2 manic-depression depressed type, 300.4 depressive neurosis, or 296.1 manic-depression manic type). One hundred and eighty-three patients had a course of ECT. These figures would indicate that approximately 1 in 15 inpatients received a course of ECT. ECT is little used as a treatment for other psychiatric conditions. At the time of the study bilateral ECT was routinely given unless the consultant specifically requested unilateral treatment. Very little outpatient ECT was given, though in a few cases ECT that had been started on an inpatient basis was continued on an outpatient basis.

ECT was given in two places in the hospital. In the main hospital a separate ECT suite was used and the patients were fasted overnight in their wards, given atropine premedication at 40 minutes, and then brought down to the ECT suite by a ward nurse at approximately 15 to 30 minutes before each treatment. There were separate waiting, treatment, and recovery rooms. In the other area (Craig House) ECT was given in the patient's ward. This usually involved clearing a side room or four-bedded ward. The ECT was given by the ward doctor and a visiting anesthetist. In both areas ECT was routinely given twice weekly but could be given three times weekly if this was specifically requested.

RESULTS

One hundred and eighty-three patients received one or more courses of ECT during 1976 and constituted the main sample. At enquiry in 1977–78, 12 were dead, 25 were over 70, and 27 had left the Edinburgh area. This left 119 people available for interview, of whom we interviewed 106 (89%). Sixty patients who had had ECT in 1971 formed a subsidiary sample. The two samples were analyzed separately but are reported here together, as no differences were found between the two. The combined sample was thus 166.

Of the 13 patients who were not interviewed, 3 were still in treatment at the hospital but refused to be interviewed for research purposes. All 3 were said by the

TABLE 1. Background Details of the Two Samples[a]

	1976	1971
Mean age	50	54
Sex ratio: M:F	1.46:1	1.4:1
Marital status		
Single	24%	21%
Married	57%	67%
Widowed	15%	8%
Divorced	4%	3%
Social class		
1	4%	16%
2	21%	23%
3	35%	23%
4	24%	25%
5	16%	13%
Bilateral ECT	81%	96.7%
Unilateral ECT	19%	3.3%
Experience of ECT during lifetime		
6 or less treatments	31%	25%
7–24 treatments	52%	49%
25–50 treatments	12%	21%
51 or more treatments	5%	5%
Range of experience	1–75	1–93
Mean total of treatments ever received	16	18

[a] $n = 183$ for 1976, but only 106 interviewed; $n = 60$ for 1971.

doctors treating them to be somewhat hostile to doctors in general, but they had not made any specific comments about ECT. The remaining 10 patients could not be traced.

The Treatments

Many subjects had little idea how many treatments or how many courses of ECT they had had, and the information they gave was quite unreliable when checked against case-note records. The details of background variables and actual experience of ECT are summarized in TABLE 1. It can be seen that there was a wide range of experience. A few people had had only a single ECT treatment and one lady had had as many as 93 treatments in her lifetime, spread over 14 courses. The average number of treatments of those interviewed were 16 for the 1976 group and 18 for the 1971 group.

TABLE 2. Percentage Distribution of Diagnosis for First Course of ECT[a]

	1976	1971
Unipolar depression	67.6	62.3
Bipolar illness depressed	14.5	16.4
Bipolar illness manic or hypomanic	3.9	1.6
Schizophrenic	5.0	16.4
Puerperal psychosis	3.4	0
Miscellaneous or unspecified psychosis	1.1	1.6
Other diagnoses	3.9	1.6

[a] $n = 243$ for 1976; $n = 60$ for 1971.

TABLE 3. Reason in Case Notes for ECT Ending[a]

Sufficient or satisfactory improvement	73.7%
Not sufficient improvement to justify continued treatment	13.6%
Hypomanic reaction	3.7%
Side effects	2.9%
Patient refused further treatment and/or took own discharge	1.6%
Death	0.5%
Major complication	0.0%
Other reason or not specified	3.3%

[a]$n = 183 + 60$.

The distribution about the mean was skewed. Over half those interviewed had had only a single course of ECT, usually of five to eight treatments. Details of the diagnoses obtained from the case notes are given in TABLE 2. The main difference between the two years is that fewer schizophrenic patients were given ECT in 1976.

The reasons given in the case notes for treatment being stopped are given in TABLE 3. In 74% this was because improvement was felt to be satisfactory or sufficient.

Causes of Death

Twelve patients had died before they could be interviewed. Four had committed suicide. In two there was a good response to ECT and the suicide occurred during a subsequent illness, and in two there was only a partial response, the depression continued, and suicide occurred 9 months and 11 months later.

In six cases death appeared to have been from causes entirely unrelated to ECT. They all occurred six months or more after treatment. In the remaining two cases death may have been related to ECT. A 69-year-old woman died 24 hours after her 13th treatment. Postmortem showed a myocardial infarction. She had had one previous infarct. A 76-year-old woman also died 48 hours after her 13th ECT. Postmortem showed a myocardial infarction 24–48 hours old. Both patients were taking a tricyclic drug at the time.

Patients' Experiences of the Treatment

Details of this are given in TABLE 4. Only 21% of patients felt they had been given an adequate explanation of the treatment before it began. Forty-nine percent were sure

TABLE 4a. Adequacy of Explanation Given before Treatment[a]

	Percent
Adequate	20.6
No explanation	49.1
Inadequate	8.5
Misleading	0
Can't remember if any explanation given	12.1
Other	3
Don't know	6.6

[a]$n = 166$.

TABLE 4b. Do You Remember How You Felt before Your First Treatment?[a]

	Percent
Very anxious and frightened	16.3
Slightly anxious and frightened	23.5
No particular feelings	22.9
Reassured; pleased that treatment was starting	22.9
Can't remember	5.4
Other	5.4

[a]$n = 166$.

they had been given no explanation at all and stuck to this view even when it was suggested to them that they might have forgotten. Twelve percent said that they couldn't remember being given any explanation but one might have been given.

When asked how they felt before their first ECT treatment, 16% described feeling very anxious or frightened and a further 23.5% feeling slightly anxious. Forty-six percent said that they either had no particular feelings one way or the other or felt reassured that some new action was being taken, or an effective treatment instigated. Most found it difficult to say why they had been afraid, though a few said spontaneously they were afraid of the unknown or afraid of the anesthetic.

The responses to specific questions about brain damage, fear of epilepsy, worry about electricity, worry about being made unconscious, etc., are listed in TABLE 5. It can be seen that worry about possible brain damage was the most common fear, but even then 77% of patients had not thought about this at all. We did not come across anybody who had bizarre ideas about what happened during ECT, and our general impression was that patients did not find it particularly frightening. When asked to compare it with a trip to the dentist (see TABLE 4d), 50% of subjects felt that going to the dentist was more upsetting or frightening.

Specific parts of the treatment procedure, listed in TABLE 4c, seemed to arouse little feeling in subjects, and most found them neutral. We optimistically asked whether any aspect of the treatment was pleasant. Thirty-two percent of subjects thought that the sensation of falling asleep was a pleasant one, and 27% commented on the staff being pleasant. No aspect of the treatment was rated as unpleasant by more than 30% of the subjects.

Side Effects

Details of the side effects are given in TABLE 6. It should be noted that these are side effects remembered approximately a year afterwards.

TABLE 4c. Experience of Various Parts of the Treatment (Percentages)[a]

Aspect of Treatment	Pleasant	Neutral	Unpleasant	Don't Know
Premedication	2.4	77.1	15.7	4.8
Waiting for treatment in the morning	1.2	74.7	19.9	4.2
ECT staff	26.5	65.7	3.0	4.8
Anesthetic injections	5.4	83.7	6.6	4.2
Falling asleep	31.9	54.8	8.4	4.8
Waking up	10.8	63.9	20.5	4.8
Recovery period for a few hours after each treatment	6.0	69.9	17.5	6.6

[a]$n = 166$.

TABLE 4d. Response to Statements about Experience of ECT

Statement	Percentage Answering		
	Agree	Disagree	Don't Know
1. I was so upset by the treatment I'd be reluctant to have it again	13.1	80.0	6.9
2. If necessary I'd readily have the treatment again	59.4	34.4	6.2
3. More explanation should be given to patients about the treatment	51.2	30.6	18.1
4. ECT is a frightening treatment to have	38.7	45.0	15.6
5. How did ECT compare with going to the dentist?	More upsetting		18.3
	Less upsetting		49.4
	About the same		32.3
6. How frightening or upsetting was ECT compared with what you expected?	More		3.0
	Less		52.7
	About the same		32.1
	Not upsetting at all		9.7
	Don't know		2.4

Twenty percent reported remembering no side effects whatsoever. Memory impairment was clearly the most troublesome, with 50% of the total sample mentioning this as the worst side effect. Forty-one percent mentioned memory impairment spontaneously when asked about side effects, and a further 23% when prompted, making 74 percent of the whole sample who reported some memory disturbance.

The only other side effect commonly reported was headache occurring at the time of treatment. This was reported by 48% of subjects. Fifteen percent of the total sample thought it was the most troublesome unwanted effect.

When asked to respond to a series of statements about ECT, 30% agreed with the statement that their memory had never returned to normal afterwards though 12% felt their memory was better now than it had ever been. Twenty-eight percent felt that ECT caused permanent change to memory, and 22% that ECT had no effect on memory at all. (See TABLES 7 and 8.)

There were single complaints of neck stiffness, skin burns, increased sweating, and

TABLE 5. Fears and Worries about ECT[a]

Worry or Fear	Not at All	A Little	A Lot
About being made unconscious	80.6%	11.9%	7.5%
About losing control of bladder, or embarrassing things happening while unconscious	83.7%	9.4%	6.9%
That electricity was used in the treatment	76.9%	13.1%	10.0%
About having a fit or a turn	90.9%	4.2%	3.8%
Of possible brain damage as a result of the treatment	76.9%	13.1%	10.0%

[a] $n = 166$.

TABLE 6. Side Effects Remembered

Patients' Reports of Worst Side Effect	$n = 166$		$n = 243$[a]
	n	Percentage	Percentage
Memory impairment	83	50	7
Headache	26	15.6	16
Other side effects	8	4.8	14
Confusion	6	3.6	9
Dizziness	3	1.8	
Vomiting	2	1.2	
Don't know	4	2.4	
No side effects at all	33	19.8	

[a]This column is side effects recorded at the time by the staff, for comparison.

muscle aches. One man complained of choking and said he had been too lightly anesthetized on one occasion.

Did Patients Find the Treatment Helpful?

Details regarding helpfulness of treatment are given in TABLE 9. Altogether 78% of subjects thought that ECT had helped them either a little or a lot. Only one person thought that ECT had made him much worse. He was a young electrical engineer who had developed a schizophrenic illness. Because of his trade he had considerable respect for electricity and had found the whole experience quite upsetting and blamed his present state on ECT.

Although 78% of people said it had helped them, only 65% were willing to say that they would have ECT again. This discrepancy appeared to be due to two factors. A number could not imagine themselves getting depressed again and therefore could not believe that they would ever need more ECT. Others had clearly been put off by the side effects, and 13% said so. When asked if they would recommend it to a friend if a psychiatrist advised the friend to have it, 65% said yes, but 24% didn't know, and 11.4% said definitely no.

Few people believed that the effect of ECT had been permanent. Thirty-five percent believed the beneficial effects had lasted for a year or more, 15% that they had

TABLE 7. Patients' Estimates of Severity

	Total Percentage Reporting Symptom	Percentage Who Reported Symptom Spontaneously	Percentage Who Reported When Prompted	Percentage Who Thought Symptom Severe	Percentage Who Thought Symptom Mild
Memory impairment	63.9	41	22.9	25.3	38.6
Headache	47.6	24.7	22.9	19.2	28.4
Confusion	26.5	4.8	21.7	9.0	17.5
Clumsiness	9.0	2.4	6.6	3.6	5.4
Nausea or vomiting	4.2	2.4	1.8	2.8	1.4
Eyesight problems	4.2	2.2	2.0	2.2	2.0
Other side effects	12.0	10.8	1.2	3.6	8.4

TABLE 8. Opinions on Memory Impairment

Statement	Responses		
	Agree	Disagree	Don't Know
My memory has never returned to normal after ECT	30%	61.3%	6.9%
My memory now is better than ever it has been	11.9%	84.4%	3.7%
ECT is helpful but the side effects are severe	15.6%	77.5%	6.9%
ECT has no effect on memory at all	21.9%	73.7%	4.3%
ECT causes permanent changes to memory	28.1%	63.7%	8.1%

TABLE 9. How Helpful Was the Treatment?[a]

How much did ECT help you?	A lot	57.2%
	A little	20.5%
	No change	18.7%
	A little worse	2.4%
	Much worse	0.6%
In what way did it help?	Less depressed	50.6%
	Less anxious	6.0%
	Made me forget	1.2%
	Gave me a jolt	0.6%
	Other explanation	19.3%
	Didn't help	21.1%
	Don't know	1.2%
Has the effect lasted?	Permanently	9.0%
	1 year or more	34.9%
	6–12 months	15.1%
	Less than 6 months	12.7%
	Immediate relapse	2.4%
	Not applicable	24.7%
	Don't know	1.2%
ECT is a helpful and useful procedure	Agree	79.5%
	Disagree	14.3%
	Don't know	6.2%
ECT works for a short while but the effects don't last	Agree	65.6%
	Disagree	14.4%
	Don't know	20.0%
ECT gets you better quicker than drugs	Agree	65.6%
	Disagree	14.4%
	Don't know	19.4%

[a] $n = 166$.

lasted from six months to a year, 13% less than six months, and 2.4% thought they had relapsed immediately.

Did Patients Understand the Treatment?

Fifteen percent of those interviewed appeared to have a full understanding of what the treatment involved (see TABLE 10). They knew about the anesthetic, that the electrodes were applied to the head, and that the object was to produce an epileptic fit. Thirty percent had a partial understanding. They knew about the anesthetic, they knew that electricity was used and that it was applied somewhere around the head. They said they were put to sleep but then had no idea of what happened to them while they were asleep. Only four patients described false ideas. One believed that patients were naked when they had the treatment and another that some sort of medical electrode was implanted in the head during the treatment.

TABLE 10. Patients' Understanding of Treatment[a]

1. What does the treatment involve?	
No understanding	30.1%
Partial understanding	43.4%
Full understanding	22.9%
False ideas	2.4%
Wouldn't answer	1.2%
2. Why is the treatment given?	
No idea	16.4%
For depression	61.2%
For anxiety	5.5%
Other reasons	14.5%
Wouldn't answer	2.4%
3. How does the treatment work?	
No idea	38.8%
Gives you a jolt or a shock	32.7%
Makes you forget	7.3%
Other explanation	14.5%
Doesn't work	5.5%
Wouldn't answer	1.2%

[a] $n = 166$.

Patients' Consent to ECT

From the medical case notes, we determined that 76% of patients had signed the consent form themselves (TABLE 11). We tried to determine whether patients felt they had been coerced into having ECT, persuaded against their judgment, or compelled to have ECT when they definitely did not want it. Some patients (7.8%) felt that they shouldn't have been given ECT but in most of these this was because they felt the treatment did them little or no good. Only two patients said that they clearly remembered being given ECT against their specific wishes. One of these had been helped by the treatment and was now glad she had received it. We also asked everyone whether they thought their decision would have been respected by their doctors. A third said they could have said no and they felt they would have been obeyed. Twenty-three percent said that they wouldn't have been able to say no, either because they couldn't imagine themselves saying no to a doctor or because they were in no fit state at the time to make a decision. Forty percent said that they didn't know what would have happened or didn't understand the question. We then asked an open-ended question about whether in general they felt the consent procedures for ECT were adequate. In 90% of cases the reply was yes or that it wasn't really the patient's decision, i.e., that it was up to the doctor to decide and for the patient to do as the doctor recommended.

Two people said they had been pressured into signing the consent form. One man said he was "conned." "They said I wouldn't get out if I didn't have it!" The other, a woman, said she was going to get ECT and it was futile her resisting.

We found this area of the questionnaire the most unsatisfactory, and we were left with the clear impression that patients would agree to almost anything a doctor suggested. Many people could not remember ever having signed a consent form, didn't regard it as particularly important, and seemed quite happy to have other people, such as relatives, give consent on their behalf.

TABLE 11. Consent Procedure

1. Who signed the consent form?	
(n = 166)	
Information on whole sample from notes.	
Patient alone	76.1%
Relative alone	11.9%
Both relative and patient	11.5%
No form could be found in notes for one patient.	
2. Do you think you could have refused to have ECT if you had wanted to?	
Yes	33.7%
No	23.1%
Don't know	40.0%
Other replies	3.1%

Factors Affecting Attitudes

More women than men found the treatment very frightening, 20% as against 8%. Slightly more men than women said that their memory had not been impaired at all (41% as against 32%), otherwise there were no sex differences. The amount of previous experience of ECT did not appear to alter attitudes, nor did attitudes either mellow or harden with time. The 1971 group did not complain either more or less than the 1976 group, and they did not report that ECT had been any more or less helpful.

The number of people who had unilateral ECT was small and some of them had had bilateral treatment on other occasions. Their views differed markedly from the bilateral group. Fifty percent said they wouldn't have ECT again (26% in bilateral group), 33% said it helped them a lot (61% in bilateral group), 28% thought they shouldn't have been given ECT (9% in bilateral group). We think that the most likely explanation for this negative view is not that unilateral ECT is a more unpleasant treatment but that these patients already had adverse views and were therefore selected by their consultants for unilateral treatment although in this hospital bilateral ECT is the usual procedure.

An alternative explanation is that unilateral ECT doesn't work as well, and therefore more people complained; however, the numbers of treatments given and the therapeutic outcome recorded in the notes did not differ between unilateral and bilateral groups.

Finally, patients were asked the following:

1. ECT is dangerous and shouldn't be used: agree 6.9%, disagree 76.9%, don't know 16.2%
2. ECT is given to too many people: agree 6.2%, disagree 30.6%, don't know 63.1%
3. ECT is often given to people who don't need it: agree 8.7%, disagree 29.4%, don't know 61.9%.

The commonest reply to the second and third questions was in fact that it was "up to the doctors, and I'm not qualified to say."

DISCUSSION

We are aware that the main criticism of this study is that it was carried out by psychiatrists in a psychiatric hospital. It is obviously going to be difficult to come back to a hospital where you have been treated and criticize the treatment that you were given in a face-to-face meeting with a doctor. It is not easy to see a way round this. It would clearly not be possible to release details of a group of patients' treatments to lay persons so that they could undertake such a study. Even if this were possible we imagine that the response rate to a questionnaire administered by strangers would be much lower. It was our impression that those patients who had strong views spoke out with little inhibition. What is less certain is whether there was a significant number of people in the midground who felt more upset by ECT than they were prepared to tell us.

Given these reservations, a number of definite results are apparent. The majority of patients did not find the treatment unduly upsetting or frightening, nor was it a painful or unpleasant experience. Most felt it helped them, and hardly any felt it had made them worse. In general, then, most patients had very positive views about ECT.

We were surprised by the large number who complained of memory impairment. Many of them did so spontaneously without being prompted, and a striking 30% felt that their memory had been permanently affected, although the majority meant by this that they had permanent gaps in their memory around the time of treatment, not that their ability to learn new material was impaired. It may be that this high level of memory complaint is due to most people having had bilateral ECT. It would certainly be well worthwhile repeating the study now that nearly all of the patients in our hospital get unilateral, nondominant ECT.

We feel more confident about our results than we did in 1980 because two further studies have found strikingly similar results. Kerr *et al.* (1982) interviewed 178 subjects and compared three groups: patients who had had ECT, individuals visiting patients in hospital who had had ECT, and individuals visiting non-ECT patients.[6] Many of the results were similar to ours, and there was a general tendency for those patients who had had ECT to be less afraid and feel more positive about the treatment than either of the visitor groups. Hughes and Barraclough (1981) used a questionnaire based on our own and interviewed a sample in Southampton, United Kingdom, at the opposite end of the country to Edinburgh.[5] Their results were strikingly similar to ours.

It is clear that patients wish to be told more about the treatment. It so happened that one of us had interviewed a number of these patients before they started ECT in

1976 in connection with another study[2] and had given them quite detailed explanations of what the treatment involved, yet several of these were adamant that they had never been given any explanation. It might, therefore, be beneficial to patients to give them a second explanation of the treatment after they have completed the course and are symptomatically improved.

It is worrying that two patients from the 1976 sample died during a course of ECT. Both were elderly females, had preexisting cardiac disease, were taking tricyclic antidepressants, had longer than usual courses of ECT, and died of myocardial infarctions which were clinically silent until death. It is not possible to draw firm conclusions from two cases, but they raise the question whether in such "at risk" patients ECT and tricyclics should be given together.

Finally, we would like to emphasize the great trust that patients put in doctors. The majority of subjects in this study were more than happy to leave all decisions about their treatment to a doctor. There was hardly any concern about consent procedures being inadequate. This is perhaps best illustrated by two patients who misunderstood the initial appointment letter and came fully prepared to commence a course of ECT. Neither had been near the hospital for nine months and both were quite symptom free.

REFERENCES

1. Bird, J. M. 1979. Effects of the media on attitudes to electroconvulsive therapy. Br. Med. J. **ii:** 526–527.
2. Freeman, C. P. L., J. Basson & A. Crighton. 1978. Double blind controlled trial of ECT and simulated ECT in depressive illness. Lancet **ii:** 738–740.
3. Gomez, J. 1975. Subjective side effects of ECT. Br. J. Psychiatry **127:** 609–611.
4. Hillard, R. J. & R. Folger. 1977. Patients' attitudes and attributions to electroconvulsive shock therapy. J. Clin. Psychol. **33:** 855–861.
5. Hughes, J., B. M. Barraclough & W. Reeve. 1981. J. R. Soc. Med. **74**(4): 283–285.
6. Kerr, R. A., J. T. McGrath, R. T. O'Kearney & J. Price. 1982. ECT: misconceptions and attitudes. Aust. N. Zealand J. Psychiatry **16:** 43–49.
7. Mounter, J. 1977. The right to refuse ECT. Listener **98**(2518): 66–67.

The Cognitive Side Effects of Electroconvulsive Therapy[a]

Discussion of Part VI

STEPHANIE PORTNOY

Department of Biological Psychiatry
New York State Psychiatric Institute
722 West 168 Street
New York, New York 10032

It is a well-documented fact that electroconvulsive therapy (ECT) produces cognitive impairment. This type of side effect has been a major concern of both practitioners and their patients since the treatment was first introduced in 1938. Interest in finding ways to reduce these cognitive deficits has been at the core of research efforts in more recent years, and modification of the parameters of ECT, e.g., modality, stimulus waveform, and dosage, have met with apparent success. Research into the specificities of these cognitive deficits, and how they relate to the parameters of treatment, will not only aid us in dealing with the deficits directly, but will enable us to better understand how the treatment affects a wide range of neuropsychological functions, thereby providing data on the possible mechanisms of action of ECT as well as on the neuropsychological aspects of depression.

The papers presented in this session are primarily devoted to further exploration of the ways in which the parameters of treatment relate to cognitive dysfunction. Research advances in this area have pointed to the fact that the associated side effects of ECT are not general, but specific. They are specific to the direct effects of the stimulation, to the characteristics of the behaviors being studied, and to the time at which these assessments are made.

A wide range of research interests are presented. In some cases the data support previously reported findings, while in other cases the data are representative of new areas of study. I will briefly review the major findings in the area of ECT-related cognitive functions as they are presented in this session, and show, where possible, how these deficits relate directly to the parameters of the treatment.

The first major parameter to undergo study was that of electrode placement. It was clearly observed that the memory loss often associated with bilateral placement of electrodes was markedly reduced when the electrodes were placed on one side of the head (nondominant side). This reduction in cognitive impairment, with unilateral treatment, was primarily for verbal memory, although early studies suggested that nonverbal memory was similarly affected. The differential effects of treatment modality on verbal memory are a robust finding, which has held up through many experimental trials. We see from the data presented in this session that the differences between bilateral and unilateral electrode placement for verbal materials hold for the different stimulus waveforms (Weiner's study) and for low-dosage treatment (Sackeim's study).

[a]The preparation of this paper was supported in part by National Institute of Mental Health Grant No. MH 35636.

The differential effects of electrode placement on memory for nonverbal materials are not as clear-cut. This may be due, in part, to the difficult task of selecting stimulus materials that are sensitive to right hemisphere processing. The geometric shapes, for example, in the Sackeim *et al.* study were verbally encodable, and were, in fact, processed like verbal materials, while the nonsense shapes, which were not as easily encodable, showed treatment effects suggesting that they were being processed by the right hemisphere.

Pure nonverbal materials might be equally affected by the two treatment modalities, since the right hemisphere is being stimulated in both bilateral and unilateral electrode placements. It is interesting to note that the processing of the nonsense shapes in the Sackeim *et al.* study was sensitive to response to treatment, e.g., early in the course of treatment individuals who were later classified as responders showed greater deficit in their retrograde memory for nonsense shapes than did individuals who did not respond to the treatment. These data suggest that right hemisphere processing is differentially affected by the therapeutic aspects of the treatment. It is possible that tests of this kind could be used to predict ultimate response to treatment early in its course, and thereby restrict treatment to patients likely to respond.

Recent interest in the postictal period, i.e., the time immediately following the occurrence of the seizure, has revealed substantial differences in orientation for the two treatment modalities. Daniel and Crovitz, using a 12-item questionnaire, report marked differences between the two modes for both traditional sine-wave stimulation and for brief pulse. Greater cumulated disorientation, over the course of treatment, was observed in the bilateral groups. Similar modality differences are reported by Sackeim *et al.*, using low-dosage, titrated energy levels. Use of low-dosage treatment, however, apparently eliminates the cumulative disorientation effects for the bilateral group, while resulting in cumulative improvement in orientation times for the unilateral group. It may be that the shorter orientation times in the unilateral group at the end of the treatment course were related to the decreases in seizure durations observed in this group. Correlations between seizure duration and time to orient were found to be significant for this group.

Modifications of the stimulus waveform used to elicit the therapeutic seizure were first introduced in the 1940s. It was believed that the amount of energy needed to elicit a seizure, using a brief pulse, was substantially lower than that needed to elicit a seizure using a sine wave, and that this reduction in amount of energy might have a significant effect on cognitive impairment. Weiner and his associates report in this session that sine-wave stimulation causes greater cognitive impairment than does brief-pulse stimulation without compromising clinical benefit. Using a wide variety of carefully selected neuropsychological tests, they concluded that stimulus waveform has a more potent effect on cognitive functioning than does modality, although modality differences were also apparent in both stimulus waveform groups.

It is possible that it is not the absolute amount of energy applied to the brain that produces the cognitive impairment, but rather the amount in excess of an individual's threshold. Recent efforts (Sackeim *et al.*) have been made to develop a procedure for titrating energy levels for individuals, thereby reducing the amount of energy applied. The lower levels of energy have resulted in reduced impairment in both immediate and short-term cognitive functioning. In addition, there is no evidence for cumulative impairment over the course of the treatment, for either postictal orientation time or retrograde amnesia. While the cognitive impairment associated with the low-dosage treatment shows typical modality effects, low-dosage unilateral treatment was not found to be as effective a treatment as low-dosage bilateral treatment, despite the fact that available characteristics of the seizure obtained appeared to be equivalent.

The substantially shorter postictal orientation times for the low-dosage treatment group have definite advantages for the patient. Most of the patients oriented within a 45-minute period following their treatment, and were able to return to their wards and participate in ward activities by lunchtime. For outpatients, this shorter recovery time enabled them to return to their homes and to resume their domestic responsibilities by early afternoon, if they wished.

Short orientation times also make it possible to gather data on a wide variety of neuropsychological functions, closer in time to the actual seizure than is possible with the more traditional forms of treatment and their prolonged orientations. These data will be more sensitive to the treatment parameters and provide better insight into possible mechanisms of action.

At one time the confusion produced by the treatment was believed to be a mechanism of action. It was thought that patients became disoriented and "forgot" what was bothering them. Recent research, however, has offered little support for this notion. Degree of cognitive impairment, per se, has not been found to be related to response to treatment.

The specificity of the treatment on cognitive functioning was first observed when comparisons of the effects of bilateral and unilateral treatment on verbal and nonverbal memory revealed that bilateral placement had a more profound effect on verbal functioning than did unilateral placement. The fact that materials processed by the different hemispheres would be differently affected by the treatment parameters has resulted in the selection of stimuli sensitive to brain lateralization. As mentioned above, early attempts to select nonverbal stimuli were not successful since nonverbal stimuli that can be easily verbally encoded are processed by the left hemisphere. Since then researchers have explored the effects of the treatment on a wide range of neuropsychological tasks. Just reviewing the materials utilized in the studies reported in this session, we see an extensive list including memory for words, paragraphs, geometric shapes (for verbal materials), and facial recognition (affective and neutral), form reproduction and memory for nonsense shapes (for nonverbal materials).

With the use of more appropriate nonverbal materials it now appears that the differences between the bilateral and unilateral treatments, previously reported for nonverbal materials were probably more a function of the stimulus properties than of the treatment modality, and that the effects of the two treatment modalities on nonverbal tasks are about equivalent (the Weiner and Sackeim studies).

Interest in the effects of the treatment on different kinds of memory has led to comparisons of retrograde amnesia (memory loss for material learned before treatment) with anterograde amnesia (inability to learn new material). Results have indicated that following ECT, anterograde amnesia is less pronounced than retrograde amnesia. Recovery of anterograde memory (Squire's study) seems to progress at a regular pace from time of last treatment and is usually back to normal at about six months, depending, of course, on the nature of the task. Retrograde memory loss often displays a temporally limited gradient, e.g., loss of more recently acquired information and less or no loss of material more remote in time. While retrograde amnesia also returns to normal by the end of six months, many individuals report losses persisting many months after treatment, and some patients report that this gap is never filled. Memory losses are often for the events immediately surrounding the treatment experience, and these losses are often the most frequent of patient complaints.

The magnitude of the memory loss is often directly related to the time from the last treatment, and seems to be a direct response to the treatment. With time, some of the loss is dissipated. Dr. Squire reports that anterograde learning is most impaired within the 45 minutes following the treatment, and then improves with increases in time. This gradient was found for the bilateral group, but not for the unilateral group, where only minimal deficits were observed shortly after the treatment. While these findings were clearly reported for the verbal materials (paired associate word learning), his data for the nonverbal materials (faces and nonsense shapes) suggest that the unilateral and bilateral groups were similarly affected.

There is a general claim in the literature that the learning of new materials is not as affected by ECT as the ability to retain this information, e.g., retention is more strongly affected than acquisition, particularly when a substantial delay is imposed between the acquisition and retention of the materials.

Results from the Sackeim *et al.* study provide additional support for this hypothesis. Using paired-word and paired-face tasks, they reported that depressed patients differed from normal controls in their ability to acquire information prior to treatment, and that the ECT produced deficits in retention for both the verbal and nonverbal stimuli, suggesting that these two neuropsychological processes are differently affected by the treatment.

Along a different dimension, Weiner and his associates report that memory loss for personal information is affected by the treatment to a greater extent than is memory for impersonal material, the latter being measured in terms of recall for famous events and famous faces. Most important is the finding that bilateral treatment produced greater impairment for personal memory than did unilateral treatment. While Weiner's data lack corroborative control, this is probably an important step in the finer differentiation of the kinds of memory losses often complained about.

Freeman's paper on patients' attitudes towards ECT lends additional support to the importance of memory losses, since close to 75% of the patients reported that memory loss was the worst side effect experienced, with 30% stating that their memories have never returned to normal. He reported that those patients who had received unilateral treatment were more likely to report that they would not want to have ECT again. At first this seems contradictory, since bilateral treatment produces greater cognitive impairment. However, it is possible that the unilateral treatment was not as effective a treatment and that the patients were disappointed in the therapeutic effects of this treatment. It would have been interesting to compare the bilateral nonresponders to the bilateral responders to see if attitude towards ECT is related to response to treatment.

The lack of a relationship between subjective reports of memory loss and objective measures reported in the Weiner *et al.* study suggests that the former are more a function of the mood state of the patient (in fact correlations between Hamilton Rating Scale scores and the reports of subjective memory loss were high), while the latter are more a function of the "organic" state of the patient (no correlation with depression scores). It is possible that patients' complaints of memory loss are of a specific kind, a kind not reflected in the objective scores, and a kind exacerbated by depressive symptomatology.

In summary, the papers presented at this session represent current research efforts in the study of the cognitive effects of ECT. While many of the previously reported findings have been supported, new ones have been offered and have contributed to a better understanding of the specific effects of the treatment on cognitive functioning. Hopefully, research efforts will continue in this vein and the data culled from these efforts will help to further reduce the undesirable side effects of the treatment, enabling more patients to seek and utilize ECT as an effective treatment for depression.

Clinical Perspectives on Mechanism of Action

JAN-OTTO OTTOSSON

Department of Psychiatry
Sahlgrenska Hospital
University of Göteborg
413 45 Göteborg, Sweden

While more exact knowledge of the mechanism of action of electroconvulsive therapy (ECT) only can be obtained from studies on the cellular or molecular level, mere clinical observations can give valuable information on the mode of action in different conditions.

The issue to be elucidated is specific and unspecific effects of ECT. To be specific a psychiatric treatment should fulfill the following criteria.

1. Be effective on one psychopathological syndrome but not on another (selective effect).
2. Be effective on the same psychopathological syndrome without interfering with normal mental functions (target effect).
3. Be effective on the total psychopathological syndrome and not only on single symptoms (syndromatic effect).

SELECTIVE EFFECT

Clinical experience shows that the number and spacing of ECT treatments that must be given to achieve a therapeutic effect vary in different psychopathological syndromes. Most melancholic syndromes respond to six to eight treatments with a frequency of two to three per week. Manic syndromes, on the other hand, require daily treatments or even several treatments a day en bloc. Schizophrenic syndromes in comparison to melancholic ones require considerably more and closer spaced treatments without attaining the same degree of remission. Psychogenic confusional psychoses with agitation or stupor may clear up after one to two treatments. Hysteric conversion reactions which were sometimes treated with ECT could be reversed, at least temporarily, after a single treatment. These circumstances do not indicate a selectivity of the action of ECT in the sense that only one psychopathological syndrome can be improved but rather that there are several therapeutic effects and several different mechanisms of action. A selective action on melancholic syndromes may be claimed in the sense that they respond more reliably to ECT than other syndromes do.

TARGET EFFECT

Another clinical observation is the varying degree of interference with other mental functions than those that are the target of the treatment. When treating melancholia with ECT the melancholic syndrome is improved whereas other mental functions are largely intact, disregarding an immediate confusion and memory disturbance for a limited period of time. Treatment of chronic schizoprenic syndromes with ECT may also cause alleviation of conspicuous symptoms but only at the price of affective blunting, amnesia, decrease of initiative and interest, and in extreme cases long-lasting confusion, incontinence, and ataxia. These symptoms belong to an organic brain syndrome which is most obvious after many and closely spaced treatments. When the organic syndrome recedes, the schizophrenic symptoms tend to reappear. Thus, a target effect of ECT is seen in melancholic but not in schizophrenic syndromes. The response of manic syndromes to ECT seems to occupy an intermediate position.

SYNDROMATIC EFFECT

A third clinical observation is that ECT sometimes results in improvement or recovery of the total psychopathological syndrome whereas in other conditions the effect is restricted to single symptoms. Thus, all the components of the melancholic syndrome—the distinct quality of depression, retardation, vital symptoms, and non-reactivity to external stimuli—improve parallelly. The retardation may have various modes of expression—cognitive, emotional, conative, or psychomotor—which, however, respond equally well. In contrast, in the treatment of schizophrenia there is an influence on some symptoms, mainly catatonic and affective, whereas Schneider's first-rank symptoms do not respond at all or, if they do, only as a part of an organic brain syndrome. The conclusion is that ECT has a syndromatic effect in melancholic syndromes and symptomatic effects in schizophrenia.

Also here, treatment of manic syndromes with ECT occupies an intermediate position.

SPECIFIC ANTIMELANCHOLIC EFFECT

Taken together, these observations indicate that ECT has both specific and unspecific effects. For the following reasons the antimelancholic effect may be regarded as specific:

1. It has a certain selectivity since it is stronger and more reliable than other effects, e.g., antimanic and antipsychotic.
2. It is obtained with minor interference with normal mental function (target effect).
3. It is syndromatic, i.e., the whole melancholic syndrome is improved and not only single symptoms. It is reasonable to assume that syndromatic effects interfere with more basic or fundamental processes in the pathogenesis than symptomatic effects.

UNSPECIFIC EFFECTS

Apart from the specific antimelancholic effect, ECT has several unspecific effects. These fulfill the opposite criteria to specific effects: they are nonselective, they hit more than the target, and they are symptomatic. One unspecific effect of ECT is the organic brain syndrome which via a general reduction of mental functioning may alleviate some of the schizophrenic symptoms and, probably also in this way, some of the manic symptoms.

Another unspecific effect is coma followed by sleep. It is reasonable to assume that this mechanism of action explains the good effect in psychogenic psychoses with agitation or stupor which are often preceded by long insomnia. The lifesaving effect of ECT in the catatonic excitement state (acute lethal catatonia) may also be explained by induction of sleep which brings the exhausted and dehydrated state to an end.

A final unspecific effect is suggestion which is part of every treatment with a dramatic nimbus. This effect probably explains why a hysteric paresis or blindness may cease after a single treatment, which in these cases might have been a sham treatment as well.

UNSPECIFIC ECT EFFECTS IN MELANCHOLIA

The circumstance that the antimelancholic effect is specific does not imply that the treatment of melancholia with ECT only utilizes specific effects. In fact, also in this treatment an organic brain syndrome is induced which can be shown with psychological tests and EEG. It may even be argued that the antimelancholic effect is part of an organic syndrome, as is probably the antipsychotic effect.

However, three sets of data argue against that view.

Clinical Observations

Negative life events and memories from the past may be ascribed a causal significance by the melancholic patient. ECT does not extinguish these memories. When recovered, the patient remembers them but they have lost their emotional significance, and they do not cause a relapse.

Systematic Studies

The most sensitive sign of an organic syndrome is memory disturbance. The typical memory disturbance after ECT is diminished capacity to consolidate. Learning as measured by immediate reproduction is normal, but the learned material does not stick and is forgotten quicker than normally. Accordingly, delayed reproduction is decreased.[1]

Experiments where the energy of the electrical stimulation and the cerebral seizure—recorded with EEG—were systematically and independently manipulated have shown that the memory disturbance and the antimelancholic effect do not run a parallel course.[2–4]

When a bilateral stimulation is augmented above the grand mal seizure threshold, the memory disturbance is increased whereas the antimelancholic effect is unchanged. The EEG seizure or postseizure pattern does not change, which shows that the seizure follows an all-or-none law when the grand mal threshold has been reached.

On the other hand, when the electrical stimulation is decreased by using unilateral stimulation, the memory disturbance is decreased whereas the antimelancholic effect still is unchanged provided a grand mal seizure has been evoked.

Finally, when the cerebral seizure activity is reduced with the administration of an anticonvulsive drug, lidocaine, the antimelancholic effect is markedly reduced, whereas the memory disturbance is only slightly less.

Correlational Analysis

An untreated melancholic syndrome is characterized by disturbance of the capacity of learning but not of consolidation. On recovery the learning is restituted to the normal level whereas a disturbance of consolidation may have been induced with ECT. The improvement of the melancholic syndrome is positively related to the improvement in learning but there is no relation with the impairment of consolidation. Thus, no support is obtained that the organic syndrome, of which decreased consolidation is a marker, is relevant for the recovery.[5,6]

These experiments show that the antimelancholic and organic effects may be dissociated from each other. Besides, the two effects have different origin, the antimelancholic effect being dependent on the cerebral seizure activity and not on direct effects of the stimulation, the organic syndrome conversely being dependent both on direct effects of the stimulation and on the seizure. Other observations indicate that both cerebral and peripheral seizure manifestations, such as hypoxia, hypercapnia, and blood pressure elevation, contribute to the memory disturbance. The mechanisms of action are shown in FIGURE 1.

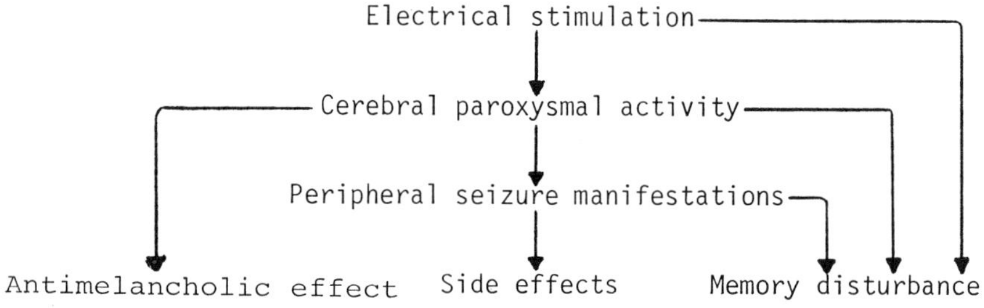

FIGURE 1. Mechanism of antimelancholic action of ECT.

Since the antimelancholic effect may be obtained without or at least only with a minor memory disturbance, the organic brain syndrome should be regarded as an undesirable side effect in the treatment of melancholic syndromes with ECT. In schizophrenic syndromes, on the other hand, clinical experience indicates that the organic syndrome is a prerequisite for the antipsychotic effect of ECT.

PRACTICAL IMPLICATIONS

If a specific antimelancholic effect of ECT is not acknowledged, a silent approval is given of the justification in inducing an organic brain syndrome in the treatment of mental disorders with ECT. The motivation to reach an exact diagnosis will be poor since, according to the unspecific view, ECT has reasonable prospects of improving the condition, irrespective of diagnosis. It is merely a matter of intensity and endurance. As a not too remote history of psychiatry has shown, the road is open to long series of closely spaced treatments ending up with a confused, incontinent, and blunted state—annihilation. Resurrection usually occurs; in fact, the brain has an astonishing resistance and capacity to recover. However, the induction of long-lasting organic brain syndromes is a high price for short-lasting effects on schizophrenic symptoms.

Since there is no support for specific antipsychotic effects but rather that they are part of an organic syndrome, it should strongly be questioned if ECT should be used in schizophrenia at all. The only exceptions are affective and catatonic symptoms and life-threatening catatonic excitement states which do not respond to conventional antipsychotic therapy but may be alleviated with a reasonable number of ECT treatments. The use of ECT with intentional or unintentional induction of organic syndromes puts a powerful weapon in the hands of our critics.

Even the treatment of melancholic syndromes may degenerate to a more or less unspecific treatment if available knowledge of the origins of specific and unspecific effects is not utilized. Measures should be taken to reduce the unspecific organic side effects and promote the specific antimelancholic effect. The principle is attainment of maximal cerebral seizure activity with minimal electrical stimulation and, besides, to minimize the peripheral seizure manifestations. The major factors for attainment of maximal cerebral seizure activity are abundant supply of oxygen, superficial narcosis, no concomitant bensodiazepine medication, and seizure monitoring to control for maximal seizure activity. The major factors for minimizing the unspecific organic effect are tailored number of treatments, adequate recovery between them, and unilateral nondominant threshold stimulation with brief pulses. In treatment centers where these principles are not adhered to, unspecific may dominate over specific effects. The first sign is short seizures, correspondingly prolonged treatment series, and, in spite of that, suboptimal antimelancholic effect. Such practice also contributes to the bad reputation of ECT.

PROMOTION OF THE SPECIFIC ANTIMELANCHOLIC EFFECT OF ECT

Is it possible to increase the antimelancholic specificity of ECT further and even to purify the antimelancholic effect? Three attempts will be commented upon.

ALTERNATIVE APPLICATION OF ELECTRICAL STIMULATION

The typical memory disturbance after ECT is of the same type as in Korsakoff's psychosis. In fact, the memory disturbance is a mild and transient Korsakoff syndrome. Anatomical lesions in Korsakoff's psychosis are located in Papez' circuit including the mamillary bodies, fornix, hippocampus, and adjacent parts of the cingulate cortex.[7] Therefore, it is reasonable to assume that the disturbance of consolidation after ECT is due to interference with Papez' circuit.

Up until now, the electrical stimulation has been modified in three ways which all have in common that the input of electrical energy to the brain is reduced.

1. Substitution of the sine-wave stimulation with short discrete pulses.[8–10]
2. Threshold doses of stimulation.[4]
3. Unilateral stimulation (survey in References 11 and 12).

A fourth way would be to change the site of stimulation.

The hippocampus is projected in the temporal part of the head exactly where one of the electrodes is applied in most techniques (FIGURE 2). With this location it is conceivable that the hippocampus receives an inappropriate density of current which may contribute to the Korsakoff syndrome. Alternative electrode positions have been recommended.[13] However, the memory disturbance has turned out to be equal with temporoparietal, frontoparietal, and frontotemporal unilateral positions.[14] This is due

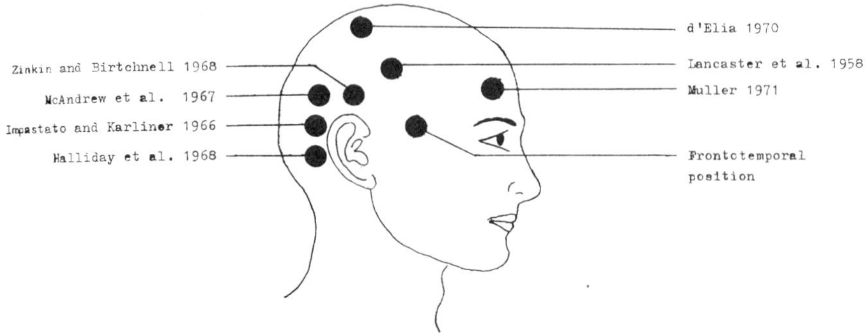

FIGURE 2. Unilateral electrode placements. The frontal temporal electrode is common to all placements. The placement according to Lancaster *et al.* (1958) is the most commonly used. (Reproduced from Reference 11 with permission from the publisher.)

to the conductivity of the scalp and the resistivity of the skull, which interact to distribute the current widely within the hemisphere.[15] Thus, it does not seem possible to reduce the memory disturbance further with new applications of the stimulation. Crossing over from the nondominant to the dominant hemisphere only leads to a changed pattern of memory disturbance, from nonverbal to verbal, but not to a changed degree.[16]

PHARMACOLOGICAL SEIZURES

By substituting the electrical stimulation with chemical induction, the organic effects from the current are eliminated. As expected, the organic syndrome, as measured by retrograde amnesia, is less after a flurothyl (Indoklon) induced seizure than after an electrically induced one.[17] However, after a full series of treatments the difference between the methods is leveled out. This is probably due to the fact that flurothyl-induced seizures are longer—about 70%—the brain being forced to seizure activity beyond the point where electrically induced seizures would have stopped. Forced prolongation has probably an adverse effect on the hippocampus. The hippocampus has a lower epileptogenic threshold than the rest of the brain and is involved with a higher metabolic rate in the seizure.[18,19] Due to the higher oxygen demand a relative hypoxia may develop in the hippocampus in spite of an unaltered arteriovenous oxygen difference over the whole brain in ECT.[20] A putative local hypoxia in flurothyl-induced seizures outweighs the gain from eliminating the electrical stimulation. One way of inducing an organic syndrome is merely replaced by another. Under such circumstances ECT is preferred as technically more simple and reliable.

PARTIAL SEIZURES

The question may be raised whether the whole nervous system must be involved in the seizure in order to obtain an optimal antimelancholic effect. A priori it seems hardly likely that seizure activity in, e.g., the motor cortex or the visual area is essential. If it were possible to induce a partial seizure, a more specific antimelancholic effect might be obtained. Two types of partial seizures have been studied regarding their antimelancholic effect.

Unilateral Seizures

The usual meaning of unilateral treatment is unilateral stimulation to induce bilateral seizures. This is contrary to unilateral seizures, which are confined to one hemisphere. Nobody has succeeded in producing unilateral seizures intentionally in order to study left and right cerebral specialization.[21] However, in ECT unilateral seizures are sometimes produced unintentionally. In one study one-third of the

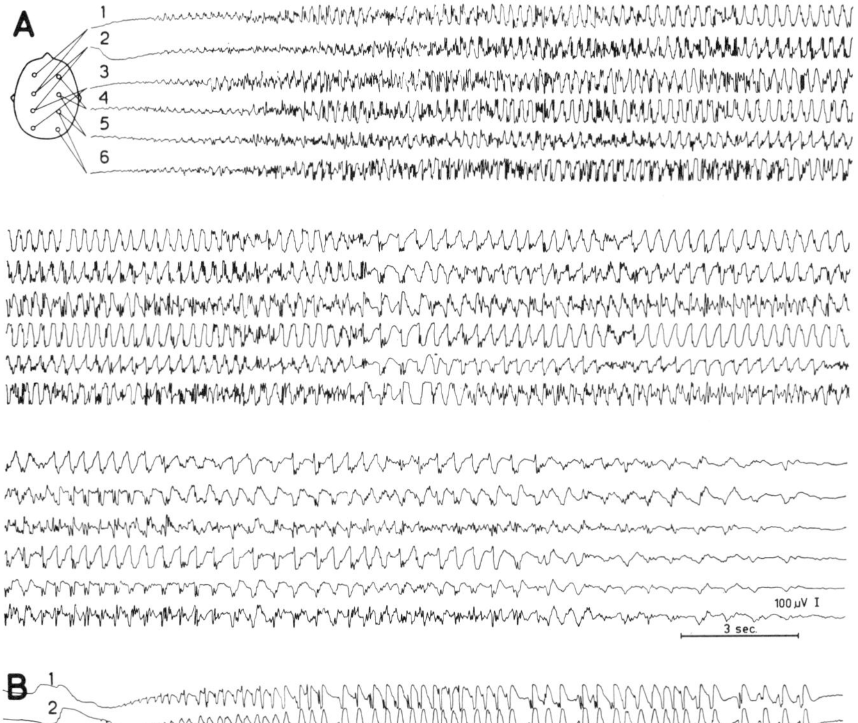

FIGURE 3. **A:** Seizure discharge in light narcosis and full muscular relaxation. First 3 seconds omitted. **B:** Seizure discharge modified by 3 mg/kg lidocaine but under otherwise identical conditions. The seizures were recorded at the second and fourth treatment to a woman of 54. Electrode positions according to the 10/20 system. Leads: 1, F3-C3; 2, C3-P3; 3, P3-O1; 4, F4-C4; 5, C4-P4; and 6, P4-O2. (Reproduced from Reference 4 with permission from the publisher.)

unilaterally induced seizures were wholly or predominantly unilateral but there was no analysis of their efficacy compared to bilateral seizures.[22] Due to the lack of a reliable method to induce unilateral seizures the issue of possibly different effects of dominant and nondominant seizures seems to remain unresolved. However, seizures, most of which were generalized, elicited by stimulation of the dominant hemisphere had lower efficacy than when they were elicited from the nondominant hemisphere.[22]

Brain-Stem Seizures

ECT modified by drugs may be another possibility to induce localized seizures. A lidocaine-modified seizure is shorter than an unmodified one, has a wave-and-spike pattern without fast cortical activity, and does not extinguish the α-activity[23] (FIGURE 3). All these circumstances indicate that such seizures mainly take place in the brain stem. The duration of this brain-stem-dominated seizure is positively related to the antimelancholic effect, which is not the case with the unmodified seizure.[24] Another EEG observation indicating the importance of the brain stem is that the barbiturate-induced slow, bilaterally synchronous posttreatment EEG activity, which presumably is of diencephalic origin, is positively related to the outcome of the therapy.[25,26] These circumstances indicate that the relevant antimelancholic processes take place in the brain stem, comprising among other structures the hypothalamus. However, the lidocaine method is not practically applicable since the antimelancholic effect of the modified seizure is lower than of the unmodified.

CONCLUSION

Specificity of a therapeutic action gives promise to identify the therapeutic agent. Although many data point at the hypothalamus, it has not been possible up until now to identify the antimelancholic factor of ECT, nor has it been possible to establish the utmost cause or exact pathogenesis of the melancholic syndrome. A hypothesis supported by several observations is that, in melancholia, inherited or acquired deficiencies in monoaminergic tramission disturb the release of hypothalamic peptides with behavioral effects. ECT and antidepressive drugs may exert their antimelancholic effects by restoring aminergic transmission at which hypothalamic function is normalized.[27]

Until we have more exact knowledge of the mechanism of action, ECT should be used with the goal to produce the antimelancholic effect in as pure a culture as possible—free from unspecific organic side effects. When we have got that knowledge, the antimelancholic treatment par preference will probably no longer be ECT.

REFERENCES

1. CRONHOLM, B. & L. MOLANDER. 1957. Memory disturbances after electroconvulsive therapy. I. Conditions 6 hours after electroshock treatment. Acta Psychiatr. Scand. **32:** 280–306.
2. KIRSTEIN, L. & J.-O. OTTOSSON. 1960. Experimental studies of electroencephalographic changes following electroconvulsive therapy. Acta Psychiatr. Scand. Suppl. **145:** 49–68.
3. CRONHOLM, B. & J.-O. OTTOSSON. 1960. Experimental studies of the therapeutic action of electroconvulsive therapy in endogenous depression. Acta Psychiatr. Scand. Suppl. **145:** 69–101.

4. OTTOSSON, J.-O. 1960. Experimental studies of memory impairment after electroconvulsive therapy. Acta Psychiatr. Scand. Suppl. **145:** 103–131.
5. CRONHOLM, B. & J.-O. OTTOSSON. 1961. Memory functions in endogenous depression. Before and after electroconvulsive therapy. Arch. Gen. Psychiatry **5:** 193–199.
6. OTTOSSON, J.-O. 1968. Memory disturbance after ECT: a major or minor side effect? Excerpta Med. Int. Congr. Ser. Psychosom. Med. **124:** 161–168.
7. BARBIZET, J. 1963. Defect of memorizing of hippocampal–mamillary origin: a review. J. Neurol. Neurosurg. Psychiatry **26:** 127–135.
8. LIBERSON, W. T. 1953. Current evaluation of electric convulsive therapy. Correlation of the parameters of electric current with physiologic and psychologic changes. Res. Publ. Assoc. Res. Nerv. Ment. Dis. **31:** 199–231.
9. VALENTINE, M., K. M. G. KEDDIE & D. DUNNE. 1968. A comparison of techniques in electro-convulsive therapy. Br. J. Psychiatry **114:** 989–996.
10. WEAVER, L., C. RAVARIS, S. RUSH & R. PAANANEN. 1974. Stimulus parameters in electroconvulsive shock. J. Psychiatr. Res. **10:** 271–281.
11. D'ELIA, G. & H. RAOTMA. 1975. Is unilateral ECT less effective than bilateral ECT? Br. J. Psychiatry **126:** 83–89.
12. HESHE, J., E. RÖDER & A. THEILGAARD. 1978. Unilateral and bilateral ECT. Acta Psychiatr. Scand. Suppl. **275.**
13. INGLIS, J. 1970. Shock, surgery and cerebral asymmetry. Br. J. Psychiatry **117:** 143–148.
14. D'ELIA, G. 1976. Memory changes after unilateral electroconvulsive therapy with different electrode positions. Cortex **12:** 280–289.
15. WEAVER, L., R. WILLIAMS & S. RUSH. 1976. Current density in bilateral and unilateral ECT. Biol. Psychiatry **11:** 303–312.
16. D'ELIA, G., S. LORENTZSON, H. RAOTMA & K. WIDEPALM. 1976. Comparison of unilateral dominant and non-dominant ECT, on verbal and non-verbal memory. Acta Psychiatr. Scand. **53:** 85–94.
17. LAURELL, B., Ed. 1970. Fluorothyl convulsive therapy. Acta Psychiatr. Scand. Suppl. **213:** 1–79.
18. LIBERSON, W. T. & J. G. CADILHAC. 1953. Electroshock and rhinencephalic seizure states. Confin. Neurol. **13:** 278–286.
19. BERLYNE, N. & M. STRACHAN. 1968. Neuropsychiatric sequelae of attempted hanging. Br. J. Psychiatry **114:** 411–422.
20. BRODERSEN, P., O. B. PAULSON, T. G. BOLWIG, Z. E. ROGON, O. J. RAFAELSEN & N. A. LASSEN. 1973. Cerebral hyperemia in electrically induced epileptic seizures. Arch. Neurol. **28:** 334–338.
21. GALIN, D. 1964. Implications for psychiatry of left and right cerebral specialization. A neurophysiological context for unconscious processes. Arch. Gen. Psychiatry **31:** 572–583.
22. HALLIDAY, A. M., K. DAVISON, M. W. BROWNE & L. C. KREEGER. 1968. A comparison of the effects on depression and memory of bilateral ECT and unilateral ECT to the dominant and non-dominant hemispheres. Br. J. Psychiatry **114:** 997–1012.
23. OTTOSSON, J.-O. 1960. Effects of lidocaine on the seizure discharge in electroconvulsive therapy. Acta Psychiatr. Scand. Suppl. **145:** 7–32.
24. OTTOSSON, J.-O. 1962. Seizure characteristics and therapeutic efficiency in electroconvulsive therapy: an analysis of the antidepressive efficiency of grand mal and lidocaine-modified seizures. J. Nerv. Ment. Dis. **135:** 239–251.
25. ROTH, M. 1951. Changes in the EEG under barbiturate anaesthesia produced by electro-convulsive treatment and their significance for the theory of ECT action. EEG Clin. Neurophysiol. **3:** 261–280.
26. ROTH, M., D. W. K. KAY, J. SHAW & J. GREEN. 1957. Prognosis and pentothal induced electroencephalographic changes in electro-convulsive treatment. EEG Clin. Neurophysiol. **9:** 225–237.
27. FINK, M. & J.-O. OTTOSSON. 1980. A theory of convulsive therapy in endogenous depression: significance of hypothalamic functions. Psychiatry Res. **2:** 49–61.

Neurochemical Mechanisms of Mood Stabilization

Focus on Electroconvulsive Therapy

BERNARD LERER AND BARUCH SHAPIRA

Jerusalem Mental Health Center
Post Office Box 140
Jerusalem, Israel

The possible neurochemical bases of abnormal mood states have been a central focus of interest in biological psychiatry for over three decades. The major input of research data into this area has been from preclinical studies on the mechanism of action of mood-stabilizing treatments, particularly antidepressants. Observed effects of such treatments on neurochemical parameters in rodent brain have formed the basis for most of the major hypotheses regarding the pathogenesis of affective disorders and their biological treatment. The most widely studied of these theories are the catecholamine,[1,2] indoleamine,[3,4] and cholinergic[5] hypotheses and theories that suggest an interplay between the activity of two or more neurotransmitters such as noradrenaline (NA) and serotonin[6] or NA and acetylcholine.[7]

The neurochemical mechanisms that underlie as effective an antidepressant treatment as electroconvulsive therapy (ECT) have an important bearing on the scientific basis of theories of affective disorder and mood stabilization. The fact that ECT is devoid of pharmacodynamic interactions, which complicate studies with chemical antidepressants, lends additional significance to its observed central effects. Furthermore, ECT is effective in alleviating manic as well as depressive symptoms[8] and may also prevent affective relapses when administered prophylactically.[9] This bidirectional clinical spectrum presents unique opportunities for interpreting neurochemical findings but also demands caution in focusing too narrowly on a single mechanism of action. Parallels and contrasts in the basic mechanisms of ECT, tricyclic antidepressants (TCA), monoamine oxidase inhibitors (MAOI), and lithium have therefore assumed considerable importance.

Other papers in this volume deal in a more specific fashion with the neurochemical and functional effects of repeated electroconvulsive shock (ECS) on brain noradrenergic, serotonergic, γ-aminobutyric acid (GABA)-ergic, neuropeptide, and cholinergic systems. The purpose of the present paper is to review relevant findings in the context of some of the major neurochemical theories of affective disorder, to consider the extent to which observed effects of ECS provide critical support for these theories, and to outline potential strategies for future research.

THE CATECHOLAMINE HYPOTHESIS

The postulated association between disturbed noradrenergic neurotransmission and abnormal mood[1,2] has been one of the seminal theories of biological psychiatry and has had a major heuristic impact on research in this area. The original hypotheses were based on the observation that drugs (e.g., TCA and MAOI) that enhance availability of NA at central synapses alleviate depression, whereas drugs (e.g., reserpine) that deplete NA may induce depressive states. A corollary to this hypothesis was that manic states are associated with a relative excess of NA or abnormally enhanced noradrenergic neurotransmission.

Intensive research in affectively disturbed or euthymic patients with unipolar and bipolar affective disorder has yielded little definitive clinical evidence for these postulated abnormalities (e.g., Reference 10). At the same time, a shift in emphasis from neurotransmitter levels and turnover to pre- and postsynaptic receptors has been brought about by further preclinical studies with antidepressant agents. Vetulani and Sulser demonstrated that chronic but not acute TCA, MAOI, and ECS administration reduced NA-sensitive adenylate cyclase activity in rat limbic forebrain.[11] Cortical beta-adrenergic receptor number has been shown by a number of groups to be similarly reduced following chronic antidepressant and ECS administration to rodents (e.g., References 12 and 13). These findings are of considerable importance in that they are induced by chronic treatment and follow a time course that parallels clinically observed antidepressant effects in humans. It has therefore been hypothesized that depressive states may be associated with supersensitivity of postsynaptic beta-adrenergic receptors and that induction of receptor subsensitivity, even by agents that do not appreciably affect NA turnover, may underlie clinical antidepressant effects.[11]

Preclinical findings with regard to repeated ECS administration are clearly compatible with both the original catecholamine hypothesis and its revised form. Repeated ECS has been shown to enhance synthesis and utilization of NA in rat brain,[14] to enhance the activity of tyrosine hydroxylase, the rate-limiting enzyme in catecholamine biosynthesis,[15] and to reduce the uptake of NA into synaptosomal preparations.[16] Although small in magnitude, all these effects would result in enhanced synaptic availability of the neurotransmitter. Postsynaptic receptor effects of repeated ECS are in line with those of repeated TCA administration, and the observed reductions in beta-adrenoceptor number and beta-adrenoceptor-linked adenylate cyclase activity are of a similar order of magnitude.[11,13,17] Furthermore, beta-adrenoceptor down regulation is also induced by ECS administered according to a spaced paradigm paralleling clinical ECT[18] and is persistent up to seven days following the last treatment.[19] Repeated ECS also reverses beta-adrenoceptor supersensitivity induced by reserpine treatment.[19] Effects of repeated ECS on presynaptic alpha-2 adrenergic receptors, which putatively inhibit NA release, have been studied by functional,[20] behavioral,[21] and biochemical methodologies.[21,22] Findings from all these studies indicate presynaptic alpha-2 adrenoceptor subsensitivity after chronic ECS and therefore consistence with reduced inhibition of NA release.

Thus, preclinical studies with repeated ECS support the suggestion that depressed mood is alleviated by treatments that enhance NA availability and reduce postsynaptic beta-adrenoceptor number and function. Critical evidence that these processes are of therapeutic importance in depressed patients treated with ECT is, however, still conspicuously lacking. In part, this deficiency is due to the lack of appropriate research strategies for studying central noradrenergic function in humans. Studies of the NA metabolite MHPG in cerebrospinal fluid have, however, yielded inconsistent results.[23] Studies of adrenergic receptor number and function on peripheral blood cells may, however, yield important clues as to central effects. Smith *et al.* have demonstrated that both antidepressants and ECT reduce radioligand binding to alpha-2 receptors in platelets,[24] which is in line with functional changes in these receptors reported in rat brain following repeated ECS (see above). Neuroendocrine strategies directly referable to central beta-adrenoceptor function are, however, still lacking; one study employing clonidine-induced growth hormone secretion showed no effect for ECT but is referable to postsynaptic alpha-2 adrenoceptors rather than beta-adrenoceptors.[25]

Thus, in regard to the catecholamine hypothesis, both ECT and other antidepressant treatments await confirmatory human evidence before promising preclinical findings can be regarded as definitely established.

INDOLEAMINE HYPOTHESIS

The original serotonin hypothesis of affective disorders was based on indirect evidence derived from studies on the effect of TCA on serotonin uptake and turnover.[3,4] A selective deficiency of brain serotonin in depression was postulated. This suggestion has since been supported by a number of converging lines of evidence derived from human studies. Levels of serotonin or its metabolites have been found to be reduced in postmortem brain specimens from suicides and in the cerebrospinal fluid (CSF) of some depressed patients.[26] Reduced [^{3}H]imipramine binding[27] and increased serotonin binding sites of the 5-hydroxytryptamine (5-HT_2) subtype[28] have been reported postmortem in suicide brains. Reductions in serotonin uptake in platelets of depressed patients[29] have been reported and linked to reduced numbers of platelet [^{3}H]imipramine binding sites.[30] Parachlorophenylalanine, a drug that decreases serotonin synthesis, has been shown to reverse the antidepressant effects of imipramine.[31] Conversely, serotonin precursors such as tryptophan and 5-hydroxytryptophan have been shown to have antidepressant effects, alone[32] or in combination with antidepressant drugs.[33]

ECS effects on serotonin synthesis and turnover in rodent brain are inconsistent; while single ECS enhances these parameters,[34] repeated treatments have yielded results that suggest no change.[35] However, the effects of ECS on serotonergic receptors in rat brain suggest that chronic administration of the treatment may correct a relative serotonergic deficit in depression. Both the functional activity and binding characteristics of postsynaptic serotonin receptors are up regulated by repeated ECS administration. Behavioral supersensitivity has been demonstrated using pharmacological manipulations that stimulate central serotonin receptors (e.g., tranylcypromine + L-tryptophan or serotonin agonists such as quipazine).[35,36] Repeated ECS has also been shown to enhance serotonin-mediated head twitch in mice[37] and hyperthermic responses in heat-adapted rats.[38] Although radioligand binding to receptors of the 5-HT_1 subtype is unchanged by repeated ECS, up regulation of [^{3}H]spiperone binding to 5-HT_2 receptors in the cerebral cortex has been consistently demonstrated.[38,39] It has been suggested that most of the stimulatory serotonergic effects, such as those enhanced by ECS, are mediated via 5-HT_2 receptors.[40] Up regulation of [^{3}H]spiperone-labeled 5-HT_2 receptor sites by ECS may therefore represent the biochemical correlate of ECS-enhanced, serotonergically mediated responses.[41] CPP (3 chlorophenylpiperazine) induced hypothermia, an inhibitory serotonergic response putatively mediated via 5-HT_1 receptors, is reported unchanged by ECS, matching the lack of effect of ECS on radioligand binding to this serotonin receptor subtype.[42]

While chronically administered ECS has been found to up regulate serotonin receptors of the 5-HT_2 subtype, antidepressant treatments other than ECS reduce 5-HT_2 receptor number,[39] thus complicating interpretation of this finding. The reported down regulation of 5-HT_2 receptor density by tricyclic antidepressants is not, however, paralleled by functional inhibition. On the contrary, as reported for ECS, enhanced serotonergic behavioral and electrophysiological responses have been reported following chronic tricyclic antidepressant administration.[43,44]

An explanation for this discrepancy is not immediately apparent. However, human studies that have examined the effects of antidepressants and ECT on neuroendocrine parameters reflecting central serotonergic function also suggest up rather than down regulation. Coppen *et al.* have shown that the prolactin (PRL) response to thyrotropin releasing hormone (TRH), which appears to be serotonergically mediated, is potentiated by ECT.[45] More recently, Heninger *et al.* demonstrated a marked blunting of the maximal PRL response to intravenous tryptophan in depressed patients compared to healthy controls.[46] In a further study, Charney *et al.* reported that chronic administration of both desipramine and amitriptyline significantly increased the serum PRL response to tryptophan.[47] These findings support the hypothesis that central serotonergic function is reduced in depressed patients and suggest that TCA therapy is associated with an up regulation of central serotonin receptor sensitivity, as suggested by behavioral and electrophysiological studies in rats, and not with a reduction in central serotonin receptor sensitivity, as suggested by radioligand binding studies (see above). The effect of ECT on the plasma PRL response to intravenous tryptophan remains to be evaluated. Peripheral strategies including serotonin receptors on blood platelets, platelet imipramine binding, and platelet serotonin uptake all remain to be definitely investigated in depressed patients following ECT administration.

NORADRENALINE-SEROTONIN INTERACTIONS: "PERMISSIVE" OR "BALANCE" HYPOTHESES

It is perhaps remarkable that "single amine" hypotheses have been so widely accepted by researchers studying the chemical pathogenesis of affective disorders. This approach presupposes that neurotransmitters function in an independent fashion and also ignores the fact that almost all the major antidepressant treatments affect multiple rather than single systems. An increasing number of studies are now seeking to define the interrelationship between brain noradrenergic and serotonergic function and the role of each system in modulating and influencing antidepressant- and ECS-induced changes in the other.

In one such study, Janowsky *et al.* demonstrated that lesioning of the raphe nuclei with the serotonergic neurotoxin 5.7-dihydroxytryptamine (5.7-DHT) attenuated the reduction in cortical beta-adrenoceptor binding induced by the tricyclic antidepressant desipramine.[48] The role of brain NA pathways in ECS-induced alterations in brain serotonergic function has been elegantly studied by Green and colleagues.[49,50] Using localized injections of 6-hydroxydopamine, rats were bilaterally lesioned in the dorsal and ventral NA bundles and locus coeruleus.[49] This destruction did not alter the locomotor responsiveness of the animals to the serotonin agonist quipazine. It did, however, prevent the development of enhanced locomotor responses to quipazine after five alternate-day ECS over 10 days. These findings are supported by additional data from Green *et al.* showing that inhibition of NA synthesis by alpha-methyl-*p*-tyrosine also abolished the enhancement of serotonin-mediated behaviors induced by ECS.[50] Green and Deakin concluded that changes that occur in the NA system following ECS are essential to the development of behavioral supersensitivity of serotonin receptors.[49]

These findings have an important bearing upon theories of affective disorder that take into account an interaction between brain NA and serotonergic function. The so-called permissive hypothesis of affective disorder suggests that a deficit in cerebral indoleaminergic neurotransmission "permits" both the depressive and manic phases of affective disorder but is insufficient for its cause.[6] Alterations in central NA function in the context of indoleamine deficiency would then determine the quality of the affective episode. While these formulations may be overly simplistic, an approach to ECT mechanisms that takes into account possible interactions between the two major brain amines as well as other central neurotransmitters and neuromodulators is clearly indicated. Thus, preclinical studies should ideally examine both parameters in the models studied. Clinical studies should focus on peripheral and central strategies reflecting neurotransmitter levels and receptor function referable to both systems in the same patients. Furthermore, studies on the antimanic and prophylactic mechanisms of ECT are strongly indicated, ideally in parallel with studies on other treatments (such as lithium and possibly carbamazepine) that also have a bidirectional clinical spectrum.

CHOLINERGIC AND NORADRENERGIC-CHOLINERGIC BALANCE HYPOTHESES

In contrast to the catecholamine and indoleamine hypotheses of affective disorder, theories implicating acetylcholine in abnormal mood states have been primarily derived from clinical observations rather than preclinical findings on the neurochemical effects of mood-stabilizing treatments. A number of reports, in normals, depressives, and manics, indicate that cholinesterase inhibitors exert anergic-inhibitory effects in man (e.g., References 51 and 52), inducing lethargy, tiredness, psychomotor retardation, and social withdrawal. These effects were demonstrated by Janowsky and colleagues to be present in spite of administration of a peripherally acting anticholinergic agent, were not induced by the peripheral cholinesterase inhibitor neostigmine, and were inhibited by the centrally acting anticholinergic atropine.[53,54] Antimanic effects of the irreversible cholinesterase inhibitor diisopropylfluorophosphate (DFP) were reported by Rowntree *et al.*[51] Janowsky *et al.* subsequently reported a rapid reduction in manic symptoms following administration of the centrally acting cholinesterase inhibitor physostigmine (1–4 mg intravenously).[53] More recent studies have suggested that cholinergic supersensitivity may be a trait marker for depressive illness. Thus, Sitaram and Gillin demonstrated accelerated rapid eye movement (REM) sleep induction by cholinomimetic agents in untreated and also in recovered depressed patients.[5]

ECS induces changes in brain cholinergic systems that are compatible with acute release of acetylcholine during the seizure. Ictal and postictal reductions in brain acetylcholine levels have been reported (e.g., References 55 and 56) as well as increases in choline acetyltransferase activity.[56] Acute release of acetylcholine during seizures is supported by human data showing increased CSF acetylcholine levels following pentyleneterrazol-induced or epileptic seizures and evidence for cholinergically related EEG slowing following ECT.[57]

Lerer and colleagues have shown that repeated but not single ECS induces a 13–15% reduction in [^{3}H]quinuclidinyl benzilate ([^{3}H]QNB) labeled muscarinic cholinergic receptors in rat cerebral cortex.[58–60] Lerer *et al.* also demonstrated that concurrent ECS administration reversed the significant increase in cortical [^{3}H]QNB binding caused by chronic atropine administration.[58] Earlier, Dashieff *et al.* had found a 19–25% reduction in [^{3}H]QNB binding in the hippocampus following repeated ECS.[61] A possible functional correlate of ECS-induced reductions in muscarinic receptor binding had been demonstrated by Green *et al.*[62] and was confirmed by Stanley and Lerer.[63] Repeated ECS was shown by both groups to induce subsensitive cataleptic responses to the muscarinic agonist pilocarpine. Further studies are, however, needed to more clearly define the nature of the muscarinic receptor binding sites that are influenced by repeated ECS.

Down regulation of brain muscarinic receptors by ECT is potentially relevant to the suggestion that depressive states are associated with supersensitivity of brain cholinergic systems. Reversal of cholinergic supersensitivity, as demonstrated preclinically by Lerer *et al.*,[58] might thus explain the antidepressant action of the treatment. An explanation of how ECT acts in mania is not, however, as readily forthcoming in this context. A similar discrepancy exists in the case of lithium, which has been shown to enhance functional responses to cholinergic agents.[64] This effect might explain the antimanic action of lithium but not its antidepressant effect.

There is little evidence to date regarding ECT effects on cholinergic receptor systems in man. Potential neuroendocrine challenges and peripheral biochemical marker strategies have not been applied to this question, and physiological responses reflecting central cholinergic function have yet to be evaluated following ECT.[65] For example, it is not known how supersensitive REM sleep response to cholinergic agonists[5] is affected by ECT in depressed patients. It also remains to be investigated whether behavioral responses to the depressogenic effects of cholinomimetics are altered by ECT administration. Further research on these issues would answer critical questions relevant not only to the basic mechanisms of ECT but to theories suggesting a role for acetylcholine or cholinergic-noradrenergic balance in the pathogenesis of affective disorders.

OTHER THEORIES AND FINDINGS

The neurochemical effects of ECS are not limited to NA, serotonin, and acetylcholine, as is abundantly clear from this volume and from other reviews on the topic (e.g., References 66 and 67).

1. Although less closely linked to the putative chemical pathogenesis of affective disorders, brain dopamine (DA) systems are functionally affected by repeated ECS.[66,68] The finding that repeated ECS enhances the functional sensitivity of striatal DA receptors has had an important clinical correlate in the treatment of Parkinson's disease.[68] Human studies utilizing growth hormone release by DA agonists as a measure of DA receptor sensitivity have yielded mixed results.[69,70] However, other potential biochemical and psychophysiological strategies remain to be explored.[65]
2. ECS has significant effects on brain GABA systems with increased GABA concentrations and inhibition of GABA synthesis, suggesting enhanced GABA function.[71] GABA-ergic effects of ECT may be related to the increase in seizure threshold induced by ECT.[71] Altered GABA function may also play a role in ECT effects on brain NA and serotonin.[72]
3. ECS has been shown to induce a spectrum of opiatelike responses in rats which are attenuated by pretreatment with an opiate antagonist. Chronic ECS sensitizes rats to opioid effects and enhances opioid receptor binding.[73] These findings suggest activation of endogenous opioid systems by ECS and are supported by human studies showing increased plasma beta-endorphin levels following ECT.[74] If putative antidepressant effects of opioids are confirmed, an antidepressant mechanism of ECT via endogenous opioid systems would be plausible.

CONCLUSIONS

This paper has focused on the neurochemical effects of ECT in the noradrenergic, serotonergic, and cholinergic systems and has attempted to relate relevant findings to theories of affective disorder implicating these neurotransmitters. A wealth of data are available on the effects of ECT on these systems, particularly on the basis of animal studies. Such studies are likely to generate further data as newer techniques in neurochemistry, neuropharmacology, and neurophysiology are applied to ECT mechanisms. The phylogenetic gap between rodents and humans is an obvious shortcoming in attempting to interpret these findings. To this may be added the fact that normal animals have been studied while ECT is administered to depressed or otherwise ill patients. Studies employing pharmacological models of "pathological" neurotransmitter and receptor states (e.g., References 58 and 19) are therefore of considerable importance. Studies employing behavioral models of depression (cf. McKinney, this volume) are a further step in this direction and can provide the opportunity to examine directly ECS effects on the neurochemical correlates of abnormal mood states.

As has been stressed throughout this paper, human studies seeking support for a relationship between ECS effects in animals and the clinical efficacy of the treatment in humans represent a critical but relatively unexplored strategy. Further development of brain imaging techniques to permit *in vivo* receptor binding studies will represent a quantum jump in this direction. In the final analysis, a close interaction between basic and clinically oriented researchers holds the key to understanding the neurochemical mechanisms that underlie abnormal mood states and their correction by ECT and other biological treatments.

REFERENCES

1. Schildkraut, J. J. 1965. The catecholamine hypothesis of affective disorders: a review of supporting evidence. Am. J. Psychiatry **122:** 509–522.
2. Bunney, W. E., Jr. & J. M. Davis. 1965. Norepinephrine in depressive reactions. Arch. Gen. Psychiatry **13:** 483–494.
3. Lapin, I. P. & G. F. Oksenkrug. 1969. Intensification of the central serotonergic processes as a possible determinant of the thymoleptic effect. Lancet **1:** 132–136.
4. Coppen, A., A. J. Prange, Jr., P. C. Whybrow & R. Noguera. 1972. Abnormalities of indoleamines in affective disorders. Arch. Gen. Psychiatry **26:** 474–478.
5. Sitaram, N. & J. C. Gillin. 1980. Development and use of pharmacological probes of the CNS in man: evidence of cholinergic abnormality in primary affective illness. Biol. Psychiatry **15:** 925–955.
6. Prange, A. J., Jr., I. C. Wilson, C. W. Lynn, L. B. Alltop & R. A. Stikeleather. 1974. L-Tryptophan in mania: contribution to a permissive hypothesis of affective disorders. Arch. Gen. Psychiatry **30:** 56–62.
7. Janowsky, D. S., M. K. El-Yousef, J. M. Davis & H. J. Sekerke. 1972. A cholinergic-adrenergic hypothesis of mania and depression. Lancet **ii:** 6732–6735.
8. Fink, M. 1979. Convulsive Therapy: Theory and Practice. Raven Press. New York, N.Y.
9. Stevenson, G. H. & J. J. Geoghegan. 1951. Prophylactic electroshock. Am. J. Psychiatry **107:** 743–748.
10. Charney, D. S., D. Menkes & G. R. Heninger. 1984. Receptor sensitivity and the mechanism of action of antidepressant treatment. Arch. Gen. Psychiatry **41:** 398–402.
11. Vetulani, J. & F. Sulser. 1975. Action of various antidepressant treatments reduces reactivity of noradrenergic cyclic AMP-generating system in limbic forebrain. Nature **27:** 495–496.
12. Banerjee, L. P., L. S. Kung, S. T. Riggi & S. K. Chanda. 1977. Development of beta-adrenergic receptor subsensitivity by antidepressants. Nature **268:** 455–456.
13. Bergstrom, D. A. & K. J. Kellar. 1979. Effect of electroconvulsive shock on monoaminergic receptor binding sites in rat brain. Nature **278:** 464–466.
14. Kety, S. S., F. Javoy, A.-M. Thierry, L. Julou & J. Glowinski. 1967. A sustained effect of electroconvulsive shock on the turnover of norepinephrine in the central nervous system of rat. Proc. Nat. Acad. Sci. USA **58:** 1249–1254.
15. Musacchio, J. M., L. Julou, S. S. Kety & J. Glowinski. 1969. Increase in rat brain tyrosine hydroxylase activity produced by electroconvulsive shock. Proc. Nat. Acad. Sci. USA **63:** 1117–1119.

16. Hendley, E. D. & B. L. Welch. 1975. Electroconvulsive shock: sustained decrease in norepinephrine uptake affinity in a reserpine model of depression. Life Sci. **16:** 45–54.
17. Pandey, G. N., W. J. Heinze, B. D. Brown & J. M. Davis. 1979. Electroconvulsive shock treatment decreases beta-adrenergic receptor sensitivity in rat brain. Nature **280:** 234–235.
18. Belmaker, R. H., B. Lerer, J. Bannet & B. Birmaher. 1982. The effect of repeated electroconvulsive shock at a clinically equivalent schedule on rat cortical adrenoceptors. J. Pharm. Pharmacol. **34:** 275.
19. Kellar, K. J., C. S. Cascio, D. A. Bergstrom, J. A. Butler & P. Iadarola. 1981. Electroconvulsive shock and reserpine: effects on beta-adrenergic receptors in rat brain. J. Neurochem. **37:** 830–836.
20. Pilc, A. & J. Vetulani. 1982. Depression by chronic electroconvulsive treatment of clonidine hypothermia and ^{3}H-clonidine binding to rat cortical membranes. Eur. J. Pharmacol. **80:** 109–113.
21. Heal, D. J., H. Akagi, J. M. Bowdler & A. R. Green. 1981. Repeated electroconvulsive shock attenuates clonidine-induced hypoactivity in rodents. Eur. J. Pharmacol. **75:** 231–237.
22. Ebstein, R. P., B. Lerer, M. Shlaufman & R. H. Belmaker. 1983. The effect of repeated electroconvulsive shock treatment and chronic lithium feeding on the release of norepinephrine from rat cortical vesicular preparations. Cell. Mol. Neurobiol. **3:** 191–201.
23. Lerer, B. & R. H. Belmaker. 1982. Receptors and the mechanism of action of ECT. Biol. Psychiatry **17:** 497–511.
24. Smith, C. B., P. J. Hollingsworth, J. A. Garcia-Sevilla & P. Z. Athanasios. 1983. Platelet alpha$_2$ adrenoreceptors are decreased in number after antidepressant therapy. Prog. Neuro-Psychopharmacol. Biol. Psychiatry **7:** 241–247.
25. Checkley, S. A., B. S. Meldrum & J. McWilliam. 1983. Neuroendocrine studies of the mechanism of action of ECT. *In* ECT: Basic Mechanisms. B. Lerer, R. D. Weiner & R. H. Belmaker, Eds.: 101–106. John Libbey. London, England.
26. Murphy, D. L., I. Campbell & J. L. Costa. 1978. Current status of the indoleamine hypothesis of affective disorders. *In* Psychopharmacology: a Generation of Progress. M. A. Lipton, A. DiMascio & K. F. Killam, Eds.: 1235–1247. Raven Press. New York, N.Y.
27. Stanley, M., J. Virgilio & S. Gershon. 1982. Tritiated imipramine binding sites are decreased in frontal cortex of suicides. Science **216:** 1337–1339.
28. Stanley, M. & J. J. Mann. 1983. Serotonin alpha binding sites are increased in the frontal cortex of suicide victims. Lancet **i:** 214–216.
29. Tuomisto, J. & E. Tukianen. 1976. Decreased uptake of 5-hydroxytryptamine in blood platelets from depressed patients. Nature **262:** 596–598.
30. Briley, M. S., S. Z. Langer, R. Raisman, D. Sechter & E. Zarifian. 1980. Tritiated imipramine binding sites are decreased in platelets of untreated depressed patients. Science **209:** 303–305.
31. Shopsin, B., E. Friedman & S. Gershon. 1974. Parachlorophenylalanine reversal of tranylcypromine effects in depressed patients. Arch. Gen. Psychiatry **33:** 811–819.
32. Van Praag, H. M. 1981. Management of depression with serotonin precursors. Biol. Psychiatry **16:** 290–310.
33. Walinder, J., A. Skott, A. Carlson, A. Nagy & B.-E. Roos. 1976. Potentiation of the antidepressant action of clomipramine by tryptophan. Arch. Gen. Psychiatry **33:** 1384–1389.
34. Engel, J., L. C. F. Hanson & B.-E. Roos. 1971. Effect of electroshock on 5-HT metabolism in rat brain. Psychopharmacologia **20:** 197–200.
35. Evans, J. P. M., D. G. Grahame-Smith, A. R. Green & A. F. C. Tordoff. 1976. Electroconvulsive shock increases the behavioral responses of rats to brain 5-hydroxytryptamine stimulation and central nervous system stimulant drugs. Br. J. Pharmacol. **56:** 193–199.
36. Green, A. R., M. R. Bloomfield, C. K. Atterwill & D. W. Costain. 1979. Electroconvulsive shock reduces the cataleptogenic effects of both haloperidol and arecoline in rats. Neuropharmacology **18:** 447–451.

37. Lebrecht, U. & J. Z. Nowak. 1980. Effect of single and repeated electroconvulsive shock on serotonergic system in rat brain. II. Behavioral studies. Neuropharmacology **19:** 1055–1061.
38. Vetulani, J., U. Lebrecht & A. Pilc. 1981. Enhancement of responsiveness of the central serotonergic system and serotonin-2 receptor density in rat frontal cortex by electroconvulsive treatment. Eur. J. Pharmacol. **76:** 81–85.
39. Kellar, K. J., C. S. Cascop, J. A. Butler & R. N. Kurtzke. 1981. Differential effects of electroconvulsive shock and antidepressant drugs on serotonin-2 receptors in rat brain. Eur. J. Pharmacol. **69:** 515–518.
40. Peroutka, S. J., R. M. Lebovitz & S. H. Snyder. 1981. Two distinct central serotonin receptors with different physiological functions. Science **212:** 827–829.
41. Green, A. R., P. Johnson & V. L. Nimgaonkar. 1983. Increased 5-HT receptor number in brain as a probable explanation for the enhanced 5-hydroxytryptamine-mediated behaviour following repeated electroconvulsive shock administration to rats. Br. J. Pharmacol. **80:** 173–177.
42. Vetulani, J. 1983. Changes in responsiveness of central aminergic structures after chronic ECS. *In* ECT: Basic Mechanisms. B. Lerer, R. D. Weiner & R. H. Belmaker, Eds.: 33–45. John Libbey. London, England.
43. Friedman, E. & A. Dallob. 1979. Enhanced serotonin receptor activity after chronic treatment with imipramine or amitriptyline. Commun. Psychopharmacol. **3:** 89–92.
44. deMontigny, C. & G. K. Aghajanian. 1978. Tricyclic antidepressants: long-term treatment increases responsivity of rat forebrain neurons to serotonin. Science **202:** 1303–1306.
45. Coppen, A., V. A. Rao, M. Bishop, M. T. Abou-Saleh & K. Wood. 1980. Neuroendocrine studies in affective disorder. II. Plasma thyroid stimulating hormone response to thyrotropin-releasing hormone in affective disorders: effect of ECT. J. Affect. Disord. **2:** 317–320.
46. Heninger, G. R., D. S. Charney & D. E. Sternberg. 1984. Serotonergic function in depression: prolactin response to intravenous tryptophan in depressed patients and healthy subjects. Arch. Gen. Psychiatry **41:** 398–402.
47. Charney, D. S., G. R. Heninger & D. E. Sternberg. 1984. Serotonin function and the mechanism of action of antidepressant treatment: effects of amitriptyline and desimipramine. Arch. Gen. Psychiatry **41:** 359–365.
48. Janowsky, A., O. Fumihiko, O. H. Manier, C. D. Applegate, F. Sulser & L. R. Steranka. 1982. Role of serotonergic input in the regulation of the beta-adrenergic receptor-coupled adenylate cyclase adenylate cyclase system. Science **218:** 900–901.
49. Green, A. R. & J. F. W. Deakin. 1980. Depletion of brain noradrenaline prevents electroconvulsive shock induced enhancement of 5-hydroxytryptamine and dopamine mediated behavior. Nature **285:** 232–233.
50. Green, A. R., D. W. Costain & J. F. W. Deakin. 1980. Enhanced 5-hydroxytryptamine and dopamine-mediated behavioral responses following convulsions. III. The effects of monoamine and agonists and synthesis inhibition on the ability of electroconvulsive shock to enhance responses. Neuropharmacology **19:** 907–914.
51. Rowntree, D. W., S. Neven & A. Wilson. 1950. The effects of diisopropylfluorophosphonate in schizophrenia and manic depressive psychosis. J. Neurol. Neurosurg. Psychiatry **13:** 47–62.
52. Gershon, S. & F. H. Shaw. 1961. Psychiatric sequelae of chronic exposure to organophosphorous insecticides. Lancet **i:** 1371–1374.
53. Janowsky, D. S., J. M. Davis, M. K. El-Yousef & H. J. Sekerke. 1973. Acetylcholine and depression. Psychosom. Med. **35:** 459.
54. Janowsky, D. S., M. K. El-Yousef, J. M. Davis & H. J. Sekerke. 1973. Parasympathetic suppression of manic symptoms by physostigmine. Arch. Gen. Psychiatry **28:** 542–547.
55. Takahashi, R., T. Nasu, T. Tamura & T. Koriya. 1961. Relationship of ammonia and acetylcholine levels to brain excitability. J. Neurochem. **7:** 103–112.
56. Longoni, R., A. Mulas, B. O. Novak, I. M. Pepeu & G. Pepeu. 1976. Effect of single and repeated electroshock applications on brain acetylcholine levels and choline acetyltransferase activity in the rat. Neuropharmacology **15:** 283–286.

57. FINK, M. D. 1966. Cholinergic aspects of convulsive therapy. J. Nerv. Ment. Dis. **142:** 475–484.
58. LERER, B., M. STANLEY, S. DEMETRIOU & S. GERSHON. 1983. Effect of electroconvulsive shock on muscarinic cholinergic receptors in rat cerebral cortex and hippocampus. J. Neurochem. **41:** 1680–1683.
59. LERER, B., M. STANLEY, I. MCINTYRE & H. ALTMAN. 1984. Electroconvulsive shock and brain muscarinic receptors: relationship to anterograde amnesia. Life Sci. **35:** 2659–2664.
60. LERER, B. 1985. Studies on the role of brain cholinergic systems in the therapeutic mechanisms and adverse effects of ECT and lithium. Biol. Psychiatry **20:** 20–40.
61. DASHIEFF, R. M., D. P. SAVAGE & J. O. MCNAMARA. 1982. Seizures down-regulate muscarinic cholinergic receptors in hippocampal formation. Brain Res. **235:** 327–334.
62. GREEN, A. R., D. J. HEAL & D. G. GRAHAME-SMITH. 1977. Further observations on the effect of repeated electroconvulsive shock on behavioral responses of rats produced by increases in the functional activity of brain 5-hydroxytryptamine and dopamine. Psychopharmacology **52:** 195–200.
63. LERER, B. & M. STANLEY. 1985. Effect of chronic lithium on cholinergically-mediated responses and [^{3}H]QNB binding in rat brain. Brain Res. **344:** 211–219.
64. STANLEY, M. & B. LERER. 1985. Electroconvulsive shock and brain cholinergic function: role of striatal muscarinic receptors. Convulsive Ther. **1:** 158–166.
65. LERER, B. & N. SITARAM. 1983. Clinical strategies for evaluating ECT mechanisms: pharmacological, biochemical and psychophysiological approaches. Prog. Neuropsychopharmacol. Biol. Psychiatry **7:** 309–333.
66. GRAHAME-SMITH, D. G. A. R. GREEN & D. W. COSTAIN. 1978. Mechanism of the antidepressant action of electroconvulsive therapy. Lancet **1:** 245–256.
67. LERER, B., R. D. WEINER & R. H. BELMAKER, Eds. 1984. ECT: Basic Mechanisms. John Libbey. London, England.
68. MODIGH, K., J. BALLDIN, E. ERIKSSON, A.-K. GRANERUS & J. WALINDER. 1984. Increased responsiveness of dopamine receptors after ECT: a review of experimental and clinical evidence. *In* ECT: Basic Mechanisms. B. Lerer, R. D. Weiner & R. H. Belmaker, Eds.: 18–27. John Libbey. London, England.
69. COSTAIN, D. W., P. J. COWEN, M. G. GELDER & D. G. GRAHAME-SMITH. 1982. Electroconvulsive therapy and the brain: evidence for increased dopamine-mediated responses. Lancet **ii:** 400–404.
70. CHRISTIE, J. E., L. J. WHALLEY, N. S. BROWN & H. DICK. 1982. Effect of ECT on the neuroendocrine response to apomorphine in severely depressed patients. Br. J. Psychiatry **133:** 416.
71. NUTT, D. J., P. J. COWEN & A. R. GREEN. 1981. Studies on the post-ictal rise in seizure threshold. Eur. J. Pharmacol. **71:** 287–295.
72. GREEN, A. R., P. JOHNSON, J. A. MOUNTFORD & V. L. NIMGAONKAR. 1985. Some anticonvulsant drugs alter monoamine-mediated behaviour in mice in ways similar to electroconvulsive shock; implications for antidepressant therapy. Br. J. Pharmacol. **84:** 337–346.
73. BELENKY, G., F. C. TORTELLA, R. J. HITZEMANN & J. W. HOLADAY. 1984. The role of endorphin systems in the effects of ECS. *In* ECT: Basic Mechanisms. B. Lerer, R. D. Weiner & R. H. Belmaker, Eds.: 89–97. John Libbey. London, England.
74. ALEXOPOULOS, G. S., C. E. INTURRISI, R. LIPMAN, R. FRANCES, J. HAYCOX, J. H. DOUGHERTY & J. ROSSIER. 1983. Plasma immunoreactive beta-endorphin levels in depression. Arch. Gen. Psychiatry **40:** 181–183.

Electroconvulsive Therapy as an Anticonvulsant

Implications for Its Mechanism of Action in Affective Illness

ROBERT M. POST, FRANK PUTNAM, THOMAS W. UHDE, AND SUSAN R. B. WEISS

Biological Psychiatry Branch
National Institute of Mental Health
Building 10, Room 3N212
9000 Rockville Pike
Bethesda, Maryland 20205

INTRODUCTION

The rationale for the introduction of the use of electroconvulsive therapy (ECT) in the treatment of major psychiatric illness contained the latent idea that is the major focus of this manuscript—that ECT may paradoxically be an effective anticonvulsant. Based on the observations of many investigators that there was an inverse relationship between seizures and psychosis, von Meduna introduced convulsive therapy as a potential treatment strategy for major psychiatric illnesses.[1] The use of major motor seizures themselves as an effective treatment modality, particularly for the major affective disorders, obscured the possibility that the repeated seizures might be effective not because of the convulsions but because of their anticonvulsant effects. It has largely been forgotten that ECT has in fact been used to treat seizure disorders and some of their associated behavioral problems[2–3] (also S. Sato, personal communication, 1982). More recently, Sackeim *et al.* have again reported success in the use of ECT as an anticonvulsant for epileptic patients resistant to pharmacotherapy.[6]

In light of our experience that anticonvulsant treatments, particularly carbamazepine, are effective in the treatment of both manic and depressive episodes, we became increasingly interested in the perspective that electroconvulsive shock (ECS) in animals is a potent anticonvulsant.[7,8] Examining the anticonvulsant effects of ECS provides a new conceptual approach to the study of its possible mechanism of action. One can explore similarities and differences between the effects of ECS and psychotropic and anticonvulsant drugs effective in manic-depressive illness[9–14] on biochemistry and behavior. In addition, the anticonvulsant effects of ECS are an easily measurable index of the efficacy of this treatment, so that the time course and mechanisms of effects can be delineated in relationship to biochemistry. Finally, one can use appropriate biochemical and pharmacological dissection to elucidate the possible factors that account for the anticonvulsant effects of ECS as a first step to assessing whether these factors then are important to its effects in affective disorders.

Thus, in this manuscript we review the available data on the anticonvulsant effects of ECS and begin a discussion of these findings and their mechanistic implications. We also briefly review our experience with the effects of more traditional anticonvulsants in manic-depressive illness and the comparative ability of these anticonvulsants to inhibit kindled seizures.

THE ANTICONVULSANT EFFECTS OF ECS ON COMPLETED AMYGDALA-KINDLED SEIZURES

As summarized in TABLE 1, a substantial body of evidence suggests that single or multiple ECS in rats exerts substantial anticonvulsant effects against amygdala-kindled seizures. Babington reported that a single ECS administered up to 120 minutes prior to an amygdala-kindled seizure reduced seizure duration by more than 50% of control.[15] With longer intervals, the effect was less robust. Handforth indicated that multiple ECS administered 12 to 24 hours prior to amygdala-kindled seizures exerted long-lasting anticonvulsant effects for a period of 24–48 hours.[16] In our study, we observed that a single ECS followed by a six-day delay did not significantly affect amygdala-kindled seizures. However, a series of seven once-daily ECS significantly reduced amygdala-kindled seizure durations for up to five days following the termination of ECS. These data are illustrated in FIGURE 1. The top part of the figure indicates that afterdischarge duration in established amygdala-kindled seizures was not significantly affected by either real or sham ECS administered once or for seven consecutive days. In contrast, seizure stage and seizure duration were substantially reduced for five days by the series of seven ECS. The fact that afterdischarge was not significantly affected indicates that the animals were not refractory to further excitatory effects of the amgydala-kindled stimulation, but that the prior chronic ECS treatment was significantly affecting the mechanisms and pathways involved in converting this excitatory process into a full-blown seizure.

TABLE 1. Effects of ECS on Completed Amygdala-Kindled Seizures

	Interval	Type	Seizures	Duration
Babington & Wedeking[15]	15 minutes	Single	↓ ↓ ↓	
	30 minutes	Single	↓ ↓ ↓	
	60 minutes	Single	↓ ↓	
	120 minutes	Single	↓ ↓	
	180 minutes	Single	(↓)	
	240 minutes	Single	(↓)	
Urca & Frenk[26,a]	—		—	
Handforth[16]	12–24 hours	Multiple	↓ ↓ ↓	24–48 hours
Post *et al.*[8]	24 hours	Single (6-day delay)	—	1–5 days
		Multiple (×7)	↓ ↓ ↓	

[a]Eighteen or twenty days of prior ECS had no effect on *development* of kindling.

The paradigm of one ECS followed by a six-day delay in comparison to seven chronic ECS was employed in order to assess the possible effects of dopamine autoreceptor desensitization as a potential mechanism for the effects of ECS on amygdala kindling. Chiodo and Antelman had reported that a single ECS followed by a seven-day delay was as effective as six chronic ECS with a two-day delay in producing dopamine autoreceptor subsensitivity,[17] a mechanism they postulated was important to the antidepressant effects of ECS and tricyclic antidepressants. The fact that a single ECS with a six-day delay in our paradigm was not sufficient to inhibit amygdala kindling suggests that dopamine autoreceptor desensitization is not important, at least to the anticonvulsant mechanisms of ECS.

Anticonvulsants such as carbamazepine, valproic acid, and diazepam are also

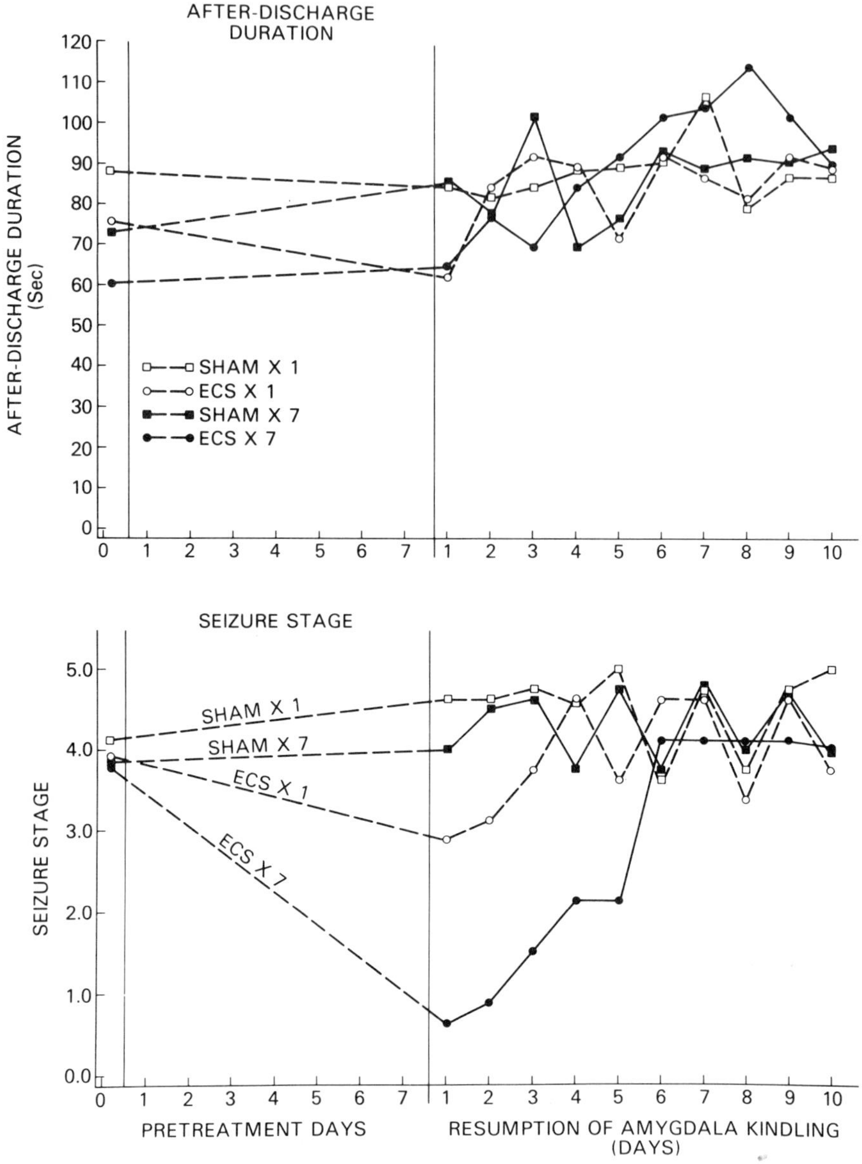

FIGURE 1. Electroconvulsive seizures inhibit amygdala-kindled seizures without affecting afterdischarges. Animals were amygdala kindled until the first stage 3 or 4 seizure was observed. During the next seven days rats received only real or sham electroconvulsive seizures (ECS). Compared with sham ECT controls, seven daily ECS, but not a single ECS followed by a six-day delay, markedly suppressed kindled seizures when amygdala stimulation was resumed ($p < 0.0001$; $F = 3.59$; df = 19,92). Afterdischarge duration was not significantly affected. The suppressive effects of repeated ECS persisted for five days. On day five, kindled seizure stage was significantly reduced ($p < 0.04$; $t = -2.40$; df = 9) as was seizure duration ($p < 0.005$; $t = -3.65$).

highly effective in inhibiting seizure stage and seizure duration, while the afterdischarge component of amygdala-kindled seizures is more difficult to suppress. As revealed in the studies of Albright and Burnham, carbamazepine is the most potent of the anticonvulsants in decreasing amygdala-kindled afterdischarge duration compared to that kindled from the cortex,[18] suggesting that carbamazepine has the best ratio of effects on ability to suppress limbic compared to neocortical afterdischarge excitatory foci. Carbamazepine was able to decrease amygdala afterdischarge duration to 55% of that seen in the cortex, and was followed by the other anticonvulsants in decreasing order of efficacy: valproate (37%), phenobarbital (33%), phenytoin (30%), methsuximide (25%), clonazepam (22%), ethosuximide (14%), and surprisingly last, diazepam (0%). While Ashton and Waugquier[19] and many other studies reviewed elsewhere[13] also found potent anticonvulsant effects of carbamazepine (ED_{50} of 5 mg/kg, intraperitoneally), Albertson *et al.* reported a different rank order of anticonvulsant efficacy to that reviewed above.[20]

In addition to the typical anticonvulsants, Horovitz[21] and Babington[22] reported that the tricyclic antidepressants nortriptyline, amitriptyline, and imipramine significantly suppressed amygdala-kindled seizures. Moreover, a dose of amitriptyline that was not effective acutely, after 14 days of treatment did reduce seizure duration, suggesting some parallelism to the lag in onset of antidepressant effects. Other investigators have replicated some aspects of these findings but not others. For example, Knobloch *et al.* found that the antidepressant amitriptyline acutely inhibited amygdala-kindled seizures better than those kindled from the cortex;[23] neither amitriptyline nor imipramine showed this selective effect following subacute administration. Moreover, as observed by Babington, the antidepressant iprindole did not alter seizures kindled from either site.[22] High doses of mianserin, when given acutely or subacutely, did show selective attenuation of amygdaloid seizures.

In contrast to the dose-related effects of imipramine on amgydala-kindled seizures, Lange *et al.* reported a biphasic effect of imipramine against ECS and pentylene tetrazol seizures in mice.[24] This anticonvulsant effect at low doses and proconvulsant effect at high doses (like that of lidocaine) on "classical" motor seizure models could account for the clinical observations of seizures during tricyclic treatment, even in the face of dose-related anticonvulsant effects on the amygdala-kindled type.

It is noteworthy that Babington and Wedeking found that ECS in the rat produced a greater magnitude and duration of anticonvulsant effects on amygdala-kindled seizures compared to those produced in the septum or sensorimotor cortex.[25] However, the ultimate utility of the amygdala kindling model for assessing potential antidepressant and antimanic effects of somatic treatments requires further study.

EFFECT OF ECS ON THE DEVELOPMENT OF KINDLING

The effects of ECS on the development of kindling are summarized in TABLE 2. Babington found profound effects of ECS administered ½ hour or 20 hours prior to amygdala stimulation. In his series, he also found that ECS administered 24 hours prior to kindling was moderately effective in suppressing the development of seizures; afterdischarges were not measured. We found that ECS administered 6 hours prior to each once-daily amygdala-kindled stimulation using suprathreshold stimulation with 50 Hz biphasic square waves for one second duration completely inhibited the development of amygdala kindling, as illustrated in FIGURE 2. In contrast, ECS administered immediately after amygdala kindling (i.e., 24 hours prior to the next stimulation) was not effective under these conditions. These data are similar to those of Urca and Frenk, who found that ECS five minutes prior to kindling potently suppressed the development of amygdala seizures, while a 24-hour interval was without effect.[26] However, Tsuru *et al.*[27] and Handforth[16] did find that ECS administered 24 hours prior to kindling was effective in suppressing the development of seizures, at least to a mild to moderate extent.

As illustrated in FIGURE 3, when ECS treatment was terminated, amygdala kindling proceeded at a relatively normal rate. These data are consistent with those of Babington,[22] indicating that the ECS appeared to suppress the development of amygdala-kindled seizures but that the process would proceed normally once the ECS was discontinued.

The highly potent effects of ECS in inhibiting the development of amygdala kindling raise the question of the relative efficacy of this approach to that achieved by more traditional anticonvulsant treatments. In fact, there are considerable data that ECS may be a more potent anticonvulsant for amygdala-kindled seizure development

TABLE 2. Effects of ECS on Development of Amygdala Kindling

	Interval between ECS and Kindling	Effect on After Discharges	Effect on Seizures
Babington & Wedeking[15]	0.5 hours	NA[a]	↓ ↓ ↓
	20 hours	NA	↓ ↓ ↓
	24 hours	NA	↓ ↓
Post *et al.*[7] and	6 hours	—	↓ ↓ ↓
Post *et al.*[8]	24 hours (~1 minute post)	—	—
Tsuru *et al.*[2]	24 hours (5 minutes post)	—	↓ ↓
	ECS alone (20 days)		—
Urca & Frenk[26]	5 minutes	(↓)	↓ ↓ ↓
	(0.3 second post)	—	↓
	24 hours	—	—
	ECS alone (18 days)	—	—
Handforth[16]	22 hours	—	↓ ↓
	24 hours (immediately post)	—	↓ ↓

[a]NA means not ascertained.

in the rat than is the drug carbamazepine. While carbamazepine is extremely effective in inhibiting completed kindled seizures, and does inhibit the process or development of kindling in the cat and monkey,[28,29] data from our laboratory[30] and those of Wada *et al.*,[28] Baltzer *et al.*,[31] and Albertson *et al.*[32] indicate that carbamazepine is not effective in inhibiting the development of kindling in the rat. These findings are consistent with others indicating that differential biochemical and pharmacological processes may underlie the development of kindled seizures compared to those maintaining completed kindled seizures. Moreover, there may be important species differences in the responsivity to different anticonvulsant agents. Nonetheless, at least in the rat, ECS would appear to be a more potent anticonvulsant than carbamazepine in the development phase of amygdala kindling. It is noteworthy that another agent used in the treatment of manic-depressive illness—lithium carbonate—is not effective in inhibiting either completed kindled seizures or their development.[30]

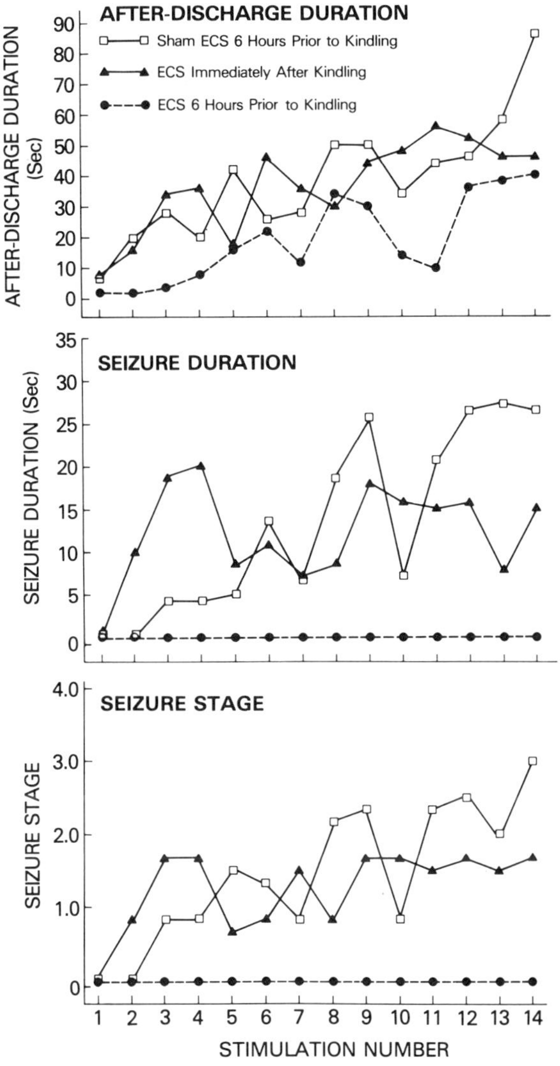

FIGURE 2. Electroconvulsive seizures inhibit the development of amygdala kindling. Electroconvulsive-seizures (ECS) 6 hours prior to amygdala kindling markedly inhibited seizure stage development ($p < 0.0001$; $F = 3.00$; df = 27,154) and seizure duration ($p < 0.0001$; $F = 2.92$; df = 27,154), while they had a lesser but significant suppressive effect on afterdischarge duration ($p < 0.0018$; $F = 2.16$; df = 27,154; analysis of variance, group differences). ECS administered after kindling (or 24 hours prior to the next amygdala stimulation) did not significantly alter seizure development. Values represent means of all animals in each group. Standard errors are omitted for clarity of presentation, although there was no variability in the lack of seizure development in the group receiving ECS 6 hours prior to kindling.

CLINICAL AND MECHANISTIC IMPLICATIONS OF ANTICONVULSANT EFFECTS OF ECS

Sangdee *et al.* reported that a kindling-like effect (i.e., proconvulsant) of ECS itself could be induced in mice.[33] Ramer and Pinel indicated that the interval between ECS (one hour vs. three days) was important to whether seizure thresholds increased or decreased following ECS.[34] Whether ECS treatment of patients can, in some instances, facilitate subsequent seizure development remains controversial.[35–38] If seizure facilitation or sensitization does occur, it would appear to be a very uncommon outcome and of

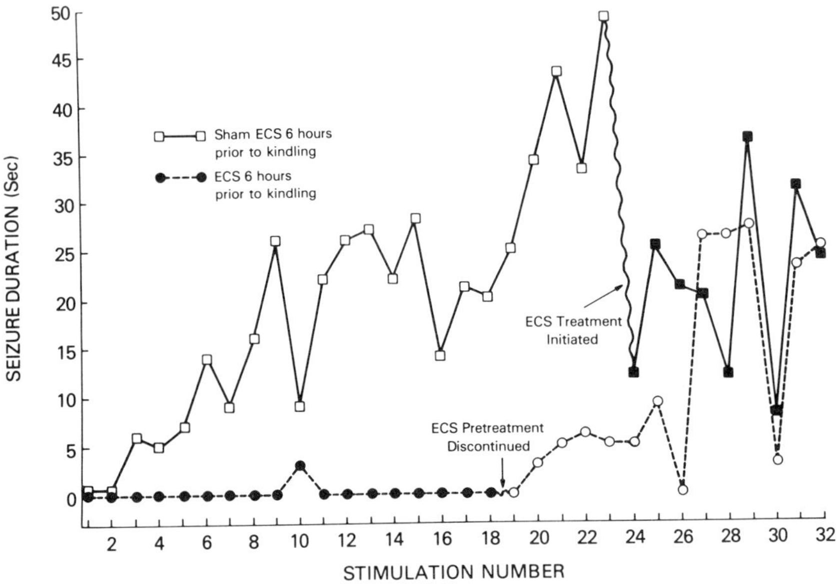

FIGURE 3. Electroconvulsive seizures (ECS) inhibit the development of amygdala kindling and suppress completed kindled seizures. ECS administered six hours prior to each amygdala stimulation blocks the development of kindling. However, when ECT treatment was discontinued on day 19, the remaining animals showed a relatively normal rate of kindling development. When active ECT was given to the previously sham-treated group on day 24, acute anticonvulsant effects of ECS were again evident. Data in the first two weeks parallel those in FIGURE 2 but include additional animals in each group which did not have histologically confirmed electrode placements.

unknown relationship to the clear anticonvulsant effects of ECS, at least on amygdala-kindled seizures.

Taken together, the studies summarized in TABLES 1 and 2 and FIGURES 1–3 suggest that ECS exerts potent acute and long-term effects on amygdala-kindled seizures and their development. The anticonvulsant effects of electroconvulsive shock appear to be of a magnitude comparable to that produced by more typical anticonvulsants. Albright and Burnham found that carbamazepine and valproic acid were the most effective in inhibiting the amygdala-kindled compared to cortical-kindled afterdischarge.[18] These two anticonvulsants appear to have the best efficacy in providing acute and prophylactic treatment for bipolar disorder.[13,39] These data raise many questions for further discussion. Are the anticonvulsant effects of these drugs and of ECS related to their clinical efficacy in the mood disorders? Elsewhere we have discussed whether or not the limbic mechanisms of action of carbamazepine are related to its clinical efficacy in manic-depressive illness.[40] Carbamazepine has multiple biochemical effects[13,41–43] and potently suppresses excitability in many seizure models and in many areas of brain outside the limbic system that could also be important to its clinical effects.[40] The potent anticonvulsant effects of ECS against amygdala kindling and possibly other seizures are provocative and suggest the importance of exploring possible mechanisms of this action of ECS in its own right and in relationship to its efficacy in affective illness.

There are numerous classical and peptide neurotransmitter candidates for the anticonvulsant effects of ECS.[44,45] As reviewed by Sackeim *et al.*[6] and Green and collaborators in this volume, there is evidence that ECS, like many pharmacological anticonvulsants, may also increase γ-aminobutyric acid (GABA) effects and decrease GABA turnover. Are these common effects also related to the psychotropic properties of these treatments? We suggest that this is a particularly important area of investigation. Based on the data that treatment with a variety of agents effective in manic-depressive illness (carbamazepine, lithium, valproic acid, progabide, and ECT) appears to increase GABA turnover[13,43] and the mounting evidence of GABA defects in affectively ill patients, we would propose this system as a candidate for the psychotropic effects of ECT. In a similar vein, one might ask whether the effects of ECS on catecholamine release and turnover are important to either its anticonvulsant or psychotropic properties, especially since noradrenergic mechanisms have been linked to the anticonvulsant effects of carbamazepine[13] and noradrenergic alternatives have long been hypothesized in the affective disorders.

Recent evidence suggests that ECS may transiently increase benzodiazepine receptors,[46] a phenomenon that could be important to its anticonvulsant and/or psychotropic properties, although other data suggest that these changes in benzodiazepine receptor binding may not persist for 24 hours after a series of ECS and thus may not be clinically relevant.[44] Moreover, the anticonvulsant effects of carbamazeprine, in contrast to those of diazepam, do not appear to involve the classical "central" benzodiazepine receptor site, but may involve the so-called peripheral benzodiazepine receptor site in brain, as is evidenced by the reversal of the anticonvulsant effects of carbamazepine by Ro5-4864.[47]

As reviewed in this volume (Fink; Holaday; Cowen) and elsewhere, there is evidence that ECS influences a variety of neural peptides including endogenous opiate substances,[48,49] thyrotropin releasing hormone (TRH), adrenocorticotropin releasing hormone (ACTH), α-melanotropic stimulating hormone (αMSH),[50] prolactin,[51] vasopressin, and, potentially, corticotropin releasing factor (CRF) and somatostatin. Each one of these peptide systems requires exploration as a possible mediator or modulator of anticonvulsant and/or psychotropic effects. The endogenous opiates are also candidates at least for the anticonvulsant effects of ECS.[52] Altered response to CRF has been closely linked to both affective illness[53] and kindled seizures,[54] further suggesting the possible importance of this peptide in the modulation of the endocrine and/or therapeutic responsivity following ECT.

A novel approach to the study of the mechanisms underlying the long-lasting anticonvulsant effects of ECS has been explored by Isaac and Swager.[55] These investigators observed that daily ECS for 22 days in the cat resulted in a progressive elevation of electroconvulsive threshold. This phenomenon lasted for approximately 20 days. Cerebrospinal fluid (CSF) collected from cats with these elevated thresholds, when transferred into the ventricular space of untreated animals, conferred an elevated threshold to the recipient animal. These data suggest that a substance present in CSF of cats receiving repeated ECS may confer the altered threshold to untreated animals. Long and Tortella have made similar observations in the rat that following ECS a substance is released into CSF that has anticonvulsant effects;[52] the effects are naloxone reversible, suggesting that it is an opiate peptide, possibly beta-endorphin.

Somatostatin may also deserve study as a potential mediator of the effects of ECS. The anticonvulsant carbamazepine decreases somatostatin in the CSF of affectively ill patients,[56] and the depletion or inactivation of somatostatin (with cysteamine or antibodies, respectively) is anticonvulsant to kindled seizures.[57] Moreover, seizures induced by amygdala kindling produce long-lasting (at least two months) increases in brain somatostatin in the rat.[58] These data suggest a possible role of somatostatin in anticonvulsant mechanisms, and six studies reporting decreases in somatostatin in the CSF of depressed patients[59] suggest a possible role in affective illness.

In addition to the common effects on GABA turnover of three treatments (ECT, carbamazepine, and lithium) that are effective in both phases of manic-depressive illness, these agents also share common effects on thyroid. Surprisingly, ECT, carbamazepine, and lithium all decrease plasma thyroxine,[60] and this hormone thus remains a possible candidate for the psychotropic (but not anticonvulsant) effects of these agents.

Engel *et al.* reported that electroconvulsive treatment in patients produced diffuse increases in cerebral glucose metabolism and postictal decreases.[61] These findings have been replicated in animal studies, although additional ECT patients have only shown the pattern of postictal decreases in glucose consumption.[62] This pattern of ECT in man and that reported by Blackwood *et al.* in the rat[37] are very different from the regional selective changes in glucose utilization produced by amygdala-kindled[63] or lidocaine-kindled[64] seizures and could be important to the interpretation of the anticonvulsant effects of ECS.

As noted above, it is possible that the anticonvulsant and psychotropic effects of ECS and the anticonvulsants may be mediated through different mechanisms. This would considerably complicate the elucidation of the important mechanisms for the psychotropic effects of ECS, particularly since there is at present no clear index or end point measurable in animals for the psychotropic effect. The possibility of dissociating anticonvulsant, psychotropic, and side effects is highlighted by the finding that the anticonvulsant carbamazepine may reverse the amnesic effects of electroconvulsive shock in mice. Mondadori and Classen found that carbamazepine was the only anticonvulsant capable of reversing ECS-induced amnesia in mice.[65] Indirect evidence suggests that carbamazepine may be acting as an agonist at vasopressin receptors.[66,67,13] It is possible that this unique action of carbamazepine among the anticonvulsants accounts for its ability to counter ECS-induced amnesia. If this were borne out in further experiments it might suggest that ECS and carbamazepine have opposing effects on vasopressin function that are not directly related to their psychotropic properties, but may be closely related to their effects on cognitive processes.

CONCLUSIONS

Our conceptualization of ECS as an anticonvulsant treatment may facilitate studies of the mechanism of action of this treatment, especially since this provides an easily measurable effect of ECS. It may also help focus on the questions of why seizures stop and what endogenous anticonvulsant mechanisms are ECS enhancing. However, at this time it remains only a working hypothesis for further exploration that the anticonvulsant effects of ECS and the anticonvulsant agents are related to their psychotropic efficacy in the treatment of manic and depressed patients. The biochemical and physiological mechanisms underlying their anticonvulsant effects may be differentiable from those related to their therapeutic efficacy in affective illness. Moreover, even the demonstration that common mechanisms of ECS and other anticonvulsant agents were closely related to their psychotropic efficacy in affective illness would not imply that a seizure disorder was an underlying pathophysiological process in affective illness. Carbamazepine and other anticonvulsants are effective in the treatment of pain syndromes and a variety of other paroxysmal syndromes[13] that do not appear to involve an ictal process. Nevertheless, it remains an intriguing proposition that mechanisms common to ECS and anticonvulsants such as carbamazepine and valproic acid (and either similar to or different from the prototypic treatment for manic-depressive illness, i.e., lithium carbonate) are related to their efficacy in the treatment of both the manic and depressive phases of affective disorders.

REFERENCES

1. VON MEDUNA, L. J. 1935. Die konvulsionstherapie der schizophrenie. Psychiatr. Neurol. Wochenschr. **37:** 317–319.
2. KALINOWSKI, L. B. & F. KENNEDY. 1943. Observations in electric shock therapy applied to problems of epilepsy. J. Nerv. Ment. Dis. **98:** 56.
3. CAPLAN, G. 1946. Electrical convulsion therapy in the treatment of epilepsy. J. Ment. Sci. **92:** 784–793.
4. TAYLOR, J. H. 1946. Control of grand mal epilepsy with electro-shock. Dis. Nerv. Syst. **7:** 284–285.
5. WOLFF, G. E. 1956. Electro-convulsive therapy: a help for epileptics. Am. Prac. Dig. Treat. **7:** 1791–1793.
6. SACKEIM, H. A., P. DECINA, S. MALITZ, S. R. RESOR & I. PROHOVNIK. 1983. Anticonvulsant and antidepressant properties of electroconvulsive therapy: a proposed mechanism of action. Biol. Psychiatry **18:** 1301–1310.
7. POST, R. M., F. W. PUTNAM & N. R. CONTEL. 1981. Electroconvulsive shock inhibits amygdala kindling. *In* Proceedings of Society for Neuroscience, 11th Annual Meeting, Los Angeles, Calif. (Abstr. No. 187.13, page 587).
8. POST, R. M., F. PUTNAM, N. R. CONTEL & B. GOLDMAN. 1984. Electroconvulsive seizures inhibit amygdala kindling: implications for mechanisms of action in affective illness. Epilepsia **25:** 234–239.
9. BALLENGER, J. C. & R. M. POST. 1980. Carbamazepine (Tegretol) in manic-depressive illness: a new treatment. Am. J. Psychiatry **137:** 782–790.
10. BALLENGER, J. C. & R. M. POST. 1978. Therapeutic effects of carbamazepine in affective illness: a preliminary report. Commun. Psychopharmacol. **2:** 159–178.
11. POST, R. M., T. W. UHDE, J. C. BALLENGER, D. C. CHATTERJI, R. F. GREEN & W. E. BUNNEY, JR. 1983. Carbamazepine and its -10,11-epoxide metabolite in plasma and CSF: relationship to antidepressant response. Arch. Gen. Psychiatry **40:** 673–676.
12. POST, R. M., T. W. UHDE, J. C. BALLENGER & K. M. SQUILLACE. 1983. Prophylactic efficacy of carbamazepine in manic-depressive illness. Am. J. Psychiatry **140:** 1602–1604.
13. POST, R. M., J. C. BALLENGER, T. W. UHDE & W. E. BUNNEY, JR. 1984. Efficacy of carbamazepine in manic-depressive illness: implications for underlying mechanisms. *In* Neurobiology of Mood Disorders. R. M. Post & J. C. Ballenger, Eds.: 777–816. Williams & Wilkins. Baltimore, Md.
14. POST, R. M., T. W. UHDE, W. BERRETTINI & C. KELLNER. 1984. Selective response to the anticonvulsant carbamazepine in manic-depressive illness: a case study. J. Clin. Psychopharmacol. **4:** 178–185.
15. BABINGTON, R. G. & P. W. WEDEKING. 1975. Blockade of tardive seizures in rats by electroconvulsive shock. Brain Res. **88:** 141–144.
16. HANDFORTH, A. 1982. Postseizure inhibition of kindled seizures by electroconvulsive shock. Exp. Neurol. **78:** 483–491.

17. Chiodo, L. A. & S. M. Antelman. 1980. Electroconvulsive shock: progressive dopamine autoreceptor subsensitivity independent of repeated treatment. Science **210:** 799–801.
18. Albright, P. S. & W. M. Burnham. 1980. Development of a new pharmacological seizure model: effects of anticonvulsants on cortical- and amygdala-kindled seizures in the rat. Epilepsia **21:** 681–689.
19. Ashton, D. & A. Wauquier. 1979. Behavioral analysis of the effects of 15 anticonvulsants in the amygdaloid kindled rat. Psychopharmacology **65:** 7–13.
20. Albertson, T. E., S. L. Peterson & L. G. Stark. 1980. Anticonvulsant drugs and their antagonism of kindled amygdaloid seizures in rats. Neuropharmacology **19:** 643–652.
21. Horovitz, Z. P. 1966. The amygdala and depression. *In* Anti-Depressant Drugs. S. Garattini, M. Milan & N. G. Dukes, Eds.: 121–129. Excerpta Medica. Amsterdam, Holland.
22. Babington, R. G. 1977. The pharmacology of kindling. *In* Animals Models of Psychiatry and Neurology. I. Hanin & E. Usdin, Eds.: 141–149. Pergamon Press. Oxford & New York.
23. Knobloch, L. C., J. M. Goldstein & J. B. Malick. 1982. Effects of acute and subacute antidepressant treatment on kindled seizures in rats. Pharmacol. Biochem. Behav. **17:** 461–465.
24. Lange, S. C., R. M. Julien & G. W. Fowler. 1976. Biphasic effects of imipramine in experimental models of epilepsy. Epilepsia **17:** 183–196.
25. Babington, R. G. & P. W. Wedeking. 1973. The pharmacology of seizures induced by sensitization with low intensity brain stimulation. Pharmacol. Biochem. Behav. **1:** 461–467.
26. Urca, G. & H. Frenk. 1982. Electroconvulsive shock disrupts amygdaloid kindling: dissociation between behavioral and electrographic events. Exp. Neurol. **78:** 492–502.
27. Tsuru, N., H. Ninomiya, H. Fukuoka & D. Nakahara. 1981. Alterations of amygdaloid kindling phenomenon following repeated electroconvulsive shocks in rats. Folia Psychiatr. Neurol. Jpn. **35:** 167–174.
28. Wada, J. A., D. P. Cain & E. Jung. 1977. Pharmacological prophylaxis of amygdaloid kindling in Senegalese baboons. Electroencephalogr. Clin. Neurophysiol. **43**(E108).
29. Wada, J. A., M. Sato, A. Wake, J. R. Green & A. S. Troupin. 1976. Prophylactic effects of phenytoin, phenobarbital, and carbamazepine examined in kindled cat preparations. Arch. Neurol. **33:** 426–434.
30. Post, R. M., S. R. B. Weiss & A. Pert. 1984. Differential effects of carbamazepine and lithium on sensitization and kindling. Prog. Neuropsychopharmacol. Biol. Psychiatry **8:** 425–434.
31. Baltzer, V., K. Klebs & M. Schmutz. 1981. Effects of oxcarbazepine, a compound related to carbamazepine, and of GP47 779, its main metabolite in man, on the evolution of amygdaloid-kindled seizures in the rat. Paper presented at the Epilepsy International Congress, Kyoto, Japan, Sept. 17–21.
32. Albertson, T. E., R. M. Joy & L. G. Stark. 1984. Carbamazepine. A pharmacological study in the kindling model of epilepsy. Neuropharmacology **23:** 1117–1124.
33. Sangdee, P., S. A. Turkanis & R. Karler. 1982. Kindling-like effect induced by repeated corneal electroshock in mice. Epilepsia **23:** 471–479.
34. Ramer, D. & J. P. J. Pinel. 1976. Progressive intensification of motor seizures produced by periodic electroconvulsive shock. Exp. Neurol. **51:** 421–433.
35. Devinsky, O. & M. S. Duchowny. 1983. Seizures after convulsive therapy: a retrospective case survey. Neurology **33:** 921–925.
36. Small, J. G., V. Milstein, I. F. Small & P. H. Sharpley. 1981. Does ECT produce kindling? Biol. Psychiatry **16:** 773–778.
37. Blackwood, D. H. R., R. E. Cull, C. P. L. Freeman, J. I. Evans & C. Mawdsley. 1980. A study of the incidence of epilepsy following ECT. J. Neurol. Neurosurg. Psychiatry **43:** 1098–1102.
38. Fink, M. 1978. Efficacy and safety of induced seizures (EST) in man. Compr. Psychiatry **19:** 1–18.
39. Post, R. M., T. W. Uhde, R. T. Joffe, P. P. Roy-Byrne & C. Kellner. 1985. Anticonvulsants in psychiatric illness: new treatment alternatives and theoretical impli-

cations. *In* The Neuropharmacology of Epilepsy. M. R. Trimble, Ed.: 141–171. John Wiley & Sons, Ltd. Chichester, England.
40. POST, R. M. & T. W. UHDE. Are the psychotropic effects of carbamazepine in manic-depressive illness mediated through the limbic system? Psychiatr. J. Univ. Ottawa **10**(4). (In press.)
41. POST, R. M., T. W. UHDE, J. C. BALLENGER & W. E. BUNNEY, JR. 1982. Carbamazepine, temporal lobe epilepsy, and manic-depressive illness. Adv. Biol. Psychiatry **8:** 117–156.
42. POST, R. M., T. W. UHDE & J. C. BALLENGER. 1984. Efficacy of carbamazepine in affective disorders: implications for underlying physiological and biochemical substrates. *In* Anticonvulsants in Affective Disorders. H. M. Emrich, T. Okuma & A. A. Muller, Eds.: 93–115. Elsevier Science Publishers. Amsterdam, Holland.
43. POST, R. M., D. R. RUBINOW & T. W. UHDE. 1984. Biochemical mechanisms of action of carbamazepine in affective illness and epilepsy. Psychopharmacol. Bull. **20:** 585–589.
44. GRAHAME-SMITH, D. G. 1984. The neuropharmacological effects of electroconvulsive shock and their relationship to the therapeutic effect of electroconvulsive therapy in depression. *In* Frontiers in Biochemical and Pharmacological Research in Depression. E. Usdin *et al.*, Eds.: 327–343. Raven Press. New York, N.Y.
45. LERER, B. 1984. Electroconvulsive shock and neurotransmitter receptors: implications for mechanism of action and adverse effects of electroconvulsive therapy. Biol. Psychiatry **19:** 361–383.
46. PAUL, S. M. & P. J. SKOLNICK. 1978. Rapid changes in brain benzodiazepine receptors after experimental seizures. Science **202:** 892–894.
47. WEISS, S. R. B., R. M. POST, J. PATEL & P. S. MARANGOS. 1985. Differential mediation of the anticonvulsant effects of carbamazepine and diazepam. Life Sci. **36:** 2413–2419.
48. BELENKY, G. L. 1983. Electroconvulsive shock and endogenous opioids. Abstr. Am. Psychiatr. Assoc. No. 103.
49. HOLADAY, J. W., F. C. TORTELLA, J. B. LONG, G. L. BELENKY & R. J. HITZEMAN. 1986. Endogenous opioids and their receptors: evidence for involvement in the postictal effects of electroconvulsive shock. Ann. N.Y. Acad. Sci. (This volume.)
50. VARGAS, L. 1983. Hormone patterns after electroconvulsive therapy. Lancet **1:** 365.
51. WHALLEY, L. J., H. DICK, A. G. WATTS, J. E. CHRISTIE, R. ROSIE, G. LEVY, W. J. SHEWARD & G. FINK. 1982. Immediate increases in plasma prolactin and neurophysin but not other hormones after electroconvulsive therapy. Lancet **2:** 1065–1068.
52. LONG, J. B. & F. C. TORTELLA. 1984. Cerebrospinal fluid from convulsed rats causes a naloxone-reversible increase in the seizure threshold of recipient animals: regulation of postseizure inhibition by endogenous opioid systems. Soc. Neurosci. Abstr. (145th Annual Meeting, Anaheim, Calif., Oct. 10–15, Abstract No. 273.6, page 929).
53. GOLD, P. W., G. P. CHROUSOS, C. K. KELLNER, R. M. POST, A. ROY, P. AVGERINOS, H. M. SCHULTE, E. OLDFIELD & D. L. LORIAUX. 1984. Psychiatric implications of basic and clinical studies with corticotropin-releasing factor. Am. J. Psychiatry **141:** 619–227.
54. WEISS, S. R. B., R. M. POST, P. W. GOLD, G. CHROUSOS, T. L. SULLIVAN, D. WALKER & A. PERT. 1984. CRF-induced aggressive behavior and seizures: facilitation of amygdala kindling. Soc. Neurosci. Abstr. (145th Meeting, Anaheim, Calif., Oct. 10–15, Abstract No. 55.9, page 178).
55. ISAAC, L. & J. SWANGER. 1983. Alteration of electroconvulsive threshold by cerebrospinal fluid from cats tolerant to electroconvulsive shock. Life Sci. **33:** 2301–2304.
56. RUBINOW, D. R., P. W. GOLD, R. M. POST, J. C. BALLENGER, R. COWDRY, J. BOLLINGER & S. REICHLIN. 1983. Somatostatin in affective illness. Arch. Gen. Psychiatry **40:** 403–412.
57. HIGUCHI, T., G. S. SIKAND, N. KATO, J. A. WADA & H. G. FRIESEN. 1983. Profound suppression of kindled seizures by cysteamine: possible role of somatostatin to kindled seizures. Brain Res. **288:** 359–362.
58. KATO, N., T. HIGUCHI, H. G. FRIESEN & J. A. WADA. 1983. Changes of immunoreactive somatostatin and beta-endorphin content in rat brain after amygdala kindling. Life Sci. **32:** 2415–2422.
59. POST, R. M., P. W. GOLD & D. R. RUBINOW. Neuropeptides in manic-depressive illness. *In*

Neuropeptides in Psychiatric and Neurological Disease. C. B. Nemeroff, Ed. Johns Hopkins University Press. Baltimore, Md. (In press.)

60. JOFFE, R. T., P. P. ROY-BYRNE, T. W. UHDE & R. M. POST. 1984. Thyroid function and affective illness: a reappraisal. Biol. Psychiatry **19:** 1685–1691.

61. ENGEL, J., D. E. KUHL & M. E. PHELPS. 1982. Patterns of human local cerebral glucose metabolism during epileptic seizures. Science 218: 64–66.

62. ACKERMANN, R. F., J. ENGEL, JR. & L. BAXTER. 1986. Positron emission tomography and autoradiographic studies of glucose utilization following electroconvulsive seizures in humans and rats. Ann. N.Y. Acad. Sci. (This volume.)

63. ENGEL, J., JR., L. WOLFSON & L. BROWN. 1978. Anatomical correlates of electrical and behavioral events related to amygdaloid kindling. Ann. Neurol. **3:** 538–544.

64. POST, R. M., C. KENNEDY, M. SHINOHARA, K. SQUILLACE, M. MIYAOKA, S. SUDA, D. H. INGVAR & L. SOKOLOFF. 1984. Metabolic and behavioral consequences of lidocaine-kindled seizures. Brain Res. **324:** 295–304.

65. MONDADORI, C. & W. CLASSEN. 1984. The effects of various antiepileptic drugs on E-shock-induced amnesia in mice: dissociability of effects on convulsions and effects on memory. Acta Neurol. Scand. **99:** 125–129.

66. BERRETTINI, W., R. M. POST, E. K. WORTHINGTON & J. B. CASPER. 1982. Human platelet vasopressin receptors. Life Sci. **30:** 425–432.

67. GOLD, P. W., G. L. ROBERTSON, J. C. BALLENGER, W. KAYE, J. CHEN, D. R. RUBINOW, F. K. GOODWIN & R. M. POST. 1983. Carbamazepine diminishes the sensitivity of the plasma arginine vasopressin response to osmotic stimulation. J. Clin. Endocrinol. Metab. **57:** 952–957.

Electroconvulsive Therapy and Lateralized Affective Systems

PIERRE FLOR-HENRY

Alberta Hospital, Edmonton
Box 307
Edmonton, Alberta, Canada T5J 2J7
and
Department of Psychiatry
University of Alberta
Edmonton, Alberta, Canada

It is now well established that artificially induced generalized seizures, irrespective of the mode of induction, be it convulsant anesthetic gas such as Indoklon (hexofluorodiethyl ether), intravenous Metrazol, or electrical energy, has a beneficial effect on endogenous depressive psychoses and catatonic states, either of pure motility type or with affective and/or schizophrenic symptomatology. Generalized seizures, however, are without effect on the schizophrenic syndrome, "stricto sensu." It should be noted that those syndromes of psychosis that are ECT responsive are fundamentally bipolar types of syndromes with associated disturbances of motility regulation: the psychomotor retardation of depression which may progress to the functional motor paralysis of depressive stupors; the hypermotility of manic or of excited schizomanic states or—at the opposite pole—the slowing seen in schizodepressive syndromes. Similarly we have the excited and stuporous catatonias, both of which are usually dramatically cured by induced (or spontaneous) generalized seizures.

Considering a special case, schizophrenic psychoses associated with temporal lobe epilepsy, it has been shown that the emergence of psychosis is *inversely* correlated with the presence and frequency of frontotemporal limbic seizures but independent of the generalized seizure system activity.[1,2] Conversely, the epileptic evidence suggests that a manic depressive modulation hinges, in an inverse relationship, on activation of the generalized seizure system with secondary bilateral synchrony.

These various considerations have important theoretical implications for they suggest, on the one hand, that seizures and psychosis are antithetical manifestations of the same underlying disturbance of cerebral function and, on the other, that the frontotemporal neuronal limbic circuit underlies schizophrenic symptomatology while the neuronal systems responsible for generalized seizures are critical in determining the appearance, or dissolution, of manic-depressive states.

Thus it becomes important to define more precisely the neurophysiological systems involved. Clinical and experimental evidence derived from studies of the propagation of the seizure discharge with depth electrodes shows that the limbic and generalized seizure systems are largely independent of each other. The majority of psychosensory or psychomotor attacks do not proceed to generalized seizures and generalized seizures do not end with psychomotor fits, although occasionally the latter may be followed by postictal automatisms and nonconvulsive "absence" epilepsy may be associated with psychomotor phenomena. The tendency of limbic discharges to be restricted to the limbic system in experimental animals led McLean to describe the "schizophysiology" of the limbic system. Furthermore depth-electrode studies in man confirm that generalized seizures, in their propagation, bypass limbic structures, although rarely these may become activated at the end of the discharge (Bancaud, Gloor, personal communications).

To explain the sudden onset without warning and with immediate loss of consciousness and the symmetrical features, both clinical and electrographic, of convulsive and nonconvulsive generalized epilepsies, Penfield and Jasper introduced the hypothesis of "centrencephalic" epilepsy.[3] This was because in experimental animals stimulation of intralaminar thalamic nuclei, with or without stimulation of the mesencephalic reticular formation, could evoke bilateral synchronous spike and wave discharges and a diencephalic origin seemed to account satisfactorily for the characteristics of generalized epilepsies. However Walshe in 1965, in a very critical analysis of the concept "centrencephalic," argued that, reminiscent of the mid–19th century "automatic apparatus" of Carpenter, it lacked virtually all empirical foundations.[4]

Bancaud *et al.* in Paris described how in patients presenting with primary generalized epilepsy, unilateral electrical stimulation of the mesial frontal cortex reproduced these seizures:[5–7] either simple electroclinical "absences," complex absences, generalized tonic-clonic attacks, or bilaterally synchronous spike and wave discharges. The observations of Bancaud and his collaborators do not implicate thalamic or diencephalic structures but suggest a very rapid propagation from either mesial frontal-orbital cortices to the contralateral mesial frontal region via the corpus callosum, followed by secondary irradiation of the brain stem. Of interest is the report that symmetrical synchronous frontocentral spike and waves induced by stimulation of the mesial frontal cortex propagate rapidly to the dorsomedial nucleus of the thalamus.[6] Gloor at the Montreal Neurological Institute confirmed and amplified these findings.[8,9]

Having been established in the monkey with experimental epilepsy,[10] the technique of intracarotid amobarbital and metrazol injections for the study of epilepsy in man was developed.[11] The technique is based on the fundamental observation that in man each internal carotid artery irrigates the ipsilateral cortex and basal ganglia with virtually no overlap across the midline, while the thalamus, except for a very small lateral shell, lies in the territory of the vertebrobasilar system. Studying patients with primarily generalized seizures of presumed "centrencephalic" origin, Gloor found that unilateral intracarotid injection of metrazol "elicited a fully developed bilateral electrographic and clinical pattern of 'centrencephalic' epileptic discharge";[8] the threshold of response being the same on both sides. Unilateral injection of intracarotid amytal abolished the epileptic discharge simultaneously and bilaterally. In addition not only did intravertebral metrazol fail to evoke a "centrencephalic" seizure: it had the opposite effect and inhibited the discharge. To explain these phenomena Gloor introduced the model of "corticoreticular" generalized epilepsies. The pathophysiology of generalized seizures would hinge on a perturbation of the brain-stem reticular stabilizing action on the mesial-orbital frontal cortex. The report of Rodin *et al.* investigating fast frequencies (over 1000 Hz) in cats subjected to metrazol- and megimide-induced generalized seizures[12] is congruous with Gloor's model. Rodin notes that spike and wave activity is usually associated with high-frequency discharges occurring in the pons.

In this way it is seen that, at the cortical level, generalized seizures are determined by events in the mesial frontal cortex, itself closely associated with the orbital frontal cortex, which in a functional sense is the regulating and modulating component of the limbic system. Subcortically the generalized seizure system is subtended by the dorsomedial nucleus of the thalamus (functionally coextensive with the orbital frontal cortex) and the brain stem, notably the pontine reticular formation. This last, in turn, establishes links with the mesencephalic limbic projections of Nauta. The orbital-mesial frontal region and the dorsomedial nucleus of the thalamus—in other words the frontal extension of the limbic system—are the common link between the generalized and limbic seizure systems. That such a link exists is shown by the fact that the interruption of the connections between the mammillary bodies and the anterior thalamus by very discrete stereotactic lesions of the mammillothalamic tracts in the guinea pig results in complete protection from the behavioral, electroencephalographic, and lethal effects of the convulsant pentylenetetrazol.[13] Conversely these investigators had found that in states of prolonged minimal seizure activity induced by the simultaneous infusion of a convulsant and anticonvulsant, selective metabolic activation of the mammillary bodies, mammillothalamic tracts, anterior nuclei of the thalamus, and ventral tegmental nuclei occurred. Mesial frontal seizures, or "supplementary motor seizures," are characterized by automatic behavior, vocalization, tonic adversive movements, and posturing of limbs with retention of consciousness. Orbital frontal seizures, on the other hand, are manifested by signs of autonomic dysfunction: flushing of face, mydriasis, piloerection, epigastric sensations, automatisms with an expression of fear, vocalization, and amnesia. Generalized convulsive seizures do not occur.[14] The elements common to orbital frontal and mesial frontal seizures and catatonic states are clear.

Let us now return to those psychotic syndromes that are favorably influenced by generalized seizures: the endogenous affective psychoses, the periodic schizoaffective psychoses, and catatonic syndromes. Common to all these are pathology of mood and motility. Is it a coincidence that the mesial frontal cortex is the "supplementary motor cortex" and that the orbital frontal cortex–dorsomedial thalamic network is the cerebral region specifically implicated in pathological mood disturbances? It is barely necessary to recall here the beneficial effects of mesial frontal and orbital frontal lesions in chronic depressive states, or of the similar efficacy of dorsomedial frontal disconnection. Noteworthy also is the fact that these frontal limbic lesions, like generalized seizures, are without effect on the essential features of the schizophrenic syndrome. It would thus seem that it is only when the latter has "spilled over," so to speak, from the temporal limbic system to the mesial orbital frontal system (thereby acquiring affective and/or motor accretions) that it becomes susceptible to modifications induced by activation of the generalized seizure system.

Although the relative independence of the limbic seizure system and of the generalized seizure system has been emphasized, that there are reciprocal interactions existing between these two neural systems has recently been fascinatingly confirmed by Post *et al.*[15] In the rat, generalized convulsive seizures given six hours prior to amygdaloid kindling significantly delay the development of subsequent amygdaloid-limbic afterdischarges and seizures.

Le Gal La Salle has shown that potentiation of γ-aminobutyric acid (GABA)-ergic transmission by aminooxyacetic acid inhibits kindling-induced generalized discharges.[16] There are reports that indicate that valproic acid exacerbates schizophrenic symptomatology,[17,18] while there is evidence, on the other hand, that major depressive disorders (see Sackeim *et al.*)[19] and bipolar psychoses (Berrettini *et al.*)[20] exhibit a functional reduction of GABA-ergic activity. Thus, keeping in mind the reciprocal relationship existing between schizophrenic symptomatology and the limbic seizure system and that between the bipolar psychoses and the generalized seizure system, it would appear that in schizophrenia a hyperfunctional GABA-ergic–dopaminergic state restricted to the limbic structures leads to *diminished* neural excitability, while in the manic-depressive syndrome there is *increased* neural excitability in the anterior limbic regions.

Since d'Elia and Raotma published their review on the effects in depression of unilateral nondominant and bilateral electroconvulsive therapy (ECT),[21] it is generally accepted that the antidepressant efficacy of bilateral and unilateral nondominant ECT is equivalent. A number of studies in fact find unilateral nondominant ECT superior to bilateral ECT. Halliday *et al.* in the analysis of 52 patients with endogenous depression, all dextrals, who were randomly allocated to bilateral, unilateral dominant, and unilateral nondominant ECT note that the induced seizures were "wholly or predominantly contralateral in one third."[22] This fact gives particular significance to their observation that in their cases there is a trend whereby, at three months follow-up, the nondominant ECT group showed a greater degree of recovery from depression than did either the bilateral or dominant ECT groups. Galin analyzed in detail Halliday's data from this perspective and showed that the group receiving dominant ECT was significantly worse that the other two groups.[23] Deglin and Nikolaenko in Moscow confirmed these relationships, demonstrating in depressed and schizophrenic patients that, irrespective of psychiatric diagnosis, dominant ECT induced dysphoric mood and an aggravation of preexisting melancholia while nondominant ECT evoked euphoric or even a hypomanic mood shift.[24] Other investigations have also demonstrated the superiority of nondominant over bilateral ECT in the relief of depression. There was a trend in this direction in the study of Zinkin and Birtchnell, since 30% of the unilateral and only 10% of the bilateral group showed the maximal decrease in depression scores in the pre- and posttreatment evaluations.[25] Cronin *et al.* found unilateral nondominant ECT superior to dominant ECT (but equivalent to bilateral ECT) in a series of 51 endogenous and reactive depressions, all of whom were female.[26] Cohen *et al.* found a significant superiority for right hemisphere ECT in a group of 40 depressed women subjected to left, right, and bilateral ECT and whose initial level of depression before treatment was of the same intensity.[27] Kronfol *et al.* described a differential pattern of neuropsychological functions with unilateral dominant, unilateral nondominant, and bilateral ECT, administered with relatively high voltage so that in all cases a bilaterally generalized seizure supervened.[28] Neuropsychological tests showed that right hemispheric functions were more frequently abnormal than left hemispheric functions before ECT and after ECT; with recovery from depression there was an improvement in right hemispheric functions. Studies that have compared neuropsychological scores of depressed patients before and after ECT (bilateral, unilateral left and right) have the same implication. Fromm-Auch has reviewed in detail all studies published after 1965 that have compared the effects on neuropsychological scores of either bilateral ECT versus unilateral ECT, or unilateral left versus unilateral right ECT in depression.[29] A total of 21 studies providing quantitative memory measurements were collected. In all instances unilateral left ECT was followed by an impairment in verbal functions. Bilateral and unilateral left ECT inconsistently led to an improvement in visuospatial nondominant hemispheric functions. The vast majority of studies using unilateral nondominant ECT were associated with improvement or complete normalization of neuropsychological indices of nonverbal memory after a minimum of five seizure inductions. Some findings in the older literature are surprisingly consistent. For example, Small *et al.* found that unilateral right ECT produced a significant improvement in contralateral left-hand finger oscillations, whereas no corresponding effect appeared after unilateral left ECT.[30] The more recent experience of Small and collaborators is also consistent with these general trends.[31] Comparing on Halstead-Reitan and Wechsler parameters a large, previously studied sample of bilateral ECT, with 28 patients given unilateral right ECT, after the fifth treatment and after two or three weeks, they find a comparable improvement in the two populations. However the cognitive measures follow different curves: they are U shaped through time, worsening around the fifth period in the bilateral group, then gradually returning to baseline whereas the unilateral right ECT group shows a gradual and continuous improvement for most neuropsychological scores. Of the Wechsler subtests, only Object Assembly, a visuospatial subtest, is significantly improved at three weeks compared to pre-ECT values. Thus the neuropsychological consequences of bilateral and unilateral nondominant ECT differ, but in both the antidepressant effect is linked to a normalization of disrupted nondominant hemispheric functions. It is also well known that the neurophysiological sequellae of bilateral and unilateral ECT are quite different. At the end of a lateralized induced seizure sensorimotor cortical functions are transiently depressed as is shown by the brief contralateral hemiparesis and by the elevation of the acoustic threshold to short tones in the contralateral ear. These changes do not occur with bilateral ECT. Kriss *et al.* for example examined 29 dextral patients before and after 62 unilateral ECTs (47 to the right and 15 to the left hemisphere).[32] Contralateral deep tendon reflex asymmetry, hemiparesis, tactile and visual inattention, and homonymous hemianopia occurred. Nondominant ECT induced left visuospatial neglect and dominant ECT aphasia. All neurological abnormalities resolved within 20 minutes. This pattern of lateralized hemispheric inactivation after unilateral ECT is similar to that which follows intracarotid barbiturization. Furthermore the induced emotional shifts that follow lateral hemispheric inactivation, be they induced by unilateral ECT or by carotid barbiturization, are, statistically, identical: inactivation of the left hemisphere evokes dysphoric mood or depression, inactivation of the right hemisphere evokes euphoria or hypomania. Thus logically the antidepressant action of bilateral and unilateral nondominant ECT is the consequence of the seizure discharge in critical regions of the right hemisphere. Two investigations undertaken by Sackeim and his co-workers at the New York State Psychiatric Institute support this conclusion. In the first study it was found that patients with severe depression who responded to ECT showed greater left-sided visual neglect (tested 30–60 minutes after the end of the seizure) than those who failed to respond, the left-sided visual neglect being identical in bilateral or unilateral nondominant conditions.[33] In the second investigation Sackeim *et al.* observed a significant elevation of the acoustic threshold in the left ear of severely depressed dextral patients.[34] With either unilateral nondominant or bilateral ECT those patients who recovered from depression showed a decrease in *left* ear acoustic threshold (hence a contralateral right hemisphere implication), which returned toward normal values. The acoustic investigations of depressive states undertaken by Bruder *et al.* also demonstrate right hemispheric disturbance since patients with major, typical depressive disorders show on dichotic stimulation the expected pattern of marked right-ear advantage of consonant-vowels, but fail to show a left-ear advantage for complex tones discrimination.[35]

The neuropsychological, neurological, and acoustic evidence then is quite consistent and indicates that the beneficial effects of induced seizures in depression, be they bilaterally symmetrical or asymmetrical nondominant, are mediated through the repercussions of the seizure discharge in critical neural networks in the right hemisphere which are thereby normalized. This phenomenon in depression is quite general, as Fromm and Schopflocher have shown in a study of 60 patients with psychotic and neurotic forms of depression tested with an extensive neuropsychological test battery before and after treatment with tricyclic antidepressants or monoamine-oxidase inhibitors (MAOI) that:[36]

1. Before treatment both the neurotic and psychotic depressions had a selective impairment of visuospatial processing and retention and of short-term memory (verbal and nonverbal), more severe in psychotic than neurotic depressions.
2. After treatment and with recovery from depression there was a significant improvement in these functions (essentially bitemporal–right hemispheric) and the two depressive groups were no longer statistically different from age- and sex-matched controls.

Thus the antidepressant action of bilateral ECT, unilateral nondominant ECT, tricyclic agents, and MAOIs appears to be the consequence of right hemisphere interactions. At the biochemical level the neurotransmitters noradrenaline and serotonin are considered to play a crucial part in the pathogenesis of pathological depressions. There is evidence that the distribution of these neurotransmitters in a functional sense is bilaterally asymmetric. Gottfries *et al.* reported a correlation between the amplitude of evoked responses in the right hemisphere and cerebrospinal fluid (CSF) concentrations of 5-HIAA.[37] Laurian *et al.* found a preponderance of right hemispheric spectral EEG indicators in depression after 25 mg of amitriptyline,[38] a tricyclic interacting principally with serotoninergic systems, and, in a remarkable investigation, Sai-Halasz *et al.* found that intravenous injection of the hallucinogen dimethyltryptamine (chemically related to serotonin) produced in normal volunteers transient neurological signs: hyperreflexia and Babinski on the *left* side.[39] Oke *et al.* noted significant neurochemical asymmetries in noradrenaline distribution in the human thalamus: higher concentrations on the left side posteriorly and higher concentrations on the right side anteriorly.[40] More recently Oke describes three variations on the above pattern, the first of right lateralized distribution of noradrenaline throughout the midthalamus and pulvinar; the second of a diagonal pattern such as left ventral and right dorsal; and the third consisting of combinations of the above patterns.[41] It should be noted that the basic pattern of higher noradrenaline concentrations anteriorly on the right side and posteriorly on the left side establishes a particular right-lateralized link with limbic physiology. For the afferent inputs into the anterior/medial specific thalamic nuclei are from the mammillary bodies and amygdaloid, the efferent cortical projections being to the cingulate, orbital frontal, and frontal zones. The relations of the posterior thalamus are more essentially concerned with sensory-motor functions. Von Knorring *et al.* administered imipramine to normal subjects and found a significant consequent increase in left frontal alpha power,[42] i.e., corresponding to right hemisphere activation, which again implies the presence of a right hemisphere bias for noradrenergic systems.

In conclusion the evidence reviewed suggests that the "modus operandi" of both bilateral and unilateral nondominant ECT is that, through the repercussion of the generalized seizure discharge, dysfunctional neural systems in the nondominant hemisphere determining pathological depressions are normalized. The pathological anatomy implicated is mesialorbital frontal and the subcortical mammillothalamic–dorsomedial thalamic components of the limbic system but largely independent of the temporal-limbic system. The functional bias to the right hemisphere in the bilaterally asymmetrical distributions of the neurotransmitters noradrenaline and serotonin especially implicated in depression[43] is consistent with the fundamental importance of the nondominant hemisphere in the genesis of depressive mood psychoses.

SUMMARY

The neurophysiological systems subtending generalized seizures (activated by ECT) and temporal-limbic seizures are described as well as the interactions existing between the two seizure systems. There are correlations between schizophrenia and the limbic seizure system on the one hand and the manic-depressive or bipolar syndromes and the generalized seizure system on the other which are theoretically related to the different (although overlapping) neural substrates underlying the two major syndromes of psychosis. Evidence is reviewed that indicates that in ECT-responsive depression (with both bilateral and unilateral nondominant ECT) the *modus operandi* hinges on right-hemispheric neural events. Neurophysiological, neurological, and acoustic threshold evidence is discussed: all of which emphasizes the importance of the nondominant hemisphere in the genesis of endogenous depressions and in their treatment with convulsive therapies. In addition, studies showing that psychotropic agents with specific antidepressant effects produce asymmetric activation of the right hemisphere (EEG) are related to the above issues.

REFERENCES

1. FLOR-HENRY, P. 1969. Psychosis and temporal lobe epilepsy—controlled investigation. Epilepsia **10:** 363–395.
2. KRISTENSEN, O. & E. H. SINDRUP. 1978. Psychomotor epilepsy and psychosis. I. Physical aspects. II. Electroencephalographic findings (sphenoidal electrode recordings). Acta Neurol. Scand. **57:** 361–379.
3. PENFIELD, W. & H. H. JASPER. 1954. Epilepsy, and the Functional Anatomy of Human Brain. Little, Brown. Boston, Mass.
4. WALSHE, F. 1965. Further Critical Studies in Neurology and Other Essays and Addresses (Chapter 3): 61–95. Livingston. Edinburgh & London.
5. BANCAUD, J., J. TALAIRACH, A. BONIS, C. SCHAUB, G. SZIKLA, P. MOREL & M. BORDAS-FERRER. 1965. La Stéreo-Electroencéphalographie dans l'Épilepsie: 321. Mason. Paris, France.
6. BANCAUD, J. 1972. Mechanisms of cortical discharges in 'generalized' epilepsies in man. *In* Synchronization of EEG Activity in Epilepsies. H. Petsche & M. A. B. BRAZIER, Eds. Springer Verlag. New York, N.Y.
7. BANCAUD, J., J. TALAIRACH, P. MOREL, M. BESSON, A. BONIS, S. GRIER, E. HOMON & P. BUSER. 1974. 'Generalized' epileptic seizures elicited by electrical stimulation of the frontal lobe of man. Electroencephalogr. Clin. Neurophysiol. **37:** 275–282.
8. GLOOR, P. 1968. Generalized cortico-reticular epilepsies: some considerations on the pathophysiology of generalized bilaterally synchronous spike and wave discharge. Epilepsia **9:** 249–263.
9. GLOOR, P. 1972. Generalized spike and wave discharges: a consideration of cortical and subcortical mechanisms of their genesis and synchronization. *In* Synchronization of EEG Activity in Epilepsies. H. Petsche & M. A. B. Brazier, Eds. Springer Verlag. New York, N.Y.
10. COCEANI, F., I. LIBMAN & P. GLOOR. 1966. The effect of intracarotid amobarbital injections upon experimentally induced epileptiform activity. Electroencephalogr. Clin. Neurophysiol. **20:** 542–558.
11. GARRETSON, H., P. GLOOR & T. RASMUSSEN. 1966. Intracarotid amobarbital and metrazol test for the study of epileptiform discharges in man: a note on its technique. Electroencephalogr. Clin. Neurophysiol. **21:** 607–610.
12. RODIN, E., T. ONUMA, S. WASSON, J. PORZAK & M. RODIN. 1971. Neurophysiological mechanisms involved in grand mal seizures induced by metrazol and megimide. Electroencephalogr. Clin. Neurophysiol. **30:** 62–72.
13. MIRSKI, M. A. & J. A. FERRENDELLI. 1984. Interruption of the mammillothalamic tract prevents seizures in guinea pigs. Science **226**(4670): 72–74.
14. THARP, B. R. 1972. Orbital frontal seizures: an unique electroencephalographic and clinical syndrome. Epilepsia **13:** 627–642.
15. POST, R. M., F. PUTNAM, N. R. CONTEL & B. GOLDMAN. 1984. Electroconvulsive seizures inhibit amygdala kindling: implications for mechanisms of action in affective illness. Epilepsia **25**(2): 234–239.
16. LE GAL LA SALLE, G. 1979. Inhibition of kindling-induced generalized seizures by amino-oxyacetic acid. Can. J. Physiol. Pharmacol. **58:** 7–11.
17. LAUTIN, A., B. ANGRIST, M. STANLEY, S. GERSHON, *et al.* 1980. Sodium valproate in schizophrenia: some biochemical correlates. Br. J. Psychiatry **137:** 240–244.
18. STEVENS, J. R., L. BIGELOW, D. DENNEY, *et al.* 1979. Telemetered EEG-EOG during psychotic behaviors of schizophrenia. Arch. Gen. Psychiatry **36:** 251–262.

19. SACKEIM, H. A., P. DECINA, S. MALITZ, *et al.* 1983. Anticonvulsant and antidepressant properties of electroconvulsive therapy: a proposed mechanism of action. Biol. Psychiatry **18**(11): 1301–1310.
20. BERRETTINI, W. H., B. UMBERKOMAN-WIITA, J. I. NURNBERGER, *et al.* 1982. Platelet GABA-transaminase in affective illness. Psychiatry Res. **7:** 255–260.
21. D'ELIA, G. & H. RAOTMA. 1975. Is unilateral ECT less effective than bilateral ECT? Br. J. Psychiatry **126:** 83–89.
22. HALLIDAY, A. M., K. DAVISON, M. W. BROWNE, *et al.* 1968. A comparison of the effects on depression and memory of bilateral ECT and unilateral ECT to the dominant and nondominant hemispheres. Br. J. Psychiatry **114:** 997–1012.
23. GALIN, D. 1974. Implications for psychiatry of left and right cerebral specialization: a neuropsychological context for unconscious processes. Arch. Gen. Psychiatry **31:** 572–583.
24. DEGLIN, V. L. & N. N. NIKOLAENKO. 1975. Role of the dominant hemisphere in the regulation of emotional states. Hum. Physiol. **1**(3): 394–402.
25. ZINKIN, S. & J. BIRTCHNELL. 1968. Unilateral electroconvulsive therapy: its effects on memory and its therapeutic efficacy. Br. J. Psychiatry **114:** 973–988.
26. CRONIN, D., P. BODLEY, L. POTTS, *et al.* 1970. Unilateral and bilateral ECT: a study of memory disturbance and relief from depression. J. Neurol. Neurosurg. Psychiatry **33:** 705–713.
27. COHEN, B. D., S. B. PENICK & R. E. TARTER. 1974. Antidepressant effects of unilateral electric convulsive shock therapy. Arch. Gen. Psychiatry **31:** 673–675.
28. KRONFOL, Z., K. DES. HAMSHER, K. DIGRE & R. WAZIRI. 1978. Depression and hemispheric functions: changes associated with unilateral ECT. Br. J. Psychiatry **132:** 560–567.
29. FROMM-AUCH, D. 1982. Comparison of unilateral and bilateral ECT: evidence for selective memory impairment. Br. J. Psychiatry **141:** 608–613.
30. SMALL, I. F., J. G. SMALL, V. MILSTEIN & J. E. MOORE. 1972. Neuropsychological observations with psychosis and somatic treatment. J. Nerv. Ment. Dis. **155:** 6–13.
31. SMALL, I. F., V. MILSTEIN & J. G. SMALL. 1981. Relationship between clinical and cognitive change with bilateral and unilateral ECT. Biol. Psychiatry **16**(8): 793–794.
32. KRISS, A., A. M. HALLIDAY & R. T. C. PRATT. 1975. Asymmetries in the flash evolved response following unilateral electroconvulsive therapy. Electroencephalogr. Clin. Neurophysiol. **39**(4): 430.
33. SACKEIM, H. A., S. PORTNOY, P. DECINA, S. MALITZ, V. WARMFLESH, W. A. VINGIANO & S. C. YUDOFSKY. 1983. Left-side visual neglect in ECT patients. Psychopharmacol. Bull. **19**(1): 83–85.
34. SACKEIM, H. A., S. PORTNOY, P. DECINA, I. PROHOVNIK. S. MALITZ, D. EPSTEIN & W. VINGIANO. 1984. Clinical response to ECT: alterations in functional asymmetries. Paper presented at the 92nd Annual Meeting of the American Psychological Association, Toronto, Canada, August.
35. BRUDER, G., C. MARTIN, F. QUITKIN, J. STEWART, P. MCGRATH & W. HARRISON. 1984. Perceptual asymmetry in depressed patients before and after antidepressant treatment. Paper presented at the 92nd Annual Meeting of the American Psychological Association, Toronto, Canada, August.
36. FROMM, D. & D. SCHOPFLOCHER. 1984. Neuropsychological test performance in depressed patients before and after drug therapy. Biol. Psychiatry **19**(1): 55–72.
37. GOTTFRIES, C. G., C. PERRIS & B. E. ROOS. 1974. Visual averaged evoked responses (AER) and monoamine metabolites in cerebrospinal fluid (CSF). Acta Psychiatr. Scand. Suppl. **255:** 135–157.
38. LAURIAN, S., J. -M. GAILLARD, P. K. LE & J. SCHOPF. 1983. Topographic aspects of EEG profile of some psychotropic drugs. Adv. Biol. Psychiatry **13:** 165–171. (Also *In* Neurophysiological Correlates of Normal Cognition and Psychopathology. C. Perris, D. Kemali & M. Koukkou-Lehmann, Eds. Karger. Basel, Switzerland.)
39. SAI-HALASZ, A., G. BRUNECKER & S. SZERA. 1958. Dimethyltryptamin: ein neues psychoticum. Psychiatr. Neurol. **135:** 285–301.
40. OKE, A., R. KELLER, J. MEFFORD & R. M. ADAMS. 1978. Lateralization of norepinephrine in human thalamus. Science **200:** 1411–1413.

41. OKE, A. 1983. Norepinephrine distribution patterns in human thalamus. Int. J. Psychophysiol. **1:** 109.
42. VON KNORRING, L. 1983. Interhemispheric EEG differences in affective disorders. *In* Laterality and Psychopathology. P. Flor-Henry and J. Gruzelier, Eds.: 315–338. Elsevier-North Holland. Amsterdam, Holland.
43. FLOR-HENRY, P. 1985. Observations, reflections and speculations on the cerebral determinants of mood and on the bilaterally asymmetrical distributions of the major neurotransmitter systems. *In* The Pharmacotherapy of Affective Disorders: Theory and Practice. W. G. Dewhurst & G. B. Baker, Eds.: 151–184. Croom Helm Ltd. London, England.

Dosage, Seizure Threshold, and the Antidepressant Efficacy of Electroconvulsive Therapy[a]

HAROLD A. SACKEIM,[b,c,d] PAOLO DECINA,[b,c,d]
ISAK PROHOVNIK,[b,c,d] STEPHANIE PORTNOY,[b,c,d]
MAUREEN KANZLER,[b,c] AND SIDNEY MALITZ[b,c]

[b]*Department of Biological Psychiatry*
New York State Psychiatric Institute
722 West 168 Street
New York, New York 10032

[c]*Department of Psychiatry*
College of Physicians and Surgeons
Columbia University
722 West 168 Street
New York, New York 10032

[d]*Department of Psychology*
New York University
6 Washington Place
New York, New York 10003

In accounting for the mechanisms of action of electroconvulsive therapy (ECT), considerable attention has been paid to the seizure. Generalized tonic-clonic seizures are hypermetabolic states. They result in pronounced electrical discharge and in pronounced increases in cerebral blood flow (CBF), cerebral oxygen, and glucose consumption. These effects are robust and have been observed in studies of spontaneous or induced seizures in epileptic patients,[1-4] in ECT patients,[5,6] and in animals.[7,8] The increase in circulatory and metabolic rates may be on the order of 200 to 300%. CBF will increase markedly, with or without adequate oxygenation, and under conditions of constant cardiac output. As the magnitude of the CBF increase typically exceeds the increased metabolic demands, with modified ECT clinically significant changes are not expected in cerebral arteriovenous (A-V) oxygen pressure (pO_2), carbon dioxide pressure (pCO_2), and lactate gradients, or in tissue pO_2, accumulation of tissue lactate and CO_2, or hypoxia.[6,7,9,10]

We have suggested that despite the marked neurophysiological changes that accompany the seizure, these are not central to the therapeutic consequences of ECT.[11] Rather, we suggested that the processes that terminate the seizure are more reflective of the state of the brain following ECT and are more critical in accounting for the antidepressant properties of the treatment. Specifically, we suggested that ECT has marked anticonvulsant properties and that these anticonvulsant properties provide the basis for the antidepressant effects of the treatment.[11,12]

At this point we know that it is not true that the seizure ends because the brain runs out of carbohydrate supplies, or because of acidosis or hypoxia. Such events either do

[a]This work was supported in part by National Institute of Mental Health Grant MH 35636.

not occur or do not account for termination. Neuronal exhaustion models do not appear to be consistent with the neurophysiological effects of seizure elicitation. Indeed, the disruption of the processes that terminate seizures in cases of status epilepticus testifies that the brain is capable of sustaining seizure activity for much longer periods than the typical 60 seconds following electrical inductions in depressed patients. Instead, we have suggested that an active inhibitory process is potentiated by seizure elicitation. In this light, the goal in ECT is not so much the elicitation of a generalized seizure, but rather the potentiation of the process that ends the seizure.

This paper has two main aims. The first is to review the anticonvulsant properties of ECT and to suggest how each property might or might not be related to the antidepressant effects of the treatment. The second aim is to discuss the issue of dosage in ECT. Here our purpose is to discuss how dosage might be best measured, how dosage relates to seizure threshold, and to speculate about why generalized seizures may be elicited with right unilateral ECT at threshold dosage and yet have notably weak therapeutic properties.[13]

TABLE 1. Anticonvulsant Properties of ECT

1. Progressive increase in seizure threshold
2. Progressive decrease in seizure duration
3. Acute reduction in neurometabolic rate and blood flow
4. Inhibition of kindled and spontaneous seizures
5. Enhanced transmission of inhibitory neurotransmitters and peptides

ANTICONVULSANT PROPERTIES OF ECT

There are five areas of evidence that indicate that ECT has anticonvulsant properties (see TABLE 1). These include the effects of ECT on seizure threshold, on seizure duration, on neurometabolic rates, on kindled seizures and on spontaneous epileptic seizures, and on inhibitory neurotransmitters and peptides.

Seizure Threshold

Chemical or electrical inductions of seizure will raise the threshold for subsequent inductions in both animals and man.[14,15] In the random-assignment, double-blind efficacy study we just completed, contrasting titrated, relatively low-dosage right unilateral and bilateral ECT, we used an ECT administration procedure that permitted for quantification and tracking of seizure threshold over the course of treatment.[16] Across the sample of 52 patients with primary, major depressive disorder, seizure threshold increased on average by 65% from the beginning to the end of the course. This change within patients must reflect a major alteration in the state of neural excitability.

We found in this study that 70.37% of patients who received titrated, bilateral ECT met conservative criteria for therapeutic response, whereas only 28% of patients receiving titrated, right unilateral ECT were classified as responders.[13] With respect to seizure threshold, parallel differences were observed. Seizure threshold increased more substantially in the bilateral than unilateral group. At the end of the treatment course, threshold had increased on average 87% in the bilateral group and only 40% in the unilateral group.

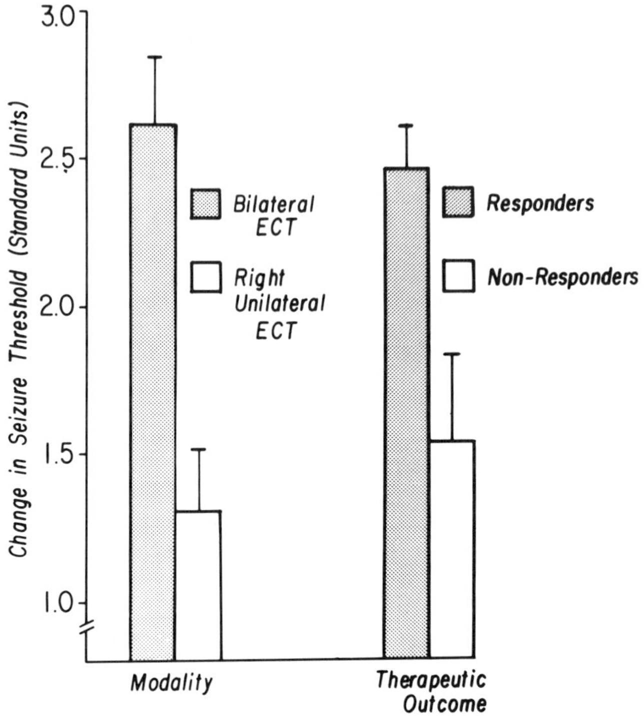

FIGURE 1. Change in seizure threshold from beginning to end of treatment course as a function of modality and therapeutic outcome.

We computed a standard units measure of the seizure threshold increase by dividing for each patient the magnitude of their change in threshold in millicouloumbs by their standard deviation in the stimulus intensity necessary to produce seizure, computed across all their treatment sessions. Again, seizure threshold increased more in the bilateral than unilateral group (see FIGURE 1). When the data were analyzed in relation to treatment response, seizure threshold increased more in responders than nonresponders. Likewise, this held for the proportionate increase in seizure threshold.

Of note, the magnitude of the threshold increase was similar for patients in the bilateral groups regardless of whether they responded to treatment and for patients who responded to titrated right unilateral ECT. Nonresponders to right unilateral ECT displayed a weak seizure threshold increase. Indeed, of nine patients who evidenced an increase of 12 millicoulombs or less, none responded to treatment, and all of these patients received titrated, right unilateral ECT.

At the clinical level, we are suggesting that if a substantial increase in seizure threshold is not observed, patients will have weak or no therapeutic response to ECT. There is a small percentage of patients who will evidence a large increase, but fail to respond. Presumably in this minority of cases, the anticonvulsant properties of ECT are irrelevant to the pathophysiology of their depressions. The suggestion then is that a large increase in seizure threshold is not particularly predictive of therapeutic response. No increase or a very small increase is predictive of nonresponse.

Seizure Duration

It is well accepted that the seizure elicited in the first ECT treatment tends to be the longest in duration relative to remaining treatments.[17] Small *et al.* recently demonstrated this by contrasting seizure duration in the first and fifth treatments.[18] TABLE 2 displays from our data set mean seizure duration over the first eight treatments. There is a steady and progressive decline in seizure duration until the fifth or sixth treatment, after which there is a plateau. These findings with an EEG measure are fully in line with what Holmberg reported in the 1950s for an EMG measure of motor manifestations of convulsion.[17] On average, seizure duration decreased 24% from beginning to end of the treatment course. This anticonvulsant effect was highly consistent. Of the 52 patients, 44 had shorter durations in their last two treatments than in their first two treatments.

The decrease in seizure duration does not appear to be associated with the antidepressant properties of the treatments. As seen in TABLE 2, both treatment modalities had comparable durations at the beginning and end of the treatment course and comparable decreases in duration, both in terms of absolute magnitude and percentage decrease.

In our hands, no aspect of seizure duration was related to therapeutic outcome, whether assessed in terms of mean duration per treatment, total seizure time, or in terms of the decrease in duration. At best, the increase in seizure threshold and the decrease in seizure duration are only partially overlapping phenomena. Threshold increased progressively over the course of treatment, whereas the decrease in seizure duration plateaued after the fifth or sixth treatment. There did not appear to be an association between the changes in threshold and in seizure duration. Threshold changes were more marked in the bilateral group and in ECT responders. Changes in seizure duration did not discriminate.

The absence of associations between changes in seizure duration and antidepressant effects may be a reflection of the crudeness of the seizure duration measure based on a left frontal EEG lead. In pilot work, using 20 leads, conducted in collaboration

TABLE 2. Seizure Duration as a Function of Treatment Number and Modality

	Total Sample ($n = 52$)[a]	Right Unilateral ($n = 25$)[a]	Bilateral ECT ($n = 27$)
Treatments 1–2			
Mean	72.63	70.62	74.42
SD[b]	26.01	26.70	25.24
Treatments 3–4			
Mean	62.92	59.94	65.67
SD	27.85	31.38	23.81
Treatments 5–6			
Mean	57.18	55.47	58.77
SD	20.79	18.51	22.58
Treatments 7–8			
Mean	54.36	53.61	55.05
SD	21.47	19.65	23.01
Last Two Treatments			
Mean	52.63	52.29	52.94
SD	24.45	24.57	24.33

[a]Data missing for treatments 1–2 of one unilateral right ECT patient.
[b]SD is standard deviation.

with Dr. John Morihisa from the National Institute of Mental Health, we observed, at times, marked regionality in the offset of seizures. At times seizure activity disappeared notably earlier in some brain regions than others. Furthermore, the lack of association may further indicate that the seizure is not a unitary phenomenon. It is our impression, which we hope soon to test topographically, that with increases in threshold the tonic phase of the seizure may shorten or even drop out completely, while there are variable effects on the duration of the clonic phase.

Neurometabolic Rates

Turning to neurometabolic rates and cerebral circulation, at the beginning of our work we had hypothesized that following the electrically induced seizure, there is a decrease in neural metabolic activity.[16] We interpreted such a phenomenon as reflecting the potentiation of the endogenous inhibitory processes that terminated the seizure.

The studies reported by Prohovnik[19] and Silfverskiöld[20] in this volume indicate that 50 minutes to two hours following ECT there is a marked reduction in cerebral flood flow when contrasted with pretreatment baselines. Further, in our laboratory, Prohovnik has been able to demonstrate both marked laterality and regionality in the reductions of cerebral blood flow as a function of electrode placement. Bilateral ECT produced largely symmetric changes in CBF. The area of greatest reduction was in the frontal cortex, and the extent of reduction diminished as one moved more posteriorly on the caudality dimension. Compared to pre-ECT baseline, bilateral ECT patients averaged a 10 to 15% reduction in gray matter flow rates in anterior frontal regions, with little change in occipital cortex. In contrast, right unilateral ECT resulted in significantly greater reductions in the right than left hemisphere. The reductions within the right hemisphere were more diffuse than with bilateral ECT. In particular, an area surrounding the central sulcus seemed markedly reduced.

These differences between modalities in the patterns of acute CBF reduction highlight the general fact that with standard electrode placements, bilateral and unilateral ECT differ not only in lateralized effects but also in regionalized effects. Specifically, we offer the suggestion that the regional patterns of CBF reductions are related to current density paths. On the basis of theoretical models and empirical work with animals and cadavers it is largely agreed that within the cortex current density is greatest in the anterior frontal pole with the standard bifrontotemporal electrode placement. Current density with right unilateral ECT is substantially greater in the right than left hemisphere and is more diffusely distributed over right cortical tissue than with bilateral ECT.[21–24] We do not mean by this that the suppression of neurometabolic activity following ECT is a direct effect of current. Rather, we speculate that the current paths are intimately related to the neural regions that trigger and lead to propagation of the seizure. Specifically, we suggest that the endogenous inhibitory process that terminates the seizure is particularly directed at regions responsible for elicitation of the seizure.

Such a pattern of neurometabolic changes appears to occur with focal epilepsy. It has now become a standard observation reported in a number of laboratories that functional neurometabolic activity is often suppressed interictally in regions surrounding foci in cases of focal epilepsy.[5,25–27] The metabolic suppression cannot be readily attributed to cerebral cicatrix or scarring of tissue since the functional suppression is larger in extent than the structural damage identified by light microscopy of resected tissue. Further, the same area is capable of sustaining profound hypermetabolic activity during the ictal state.[26]

The physiological determinants of the interictal hypometabolic zones are unknown. One suggestion is that the hypometabolism reflects the marshaling of inhibition directed at the neuronal aggregates critical to seizure generation. Applying this to ECT, we suggest that bilateral and right unilateral ECT differ markedly in current density paths both on dimensions of lateralization and regionalization.[21-24] Seizures are, therefore, triggered in different loci in the cortex as a function of electrode placement. The subsequent pattern of postictal neurometabolic suppression may reflect the potentiation of the endogenous inhibitory process directed at the regions that trigger and lead to propagation of the seizure.

It should be noted that while this view is speculative, it can be tested with autoradiographic methods in animals. If this view is correct, it suggests that ultimately particular configurations of electrode placements may be selected in relation to the abnormalities in neural activity characteristic of individual patients.

More broadly, at this point we now can feel more confident in stating that in the acute postictal period following ECT a profound reduction is observed in neurometabolic activity. Whether neurometabolic measures are related to the increase in seizure threshold and to therapeutic outcome measures is unknown at this time. It will be critical to observe the more long-term effects of ECT on CBF and metabolism measures. Our own data on the CBF changes over the course of ECT are quite preliminary. Further, it may be useful at this point to raise a cautionary note. We are on relatively safe ground when we interpret reductions in CBF and in metabolic rates as reflecting decreased neural excitability. However, increased inhibitory neural transmission can also result in increased metabolic activity. The inhibition of neural transmission certainly involves metabolic demands. Engel and colleagues recently demonstrated this principle in 2-deoxyglucose (2-DG) autoradiography with animals. Selective stimulation of inhibitory tracts to the hippocampus resulted in enhanced postsynaptic inhibition and led to local increases in metabolic rates.[26] Therefore, we may be in a circumstance where decreased metabolic rates are interpretable as reflecting a decrease in neural excitability and, possibly, enhanced inhibitory transmission, but where increased metabolic rates can reflect either increased or decreased neural excitability. Nonetheless, it will be critical over the next few years to determine what relations, if any, alterations in cerebral circulation and metabolism have with changes in seizure threshold, the development of regional EEG slow wave activity, localized neuropsychological deficits, and therapeutic outcome following ECT.

Kindling and Spontaneous Seizures

Virtually simultaneous with the introduction of the kindling paradigm as a method for eliciting seizures in animals, the concern was raised that ECT in humans is a method of kindling and ECT puts patients in danger of developing a seizure disorder.[28] Likewise, since the introduction of ECT there has been concern as to whether the treatment enhances the likelihood of manifestation of spontaneous seizures.[18,29]

Of consequence for the theoretical framework offered here, elegant work by Post[30] and others[31] has demonstrated that electroconvulsive shock (ECS) in animals will retard the development of kindled seizures or reduce or block the expression of kindled seizures. In this respect ECS has effects similar to anticonvulsant medications, such as carbamazepine, that are powerful inhibitors of kindled seizures.[32]

With respect to human seizure disorders there is also evidence that ECT can be a powerful anticonvulsant. In 1946, Caplan administered ECT on a regular basis to a large sample of psychotic patients who were actively epileptic.[33] In a substantial proportion, the frequency of spontaneous and ECT-induced seizures was considerably below the baseline of spontaneous seizures. In a fair proportion, spontaneous seizures stopped completely. When ECT was discontinued spontaneous seizure activity returned.

We have reported a similar experience, treating with ECT a 19-year-old patient with intractable, idiopathic secondary generalized epilepsy since the age of eight months.[12] Despite treatments with all conventional anticonvulsants, she continued to have spontaneous seizures at virtually a daily rate. Eight days after ECT was instituted at a three per week schedule without change in her medication regimen, the patient became free of spontaneous seizures for 25 days. This was the longest period since the onset of her seizure disorder that the patient was free of spontaneous convulsions. Since this report, we have heard from clinicians who have used ECT successfully to break up status epilepticus. A fairly high proportion of patients in status, some estimate as many as 40%, do not respond to anticonvulsant medications and die.

It would seem, therefore, that ECT has powerful anticonvulsant effects in the kindling model of epilepsy and in some cases of human seizure disorders. There is insufficient space to discuss the possible reasons why exogenous electrically induced seizures may be more potent as anticonvulsants than endogenously elicited spontaneous seizures. At the clinical level, there would seem ample reason to investigate the extent to which the electrical induction of seizures under medically controlled and predictable circumstances has a role in the care of pharmacologically intractable seizure disorders. Indeed, one wonders whether the controversy concerning the use of ECT would be so intense had the early study of its application to neurological disorders advanced to the extent that it has in psychiatric disorders.

Effects on Inhibitory Neurotransmitters and Peptides

The potentiation by ECT of an endogenous inhibitory process must have a biochemical basis. Recently, Isaac and Swanger demonstrated that injection of CSF from cats that underwent ECS into the ventricular system of host cats raised the seizure threshold of the hosts.[34] Presently, a number of neurotransmitter and peptide systems are possibilities in accounting for the effects of ECT on seizure threshold, neurometabolic rates, and kindling. For example, it has been demonstrated that concurrent administration of opioid antagonists will block the rise in seizure threshold following ECS[35] and will also partially block the action of ECS in inhibiting the expression of kindled seizures.[36] There is also evidence that administration of enkephalin analogues will have anticonvulsant effects on kindled seizures and protect against ECS-elicited seizures.[37] As Holaday has reviewed in this volume, ECS has notable effects in altering various aspects of endogenous opioid systems.[38]

We have been particularly intrigued by ECT effects on the transmission of gamma-aminobutyric acid (GABA). Green and colleagues have found that previous ECS raises the seizure threshold for bicuculine, pentylenetetrazol (PTZ), and IPTBO,[14] agents whose convulsant properties appear to be related to antagonism of GABA-ergic transmission. On the other hand, ECS does not raise the threshold for the convulsant strychnine, a glycine antagonist, or quipazine, a 5-hydroxytryptamine agonist. Therefore, there appears to be selectivity in that ECT will raise the threshold for convulsants acting primarily on GABA and not for convulsants acting in some other systems.

In line with this evidence, Loscher has shown that a variety of agents that increase whole brain and synaptosome GABA levels also increase the minimal ECS and PTZ seizure thresholds.[39] However, as a cautionary note, Loscher also reported that there were strong associations between brain GABA levels and the relative increase in PTZ threshold but not the increase in ECS threshold.

Green's group was the first to demonstrate that a single ECS will raise concentrations of GABA in various brain regions.[40,41] If indeed alterations in GABA-ergic transmission are responsible for the steady increase in seizure threshold observed in ECT patients, one would hope to see that repeat ECS has a cumulative effect in increasing GABA concentrations. To date, using a schedule of one ECS a day for 10 days, Green's group has been able to demonstrate some relatively long-term enhancement of GABA levels in the striatum, but higher concentrations have not been observed than that elicited by a single seizure.[42]

Our group has suggested that repeat ECS schedules as frequent as one a day may be inappropriate models for what occurs in human ECT.[11] At treatment rates of three times a week in humans, there is a steady and continuous increase in seizure threshold. Therefore, threshold does not recover fully to baseline with intervals of 48 hours between treatments. In rats there is a more rapid recovery and thresholds for electrical or chemical induction of seizures may often return to baseline within approximately 2 hours of seizure induction.[14] To mimic the changes in seizure threshold in humans we have suggested that more massed ECS must be used. This is supported by findings described by Holaday *et al.* that massed ECS, unlike spaced ECS, results in progressive shortening in duration and reduced severity of seizures and that the reversal of anticonvulsant properties by opioid antagonists appears more powerful in massed than spaced models.[38]

There is insufficient space to review the body of evidence implicating disturbances in GABA transmission in affective disorders and the interactions of GABA with other transmitter systems. It should be noted, however, that in the recent report by Gerner and colleagues GABA levels as well as 3-methoxy-4-hydroxyphenylglycol (MHPG), homovanillic acid (HVA), 5-hydroxyindoleacetic acid (5-HIAA), and other substances were assayed from CSF of relatively large samples of drug-free depressed, schizophrenic, and manic patients as well as normal controls.[43] GABA was the only substance to distinguish the groups, with low concentrations being found in depression. This supports other claims of reduced CSF and plasma GABA in affective disorders.[44–47] Berrettini and colleagues have reported low levels of plasma GABA in normothymic, unmedicated bipolars, which normalized with lithium therapy.[48] It should be noted as well that animal studies suggest that reduced levels of GABA-ergic transmission are associated with reduced release of serotonin and catecholamines.[49,50]

This view may also have implications for the pharmacological treatment of depression. In the learned helplessness animal model there appears to be a decrease in calcium-stimulated GABA release in the hippocampus. Chronic imipramine treatment can reverse this. Behaviorally, standard antidepressant medications such as imipramine will reduce learned helplessness deficits in escape responses. Progabide, an anticonvulsant and GABA agonist, has shown equivalent power in deficit reduction as imipramine.[51–52] In human depression, progabide was found to have the same antidepressant potency as imipramine in a double-blind clinical trial.[51,53] More generally, it is noteworthy that claims are emerging that a variety of anticonvulsant medications, particularly sodium valproate and carbamazepine, have therapeutic properties in some cases of affective disorders.[54] If indeed the antidepressant potency of ECT is related to its anticonvulsant properties, then we might progress in identifying agents that mimic these properties. For instance, by this view, progabide, a GABA agonist, or sodium valproate, which is believed to inhibit the catabolism of GABA, may be useful for continuation therapy to prevent relapse following remission of acute episodes with ECT in patients resistant to standard antidepressants.

NEURAL EXCITABILITY AND DEPRESSION

We have seen that at the behavioral, neurophysiological, and biochemical levels there is considerable evidence that ECT has anticonvulsant properties. In this framework, one must wonder why the potentiation of an endogenous inhibitory process may be associated with antidepressant response.

One model that is harmonious with this position states simply that disturbed affective states reflect the disinhibition of the neuronal aggregates that subserve depression or mania. At the level of the cerebral cortex, there is increasing evidence, for instance, for localization in the functional systems that regulate mood. As Flor-Henry has reviewed in this volume, some type of right hemisphere dysfunction seems to characterize depressed states.[55] Our group and others have suggested that depression is accompanied by relative hyperexcitability in right frontal cortex.[16,56] In this context, it would not be surprising that treatments that enhance inhibitory neural transmission have antidepressant properties. ECT may present a particularly useful method for contributing to our understanding of lateralization and regionalization in affective systems. It is noteworthy that, of the six comparative clinical trials in depression of left unilateral and right unilateral ECT,[57–62] when differences were observed they were all in the direction of superior results with right unilateral ECT. Likewise the equivalence in efficacy between bilateral and right unilateral ECT in the large bulk of studies using traditional forms of administration[63,64] may be interpreted as suggesting equivalence in suppression of relative right-side hyperactivity.

UNITS OF DOSAGE

What clearly stands out as problematic for us is why in our clinical trial titrated, relatively low-dosage right unilateral ECT was so inferior in efficacy to titrated, bilateral ECT. As Malitz *et al.* indicated in this volume,[13] we are suggesting that electrical stimulus dosage may be more critical to the efficacy of unilateral ECT than the efficacy of bilateral ECT. Briefly, three issues need mention.

To conduct research on dose-response relations there should be an adequate unit of ECT dosage. In this volume we presented dosage data in terms of the unit of charge or millicoulomb rather than the more traditional unit of watt-second or joule. We have suggested that at least with brief pulse, constant current administration the unit of charge is both a more reliable and valid measure of dosage.[65] Empirically there are several indications of this. Perhaps the most important is that there are strong negative relations between the charge necessary to elicit seizure and dynamic impedance to the passage of current. The watt-second unit is determined by the multiplicative relation between charge and impedance. However, these two factors are far from independent so that the greater the stimulus intensity required to elicit seizures in units of charge, the greater the underestimation of dosage in units of joules.[65] Similar reservations have been offered by Gordon concerning the utility of the watt-second unit.[66]

Secondly, in characterizing the nature of the stimulus given to patients we believe it is important to distinguish among the absolute dosage administered, the dosage relative to seizure threshold, and the dosage relative to the efficiency of the seizure-eliciting properties of the stimulus waveform. To illustrate, we have hypothesized in our ongoing study that the extent to which dosage exceeds threshold is more critical in terms of acute side effects than the absolute dosage per se. We predict, for instance, that patients with low thresholds who are treated at 2.5 times the initial threshold level will display more severe side effects than will patients with high thresholds treated with higher dosages in absolute terms, but at threshold levels. A further complication of course is that stimulus waveforms differ markedly in their efficiency as seizure eliciters.[67] We have referred to the administration procedure we used in the first study as a titrated, relatively low-dosage technique. We believe, however, that had the pulse width been reduced from 1.5 to 1.0 msecond, absolute dosages at threshold would also have been lower. As Weiner has shown, considerably higher dosage is needed with a constant voltage sine-wave stimulus to elicit seizures relative to constant current pulse administration.[67] It is a complete mystery at this point whether there are different patterns of cognitive and therapeutic effects when excess stimulation is given due to an inefficient waveform or when stimulation exceeds seizure threshold with an efficient waveform.

Thirdly, in relation to our efficacy findings we can offer the following speculations. As mentioned earlier, current density paths differ markedly for bilateral and right unilateral ECT both in terms of lateralization and regionalization. In the cortex current density with bilateral ECT appears to be greatest at the frontal pole. There is more even diffusion of current across the right hemisphere with the d'Elia placement.[68–71] There is evidence that the cortex is not a homogenous medium in terms of seizure threshold. In particular more posterior regions may have lower thresholds than frontal cortex.[72,73] With unilateral ECT given at threshold dosage we may have triggered seizures from the areas surrounding the central sulcus, due to low thresholds. With bilateral ECT frontal cortex was prominently involved in the triggering and propagation of seizures due to the nature of current density paths. It is noteworthy here that higher dosages were necessary to elicit seizures with bilateral ECT from the start of ECT. We have suggested that inhibition following the seizure may be directed at regions critical in seizure elicitation. We observed in our preliminary CBF results differences in the landscape of acute regional reductions within the right hemisphere as a function of modality. Presumably, such differences may contribute to the modality effects on efficacy and the increase in seizure threshold. We suspect that when the dosage of right unilateral ECT is increased above threshold, frontal regions with higher seizure threshold will become more involved in the triggering and propagation of the seizure with a consequent gain in efficacy.

REFERENCES

1. BRODERSEN, P., O. B. PAULSON, T. G. BOLWIG, *et al.* 1973. Cerebral hyperemia in electrically induced epileptic seizures. Arch. Neurol. **28:** 334–338.
2. INGVAR, D. H. 1973. Regional cerebral blood flow in focal cortical epilepsy. Stroke **4:** 359–360.
3. KUHL, D. E., J. ENGEL, JR. M. E. PHELPS, *et al.* 1980. Epileptic patterns of local cerebral metabolism and perfusion in humans determined by emission computed tomography of ^{18}FDG and $^{13}NH_3$. Ann. Neurol. **8:** 348–360.
4. GIBBS, F. A., W. G. LENNOX & E. L. GIBBS. 1934. Cerebral blood flow preceding and accompanying epileptic seizures in man. Arch. Neurol. Psychiatry **32:** 257–272.
5. ENGEL, J., D. E. KUHL & M. E. PHELPS. 1982. Patterns of human local cerebral glucose metabolism during epileptic seizures. Science **218:** 64–66.
6. POSNER, J. B., F. PLUM & A. VAN POZNAK. 1969. Cerebral metabolism during electrically induced seizures in man. Arch. Neurol. **20:** 388–395.
7. PLUM, F., D. C. HOWSE & T. E. DUFFY. 1974. Metabolic effects of seizures. Res. Publ. Assoc. Res. Nerv. Ment. Dis. **53:** 141–157.
8. GIBB, F. A. 1933. Cerebral blood flow preceding and accompanying experimental convulsions. Arch. Neurol. Psychiatry **30:** 1003–1010.

9. BERESFORD, H. R., J. B. POSNER & F. PLUM. 1969. Changes in blood lactate during induced cerebral seizures. Arch. Neurol. **29:** 243–248.
10. PITTS, F. N. 1982. Medical physiology of ECT. *In* Electroconvulsive Therapy: Biological Foundations and Clinical Applications. R. Abrams & W. B. Essman, Eds.: 57–89. SP Medical. New York, NY.
11. SACKEIM, H. A., I. PROHOVNIK, P. DECINA, S. MALITZ & S. RESOR. 1983. Anticonvulsant and antidepressant properties of ECT: a proposed mechanism of action. Biol. Psychiatry **18:** 1301–1310.
12. SACKEIM, H. A., I. PROHOVNIK, P. DECINA, S. MALITZ & S. RESOR. 1983. Anticonvulsant properties of electroconvulsive therapy: theory and case report. *In* Current Problems in Epilepsy: Cerebral Blood Flow, Metabolism and Epilepsy. M. Baldy-Moulinier, D.-H. Ingvar & B. S. Meldrum, Eds. Libbey. London, England.
13. MALITZ, S., H. A. SACKEIM, P. DECINA, M. KANZLER & B. KERR. 1986. The efficacy of electroconvulsive therapy: dose-response interactions with modality. Ann. N.Y. Acad. Sci. (This volume.)
14. GREEN, A. R., D. J. NUTT & P. J. COWEN. 1982. Increased threshold following convulsion. *In* Psychopharmacology of Anticonvulsants. M. Sandler. Ed.: 16–26. Oxford University Press. Oxford, England.
15. GREEN, M. A. 1960. Relation between threshold and duration of seizures and electrographic change during convulsive therapy. J. Nerv. Ment. Dis. **131:** 117–120.
16. MALITZ, S., H. A. SACKEIM & P. DECINA. 1982. ECT in the treatment of major affective disorders: clinical and basic research issues. Psychiatr. J. Univ. Ottawa **7:** 127–134.
17. HOLMBERG, G. 1954. Effect on electrically induced convulsion of the number of previous treatments in a series. Arch. Neurol. Psychiatry **71:** 619–623.
18. SMALL, J. G., V. MILSTEIN, I. F. SMALL, *et al.* 1981. Does ECT produce kindling? Biol. Psychiatry **16:** 773–778.
19. PROHOVNIK, I., H. A. SACKEIM, P. DECINA & S. MALITZ. 1986. Acute reductions of regional cerebral blood flow following electroconvulsive therapy: interactions with modality and time. Ann. N.Y. Acad. Sci. (This volume.)
20. SILFVERSKIÖLD, P., L. GUSTAFSON, J. RISBERG & I. ROSÉN. 1986. Acute and late effects of electroconvulsive therapy: clinical outcome, regional cerebral blood flow, and electroencephalogram. Ann. N.Y. Acad. Sci. (This volume.)
21. HAYES, K. J. 1950. The current path in electric convulsive shock. Arch. Neurol. Psychiatry **63:** 102–109.
22. RUSH, S. & D. A. DRISCOLL. 1968. Current distribution in the brain from surface electrodes. Anesth. Analg. **47:** 717–723.
23. SMITT, J. & C. F. WEGNER. 1944. On ECT: with particular regard to a parietal application of electrodes, controlled by intracerebral voltage measurements. Acta Psychiatr. Neurol. Scand. **19:** 529–549.
24. WEAVER, L., R. WILLIAMS & S. RUSH. 1976. Current density in bilateral and unilateral ECT. Biol. Psychiatry **11:** 303–312.
25. BERNARDI, S., B. GALLHOFER, M. R. TRIMBLE, R. S. J. FRACKOWIAK, R. J. S. WISE & T. JONES. 1983. An inter-ictal study of partial epilepsy using the oxygen-15 inhalation technique and positron emission tomography, with special reference to psychosis. *In* Current problems in Epilepsy I. Cerebral Blood Flow, Metabolism and Epilepsy. M. Baldy-Moulinier, D. H. Ingvar & B. S. Meldrum, Eds.: 44–50. Libbey. London, England.
26. ENGEL, J. 1983. Metabolic patterns of human epilepsy: clinical observations and possible physiological correlates. *In* Current Problems in Epilepsy I. Cerebral Blood Flow, Metabolism and Epilepsy. M. Baldy-Moulinier, D. H. Ingvar & B. S. Meldrum, Eds.: 6–18. Libbey. London, England.
27. YAMAMOTO, Y. L., R. OCHS, P. GLOOR, W. AMMANN, E. MEYER, A. C. EVANS, B. COOKE, K. SAKO, J. GOTMAN. W. H. FEINDEL, M. DIKSIC, C. J. THOMPSON & Y. VON ROBITAILLE. 1983. Patterns of rCBF and focal energy metabolic changes in relation to electro-encephalographic abnormality in the inter-ictal phase of partial epilepsy. *In* Current Problems in Epilepsy I. Cerebral Blood Flow, Metabolism and Epilepsy. M. Baldy-Moulinier, D. H. Ingvar & B. S. Meldrum, Eds.: 51–62. Libbey. London, England.

28. GODDARD, G. V., D. C. MCINTYRE & C. K. LEECH. 1969. A permanent change in brain function resulting from daily electrical stimulation. Exp. Neurol. **25:** 295–330.
29. DEVINSKY, O. & M. S. DUCHOWNY. 1983. Seizures after convulsive therapy: a retrospective case survey. Neurology **33:** 921–925.
30. POST, R. M., F. PUTNAM, N. R. CONTEL & B. GOLDMAN. 1984. Electroconvulsive seizures inhibit amygdala kindling: implications for mechanisms of action in affective illness. Epilepsia **25:** 234–239.
31. BABINGTON, R. G. & P. W. WEDEKING. 1975. Blockade of tardive seizures in rats by electroconvulsive shock. Brain Res. **88:** 141–144.
32. POST, R. M., F. PUTNAM, T. W. UHDE & S. R. B. WEISS. 1986. Electroconvulsive therapy as an anticonvulsant: implications for its mechanism of action in affective illness. Ann. N.Y. Acad. Sci. (This volume.)
33. CAPLAN, G. 1946. Electrical convulsion therapy in treatment of epilepsy. J. Ment. Sci. **92:** 784–793.
34. ISAAC, L. & J. SWANGER. 1983. Alteration of electroconvulsive threshold by cerebrospinal fluid from cats tolerant to electroconvulsive shock. Life Sci. **33:** 2301–2304.
35. TORTELLA, F. C. & A. COWAN. 1982. Studies on opioid peptides as endogenous anticonvulsants. Life Sci. **31:** 2225–2228.
36. CHUGANI, H. T., R. F. ACKERMANN, D. C. CHUGANI & J. ENGEL, JR. 1984. Opioid-induced epileptogenic phenomena: anatomical, behavioral, and electroencephalographic features. Ann. Neurol. **15:** 361–368.
37. PUGLISI-ALLEGRA, S., C. CASTELLANO, V. CSANYL, A. DOKA & A. OLIVERIO. 1984. Opioid antagonism of electroshock-induced seizures. Pharmocol. Biochem. Behav. **20:** 767–769.
38. HOLADAY, J. W., F. C. TORTELLA, J. B. LONG, G. L. BELENKY & R. J. HITZEMANN. 1986. Endogenous opioids and their receptors: evidence for involvement in the postictal effects of electroconvulsive shock. Ann. N.Y. Acad. Sci. (This volume.)
39. LOSCHER, W. 1981. Biochemical pharmacology of inhibitors of GABA metabolism and valproic acid. *In* Neurotransmitters, Seizures, and Epilepsy. P. L. Morselli, K. G. Lloyd, W. Loscher, B. S. Meldrum & E. H. Reynolds, Eds.: 93–102. Raven. New York, N.Y.
40. BOWDLER, J. M. & A. R. GREEN. 1982. Regional rat brain benzodiazepine receptor number and -aminobutyric acid concentration following a convulsion. Br. J. Pharmacol. **76:** 291–298.
41. GREEN, A. R. 1986. Changes in α-aminobutyric acid biochemistry and seizure threshold. Ann. N.Y. Acad. Sci. (This volume.)
42. BOWDLER, J. M., A. R. GREEN, M. C. W. MINCHIN & D. J. NUTT. 1983. Regional GABA concentration and [^{3}H]-diazepam binding in rat brain following repeated electroconvulsive shock. J. Neural Transm. **56:** 3–12.
43. GERNER, R. H., L. FAIRBANKS, G. M. ANDERSON, J. G. YOUNG, M. SCHEININ, M. LINNOILA, T. A. HARE, B. A. SHAYWITZ & D. J. COHEN. 1984. CSF neurochemistry in depressed, manic, and schizophrenic patients compared with that of normal controls. Am. J. Psychiatry **141:** 1533–1540.
44. GERNER, R. H. & T. A. HARE. 1981. CSF GABA in normals, depression, schizophrenia, mania and anorexia nervosa. Am. J. Psychiatry **138:** 362–364.
45. GOLD, B. I., M. B. BOWERS, R. H. ROTH & D. W. SWEENEY. 1980. GABA levels in CSF of patients with psychiatric disorders. Am. J. Psychiatry **137:** 362–364.
46. PETTY, F. 1985. Plasma GABA abnormalities in psychiatric illness. Paper presented at the Annual Meeting of the Society of Biological Psychiatry, Dallas, Texas, May 15–19.
47. PETTY, F. & M. A. SCHLESSER. 1981. Plasma GABA in affective illness. J. Affective Dis. **3:** 339–343.
48. BERRETINI, W. H., J. I. NURNBERGER, JR., T. A. HARE, S. SIMMONS-ALLING, E. S. GERSHON & R. M. POST. 1982. Plasma and CSF GABA in affective illness. Br. J. Psychiatry **141:** 483–487.
49. ARBILLA, S. & S. Z. LANGER. 1979. Facilitation by GABA of the potassium evoked release of ^{3}H-noradrenaline from the rat occipital cortex. Naunyn Schmiedebergs Arch. Pharmacol. **306:** 161–168.
50. BISWAS, B. & A. CARLSSON. 1977. The effect of intracerebroventricularly administered GABA on brain monoamine metabolism. Naunyn Schmiedebergs Arch. Pharmacol. **299:** 41–46.

51. LLOYD, K. G., B. ZIVKOVIC, B. SCATTON & G. BARTHOLINI. 1984. Evidence for functional roles of GABA pathways in the mammalian brain. *In* Actions and Interactions of GABA and Benzodiazepines. N. B. Bowery, Ed.: 59–80. Raven. New York, N.Y.
52. SHERMAN, A. D. & F. PETTY. 1980. Neurochemical basis of the action of antidepressants on learned helplessness. Behav. Neural Biol. **30:** 119–134.
53. LLOYD, K. G., P. L. MORSELLI, H. DEPOORTERE, V. FOURNIER, B. ZIVKOVIC, B. SCATTON, C. BROEKKAMP, P. WORMS & G. BARTHOLINI. 1983. The potential use of GABA agonists in psychiatric disorders evidence from studies with progabide on animal models and clinical trials. Pharmacol. Biochem. Behav. **18:** 957–966.
54. POST, R. M., J. C. BALLENGER, T. W. UHDE & W. E. BUNNEY, JR. 1984. Efficacy of carbamazepine in manic-depressive illness: implications for underlying mechanisms. *In* Neurobiology of Mood Disorders. R. M. Post & J. C. Ballenger, Eds.: 777–816. Williams & Wilkins. Baltimore, Md.
55. FLOR-HENRY, P. 1986. Electroconvulsive therapy and lateralized affective systems. Ann. N.Y. Acad. Sci. (This volume.)
56. SACKEIM, H. A., M. S. GREENBERG, A. L. WEIMAN, R. C. GUR, J. HUNGERBUHLER & N. GESCHWIND. 1982. Hemispheric asymmetry in the expression of positive and negative emotions. Arch. Neurol. **39:** 210–218.
57. COHEN, B. D., S. B. PENICK & R. E. TARTER. 1974. Antidepressant effects of unilateral electric convulsive therapy. Arch. Gen. Psychiatry **31:** 673–675.
58. COSTELLO, C. G., C. P. BELTON, J. C. ABRA & B. E. DUNN. 1970. The amnesic and therapeutic effects of bilateral and unilateral ECT. Br. J. Psychiatry **116:** 69–78.
59. CRONIN, D., P. BODLEY, L. POTTS, M. D. MATHER, R. K. GARDNER & J. C. TOBIN. 1970. Unilateral and bilateral ECT: a study of memory disturbance and relief from depression. J. Neurol. Neurosurg. Psychiatry **33:** 705–713.
60. DEGLIN, V. L. 1973. A clinical study of unilateral electroconvulsive seizures. Zh. Nevropatol. Psikhiatr. **73:** 1609–1621.
61. FLEMINGER, J. J., D. J. DE L. HORNER, N. P. V. NAIR & P. N. NOTT. 1970. Differential effect of unilateral and bilateral ECT. Am. J. Psychiatry **127:** 430–436.
62. HALLIDAY, A. M., K. DAVIDSON, M. W. BROWNE & L. C. KREEGER. 1968. A comparison of effects on depression and memory of bilateral ECT and unilateral ECT to the dominant and nondominant hemispheres. Br. J. Psychiatry **114:** 997–1012.
63. D'ELIA, G. & H. RAOTMA. 1975. Is unilateral ECT less effective than bilateral ECT? Br. J. Psychiatry **126:** 83–89.
64. FINK, M. 1979. Convulsive Therapy: Theory and Practice. Raven. New York, N.Y.
65. SACKEIM, H. A., P. DECINA, I. PROHOVNIK & S. MALITZ. Units of dosage in ECT: effects of sex, age, electrode placement, and treatment number on seizure threshold. (Manuscript submitted for publication.)
66. GORDON, D. 1982. Electro-convulsive therapy with minimum hazard. Br. J. Psychiatry **141:** 12–18.
67. WEINER, R. D. 1980. ECT and seizure threshold: Effects of stimulus wave form and electrode placement. Biol. Psychiatry **15:** 225–241.
68. HAYES, K. J. 1950. The current path in electric convulsive shock. Arch. Neurol. Psychiatry **63:** 102–109.
69. LORIMER, F. M., M. M. SEGAL & S. N. STEIN. 1949. Path of current distribution in brain during electro-convulsive therapy. Electroencephalogr. Clin. Neurophysiol. **1:** 343–348.
70. RUSH, S. & D. A. DRISCOLL. 1968. Current distribution in the brain from surface electrodes. Anesth. Analg. **47:** 717–723.
71. WEAVER, L., R. WILLIAMS & S. RUSH. 1976. Current density in bilateral and unilateral ECT. Biol. Psychiatry **11:** 303–312.
72. ERMAN, M. K., C. A. WELCH & M. R. MANDEL. 1979. A comparison of two unilateral ECT electrode placements: efficacy and electrical energy considerations. Am. J. Psychiatry **136:** 1317–1319.
73. GOTTESFELD, B. H., S. M. LESSE & H. HERSKOVITZ. 1944. Studies in electroconvulsive shock therapy of varied electrode applications. J. Nerv. Ment. Dis. **99:** 56–64.

What Have We Learned?

FRED H. FRANKEL

Clinical Psychiatry
Beth Israel Hospital and
Harvard Medical School
330 Brookline Avenue
Boston, Massachusetts 02215

I imagine I was invited to discuss what we have learned since the American Psychiatric Association Task Force deliberated these issues just 10 years ago. Those who planned this meeting did not expect me in the time allotted to distil the quintessentials from this unceasingly rich three-day presentation. They invited me to discuss this session, with which honor I am delighted. But how to do that without being anticlimactic? I am expected to touch on only a few of the highlights, but in so doing intend no disrespect for those aspects that I must either leave out altogether or attend to perfunctorily. I might also find myself dwelling ever so slightly on topics that surfaced elsewhere in the conference.

We have learned much from this session's challenging presentations. Most importantly I believe, we have learned how very limited still is our understanding of the psychoses and our treatment of them. It is invariably a humbling experience to find that what seems to be an important breakthrough turns out to be like a single tree in the fall—impressive but minute in comparison to the whole. We have learned that we are only at the threshold of the knowledge that we seek. I labor this point because the past and recent history of our field is burdened by the claims of many different experts jealous of the importance of their own discoveries, their practices, and their theories. Our effectiveness as clinicians and our reputation abroad bear the scars. Even as we deliberate and in our midst, there are those who so favor one approach to mental illness over the other that they would dispense totally with either the psychological or the biological in the firm belief that theirs is the only true system.

Let me dwell here for a moment on the psychological. I was struck by the surprise and even impatience evoked in many by the idea that sham electroconvulsive therapy (ECT) could, in the least way, be effective. We fail to integrate the importance of the psychological when we denigrate the placebo effect. We might be reminded that the stronger and more effective a treatment is, so is the placebo effect it generates.[1] There are studies that prove that a placebo masquerading as morphine will have approximately 50% of the effect of morphine, one pretending to be codeine will be roughly half as effective as codeine, and one presented as aspirin will be only half as effective as aspirin. If we value the efficacy of ECT, we must at least consider the results of sham ECT in the light of this knowledge that is embedded in the psychological understanding of reassurance, of being cared for, of positive expectations, and of demand characteristics. We should be delighted that in some ways sham ECT achieves positive results. Let me now return to the status of our biological competence.

Here we need to be reminded that although we have refined our biological therapies and our understanding of their implications, we still depend in the main on the neuroleptics and the tricyclic antidepressants that were available and in use 25–30 years ago, and in most centers of the world ECT is still administered in much the same way as it was then. Thus, despite the major promise of the exciting and dramatic discoveries of the past decade, the credit for which belongs to many of you, the direct impact of that new knowledge on how we will treat the patient admitted to our hospital unit tomorrow is as yet not very noticeable. As I move toward what we have learned here, let me briefly revisit a few familiar guidelines.

Since Ottosson's very clear demonstration in 1962 that the cerebral seizure was the central therapeutic event in treatment with ECT,[2] the electrical energy has been viewed largely as a necessary evil—the agent responsible for producing the seizure but of itself not worthy of attention other than as a factor responsible for the subsequent memory impairment.

A second very firm plank in the platform on which clinical practice has depended for several years has been the advantages of unilateral over bilateral ECT in containing memory impairment.[3,4] Although several studies have reported equal efficacy for unilateral placement,[5–7] others have challenged the findings with reports of unilateral courses requiring more treatments, and reports of cases that did not respond until bilateral placement was introduced.[8] As we are well aware, the debate has not yet been settled.

A third factor that has shaped the practice of ECT has been the lack of persuasive data regarding the stimulus waveforms. Sine-wave stimuli were chosen by the great majority of those who responded to the questionnaire distributed by the American Psychiatric Association Task Force on ECT in 1976.[9] We have known that for brief-pulse stimuli, unilateral ECT was associated with a slightly lower seizure threshold than was bilateral electrode placement.[10] There have been no compelling data leading to a preference for one stimulus waveform over another, but it has been generally agreed upon that the less electrical energy used, the better.

NEUROPHYSIOLOGICAL MECHANISMS

The presentations in this session emphasize the dimensions that have been added to the task of understanding the mechanisms. Varied, overlapping, and at times contradictory neurophysiological data must now be considered. Central to more than one of the papers has been the importance of the seizure. Both clinical experience and careful study attest to the therapeutic advantages of convulsions in the treatment of mental illness, particularly severe depressive illness.[11] Flor-Henry has not only captured the essential theme in his description of the depression-epilepsy axis; he has explained the seesaw effect of the relationship by linking it to neural excitability.[12] His original hypothesis of reduced excitability in depression and increased excitability in epileptic states is challenged by Post in his finding that the anticonvulsant carbamazepine is also effective in the treatment and prophylaxis of mania and depression.[13]

As if that were not enough to remind us that there will probably be few simple answers to the complex questions, we also have to integrate the findings of Malitz, Sackeim, and their co-workers which point to the anticonvulsant properties of ECT.[14] This requires at least a revised perspective on the theory of kindling which points in a different direction.[15,16] Let me return here to the depressive-epileptic axis, and then proceed to the Columbia findings.

Flor-Henry has assembled and added to the evidence in support of systems lateralized to one or the other of the cerebral hemispheres.[17] Both biochemical and neurophysiological evidence points to the lateralization of schizophrenia in changes in the left hemisphere, and bipolar psychoses in changes in the right hemisphere. Flor-Henry subsumes an intricate and delicate balance within the hemispheres and between them. He states that "the evidence on the modus operandi of ECT therefore suggests that its antidepressant action is the result of several interacting influences: at the most general neurobiological level it increases neural excitability, thereby reversing the reduced neural excitability that is one of the fundamental parameters of psychosis. Furthermore, unilateral non-dominant ECT, by transiently inactivating the non-dominant hemisphere, produces a euphoric mood change through the consequent dominant hemispheric activation . . . moreover, both bilateral and unilateral non-dominant ECT by activating the reticulofrontal generalized seizure system—through the neural repercussions of the seizure discharge—normalize the functional impairment of non-dominant hemispheric systems that underlies endogenous depressions of psychotic type."[12] He continues, "The neurophysiological activation of the non-dominant frontal component of the generalized seizure system which is the common denominator for both bilateral and non-dominant ECT is the critical region in question here."[12]

The inverse relationship between depression and epilepsy, appealing because it is easy to follow when stated in terms of reduced or increased neural excitability, must now take into account Post's findings with carbamazepine.[13] He and his co-workers have demonstrated the value of anticonvulsants in the treatment and prevention of bipolar illness in specific groups of patients. What can convulsive seizures and pharmacological anticonvulsants have in common? A possible explanation lies in another study by Post and his group in which it was found that electric convulsive seizures in animals inhibited amygdala kindling. That means that the seizures, too, had anticonvulsant effects. Whatever the specific mechanisms are that account for the therapeutic effects of seizures in affective illness, the anticonvulsant effects of both seizures and pharmacological agents appear to be playing a part.

Somewhat in keeping with these seemingly paradoxical developments are the findings of Malitz, Sackeim, and their co-workers.[14] In their series, they found that:

1. Using the lowest intensity of energy (brief pulse) necessary to produce seizures in comparable groups treated with bilateral and unilateral placement, unilateral treatment was significantly and disturbingly less effective.
2. Seizure threshold increased drastically more in the bilateral groups, and the increase in threshold was associated (in both bilateral and unilateral) with a clinical response.
3. Seizure duration decreased with the course of treatment, and regional cerebral blood flow was reduced.
4. With low-dosage ECT they did *not* observe cumulative deterioration with advancing treatment number in orientation recovery, on a variety of memory function tests.

This forces us again to take into account the anticonvulsant component in ECT and acknowledge that in some way it is involved in or associated with the therapeutic effect. There are here, however, two added dimensions. In addition to the importance of the seizure, it seems that the dosage of energy must be noticeably higher relative to threshold for the clinical response to unilateral ECT to be comparable to low-dose bilateral ECT. Increase in threshold is thus seen to be associated with clinical response. It is as if the more ECT is used, the higher the intensity of the electrical energy needed to produce a seizure—and that in some way in overcoming the increasing resistance to the production of the seizure, some therapeutic benefit is unleashed. Secondly, when there was no dramatic increase in threshold in unilateral treatment, and therefore no need to use high-intensity energy to produce a seizure, the clinical response was poor.

These findings not only add an interesting dimension to the long-standing deduction of Ottosson that the seizure is the all-important factor,[2] they also might throw light on why some workers continue to find unilateral treatments less effective.

In other words, could we have learned that the intensity of the energy in some way modifies the therapeutic value of the seizure that is produced, and that in some way not clearly understood more is better than less? This will of course be investigated, and with it the nature of the electrical stimulus, the placement of the electrodes, and the importance of cerebral blood flow.

NEUROTRANSMITTERS AND RECEPTORS

Neurotransmitter and receptor technology has made possible the measurement of transmitters and the sensitivity of receptors. As we have learned from Lerer's masterful review, studies have yielded evidence for significant effects in a number of systems including the noradrenergic, the serotonin, and the opioid systems. From the comments in this section and throughout this conference, it is apparent that a general receptor theory of ECT action does not yet seem possible. The most exciting finding is probably that of postsynaptic β-adrenoceptor subsensitivity.[18] This could place ECT in line with other effective antidepressant treatments such as the tricyclic antidepressants and the monoamine oxidase inhibitors. While some of the animal findings referred to above have been supported by clinical evidence, considerable additional clinical support must still be found for most of them.[19]

Possibly the most pressing demand reiterated these past few days is the need for further study. The data on gamma-aminobutyric acid (GABA), for instance, met-enkephalin, and acetylcholine, although promising in some instances, are still too sparse for evaluation. The down regulation of muscarinic cholinergic receptors by electric shocks in animals suggests a possible explanation for ECT-induced amnesia, and the central cholinergic depletion in Alzheimer's disease could be seen as a parallel finding.[20]

But the relevance of the observation on the cholinergic system is a matter for speculation, as is much of what we are discussing. That does not gainsay that what we have learned about the neurotransmitters since our deliberations on the American Psychiatric Association Task Force 10 years ago is considerable. Statements were made then that by 1985 we would understand the mechanisms of ECT so well that we would have dispensed with the electrical energy to achieve them. It is an irony that the electrical stimulus itself is demanding such renewed attention since the work of Malitz and his colleagues[14] and that of Post and his co-workers.[13]

In essence, the lesson we have learned then, in addition to the clear-cut demand for humility, is that although we still lack most of the answers, we have uncovered many new questions that have to be asked.

REFERENCES

1. EVANS, F. J. 1984. Unravelling placebo effects: expectations and the placebo response. Adv. Inst. Adv. Health **1**(3): 11–20.
2. OTTOSSON, J. O. 1962. Seizure characteristics and therapeutic efficiency in electroconvulsive therapy: an analysis of the antidepressive efficiency of grand mal and lidocaine-modified seizures. J. Nerv. Ment. Dis. **135:** 239–251.
3. D'ELIA, G. 1970. Unilateral electroconvulsive therapy. Acta Psychiatr. Scand. Suppl. **215:** 5–98.
4. SQUIRE, L. R. & P. C. SLATER. 1978. Bilateral and unilateral ECT: effects on verbal and nonverbal memory. Am. J. Psychiatry **135:** 1316–1320.
5. D'ELIA, G. 1974. Unilateral electroconvulsive therapy. *In* Psychobiology of Convulsive

Therapy. M. Fink. S. Kety, J. McGaugh & T. Williams, Eds.: 21–34. V. H. Winston & Sons. Washington, D.C.
6. SAND-STROMGREN, L. S. 1973. Unilateral vs. bilateral electroconvulsive therapy. Acta Psychiatr. Scand. Suppl. **240:** 1–65.
7. D'ELIA, G. & H. RAOTMA. 1975. Is unilateral ECT less effective than bilateral ECT? Br. J. Psychiatry **126:** 83–89.
8. ABRAMS, R. 1982. Technique of electroconvulsive therapy. *In* Electroconvulsive Therapy: Biological Foundations and Clinical Applications. R. Abrams & W. B. Essman, Eds.: 50–51. Spectrum Publications. Jamaica, N.Y.
9. APA. 1978. American Psychiatric Association Task Force Report No. 14. Electroconvulsive Therapy: 6. American Psychiatric Association. Washington, D.C.
10. WEINER, R. D. 1980. ECT and seizure threshold: effects of stimulus wave form and electrode placement. Biol. Psychiatry **15:** 225–241.
11. FINK, M. 1979. Convulsive Therapy: Theory and Practice: 5–17. Raven Press. New York, N.Y.
12. FLOR-HENRY, P. 1983. Cerebral Basis of Psychopathology: 132–133. John Wright/PSG Inc. Boston, Mass.
13. POST, R. M., F. PUTNAM, N. R. CONTEL & B. GOLDMAN. 1984. Electroconvulsive seizures inhibit amygdala kindling: implications for mechanism of action in affective illness. Epilepsia **25:** 234–239.
14. SACKEIM, H. A., P. DECINA, I. PROHOVNIK, S. MALITZ & S. R. RESOR. 1983. Anticonvulsant and antidepressant properties of electroconvulsive therapy: a proposed mechanism of action. Biol. Psychiatry **18:** 1301–1310.
15. GODDARD, G., D. MCINTYRE & C. LEECH. 1969. A permanent change in brain function resulting from daily electrical stimulation. Exp. Neurol. **25:** 295–330.
16. PINEL, J. P. J. & P. H. VAN OOT. 1975. Generality of the kindling phenomenon: some clinical implications. Can. J. Neur. Sci. **2:** 467–475.
17. FLOR-HENRY, P. 1983. Cerebral Basis of Psychopathology: 47–57. John Wright/PSG Inc. Boston, Mass.
18. VETULANI, J. & F. SULSER. 1975. Action of various antidepressant treatments reduces reactivity of noradrenergic cyclic AMP–generating system in limbic forebrain. Nature **257:** 495–496.
19. LERER, B. & R. H. BELMAKER. 1982. Receptors and the mechanisms of action of ECT. Biol. Psychiatry **17:** 497–511.
20. LERER, B. 1984. Electroconvulsive shock and neurotransmitter receptors: implications for mechanism of action and adverse effects of electroconvulsive therapy. Biol. Psychiatry **19:** 361–383.

Mechanisms of Action

Discussion of Part VII

JACK D. BLAINE[a] AND SIDNEY MALITZ[b]

[a]*Pharmacologic and Somatic Treatments Research Branch*
National Institute of Mental Health
Rockville, Maryland 20857

[b]*Department of Biological Psychiatry*
New York State Psychiatric Institute
722 West 168 Street
New York, New York 10032

The mechanism of action of convulsive therapy has been questioned and investigated since the first therapeutic use of induced seizures by Meduna in 1935.[1] Meduna believed that biological antagonism existed between the process that produces epilepsy and the process that produces schizophrenia. Thus, he thought that an induced convulsion in man would change brain chemistry in a therapeutic manner. When, in 1938, Cerletti and Bini introduced the use of electrically induced convulsions,[2] they believed that the seizure was the fundamental therapeutic factor while the electricity was only the epileptogenic stimulus.

In 1960, Ottosson and associates reported on a series of studies in which energy of electrical stimulation and cerebral seizure activity were systematically and independently manipulated experimentally to carefully delineate the specific effects of the electrical stimulation and seizure activity.[3] They concluded that the therapeutic and cognitive effects of electroconvulsive therapy (ECT) arise through different mechanisms. The therapeutic effect "is due to seizure activity and not, or only slightly, to the other effects of the current."[3] The memory disturbance is to a great extent accounted for by the effects of the electrical stimulation other than the seizure.

Over the years of extensive ECT usage, a variety of theories or explanations have been forthcoming to attempt to ascribe the therapeutic effect of ECT to other causes including the occurrence of structural brain changes and psychological theories focusing on fear, punishment, amnesia, denial, repression, and ego adaptation.[4] No evidence is available supporting any of these theories. However, primacy of the generalized seizure itself has been confirmed clearly and repeatedly over the last 10 years in a series of controlled clinical trials comparing ECT and sham ECT (simulated ECT in which all elements of the treatment, including general anesthesia and muscle relaxant, are given except for the electrical stimulation).[5–10]

Contemporary clinical therapy and most research on ECT have been guided by these basic assumptions. In recent years, basic and clinical scientists have intensified research efforts to better understand the mechanism of action of ECT by delineating the specific alterations in brain biological functioning brought about by a series of electrically induced generalized seizures that serve to relieve depression in man. As a result, a wealth of information is available on the effects of ECT on brain biological function from a multitude of vantage points including the neurophysiology, neuroendocrinology, neurochemistry, and neuroreceptorology. Much of this work, which has been presented earlier in this volume, has been based on basic studies employing electroconvulsive shocks in rodents. Human clinical studies attempting to clarify the relationship between these alterations and therapeutic efficacy and side effects in depressed patients are few in number. However, these types of studies are increasing as contemporary techniques and methodologies such as photon emission tomography, and regional cerebral blood flow and electrical activity permit their utilization in humans as evidenced by papers presented earlier in this volume.

Taken together with the diverse series of papers presented in this session on mechanism of action, which have been well reviewed and discussed by Dr. Frankel, this conference has provided an extensive review of the current status of knowledge of ECT mechanisms of action from a wide variety of currently divergent viewpoints. The fact that these diverse findings do not as yet fit neatly together to provide a definitive unified understanding of the mechanisms of action should not be seen as a failing of ECT, as is often portrayed by those opposed to ECT. While ECT is in a sense an empirical treatment in that it lacks a proven mechanism of action, its effectiveness is proven. From this perspective, ECT is at least comparable with many general medical treatments and other psychiatric treatments including psychopharmacological agents used to treat depression, mania, and schizophrenia.

Furthermore, a better understanding of the similarities and differences in mechanism of action between ECT and psychotropic medications might also provide important information about the nature of the affective disorders being treated. Although tricyclic antidepressants are effective therapy for most endogenous depression, a significant patient subgroup only responds to subsequent ECT. The identification of specific biological parameters correlated with therapeutic efficacy in these different subgroups of patients could potentially lead to better diagnosis and treatment.

Hopefully, research on mechanisms of therapeutic effect and cognitive side effects of ECT will be advanced further over the next decade. Increasingly more sophisticated technologies are becoming available and applied in conjunction with clinical treatment. In this way neurochemical and physiological measures of relevance to mechanism of action can be studied in patient groups including responders and nonresponders to treatment. One of the objectives of this conference was to bring together basic and clinically oriented researchers to provide cross-fertilization and promote cooperation and collaboration in the design and conduct of studies to answer critical questions on mechanism of action of ECT. The organizers of the conference have very successfully accomplished the first objective. We will have to wait 5 to 10 years to judge the outcome of the second objective based on the progress of research on mechanism of action of ECT.

REFERENCES

1. Meduna, L. J. 1935. Versuche uber die biologische beeinflussung des abaufes der schizophrenia: camphor und cardiozolkrampbe. Z. Ges. Neurol. Psychiat. **152:** 235–262.
2. Cerletti, U. & L. Bini. 1938. Un neuro metodo di schockterapie 'L elettro-shock.' Boll. Acad. Med. Roma **64:** 136–138.
3. Cronholm, B. & J. O. Ottosson. 1960. Experimental studies of the mode of action of electroconvulsive therapy in endogenous depression. Acta Psychiatr. Scand. **35**(Suppl. 145): 3–141.
4. Fink, M. 1979. Review of theories. *In* Convulsive Therapy: Theory and Practice (Chapter 13): 161–170. Raven Press. New York, N.Y.
5. Freeman, C. P. L., J. V. Basson & A. Crighton. 1978. Double-blind controlled trial of electroconvulsive therapy (ECT) and simulated ECT in depressive illness. Lancet **i:** 738–740.

6. LAMBORN, J. & D. GILL. 1978. A controlled comparison of simulated and real ECT. Br. J. Psychiatry **133:** 514–519.
7. JOHNSTONE, E. C., J. F. W. DEAKIN, P. LAWLER, C. D. FRITH, M. STEVENS, K. MCPHERSON & T. J. CROW. 1980. The Northwick Park electroconvulsive therapy trial. Lancet **ii:** 1317–1320.
8. WEST, E. D. 1981. Electroconvulsive therapy in depression: a double-blind controlled trial. Br. J. Med. **282:** 355–357.
9. BRANDON, S., P. COWLEY, C. MCDONALD, P. NEVILLE, R. PALMER & S. WILLSTONE-EASON. 1984. Electroconvulsive therapy: results in depressive illness from the Leicestershire trial. Br. Med. J. **288:** 22–25.
10. GREGORY, S., C. R. SHAWCROSS & D. GILL. 1985. The Nottingham ECT study. A double-blind comparison of bilateral, unilateral and simulated ECT in depressive illness. Br. J. Psychiatry **146:** 520–524.

Index of Contributors

Subject Index